THE WHEELS OF COMMERCE

Fernand Braudel

CIVILIZATION AND CAPITALISM
15th–18th Century

VOLUME II

THE WHEELS OF COMMERCE

Translation from the French
by Siân Reynolds

1817

HARPER & ROW, PUBLISHERS, New York
Cambridge, Philadelphia, San Francisco, London,
Mexico City, São Paulo, Sydney

First published in France under the title *Les Jeux de l'Echange*, 1979
Copyright © 1979 by Librairie Armand Colin, Paris

First U.S. Edition

Library of Congress Cataloging in Publication Data

Braudel, Fernand.
   Civilization and capitalism, 15th-18th century.

   Rev. translation of: Civilisation matérielle, économie et capitalisme: XVe-
XVIIIe siècle.
   Includes bibliographical references and index.
   Contents: V. 1. The structures of everyday life: the limits of the possible—v.
2. The wheels of commerce.
   1. Economic history. 2. Social history. 3. Civilization, Modern history.
HC51.B67413 1982   909.08   81-47653
ISBN 0-06-014845-4 (v. 1)   82-48109 (v. 2)
ISBN 0-06-015091-2 (v. 2)

83 84 85 86 87 10 9 8 7 6 5 4 3 2

To Pierre Gourou
in token of a double affection

Contents

7

Maps and Graphs

Illustrations

Foreword

If I were to look for a simple image, I would say that the present volume takes us upstairs from the ground-level of material life – the subject of the first volume of this book – and explores the upper storeys, representing what I have called 'economic life', before moving to the highest level of all, the action of capitalism. This metaphor of a house with several floors is a reasonable translation of the reality of the things we shall be considering, though it does rather strain their concrete meaning.

Between 'material life' (in the sense of an extremely elementary economy) and 'economic life', the contact surface is not continuous, but takes the form of thousands of humble points of intersection: markets, stalls, shops. Each point marks a break: on one side is economic life with its commerce, its currencies, its nodal points and its superior equipment – great trading cities, Stock Exchanges and fairs; on the other 'material life', the non-economy, imprisoned within self-sufficiency. The economy begins at the fateful threshold of 'exchange value'.

In this second volume, I have tried to analyse the machinery of exchange *as a whole*, from primitive barter up to and including the most sophisticated capitalism. Starting from as careful and neutral a description as possible, I have tried to grasp regularities and mechanisms, to write a sort of *general economic history* (as we have 'general principles of geography'); or, to use a different set of terms, to construct a *typology*, a *model*, or perhaps a *grammar* which will help us at least to pin down the meaning of certain key words, or of certain evident realities, without however assuming that the general history can be totally rigorous, the typology definitive or at all complete, the model in any sense mathematically verifiable, or that the grammar can give us the key to an economic language or form of discourse – even supposing that one such exists or is sufficiently consistent through time and space. In sum, what follows is an attempt at intelligibility, at uncovering certain articulations and developments – and, no less, the powerful forces which have maintained the traditional order, 'inert violence' as Jean-Paul Sartre called it. This then is a study on the borderlines of the social, the political and the economic.

For such a project, the only possible method was observation – repeated until the eyes ached; then a call for assistance from the different human sciences; and above all systematic comparison, the bringing together of experiences of the same nature, without being afraid, when dealing with systems that changed so little, that anachronism would lay too many traps for us during these necessary confrontations. This is the comparative method particularly recommended by Marc Bloch, and I have practised it using the perspectives of the long term, *la longue durée*. In the present state of knowledge, so many comparable phenomena are available to us over time and space that one can feel one is undertaking not merely a set of comparisons dictated by chance, but virtually a series of experiments. So I have built a book which is halfway between history, its onlie begetter, and the other human sciences.

In this confrontation between model and observation, I found myself constantly faced with a regular contrast between a normal and often routine exchange economy (what the eighteenth century would have called the *natural* economy) and a superior, sophisticated economy (which would have been called *artificial*).[1] I am convinced that this distinction is tangible, that the *agents* and men involved, the actions and the mentalities, are not the same in these different spheres; and that the rules of the market economy regarding, for instance, free competition as described in classical economics, although visible at some levels, operated far less frequently in the upper sphere, which is that of calculations and speculation. At this level, one enters a shadowy zone, a twilight area of activities by the initiated which I believe to lie at the very root of what is encompassed by the term capitalism: the latter being an accumulation of power (one that bases exchange on the balance of strength, as much as, or more than on the reciprocity of needs) a form of social parasitism which, like so many other forms, may or may not be inevitable. In short, there is a hierarchy in the world of trade, even if, as in all hierarchies, the upper storeys could not exist without the lower stages on which they depend. And we should not of course forget that below even the simplest forms of trade, what I have for want of a better expression called *material life* constitutes, throughout the *ancien régime*, the broadest layer of all.

But will the reader find questionable – more questionable even than this contrast between different layers of the economy – my use of the word *capitalism* to describe the top layer? The word *capitalism* did not emerge in its full maturity and with explosive force until very late – the very beginning of the twentieth century. That its meaning should have been profoundly marked by the date of its 'true' birth is indisputable; by parachuting it into the period 1400–1800, am I not committing the cardinal sin for a historian – anachronism? To tell the truth, this does not bother me overmuch. Historians invent words and labels to identify retrospectively problems and periods in history: the Hundred Years' War, the Renaissance, Humanism, the Reformation. I needed a special word to describe this zone which is not the true market economy, but indeed often its exact opposite. And the word that irresistibly suggested itself was precisely *capitalism*. Why not make use of this word, evocative as it is of so many images, and forget the heated debates it has raised in the past and is raising still?

Observing the rules governing any exercise in model-building, I have in this volume prudently moved from the simple to the complex. What is visible on first observation without difficulty, in past economic societies, is what is usually called the circulation of goods, or the market economy. In the first two chapters, *The instruments of exchange* and *Markets and the economy*, I have concentrated on describing markets, pedlars, shops, fairs, Stock Exchanges – perhaps in too much detail. And I have tried to identify the rules of exchange, if such there be. The next two chapters, *Capitalism away from home* and *Capitalism on home ground*, will tackle the different problems of production, which lie alongside those of circulation. They will also clarify the precise meaning of the crucial words in the debate upon which we have embarked: *capital, capitalist, capitalism*; and lastly, they will try to situate capitalism by sector. Such a topology should be able to reveal the limits of capitalism, and logically therefore to uncover its nature. We shall by then have arrived at the heart of our difficulties, but not at the end of our problems. One last chapter, arguably the most necessary of all, *Society* or the *'set of sets'*, seeks to replace the economy and capitalism in the overall context of social reality, outside which nothing can have full meaning.

To describe, analyse, compare and explain usually means standing aside from historical narrative: it means ignoring or wilfully chopping up the continuous flow of history. But this flow does exist: and we shall find it again in the final volume of this work: *The Perspective of the World*. In the present volume then, we are at an earlier stage, in which time is not respected in its chronological continuity, but used as a means of observation.

Not that this made my task any easier. I have started the chapters you are about to read four or five times over. I have delivered them as lectures at the Collège de France and at the Ecole des Hautes Etudes. I have written and rewritten them from start to finish. Henri Matisse, according to a friend of mine who once sat for him, used to begin his drawings ten times over, throwing them into the wastepaper basket day after day, and only keeping the last in which he thought he had achieved purity and simplicity of line. Sadly, I am not Matisse. And I am not at all sure that my final version is the clearest, or the closest to what I think, or am trying to think. I console myself with a remark by the English historian Frederick W. Maitland (1887) that 'simplicity is the outcome of technical subtlety; it is the goal, not starting point'.[2] With luck, we may achieve it in the end.*

---

* Notes to the text will be found on pages 603–49.

I

The Instruments of Exchange

AT FIRST SIGHT, the economy consists of two enormous areas: production and consumption. One completes and destroys; the other renews and starts afresh. 'A society cannot leave off producing any more than it can leave off consuming', wrote Marx.[1] This seems a self-evident truth. Proudhon says much the same thing when he asserts that working and eating are the two apparent purposes of man's existence. But between these two worlds slides another, as narrow but as turbulent as a river, and like the others instantly recognizable: exchange, trade, in other words the market economy – imperfect, discontinuous, but already commanding in the centuries studied in this book, and without a doubt revolutionary. In an overall structure which had an obstinate tendency towards a routine balance, and which left it only to revert to it, this was the zone of change and innovation. Marx called it the sphere of circulation[2] a term I persist in finding a happy one. The word circulation, transferred from physiology to economics,[3] does, it is true, cover a multitude of things. According to G. Schelle,[4] the editor of the complete works of Turgot, the latter once thought of writing a *Treatise on Circulation* which would have dealt with banks, Law's system, credit, exchange and trade, and luxury – in other words practically the entire economy as then conceived. But has not the expression *market economy* today, in turn, taken on a wider meaning which goes far beyond the simple notion of circulation and exchange?[5]

Three worlds then. In the first volume of this book, I gave pride of place to consumption. In the pages which follow, we shall be looking at circulation. The difficult problems of production will be tackled last of all.[6] Not that I would challenge the views of Marx and Proudhon that they are essential. But for the historian, looking backward in time, it is hard to begin with production, a baffling territory, difficult to locate and as yet inadequately charted. Circulation, by contrast, has the advantage of being easily observable. It is constantly in movement and draws attention to its movement. The clamour of the marketplace has no difficulty in reaching our ears. I can without exaggeration claim to see the dealers, merchants and traders on the Rialto in the Venice of 1530, through the very window of Aretino, who liked to look down at this daily scene.[7]

I can walk into the Amsterdam Bourse of 1688 or even earlier and feel quite familiar – I almost wrote 'free to speculate'. Georges Gurvitch would immediately object that the *easily observable* may well be the secondary or the negligible. I am not so sure; and I do not believe that Turgot, who had to tackle the whole of the economy of his time, was so very mistaken in paying special attention to circulation. After all, the genesis of capitalism is strictly related to exchange – is that negligible? Finally, production means division of labour and therefore forces men to exchange goods.

In any case, who would seriously think of minimizing the role of the *market*? Even in an elementary form, it is the favoured terrain of supply and demand, of that appeal to *other people* without which there would be no economy in the ordinary sense of the word, only a form of life 'embedded' as English economists say, in self-sufficiency or the non-economy. The market spells liberation, openness, access to another world. It means coming up for air. Men's activities, the surpluses they exchange, gradually pass through this narrow channel to the other world with as much difficulty at first as the camel of the scriptures passing through the eye of a needle. Then the breaches grow wider and more frequent, as society finally becomes a 'generalized market society'.[8] 'Finally': that is to say with the passage of time, and never at the same date or in the same way in different regions. So there is no simple linear history of the development of markets. In this area, the traditional, the archaic and the modern or ultra-modern exist side by side, even today. The most significant images are undoubtedly easy to find and collect, but not, even in the favoured case of Europe, to situate with precision in relation to one another.

Could it be that this lurking problem is also a consequence of the restriction of our field of observation – even though it runs from the fifteenth to the eighteenth century? The ideal field of observation would cover all the markets in the world, from the very beginnings to our own time – the huge area tackled with iconoclastic zeal by Karl Polanyi.[9] But how can one include in the same explanation the pseudo-markets of ancient Babylon, the primitive exchange habits of the Trobriand Islanders in our own time, and the markets of medieval and pre-industrial Europe? I am not convinced that such a thing is possible.

In any case, we shall not begin by immersing ourselves in general explanations. We shall begin with description: first of Europe, a vital witness and better known than any other. Then of countries outside Europe, for no description can even begin to lead to a valid explanation if it does not effectively encompass the whole world.

Europe: the wheels of commerce at the lowest level

Let us begin then with Europe. By the fifteenth century, the most archaic forms of exchange had already been eliminated there. All the evidence relating to prices

Venice, the Rialto. Painting by Carpaccio, 1494. (Academy, Venice. Photo Giraudon.)

as early as the twelfth century indicates that they were already fluctuating,[10] evidence that by then 'modern' markets existed and might occasionally be linked together in embryonic systems, town-to-town networks. For effectively only towns (or very large villages) had markets. Small villages might very occasionally possess a market in the fifteenth century[11] but their number was negligible. The western town swallowed everything, forced everything to submit to its laws, its demands and its controls. The market became one of its mechanisms.[12]

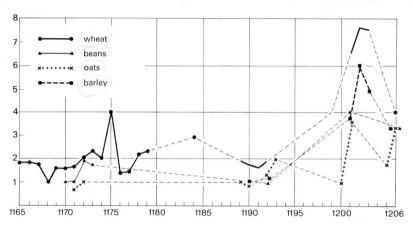

1   EARLY PRICE FLUCTUATIONS IN ENGLAND
From D.L. Farmer, 'Some Price Fluctuations in Angevin England' in *The Economic History Review*, 1956-1957, p. 39. Note how the prices of the different cereals went up in unison following the bad harvest of the year 1201.

Ordinary markets like those of today

In their elementary form, markets still exist today. Survivals of the past, they are held on fixed days, and we can see them with our own eyes on our local market-places, with all the bustle and mess, the cries, strong smells and fresh produce. In the past, they were recognizably the same: a few trestles, a canopy to keep off the rain; stallholders, each with a numbered place,[13] duly allotted in advance, registered, and to be paid for as authorities or landlords decreed; a crowd of buyers and a multitude of petty traders – a varied and active proletariat: pea-shellers, who had a reputation for being inveterate gossips; frog-skinners (the frogs came in mule-loads from Geneva[14] or Paris[15]), porters, sweepers, carters, unlicensed pedlars of both sexes, fussy controllers who passed on their derisory offices from father to son; secondhand dealers, peasants and peasant women recognizable by their dress, as were respectable townswomen looking for a bargain, servant-girls who had worked out, so their employers complained, how to make something out of the shopping-money (to shoe the mule, *ferrer la mule* as they said);[16] bakers selling coarse bread on the market-place, butchers whose displays of meat encumbered the streets and squares, wholesalers ('grossers') selling fish, butter and cheese in large quantities);[17] tax-collectors. And everywhere of course were the piles of produce, slabs of butter, heaps of vegetables, pyramids of cheeses, fruit, wet fish, game, meat which the butcher cut up on the spot, unsold books whose pages were used to wrap up purchases.[18] From the countryside there also came straw, hay, wood, wool, hemp, flax and even fabrics woven on village looms.

If this elementary market has survived unchanged down the ages, it is surely because in its robust simplicity it is unbeatable – because of the freshness of the perishable goods it brings straight from local gardens and fields. Because of its low prices too, since the primitive market, where food is sold 'at first hand'[19] is the most direct and transparent form of exchange, the most closely supervised and the least open to deception. Is it the most equitable? Boileau's *Livre des Métiers* (Book of Trades), originally written in 1270,[20] insists that it is: 'For it is clear that the goods come to the open market and there it can be seen if they are good and fair or not … for of things … sold on the open market, all may have a share, poor and rich.' The German expression for this is *Hand-in-Hand, Auge-in-Auge Handel* – selling hand to hand, eyeball to eyeball;[21] in other words immediate exchange: the goods are sold on the spot, the purchases are taken and paid for there and then. Credit is hardly used between one market and another.[22] This very ancient form of exchange was already being practised at Pompeii, Ostia or Timgad, and had been for centuries or millennia before that: ancient Greece had its markets, as did classical China, or the Egypt of the Pharaohs, or Babylonia where exchange made its very earliest appearance.[23] European travellers have described the multi-coloured splendours and the organization of the market 'of Tlalteco next to Tenochtitlan' (Mexico City)[24] and the 'regulated and policed' markets of Black Africa, where they were struck by the orderliness of the market, if not by the abundance of goods on offer.[25] The origins of the markets of Ethiopia go back into the mists of time.[26]

Towns and markets

Markets in towns were generally held once or twice a week. In order to supply them, the surrounding countryside needed time to produce goods and to collect them; and it had to be able to divert a section of the labour force (usually women) to selling the produce. In big cities, it is true, markets tended to be held daily, in Paris for instance, where in theory (and often in practice) they were supposed only to be held on Wednesdays and Saturdays.[27] In any case, whether intermittent or continuous, these elementary markets between town and countryside, by their number and indefinite repetition represent the bulk of all known trade, as Adam Smith remarked. The urban authorities therefore took their organization and supervision firmly in hand: it was a matter of vital necessity. And these were on-the-spot authorities, prompt to react or devise regulations, and always keeping a sharp eye on prices. In Sicily, if a vendor asked a price a single *grano* over the fixed tariff, he could be sent straight to the galleys! (One such case occurred on 2 July 1611 at Palermo.)[28] At Châteaudun,[29] bakers who were third-time offenders were 'brutally tipped out of tumbrils, trussed up like sausages'. This practice dated back to 1417, when Charles d'Orléans granted aldermen the right to inspect the bakeries, and the community did not succeed in having the torture banned until 1602.

But supervision and penalties did not prevent the market from growing to meet demand and taking its place at the heart of urban life. Since people went there on set days, it was a natural focus for social life. It was at market that the townspeople met, made deals, quarrelled, perhaps came to blows; the market was the source of incidents later reflected in court cases which reveal patterns of complicity, and it was the scene of the infrequent interventions of the watch, sometimes spectacular, sometimes prudent.[30] All news, political or otherwise, was passed on in the market. In 1534, the actions and intentions of Henry VIII were criticized aloud in the market-place of Fakenham in Norfolk.[31] And was there any English market down the ages where one would not have heard the vehement pronouncements of preachers? The impressionable crowd was there to hear all sorts of causes, good and bad. The market was also the favourite place for all business or family agreements. 'At Giffoni, in the province of Salerno, in the fifteenth century, we see from the lawyer's records that on market days, apart from the sale of produce and local artisans' wares, a higher percentage [than on other days] is recorded of land sale agreements, emphyteutic leases [i.e. those providing for fixed perpetual rent] donations, marriage contracts and dowry settlements.'[32] The market was a stimulus to everything – even, logically, the trade of the local shops. William Stout, a Lancaster shopkeeper at the end of the seventeenth century, hired extra help 'on market and fair days'.[33] This was no doubt a general rule – unless that is the shops were officially closed, as was often the case, on fair or market days.[34]

One has only to sample the wisdom of proverbs to see how central the market was to a whole world of relationships. Here are a few examples:[35] 'One can buy anything in the market but silent prudence and honour'; 'a man who buys fish while it is still in the sea may only get the smell in the end'. If you are unskilled in the arts of buying and selling, 'the market will teach you'. Since no man is an island in the market, 'think of yourself but think of the market too', that is of other people. The wise man, says an Italian proverb, *'val più avere amici in piazza che denari nella cassa'*, will prefer to have friends on the market-place than money in a chest. To resist the temptations of the market-place is the image of wisdom in the folklore of Dahomey of today: 'When a seller calls "Come and buy", reply if you are wise: "I spend only what I have".'[36]

Markets increase in number and become specialized

Taken over by the towns, the markets grew apace with them. More and more markets appeared, overflowing from the small town squares which could no

Paris, the bread market and the poultry market, quai des Augustins, about 1670. (Paris, Musée Carnavalet. Photo Giraudon.)

longer contain them. And since they represented modernity on the march, their growth allowed no obstacle to bar their way: they could with impunity impose on their surroundings their congestion, their rubbish and their obstinate gatherings of people. The solution adopted was to send them to the outskirts of the towns, outside the walls and towards the suburbs. This was often done if a new market was to be set up: as one was in Paris on the Place St Bernard in the Faubourg Saint-Antoine (2 March 1643); or in October 1660 'between the Porte Saint-Michel and the moat of the city of Paris, the rue d'Enfer and the Porte Saint-Jacques'.[37] But the old rendez-vous in the city centres survived: indeed it was already quite a business even to shift them a little distance, for instance from the Pont Saint-Michel to the far end of the same bridge in 1667,[38] or fifty years later from the rue Mouffetard to the nearby courtyard of the Hôtel des Patriarches (May 1718).[39] The new did not chase out the old. And since city walls also moved as the urban centres expanded, markets which had been placed sensibly on the outskirts found themselves locked inside the towns, and remained there.

In Paris, the *Parlement*, aldermen and (after 1667) the Lieutenant of Police, tried desperately to keep the markets within reasonable bounds: in vain. The rue Saint-Honoré was impassable in 1678 because of 'a market which has unlawfully set itself up near and in front of the Quinze-Vingts butcher's in the rue Saint-Honoré, where on market days several women and stallholders, from the fields as well as from the city, spread out their produce right on the street and prevent free passage which should always be unhindered as [it is] one of the most frequented and considerable streets in Paris'.[40] This was an obvious abuse, but how could it be remedied? To clear one place meant filling up another. Almost fifty years later, the little Quinze-Vingts market was still there, since we find the *commissaire* Brussel writing to his superior at the Châtelet: 'Today sir, I received a complaint from the townspeople at the little market of the Quinze-Vingts, where I had gone for bread, about the mackerel-sellers who throw away the heads of their mackerel, which is most unpleasant by the infection it spreads in the market. It would be a good thing if these women were told to put the fish-heads in baskets, which could then be emptied into a cart, as the pea-shellers have to.'[41] Even more scandalous, because it took place on the *parvis* of Notre-Dame during Holy Week, was the *Bacon Fair*, which was really a large market where the poor and not-so-poor of Paris came to buy hams and flitches of bacon. The public weighing-scales were set up under the very porch of the cathedral: which was therefore the scene of incredible jostling, as people tried to get their meat weighed before anyone else, as well as of much banter, practical jokes, and petty thieving. The *gardes-françaises* themselves, who were supposed to keep order were no better than the rest and the undertakers from the nearby Hôtel-Dieu permitted themselves many ludicrous pranks.[42] None of this however prevented permission being given to the chevalier de Gramont in 1669 to establish a 'new market between the church of Notre-Dame and the *isle du Pallais*'. Every Saturday, there were catastrophic traffic jams. The square was thick with people: how were religious processions or the queen's carriage to get through?[43]

When an open space became available of course, a market took it over. Every winter in Moscow when the Moskva river froze, shops, booths and stalls were set up on the ice.[44] It was the time of year when goods could be easily transported over the snow by sled, and when meat and slaughtered animals were deep-frozen by the open air: just before and after Christmas, the volume of trade regularly increased.[45] During the abnormally cold winters of the seventeenth century in London, people rejoiced to be able to hold on the frozen Thames all the festivities of Carnival which 'throughout England lasts from Christmas until after Twelfth Night'. 'Sheds which are taverns', huge sides of beef roasting over a fire in the open air, Spanish wine and spirits attracted the whole population, even the king himself on occasion (13 January 1677).[46] In January and February 1683, however, things were not so gay. Unprecedented cold gripped the city: at the mouth of the Thames, huge ice-floes were threatening ships which were frozen in. Food and goods ran short, prices tripled and quadrupled, and the roads were impassable with ice and snow. City life took refuge on the frozen river: it became the route for provision carts and hired carriages; merchants, shopkeepers and artisans set up their stalls on the ice. A huge market sprang into existence, showing how great was the force of number in the enormous capital – so huge that a Tuscan observer called it a '*grandissimo* fair'. There immediately flocked to it of course

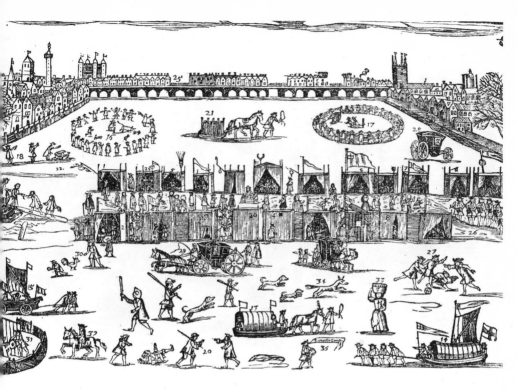

The Fair on the Thames 1683. This engraving, reproduced in Edward Robinson's book, *The Early History of Coffee Houses in England* shows all the activities of the fair held on the frozen river. On the left, the Tower of London, in the background London Bridge. (Photothèque Armand Colin.)

'charlatans, clowns and all the inventors of tricks to wheedle money out of purses'.[47] And the whole extraordinary gathering *did* leave in people's minds the memory of a fair: 'The Fair on the Thames' 1683. A rather clumsy engraving commemorates the event without communicating all the picturesque bustle.[48]

The growth of trade everywhere led towns to construct covered markets (halls or *halles*), sometimes surrounded by open-air markets. The covered markets were usually permanent and specialized institutions. There were countless cloth halls.[49] Even a minor town like Carpentras had one.[50] Barcelona built its *ala dels draps* over the Exchange (the *Lonja*).[51] Blackwell Hall,[52] the cloth market of London, was built in 1397, rebuilt in 1558, burnt down in the Fire of London in 1666, rebuilt again in 1672, to huge dimensions. Sales were for a long time confined to certain days of the week, but became daily in the eighteenth century, and the 'country clothiers' fell into the habit of leaving unsold cloth there to be held over until the next market. In about 1660, the hall had its factors, full-time employees, and a whole complicated administration. But even before this expan-

The *halles* of Le Faouët, Brittany (late sixteenth century). (Photo Giraudon.)

sion, Basinghall Street, where this complex building stood, was already 'the heart of the business quarter', even more so than the *Fondaco dei Tedeschi* in Venice.[53]

There were of course different halls representing various goods. There were cornmarkets (in Toulouse as early as 1203)[54] and halls selling wine, leather, shoes, furs (the *Kornhaüser*, *Pelzhaüser* and *Schuhhaüser* of German towns); in Görlitz, in a region which produced the precious dyestuff, there was even a woad market.[55] In the sixteenth century, the towns and cities of England saw a series of markethalls with different names spring up, often at the expense of a wealthy local merchant disposed to be generous.[56] In Amiens in the seventeenth century, the yarn market stood in the town centre, behind the church of Saint-Firmin-en-Castillon, a stone's throw from the central or corn market: the weavers came every day there to fetch the yarn known as *sayette*, 'combed and degreased, and usually spun on a small wheel'; this commodity was brought into town by the spinners from the nearby countryside.[57] And in many places the butcher's stalls, lined up under a roof, were virtually covered markets too, in Evreux for instance;[58] in Troyes, where they were in a dark warehouse;[59] in Venice where the *Beccarie*, the principal butchers' shops of the city, were brought together after 1339 a few steps from the Rialto square, in the former Ca' Querini. The street and the canal were both renamed Beccarie after them, and the church of San Matteo, the butchers' church, stood here until it was destroyed in the early nineteenth century.[60]

The word *halle* could mean several things then, from a simple covered market to the mighty buildings and complicated organization of the Halles which were from a very early date 'the belly of Paris'. The immense machinery dates back to Philip Augustus.[61] It was in his time that a great market was built on the Champeaux, near the churchyard of the Innocents which was not deconsecrated until very late, in 1786.[62] But during the great recession between 1350 and 1450, the Halles clearly deteriorated – because of the recession, undoubtedly, but also because of competition from neighbouring shops. In any case the decline of the Halles was not a merely Parisian phenomenon. It was clear to see in other cities in the kingdom. Disused market buildings fell into ruins; some became rubbish dumps for the neighbourhood. The weavers' hall in Paris, 'according to the accounts of 1484 to 1487 was used at least in part as a garage for the King's gun-carriages'.[63] Roberto S. Lopez's theory that religious buildings are a good economic indicator is well known:[64] if the building of a church is interrupted, as was Bologna cathedral in 1223, Siena Cathedral in 1265 or the Santa Maria del Fiore in Florence in 1301-1302, this is a sure sign of economic crisis. Can we promote market halls, whose history has never been written, to the dignified status of economic indicators? If so, one could suggest that business picked up in Paris from about 1543-1572, rather more towards the end than the beginning of this period. François I's edict of 20 September 1543, registered by the *Parlement* on 11 October following, was only the first move in the new direction. Others followed. Their apparent aim was to make Paris more beautiful rather than to provide it with a powerful trading organism. And yet the return to a more active commercial life, the growth of the capital and the subsequent reduction, as the Halles were rebuilt, of the number of shops and selling-points in its neighbour-hood, made the operation an exceptional commercial enterprise. By the end of the sixteenth century at any rate, the Halles, now newly reconstructed, were restored to their old level of activity of the days of Saint Louis. This was another 'Renaissance' of a sort.[65]

No map of the Halles can convey a faithful image of this huge combination of covered spaces and open spaces, its pillars holding up the arcades of neigh-bouring houses, and surrounded by a bustling commercial life on the fringes of the central market, taking advantage of the disorder and sprawl and creating more of both to its own profit. Savary (1761)[66] says that the whole complex was no further modified after the sixteenth century: we should not take this literally: there were constant internal movements and shifts. And there were two inno-vations in the eighteenth century: in 1767, the corn hall was taken down and put up again on the site of the former Hôtel de Soissons; at the end of the century, the seafood hall and the leather hall were rebuilt, and the wine hall was transferred beyond the Saint-Bernard gate. And plans were always being put forward to improve and – already – to relocate the Halles. But the huge complex (50,000 square metres of land), stayed not unreasonably where it was.

Only the wool and cloth halls, saltfish and fresh seafood stalls were under covered markets. But all round these buildings, clustering against them, were open-air markets in corn, flour, butter, candles, tow, and well-ropes. Near the 'pillars' which stood all round, secondhand-clothes dealers, bakers, shoemakers and 'other poor masters of the trades of Paris who have the right to the halls' would dispose themselves as best they could. 'On 1st March 1657,' say two Dutch travellers,[67] 'we saw the second-hand clothes market, (*la Friperie*) near the Halles. This is a large gallery, held up by stone pillars under which all the sellers of old clothes have their stalls ... There is a public market twice a week ... and it is then that all these dealers, among whom there are it seems a number of Jews, spread out their goods. At any hour going past there, one is assailed by their continual cries, "Here's a good country coat!" "Here's a fine jerkin!" and by the patter about their merchandise with which they seek to draw people into their stalls ... One can hardly believe the prodigious quantity of clothes and furniture they have: one sees some very fine things, but it is dangerous to buy unless one knows the trade well, for they have marvellous skill in restoring and patching up what is old so that it appears new.' As the stalls are badly lit, 'you think you have bought a black coat, but when you take it into the daylight, it is green or purple or spotted like leopard-skin'.

A collection of different markets one alongside another, surrounded by heaps of rubbish, dirty water and rotten fish, the splendid Halles were 'also the most vile and unhealthy quarter of Paris', says Piganiol de la Force (1742).[68] They were equally the capital of loud-mouthed quarrels and strong language. The market wives, more numerous than the men, set the tone: they had the reputation of having 'the foulest mouths in Paris'. '*Hée! Madame l'impudente! Parle donc! Hé, grande putain! T'es la garce des écoliers! Va! Va au collège de Montaigu! Ne devrois-tu pas avoir honte? Vieille carcasse! Dos fouetté! Impudente! Double vilaine, t'es soule jusqu'au gosier*' – such were the insults hurled by the fishwives of the seventeenth century – and in later times too no doubt.[69]

Intervention by the towns

Complicated and unique as the central market of Paris may have appeared, it was but a reflection of the complexity and supply requirements of a big city, which had quickly grown beyond all normal proportions. When London began its celebrated expansion, the same causes produced the same effects and the English capital was invaded by a multitude of uncontrolled markets. Unable to fit into the original spaces reserved for them, they spilled over into the nearby streets, which each became a sort of specialized market: fish, vegetables, poultry. By Elizabethan times, they were expanding daily, and blocking up the busiest thoroughfares of the capital. The great fire of 1666 finally made reorganization

The herring-seller and other fishwives in action on the floor of the Halles; in the foreground, a sweetmeat-seller. Anonymous engraving from the time of the Fronde. (Cabinet des Estampes, B.N., Paris.)

possible. The city authorities, in order to clear the streets, put up large new buildings around huge courtyards: these were closed markets, but open to the air, some specialized and really wholesale markets, others more diversified.

Leadenhall, the biggest of all – some said it was the biggest in Europe – was the one which afforded a sight most nearly comparable to the Paris Halles. It was undoubtedly more orderly. Leadenhall absorbed into its four buildings all the street-markets that had flourished before 1666 around its former site, those of Gracechurch Street, Cornhill, The Poultry, New Fish Street, Eastcheap. In one courtyard, a hundred butchers' stalls sold beef; in another, a further 140 stalls were reserved for other meats; elsewhere butter, fish, cheese, nails, ironmongery was sold. It was a 'monster market, an object of civic pride and one of the showpieces of the town'. The orderliness of which Leadenhall was a symbol did not of course last long. As it continued to expand, the city outgrew these wise solutions and found itself faced with the same old problems. By 1699, and probably earlier, the stalls were once more spilling out on to the streets, taking up their positions under the porches of houses, and pedlars were spreading throughout the city, despite the prohibition on travelling salesmen. The most picturesque of the street criers of London were probably the fishwives, carrying their merchandise in baskets on their heads. They had a bad reputation, and were both reviled and exploited. After a good day, one was fairly sure of finding them in the tavern at night. And they were probably just as foul-mouthed and aggressive as their counterparts in the Halles,[70] to return to the subject of Paris.

To be assured of supplies, Paris had to organize a huge region around the capital. Oysters and fish came from Dieppe, Crotoy, Saint-Valéry. 'We meet nothing but catches of fish (*des chasses marées*),' writes a traveller who passed by these two towns in 1728. But it was impossible 'to get hold of any of this fish which follows us on all sides ... It is all bound for Paris'.[71] Cheeses came from Meaux; butter from Gournay, near Dieppe, or from Isigny; beasts for slaughter from the markets of Poissy, Sceaux and further afield from Neubourg; good bread from Gonesse; pulses from Caudebec in Normandy, where a market was held every Saturday.[72] Hence a series of regulations, forever undergoing change and revision. Their object was to protect the area which directly supplied the city, to allow free rein to its producers, transporters and dealers, all the modest agents who saw to it that the great city's markets were kept constantly supplied. Professional merchants were therefore allowed to trade freely only outside this area. A police order from the Châtelet in 1622 extended to a radius of ten leagues the zone outside which merchants could handle corn supplies; the distance was seven leagues for meat on the hoof (1635); and twenty leagues for calves 'on grass' and hogs (1665); for freshwater fish it was four leagues, from the beginning of the seventeenth century;[73] and twenty for large-scale wine purchases.[74]

There were other problems too: one of the thorniest was the supply of horses – and of livestock. This was handled by noisy markets which were as far as possible kept on the outskirts of the city or outside it altogether. What eventually became the Place des Vosges, a piece of wasteland near the Tournelles, was for many years the site of a horse-market.[75] Paris was thus permanently surrounded by a ring of markets, virtually a series of fatstock fairs. No sooner did one end than another opened the next day, with the same throng of people and animals. At one of these markets, probably Saint-Victor, eyewitnesses in 1667 reported seeing 'over three thousand horses [at a time] and it is most remarkable that there should be so many, since markets are held twice a week'.[76] In fact the horse trade penetrated the entire city: there were 'new' horses from the provinces or abroad, but mostly there were 'old horses . . . that is, which have already served' – secondhand beasts in other words, 'which the bourgeois [sometimes] wish to get rid of without sending them to market'; as a result there was a whole network of brokers and smiths, who acted as go-betweens for horse-dealers and stable-owners. And every district had its livery stables.[77]

The big livestock markets were huge gatherings too, at Sceaux on Mondays, at Poissy on Thursdays at the four gates of the little town: (the Ladies' Gate, the Bridge Gate, the Conflans and Paris gates).[78] A very active meat trade went on there through a chain of *traitants*, middlemen who paid in advance at the market (and were reimbursed later) go-betweens, rounders-up (*griblins* or *bâtonniers*) who went all over France buying up stock, and lastly butchers, who were by no means all poor shopkeepers: some founded bourgeois dynasties.[79] According to the records, in 1707, there were sold weekly on the Paris markets (in round figures) 1300 oxen, 8200 sheep and almost 2000 calves (100,000 per annum). In 1707, the *traitants* or wholesalers 'who have taken hold both of the market at Poissy and the market at Sceaux, complain that sales take place [outside their control] all round Paris, at Petit-Montreuil for instance'.[80]

It should be noted that the market for Paris's meat supply extended over a large area of France, as did the zones from which the capital regularly or irregularly drew its grain.[81] This wide radius raises the question of routes and communications – such an enormous question that it is difficult in a few words to suggest even its main lines. The most important feature of the system was probably the organization of the waterways to supply Paris: the Yonne, the Aube, the Marne, the Oise running into the Seine, and the Seine itself. On its course through the city, the Seine had 'ports' – a total of 26 in 1754 – which were at the same time large and extraordinary markets, giving the best value. The two most important were the *port de Grève*, where the downstream goods were landed: grain, wine, wood, hay (though for the latter the Tuileries port seems to have been more significant); and the *port Saint-Nicolas*[82] where the upstream traffic landed. The river was alive with craft of all kind: ferries, or in the time of Louis XIV, *bachoteurs*, little boats for hire to clients, rather like the water-taxis[83] or 'gondolas' which plied on the Thames upstream from London Bridge and which were often preferred to the bumpy ride of carriages.[84]

Complicated though it may appear, the case of Paris is not unlike that of several other cities. Any town of importance required a supply zone suited to its own dimensions. Thus Madrid in the eighteenth century drew to excess on the means of transport of Castile, to the point of disrupting the country's entire economy.[85] In Lisbon, if one is to believe Tirso de Molina (1625) everything was simplicity itself: fruit, snow from the Serra d'Estrela, and food arrived by the all-providing sea: 'The inhabitants, as they sit eating at table, can see the fishermen's nets fill with fish ... caught on their doorsteps.'[86] It is a pleasure to the eyes, says an account of July–August 1633, to see the hundreds and thousands of fishermen's barks on the Tagus.[87] Lazy, greedy, perhaps indifferent, the city seems from these accounts to be swallowing the sea. But the picture is too good to be true: in fact Lisbon had to labour endlessly to find enough grain for her daily bread. And the larger the population, the higher the degree of risk to supplies. Venice was already having to buy cattle for consumption from Hungary in the fifteenth century.[88] Istanbul, which had a population in the sixteenth century of perhaps 700,000, ate flocks of sheep from the Balkans, and grain from the Black Sea and Egypt. But if the harsh government of the Sultan had not kept things firmly in hand, the huge city would have been struck by shortages, breakdowns in supply and famines of tragic dimensions – and indeed over the years it was not entirely spared such misfortunes.[89]

The example of London

In its way, London is an exemplary case. It demonstrates, *mutatis mutandis*, everything we might have to say about these precociously tentacular metropolises. And more historical research has been done on London than elsewhere, which enables us to draw conclusions going beyond the picturesque or the anecdotal.[90] N. S. B. Gras[91] was right to see in London a typical example of Von Thünen's rules on the zonal organization of economic space. Such an organization had even appeared around London a century earlier than it had around Paris.[92] The zone drawn upon by London was soon tending to cover virtually the entire area of production and trade in Britain. By the sixteenth century, at any rate, it stretched from Scotland in the north to the Channel in the south, from the North Sea in the east – where the coastal shipping was essential to the capital's daily life – to Wales and Cornwall in the west. But within this space, there were some regions hardly or ineffectively exploited – resistant even – such as Bristol and the surrounding countryside. As in the case of Paris (and as in Von Thünen's schema) the farthest regions sent livestock: Wales had been drawn into the net by the sixteenth century and much later, after the Act of Union of 1707, so was Scotland.

The beating heart of the London market was of course the Thames Valley, the area near the capital, with its easy access by waterway and a ring of staging-post towns (Uxbridge, Brentford, Kingston, Hampstead, Watford, St Albans, Hertford, Croydon, Dartford) which busied themselves in the city's service, grinding grain and sending in flour, preparing malt, dispatching food-stuffs and manufactured goods towards the Great Wen. If we could look at a

The Eastcheap market in London in 1598, described by Stow in his *Survey of London* as a meat market. The houses on either side of the street were inhabited by butchers and by roasting-cooks who sold meat ready to eat. (Photothèque Armand Colin.)

series of pictures of this 'metropolitan' market, we should see it extending and expanding year by year, at the same pace as the growth of the town itself (250,000 inhabitants at most in 1600, 500,000 or more by 1700). The overall population of England was also growing at the time, but not as fast. So as one historian puts it, London 'is going to eat up all England'.[93] And King James I himself said, 'With time England will be only London'.[94] Such statements are both true and false: they underestimate and overestimate. What London was really 'eating up' was not merely the English interior, but also so to speak its exterior – at least two-thirds, possibly three-quarters or four-fifths of its foreign trade.[95] But even assisted by the triple appetite of the Court, the Army and the Navy, London did not swallow absolutely everything, nor draw everything irresistibly towards its wealth and high prices. Indeed national production even increased under its influence, in the English countryside as well as in the small towns 'which distributed more than they consumed'.[96] The flow of services ran both ways, to some extent.

What was in fact being built under pressure from London, was the modernity of English life. The increasing prosperity of the surrounding countryside struck all travellers, who remarked on the servant-girls at the inns ('they could be mistaken for ladies of condition, being very neatly dressed') and the well-clothed peasants, who ate white bread, did not wear clogs like the French peasant, and even rode on horseback.[97] But the whole of England, as well as distant Scotland and Wales, was touched and transformed by the tentacles of the urban octopus.[98] Any region affected by London tended to specialize, to change and become more commercially-minded, in limited sectors as yet it is true, for between the modernized regions there still lay expanses of the old rural régime with its traditional farms and crops. Kent for instance, south of the Thames and close to London, saw orchards and hops cover its fields to supply the capital, but Kent still retained its identity, with its peasant-farmers, its cornfields, livestock, thick forests (the haunt of highwaymen) and – an unmistakable index – its abundant wildfowl: pheasant, partridge, quail, teal, wild duck and the wheatear or English ortolan, 'the most delicious taste for a creature of one mouthful, for 'tis little more, that can be imagined'.[99]

Another effect of the organization of the London market was the dislocation (inevitably, in view of the scale of the enterprise) of the traditional open market, the public market where nothing could be concealed, where producer-vendor and buyer-consumer met face to face. The distance between the two was becoming too great to be travelled by ordinary people. The merchant, or middleman, had already, from at least the thirteenth century, made his appearance in England as a go-between for town and country, in particular in the corn trade. Gradually, chains of intermediaries were set up between producer and merchant on one hand, and between merchant and retailer on the other; along these chains passed the bulk of the trade in butter, cheese, poultry produce, fruit, vegetables and milk. Traditional habits and customs were lost or smashed. Who would have thought that the belly of London or the belly of Paris would cause a revolution? Yet they did so simply by growing.

Some statistics

Developments such as these would be much clearer to see if we had some figures, serial documents or overall balance-sheets. In fact it is possible to find such material and synthesize it, as is demonstrated by the map taken from Alan Everitt's excellent article (1967) on markets in England and Wales from 1500 to 1640;[100] by the map I have compiled of the markets in the *généralité* of Caen in 1722; or by the figures relating to Bavarian markets in the eighteenth century worked out by Eckhart Schremmer.[101] But these studies and others like them are only beginning to open up a promising area of research.

Setting aside the five or six exceptional villages which kept their markets, there were in the sixteenth and seventeenth century some 760 towns with one or more markets in England, and a further 50 in Wales, a total of about 800 localities with regular markets. Supposing the total population of the two countries to have been about 5.5 million inhabitants, each market town must have concerned on average the trading activities of 6000 to 7000 people, while the average population of the locality itself was about 1000. So a market town might animate trade within a community six or seven times the size of its own population. Similar proportions can be found in Bavaria at the end of the eighteenth century: there was one market for every 7300 inhabitants.[102] But this coincidence should not lead us to suppose that there is some sort of law. The proportions must surely have varied with region and period. And one must always check the method of calculation used.

We do know that there were probably more markets in England in the thirteenth century than in Elizabethan England, although the population was much the same size. The explanation must be either increased activity, and therefore a larger radius of influence for each locality in Elizabethan times, or a superabundance of markets in medieval England, possibly because noblemen, either as a point of honour or in hope of gain, set out to create markets. Everitt comments that 'perhaps the history of England's vanished market towns would be as interesting a study as its lost villages'.[103]

With the economic growth of the sixteenth century, especially after 1570, new markets were set up, rising from their former ashes, or rather slumber. And what disputes they caused! Old charters were looked out to see who had or would have the right to collect market dues, who would be responsible for the equipment: 'lanthorne and market bell', cross, weighing-scales, the stalls, cellars or sheds to be hired, and so forth.

At the same time, on a national scale, a division of trade was becoming apparent between markets, according to the nature of the goods on offer, the distances involved, the ease of access to transport or the lack of it, according, in short, to the geography both of production and of consumption. The 800 or so market towns counted by Everitt had an influence over an average radius of about seven miles. In about 1600, grain transported *overland* did not travel more than 10 miles, and 5 was more usual; cattle could be driven up to about 11 miles; sheep 40 to 70 miles; wool and woollen cloth would travel between 20 and 40 miles. Doncaster in Yorkshire, one of the biggest wool markets, had buyers coming, in the time of Charles I, from Gainsborough (21 miles), Lincoln (40 miles), 'Warsop' (25 miles), Pleasley (26 miles), Blankney (50 miles). John Hatcher of Careby in Lincolnshire sold 'his wethers at Stamford, and his cows and oxen at Newark while he bought his steers at Spilsby, his fish at Boston, his wine at Bourne, and his luxuries in London'.

This dispersion indicates how markets were gradually becoming more specialized. Of the 800 market towns of England and Wales, at least 300 confined themselves to single trades: 133 to the grain trade; 26 to malt; 6 to fruit; 92 to cattle markets; 32 to sheep; 13 to horses; 14 to swine; 30 to fish; 21 to wildfowl and poultry; 12 to butter and cheese; over 30 to wool or yarn; 27 or more to woollen cloth; 11 to leather; 8 to linen; at least 4 to hemp – not to mention some very precise and idiosyncratic specialities: Wymondham dealt exclusively in 'wooden spoons, taps and handles'.

The specialization of the markets was of course accentuated in the eighteenth century, and not just in England. If we had the data to mark its statistical progress in the rest of Europe, we should have some kind of map of European growth to replace the purely descriptive information which is all we possess.

However, and this is the most important conclusion to be drawn from Everitt's work, with the increased population and economic growth of sixteenth- and seventeenth-century England, the existing network of regular markets became inadequate, in spite of specialization and concentration and despite the considerable contribution added by fairs – another traditional instrument of exchange, of which more later.[104] The increase in trade encouraged the

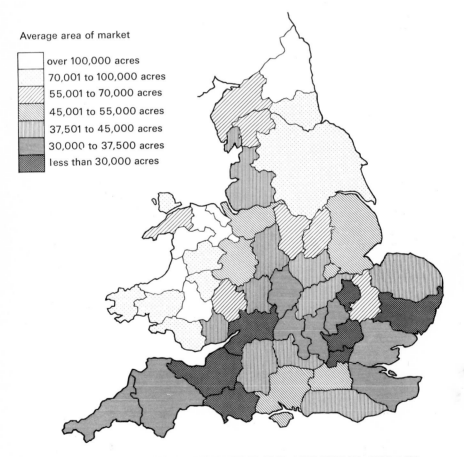

Average area of market

over 100,000 acres
70,001 to 100,000 acres
55,001 to 70,000 acres
45,001 to 55,000 acres
37,501 to 45,000 acres
30,000 to 37,500 acres
less than 30,000 acres

2   DENSITY OF MARKET-TOWNS IN ENGLAND AND WALES, 1500-1680

Calculating the average area served by each market-town, by county, Alan Everitt has obtained figures ranging from over 100,000 acres in the extreme north and west, to less than 30,000 acres. The more densely populated the region, the smaller the area covered by the market. From A. Everitt, "The Market Town" in *The Agrarian History of England and Wales*, vol. IV, ed. J. Thirsk, 1967, p. 497.

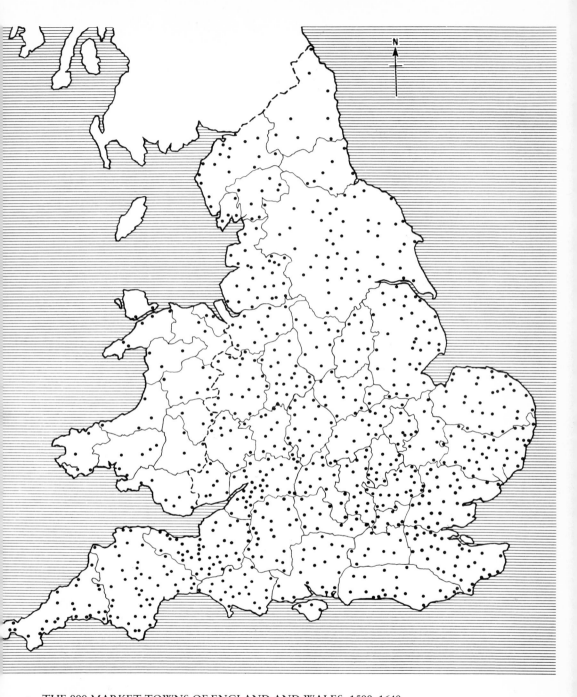

3   THE 800 MARKET TOWNS OF ENGLAND AND WALES, 1500–1640
Each town had at least one market, usually several; and to the markets must be added the fairs.
From the same source as Figure 2, pp. 468–473.

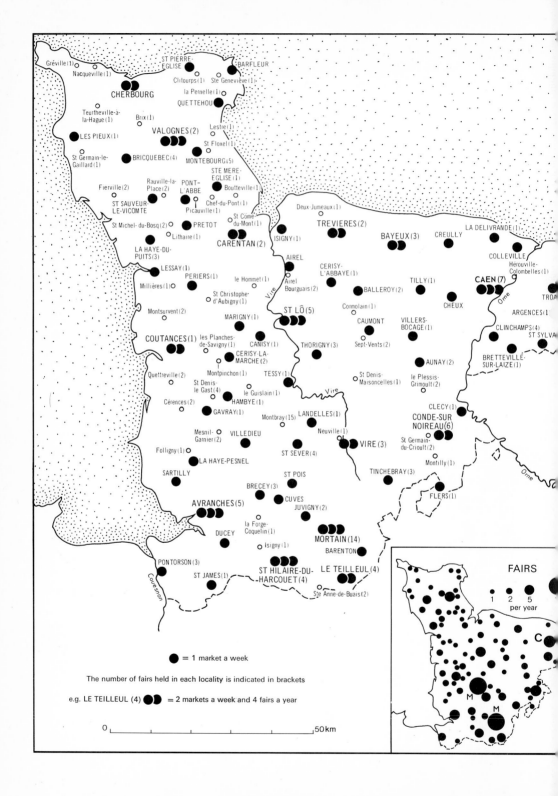

Gréville(1) ○   ○
Nacqueville(1) ○

ST PIERRE-
EGLISE ● BARFLEUR ○

CHERBOURG

Clitourps(1) ○   ○ Ste Geneviève(1)
la Pernelle(1) ○
QUETTEHOU ●

Teutheville-à- ○
la-Hague(1)   Brix(1) ○
LES PIEUX(1) ●   VALOGNES(2) ●●   Lestre(1) ○
St Germain-le- ○ BRICQUEBEC(4) ●●●   St Floxel(1) ○
Gaillard(1)   MONTEBOURG(5) ●

STE MERE-
EGLISE(1) ○
Fierville(2) ○   Rauville-la- ○ PONT- ●   Boutteville(1) ○
                 Place(2)   L'ABBE
ST SAUVEUR- ●   ○ Chef-du-Pont(1)
LE-VICOMTE   Picauville(1) ○

St Michel-du-Bosq(2) ○   PRETOT ●   St Côme- ○
                                     du-Mont(1)
Lithaire(1) ○
LA HAYE-DU-   CARENTAN(2) ●   ISIGNY(1) ○   Deux-Jumeaux(1) ○   TREVIERES(2) ●●   BAYEUX(3) ●   CREULY ●   LA DELIVRANDE(1) ●
PUITS(3)   AIREL ●   COLLEVILLE ●
LESSAY(1) ●   CERISY-   Hérouville-
PERIERS(1) ●   L'ABBAYE(1) ●   Colombelles(1) ●
Millières(1) ○   le Hommet(1) ○ Airel ○   TILLY(1) ●   CAEN(7) ●●   TROA
                  Bourguais(2)   BALLEROY(2) ●   Orne
St Christophe- ○   CHEUX ●   ARGENCES(1)
Montsurvent(2) ○ d'Aubigny(1)   Cormolain(1) ○   CLINCHAMPS(4) ●●
                  MARIGNY(1) ●   ST LÔ(5) ●●   CAUMONT ●   VILLERS-   ST SYLVA
                                                    Sept-Vents(2) ○ BOCAGE(1) ●   BRETTEVILLE-
COUTANCES(1) ●   les Planches- ○   THORIGNY(3) ●   SUR-LAIZE(1) ●
                 de-Savigny(1)   CANISY(1) ●
                 CERISY-LA- ●   AUNAY(2) ●
                 MARCHE(2)   St Denis- ○   le Plessis- ○
Quettreville(2) ○ Montpinchon(1) ○ TESSY(1) ●   Maisoncelles(1) Grimoult(2)
                 St Denis- ●   CLECY(1) ●
Cérences(2) ○   le Gast(4)   HAMBYE(1) ●   CONDE-SUR-
                 le Guislain(1) ○   NOIREAU(6) ●●
                 GAVRAY(1) ●   Montbray(15) ○ LANDELLES(1) ●   St Germain- ○
Folligny(1) ○   Mesnil- ○   Neuville(1) ○   du-Crioult(2)
                 Garnier(2) VILLEDIEU ●   Montilly(1) ○
LA HAYE-PESNEL ● ST SEVER(4) ●   VIRE(3) ●
SARTILLY ○   ST POIS ○   TINCHEBRAY(3) ●
                 BRECEY(3) ●   FLERS(1) ●
AVRANCHES(5) ●●● CUVES ○
                 JUVIGNY(2) ○
DUCEY ○   la Forge- ○
                 Coquelin(1)   MORTAIN(14) ●●●
                 Isigny(1) ○   BARENTON ●
PONTORSON(3) ●
                 ST HILAIRE-DU- LE TEILLEUL(4) ●
ST JAMES(1) ○   HARCOUET(4) ●
Couesnon   Ste-Anne-de-Buais(2) ○

● = 1 market a week

The number of fairs held in each locality is indicated in brackets

e.g. LE TEILLEUL (4) ●● = 2 markets a week and 4 fairs a year

0   50km

FAIRS
1 2 5
per year

use of new channels of communication, freer and more direct. The growth of London contributed to this as we have seen. Hence the rise in the fortunes of what Alan Everitt calls, for want of a better term, *private trading*. This was simply a way of getting round the open or public market which was closely supervised. The initiators of such private trading were 'substantial' travelling merchants, pedlars and salesmen: they went round to the kitchen doors of farms to buy up *in advance* wheat, barley, sheep, wool, poultry, rabbit-skins and sheepskins. In this way, the market was reaching out into the villages. Sometimes the newcomers would hold court in inns, which were beginning a long career as substitutes for the market. They travelled about from county to county, making deals with a shopkeeper here, a pedlar or a wholesaler there. And they acted as wholesalers themselves or as middlemen of every description, willing to deliver barley to brewers in the Netherlands or to buy up rye in the Baltic to supply Bristol. Sometimes two or three of them would join together to share the risks.

That the newcomer with the many faces was detested, hated for his cunning, intransigence and hard-heartedness is abundantly clear from the court cases that cropped up. This new kind of trade, carried on by a simple written note binding upon the vendor (who was often illiterate) led to all kinds of misunderstandings and dramas. For the trader himself though, driving his pack-horses, or supervising grain being embarked on the waterways, the hard travelling life had its charms. He could cross the whole country from Scotland to Cornwall, finding at every inn friends or fellow-traders, and feeling that he belonged to a tough and intelligent confraternity – while making a very good living for himself. This was a revolution which went beyond the economy, into social behaviour. It is no accident, Everitt thinks, that these new trading activities developed at the same time as the appearance of the new political phenomenon of the *Independents*. At the end of the civil war, when roads and highways were once more open to traffic, in about 1647, Hugh Peter, a leading Independent divine, exclaimed:

> Oh, the blessed change we see that can travel now from Edinburgh to the Land's End in Cornwall, who not long since were blocked up at our doors. To see the highways occupied again; to hear the carter whistling to his toiling team; to see the weekly carrier attend his constant mart; to see the hills rejoicing, the valleys laughing.[105]

---

4 MARKETS AND FAIRS IN THE *GÉNÉRALITÉ* OF CAEN IN 1725

Map drawn by G. Arbelot, from information in the Departmental Archives of the Calvados (c 1358). J.-C. Perrot has told me about an extra 6 fairs not shown here (Saint-Jean-du-Val 1, Berry 2, Mortain 1, Vassy 2). The total number of fairs was 197, most of which lasted one day, some 2 or 3, and the great fair of Caen for 15 days. The total number of fair days in a year was 223. There were in addition, a total of 85 markets a week. There were 4420 market days in all in a year. The population of the *généralité* at this time was between 600,000 and 620,000 people; its area was about 11,524 sq. km. Comparable statistics for other areas would enable useful comparisons to be made with other regions of France.

Farmer's wife bringing live fowls to market. Illustration from a manuscript in the British Museum, 1598 (Eg. 1222, f. 73). (Photothèque Armand Colin.)

From England to Europe

Private trading was not confined to England. On the continent too, it seems that merchants were taking to the roads again. The shrewd and active merchant of Basle, Andreas Ryff, who was constantly travelling in all directions during the second half of the sixteenth century – an average of thirty trips a year – said of himself: '*Hab wenig Ruh gehabt, dass mich der Sattel nicht an das Hinterteil gebrannt hat*' (I have had so little rest that the saddle has hardly stopped burning my hindparts).[106] In the present state of our knowledge, it must be said, it is not always easy to distinguish between fair-people, travelling from fair to fair, and merchants going to purchase at the point of production. What is certain is that almost everywhere in Europe, the public market was turning out to be both inadequate and too closely controlled, and wherever observations have been made, detours and ways round the market were being used, or soon would be.

A note in Delamare's *Traité* refers in April 1693 to the fraudulent behaviour of travelling salesmen in Paris who 'instead of selling their wares in the Halles or in the public markets, have been selling them in hostelries and outside'.[107] Delamare also draws up a minute inventory of all the means employed by millers, bakers, butchers, and illegal or irregular merchants and stockpilers, to provide themselves with goods at the lowest cost and to the detriment of the normal supplies coming to market.[108] As early as 1385 in Evreux in Normandy, the defenders of public order were protesting about producers and retailers who agreed among themselves 'by whispering in each other's ear, by speaking low or by signs, and in strange or hidden words'. Another way the rules were bent was by retailers going to meet peasants and buying their produce 'before it reaches the Halles'.[109] At Carpentras in the sixteenth century, *répétières* (women vegetable-sellers) went out on the roads to buy goods being brought in to market.[110] This was frequent practice in all towns.[111] Not that that prevented it being condemned in London as late as April 1764 as fraudulent. The government, says a diplomatic report, 'ought at least to have some care for the murmurs excited among the people by the excessive cost of food; all the more because such murmurs arise from an abuse which may justly be imputed to those who govern ... for the principal cause of the high cost of food ... is the greed of the monopolists of whom there is a multitude in the capital. They have recently contrived to anticipate the market, by going down the highways in search of the countryman and relieving him of the goods he is bringing, to sell them at any price they please.'[112] 'A pernicious crew' adds the correspondent – but the crew was present everywhere.

Everywhere too, ubiquitous and many-faced, persecuted in vain, regular smuggling laughed at rules and at tolls and excise duties. Printed fabrics from India, salt, tobacco, wines, alcohol – it handled everything. At Dole in the Franche-Comté (1st July 1728) 'trade in smuggled goods was carried on openly ... since a merchant had had the temerity to bring an action to make sure he was paid his price for this kind of merchandise'.[113] 'Your worship', wrote one of his agents to Desmarets, last of the controllers-general of Louis XIV's long reign, 'could set an army along the entire coast of Brittany and Normandy but it would never stop fraud'.[114]

Markets and markets: the labour market

Markets, direct or indirect, all the many forms of trading, endlessly worked on economies, even the most quiescent, stirring them up, or as some would say bringing them to life. And the day would in any case come when logically, everything would have to pass through the market, not only the produce of agriculture and industry but land, money which travelled faster than any other merchandise, and labour: men's toil, not to say men themselves.

Transactions had of course always taken place, in town and village, over houses, building plots, lodgings, shops or homes for rent. What is interesting here is not so much the discovery, from the relevant documents, that houses were bought and sold in Genoa in the thirteenth century,[115] or that at the same period, in Florence, plots were rented out on which houses would later be built.[116] The really significant thing is that we find such transactions and exchanges increasing in number, as property markets come into being and sooner or later show bursts of speculative buying. For this to happen, the volume of transactions had to have

The vegetable-seller and her donkey: 'Who'll buy my fine beets, fresh spinach!'
Woodcut, sixteenth century. (Viollet Collection.)

reached a certain level. Such was clearly the case by the sixteenth century in
Paris, as is proved by the fluctuation of rents (including that of shops); their rates
were unmistakably caught up in the successive movements of the economy and
inflation.[117] It was also the case elsewhere as a simple detail shows: at Cesena, a
little town in the prosperous agricultural province of Emilia, the lease for a small
shop, signed on 17 October 1622 and preserved by chance in the local library,
appears in the shape of a printed form: the parties simply filled in the blanks and
signed it.[118] Speculation in these early times also has a modern ring to it:
'promoters' and their clients are not a twentieth-century phenomenon. In Paris,
it is possible to trace sixteenth-century speculation on the space near the Seine,
known as the Pré-aux-Clercs, which long stood empty,[119] or on another waste
patch, Les Tournelles, where a consortium led by *président* Harlay, in 1594 began
the profitable construction of the magnificent houses of the present Place des
Vosges: they were afterwards leased to great noble families.[120] In the seventeenth
century, speculation flourished on the edges of the Faubourg Saint-Germain, and
no doubt elsewhere as well.[121] As the capital sprouted a series of building-sites
during the reigns of Louis XV and Louis XVI, the property market was even
more buoyant. In August 1781, a Venetian informed one of his correspondents
that the fine promenade of the Palais-Royal had been destroyed and its trees cut
down '*nonnostante le mormorazioni di tutta la città*'; the Duc de Chartres had
plans to 'build houses here and offer them for rent'.[122]

The same was true of the land market: 'landed estates' ended up on the
market. In Brittany, *seigneuries* were being bought and sold by the end of the
thirteenth century,[123] as they were no doubt elsewhere, and earlier. In Europe as

a whole, there are some very revealing price series[124] on land sales, and many references to the regular rise in prices. In Spain in 1558 for instance, according to a Venetian ambassador,[125] *'i bene che si solevano lasciare a otto e dieci per cento si vendono a quatro e cinque'*: properties (i.e. land) which used to be sold at 8 to 10%, that is 12.5 or 10 times their revenue, are now selling at 4 and 5%, or 25 to 20 times their revenue; they have doubled 'with the abundance of money'. In the eighteenth century, tenancy agreements for Breton estates were being handled at Saint-Malo with its rich merchants, thanks to chains of intermediaries going all the way to Paris and the *Ferme-Générale*.[126] Advertisements of properties for sale also appeared in gazettes.[127] Advertising was already flourishing. And in any case, with or without advertisements, land was constantly changing hands all over Europe, as people bought, sold and sold again. This movement was of course everywhere linked to the economic and social transformation which was dispossessing the old landowners, whether lord or peasant, for the benefit of the new rich from the towns. Even in the thirteenth century, in the Ile-de-France, there were many 'unlanded gentry' as Marc Bloch called them (*'des seigneurs sans terre'*) and plenty of *seigneuries-croupions* 'rump (i.e. truncated) estates' (Guy Fourquin).[128]

I shall have more to say later about the money market, both long- and short-term. It was at the heart of European growth and it is significant that it did not develop everywhere at the same pace and with the same effectiveness. What was universal, by contrast, was the emergence of people willing to advance funds, and of networks of money-lenders, whether Jews or Lombards, natives of Cahors or, as in Bavaria, convents which specialized in loans to peasants.[129] Every time we come across any information about this, usury appears to be alive and well; and this was true of every civilization in the world.

The forward market in money, on the other hand, could only exist where there was already a highly-charged economy. Such was the case by the thirteenth century in Italy, Germany, and the Netherlands: everything conspired to create such a market in these countries: capital accumulation, long-distance trade, the artifices of the bill of exchange, the early creation of public-debt 'bonds', investment in craft or industrial activities, in shipbuilding, or in voyages made by ships which as they increased enormously in size by the fifteenth century were no longer individually owned. As time went on, the money market moved towards Holland, and later London.

But of all these different markets, the most important, from the point of view of this book, is the labour market. I will, as Marx did, leave aside the classic case of slavery, which was however to be prolonged and even renewed.[130] Our problem is to see how man, or at least his labour, could become a commodity. A perspicacious intellect such as Thomas Hobbes (1588–1679) could already write: 'a mans Labour also is a commodity exchangeable for benefit, as well as any other thing' – something which is normally offered for exchange in the full competition of the market[131] – but this was not a very familiar notion at the time. I find rather engaging a remark by an obscure French consul in Genoa, no doubt a little out of touch with his times: 'This is the first time, Monseigneur, that I have heard that a man may be reckoned money.' Ricardo writes without a moment's hesitation 'Labour, like all other things which are purchased and sold ...'[132]

It is perfectly clear however that the labour market – as a reality if not as a concept – was not a creation of the industrial era. The labour market was the market upon which a man offered himself, without any of his traditional means of production, if he had ever had any: a piece of land, a loom, a horse or cart. All he had to offer was his arm or hand, his 'labour' in other words. And of course his intelligence or skill. The man who hired or sold himself in this way was passing through the narrow opening of the market out of the traditional economy. The phenomenon can be seen with unusual clarity in the case of the miners of Central Europe. Having long been independent artisans, working in small groups, they were obliged in the fifteenth and sixteenth century to put themselves under the control of the merchants who alone could provide the considerable investment required for equipment to mine deep below the surface. And they became wage-earners. The crucial admission can perhaps be seen in the words of the aldermen of Joachimstal, a little mining town in Bohemia: 'One gives money, the other does the work' (*Der eine gibt das Geld, der andere tut die Arbeit*). What better formula for the early confrontation between Capital and Labour?[133] It is true that wage-earning having once been established could sometimes disappear again, as happened in the Hungarian vineyards: in Tokay in the 1570s, at Nagybanyn in 1575, in Szentgyögy Bazin in 1601, peasant serfdom was once again established.[134] But this was peculiar to Eastern Europe. In the West, the transition to wage-earning, an irreversible phenomenon here, often happened quite early and, above all, more frequently than is usually supposed.

From the thirteenth century, the Place de Grève in Paris and the nearby Place 'Jurée' by Saint-Paul-des-Champs, or the square outside Saint-Gervais 'near the *maison de la Conserve*', were the usual places for hiring labour.[135] Some curious contracts for workers at a brickworks near Piacenza in Lombardy, dating from 1288 and 1290, have been found.[136] Between 1253 and 1379, documents prove that there were wage-earners in the Portuguese countryside.[137] In 1393, at Auxerre in Burgundy,[138] workers in the vineyards went on strike (we should remember that towns were still, at this time, half-embedded in agricultural life, and that vines were a sort of industry). From this incident we learn that every day in summer, day-labourers and employers would meet on one of the town's squares at sunrise – the employers often being represented by a sort of foreman, the *closier*. This is one of the earliest labour markets of which we have *concrete* evidence. In Hamburg in 1480, the *Tagelöhner*, day-labourers, went to the *Trostbrücke* to look for a master. Here already was a 'transparent labour market'.[139] In the time of Tallemant de Réaux, 'in Avignon, labourers for hire stood on the bridge'.[140] There were other markets too, if only the 'hirings' at fairs (Mid-summer, Michaelmas, Martinmas, All Saints', Christmas and Easter)[141] when farm labourers and servant-girls offered themselves for inspection by potential masters (rich peasants or noblemen like the *sire* de Gouberville),[142] just like livestock, to have their good qualities valued and checked. 'Every small town or large village in Lower Normandy in about 1560, had its hiring-fair, a sort of cross between a slave-market and a village carnival.'[143] At Evreux, the mid-summer donkey fair (24 June) was also the day for hiring servants.[144] At reaping or grape-harvest, extra labour swarmed from all directions and was hired in the usual way for money or wages in kind. We may be sure that this represented a huge movement of people: from time to time a statistic forcefully confirms this.[145] Sometimes a tiny piece of micro-observation tells the same story: in the country-side round the little town of Château-Gontier in Anjou in the seventeenth and eighteenth centuries,[146] the 'day-labourers' came flocking in 'to cut down trees, saw or break up wood; to prune the vines or harvest the grapes; to weed, dig and garden ... to plant vegetables, bale hay, thresh grain, or clean it'. Records from Paris[147] mention in connection with the transport of hay alone, *'metteurs à port, crocheteurs, baguedeniers, chartiers, botteleurs, gens de journée'* (fork-lifters, binders, carters, balers, all hired by the day). Lists like this and other similar ones give us to reflect, for behind every term one must imagine, in town or countryside, a salaried trade, temporary or permanent. The bulk of the labour market was no doubt provided by the countryside, where the majority of the population lived. Another source of employment created by the development of the modern state was the recruitment of mercenaries for fighting. States knew where to hire them; they knew where to look for work: all according to strict market rules. The same applied to domestic servants – below stairs or above (there was a very strict hierarchy): various placing agencies already existed in Paris by the fourteenth century, and in Nuremberg certainly by 1421.[148]

As years went by, the labour markets became more official and their rules clearer. *Le Livre commode des adresses de Paris pour 1692*, by Abraham du Pradel (the pseudonym of a certain Nicolas de Blégny) gave Parisians useful tips:[149] do you require a serving-girl? Go to the rue de la Vannerie, to the 'bureau of recommenders'; you will find a manservant at the Marché Neuf, a cook at the Grève. A shop-boy or apprentice? If you are a merchant go to the rue Quincam-poix; a surgeon, rue des Cordeliers; an apothecary, rue de la Huchette; 'Limousin stone-masons and labourers' offer their services at the Grève, but 'shoemakers, locksmiths, joiners, coopers, arquebus-makers, roasting-cooks and others hire themselves by coming to the shops'.

The overall history of wage-labour is undoubtedly still poorly documented. But some of the available figures point to the growing body of wage-earning workers. In Tudor England, 'there is evidence that ... well over a half or even two-thirds of all households received some part at least of their income in wages'.[150] In the early seventeenth century, in the Hanseatic towns, notably Stralsund, the mass of wage-earners was constantly increasing, and finally came to represent at least 50% of the population.[151] In Paris, on the eve of the Revolution, the figure would have been over 50%.[152]

The development begun so long ago had not of course by any means reached its full expression by this time. Turgot complains in passing that 'there is no circulation of labour as there is of money'.[153] But the movement had begun and was launched on a course towards all the future would bring in the way of change, adaptation and suffering. That the transition to wage-earning, whatever its motivations and benefits, was accompanied by a certain loss of social standing few would deny. Evidence of this in the eighteenth century comes from the many strikes[154] and the visible impatience of workers. Jean-Jacques Rousseau spoke of the working men who, 'if one should vex them, make short work of packing: they simply fold their arms and go'.[155] Did such susceptibility and social consciousness really begin with the first developments of large-scale industry? Surely not: in Italy, painters were artisans, craftsmen, working in their studios with their employees, who were often their own children. Like merchants, they kept their account-books: those of Lorenzo Lotto, Bassano, Farinati, Guercino have survived.[156] Only the owner of the shop or studio was a merchant, in contact with the customers whose orders he accepted. His assistants, including his own sons who were already quick to rebel even in those days, were at best wage-earners. So one can understand Bernardino India, when he confides to his correspondent Scipione Cibo that although certain established artists, Alessandro Acciaioli and Baldovini, would like him to enter their service, he has refused, because he wishes to keep his liberty and not to give up his own business *per un vil salario*. And this was in 1590![157]

Markets as watersheds

Markets were in fact like watersheds between rivers. It depended which side you were on how you experienced the market. One might be forced to rely entirely upon the market for food, as were among many others the silk-workers of Messina,[158] immigrants to the town who were utterly dependent on the urban food supply (much more so than the city-dwelling nobles or bourgeois, who often had some land outside, a garden perhaps or an orchard and therefore some private resources). And if the poor workers were tired of eating the 'sea-corn', usually half-rotten from its travels, which was used to make the bread sold to them at high prices, the only alternative was to move to Catania or Milazzo changing both their jobs and their food supply – and indeed they did so in 1704.

To people who were not used to the market, to those who were usually excluded or lived far away from it, it seemed like an extraordinary treat, an outing, almost an adventure. It was an opportunity to '*presumir*' as the Spanish said, to display oneself. The sailor, says a trading manual written in the fifteenth century,[159] is generally very primitive: 'he has such a dull mind that when he drinks in a tavern, or buys bread in a market, he thinks he is important'; like the

Eighteenth-century Hungary: a pig is brought to the Debrecen College.
(Author's private collection.)

Spanish soldier[160] who found himself at Zaragoza market between two campaigns, in 1645, and stood amazed at the piles of fresh tunny, salmon-trout, and
hundreds of other fish from the sea or the nearby river. But what did he buy in
the end, with the coins in his purse? A few *sardinas salpesadas* (packed in salt),
which the landlady at the corner tavern grilled for him, a banquet which he
washed down with white wine.

The world of the peasants was of course *par excellence* the zone excluded (or
at least half-excluded) from the market: this was the world of self-sufficiency,
autarky, a self-contained life. Peasants had to be content their lives long with
what they produced with their own hands, or what their neighbours could give
them in exchange for a few goods or services. It is true that many peasants
appeared at the markets in the towns. But those who did no more than buy the
indispensable iron ploughshare, or obtain the money needed to pay their dues
and taxes by selling a few eggs, a lump of butter, a few chickens or vegetables,
were not really integrated into the business of the market. They were on the
fringes, like the Norman peasants 'who bring about 15 or 20 *sols*' worth of goods
to market and cannot enter a tavern without spending at least that'.[161] A village
often communicated with the town only by way of one of the merchants in town
or perhaps through the tenant-farmer of the local estate.[162]

Overleaf: Antwerp market. Anonymous master, late sixteenth century. Antwerp Royal Fine Arts
Museum. (Copyright A.C.L., Brussels.)

This life apart has often been pointed out, and no one can deny its existence. But there were degrees of isolation, and there were exceptions. Many richer peasants made full use of the market: English farmers in a position to sell their crops, for example, who no longer needed to spend the winter spinning and weaving their wool, hemp or flax, and who had become regular customers as well as suppliers of the market; peasants from the compact or dispersed large villages of the United Provinces (sometimes with as many as 3000 or 4000 inhabitants) who produced milk, meat, bacon, cheeses, food- and dye-plants, and bought grain and firewood; the cattle-farmers of Hungary, who exported their herds to Germany and Italy and who also bought grain, which they lacked; all the market-gardeners of the city suburbs (much studied by economists) who were drawn into the life of the city and enriched by it: the fortune of Montreuil, outside Paris, achieved through its peach orchards, astonished Louis-Sébastien Mercier[163] (1783); and who has not heard of localities outside towns like London, Bordeaux, Angoulême, which became prosperous through supplying food?[164] These are all no doubt exceptions, in a peasant world which represented 80 to 90% of the population. But we should not forget that even the poorest rural areas were contaminated by the insidious tentacles of the economy. Coins reached them in various ways outside the regular market. They found their way there through itinerant merchants, town and village moneylenders (like the Jewish moneylenders of the rural areas of Northern Italy),[165] the owners of rural industry, new rich bourgeois and tenant-farmers looking for labour to work their land, and even village shopkeepers.

For all that, the market in the narrow sense remains, for the historian of the *ancien régime* economy, an indicator which he will never be tempted to underestimate. Bistra A. Cvetkova is quite justified for instance in using it as the basis for a sort of graded scale, to measure the economic weight of the Bulgarian towns along the Danube according to the amount of tax levied on sales in the market, noting meanwhile that the taxes were paid in silver *aspres* and that specialized markets already existed.[166] Two or three references to Jassy in Moldavia show that in the seventeenth century, the town possessed 'seven places where goods were sold, some of them named after the principal products on sale, as the *hay fair*, the *flour fair*'.[167] This points to a certain division of trade. Arthur Young goes even further. Coming out of Arras in 1788, he met 'at least an hundred asses, some loaded with a bag, others a sack, but all apparently with a trifling burthen, and swarms of men and women', enough to stock the market and to spare. But 'a great proportion of all the labour in the countryside is idle in the midst of harvest, to supply a town which in England would be provided for by $\frac{1}{40}$ of the people. Whenever this swarm of triflers buz in a market', he concluded, 'I take a minute and vicious division of the soil for granted'.[168] Could it be said then that markets frequented by only a few people, where there was but little amusement and few 'triflers', were the mark of a modern economy?

Beneath the level of the market

As the commercial economy spread, pushing back the limits of neighbouring or more modest activities, the markets grew in size, boundaries were changed and elementary activities modified. Money in the countryside was only rarely used as capital, it is true: it was used for land purchases the aim of which was social promotion; and even more it was hoarded: one thinks of the coins strung on to women's necklaces in Central Europe, the chalices and patens made by village goldsmiths in Hungary,[169] or the gold crosses worn by peasant women in France before the Revolution.[170] But money still played its part in destroying old values and relationships. The peasant who was paid a wage, duly noted in his employer's account-book, even if he received so much of his pay in kind that he practically never had two coins to rub together at the end of the year,[171] had grown accustomed to reckoning in money terms. In the long run, mentalities were changing; and so were work relations, easing the passage to modern society, though never in such a way as to benefit the poorest.

A young economist studying the Basque country, Emiliano Fernandez de Pinedo[172] has succeeded better than anyone else I know in showing how rural property and population were affected by the inexorable progress of the market economy. In the eighteenth century, the Basque country was tending to become a thoroughgoing 'national market', hence the increasing commercialization of rural property; in the end even Church lands and the similarly 'untouchable' land of entailed estates went on the market. As a consequence, land ownership became concentrated in a few hands and the already poor peasants underwent further pauperization, being obliged in larger numbers than ever to pass through the narrow gateway of the labour market, in town or countryside. It was because the market had extended that such upheavals occurred, with irreversible results. *Mutatis mutandis*, this development echoes the process which, much earlier, had led to the large estates of English landowners.

So the market sailed on the tide of history. Even the most modest individual was on a rung in the economic ladder – the lowest, needless to say. Wherever the market is absent, or insignificant, wherever money is so rare that it has a virtually explosive value, one is certain to be observing the lowest plane of human existence, where each man must himself produce almost all he needs. Many peasant societies in pre-industrial Europe were still living at this level, on the margin of the market economy. A traveller among such people, with a few coins in his pocket, could procure all the riches of the earth at ridiculous prices. One did not have to go as Maestre Manrique[173] did to the land of Arakan in 1630, to encounter these surprises, to find oneself choosing thirty chickens for four *reals* or a hundred eggs for two *reals*. One had only to venture away from the main roads, to plunge into the mountain paths, to be anywhere in Sardinia, or to stop at a little-frequented port on the Istrian coast. In short, the only too visible life of the market often conceals from the historian the life going on at the level underneath, a modest but independent life of total or near self-sufficiency. It is another universe, another economy, another society, another culture. Particularly interesting therefore are attempts like those of Michel Morineau[174] or Marco Cattini[175] who both seek to show what was going on underneath the market, what failed to reach it at all, thus providing so to speak the measure of rural self-sufficiency. The procedure followed by both historians is the same: a grain market consists of, on the one hand the populated area dependent upon the market, on the other the demand of a population whose consumption can be calculated according to previously established norms. If, in addition, we know the volume of local production, the prices and quantities released on to the market, how much was consumed locally and how much was exported or imported, we can work out what was happening, or ought to have been happening, *underneath* the market. Michel Morineau based his study on a medium-sized town, Charleville; Marco Cattini took a small town near Modena, one much closer to country life in a slightly isolated region.

A similar plunge into the unknown but using different means, was made by Yves-Marie Bercé[176] in his recent thesis on the rebellions of the *croquants* in seventeenth-century Aquitaine. From a study of these risings, he has reconstituted the mentalities and motivations of a people all too often hidden from history. I particularly like what he has to say about the violent population of the village taverns, the scene of many outbursts.

In short the field is open. Methods, means and approaches may differ (as we have already seen) but it is now established that there can be no complete history, certainly no history of rural society worthy of the name, until we have systematically explored human life below the level of the market.

Shops

The first competition for the markets (though trade benefited from it) came from the shops. These innumerable small units are another elementary instrument of exchange – similar to the market, yet different, for the market is held only at intervals, while a shop is open almost all the time; at least that is the theory, but the rule, if rule there be, admits of many exceptions.

The word *souk* for instance, something peculiar to Muslim towns, is often translated as 'market'. Yet a *souk* is often simply a street lined with shops, all specializing in the same trade, just like the many such to be found in every town in the west. In Paris, the butchers' shops near St Etienne-du-Mont gave to the present-day rue de la Montagne-Sainte-Geneviève the name of *rue des Boucheries* in the twelfth century.[177] In 1656, still in Paris, 'alongside the charnel-house of Saint-Innocent [sic] . . . all the iron, tin, copper and pewter merchants have their shops'.[178] In Lyons in 1643, 'one can find poultry in special shops, at the *Poulaillerie* in the rue Saint-Jean'.[179] And there were also streets of luxury shops (see Figure 5, plan of Madrid), like the *Merceria* between St Mark's Square and

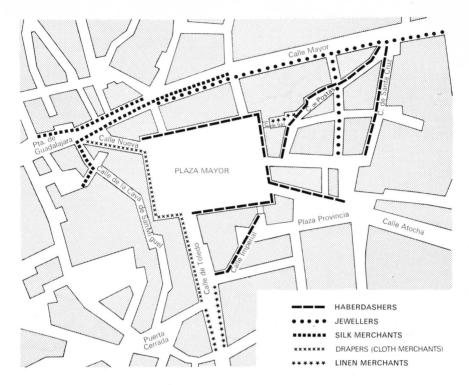

Legend:

- ▬ ▬ ▬ HABERDASHERS
- ● ● ● ● JEWELLERS
- ■■■■■■ SILK MERCHANTS
- ×××××× DRAPERS (CLOTH MERCHANTS)
- ★★★★★ LINEN MERCHANTS

Map labels: Calle Mayor, C. de Santa Cruz, C. de Postas, Pta. de Guadalajara, Calle Nueva, C. de Sal, Calle de la Cava de San Miguel, Calle de Toledo, Calle Imperial, PLAZA MAYOR, Plaza Provincia, Calle Atocha, Puerta Cerrada

5   MADRID AND ITS LUXURY SHOPS

The capital of Spain since 1560, Madrid was launched on a brilliant career in the seventeenth century. Many shops were opened. Around the Plaza Mayor, luxury shops were grouped in rows according to their wares. From M. Copella, A. Matilla Tascón, *Los Cinco Gremios mayores de Madrid*, 1957.

the Rialto, which gives, says a traveller in 1680, a grand impression of Venice,[180] or the shops on the north side of the Old Port of Marseilles, where merchandise from the Levant was sold, 'and [which] are so sought after', noted the *président* de Brosses, 'that a space twenty feet square is let at 500 *livres*'.[181] Streets like these were specialized markets of a kind.

For another exception to the rule, one can look outside Europe to two unusual examples. According to travellers, Szechwan, that is the upper basin of the Yangtse-Kiang, which had been reoccupied in force by Chinese colonization in the seventeenth century, was a zone of scattered settlements isolated from each other, whereas in China proper, the population was concentrated in centres. Yet in this area of low population density, groups of small shops, *yao-tien*, were set up in the middle of nowhere, and played the role of a *permanent* market.[182] Again according to travellers, the same was true of Ceylon in the seventeenth century: there were no markets, but there were shops.[183] And back in Europe, what should we call the booths, or hastily-erected stalls in the streets of Paris, unsuccessfully banned by ordinance in 1776? They were temporary structures as in a market – but they were open for trade every day, like shops.[184] To compound our confusion even further, in England some places, like Westerham, had their row of drapers' and grocers' shops long before they had their market.[185] And then again, there were so many shops on the market place itself: the market might open, but they continued to do business. Or, another problem of definition, when in the Halles in Lille someone owned a place to sell salt fish below the seafood merchants, was not this combining market and shop?[186]

But confusions like this do not of course prevent the shop from becoming gradually distinct from the market, a distinction that grows clearer over the years.

When in the eleventh century, towns were created or re-created all over western Europe, and the markets became busy once more, the burst of urban growth established a clear distinction between town and country. In the former were concentrated both newly-born industry and the consequently active artisan population. The first shops, which appeared immediately, were really the workshops of bakers, butchers, shoemakers, cobblers, blacksmiths, tailors and other artisans who sold their products. At first such an artisan was obliged to leave the shop, to which however his work bound him 'like a snail to its shell',[187] in order to go and sell his wares in open markets or halls. The urban authorities, who were determined to defend consumers, obliged him to do this, as the market was easier to supervise than the shop, where every man was virtually his own master.[188] But before long, the artisan was selling from his own shop 'from the window' as they said, in the *interval* between market days. So this alternating activity made the earlier shops places of intermittent business, rather like markets. In Evora in Portugal, in about 1380, the butcher would cut up the meat in his shop and sell it at one of the three markets of the week.[189] To someone from Strasbourg, it was surprising to find in Grenoble in 1643 that the butchers cut up and sold their meat in their own shops instead of at market, offering it for sale 'in a shop like other merchants'.[190] In Paris, the bakers generally sold ordinary or fancy bread in their shops, and coarse bread on the market, every Wednesday and Saturday.[191] In May 1718, yet another edict (as Law's system was being established) upset the currency; so 'the bakers, from fear or malice, did not bring the usual quantity of bread to market; by midday there was no bread to be found on the public squares; and what was worse, the same day, they put up the price by two or four sous a pound, proof', as the Tuscan ambassador, who is our informant points out, 'that there is not here that good order one finds elsewhere'.[192]

The first people to have shops then were the artisans. 'Real' shopkeepers arrived later: they were the middlemen of exchange, inserting themselves between producer and consumer, and confining their activities to buying and selling: the goods they sold were not (or not entirely at any rate) the work of their own hands. From the start, they were like the capitalist merchant as defined by Marx:

A baker's shop and a draper's side by side in Amsterdam. Painting by Jacobus Vrel, Dutch school, seventeenth century (Amsterdam, H.A. Wetzlar collection). (Photo Giraudon.)

he begins with money (M), acquires goods (G) and returns regularly to money, in a pattern MGM: 'He parts with his money only with the intention of getting it back again'. The peasant, by contrast, usually comes to sell his goods on the market in order to buy immediately whatever he needs: he begins with goods and ends with goods: GMG. And the artisan who also has to go to the market for his food, does not long remain in the position of holding money. But exceptions were possible.

The middleman, a separate and before long a very frequent figure, was the man of the future. And it is his future that most concerns us, rather than his origins, which remain obscure, although the process was probably a simple one: the travelling merchants, who had survived the decline of the Roman Empire, were surprised in the eleventh century and no doubt earlier too, by the rise of the towns: some settled down and joined urban guilds. The phenomenon cannot be precisely dated nor located. It did not happen 'in the thirteenth century' in Germany and France, for instance but some time *from the thirteenth century on*.[193] The 'dusty traveller' might, even as late as the reign of Louis XIII, give up his wandering life and set himself up alongside the artisans, in a shop similar to theirs, but with a difference – and one that became clearer with time. An eighteenth-century baker was much the same as a thirteenth-century baker or even one from an earlier century still. But between the fifteenth and eighteenth century, retail shops and retailing methods were visibly transformed.

And yet the merchant with a shop did not immediately become distinguished from the city guilds where he found himself once he had settled into the urban community. He retained from his origins and the confusions surrounding them a kind of original sin. As late as 1702, a French report argues: 'It is true that the merchants are considered as the first among the artisans, as being a little above the others, but no more.'[194] But then this was France where even if he became a '*négociant*' or wholesaler, the merchant was far from resolving *ipso facto* the problem of his social status. The representatives of commerce were still bewailing the fact in 1788 that even at this date, *négociants* were considered as 'occupying one of the lower classes of society'.[195] One would not have heard this kind of talk in Amsterdam, London or even Italy.[196]

In the early days, and often until the nineteenth century, shopkeepers would sell, indiscriminately, goods obtained at first, second or even third hand. The name they were originally given, *mercer* in English (*mercier* in French) is revealing: it comes from the Latin *merx, mercis*, merchandise in general. A French proverb says 'A shopkeeper (*mercier*) sells everything, makes nothing'. And whenever we have records of the stock in such shops, we find the strangest assortment of goods, whether in fifteenth-century Paris,[197] Poitiers,[198] Krakow,[199] Frankfurt-am-Main[200] or the shop kept by Abraham Dent in Kirkby Stephen, a small town in Westmorland, northern England, in the eighteenth century.[201]

This grocery and general store, which is known to us because its books of

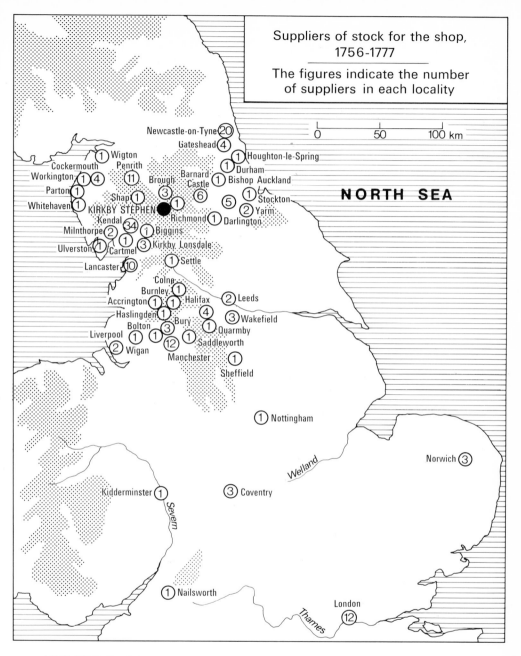

Suppliers of stock for the shop,
1756-1777

The figures indicate the number
of suppliers in each locality

0   50   100 km

Newcastle-on-Tyne (20)
Gateshead (4)
Wigton (1)
Houghton-le-Spring (1)
Cockermouth   Penrith (11)
Durham (1)
Workington (1)(4)   Brough   Barnard (1) Bishop Auckland
Parton (1)   Castle (3)(1)(6)   Stockton (1)
Shap (1)   (5)   Yarm (2)
Whitehaven (1)   KIRKBY STEPHEN ●
Kendal (34)   Richmond (1) Darlington
Milnthorpe (2) (1) Biggins
Ulverston (1)(1)(3) Kirkby Lonsdale
Cartmel
Lancaster (10)   Settle (1)

NORTH SEA

Colne
Burnley (1)
Accrington (1)(1) Halifax   Leeds (2)
Haslingden (1)   (4)   Wakefield (3)
Bury   Quarmby (1)
Bolton (3)   Saddleworth
Liverpool (1)(1)(12)(1)
(2) Wigan   Manchester (1)
Sheffield

Nottingham (1)

Welland   Norwich (3)

Kidderminster (1)   Coventry (3)

Severn

Nailsworth (1)   London
Thames   (12)

6   THE SUPPLIERS OF THE SHOPKEEPER ABRAHAM DENT OF KIRKBY STEPHEN
(From T.S. Willan, *Abraham Dent of Kirkby Stephen*, 1970.)

A Scottish 'groceress' behind her counter in 1790: she sells among other things sugar-loaves, green tea, (Hyson), fabric, lemons, candles (?). Her gold earrings and jet necklace tell us that she was a woman of substance. (People's Palace, Glasgow.) (Photo by the Museum.)

1756 to 1776 have survived, sold practically everything. One prominent item was tea (both black and green) of different qualities – and at high prices, because Kirkby Stephen was inland and thus unable to take advantage of smuggling; then came sugar, treacle, flour, wine and brandy, beer, cider, barley, hops, soap, Spanish white (a finely powdered chalk used as a pigment), lampblack, pearl ashes, beeswax, tallow, candles, tobacco, lemons, almonds, raisins, vinegar, peas, pepper, 'the usual condiments and spices', mace, cloves. And Abraham Dent also sold all kinds of haberdashery: silk, cotton and woollen fabrics, needles, pins, etc. He even stocked books, bound magazines, almanacs, and paper. In fact it is easier to list what he did not sell: viz. salt (which is hard to explain), eggs, butter and cheese (these no doubt were easy to find at market).

The chief customers of the shop were naturally the inhabitants of the town and of the surrounding villages. The suppliers (see the map in Figure 6)[202] came from a much wider area, although there were no waterways serving Kirkby

Stephen. But overland transport, although no doubt expensive, was regular, and the carriers accepted, along with the goods, the inland bills of exchange with which Abraham Dent made his payments. Credit was used on a large scale, both for the benefit of the shop's customers, and for that of the shopkeeper himself *vis-à-vis* his suppliers.

Abraham Dent was not content merely to be a shopkeeper: he bought up knitted stockings which he had made in Kirkby Stephen and the neighbourhood. This made him an industrial entrepreneur, a hosier, trading in his own products, which were usually destined for the English army, by way of the wholesalers in London. And as the latter settled their accounts by allowing him to draw bills of exchange on them, Dent became, it seems, a dealer in bills of exchange: the bills he handled far exceeded the volume of his own business. Handling bills meant, in effect, lending money.

From T. S. Willan's book, one has the impression that Dent was an unusual shopkeeper, virtually a businessman. This may be so. But I once came across a shopkeeper, in a little town in Galicia in Spain in 1958, who strangely resembled him: one could buy anything in his shop, one could order anything and even cash cheques there. In short, perhaps the general store was simply meeting the whole range of local needs? It was up to the shopkeeper to find ways of becoming successful. There was, it seems, in fifteenth-century Munich, another unusual shopkeeper, whose account-books have survived.[203] He went to fairs and markets, bought goods at Nuremberg and Nordlingen and even went to Venice. And yet he was a very ordinary small trader, to judge by his humble lodgings, a single room, poorly furnished.

Specialization and hierarchies

But although there were survivals like this, economic development was creating other forms of specialized shops. Gradually a distinction appeared between those who sold by weight: grocers, *épiciers*; those who sold by measure: drapers and tailors; those who sold objects: ironmongers; those who sold used utensils, clothes or furniture: second-hand dealers. There were huge numbers of the last: over 1000 in Lille in 1716.[204]

Special kinds of shop, encouraged by the development of 'services', were those of the apothecary, the pawnbroker, the money-changer or banker, the innkeeper who was often an intermediary for carriers, and the tavern-keepers or 'wine-merchants who keep tables and linen and serve meals'[205] who began to appear everywhere in the eighteenth century, to the horror of respectable people. It is true that some had sinister reputations, like the *cabaret* in the rue aux Ours in Paris, 'which resembles a brigands' lair or thieves' kitchen more than a place for honest folk'[206] in spite of the tempting smell of roast meat coming from the nearby roasting shops. To this list could be added the scribes and even notaries, at least in Lyons, where they could be seen 'sitting in their shops like shoemakers, waiting for trade' – according to a traveller passing through the city in 1643.[207] But there were also well-to-do notaries by the seventeenth century. And by contrast there were public scribes too poor to have their own shops, like those who sat out in the open at the Saints-Innocents in Paris, under the columns; they managed to make some money all the same, since so many valets, serving-girls and poor people were unable to read or write.[208] And the brothels, *casas de carne* as they were called in Spain, were another kind of shop. In Seville '*en la calle de la Serpiente*, the Street of the Serpent,' says the *Burlador* of Tirso de Molina,[209] 'one can see Adam go gallivanting like a true Portuguese . . . and even at a ducat a time, your purse is soon empty'.

There were shops and shops then – and traders and traders. Money soon introduced distinctions; almost immediately it led to a hierarchy in the old trade of 'shopkeeper': at the top, a few very rich merchants, specializing in long-distance trade; at the bottom, the poor pedlars of needles and oilcloth, of whom the proverb cruelly says 'small trade, small basket' (*petit mercier, petit panier*) and whom even a servant-girl, especially if she had some savings, would not stoop to marry. As a rule, everywhere one group of merchants sought to set itself above the rest. In Florence, the *Arti Maggiori* were distinguished from the *Arti Minori*. In Paris, from the ordinance of 1625 until the edict of 10 August 1776, there were six *Corps* or Guilds: in order, the drapers, the grocers, the money-changers, the goldsmiths, the haberdashers and the furriers. The top people in Madrid were the *Cinco Gremios Mayores* who played a considerable financial role in the eighteenth century. In London it was the twelve Merchant Companies. In Italy, and in the free cities of Germany, the distinction was even more clear: the wealthy merchants in fact became an aristocracy, a patriciate: they formed the government of the great trading cities.

How shops came to rule the world

The important thing from our point of view is how shops of all categories came to conquer and devour the towns – all towns and soon even villages as well, where by the seventeenth century and above all in the eighteenth, inefficient shopkeepers, third-rate innkeepers and taverners were beginning to appear. The last-mentioned, who were also small-scale usurers but at the same time 'organizers of collective festivities', were still to be found in the French countryside in the nineteenth and twentieth centuries. It was to the village inn or café that one went to 'game, to talk, to drink and find distraction . . . where debtor met creditor, merchant met client, deals were made and leases signed'. It was the poor man's inn. Café and church were the twin poles of village life.[210]

There is an abundance of evidence of this takeover by the shops. In the seventeenth century, it became a deluge, a flood: in 1606, Lope de Vega could write of Madrid, now a capital city, '*Todo se ha vuelto tiendas*' (everything has turned into shops).[211] And indeed the *tienda* became one of the favourite settings

A luxury boutique in Madrid in the latter part of the eighteenth century: the antique shop. The décor is like that described by Defoe in the new shops in London at the beginning of the century. Painting by Luis Paret y Alcazar, Madrid, Lazaro Museum. (Photo Scala.)

for the action of picaresque novels. In Bavaria, shopkeepers 'are becoming as numerous as bakers'.[212] In London in 1673, the French ambassador had had to leave his house, because it was being knocked down 'to make way for new buildings': he looked in vain for new lodgings, 'which you will find hard to credit', he writes, 'in such a big city ... But as most of the larger houses have been knocked down *since I have been here* and turned into shops and small lodgings for merchants, there are very few to let', and those at exorbitant prices.[213] According to Daniel Defoe, the spread of shops occurred 'monstrously':[214] in 1663, the 'mercers' numbered only about 50 or 60 in the whole city; by the end of the century, there were 300 or 400: luxury shops were transformed at great expense, the walls were covered in mirrors, and gilded columns, bronze ornaments and candelabra appeared, to the disgust of Defoe, who considered them extravagant. But a French visitor in 1728 was very taken with the first shop-windows: 'What we do not on the whole have in France,' he notes, 'is glass like this, generally very fine and very clear. The shops are surrounded with it and usually the merchandise is arranged behind it, which keeps the dust off, while still displaying the goods to passers-by, presenting a fine sight from every direction.'[215] At the same time, the shops were tending to move westwards, following the expansion of the city and the migration of the rich. Paternoster Row had long been their shopping street, until one day Covent Garden became fashionable for about ten years, before in turn giving way to Ludgate Hill, and later still, Round Court, Fenchurch Street and Houndsditch. But it was the same story in all cities. The shops increased in number, took over the streets for their displays, and moved from one district to another.[216] One can see how the cafés spread in Paris for instance,[217] how the banks of the Seine (where the *Petit Dunkerque* opened, a café particularly admired by Voltaire)[218] gradually supplanted the *galerie du Palais*, where the bustle of trade had been the great sight of the city in Corneille's time.[219] Even small urban centres underwent similar transformations. In the early eighteenth century, this was the case of the 'new town' of Valetta in Malta, where 'the shops of mercers and small retailers' according to a detailed report,[220] have 'proliferated so much that no single shopkeeper can make an adequate living. They have to steal, or rapidly go bankrupt. They never have well-stocked shops, and it is distressing to see so many young people going into a business which swallows up perhaps the previously untouched dowry of their wives, or their parents' inheritance, and all for a sedentary and good-for-nothing occupation' (*una occupatione sedentaria et cosi poltrona*). The same virtuous reporter indignantly points out that in many Maltese houses, gold and silver objects were becoming common, 'a useless and dead' kind of investment; that men, women and children of inferior birth drape themselves in fine cloth and lace mantles; and worst of all that the *putane*, prostitutes, parade in carriages, dressed in silk. At the very least, he suggests, without a smile, since there is a prohibition on this, they should be taxed, '*un tanto al mese per dritto d'abiti*'! Was he complaining about an early version of the consumer society?

But there were degrees of development. When in 1815, Jean-Baptiste Say revisited London after an absence of some twenty years (his first trip had been in 1796) he was amazed: strange shops offering their wares at reduced prices, hucksters everywhere, and large notices, some 'stationary' others 'walking about, so that passers-by can read them without stopping for a minute'. London had just invented the sandwich-man.[221]

Some explanations of the boom in shopkeeping

Everywhere there had been a remarkable increase in the distribution of goods, and the pace of trade had quickened (as both markets and fairs confirm). Using today's language, we might say that this marked the triumphant appearance of a *tertiary sector*, as shops provided a fixed point of sale and the number of services was extended, a trend in keeping with the overall development of the economy.

This rise could be charted with a whole range of statistics if it were possible to calculate the ratio of shops to population;[222] the respective percentages of tradesmen's shops and retail shops; or the average size and income of shops. Werner Sombart[223] has drawn attention to the evidence of Justus Möser, a reliable historian who observed with some chagrin of his home-town of Osnabrück in 1774 that 'the mercers have tripled in number over the last century, while the artisans have diminished by a half'. The historian Hans Mauersberg,[224] has recently provided some similar observations, this time with statistics, covering a series of large German towns. From a few samples taken from inventories drawn up on decease, one in Madrid during the reign of Philip IV,[225] two others from Catalan and Genoese retail shops in Sicily in the seventeenth century,[226] the picture is of poor shops, vulnerable and threatened, and usually leaving debts when the business was wound up. In this little world, bankruptcies were commonplace. One even has the impression, though it *is* only an impression, that conditions were ripe in the eighteenth century for some active type of 'Poujadism', if small shopkeepers had been able to speak their minds. In London, when the Fox administration tried to tax them in 1788, the government had to back-pedal quickly, faced with the 'general discontent [that the act had provoked] among the people'.[227] Even if the shopkeepers were not 'the people' – and they evidently were not – they could arouse popular protest on occasions. In Paris in 1793 and 1794, the *sans-culottes* were largely recruited among the semi-proletariat of small shopkeepers.[228] This may incline one to lend more credence to a report, at first sight apparently exaggerated, that in Paris in 1790, 20,000 traders were on the verge of bankruptcy.[229]

That said, from what we know so far, we can state:

1) that the population increase, the long-term upward trend of the economy, and the desire of the 'retail merchant' to have his own establishment, led to the expansion of the distribution network. The fact that there were, in the end, too many outlets proves at most that the rise in the retail trade ran ahead of economic growth, and placed too much confidence in it;
2) the fixed point of sale, the long opening hours, advertising, bargains and word of mouth all helped the shop. People went in for a chat, as much as to buy anything. It was a place of entertainment, as one can see from the amusing and realistic dialogues composed by the author of the *Bourgeois poli* of Chartres.[230] Indeed Adam Smith, in one of his rare flashes of humour, compares man, who can talk, with the animals who are deprived of this privilege: 'The propensity to truck, barter and exchange one thing for another ... [may be] as seems probable ... the necessary consequence of the faculty of reason and speech ... Nobody ever saw a dog make a fair and deliberate exchange of one bone for another with

État des dettes actives du S.r Guenée

M.e Boullanger à paris toutte causes pour
fournitures de pain par luy faittes à credit aux Sieurs
et D.es cy après nommés

Sçavoir

C.o le S.r Dupuis M.d de Vin à paris	130	" "
La D.e Renaud	20	" "
M. D. Bonneuil Conseiller au parlement	250	" "
Mad. outriquin mère	80	" "
M. Brisbare officier a la halle	10	" "
M. Joudilac commis	16	" "
M.e hovion	30	" "
M. D. Gauge Tresorier extraordinaire des guerres	200	" "
M.d Audin	100	" "
M. Dechabreul	400	" "
M. le Marquis Desfresnaire	110	" "
M. faria conseiller au parlement	40	" "
M. Bonnier Rotisseur	169	" "
M. Dutillet conseiller au parlement	115	" "
M. Samson	15	" "
M. Moulvieu	110	" "
M. outriquin fils	80	" "
M. Hivoire fournier	30	" "
M. Boines	66	" "
M.d D. Bourges	80	" "
M. Daubigny	40	" "
M. Journée	25	" "
M. Caurin M.d d'étoffes	60	" "
M. cheviny	12	" "
M.d Jallienne	10	" "
M. Savart	180	" "
M. Guillaume Notaire	30	" "
M.d La Bailliffe	160	" "
M. D. Beauripaire	160	" "
M.d Le Comte	24	" "
	2752	" "

another dog.'[231] For people, who like talking, the exchange of words is indispensable – even if the exchange of objects does not always follow;
3) but the principal reason for the development of shops was *credit*. One step up from the shops, the wholesaler granted credit; the retailer had to pay what we would today call instalments. The Guicciardini Corsi,[232] wealthy Florentine merchants, who sometimes imported Sicilian grain (and who advanced money to Galileo, as this important family still proudly remembers today) sold pepper from their warehouses to retailers with eighteen months' credit, as their order books show. And they were by no means innovators in this respect. But the shopkeeper himself granted credit to his customers – and to the rich more readily than to the poor. The tailor gave credit; the baker gave credit (recorded on two pieces of wood[233] which were marked simultaneously with chalk every day, one to be kept by the baker and the other by the customer); the tavern-keeper gave credit[234] (the drinker chalked up his bill himself on the wall); and the butcher gave credit. 'I have known a family', writes Defoe, 'whose revenue has been some thousands a year, pay their butcher, and baker, and grocer, and cheese-monger, by a hundred pounds at a time, and be generally an hundred more in each of their debts'.[235]

Or take the second-hand clothes dealer Fournerat whose name appears in the *Livre commode des adresses* (1692),[236] as under the pillars of the Halles, and who claims to be able to keep 'a man in good clothes for four *pistoles* a year': I should be very surprised if this very particular supplier of 'off-the-peg' clothes was always paid in advance by his customers. The same goes for the three associated second-hand dealers in the rue Neuve, in the parish of Sainte-Marie in Paris, who offered their services for all 'mourning-wear, cloaks, crepe, mourning-bands even black suits to be worn during the ceremonies'.[237]

The shopkeeper then, a capitalist in a very small way, lived between those who owed him money and those to whom he owed it. It was a precarious sort of living, and one was always on the verge of disaster. It only took one 'supplier' (that is a middleman acting for a wholesaler, or the wholesaler himself) to put a gun to the shopkeeper's head, for the nightmare to come true. Or a rich customer might fail to pay his bills and a fishwife would be ruined. 'I was just beginning

---

A Paris baker goes bankrupt, 28 June 1770. A certain Guesnée, a master baker in Paris, filed a statement of affairs before the consular jurisdiction of Paris, distinguishing as was the rule between the bankrupt's 'active debts' and 'passive debts' or as we would say his assets and his liabilities. The page reproduced here, the first of four sheets in the file, clearly shows a series of sales on credit. The major debtors were among others, councillors in the Paris Parlement. The passive debts were purchases of flour, again on credit. Our baker owned a shop, 'the tools of the trade', a cart and horse for deliveries, total value estimated at 6600 *livres*, while his household effects were valued at 7400 *livres*. The reader will no doubt be glad to learn that the master-baker was able to reach agreement with his creditors. Let us hope his customers paid their bills in time. (Archives of the *département* of the Seine, D4 B6, 11, file 526.)

An apothecary's shop: fresco in the castle of Issogna in Val d'Aosta, late fifteenth century. (Photo Scala.)

to earn a living', she says (1623) 'and now I am reduced to my last farthing'.[238] Any shopkeeper ran the risk of being paid late, or not at all. An armourer, François Pommerol, who also wrote poems, complained in 1632[239] of his situation in which:

> Il faut peiner et pour estre payé
> Patienter quand on est délayé.
>
> (You break your back, and to be paid
> You must be patient if delayed).

This is the most common complaint to be found in all the surviving correspondence of small traders, middlemen and suppliers. 'We write you these lines to enquire once more when you will be pleased to pay us', 28 May 1669. 'Monsieur, I am much astonished that my often repeated letters have so little effect; one should at least have the goodness to reply to an honest man', 30 June 1669. 'We should never have believed that after having assured us that you would come to the shop to settle your account, you would have gone away without saying a word', 1 December 1669. 'I do not know how one should write to you, as I see you pay no attention to the letters I write you', 28 July 1669. 'It is six months now since I asked you to send me the settlement', 18 August 1669. 'I see my letters to you are but a waste of time', 11 April 1676. All these letters were written by merchants in Lyons.[240] I could not find again for reference one in which the exasperated creditor warns the defaulter that he is on his way to Grenoble and will settle accounts himself with his fists. A merchant of Reims, who was a contemporary of Louis XIV and reluctant to lend money, quotes the proverb: 'When he borrows money, he's your cousin; when it comes to paying, he's a whoreson.'[241]

Defaulters on debts set up a long chain of difficulties and dependencies. In October 1728, at the Fair of the Holy Sacrament in Dijon, cotton fabrics sold quite well, but not wool or silk. 'It is thought that the reason is that the retail merchants complain that they do little business, and that since they are not paid by those to whom they sell, they are unable to make more purchases. And in addition, the wholesale merchants who come to the fairs refuse to give credit upon credit to most of the retailers, who do not pay them.'[242]

To counter this picture, there is the argument of Defoe, who explains at length how the chain of credit is the foundation of trade, how all debts cancel each other out, and that as a consequence there is an increase in the activity and income of traders. The drawback of archives is that they do tend to collect for the historian's attention the bankruptcies, lawsuits and disasters, rather than the regular flow of business. Happiness, whether in business or private life, leaves little trace in history.

Pedlars

Pedlars were merchants, usually poor ones, who carried on their backs their very meagre stock. Nevertheless, taken in the mass, they add up to an appreciable volume of trade. They filled in the gaps in the regular channels of distribution, even in towns, though mostly in villages and hamlets. Since the gaps were plentiful, so were the pedlars, and this too was a sign of the times. They went under a series of names: in France *colporteur* (one who carries goods literally 'on his neck'), *contreporteur*, *porte-balle*, *mercelot*, *camelotier*, *brocanteur*; in England, hawker, huckster, petty chapman, pedlar, packman; in Germany, every region had a different name for the traveller: *Hocke*, *Hueker*, *Grempler*, *Hausierer*, *Ausrufer* – and the words *Pfuscher* or *Bonhasen* still exist. In Italy, he was the *merciajuolo*, in Spain the *buhonero*. And there were special names too in Eastern Europe: *seyyar satici* in Turkish (which means both pedlar and small shopkeeper); *sergidzyja* (from the Turkish *sergi*) in Bulgarian; *torbar* (from the Turkish *torba* = a sack) or *torbar i srebar*, or *Kramar* or *Krämer* (a word of evident German origin denoting equally a pedlar, a caravan-driver or a petty-bourgeois) in Serbo-Croat,[243] etc.

This string of names shows that peddling, far from being confined to a precise social category, was a combination of different trades which refused to obey any general classification: a Savoyard knife-grinder in Strasbourg in 1703[244] was a workman who 'peddled' his services and travelled about, as did so many chimney sweeps or chair-caners; a 'Maragat'[245] a peasant from the Cantabrian mountains, was a carter who carried corn, wood, staves for casks, kegs of salt fish, coarse woollen cloth, depending on whether he was travelling from the cereal- and wine-growing plateaux of Old Castile to the coast, or vice versa; he was also, in a picturesque phrase, a vendor *en ambulancia*[246] since he had bought all or part of the merchandise he was carrying, on his own account, in order to sell it again. And one would have to describe as pedlars too the weavers from the cottage-industry village of Andrychow, near Krakow, or at least those of them who went to sell the cloth produced in the village at Warsaw, Gdansk, Lwow, Tarnopol, at the Lublin and Dubno fairs, and who even travelled as far as Istanbul, Smyrna, Venice and Marseilles. These peasants who were so ready to leave their native village sometimes became 'pioneers of navigation on the Dniestr and the Black Sea' (1782).[247] On the other hand, what is one to call the rich Manchester merchants, or the manufacturers from Yorkshire and Coventry who went on horseback all over the English countryside delivering their goods in person to the shopkeepers? 'Saving their wealth', wrote Defoe[248], they are 'a kind of pedlars'. And the term could also be applied to the merchants known in France as *forains*[249] (literally from another town) who travelled in France and elsewhere from fair to fair, but were sometimes quite comfortably-off.

Rich or poor, pedlars stimulated and maintained trade, and spread it over a distance. But where they *dominated*, it can usually be shown that the region was in some respects economically backward. Poland was economically behind western Europe: so naturally, the pedlar was an important figure. Indeed peddling can be seen as a survival of what was, for century upon century in the past, normal trading. The Syri[250] of the Late Roman Empire were pedlars. The image of the merchant, in medieval Europe, was that of a grimy and dusty traveller – the classic portrait of a pedlar. A lampoon of 1622[251] describes this old-fashioned merchant, with 'a satchel hanging at his side, shoes of which only the tips are leather'; his wife walks behind him, sheltered from the heat 'by a great hat hanging down to her waist'. But of course one day this pair of wanderers would settle down in a shop, assume a new identity and turn out to be less wretched than they had appeared. Were there not among the pedlars – those with carts at least – some potentially rich merchants? If chance took a hand, they moved up the ladder. It was nearly always the pedlars who set up the modest village shops we have mentioned, in the seventeenth century. They even tried their fortune in the big trading cities: in Munich, 50 Italian or Savoyard firms established there in the eighteenth century had been founded by pedlars who had made good.[252] Similar establishments may have been set up in the eleventh and twelfth centuries in the towns of Europe which were hardly bigger than villages at the time.

Taken all together at any rate, the activities of the pedlars had massive effects. The spread of popular literature and almanacs to the countryside was almost exclusively their doing.[253] All the glassware of Bohemia[254] was distributed by pedlars in the eighteenth century – whether to Scandinavia, England, Russia or the Ottoman Empire. The great expanses of Sweden were in the seventeenth and eighteenth centuries half-empty of human population: a few settlements lost in a mighty waste. But the persistence of the humble travelling merchants, from Vestrogothia or Småland, succeeded in distributing 'horseshoes, nails, locks, pins ... almanacs and religious books'.[255] In Poland, itinerant Jews handled about 40 to 50% of the trade[256] and were also well-entrenched in Germany, where they already dominated in part the brilliant Leipzig fairs.[257]

So pedlars were not always poor relations. More than once, they were pioneers of expansion, opening up a market. In September 1710,[258] the Paris council of commerce refused the request of two Jews from Avignon, Moyse de Vallabrege and Israel de Jasiar, who wanted to 'sell silk and woollen stuffs and other merchandise, in all the towns of the kingdom, for six weeks in every season of the year, without opening a shop'. This initiative by merchants who were obviously anything but humble pedlars, appeared 'most prejudicial to the trade and interests of the king's subjects', an undisguised threat to the shopkeepers and traders on the spot. Usually it was the other way round: wholesale merchants, and important, or even not-so-important shopkeepers, habitually pulled the strings of the pedlars' trade, loading off on to these indefatigable salesmen the unsold goods that cluttered up their stores. For the art of the pedlar was to sell in small quantities, to buy his way into poorly served areas, and persuade the hesitant: to this end, he devoted much energy and sales talk, like the street vendor of today who is one of his descendants. He was quick-witted, sharp and amusing: and was portrayed as such on the stage: in a play of 1637[259] if the young widow does not finally marry the fine talker, it is not for want of temptation:

> Lord! how he cheers one: if I were not poor,
> And wanted to wed him, he'd have me for sure,
> But the money he makes from selling his papers
> Would not even keep us in candles and tapers.

With or without permission, the pedlars found their way everywhere, under the arcades of Saint-Mark's in Venice, or on to the Pont-Neuf in Paris. The bridge of Åbo in Finland was covered with shops: so the pedlars simply occupied both ends of the bridge.[260] A special regulation had to be passed at Bologna to stop the main square, opposite the cathedral, where the market was held on Tuesdays and Saturdays, being turned by their efforts into a sort of daily market.[261] In Cologne, there were thirty-six categories of *Ausrufer* or street-criers.[262] In Lyons in 1643, there was a continual chorus: 'Anything that can be sold is carried through the streets: fritters, fruits, kindling, charcoal, raisins, celery, cooked peas, oranges, etc.; green and salad vegetables are wheeled along in handcarts and cried. Apples and pears are sold cooked. They sell cherries by weight, at so much a pound.'[263] The cries of Paris, London and Rome can be found in contemporary engravings and literature. In the paintings of the Carracci or Giuseppe Barberi, we can see the street-vendors of Rome, selling figs and melons, herbs, pretzels, biscuits, onions, loaves of bread, old clothes, rolls of

Blinyis-seller in the streets of Moscow. Engraving, 1794.
(Photo Alexandra Skarzynska.)

cloth and sacks of coal, game, frogs. One does not immediately think of elegant eighteenth-century Venice as invaded by sellers of corn-cookies – but in July 1767 they were well and truly on sale, in huge quantities 'for the tiny price of a sou'. This, observed a visitor 'is because the starving populace of the city is constantly getting poorer'.[264] How was a city to get rid of these hordes of unauthorized traders? Not one succeeded in doing so. Gui Patin wrote from Paris on 19 October 1666:[265] 'They are beginning to put into effect the previously agreed policy against the sellers, dealers and cobblers who encumber the public way, because they want to clean up the streets of Paris; the king has said he wants to do to Paris what Augustus did to Rome.' Nothing worked, of course: as well try to chase away a swarm of flies. All the city streets and country roads were travelled by those indefatigable legs. Even Holland, as late as 1778 what is more, was flooded 'with pack-carriers, pedlars and hawkers, who sell a multitude of strange goods to the rich and wealthy people who spend a large part of the year in their country residences'.[266] The late vogue of country houses was then at its height in the United Provinces, and no doubt this had something to do with the wave of invaders.

Peddling was often associated with seasonal migration: this was as true of the Savoyards[267] and the travellers from the Dauphiné who went to France and Germany, as of the Auvergnats[268] from the hills, especially from the volcanic plateau of Saint-Flour, who travelled the roads of Spain. Italians came to France to do their 'season'; some were content merely to 'tour' the kingdom of Naples; French *colporteurs* went to Germany. Correspondence between pedlars of Magland (Haute-Savoie today)[269] enables us to trace the comings and goings, between 1788 and 1834, of the travelling 'jewellers', (in fact watch-sellers) who placed their stock at the Swiss fairs (Lucerne and Zurzach)[270] and in the shops of southern Germany, in the course of long and virtually identical journeys made by father, son and grandson. With varying fortunes: at the Lucerne Fair on 13 May 1819, they took 'hardly enough to buy a glass of beer in the evening'.[271]

Sometimes there were sudden invasions, linked no doubt to the increased vagrancy in times of crisis. In Spain in 1783,[272] general measures had to be taken against the whole tribe of pedlars, packmen and travelling vendors, against 'those who display tame animals' and the strange healers 'known as *salutadores*, who carry a large cross around their necks and claim to cure the diseases of men and animals by prayer'. The targets of the general ban on packmen were in fact the Maltese, Genoese and natives of the country; the French are not mentioned, but that was no doubt an oversight. It was natural that these professional vagrants should have contacts with the vagrants of no profession they met on the roads, and sometimes take part in the ill-doings of this unscrupulous fraternity.[273] It was also natural that they should be associated with smuggling. England in 1641 was full of French pedlars, who, according to Sir Thomas Roe, a member of the King's Privy Council, were contributing to the kingdom's trade deficit![274] Surely they were in league with the sailors who secretly loaded wool and fuller's earth from the English coast, bringing spirits in exchange?

Peddling: an archaic trade?

The great days of the pedlar's trade are usually said to have declined spontaneously whenever a country reached a certain stage of economic development. In England, pedlars are supposed to have disappeared in the eighteenth century, in France in the nineteenth. And yet there was a revival in the pedlar's trade in the nineteenth century, at any rate in the suburbs of industrial towns poorly served by the ordinary distribution networks.[275] In France, any study of folk customs finds traces of it still in the twentieth century.[276] It had been thought (but this was *a priori* reasoning) that modern means of transport had dealt it a mortal blow. And yet our travelling watchmakers of Magland used carts, stage-coaches and even in 1834, with satisfaction, a steamship on Lake Geneva.[277] It must be concluded that peddling was an eminently adaptable system. Any breakdown in distribution might see it spring or return to life; as might any increase in clandestine activities like smuggling, theft and receiving; or any unexpected occurrence which reduced the usual competition, supervision and formalities of trade.

France during the Revolution and the Empire was thus the scene of an immense proliferation of peddling, as may be surmised from the words of an indignant magistrate on the commercial tribunal at Metz who on 6 February 1813 presented a long report to the members of the general council of trade in Paris:[278] 'The pedlar's trade today', he writes, 'is not the same as in the past, with a pack on his back. It has become a considerable trade and is at home everywhere – although it has no home.' In short, the pedlars were rogues, thieves, a scourge to innocent customers and a disaster for 'stay-at-home' merchants with a fixed abode. It was essential to put a stop to this, if only in the interests of public safety. The public was abused when trade was so little considered, when with the licence of the revolutionary period and the *assignats*, anybody could, by paying the modest price of a patent, set himself up as a trader in any goods. The only solution, according to our magistrate was to 're-establish the guilds!'; 'avoiding the abuses of the original institution', as he just has the grace to say. We need read no further; but it is quite true that in his time, squads, armies of pedlars are reported from every corner of the land. In Paris, in the same year, 1813, the Prefect of Police was informed that 'stall-holders' were putting up their trestles right on the streets, all over town, 'from the boulevard de la Madeleine to the boulevard du Temple'. They were quite shamelessly installing themselves in the doorways of shops, and selling the same goods, to the fury of the shopkeepers, especially the glass-, china- and enamel-dealers, and jewellers. The forces of order were unable to cope with them: 'We keep expelling these stall-holders from one place, but they keep coming back ... they are so many that there is safety in numbers. How can we arrest such a large number of individuals?' They were all moreover poverty-stricken. And the police report adds: 'this irregular trade is not perhaps as damaging to established merchants as one might suppose, since almost all the goods displayed on the streets have been sold by them to the stall-holders, who are in many cases simply their agents'.[279]

In very recent times, when France was starving, between 1940 and 1945, there was another wave of irregular peddling, with the black market. In Russia, the difficult period 1917–1922, with the civil troubles, and problems of movement round the country, saw the prompt re-appearance of the travelling salesmen, as in the old days: second-hand dealers, illegal collectors, traffickers, pedlars – the 'sackmen' as they were scornfully known.[280] Even today, the Breton farmers who come to Paris in trucks to make direct sales of the artichokes and cauliflowers unwanted by the wholesalers of the Halles, are acting as pedlars. So too are the picturesque Georgian and Armenian peasants, with their sacks of fruit and vegetables and live fowls in string bags, who are tempted by the low fares on the internal Soviet airlines to go as far as Moscow. If one day the tyranny of the supermarket became intolerable, who knows, one might see a reaction in the shape of a new wave of peddling – other things being equal. For peddling is and always has been a way of getting round the sacrosanct market, a way of cocking a snook at established authority.

Europe: the wheels of commerce at the highest level

Above the markets, the shops, and the travelling pedlars, rose a mighty super-structure of exchange in the hands of extremely skilled operators. This is the level at which one finds the major workings of the large-scale economy, and necessarily of capitalism which could not have existed without it.

In yesterday's world, the essential tools of long-distance trade were fairs and Exchanges (*Bourses*). Not that they accounted for all big business. The practices of notaries, in France and on the continent – not in England, where their role was simply to identify the parties – made it possible to settle, behind closed doors, countless transactions sometimes concerning very large sums – so many indeed that one historian, Jean-Paul Poisson[281] has suggested that they are one way of estimating the general level of business. Similarly the banks, reservoirs in which money slowly accumulated, and from which it did not always escape prudently and effectively, were playing an increasingly important role.[282] And the consular tribunals in France (to which questions and disputes relating to bankruptcies were in addition later referred) constituted a privileged form of justice for merchants, *per legem mercatoriam*, an expeditious form of justice which safeguarded class interests. Thus Le Puy (17 January 1757)[283] and Périgueux (11 June 1783)[284] applied to have consular tribunals, which would make things easier for their commercial life.

As for the French chambers of commerce in the eighteenth century (the first was formed in Dunkerque in 1700)[285] later imitated in Italy (Venice 1763[286], Florence 1770[287]) they tended to reinforce the authority of the large wholesalers to the detriment of others – as a merchant of Dunkerque frankly put it (6 January 1710): 'All the chambers of commerce ... are good for nothing but ruining general trade [i.e. everybody's business] by making 5 or 6 individuals the absolute masters of shipping and commerce wherever they have been established.'[288] So the institution was more or less successful depending on the town. In Marseilles, the chamber of commerce was the very heart of commercial life; in Lyons however, the *Echevinage* (assembly of aldermen) was all-important, so that the chamber of commerce, not greatly needed, finally stopped meeting. 'I have been informed', wrote the controller-general on 27 June 1775[289], 'that the Lyons chamber of commerce holds very few or no assemblies, that the dispositions of the Council's order of 1702 are not executed, and that everything concerning the commerce of the city is examined and decided by the syndics' (i.e. the aldermen of the city). But could an institution be brought into everyday life merely by crying for it? Saint-Malo had asked the king in vain in 1728 for a chamber of commerce.[290]

It is clear then that in the eighteenth century, the instruments of big business were becoming more numerous and diversified. Fairs and Exchanges however still remained at the heart of merchant life.

Fairs: ancient instruments forever being re-tuned

Fairs are ancient institutions: less so than markets (perhaps) but with roots going nevertheless far back into the past.[291] In France, rightly or wrongly, historical research places their origins further back than Rome, in the distant age of the great Celtic pilgrimages. The eleventh-century revival in the West, if so, would not be a completely new start, as is usually supposed, since traces might still have survived of towns, markets, fairs and pilgrimages – of habits that is which needed only to be revitalized. Of the Lendit fair at Saint-Denis, it was said that it went back at least as far as the ninth century (to the reign of Charles the Bald);[292] of the fairs of Troyes[293] that they dated from Roman times; of the Lyons fairs that they had been initiated in 172 A.D.[294] These may be wild claims and allegations, but they are not necessarily without some truth, since in all probability the fairs are even more ancient than has been claimed.

Their age did not, at any rate, prevent them from being living institutions which adapted to circumstances. Their function was to interrupt the tight circle of everyday exchanges. A village in the Meuse in 1800[295] asked for a fair to be created so that it could obtain the hardware it lacked. Even the fairs held in so many modest little towns, and which seem only to be a meeting-point for the surrounding countryside and the town craftsmen, were in fact breaking out of the usual trade cycle. As for the big fairs, they could mobilize the economy of a huge region: sometimes the entire business community of western Europe would meet at them, to take advantage of the liberties and franchises they offered which wiped out for a brief moment the obstacles caused by the numerous taxes and tolls. Everything contributed then to make a fair an extraordinary gathering. Rulers who (like the king of France[296] the king of England and the emperor) had quickly taken control of these vital points of confluence, granted large numbers of derogations, franchises, guarantees and privileges. But we should note in passing that fairs were not all automatically exempted from duties, and none, not even the fair of Beaucaire, was governed by a system of complete free trade. For example, of the three 'royal' fairs of Saumur, each lasting three days, a text says that they were 'of little use, since none of them is duty-free'.[297]

All fairs offered the appearance of temporary townships – they did not last, but the very number of their participants was equal to that of a town. From time to time, they would set up all their equipment, then when everything was over, move away. After one, two, perhaps three months' absence, they appeared again. Each one had its rhythm, its calendar and its code, different from any other. And the most important fairs were not necessarily the most frequented: more people probably went to the ordinary livestock fairs or *foires grasses* as they were called in France (fatstock fairs). Sully-sur-Loire[298] near Orleans, Pontigny in Brittany, Saint-Clair and Beaumont de Laumagne each had eight fairs a year;[299] Lectoure, in the *généralité* of Montauban had nine;[300] Auch, eleven;[301] 'the fatstock fairs held in Chenerailles, a large market-town in the Haute-Marche of the Auvergne are famous for the quantity of fattened beasts sold there, most of which are driven to Paris'. These fairs were held on the first Tuesday of the month, twelve a year then.[302] In Le Puy, 'there are twelve fairs a year, where all sorts of animals are sold, especially large numbers of mules and she-mules, many animal skins, wholesale fabrics of all kinds from Languedoc, white and red cloth from Auvergne, hemp, thread, wool and pelts of every sort'.[303] Mortain in Normandy may have held the record with fourteen fairs a year[304] but impressive as this was, it may have been bettered elsewhere.

There were of course fairs and fairs. There were country fairs like the tiny one held at Toscanella, near Siena, which was really only a large wool market. If a long winter prevented the peasants from shearing their sheep in time (as in May 1652) the fair was cancelled.[305]

True fairs were those for which a whole town opened its gates. In these cases, either the fair took everything over and became the town, or rather something more than the conquered town; or else the town was strong enough to keep the fair at arm's length – it was a question of respective weight. Lyons was to some extent a victim of its four monumental fairs.[306] Paris dominated its fairs, reducing them to the dimensions of large markets: so the ever-lively Lendit fair was held outside the walls at Saint-Denis. Nancy[307] wisely relegated its fairs outside the town, though still within reach, to Saint-Nicolas-du-Port. Falaise in Normandy exiled them to the large village of Guibray. During the intervals between these tumultous and celebrated gatherings, Guibray returned to being a sleepy little place. Beaucaire took the precaution, as other towns did, of locating the Magdalen-tide fair, to which it owed both its wealth and its reputation, on the land between the town and the river Rhône. However this had little effect: the visitors – some fifty thousand as a rule – invaded the town, and it took all the brigades of the *maréchaussée* of the province to keep a semblance of order, if that. What was more, the crowds usually turned up about a fortnight before the fair opened on 22 July, that is before the forces of order had arrived. In 1757 indeed, it was proposed to send the *maréchaussée* along on the twelfth, so that both visitors and townspeople should be 'protected'.

A town completely dominated by its fairs ceased to be itself. Leipzig, which was to make its fortune in the sixteenth century, knocked down and rebuilt squares and buildings so that the fair should have more space.[308] But Medina del Campo in Castile[309] is an even better example. It became completely identified with the fair which three times a year occupied the long *Rua*, with its houses with wooden pillars, and the great *Plaza Mayor*, opposite the cathedral, where during the fair, mass was celebrated on the balcony; buyers and sellers could follow the service without having to stop business. Saint John of the Cross, as a child, was entranced by the gaily-painted stalls on the square.[310] Today Medina is a husk, an empty shell of the old fair. Frankfurt-am-Main in the sixteenth century managed to keep its fair at a distance.[311] But by the next century it had become too prosperous and had taken over the town. Foreign merchants had

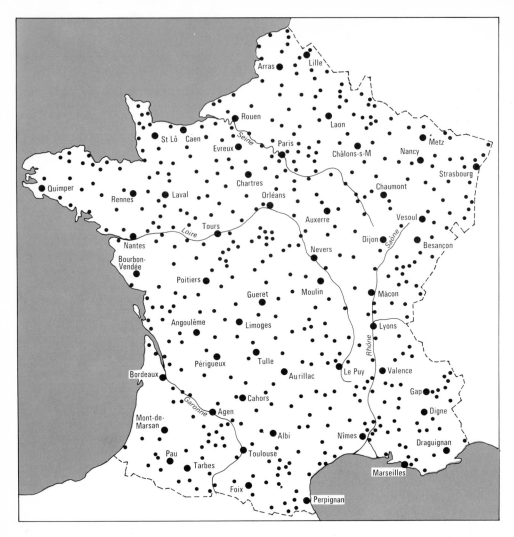

7　FRANCE IN 1841: STILL DOTTED WITH FAIRS
(From *Dictionnaire du commerce et des merchandises*, 1841, I, pp. 960 ff.)

come to settle there for good, representing firms from Italy, the Swiss Cantons, Holland. And a progressive colonization followed. The foreigners, usually the younger sons of familes, came to live in the town with a simple resident's permit, the *Beisesserschutz*; this was but a first step; then they acquired the *Burgerrecht* and soon they were laying down the law. In Leipzig, where the same process took place, the riot in 1593[312] against the Calvinists could be interpreted perhaps as a sort of 'national' reaction against the Dutch merchants. Was it wisdom then on the part of Nuremberg,[313] a great trading town if ever there was one, when having obtained from the emperor, in 1423–1424 and 1431, the necessary concessions for the establishment of fairs, it decided not to have them after all? Was this wisdom or inadvertence? The town at any rate preserved its own identity.

Fair-time, carnival-time

Fairs meant noise, tumult, music, popular rejoicing, the world turned upside down, disorder and sometimes disturbances. At Prato near Florence,[314] where the fairs dated back to the fourteenth century, every September the *trombetti* of all the towns of Tuscany would come to *suonare* in competition in the streets and on the town squares. At Carpentras, the day before the fairs of St Matthew or Saint-Siffrein, the piercing sound of trumpets would be heard at the four gates of the town, then on the squares, and finally in front of the lawcourts. 'The municipality has to pay seven *sous* per player every time' and the bells rang uninterruptedly from four o'clock in the morning; there were fireworks, bonfires, and drummers: the town certainly got its money's worth. It would then be invaded by all the jokers, sellers of miracle-cures and drugs, 'purgative spirits' or orvietan (also known as 'Venice treacle' and once held to be an antidote against poison), fortune-tellers, jugglers, tumblers, tightrope-walkers, tooth-pullers, and travelling musicians and singers. The inns were packed.[315] In Paris, the Saint-Germain fair, which opened after Lent, attracted all the low life of the capital: 'Harvest-time for us girls' as one of them said. And gambling as well as easy women attracted many takers. The 'blank' lottery was all the rage: it gave out large numbers of white or blank tickets (the losers) and a few black tickets, the winners. How many chambermaids gambled away their savings and all hopes of marriage on the blank lottery?[316] But this was as nothing compared to the discreet gaming-tables housed in certain booths of the fair, despite the frowning vigilance of the authorities. They were as attractive as the gaming-houses in Leipzig, much frequented by the Poles.[317]

And without exception, fairs were a rendezvous for travelling players. From the time when it was held in the Halles of Paris, the Saint-Germain fair had been the occasion for theatrical performances. The 'Prince of Fools' and 'Mother Foolish', which were on the programme in 1511, represent the medieval tradition of farces and satires, of which Saint-Beuve said 'this is already vaudeville'.[318] Soon to be added to them was Italian comedy which, once the great vogue for it had passed, found a last refuge in the fairs. In 1764, at the fair of Carpentras, 'Gaetano Merlani and his Florentine troupe' were putting on 'comedies', Melchior Mathieu de Piolent 'a carrousel' and Giovanni Greci some 'stage plays' during the intervals of which he took the opportunity to sell his patent medicines.[319]

The streets were full of sights to see too: there was the opening procession of the 'consuls [of Carpentras] in their hoods, followed by the furriers in their long robes, carrying masses of silver';[320] official processions, like that of the *stathouder* of the Hague,[321] the king and queen of Sardinia at the fairs of Alexandria della

The annual fair outside Arnhem. Engraving by P. de Hooghe (1645–1708).
(Photo Atlas van Stolk Foundation, Rotterdam.)

Palea;[322] the duke of Modena 'with his suite' at the fair of Reggio in Emilia and so on. Giovanni Baldi[323] a Tuscan broker who had gone to Poland to recover some unpaid debts, arrived at Leipzig fair in October 1685. What do his letters tell us about these fairs which were at their height at this time? All he can talk about is the arrival of His Highness the duke of Saxony, 'with a numerous suite of lords, ladies, and German princes, come to see the remarkable sights of the fair. The ladies, like the lords, appear in costumes so magnificent that one is quite amazed'. They were part of the spectacle. Were entertainment, escapism, and worldliness the logical culmination of these great shows? Sometimes, at any rate. At the Hague which was just becoming the political heart of Holland, the fairs provided the *stathouder* above all with an occasion to invite to his table 'ladies and gentlemen of distinction'. In Venice, the fair of the Sensa (Ascension-tide)[324] which lasted two weeks, was a ritual and theatrical occasion: foreign merchants set up their stalls on St Mark's square; men and women wore masks, and the Doge standing in front of San Nicolo, married the sea, as in the old days. But one must also remember that more than 100,000 visitors came to the Sensa fair, to enjoy themselves at the spectacle of the astonishing city.[325] Similarly at Bologna, the Porchetta fair[326] was the occasion for both popular and aristocratic festivities, and in the seventeenth century, a temporary stage set was erected on the Piazza Maggiore, every year of different design and, as one can see from the paintings of the *Insignia* preserved in the archives, of great extravagance. Along-side the theatre, the 'shops of the fair' not many in number, had been installed evidently for the amusement of the public rather than for serious business. Bartholomew fair[327] in London was also the occasion for popular amusements, 'without any serious trading'. It was one of the genuine residual fairs, designed to remind people, if they needed reminding, of the atmosphere of carnival, licence, and general reversal of everyday life which all fairs stood for, whether lively or not so lively. As the proverb rightly said, 'Coming home from the fair is not the same as coming home from market'.[328]

On the other hand, the Saint-Germain fair of Paris[329] the only one in the capital to have retained its liveliness and pleasure-seeking – with its famous huge torchlight '*nocturnes*' which were a much-frequented spectacle – also kept its trading side: massive quantities of fabric, woollen and cotton cloth went on sale to a rich clientele whose carriages were parked on a specially-reserved site. And this image is a better representation than the preceding ones of the everyday reality of these fairs, which were above all rendezvous for trade. Two Dutch visitors agape at the sight (February 1657) noted, 'It must be confessed, when one is there and considers the great diversity of merchandise of great price, that Paris is the place where one finds the rarest goods in the world.'[330]

A *kermesse* in Holland, early seventeenth century. Detail from painting by David Vinckboons (Lisbon, Museum of ancient art). (Photo Giraudon.)

Development of the fairs

It has often been remarked that the fairs were wholesale markets, where dealer met dealer.[331] This was indeed their essential activity, but only to see this is to ignore the huge scale of popular participation. For everyone had access to the fair. In Lyons, according to the tavernkeepers who no doubt knew what they were talking about, 'for one merchant who comes to the fairs on horseback and has plenty of money to spend and find good lodgings, there are ten others on foot, who are only too happy to find some modest *cabaret* to lay their heads'.[332] At Salerno or other fairs in the kingdom of Naples, crowds of peasants turned up to take the opportunity to sell a hog, a bale of raw silk or a cask of wine. In Aquitaine, cowherds and farmhands went to the fair simply in search of collective entertainment. 'They left for the fair before daybreak, and returned late at night, after dawdling in the taverns on the way home.'[333]

In fact in this essentially agricultural world, all fairs, even the very grand ones, were open to the overwhelming presence of country people. Alongside the main Leipzig fairs, large horse- and livestock fairs were also held.[334] In Antwerp, which together with Bergen-op-Zoom had four major fairs in about 1567 (two held in one town and two in the other, each lasting three weeks) there were also two horse-fairs lasting three days each, one at Whitsun, one in September. These horses were thoroughbreds, 'beautiful to see and profitable', brought in from Denmark – something like the equivalent of today's Motor Show.[335] In Antwerp at least a distinction was made between the different kinds of fair. But in Verona,[336] the outstanding town of the Venetian Terraferma, everything was mixed up together, and in April 1634, the success of the fair, according to an *habitué* was due not so much to the merchandise from abroad as to the 'quantity of animals of all sorts who were brought there'.

That said, it is still true that the real business of the fairs, economically speaking, was the activity of the great merchant houses. They it was who perfected this instrument and made the fairs the meeting-place for large-scale trade. Did the fairs invent, or re-invent credit? Oliver C. Cox[337] says on the contrary that it was an invention of the real trading-cities, not of the fairs which were only artificial towns. Since credit is probably as old as the world, the argument is perhaps not worth pursuing: it is certainly the case that the fairs developed the use of credit. No fair failed to end with a 'payment session' as at Linz, the great fair in Austria;[338] at Leipzig, from its early days of prosperity, the last week was for settling up, the *Zahlwoche*.[339] Even at Lanciano,[340] a little town in the Papal States which was regularly submerged by its fair (though the latter was only of modest dimensions), handfuls of bills of exchange converged on the fair. The same was true of Pézenas or Montagnac, whose fairs relayed those of Beaucaire and were of similar quality: a whole series of bills of exchange on Paris or Lyons travelled to them.[341] The fairs were effectively a settling of accounts, in which debts met and cancelled each other out, melting like snow in the sun: such were the miracles of *scontro*, compensation. A hundred thousand or so '*écus d'or en or*' – that is *real* coins – might at the clearing-house of Lyons settle business worth millions; all the more so as a good part of the remaining debts would be settled either by a promise of payment on another exchange (a bill of exchange) or by carrying over payment until the next fair: this was the *deposito* which was usually paid for at 10% a year (2.5% for three months). So the fair itself created credit.

If the fair is envisaged as a pyramid, the base consists of the many minor transactions in local goods, usually perishable and cheap, then one moves up towards the luxury goods, expensive and transported from far away: at the very top of the pyramid came the active money market without which business could not be done at all – or any rate not at the same pace. It does seem that the fairs were developing in such way as, on the whole, to concentrate on credit rather than commodities, on the tip of the pyramid rather than the base.

This at any rate is the pattern that emerges from the exemplary career of the old fairs of Champagne.[342] At their height, in about 1260, there was a brisk traffic in both goods and money. When the decline began, goods were touched first. The capital market survived longer and kept up an international settlement business until about 1320.[343] In the sixteenth century, an even more convincing example is that of the fairs at Piacenza (known as the Besançon fairs). These were the successors (hence their name) of the fairs originally founded by the Genoese at Besançon,[344] (which in those days belonged to the emperor) to compete with the fairs of Lyons, to which they were forbidden access by François I. In the course of the years, the fairs were transferred to Lons-le-Saulnier, Montluel, Chambéry, and finally (1579) to Piacenza[345] where they prospered until 1622.[346] One should not judge them by their appearances. Piacenza was a fair reduced to the very tip of the pyramid. Four times a year, it was the scene of decisive but discreet meetings (something like the meetings of say the International Bank of Basle in our day). No merchandise came to the fair, and very little cash, but literally masses of bills of exchange, which in fact represented the entire wealth of Europe, with payments by the Spanish Empire as the mainstream. About sixty businessmen attended, Genoese *banchieri di conto* for the most part, a few from Milan or Florence. They were members of a club to which one could not be admitted without paying a very heavy caution (3000 *écus*). These privileged men fixed the *conto*, that is the exchange rate for liquidation at the end of each fair. This was the big moment of these meetings, which were secretly frequented by foreign exchange dealers, *cambiatori* and representatives of large merchant firms.[347] There was a total of perhaps 200 initiates, behaving with great discretion and handling vast amounts of business, perhaps 30 to 40 million *écus*' worth at each fair, more if we can believe the well-documented book by the Genoese author Domenico Peri (1638).[348]

All good things come to an end however, even the ingenious and profitable Genoese clearing-house. It could only function if sufficient quantities of American silver reached Genoa. When the silver supplies began to dry up in 1610 or so, the whole structure was threatened. A not completely arbitrary date would be 1622 when the fairs were transferred to Novi[349], a decision rejected by the Milanese and the Tuscans and which is a good landmark of decline. Of these problems, more later.

Fairs and communications

The fairs were linked together, and communicated with each other. Whether handling goods or credit, they had been organized to make circulation easier. If one draws up a map of the fairs of a given region (Lombardy say,[350] or the Kingdom of Naples[351] in the fifteenth century, or the networks of fairs centred round Linz on the Danube: Krems, Vienna, Freistadt, Graz, Salzburg, Bolzano[352]) the calendar of successive gatherings shows that they accepted mutual dependence, that merchants travelled from one fair to another with their carts, their pack animals, or carrying their goods on their own backs, until the wheel came full circle again, a sort of *perpetuum mobile*. The four towns, Troyes, Bar-sur-Aube, Provins and Lagny, which shared between them the Champagne and Brie fairs in the Middle Ages, were always passing the parcel so to speak. Henri Laurent[353] claims that the first circuit was set up by the fairs of Flanders: and the Champagne fairs merely imitated them. This is possible – unless perhaps the circular movement came into being as it were spontaneously everywhere, out of a sort of logical necessity similar to that of the ordinary markets. And the calendar of fairs also had to suit the itineraries of the travelling merchants who visited them in turn.

Goods, money and credit were caught up in this circular movement. Money was of course at the same time providing the energy for other, larger circuits and usually tended towards a central point, from which it would set off again. In the West, where a clear recovery began with the eleventh century, one centre finally came to dominate the European system of payments. In the thirteenth century, it was the Champagne fairs; when they began to decline after 1320, the repercussions were felt everywhere – even in the far-away Kingdom of Naples;[354] the system reconstituted itself as best it could around Geneva in the fifteenth century,[355] then at Lyons;[356] and as the sixteenth century drew to a close, around the Piacenza fairs, that is around Genoa. Nothing so much reveals the functions of these successive systems as the breaks marking the changeover from one to another.

After 1622 however, no single fair would ever constitute the obligatory centre of economic life, dominating the rest. For it was now that Amsterdam, which had never really been a city of fairs, began to assert itself, taking over the previous superiority of Antwerp: it was becoming organized as a permanent commercial and financial centre. The fortune of Amsterdam marks the decline if not of the commodity fairs of Europe, at any rate of the great credit fairs. The age of fairs had seen its best days.

The decline of the fairs

In the eighteenth century, one is obliged to recognize that government measures which have 'for several years [granted permission] to send abroad most manu- factured goods without paying any duties, and to bring in raw materials similarly exempted, [can only] diminish from year to year the trade of the fairs, the advantage of which was that they procured such exemptions; and every year people are becoming more and more accustomed to trade directly in goods, without going through the fairs'.[357] Thus the French controller-general of Finance in a letter apropos the Beaucaire fair of September 1756.

It was at about this time that Turgot[358] wrote the article *Foires* (Fairs) which appeared in the *Encyclopédie* of 1757. For him, fairs were not 'natural' markets, arising from 'commodities', and the 'reciprocal interest which buyers and sellers have in seeking one another out ... It is not to the natural course of trade, stimulated by freedom, that we should therefore attribute these magnificent fairs, where the production of part of Europe is brought together at great expense, and which seem to be the rendezvous of nations. The interest which must compensate for these exorbitant costs does not flow from the nature of things, but is the result of the privileges and franchises granted to trade at certain places and times, whereas it is laden down elsewhere by dues and taxes.' Down with privileges then – or let privileges be extended to all trade institutions and practices. 'Should we fast the year round and feast only on certain days', asked M. de Gournay, and Turgot quotes this *mot* with approval.

But in order to feast every day, would it be enough simply to get rid of these ancient institutions? It is true that in Holland (and the aberrant case of the Hague is not important) fairs were tending to disappear; that in England, the great fair of Stourbridge, once 'beyond all comparison' was to lose its wholesale trade, and was the first to decline after 1750.[359] Turgot was right, as so often: the fair is an archaic form of exchange; it could still in its day create illusions, and even render services, but wherever it reigned without competition, the economy was not doing well. This is the true explanation of the success in the seventeenth and eighteenth centuries, of the Frankfurt fairs, still lively though past their best, or the new Leipzig fairs;[360] and that of the great Polish fairs:[361] Lublin, Sandomir, Thorun, Poznan, Gniezno, Gdansk, Leopol (Lwow), Brzeg[362] in Galicia (where in the seventeenth century one could have seen over 20,000 head of stock at a time); and the fantastic Russian fairs, among them the more-than-fantastic fair of Nijni-Novgorod which appeared in the nineteenth century.[363] The same was true, *a fortiori* in the New World, Europe's prolongation over the Atlantic. To choose a particularly striking example, could there be a fair as simple and at the same time as colossal as that of Nombre de Dios, on the Isthmus of Darien, which was moved after 1584 (still equally unique and colossal) to the nearby rather unhealthy harbour of Porto Belo? Here European goods changed hands for silver from Peru.[364] 'In a single transaction, deals worth eight or ten thousand ducats are agreed'.[365] The Irish monk, Thomas Gage, who visited Porto Belo in 1637, tells how he saw in the public marketplace piles of silver like heaps of stones.[366]

It is by a similar kind of economic backwardness that I would explain the persistent fortune of the Bolzano fair, located on the Alpine passes leading to southern Germany. As for the fairs of the Italian Mezzogiorno,[367] with all their liveliness, what a bad sign they were of its economic health! When economic life moved ahead, fairs were like old clocks which would never catch up; but if it was sluggish, they came into their own. This is how I would interpret the career of Beaucaire, a fair said to be 'exceptional' because it 'stagnated during the period of economic growth (1724–1765) and prospered when around all was stagnating',[368] from 1775 to 1790. During this grim time, which in Languedoc and no doubt elsewhere as well was no longer the 'real' eighteenth century, production unloaded on to the Magdalen-tide fair its unused surpluses, creating a 'log-jam' crisis, as Sismondi would say. But what other outlet was there for such a log-jam? To explain Beaucaire's career against the tide, I should not be inclined to invoke foreign trade so much as the economy of Languedoc itself and of Provence.

It is in this light perhaps that one should view the rather simple-minded proposal of a well-intentioned Frenchman, one Trémouillet, in 1802.[369] Business was bad. Thousands of Parisian small shop-keepers were on the verge of ruin. And yet there was a possible solution (and such a simple one!): it was to set up an enormous fair on the edge of the city, on the Place de la Révolution. The author imagines this huge vacant lot as a chequerboard of streets lined with booths, with a special space reserved for livestock and the indispensable horses. The economic advantages of the proposal were unfortunately poorly argued by its author – perhaps he thought them so obvious that he did not consider it necessary to explain them.

Warehouses, depots, stores, granaries

The slow, often imperceptible (and sometimes questionable) decline of the fairs posed many other problems. Richard Ehrenberg thought that they gave way in the face of competition from Exchanges. André E. Sayous curtly dismissed this out of hand.[370] All the same, if the Piacenza fairs were the centre of commercial life in the late sixteenth and early seventeenth century, the new centre of this world was soon to be Amsterdam: one form, one piece of machinery outstripped the other. It is quite true that Exchanges and fairs coexisted for centuries, but this does not affect the argument: a substitution on this scale could not take place overnight. And while the Amsterdam Exchange took over the vast capital market unchallenged, it also controlled from a height the movement of commodities (pepper and spices from Asia, grain and other products from the Baltic). According to Werner Sombart[371] it is at the stage of transport, storage and dispatch of

The warehouse where a Florentine merchant has stored goods landed in Palermo. Miniature by a Flemish artist illustrating a French translation by Laurent de Premierfait of the *Decameron* (1413). Bibliothèque de l'Arsenal, Paris, MS 5070, f° 314 r°. (Photo B.N.)

merchandise that the real explanation must be sought. Fairs always had been, and remained so still in the eighteenth century, concentrations of goods, which were stockpiled there. But with the increase in population, the headlong expansion of the towns, and improvements in consumption, the wholesale trade could not fail to develop too, spilling out beyond the channels offered by the fairs and becoming organized independently. This autonomous organization, through the use of depots, warehouses, granaries and stores was tending, with its regularity of supply comparable to that of the shops, to replace the periodic bustle of the fairs.

This is quite a feasible explanation. Sombart pushes it a little too far perhaps. He argues that everything depends on whether the storehouse where the goods are kept permanently, and only a short distance from the customers, will function *naturaliter* – in which case it is merely a depot; or *mercantaliter*, that is com-mercially.[371] In the latter case, the store is a shop, of a superior kind, agreed, but a shop all the same, run by the wholesaler, the *grossier* or as he later came to be called more pompously in France the *négociant*.[372] The goods are sold to retailers at the shop door, in large quantities, '*sous cordes*' (as 'roped goods')[373] – that is without opening the bales. When did this wholesale trade begin? Possibly in Antwerp in the time of Lodovico Guicciardini (1567)?[374] But it is quite impossible to agree on a precise chronology of this development.

It is however undeniable that in the eighteenth century and particularly in the northern countries dealing in the Atlantic trade, the wholesale trade was developing on an unprecedented scale. Wholesalers dominated every sector of trade in London. In Amsterdam in the early eighteenth century, 'as there arrive daily a large number of vessels ... it is easy to understand why there are a great number of warehouses and cellars to hold all the merchandise carried by these ships: so the city is well provided with them, having whole districts which consist of warehouses or granaries, from five to eight storeys high, and besides that, most houses along the canals have two or three store-rooms and a cellar'. The storage space was still not sufficient and sometimes cargoes remained on ship-board 'longer than one would wish'. So a number of new warehouses were built on the sites of old houses and 'brought in very good incomes'.[375]

In fact, the concentration of trade to the profit of warehouses and storage depots, had become a general phenomenon in eighteenth-century Europe. Raw cotton was stored in Cadiz if it came from Central America; in Lisbon if it came from Brazil (in descending order of value from Pernambuco, Maranhão and Para;[376] in Liverpool if from India;[377] and in Marseilles if from the Levant.[378] Mainz on the Rhine[379] was the great wine depot in Germany for French wines. Lille[380] even before 1715 had enormouse warehouses where spirits were stored on their way to the Netherlands. Marseilles, Nantes and Bordeaux were the principal depots in France for commodities from the islands (sugar and coffee) which brought prosperity to French trade in the age of Louis XV. Even smaller towns like Mulhouse[381] or Nancy[382] built many warehouses of all sizes. And a hundred other examples could be cited. The Europe of fairs was turning into the Europe of warehouses.

In the eighteenth century then, it looks as if Sombart is right. But what about before that? Is the distinction between the modes *mercantaliter* and *natural-iter* a plausible one? There had always been warehouses and stores, *Niederlager*, *magasins*, *entrepôts*, *magazzini di traficao*, the *khans* of the Middle East and the *ambary* of Muscovy.[383] And there had even been depot-towns of which Amsterdam was the prototype: it was their speciality and privilege to act as a store for goods which were then dispatched elsewhere: Rouen, Paris, Orleans and Lyons are French examples, from the seventeenth century;[384] so was the 'down town depot' in Dunkerque.[385] Every town had its public and private storehouses. In the sixteenth century, market-halls in general (Dijon and Beaune for instance) 'seem to have been at the same time wholesale stores, depots and halfway houses'.[386] Further back in time, how great was the number of public warehouses reserved for grain or salt! From very early on, probably before the fifteenth century, Sicily had its *caricatori* near the ports – huge warehouses where grain was piled; the owner was given a receipt known as a *cedola*, and *cedole* were negotiable.[387] In Barcelona, by the fourteenth century, in the fine merchants' houses built of Montjuich stone, 'store-rooms have been made on the ground floor, and [the merchant's] living-quarters, according to the inventories, were on the first floor'.[388] In about 1450 in Venice, round the Rialto square, right in the very trading heart of the city, shops were arranged in streets by speciality: 'above each of them is a room like the dormitory of a monastery, so every Venetian merchant has his own store-room full of goods, spices, precious fabrics and silks'.[389]

None of these details is conclusive. None helps us to distinguish with certainty between ordinary storage and the wholesale trade – which were no doubt intermingled from the start. The warehouse, an improved instrument of exchange, had existed of necessity for a long time under different forms, sometimes modest or hybrid, because it answered needs that had always been there; in sum it was a response to the weaknesses of the economy. Warehouses were necessary because of the length of the production and trade cycle, because of the slow pace of travel and communications, the risks of distant markets, the irregularities of production and the treachery of the seasons. Proof by contrast is that as soon as the speed of communications increased and the volume of transport grew, in the nineteenth century, and as soon as production became concentrated in powerful factories, the old warehousing business had to modify its ways considerably, sometimes from top to bottom, and disappear.[390]

The Exchanges

Le Nouveau Négociant (The New Businessman) by Samuel Ricard in 1681, defines the *Bourse* or (Stock) Exchange as the 'meeting-place of bankers, merchants and businessmen, exchange currency dealers and bankers' agents, brokers and other persons'. The name *Bourse* itself originated in Bruges, where such meetings were held 'near the Hôtel des Bourses, named from a nobleman of the ancient aristocratic family Van der Bourse, who had had the house built and had placed over the door his coat of arms, with three purses (*bourses*) which can still be seen on it today'. We may have one or two doubts about this explanation, but the name at any rate caught on, although other expressions were used. In Lyons, the Bourse was called the Place des Changes; in the Hanseatic towns, the College of Merchants; in Marseilles, the Loge; in Barcelona and Valencia, the Lonja. It did not always have its own building, so there was frequently confusion of the name of the building it used and the Exchange itself. In Seville, the merchants assembled every day on the *gradas*,[391] the cathedral steps; in Lisbon, on the Rua

Nova,[392] the longest and widest street in the city, which is mentioned as early as 1294; in Cadiz on the Calle Nueva, which was probably built after the sack of the town in 1596;[393] in Venice under the porticoes of the Rialto[394] and in the Loggia dei Mercanti, built on the square in Gothic style in 1459 and rebuilt in 1558; in Florence in the Mercato Nuovo[395] on what is today the Piazza Mentana;[396] in Genoa[397] 400 metres from the Strada Nuova on the Piazza dei Banchi;[398] in Lille[399] at the Beauregard; in Liège[400] at the Public Weigh-house, which was built in the late sixteenth century, or on the Quai de la Beach, or under the spacious galleries of the episcopal palace – or even in a neighbouring tavern; in La Rochelle, in the open air 'between the rue des Petits-Bacs and the rue Admyrauld' on the spot known as 'le Canton des Flamands', until a special building was erected in 1761.[401] Merchants' assemblies were also held in the open air in Frankfurt-am-Main,[402] *unter freien Himmel*, at the *Fischmarkt*, the fish market. In Leipzig,[403] the very fine Exchange was built between 1678 and 1682 *auf dem Naschmarkt*; previously the merchants had met under an arcade, in a booth of the fair or in the open air near the public scales. In Dunkerque, 'all the businessmen [meet daily] at the hour of noon, on the square in front of the town house [i.e. the town hall]. And it is there, within the sight and hearing of everyone that these bigwigs (*gros bonnets*) quarrel and insult each other'.[404] In Palermo, the *loggia* on what is today the Garafello square was the meeting-place of the merchants and, in 1610, they were forbidden to go there once the '*avemaria di Santo Antonio*' had sounded.[405] In Paris, having long been on the old Place aux Changes, by the Palace of Justice, the Bourse was moved to the Palais de Nevers in the rue Vivienne, by a ruling of the Council of 24th September 1724. In London, the 'Burse' founded by Thomas Gresham later took the name of the Royal Exchange. It was in the centre of the city, so well situated in fact that according to a foreign correspondent[406] when measures were taken against the Quakers in May 1670, the troops were stationed in this place '*dove si radunano li mercanti*' so as to be within quick reach of the various points to be covered in an emergency.

It was in fact normal that every town should have its Exchange. A Frenchman from Marseilles surveying the scene in 1685 noted that if the terms might vary, 'in several places being the market, and in the ports of the Levant the Bazaar', the reality was the same everywhere.[407] It is easy then to understand the surprise of the Englishman, Leeds Booth, who had become the Russian consul in Gibraltar[408] and wrote in his long report to the Count of Ostermann, 14 February 1782: '[In Gibraltar] we have no Exchange where the merchants meet to do business as in the great trading cities; and to speak frankly, we have only a very few merchants in this place, and yet although it is very small and does not produce anything, there is a very great amount of trade done here in peace time'. Gibraltar was, like Livorno, a town that thrived on illicit trade and contraband. What good would an Exchange have been there?

When do the first Exchanges date from? On this point, chronologies can be misleading: the date of the construction of the building may not be the same as the setting up of the institution. The building in Amsterdam dates from 1631, whereas the New Exchange was founded in 1608 and the old one went back to 1530. We shall often have to be content with traditional dates which may not be too reliable; but we cannot depend on the misleading chronology which makes it appear as if the first Exchanges appeared in the north: Bruges 1409, Antwerp 1460 (the building was constructed in 1518), Lyons 1462, Toulouse 1469, Amsterdam 1530, London 1554, Rouen 1556, Hamburg 1558, Paris 1563, Bordeaux 1564, Cologne 1566, Danzig 1593, Leipzig 1635, Berlin 1716, La Rochelle 1761 (building), Vienna 1771, New York 1772.

In spite of appearances, the list does not really represent the primacy of the north. Exchanges already existed in effect in the Mediterranean countries by at least the fourteenth century, in Pisa, Venice, Florence, Genoa, Valencia, Barcelona where the *Lonja* requested from Pedro the Ceremonious was finished in 1393.[409] The great Gothic hall which is still standing, shows how old it is. In about 1400, 'a whole squadron of brokers [could be seen] moving in and out of its pillars, and the people standing in little groups were *corredors d'orella*, the brokers by ear' whose job it was to listen, report and put interested parties in touch. Every day, the Barcelona merchant would ride his mule to the *Lonja*, settle his affairs then repair with a friend to the orchard of the Lodge, where it was pleasant to rest.[410] And this kind of Exchange activity, or what looks very much like it, was no doubt even more ancient than the usual dates suggest. In 1111 in Lucca, money-changers were already in the habit of meeting near St Martin's Church: around them were merchants and notaries – so this was already a potential Exchange, requiring only the presence of long-distance trade which soon appeared in the form of spices, pepper and later barrels of herring from the north.[411] And even this early kind of Exchange in Mediterranean Europe was not a creation *ex nihilo*. The reality, if not the word was very ancient indeed: it dated from the meetings of merchants which had taken place from earliest times in the great centres of the East and the Mediterranean, and of which there seems to be some evidence in Rome towards the end of the second century A.D.[412] Something of the sort must have happened on the curious square in Ostia, where the mosaics mark places reserved for merchants and owners of foreign ships.

All Exchanges were much alike. The scene during the short business hours was almost invariably, from the seventeenth century at least, one of noisy close-packed throngs. In 1653, the businessmen of Marseilles asked for 'a place to serve them as a lodge, and to be able to retire there from the inconvenience they suffer by remaining in the street which they have so long used as a meeting-place for their business gatherings'.[413] By 1662, they were on the ground floor of the Puget pavilion, in 'a large hall communicating by four doors with the quayside and where... on either side of the doors the bills were posted announcing the departure of ships'. But before long this had become too small. 'One has to be of the serpentine race to get in', wrote the chevalier de Gueidan to his friend

Suard; 'And what a din and tumult inside! You must confess that the temple of Plutus is a strange thing.'[414] This was because every self-respecting businessman had to look in at the Bourse at the end of the morning. Not to turn up, not to come in search of (often misleading) news might mean missing a good opportunity or even giving rise to undesirable comment on the state of one's affairs. Daniel Defoe solemnly warns the warehouse-keeper: 'To be absent from Change, which is his market ... at the time when the merchants generally go about to buy' is quite simply to court disaster.[415]

The great building of the Amsterdam Exchange was finished in 1631, on the Damplatz, opposite the Bank and the *Oost Indische Compagnie* building. Something like 4500 people were said to crush inside every day between noon and two o'clock, in Jean-Pierre Ricard's time (1722). On Saturdays it was less crowded, as the Jews were absent.[416] Very strict order was kept: every trading branch had a numbered place and there were about a thousand brokers, sworn or not. But it was never easy to find people in the throng, amid the terrible hubbub of figures being shouted aloud and the noise of continuous conversations.

An Exchange was, relatively speaking, like the top section of a fair, but one in permanent session. Because the important businessmen as well as a host of intermediaries met here, business of every sort could be transacted: operations in commodities, currency exchange, shareholding, maritime insurance where the risk was spread among several guarantors; and it was also a money market, a finance market and a stock market. It was natural that such activities should tend to become organized independently. In Amsterdam there was already by the beginning of the seventeenth century a separate Corn Exchange,[417] held three times a week, from ten o'clock until noon, in a great wooden hall where every merchant had his factor 'who is responsible for bringing there samples of the grains he wants to sell ... in bags holding about one or two pounds. As the price of grain is fixed as much by [specific] weight as by good or bad quality, there are at the back of the Exchange various little scales on which, by weighing three or four handfuls of grain ... one can estimate the weight of the sack'. Such grain would have been imported to Amsterdam for local consumption, but also for resale or re-export. Purchases on the strength of samples had very soon become the rule in England and around Paris, particularly when massive consignments of grain for the troops were being bought.

The Amsterdam stock market

The novelty at the beginning of the seventeenth century was the introduction of a stock market in Amsterdam. Government stocks and the prestigious shares in the Dutch East India Company had become the objects of speculation in a totally modern fashion. It is not quite accurate to call this the first stock market, as people often do. State loan stocks had been negotiable at a very early date in Venice,[418] in Florence before 1328,[419] and in Genoa, where there was an active market in the *luoghi* and *paghe* of the Casa di San Giorgio,[420] not to mention the *Kuxen* shares in the German mines which were quoted as early as the fifteenth century at the Leipzig fairs,[421] the Spanish *juros*,[422] the French *rentes sur l'Hotel de Ville* (municipal stocks) (1522)[423] or the stock market in the Hanseatic towns from the fifteenth century.[424] The statutes of Verona in 1318 confirm the existence of the settlement or forward market (*mercato a termine*).[425] In 1428, the jurist Bartolomeo de Bosco protested against the sale of forward *loca* in Genoa.[426] All this evidence points to the Mediterranean as the cradle of the stock market.

But what was new in Amsterdam was the volume, the fluidity of the market and the publicity it received, and the speculative freedom of transactions. Frenetic gambling went on here – gaming for gaming's sake: we should not forget that in about 1634, the tulip mania sweeping through Holland meant that a bulb 'of no intrinsic value' might be exchanged for 'a new carriage, two grey horses and a complete harness'![427] Betting on shares however, in expert hands, could bring in a comfortable income. In 1688, a curious merchant Joseph de la Vega (1650–1692) a Jew of Spanish origin, published an odd book in Amsterdam under the title *Confusión de confusiones*:[428] it is hard to follow, being written in a deliberately obscure style (the *stilo culto* of the Spanish literature of the time), but full of details, lively and unique of its kind. Its author should not perhaps be taken literally when he lets it be understood that he has been ruined five times in a row in this infernal game; nor when he laughs at things which were already of long standing: well before 1688, 'there was forward buying of herring before it had been caught and wheat and other goods before they had been grown or received'; the scandalous speculation by Isaac Le Maire in Indies shares at the very beginning of the seventeenth century was already a sign of plenty of sophisticated not to say criminal procedures;[429] and brokers had already been playing the Exchanges and growing rich while the merchants said they were becoming poorer. In every centre, Marseilles or London, Paris or Lisbon, Nantes or Amsterdam, brokers, who were little hampered by the regulations, took many liberties with them.

But is is also true that speculation on the Amsterdam Stock Exchange had reached a degree of sophistication and abstraction which made it for many years a very special trading-centre of Europe, a place where people were not content simply to buy and sell shares, speculating on their possible rise or fall, but where one could by means of various ingenious combinations speculate without having any money or shares at all. This was where the brokers came into their own. They were divided into coteries – known as *rotteries*. If one group pushed up the price, another, the 'underminers' (or 'bears' as they would be known in London) would try to bring it down. They vied with each other to try to sway the hesitating mass of speculators one way or the other. For a broker to change camps, which sometimes happened, was almost an act of treason.[430]

All shares were however nominal, and the Dutch East India Company held the certificates; a buyer could only acquire a share by having his name entered in

Inside the Amsterdam Stock Exchange in 1668. Painting by Job Berckheyde. (Photo Stedelijk Museum, Amsterdam.)

a special register kept for the purpose. The company had initially thought in this way to prevent speculation (bearer-bonds only came in later) but speculation could operate without ownership. The speculator was in fact selling something he did not possess and buying something he never would: it was what was known as 'blank' buying. The operation would be resolved by a loss or a gain. This difference would be settled by a payment one way or the other and the game would go on. The *premium*, another game, was only slightly more complicated.[431]

In fact since shares were caught up in a long-term price rise, speculation became necessarily restricted to the short term. It was on the lookout for momentary fluctuations – easily provoked by some true or false report. Louis XIV's representative in the United Provinces in 1687 was at first amazed that after all the fuss made about the fall of Bantam in Java, everything blew over as if the news had been false. But 'I am not so surprised now', he wrote on 11 August, 'that this happened: it helped to make the price of shares fall at Amsterdam, and some people gained by it'.[432] About ten years later, another ambassador reported that 'baron Jouasso, a very rich Jew of the Hague,' had boasted to him that he could make 'a hundred thousand crowns in a day . . . if he learnt of the death of the king of Spain [poor Charles II who was expected to die any minute] 5 or 6 hours before it became public news in Amsterdam'.[433] 'I am convinced this is so', the ambassador continued, 'since he and two other Jews, Texeira and Pinto, are among the most powerful people in the share market'.

All the same, such practices had not yet attained the scale they were to reach during the following century, from the time of the Seven Years' War, with the increased speculation in shares in the British East India Company, the Bank of England and the South Sea, above all in English government loans 'that ocean of annuities' as Isaac de Pinto described it (1771).[434] Share prices were not officially published until 1747 however, whereas the Amsterdam Exchange had been billing commodity prices since 1585[435] (339 items at this date, 550 in 1686).[436]

The explanation for the volume and notoriety of speculation in Amsterdam, which was relatively spectacular at first, was that small shareholders had always been associated with it, not just the big capitalists. Indeed one is sometimes reminded of present-day betting-shops or the *tiercé* in France. 'Our speculators' says Joseph de la Vega in 1688, 'frequent certain houses in which a drink is sold which the Dutch call *coffy* and the Levantines *caffé*'. These *coffy huisen* 'are of great usefulness in winter, with their welcoming stoves and tempting pastimes: some offer books to read, others gaming-tables and all have people ready to converse with one; one man drinks chocolate, another coffee, one milk, another tea and practically all of them smoke tobacco... In this way they can keep warm, be refreshed and entertained for little expense, listening to the news... There then comes into one of these houses during the opening hours of the Exchange one of the "bulls", or bidders-up. People ask him the price of shares, he adds on one or two per cent to the price of the moment, takes out his little notebook and pretends to write in it what he has only done in his mind, letting everyone believe that he has really done it, and in order to encourage in every heart the desire of buying some shares, for fear they should go up again.'[437]

What does this scene tell us? If I am not much mistaken, it illustrates how the Exchange extracted money from the pockets of small savers and small speculators. The success of the operation was made possible (1) because there was not at the time, let me repeat, any official quotation of prices to help people follow the rise and fall of the market; and (2) because the broker, who was the inevitable go-between, addressed himself to small capital-holders who did not have the right to step inside the inner sanctum of the Exchange, which was confined to merchants and brokers, although it was but two steps away from all the cafés in question, the Café François, the Café Rochellois, the Café Anglais, the Café de Leyde.[438] What was he up to? It must have been what today would be called kite-flying, going out in search of funds.

Speculation in Amsterdam was a game played by many small savers then, but the big-time speculators were there too, and some of them were extremely active. According to the supposedly impartial evidence of the Italian Michele Torcia (1782) Amsterdam was still at this late date the busiest Exchange in Europe,[439] more so than London. And no doubt the enormous volume (at least in the eyes of contemporaries) of share speculation counted for something, since it coincided at that time with the unflagging craze for subscribing to overseas loans, another kind of speculation also unparalleled in Europe, and of which we shall have more to say.

The papers of Louis Greffulhe,[440] the head of an important counting-house in Amsterdam from 1778,[441] give quite a vivid impression of this double expansion. We shall often have occasion to return to the words and deeds of this *nouveau riche*, cautious yet ready to take a risk, and a lucid observer. In 1778, on the eve of France's entering the war on the side of the English colonies in America, speculation was running riot in Amsterdam. It looked like a good moment to take advantage of the situation, from the safety of neutrality. But should one go for colonial commodities, of which it could be forecast there would be a shortage, or allow oneself to be tempted by first English, then French public stocks – or should one even back the insurgents? 'Your former clerk Bringley' writes Greffulhe to A. Gaillard in Paris, 'is up to his ass in Americans'.[442] As for himself, Greffulhe who had a finger in every promising pie, went in for speculation on the Stock Exchange in a big way, on commission. He acted for himself and for others, for Rodolphe Emmanuel Haller (who had taken over the old Thelusson-Necker bank) for Jean-Henri Gaillard, the Perrégaux, the ubiquitous Panchauds, bankers in Paris and Geneva, for Alexandre Pictet, Philibert Cramer, Turrettini – all names which are written in gold in the ledgers of Protestant banking studied by H. Lüthy.[443] The game was a difficult and risky one, and very large sums of money were at stake. But in the end if Louis Greffulhe played it with such aplomb, it was because he was staking other people's money. If they lost, it annoyed him, but it was no tragedy: 'If one could guess right about

---

8   THE RISE OF FRENCH BANKING

Map drawn by Guy Antonietti, *Une Maison de Banque à Paris au XVIIIe siècle: Greffulhe Montz et Compagnie (1789-1793)*, 1963. It should be noted that the Greffulhe bank was the largest in Paris at the time, and that the French capital had become a financial centre with a wide influence in Europe; that the cross-hatched circles correspond to what Antonietti amusingly calls the 'big business hexagon' – that is the six big centres of London, Amsterdam, Geneva, Lyons, Bordeaux and Nantes. The six peaks of the hexagon seem to have been in some sort of equilibrium.

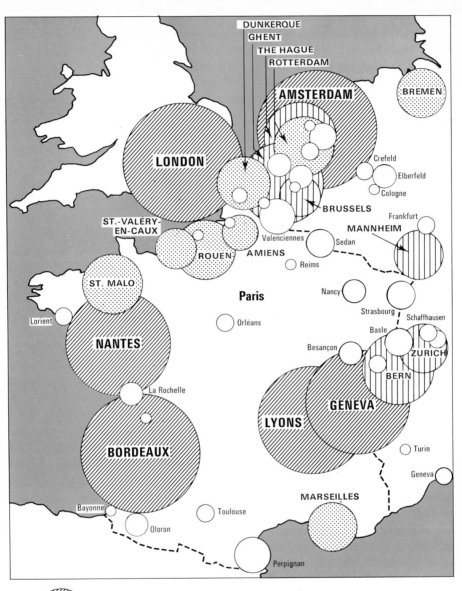

DUNKERQUE
GHENT
THE HAGUE
ROTTERDAM

AMSTERDAM

BREMEN

LONDON

Crefeld
Elberfeld
Cologne

BRUSSELS

Frankfurt

ST.-VALÉRY-
EN-CAUX

MANNHEIM

Valenciennes

Sedan

ROUEN

AMIENS

Reims

Paris

Nancy

ST. MALO

Strasbourg
Schaffhausen

Orléans

Lorient

Basle

ZURICH

NANTES

Besançon

BERN

La Rochelle

GENEVA

LYONS

Turin

BORDEAUX

Geneva

Bayonne

Toulouse

MARSEILLES

Oloron

Perpignan

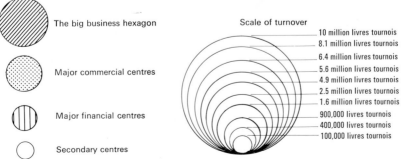

The big business hexagon

Scale of turnover

Major commercial centres

10 million livres tournois
8.1 million livres tournois
6.4 million livres tournois
5.6 million livres tournois
4.9 million livres tournois
2.5 million livres tournois
1.6 million livres tournois
900,000 livres tournois
400,000 livres tournois
100,000 livres tournois

Major financial centres

Secondary centres

stocks [English government stocks in this case] as one can in other matters', he wrote to Haller, 'one would never lose a penny; my friend'. 'The wheel may turn', he writes elsewhere, 'and there will be plenty of ups and downs still to come.' But he never bought or sold without reflection. He was not a hothead who took risks like Panchaud, but carried out his clients' instructions. When Philibert Cramer instructed him to buy '10,000 pounds' worth of Indies' (i.e. shares in the British East India Company) 'on account at 3/3 with MM. Marcet and Pictet, with the possibility of getting them at 144 to 145', Greffulhe replied: 'Impossible', on 4 May 1779, 'for in spite of the drop in these shares, they are still worth 154 for August and 152 for May. We do not at present see any possibility of this purchase being made, but we have taken note of it'.[444]

The secret of winning in Amsterdam was to guess what the price would be there, if one knew both the prices and the news from London. So Greffulhe was prepared to make sacrifices in order to have direct reports from London, which did not only arrive in the 'mails' of the official post. He was in contact with London – where he speculated on his own account – through his brother-in-law Sartoris, a modest and simple executor of instructions, as well as with the large Jewish firm of J. and Abraham Garcia, whom he used though with some misgivings.

Greffulhe's lively correspondence only offers us one narrow window on to high finance in Amsterdam. But it is enough to show how open to the outside world the Dutch Exchange was, and the extent to which international capitalism was already in place. Two of the *rescontre* books of Louis Greffulhe's accounts might tell us more:[445] a calculation of the profits to be made from these complicated operations. *Rescontre* (known as *rencontre* in Geneva) was the name given to the quarterly meeting of share brokers who arranged the compensatory payments and sorted out the profits and losses of the forward and premium market. Greffulhe's two books contain the records of the operations he was carrying out, on these occasions, for his correspondents. A stockbroker would probably be able to find his way through them quite easily – but for the historian they are a maze of some perplexity. One has to follow an operation through several *rescontres* as it is carried forward, in order to have a chance of calculating gains which did not always materialize – and I confess that I did not have the patience to take these calculations through to the end.

London: a repeat performance

London looked long and enviously at Amsterdam, copied it, and quite soon became the scene for the same activities. By 1695, the Royal Exchange was already seeing the first transactions in public stocks and shares in the Indies and the Bank of England. It almost immediately became 'the rendezvous of those who, having money already, wished to own more, as well as of the more numerous class of men who, having nothing, hoped to attract the money of those who possessed it'. Between 1698 and 1700, the stock market, finding itself cramped for space in the Royal Exchange, moved across the road to the famous Exchange or 'Change Alley.

Until the foundation of the Stock Exchange in 1773, the coffee-houses of 'Change Alley were the centre for speculation on the 'bargains for time or "the racehorses of 'Change Alley", as they were termed'.[446] Garraway's and Jonathan's were the rendezvous for share brokers and public stock brokers, while the specialists in maritime insurance frequented Edward Lloyd's coffee-house, and the fire insurance men Tom's or Carsey's. 'The limits are easily surrounded in a minute and a half', wrote a pamphleteer in about 1700. 'Stepping out of Jonathan's into the Alley, you turn your face full south; moving on a few paces, and then turning due east, you advance to Garraway's; from thence, going out at the other door, you go on still east into Birchin Lane .... and having thus boxed your compass and sailed round the stock-jobbing globe, you turn into Jonathan's again.' But this tiny universe, bursting with people at business hours, with all its regulars and excited little groups, was a web of intrigues and a centre of power.[447] Where did the French Protestants, furious at the treaty of Utrecht (1713) which restored peace between the queen of England and the king of France, go to register their protests in the hope of stirring up the business world against the treaty, and thus of helping the Whigs? They went to the Exchange and 'the coffee-houses which resound with their cries' (29 May 1713).[448]

These sensitive little worlds disturbed one another, but they were all in turn disturbed by the outside world. The news that hit prices, here and in Amsterdam, was not always invented on the spot. The War of the Spanish Succession was fertile in dramatic incidents on which everything appeared for the space of a moment to depend. A rich Jewish merchant, Medina, had the idea of sending someone to accompany Marlborough in all his campaigns, granting the illustrious and avaricious captain an annual sum of £6000 for the privilege – which paid for itself handsomely by making Medina the first to know, by express courier, the outcome of such famous battles as Ramillies, Oudenarde and Blenheim.[449] This foreshadows the famous news of the Battle of Waterloo which is said to have benefited the Rothschilds. And anecdote for anecdote, might it be that Bonaparte deliberately kept back the news of Marengo so that someone could make a sensational killing on the Paris Bourse?[450]

Like the Amsterdam equivalent, the London Stock Exchange had (and has) its own ways and its own language: the 'puts' and 'refusals' on forward transactions, the 'bulls' and 'bears' who buy and sell forward but who do so only in order to serve speculation; 'riding on horseback' which was a form of speculating in government lottery tickets, and so on.[451] But on the whole one would have found in London with a slight time-lag, just the same practices as in Holland, including the 'Rescounter days' – a literal translation of the *Rescontre-Dagen* of Amsterdam. So when government prohibitions put an end to the puts and refusals in 1734, making it impossible, for a time at least, to buy and sell fictitious

The London Royal Exchange, rebuilt after the fire of 1666. (Photo Michel Cabaud.)

shares, as in Amsterdam, the *Rescounters* – which allowed similar practices under a different name – flourished. And in London as in Amsterdam, the brokers stepped in and offered their services, both commodity brokers (in grain, dyes, spices, hemp, silk), and stockbrokers. In 1761, Thomas Mortimer protested energetically against the whole tribe: *Every man his broker* was the title of his book, and a lawsuit in 1767 was the occasion of some de-restrictive measures: it was officially declared that going through a broker was not compulsory.[452] But all this only serves to underline the importance in the stock market, of this profession – whose commission was in fact comparatively low: 1/8% from 1697. Above the brokers, one has to guess at the activity of the large merchant firms and the goldsmith-bankers, while below them came the not at all negligible swarm of 'jobbers', that is unofficial ('unsworn') intermediaries. As early as 1689, George White was accusing 'this strange species of insect known as the stock-jobbers' of making prices go up or down at will, in order to enrich themselves at others' expense and 'to devour men, in our Exchange as the locusts of old did the pasture-lands of Egypt'. Did not Defoe himself in 1701 write an anonymous little book entitled *The Villainy of Stock-jobbers Detected?*[453]

A few years later (1718) a play, *A Bold Stroke for a Wife*, by Susannah Centlivre, contained a scene set in Jonathan's coffee house, among the dealers, sworn brokers and above all jobbers. Here is an extract from the conversation:

1st Stock Jobber: South Sea at seven Eighths: who buys?
2nd Stock.: South Sea Bonds due at Michaelmas 1718. Class Lottery Tickets.
3rd Stock.: East India Bonds?
4th Stock.: What, all Sellers and no Buyers? Gentlemen, I'll buy a thousand pound for Tuesday next at three Fourths.

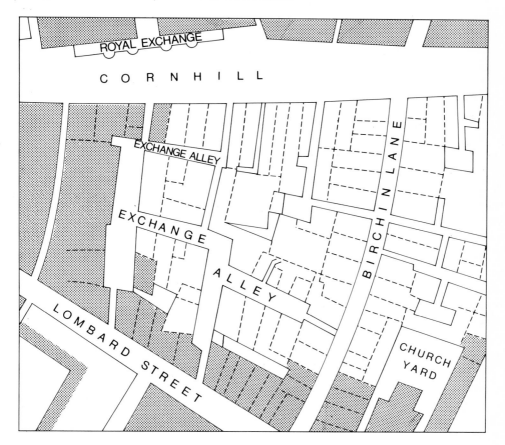

9 LONDON: THE BUSINESS QUARTER IN 1748
Detail from a sketch-map of 1748, showing famous places and buildings: Lombard Street, the Royal Exchange on Cornhill, and the celebrated Exchange Alley. Shaded areas correspond to houses burnt down in the Great Fire of 1666.

Coffee Boy: Fresh coffee, Gentlemen, fresh coffee?

Tradelove, a 'Change-Broker': Hark ye, Gabriel, you'll pay the Difference of that Stock we transacted for t' other Day.

Gabriel: Ay, Mr. Tradelove, here's a Note for the Money upon the Sword-Blade Company [gives him a note].

Coffee Boy: Bohea-Tea Gentlemen?[454]

Perhaps it should also be borne in mind that speculation was carried on in Exchequer bills, Navy bills, and the shares of about 60 companies (including the Bank of England, and the East India Company, re-united in 1709 as a single firm, which led the field.) 'The East India Company was the main point', writes Defoe. At the time the play was written, the South Sea Company had not yet given rise to the great scandal of the South Sea Bubble. The Sword Blade Company was an armaments firm.[455]

On 25 March 1748, the whole district of Exchange Alley and its coffee houses burned down in a fire. New quarters had to be found. But the brokers were still short of space and after several projects, a subscription raised the necessary funds to put up a new building, in 1773, behind the Royal Exchange. It was to be called the New Jonathan's, but was finally christened the Stock Exchange.[456] The surroundings might change and become more official, but needless to say the game went on much as before.

Paris: is a visit really necessary?

If on reflexion, one still thinks it worth going to Paris, it must be to the rue Vivienne, where the Bourse was set up in 1724 in the Hotel de Nevers, the former offices of the *Compagnie des Indes*, a site now occupied by the *Bibliothèque Nationale*. But one will find nothing there to compare with London or Amsterdam. In the time of Law, the rue Quincampoix[457] did, it is true, in a sense rival Exchange Alley, but it did so no longer after that eventful period, the aftermath of which was unhappy and inhibiting. And for some inexplicable reason, all or almost all the documents concerning the rue Vivienne have disappeared.

It was only fifty years after its creation that the Paris Bourse became a scene of much activity, in Louis XVI's capital. The passion for gaming was everywhere at its height. 'High society has fallen for pharaoh, dominoes, draughts and chess' – and the games were never innocent.[458] 'Since 1776, people have been following horse-races; they squeeze into the hundred and twelve offices that the official Lottery has opened in Paris'. And gaming-dens were everywhere. The police, who missed nothing, took care not to intervene, on the whole, even round the Bourse and at the Palais-Royal, where so many down-and-out speculators, knights of industry and financial sharks dreamed of the killing they would make. In such a climate, the example of the speculation in London and Amsterdam became irresistible – the more so as the policies of Necker and Calonne – the launching of loans – created a huge national debt, divided among some 500,000 or 600,000 bond-holders, mostly Parisians. And the Bourse was the ideal market for public debt bonds. In the narrow building in the rue Vivienne,[458] brokers and stockbrokers were reorganized: all-powerful, they now sat on a sort of platform known as the *parquet*; between them and their clients was a narrow gangway, barely wide enough for one man to pass, and known as the *coulisse*. The new vocabulary is a sign that activity was on the increase. Here public debt bonds were quoted more than anything else, but also shares (divided into *portions*) of the *Compagnie des Indes*, or those of the *Caisse d'Escompte* the predecessor of the *Banque de France*. I must confess that even with an intelligent guide like Marie-Joseph Désiré Martin[459] it is hard to make much sense at first sight of the list of share-prices which every day 'filled one page of the *Journal de Paris* and the *Affiches*'.[460]

So stock-market speculation came into existence. In 1779, the *Caisse d'Escompte* was reorganized and the shares went public. Since then, said the *Conseil d'Etat*, 'there has been such chaotic trafficking in *Caisse d'Escompte* bonds that four times as many have been sold as really exist'[461] – sold and resold effectively. I presume that the curious and lucky speculation of the young comte de Tilly,[462] of which he left only an incomplete account (speculation inspired by his mistress an actress who was at the same time granting her favours to a rich *intendant des Postes*) must have taken place at this time. The result for the fortunate young man was that 'they counted me out 22 *Caisse d'Escompte* bonds' – that is 22,000 *livres*. There can be no doubt at least that forward speculation, of a bubble-like kind, had taken more than the first steps towards taking over Paris. The judgement of 7 August 1785, the text of which was transmitted to Catherine II by her ambassador in Paris, Simolin,[463] gives a characteristic account. For some time, the text explains 'there has been introduced into the capital a type of *deal* or *compromise* [my italics] as dangerous for the sellers as for the buyers, whereby one man promises to provide at some distant date effects he does not possess, and the other commits himself to paying for them with money he does not have, with the option of being able to demand delivery before the deadline, allowing for discounting. . . . Such undertakings occasion a series of insidious manœuvres tending to have a temporary effect on the nature of prices of public bonds, giving some an exaggerated value, and using others in such a way that they are cried down. . . . The result is a disorderly kind of unscrupulous speculation, of which any wise businessman disapproves, that puts at risk the fortunes of those imprudent enough to dabble in it, diverts capital from more solid investment which would benefit national industry, excites cupidity in chasing after immoderate and suspicious profits . . . and might compromise the reputation which the Paris market so justly enjoys in the rest of Europe.' Following this judgement, the old ordinances of January 1723 and the decision of 24 September 1724 (setting up the Bourse) were renewed. Fines were stipulated of between 3000 and 24,000 *livres*. The entire project needless to say remained a dead letter and in 1787, Mirabeau could write his *Dénonciation de l'agiotage au roi*. Would the banning of *agiotage* (speculation) have saved the monarchy, which as it happens was hardly the guilty party?

This evidence notwithstanding, the French were still novices at the game. A propos the loan launched by Necker in 1781, Louis Greffulhe,[464] our banker in Amsterdam, who bought up, or rather had bought for him, large quantities of bonds, wrote to his friend and crony Isaac Panchaud (11 February 1782), 'It is a pity, a great pity, that the loan was not given a closing-date straight away. It would have gained 5 or 6%. They do not yet at all understand in your country the forms and procedures which are, in financial matters, to speculation and the circulation of funds what oil is to the workings of a watch.' What Greffulhe meant by the 'circulation' of funds meant the re-selling of bonds. Once a loan issue had been closed, it was indeed commonplace in Amsterdam or London for subscribers to buy up, at slightly raised prices, a few bonds held by others; this pushed up their price and those responsible for the operation would go on pushing it up until the point was reached when they could make large profits by selling off the bulk of the stocks they had held on to for this purpose. Yes, Paris still had a lot to learn.

Exchanges and paper money

Share speculation, an undoubted novelty, made much stir from the seventeenth century on. But to reduce the Exchanges of Amsterdam and London, or more modestly Paris, to what the Dutch themselves called *Windhandel* – trading in wind – would be absurd. Moralists were quite prepared to take the step though, damning equally credit, banking, paper-money and speculation. In France, Roland de la Platière,[465] whom the Legislative Assembly made Minister of the Interior in 1791, did not mince his words: 'Paris', he says, simplifying grandly, 'contains nothing but sellers and stirrers-up of money, bankers, people who speculate in paper, state loans and public misery'. Mirabeau and Clavière also condemned speculation and according to Couédic,[466] in 1791, '*agiotage* in order to pluck a few nobodies from obscurity, causes the ruin of several thousand citizens'. So it did. But the merit of the great Exchanges of Amsterdam and London was to have made possible the victory – a slowly-won victory – of paper money, and of all paper currencies.

There could of course be no active market economy without money. It rushed in, 'cascaded', circulated. All economic life was bent on capturing it. It increased the volume of exchange, but there was never enough of it: the mines could not produce enough precious metals, bad money drove out good over the years, and the evils of hoarding were always lurking. The solution would be to create something better than a commodity-currency, inevitably a mirror in which all other commodities were reflected and valued: the answer was to invent symbolic money. China was the first to do this, in the early eleventh century.[467] But creating paper currencies was not the same thing as getting them accepted. Paper-money did not play the role in China that it did in the West as the accelerator of capitalism.

For Europe did indeed very quickly find the solution, or rather several solutions. In Genoa, Florence and Venice, the great innovation, dating from the thirteenth century, was the bill of exchange which may only have penetrated trade slowly, but penetrate it did. In Beauvais, the first mention of bills of exchange in wills only occurs in 1685, the year of the Revocation of the Edict of Nantes.[468] But Beauvais was only a provincial centre. Another kind of currency, created very early in Venice, was the public debt bond. In Amsterdam, London and Paris, we have seen that company shares were quoted on the Exchanges. Add to this 'bank' notes of various origin and one has an enormous mass of paper money. Sages at the time said that it should not be more than three or four times the value of the mass of metal money.[469] But ratios of 1 to 15 or more are extremely probable at certain periods in Holland or England.[470] Even in a country like France, where people took some time to get used to paper money (and indeed shunned it like the plague after Law's experiment) and where bank notes from the *Banque de France* long circulated only with difficulty in later years, even here, in Paris alone, 'the bills of exchange measuring the volume of funds ... represented between five and six times the circulation of metal money before 1789'.[471]

In this invasion by the paper necessary for trading, Exchanges (and banks) played a leading role. By putting all this paper on the market, they made it possible for a public bond, or a share, to be converted, in the twinkling of an eye, into liquid cash. On this point, where the past coincides with present-day economic reality, I think there is no need for further explanation. On the other hand, a French text from the early eighteenth century – undated[472] but possibly written in about 1706, and therefore a good twenty years before the revival of the Bourse – seems to me to merit our attention. The *rentes sur l'Hotel de Ville* (Paris municipal bonds) which dated from 1552, might have played the same role in France as annuities did in England. But instead they remained a sort of gilt-edged security: a safe investment which was often immobilized in an inheritance, and was moreover difficult to negotiate. To sell them meant paying a tax and 'a whole lot of formalities' in front of a lawyer. As a result, the French text goes on, 'these *rentes* are a dead loss for trading: those who do business can no more use them than they can their houses and land. The interest of individuals, wrongly perceived, has thus injured the public interest.' This is clear to see, the writer goes on, if one compares this situation with that in Italy, Holland or England, where 'State bonds [are bought and transferred] like all buildings, with no extra cost or formality.'

To enable paper to be translated into metal, and vice versa, was undoubtedly one of the cardinal advantages of the stock markets. English annuities were not simply an opportunity for *Windhandel*. They were also an alternative currency, sufficiently guaranteed and with the advantage of carrying interest. If the holder needed liquid cash, he could obtain it immediately at the Exchange for his paper bond. And was not liquidity, free circulation of money, the secret – or one of the secrets – of the success of Dutch and English business? If we can believe an Italian enthusiast in 1782, the English possessed in 'Change Alley, *'una mina più doviziosa di quella che la Spagna possiede nel Potosi e nel Messico'*.[473] About fifteen years earlier, in 1766, in his book *Les Intérêts des Nations d'Europe*,[474] J. Accarias de Sérionne had also written 'Speculation in public stocks is one of the major methods of maintaining credit in England; the price that speculators assign them on the London stock market determines the price they fetch on foreign markets.'

The world outside Europe

To ask whether Europe was, or was not, at the same stage of exchange as the other densely-populated regions of the world – that is other privileged areas like itself – is to ask a crucial question. But production, exchange and consumption, *at the levels at which we have so far described them* are elementary obligations for all populations; they do not depend either on ancient or recent choices made by a particular civilization, or on the relationship it has with its environment, or on the nature of society, or its political structures, or on a past which continues to influence everyday life. These elementary rules have no frontiers. In theory then, at this level, the similarities ought to be more numerous than the differences.

Markets and shops: world-wide phenomena

The entire inhabited planet was dotted with markets and shops – even semi-desert areas like Black Africa, or America when the Europeans first went there.

In Latin America, images come crowding to the mind. In São Paolo in Brazil, there were already shops at the crossroads of the first streets in the town in the late sixteenth century. After 1580, taking advantage of the union of the crowns of Spain and Portugal, Portuguese middlemen literally invaded Spanish America, overwhelming it with their services. Shopkeepers and pedlars, they reached the rich centres and the towns that had sprung up overnight, whether Lima or Mexico City. Their shops, like the general stores of Europe, sold everything – everyday goods like flour, dried meat, beans, imported fabrics, but also expensive 'goods' like black slaves or fabulous precious stones. Even in the wilds of Argentina in the eighteenth century, there sprang up for the needs of the *gauchos*, the *pulperia*, a fenced-off store selling everything, especially alcohol, and providing stock for the convoys of carts and wagons.[475]

Islam is famous for its crowded markets and streets of narrow shops, grouped according to their speciality and still to be seen today in the celebrated *souks* of its big cities. Every imaginable kind of market is to be found here: some outside the city walls, spreading over a wide area and forming a gigantic traffic jam at the monumental city gates, 'on a sort of no man's land which is not quite in the city, so the peasants will venture on to it without too much fear, but not so far outside that the townspeople do not feel safe there';[476] others inside the city, finding a place for themselves as best they can in the narrow streets, unless they occupy large buildings like the Bezestan in Istanbul. Inside the towns, markets were specialized. Labour markets appeared very early in Seville and Granada during the Muslim rule – and in Baghdad. And there were countless run-of-the-mill markets for grain, wheat, barley, eggs, raw silk, cotton, wool, fish, wood, sour milk – no fewer than thirty-five different markets inside Cairo according to Maqrizi.[477] Did one of them act as an Exchange, at least for money-changers, as a recent book suggests (1965)?[478]

In short, all the characteristics of the European market are there: the peasant who comes to town, anxious to obtain the money he needs to pay his taxes, and who simply looks in at the market long enough to do so: the energetic salesman with his ready tongue and manner who pre-empts the rural seller's wares, in spite of prohibitions; the animation and the social appeal of the market, where one can always find prepared food on sale from a merchant, 'meatballs, dishes of chick peas, fritters'.[479]

In India, which very soon fell a prey to the money economy, there was not a village, strange as it may seem (less strange on reflection though) which did not have its market. The reason was that dues payable by the community to absentee landlords or to the Great Mogul – who was as voracious as the former – had to be converted into money before being paid. To do so meant selling grain or rice or dye-plants and the Banyan merchant was always on hand to facilitate the operation and make a profit for himself if possible. In the towns, there was an abundance of markets and shops. And everywhere travelling tradesmen, as in China, offered their services. Even today, there are travelling blacksmiths, who drive round in a wagon with their families, offering their services for a little rice or other food.[480] And travelling merchants, Indians and foreigners, are everywhere too. The Sherpas of the Himalayas, indefatigable pedlars, go as far as the Malacca peninsula.[481]

On the whole though, we know little about the ordinary markets of India. The hierarchy of Chinese markets, on the other hand, is plain to see. For China, more than any other society, with its great mass of humanity, preserved thousands of elements of everyday life from the past until at least 1914 – and some even until after the Second World War. Today it is of course too late to go in search of these ancient survivals. But G. William Skinner was able to observe the still-living past in 1949,[482] and his abundant and precise observations are an excellent source of information on traditional China.

A little market in Istanbul. Miniature, Museo Correr, Venice. (Photo by the museum.)

In China as in Europe, the village market was rare, and in practice non-existent. But all small towns on the other hand had their market and Cantillon's remark that you can tell a town by its market[483] was as true of China as of eighteenth-century France. These markets were held on two or three days in the week, three times when the 'week', as in southern China, meant ten days. This was the only pattern that could be supported by the peasants in the five to ten hamlets scattered round the little town, or by the customers of the markets, whose resources were limited. Normally only one peasant in five attended the market, that is one per household or family. A few rudimentary shops provided the small purchases country people needed: pins, matches, oil for lamps, candles, paper, incense, brooms, soap, tobacco. And the picture is completed by the tea-room, the taverns where rice wine was sold, the entertainers, storytellers, the public scribe, not to mention the moneylenders and pawnshops, when a local noble did not fulfil this function.

These elementary markets were interconnected, as is proved by a very precise traditional calendar which saw to it that small town markets coincided as little as possible and that none was held on the day when the local city on which they depended had its own market. The avoidance of clashes allowed the many travelling salesmen and artisans to arrange their own timetable. Pedlars, carriers, merchants and artisans, always on the move, travelled from one market to another, from city to small town, then to another and back to the city in a *perpetuum mobile*. Wretched coolies carried on their backs wares which they would sell to buy others, making their profit from the minimal, sometimes barely-existent price differences. The labour market was always in circulation; and tradesmen were often itinerant. The blacksmith, the carpenter, the lock-smith, the joiner, the barber and many others would be hired at the market itself, and make their way to their place of work during the 'cold' days that separated the 'hot' or market days. And by such encounters, the market came to govern the rhythm of village life, according to its own patterns of rest and activity. The travelling by certain economic 'agents' corresponded to elementary restraints: it was only when the artisan could not find in the town or village where he lived enough customers to enable him to work there full-time, that he moved around 'to survive'. Since he was often also the salesman for the goods he made, he needed pauses to replenish his stock, and he knew in advance from the calendar of the markets he visited, which were the days when it had to be ready.

In the large town, with its central market, trade had different dimensions. Goods and foodstuffs arrived here from the market-towns. But the town was in turn linked with other towns or cities which surrounded or dominated it. The city was the element which gradually became a foreign body in the local economy, looking beyond its narrow surroundings and out towards the greater movement of the outside world, receiving from it rare, precious goods unknown locally, which it sent in turn to smaller markets and shops. Small towns were embedded in peasant society, culture and economy; large towns and cities escaped from their context. The market hierarchy in fact described a social hierarchy. G.W. Skinner was therefore able to claim that Chinese civilization was shaped not in the villages, but in the constellations of villages, including the small market-town which was both the apex and at the same time up to a point the regulator of the whole. One should not overdo the matrix geometry, but it does have something to tell us.

The variable area of the elementary market zones

But G.W. Skinner's most important observation concerns the variable size of the average surface area of the basic unit, that is the area over which the local market wields an influence. Skinner chose to demonstrate this apropos of China in

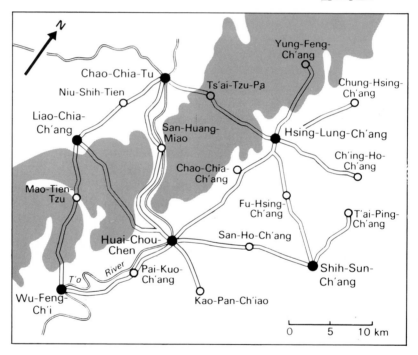

10   THE DISTRIBUTION OF MARKETS IN CHINA
Map of a region of Szechwan showing nineteen small towns, six of which are quite sizeable, lying between 35 and 90 km north-east of the city of Cheng Tu. The map and the two plans based on it are taken from G. William Skinner, 'Marketing and social structure in rural China' in *Journal of Asian Studies*, November 1964, pp. 22–23.
    In the first plan, the reader must imagine at every angle of the polygons drawn in heavy black lines a village, which is a client of the market-town at the centre. Superimposed on this simple geometry, is another set of larger polygons, drawn in dotted lines, of which the larger towns are the centres and at every angle of which is a smaller town.
    The second plan shows the same material in a simplified form, a good illustration of the theoretical model of mathematical geography propounded by Walter Christaller and August Lösch. Further explanations in the text.

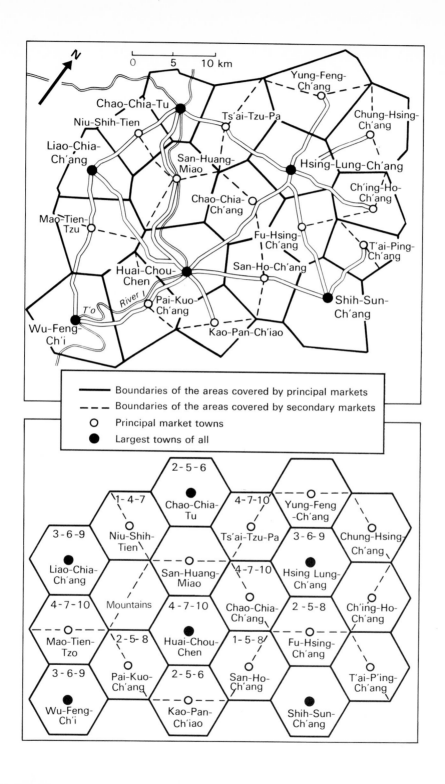

	Chao-Chia-Tu		Yung-Feng-Ch'ang
	Ts'ai-Tzu-Pa		Chung-Hsing-Ch'ang
Niu-Shih-Tien			
Liao-Chia-Ch'ang	San-Huang-Miao	Hsing-Lung-Ch'ang	
			Ch'ing-Ho-Ch'ang
Mao-Tien-Tzu	Chao-Chia-Ch'ang		
		Fu-Hsing-Ch'ang	T'ai-Ping-Ch'ang
		San-Ho-Ch'ang	
Huai-Chou-Chen			Shih-Sun-Ch'ang
Wu-Feng-Ch'i	Pai-Kuo-Ch'ang	Kao-Pan-Ch'iao	

Boundaries of the areas covered by principal markets
Boundaries of the areas covered by secondary markets
○ Principal market towns
● Largest towns of all

0   5   10 km

2 - 5 - 6 Chao-Chia-Tu
1 - 4 - 7
4 - 7 - 10 Yung-Feng-Ch'ang
3 - 6 - 9 Niu-Shih-Tien
Ts'ai-Tzu-Pa
3 - 6 - 9 Chung-Hsing-Ch'ang
Liao-Chia-Ch'ang
San-Huang-Miao
4 - 7 - 10
Hsing Lung-Ch'ang
4 - 7 - 10 Mao-Tien-Tzo
Mountains
4 - 7 - 10
Chao-Chia-Ch'ang
2 - 5 - 8
Ch'ing-Ho-Ch'ang
2 - 5 - 8
Huai-Chou-Chen
1 - 5 - 8
Fu-Hsing-Ch'ang
3 - 6 - 9 Wu-Feng-Ch'i
Pai-Kuo-Ch'ang
2 - 5 - 6
San-Ho-Ch'ang
Kao-Pan-Ch'iao
T'ai-P'ing-Ch'ang
Shih-Sun-Ch'ang

about 1930. And if the basic model is applied to the entire country of China, it becomes clear that the size of the 'hexagons' or near-hexagons, varies in relation to the density of population. If density is under 10 to the square kilometre, the area is likely to be about 185 km^2; a density of 20 per km^2 corresponds to a hexagon of about 100 km^2 and so on. This correlation makes a number of things clear; it indicates different stages of development. Depending on the density of population and the pace of the economy (I am thinking in particular of means of transport) the vital market centres will be nearer or further from each other. And perhaps this is a better way of tackling the problem which used to perplex French geographers in the days of Vidal de la Blache and Lucien Gallois. France can be divided into a number of '*pays*', elementary units which in fact consist of groups of several hexagons. Such *pays* are remarkable as much for their persistent durability as for the shifting and uncertain nature of their boundaries. Would it not be logical to suggest that their area may have varied as their population density varied over the ages?

A world of pedlars or of wholesalers?

We move into a completely different world with the merchants whom J.C. Van Leur,[484] a great historian cut down in his youth by the war, described as 'pedlars' – the merchants of the Indian Ocean and the East Indies whom I should be more inclined to see as agents of altogether higher status, sometimes even wholesalers. The difference in our estimates is so great that the reader may be surprised: it is as if in the West, one found it difficult to distinguish between a village market and an outdoor Stock Exchange. But there could be pedlars and pedlars. Were those who travelled in sailing-ships, with the monsoon behind them, from one side to the other of the great Indian Ocean and the seas bordering the Pacific, really just pedlars, as J.C. Van Leur insisted, with the immediate conclusion that trade throughout the East Indies and Asia was small-scale or even stationary? One is sometimes inclined to say yes. The appearance of these merchants, an odd one to western eyes, encourages one to compare them a little too quickly with the humble men of the peddling trade. On 22 June 1596 for instance,[485] the four ships of the Dutch captain Houtman, after sailing round the Cape of Good Hope, had reached the port of Bantam in Java after their long voyage. A swarm of merchants climbed aboard and squatted down, spreading their wares around them 'as if it were on a market'. The Javanese brought fresh foodstuffs, poultry, eggs, fruit; the Chinese brought rich silks and porcelain; Turkish, Bengali, Arab, Persian and Gujerati merchants offered all the goods of the East. One of them, a Turk, took a passage home with the Dutch flotilla to Istanbul. Van Leur sees in this an image of the Asia trade, a trade of itinerant merchants each carrying his little bundle of wares with him far from home, just as in the days of the Roman Empire. Nothing had changed. And nothing would change for many years.

Javanese boats. Note the wooden anchor, bamboo sails and the two boards of the lateral rudder. (Phototheque Armand Colin.)

This picture is probably misleading. In the first place, it does not cover all the trade 'within the Indies'. From the sixteenth century, there was a spectacular increase in this supposedly unchanging trade. Ships in the Indian Ocean were tending more and more to carry bulky but low-priced goods like grain, rice, wood, ordinary cotton textiles, being shipped to the peasants in zones of monoculture. So one is not talking about a handful of precious goods carried by a single man. And in any case, the Portuguese, then the Dutch, later on the English and French, who lived on the spot were delighted to discover the possibilities of making money by the trade 'within the Indies'. It is most instructive to read the report of D. Braems,[486] returning from the Indies in 1687 after thirty-five years service with the Dutch East Indies Company, which gives details of all the crisscrossing commercial lines, depending upon each other in a system of exchange as vast as it was varied, and into which the Dutch had successfully introduced themselves – *but which they did not invent*.

Nor should one forget that the journeyings of the merchants of the Far East had a simple and precise reason: the huge sum of free energy provided by the monsoons which themselves decided the dates of the ships' voyages and the merchants' rendezvous, with a certainty that no other sea-travel of the time could approach.

And lastly, we should pay attention to the capitalist aspects this long-distance trade was already displaying, whether one likes it or not. The merchants of all nationalities whom Cornelius Houtman saw crouching on the decks of his ships in Bantam did not all belong to the same category. Some – a minority probably – were indeed travelling on their own account and might possibly correspond to Van Leur's simple model – the dusty traveller of the Middle Ages (although even these as we shall see, if one examines individual cases, are probably more like another kind of trader). The others almost all had one feature in common, as Van Leur himself points out: behind them were large shareholders, to whom they were bound by contract; here again, the contracts could differ.

In India and the East Indies, before setting out on their endless journey, Van Leur's pedlars would have borrowed from a rich merchant or ship owner, Banyan or Muslim, or from a noble or high official, the sums of money necessary for their business. They had usually agreed to repay double the original sum to the lender, except in cases of shipwreck. Their persons and their families were their bond: either they succeeded or they became the slaves of their creditor until the debt was repaid – such were the terms of the contract. This is like the Italian contract of *commenda*, but with much harsher terms: the length of the voyage and rate of interest were enormous. But if these draconian conditions were accepted, it was evidently because price differences were so great from place to place that profits were usually very high. These were in fact very large-scale, long-distance trade circuits.

The Armenian merchants who also peopled the monsoon ships, and of whom there were many travelling between Persia and India, were often commission-agents for wealthy business men of Isfahan, with dealings in Turkey, Russia, Europe and the Indian Ocean. In their case, the contracts were different. The commission-agent received one quarter of the profit on all the transactions operated with capital (in both money and goods) entrusted to him on departure, and the rest went to his patron the *khoja*. But this simple picture in fact hides a real situation of great complexity, as is remarkably revealed by the account-book and travelling diary of one of these salesmen, which survives in the National Library in Lisbon, and of which an abridged translation was published in 1967.[487] The text is unfortunately incomplete. The final reckoning of the operation, which would have given a precise idea of the profit, is missing. But even as it stands, it is an extraordinary document.

Indeed everything about the voyage of the Armenian agent Hovhannes, son of David, seems extraordinary to us:

– the length of the trip for a start: we follow him over thousands of miles, from Julfa, the Armenian suburb of Isfahan, to Surat, then on to Lhasa in Tibet, with a series of stops and detours, and back to Surat;
– and the duration: from 1682 to 1693 – eleven years, five of which were spent without interruption in Lhasa;

– the fact that this voyage was quite normal and commonplace: the contract he signed with his *khoja* was a typical contract still to be found in 1765, almost a hundred years later, in the Code of the Armenians in Astrakhan;

– the fact that wherever the traveller stopped – in Shiraz, Surat, Agra but also more surprisingly in Patna, in the depths of Nepal, in Katmandu, and in Lhasa, he was received and assisted by other Armenian merchants, did business with them and associated himself with their affairs;

– equally extraordinary is the list of goods he handled: silver, gold, precious stones, musk, indigo and other dyestuffs, woollen and cotton cloth, candles, tea, etc; and the scale of the trade – on one occasion two tons of indigo, sent from the north to Surat and on to Shiraz; another time two hundred pounds of silver; or the ten pounds of gold obtained in Lhasa from some Armenian merchants who had travelled as far as Sining on the far-off Chinese frontier to trade silver for gold, a very profitable operation, since in China silver was overpriced by European standards: the ratio of 1 to 7 noted in Hovhannes' notebook meant a handsome profit.

Perhaps the most curious thing of all is that the traveller did not undertake all these deals with the capital entrusted to him by his *khoja*, although he remained under contract to him and noted down all his operations of every kind in the account book. He engaged himself, in his own name, with other Armenians, using his own capital (perhaps his share of the profits?), or more frequently borrowed money, and even lent it on occasion. He was constantly moving between liquid money, goods and bills of exchange which transported his wares as it were by airmail, sometimes even at cheap rates, 0.75% per month for a short distance and if dealing with merchants more or less associated with his business; at other times at very high rates when long distances were involved, for the dispatch home of money, 20 to 25% for instance for a return from Surat to Isfahan.

The precise nature of this document, and its value as a sample which is underlined by the minuteness of the detail, gives an unexpected picture of the facilities for commerce and credit in the Indies, of the very diversified local trade networks in which Hovhannes, a faithful agent, devoted servant and skilful merchant easily inserted himself, handling goods precious or commonplace, heavy or light. He certainly travelled – but did that make him a pedlar? If one absolutely insists on a comparison, he reminds me rather of the new kind of English merchant engaged in 'private trading', always on the move from inn to inn, closing a deal here and there, depending on the price and the opportunity, joining forces with one partner or another and continuing imperturbably on his way. This kind of merchant, who is always described as the modern figure who shook up the old rules of the medieval English market, seems to me the closest equivalent of the traders to be glimpsed through the pages of Hovhannes's notebook. With the difference that England does not have the dimensions of Persia, northern India, Nepal and Tibet laid end to end.

Through his example, it is easier to understand too the role of the merchants of India – certainly not pedlars in this case – who can be found from the sixteenth to the eighteenth century settled in Persia, in Istanbul,[488] Astrakhan,[489] or Moscow.[490] Or the wave at the end of the sixteenth century that brought eastern merchants to Venice,[491] Ancona,[492] Pesaro,[493] and in the following century to Leipzig and Amsterdam. These were not exclusively Armenians: in April 1589,[494] when the roundship *Ferrera* left Malamocco, the outer port of Venice, there sailed with her, alongside the Italian merchants (Venetians, Lombards and Florentines) 'Armenians, Levantines, Cypriots, Candians, Maronites, Syrians, Georgians, Greeks, Moors, Persians and Turks'. All these merchants were undoubtedly trading on the same terms as the westerners. They are to be found in the records of Venetian and Anconan notaries as well as under the columns in the Amsterdam Stock Exchange. They did not feel at all out of place.

Indian bankers

Every urban centre in India had its money-changing bankers – the *sarafs* who mostly belonged to the powerful trading caste of the Banyans. A reputable historian, Irfan Habib (1960)[495] has compared the Hindu money-changing system to that of the West. The forms are perhaps different: one has the impression of an entirely private network between one place and another, or rather one changer and another, without to my knowledge any application to public agencies such as fairs or Stock Exchanges. But the same problems were resolved by similar means: bills of exchange (*hundi*), currency exchange, payments in cash, credit, maritime insurance (*bima*).

Since the fourteenth century, India had possessed a monetary economy of some vitality, which was soon on the way towards a certain capitalism – but one that would not encompass the entire society.

These chains of money-lenders were so efficient that the factors of the English East India Company – who were allowed to trade within the Indies on their own account as well as for the Company – were always applying to the *sarafs*, just as the Dutch (and before them the Portuguese)[496] borrowed from the Japanese of Kyoto,[497] or as Christian merchants in difficulties borrowed from Muslim or Jewish moneylenders in Aleppo or Cairo.[498] Like the European 'banker', the Indian money changer was often a merchant who also invested in a big way or handled transport. Some of them were fabulously rich: Virji Vora of Surat for example was said in 1663 to possess 8 million rupees;[499] Abd ul Ghafur, a Muslim merchant,[500] with the same capital, a century later had 20 ships each of between 300 and 800 tons, and it was said that his turnover alone was equivalent to that of the powerful India Company. The Banyans acted as brokers and Europeans were obliged to use them as intermediaries in all the business they had in the

Indies; they transported and sometimes manufactured (in Ahmedabad for instance) the textiles which India exported in such massive quantities in the seventeenth and eighteenth centuries.

On Indian commercial organization and success, the French merchant Tavernier, who dealt in precious stones and who travelled far and wide in India and the East Indies, is as informative as Hovhannes who also used the *sarafs* system. The Frenchman explains how easy it was to travel through India, and even outside India, with hardly any liquid money: one simply borrowed it. Nothing was simpler for an itinerant merchant whoever he was, than to borrow in Golconda for example, and pay back in Surat, where he could transfer the debt to a third place by borrowing again, and so on. The loan moved about with the borrower, and the creditor (or rather the chain of creditors who answered for each other) would only be repaid on the last leg. Tavernier called it 'paying the old with new'. Every fresh loan which released the debtor from the old one had to be paid for of course. Such payments in the end resembled the interest payable 'on the exchanges' in Europe. They added up, and the price went higher the further the borrower travelled from the original starting-point and the usual trade routes. The Banyan network in fact extended to all the commercial points in the Indian Ocean and beyond, but 'I have always reckoned on my journeys', says Tavernier, 'that if you take money in Golconda for Livorno or Venice, exchange for exchange the cheapest rate comes to 95%, but more often it goes up to 100'.[501] 100%: this was the rate regularly paid by the travelling merchant to his supplier, in Java as in India or southern China. It was a staggering interest rate, but was only operated on the high-tension lines of economic life, for the long-distance trade circuits. The ordinary rate of interest in Canton between merchants at the end of the eighteenth century was 18 or 20%.[502] The English in Bengal could borrow locally at rates almost as low as Hovhannes was paying.

This is one more reason then not to consider the itinerant merchants of the Indian Ocean as minor figures: as in Europe, long-distance trade lay at the heart of the most advanced capitalism in the Far East.

Few Exchanges but many fairs

There were not in the East or Far East, institutionalized Stock Exchanges as in London, Amsterdam or other major trade centres in the West. But there were fairly regular meetings between large merchants. They are not always easily identifiable as such, but then the meetings between the great Venetian merchants under the porticoes of the Rialto, where they appeared to be merely walking quietly about amid the tumult of the nearby market, were equally discreet.

Fairs on the other hand, were instantly recognizable. There were any number of them in India, and played an important role in Islam and the East Indies; oddly enough they were very rare in China, although they did exist there.

It is true that a recently-published book (1968) positively affirms that 'there

A money-changer in India. Coloured drawing from the Lally-
Tollendal Collection, about 1760. (Photo Bibliothèque
Nationale.)

were practically no fairs in Islamic countries'.[503] And yet they had a word for it:
throughout the Muslim countries, *mausim* meant both fair and seasonal festival
and was also used to describe the periodic winds that blew from the Indian
Ocean.[504] After all, the monsoon unfailingly regulated sea-voyages in either
direction in the Far East and the warm seas, thus precipitating or interrupting
international encounters between merchants.

A detailed report, dating from 1621,[505] describes one of these encounters in
Mocha, the rendezvous of a limited but very profitable trade. Every year, the
monsoon brought to this Red Sea port (which was later to become the great

centre of the coffee trade) a certain number of ships from India, the East Indies and the nearby coast of Africa, laden with men and bundles of goods (similar ships make the same trips today). In that year, two ships arrived from Dabhol in India, one with 200, the other with 150 passengers, all travelling merchants coming to sell in the port small quantities of precious goods: 'pepper, gum lac, benzoin, cotton cloth [woven with gold thread or painted by hand], tobacco, cinnamon, nutmeg, cloves, mace, camphor, porcelain, musk, diamonds, indigo, drugs ... the perfumes and gums of southern Arabia'. In the other direction, from Suez to the rendezvous at Mocha, came a single ship, which for most of the voyage carried only Spanish pieces of eight; later it picked up some merchandise, woollen cloth, coral, goats-hair camlets. If the ship from Suez failed to arrive on time for one reason or another, the fair which usually marked the meeting, was threatened. The merchants from India and the East Indies deprived of their customers, would have to sell their goods at any price, for the monsoon remorselessly put an end to the fair even if it had not properly begun. Similar rendezvous with merchants from Surat or Mazulipatam took place at Basra or Hormuz, where the boats rarely loaded anything for the return trip other than silver or Shiraz wine.

In Morocco, as all over the Maghreb, local saints and pilgrimages abounded. It was under their protection that fairs were established. One of the most frequented in North Africa was among the Gouzzoûla,[506] south of the Anti-Atlas, looking out on the wastes and the gold of the desert. Leo Africanus, who had visited it himself, noted its importance at the beginning of the sixteenth century; it survived almost to the present day.

But the most active fairs of Islam were held in Egypt, Arabia and Syria, in that central area where we might expect them. From the twelfth century, the bulk of Islamic trade swung away from the dominant axis which for so long had run between the Persian Gulf and Baghdad, and transferred to the Red Sea, discovering there a major route for trade and profit. To this should be added the surge in the caravan traffic which brought prominence to the Mzebib fair in Syria, a great meeting-place for caravans. In 1503, an Italian traveller, Ludovico de Varthema,[507] left 'Mezariba' for Mecca with a caravan he claims to have consisted of 35,000 camels. And indeed the pilgrimage to Mecca was the biggest fair in Islam. As the same observer says, people came to it '*parte ... per mercanzie et parte per peregrinazione*'. As early as 1184,[508] an eyewitness was describing the incredible richness of the fair: 'No merchandise in the world is absent from this meeting.' And the fairs of the great pilgrimage had very early on fixed a calendar for merchant payments and organized their system of compensation.[509]

In Egypt, in certain towns in the Nile delta, small but lively local fairs were connected with Coptic tradition. They may even have gone back beyond Christian Egypt to pagan Egypt. As the religion changed, the protective saints simply changed their names; their festivals (the *mülid*) often continued to mark the date of an exceptional fair. At Tantah, in the delta, the annual fair corresponding to

A 'FAIR-TOWN' ON THE PERSIAN GULF THAT SPRANG TO LIFE WHEN THE BOATS CAME IN

Bandar Abass was the best port on the coast facing the island of Hormuz. Vessels from Indies unloaded merchandise here for Persia and the Levant. In Tavernier's time, after the capture of Hormuz by the Persians (1622), the town had plenty of good warehouses and lodgings belonging to European and eastern merchants. But it was only alive for three or four months a year, 'the trading season' as Tavernier calls it, the 'fair season' in fact. After it was over, in March, the town which was terribly hot and unhealthy, was emptied both of the trade and of its inhabitants – until the boats returned the following December. (Photo Armand Colin.)

the *mülid* of 'saint' Ahmad al Badawi, still draws crowds even today.[510] But the great trade gatherings were held in Cairo or Alexandria,[511] where the fairs depended on shipping in the Mediterranean and the Red Sea, as well as trying to fit in with the complicated calendar of caravans and pilgrimages. In Alexandria, it was in September and October that the favourable winds blew and 'the sea was open'. During these two months, Venetians, Genoese, Florentines, Catalans, Ragusans and Marseillais would buy their pepper and spices. The treaties signed by the sultan of Egypt with Venice or Florence laid down, as S.Y. Labib has pointed out, a kind of law for the fairs which was, *mutatis mutandis*, not unlike the regulations governing fairs in the West.

All this is not to say that *relatively* speaking, the fair had anything like the overwhelming importance it possessed in the West. To attribute this to economic backwardness would probably be wrong, for at the time of the fairs of Champagne, Egypt and Islam were certainly not lagging behind the West. Perhaps it was because of the huge scale of the Muslim city and its structure? Did it not after all have more markets and super-markets if one can use the word, than any city in the West? And above all, the quarters reserved for foreigners were like permanent international meeting-places. The fonduk of the 'Franks' in Alexandria, or that of the Syrians in Cairo served as a model for the *Fondaco dei Tedeschi* in Venice: the Venetians penned up the German merchants, just as they themselves were confined to their quarters in Egypt.[512] Prisons or not, these fonduks constituted a sort of permanent fair in Muslim cities, just as Holland, the home of free trade, was a sort of permanent fair that killed off all the other fairs prematurely as they lost their usefulness. Should one conclude that the Champagne fairs, in a still backward West, may have been a sort of drastic remedy, intended to further trade in lands as yet undeveloped?

In India, which was only part-Muslim, things were different. Fairs were such an omnipresent, obvious feature that they were part of everyday life, and the sight did not even strike travellers as unusual. Indian fairs had the disadvantage, if such it was, of being combined with the pilgrimages which brought to the banks of the rivers with their purifying waters endless processions of travellers and believers, mingling with a mass of swaying ox-carts. A country of separate races, tongues and religions, India was no doubt obliged to maintain for a long time along the borders of its hostile regions these primitive fairs, placed under the protection of tutelary divinities and religious pilgrimages and thus rescued from constant neighbourhood feuding. It is in any case a fact that many fairs, sometimes held between villages, retained the old habits of barter rather than money.

This was not of course the case with the large fairs on the Ganges, at Hardwar, Allahabad, Sonpur; or in Mathura and Batesar on the Jumna. Each religion had its own: the Hindus at Hardwar and Benares; the Sikhs at Amritsar; the Muslims at Pakpattan in the Punjab. An Englishman, General Sleeman,[513] exaggerating a little, used to say that from the beginning of the cold dry season, when the time of ritual bathing came round, the greater part of the inhabitants of India, from the Himalayan foothills to Cape Comorin, were to be found in these fairs, where one could buy anything (including horses and elephants). The pattern of everyday life was broken by the extraordinary routine that now became the rule, with days of prayer and festivity, dancing, music and pious rituals. Every twelve years, when the planet Jupiter entered into the sign of Aquarius, this heavenly event heralded an extraordinary outburst of pilgrimages and accompanying fairs. Devastating epidemics broke out as a result.

In the East Indies, the long meetings between merchants whom international shipping assembled here and there in seaports or their immediate environs, came to resemble long-drawn-out fairs.

In 'Greater' Java, until the Dutch permanently settled there with the building of Batavia (1619) and for some time after that, the chief town was Bantam[514] on the north coast, at the western tip of the island, surrounded by swamps, and huddled inside its walls of red brick with ramparts bristling with cannon which nobody really knew how to fire. Inside the walls, the town was low-lying, ugly 'and as big as Amsterdam'. Three streets led away from the royal palace towards market-places swarming with men and women selling their wares: poultry, parrots, fish, meat, hot cakes, arak (oriental liquor) silks, velvets, rice, precious stones, gold thread. Another few steps and one was in the Chinese quarter, with its shops, brick-built houses and its own market. To the east of the city, on the main square which was covered from daybreak by small pedlars, the big businessmen would meet later in the day: these were the ship insurers, pepper dealers, large-scale investors who were familiar with all kinds of currencies and languages: the square is like a Stock Exchange, a traveller wrote. Imprisoned here every year waiting for the monsoon, foreign merchants meanwhile participated in an interminable fair which lasted months. The Chinese, who had already been in Java for a long time and would remain there for many years to come, played a leading role in this international gathering. 'They have a stake in it', noted a traveller (1595) 'since they lend at interest and have acquired the same reputation as the Jews in Europe. They go about the country, scales in hand, buying up all the pepper they find, and after weighing a small amount [note the detail of buying by sample] so that they can judge approximately the quantity [i.e. weight] they offer the payment for it in a lump sum, depending on the need for money of those who are selling it, and in this way they amass such a great quantity that they can fill the ships from China when they arrive, selling fifty thousand *caixas*' [i.e. *sapekes*] worth, which has cost them no more than twelve thousand. These ships arrive in Bantam in the month of January, to the number of eight or ten, and they are of forty-five or fifty tons.' Thus the Chinese also had their 'Levant trade', and Chinese long-distance traffic was in no way inferior to the European equivalent. In Marco Polo's time, he says, China was consuming a hundred times more spice than distant Europe.[515]

Note that it was *before the monsoon*, before the arrival of the ships, that the Chinese, who were in effect resident commission agents, went round the country-side buying up stocks. The arrival of the boats meant the beginning of the fair. And indeed this was typical of the whole East Indies: long-lasting fairs, their dates governed by the monsoon. In Atjeh (Achem) in Sumatra, Davis in 1598[516] saw 'three great Market places which are every day frequented as Faires with all kinds of Marchandize'. Was he just using the word to describe an ordinary market? It seems not, since François Martin of Saint-Malo (1603) seeing the same sights, distinguished a large market from the everyday markets where curious fruits spilled from the stalls; he describes the booths of merchants from the four corners of the Indian Ocean, 'all dressed in the Turkish fashion' and who stay 'some six months in the said place to sell their goods'.[517] At the end of the six months, 'along come others'. In other words a continuous fair, ever-renewed and lazily prolonged over time without ever having the air of rapid climax of the western fairs. Dampier, who arrived at Atjeh in 1688 is even more precise.[518] 'The Chinese are the most considerable of all the merchants who do business here; some of them stay all the year round; but others only come once a year. The latter sometimes come in the month of June with 10 or 12 sailing-ships carrying cargoes of rice and various other goods … They rent houses all next to each other at one end of town, near the sea, and this quarter is known as the Chinese field … And several artisans come with the fleet, such as carpenters, joiners, painters and as soon as they arrive, they set to work and make coffers, chests, cabinets and all sorts of little Chinese objects.' So for two months on end there is a 'Chinese fair', where everyone goes to buy, or to play games of chance. 'As their merchandise is sold, they occupy less room, and rent fewer houses. As sales fall, the gaming increases.'

In China itself,[519] things were different. Since everything was controlled by a ubiquitous, efficient and bureaucratic government, in theory opposed to economic privilege, the fairs were closely supervised, while markets were comparatively free. Fairs appeared there early on though, at a time of rapid expansion in trade and traffic, towards the end of the T'ang period (eleventh century). Here too, they were generally associated with a Buddhist or Taoist temple and were held at the same time as the festival of the divinity, hence the generic name of temple assemblies – *miao-hui* – given to them. They had a pronounced atmosphere of popular rejoicing. But they had other names too. Thus the new silk fair, held at Nan-hsün-chen, on the frontier between Tchö-Kiang and Kiang-Su provinces, was known as *hui-ch'ang* or *lang-hui*. Similarly, the term *nien-shih*, is the equivalent, word for word of the German *Jahrmärkte* – annual markets, and may have indeed referred to large seasonal markets (for salt, tea or horses etc.) rather than to a fair in the proper sense of the word.

Etienne Balazs used to think[520] that these large markets or exceptional fairs appeared particularly at moments when China was divided between dynasties foreign to each other; since each half had to make some contact with the other, fairs and large markets sprang up just as in medieval Europe, perhaps for similar reasons. But when China was once again a political unit, it regained its bureaucratic structure, its efficient hierarchies of markets, and the fairs disappeared *from the interior*. They only survived on the external frontiers. Thus under the Sung dynasty (960–1279) who controlled only southern China, 'mutual markets' were held looking towards the north, conquered by the Barbarians. Once unity was restored under the Mings (1368–1644), and maintained by the Tsings (1644–1911) China's windows and lookout posts were to be found only on the circumference, turned to the outside world. There were horse fairs for instance on the Manchurian frontier from 1405, which opened or closed depending on relations between the frontier and the Barbarians who threatened it. Sometimes a fair might be held at the very gates of Peking, when a caravan arrived there from Moscow. But this was exceptional, since caravans from the West were preferably stopped by the fairs of Han Chu and Cheng Tun. In 1728[521] similarly, the very curious and important Kiatka fair, where the Chinese merchants obtained their

Dutch illustration of an account of a journey to the East Indies (1598). In the centre, one of the Chinese merchants who regularly settled in the town of Bantam during the season of commercial activity; on the left the Javanese woman who became his 'wife' during his stay; on the right, one of the resident Chinese agents who went round the island with his scales, buying up pepper in the off-season. (Photo F. Quilici.)

precious Siberian furs, was held south of Irkutsk. Finally in the eighteenth century, Canton, faced with the trade of the Europeans, was granted two fairs.[522] Like the other great seaports more or less open to international trade (Ningpo, Amoy) Canton thus acquired one or more trade 'seasons'. But these were not the same as the great free-for-all encounters of Islam or the Indies. In China, the fair remained a limited phenomenon, confined to certain particular trades, usually foreign. Either because China was afraid of the effects of such fairs and sought to protect herself against them; or more probably because she did not need them: with her administrative and governmental unity, her active chains of markets, she could do well enough without them.

As for Japan, where markets and shops were organized on a regular basis by the thirteenth century, becoming larger and more widespread later on, there does not seem to have been a system of fairs. After 1638 however, when Japan was closed to foreign trade, apart from a few Dutch and Chinese ships, a kind of fair was held in Nagasaki, every time a Dutch vessel of the East India Company arrived there 'on permission', or when the similarly 'permitted' Chinese junks sailed in. Such 'fairs' were infrequent. But like those which were held in Archangel or in Moscow when English or Dutch ships had arrived, they were a way of restoring balance, of vital importance for Japan: it was the only way, after the voluntary 'closed door' policy, of breathing the outside air – and also of playing its role, for Japan's contribution to the outside world, its exports of silver and copper in particular, handled by these ships alone, had their effect on the cycles of the world economy: the silver cycle before 1665, the brief gold cycle between 1665 and 1668 (or 1672); and finally the copper cycle.

Europe versus the rest of the world?

Images are only images. But if they are numerous, repeated, identical, they cannot all be wrong. They show us that in a varied universe, forms and performances can be similar: there are towns, routes, states, patterns of trade which in spite of everything resemble each other. We are indeed told that there are as many 'means of exchange as there are means of production'. But in any case these means are limited in number, since they are directed to solving elementary problems, the same the whole world over.

Rome, a wild-fowler's stall. (Photo Oscar Salvio.)

So we have a first impression to go on: in the sixteenth century, the *populated* regions of the world, faced with the demands of numbers, *seem* to us to be quite close to each other, on terms of equality or nearly so. No doubt a slight gap would be enough for advantages to emerge and be confirmed on one side, leading in time to superiority, while on the other side there would necessarily be inferiority and subjection. Is this what happened between Europe and the rest of the world? It is difficult to give a hard and fast answer or explain everything in a few words. There is for one thing a 'historiographical' inequality between Europe and the rest of the world. Europe invented historians and then made good use of them. Her own history is well-lit, and can be called as evidence or used as a claim. The history of non-Europe is still being written. And until the balance of knowledge and interpretation has been restored, the historian will be reluctant to cut the Gordian knot of world history – that is the origin of the superiority of Europe. This uncomfortable situation has been encountered by Joseph Needham[523] the expert on China, who found it difficult, even on the comparatively clear plane of science and technology, to locate his huge subject with precision on the world stage. One thing seems clear to me: the gap between the West and the other continents appeared *late in time*, and to attribute it simply to the 'rationalization' of the market economy, as too many of our contemporaries are still inclined to do, is obviously over-simplifying.

But in any case, to explain this gap, which was to grow wider over the years, is to tackle the essential problem of the history of the modern world. It is a problem we shall keep encountering throughout this long book, without pretending to come up with a clear-cut answer. At least we shall have tried to pose it under as many lights as possible, and to have wheeled up our explanations, as in the old days generals would wheel up their bombards to the walls of the city they hoped to take by force.

Concluding hypotheses

All the different mechanisms of trade I have presented, from the simplest market to the Stock Exchange, are easy to recognize and describe. But it is not so easy to mark with precision their relative position in economic life, to consider what they have to tell us as a whole. Do they date from the same time? Are they connected with each other or not? And if so, how? Have they been forces for growth or not? It is probably impossible to give a categorical answer to such questions, since some of the wheels of trade must have worked faster and some slower, depending on the flow of the economy that turned them. First one set, then another seems to have had its day, and each century has a particular physiognomy of trade. If we are not the victims of a simplifying illusion, this differential history may shed light on the course of economic development in

Europe and may also perhaps serve as a means of comparative interpretation for the rest of the world.

The fifteenth century prolonged the disasters and deficiencies of the latter half of the fourteenth. Then after about 1450, a recovery began. But the West would take years and years to return to the level of its former prosperity. France under Saint Louis, unless I am much mistaken, was a very different place from the active, though still suffering France of Louis XI. Outside certain privileged zones (parts of Italy, the bustling world of the Netherlands) economic communications had fallen into decay; economic agents – individuals or groups – were more or less left to themselves, and took advantage of the situation consciously or unconsciously. In such circumstances, fairs and markets – markets more than fairs – were sufficient to reanimate trade and set communications going again. The way in which the towns of the West came to dominate the countryside foreshadows the recovery of the urban markets, as instruments which would achieve unaided the regular subjection of the surrounding area. 'Industrial' prices were rising, and agricultural prices falling. Towns were getting their way.

As for the sixteenth century, Raymond de Roover,[524] (a historian who has however always eschewed easy explanations) thinks that this was the great age of the fairs. According to him they explain everything. They became more frequent; they were in blooming health; and they were soon everywhere, to be counted in hundreds if not thousands. If this was indeed the case – and I am inclined to agree that it was – then progress forward in the sixteenth century must have been achieved from *above*, under the impact of the top-level circulation of money and credit, from one fair to another. Everything else would have depended upon these international monetary movements at a high level ('flying through the air').[525] Then, as they slowed down or ran into complications, the machine would begin to hiccup. By about 1575, the Antwerp–Lyons–Medina del Campo circuit was in trouble. The Genoese, with their so-called Besançon fairs, managed to put the pieces together again but not for long.

In the seventeenth century, *commodities* led the way to recovery. I am not inclined to attribute this revival entirely to the intervention of Amsterdam and its Exchange, although they played a part in it: I prefer to explain it by the increase of trading at the lower levels, within the modest circle of the local, sometimes very localized economy: was not the crucial instrument or machine or revival the shop? If this view is correct, the price rise of the sixteenth century would correspond to the reign of the superstructure; while the decline and stagnation of the seventeenth century would have witnessed the primacy of the infrastructures. This is, if not a completely watertight explanation, at least a plausible one.

But how are we then to account for the advance, indeed the rapid take-off of the Age of Enlightenment? After 1720, there was in all likelihood movement at every level. But the important point is that this marked an increasingly obvious split within the *system* as it had hitherto existed. Increasingly, the market was faced with the *anti-market* (a stronger term which I prefer to that of *private trading*, used up till now); and the fair was confronted with the rise of the warehouse and the wholesale trade. Fairs tended to move back to the level of elementary exchange. Similarly the Exchanges and Bourses witnessed the rise of the banks which were bursting through like so many plants, if not new varieties at any rate more numerous and independent ones. We could do with a word to describe these breakthroughs, innovations and changes of scale. But there is no word that can do justice to all the external forces which were surrounding and crushing the ancient nucleus of trade: the whole range of *parallel* activities, now gathering speed and clearly visible at the summit, along the major axes of banking and the stock market, criss-crossing Europe and effectively reducing it to obedience, but which were also clearly visible at the base, with the revolutionary spread of the travelling salesman or 'pedlar'.

If these explanations, have, as I believe, a certain amount of truth in them, they bring us back once more to the mysterious but constant interaction of the superstructures and infrastructures of economic life. Can what goes on at the top have repercussions at a lower level? If so what? And by the same token, can what is happening at the level of the village market and the simplest forms of trading have an effect on the upper end of the scale? If so how does this happen? For the sake of brevity, let me give an example. When the eighteenth century was twenty years old, two simultaneous events occurred: the South Sea Bubble, the scandal which hit English financial circles; and Law's system in France, that extraordinary episode which lasted no more than eighteen months. If we accept that the experience in the rue de Quincampoix was not unlike that of 'Change Alley, we have here proof that the economy as a whole, while it might be upset by turbulence at high altitudes, was not entirely governed from these august heights over a period of years. Capitalism had not yet succeeded in imposing its rule. All the same, while I agree with Jacob Van Klaveren[526] that Law's failure is obviously explained by the interested hostility of a section of the high nobility, it is also equally to be explained by the French economy itself, which was unable to follow suit, to jump on to the infernal bandwagon. England managed to recover from its scandal more successfully than France, in economic terms. It did not suffer from that traumatic fear of paper-money and banking which was to mark France for decades afterwards. Is this not evidence of a certain politico-socio-economic maturity in England, which was now too committed to modern forms of finance and credit to be able to retreat?

The model outlined in the preceding lines holds good only for the West. But now that it has been drawn, does it help us to read developments in the rest of the world? The two outstanding features of western development were first the establishment of the higher mechanisms of trade, then in the eighteenth century, the proliferation of ways and means. What was happening outside Europe in this respect? The most aberrant case is that of China, where the imperial administration blocked any attempts to create an economic hierarchy. Only the very lowest levels of trading worked effectively, the shops and markets of city and small town. The cases most resembling Europe were those of Islam and Japan. We shall of course have to return to this comparative history of the world which is the only scale on which our problems can be solved or at any rate correctly posed.

2

Markets and the Economy

THE WORLD OF TRADE remains the subject of this second chapter, in which I hope to suggest a number of models and regularities or trends.[1] This will mean moving away from the sequence of single images offered in Chapter 1, in which we looked at the local market, the shop, the fair and the Stock Exchange as a series of individual units. Our problem now is to see how these units were related to each other, how trade circuits became established, how the merchant built up his connections, and how such connections, although completely by-passing many areas still untouched by trade, came to create coherent trading zones. Our imperfect vocabulary calls such zones 'markets' – an intrinsically ambiguous term. But we must bow to usage.

The question will be approached from two separate perspectives. First, standing alongside the merchant, we shall try to imagine his everyday activity and tactics. Then moving on to an area broadly outside the individual's control, we shall consider these trading zones in themselves, markets, that is, in the wide sense. Whether they were urban, regional, national or even international, these markets were the reality the merchant had to reckon with, the context of his actions, furthering them or holding them back. What is more, they were transformed over the centuries. And the changing geography and economy of the markets (at which we shall look more closely in Volume III) were of course constantly reshaping and redirecting the individual action of the merchant.

Merchants and trade circuits

The merchant's viewpoint and his actions are already familiar to us: we can consult his papers.[2] Nothing is easier than to sit ourselves down at his desk, reading his correspondence, checking his accounts and following the fortunes of his business. But we are here more concerned to understand the rules within which his profession enclosed him, rules he knew through experience, but to which, precisely because he did know them, he paid little attention in his day-to-day affairs. We have to build a systematic picture.

The hands of the merchant Georg Gisze. Detail of a painting by Holbein. (Staatliche Museum Preussischer Kulturbesitz, Berlin.)

Return journeys

Since exchange by definition means reciprocity, any journey from A to B must be balanced by a return journey – however complicated and roundabout – from B to A. The round trip, once complete, forms a circuit. Trade circuits are like electrical circuits: they only work when the connection is unbroken. As a merchant of Reims in the days of Louis XIV succinctly put it: 'Sale governs purchase.'[3] He meant of course that it did so, or ought to, at a profit.

Let A be Venice and B Alexandria in Egypt (since we may as well choose a grand example). A voyage from A to B should be followed by a trip from B to A. If our imaginary merchant of Venice was living there in say 1500, we might suppose that he had to hand for the outward journey several *groppi* of silver coins, mirrors, glass beads, woollen cloth. These goods, bought in Venice, would be dispatched to Alexandria and sold there; in exchange the most likely purchases in Egypt would be *colli* of pepper, spices, and drugs, to be sent back to Venice and sold there – probably at the *Fontego dei Todeschi* (to use the Venetian name: the Italian term was the *Fondaco dei Tedeschi*).

Let us suppose that our merchant is fortunate and that the *four* buying and selling operations pass off without undue delay – a critical point, since long before it became an English proverb, 'Time is money' was the motto of all traders. Never leave '*li danari mortti*',[4] money lying dead; sell quickly, even at a lower price, in order to '*venier presto sul danaro per un altro viaggo*',[5] were the orders given to his agent by the wealthy Venetian merchant Michiel da Lezze, in the early years of the sixteenth century. If there is no hitch then, the merchandise is no sooner bought in Venice than loaded on board ship. The boat leaves on the appointed day (this seldom happened in real life); in Alexandria, the goods find a buyer straight away, and the articles requested in return are available; once these are unloaded at Venice, they are easily disposed of. Needless to say, such ideal circumstances for closing the circuit were far from being the rule. Sometimes the cloth lay for months in Alexandria, in the warehouse of a relation or an agent; it was the wrong colour perhaps, or of inferior quality. Sometimes the spice caravans had not arrived on time. Or when the ship returned to Venice it was to find the Venetian market already flooded with goods from the Levant so that prices were unusually low.

That said, immediate interest in this hypothetical case is:

1 that this circuit consists of four successive deals – as indeed will any return trade operation;

2 that depending on whether one is in A or B, the process will have had different phases: two supply and demand operations will have taken place in A, two in B: the merchant will create a demand for the original goods in Venice before setting off; these will be supplied in Alexandria for sale; a new demand will be made for the next purchase, and this will be supplied in Venice to terminate the affair;

3 the whole operation can only be concluded and valued on completion. The fortunes of the merchant remain in the balance until the very end. This is his daily worry: the moment of truth comes at the end of the journey. The profits, expenses, payments and losses entered from day to day in various currencies throughout the operation are converted into a single monetary unit – Venetian currency say. Only then will the merchant be able to set off assets against liabilities and learn whether the round trip was worth it. Perhaps, as was quite often the case, only the return trip made a profit. The China trade in the eighteenth century is a classic example.[6]

All this may seem too simple to be true. But there is nothing to stop us complicating the model. A trading operation need not be a merely two-way process. What was known as the triangular circuit was the classic pattern in the Atlantic in the seventeenth and eighteenth centuries: from Liverpool, for example, to the coast of Guinea, then to Jamaica and back to Liverpool; or from Bordeaux to the Senegal coast, then to Martinique and back to Bordeaux. Captain de la Roche Couvert was asked by the owners of the vessel *Saint-Louis* to make a roundabout voyage in 1743: to sail to Acadia (Canada) and pick up a cargo of cod; to sell it in Guadeloupe and here take on sugar, which he was to bring back to Le Havre.[7] The Venetians were doing much the same thing, even before the fifteenth century, with the convenient *galere da mercato*, regularly equipped by the Signoria. In 1505 for instance, the patrician Michiel da Lezze[8] gave very detailed instructions to Sebastian Dolfin, who was taking the galleys on 'the Barbary run': on the first leg, Venice–Tunis, he was to carry specie – silver *mocenighi*; in Tunis, this would be exchanged for gold dust; in Valencia, the gold was to be melted down and coined in the city mint; or exchanged for wool; or brought back to Venice, depending on the circumstances. The same merchant had another speciality: selling in London cloves bought in Alexandria, and selling cloth from London in the Levant. The English merchantman that sailed out of the Thames in the seventeenth century, with a cargo of lead, copper and salt fish bound for Leghorn, was also engaged in a three-cornered trade: it was to pick up in the Italian port the specie which enabled goods to be bought in the Levant, in Zante, Cyprus, or Tripoli in Syria – raisins, raw cotton, spices (if there were any left), bales of silk, or even malmsey wine.[9] And voyages of four or more legs were contemplated. French ships based in Marseilles sometimes called at several Italian ports in succession, on the way home from the Levant.[10] The 'warehouse trade' practised by the Dutch in the seventeenth century was many-sided in principle, and the trade they carried on between different parts of the Far East was evidently constructed on the same pattern. The Dutch East India Company[11] only took the trouble to hold on to Timor in the East Indies for example because of the sandalwood it obtained there to use as an exchange currency in China where it was highly prized. The company brought many goods, to Surat in India, and exchanged them for silks, cottons and above all silver coins (indispensable for trade with Bengal); on the coast of Coromandel, where the company bought many fabrics (but no early pumpkins) its exchange currency was spice from the Moluccas or Japanese copper in which it had the monopoly; in densely-populated Siam, it sold large quantities of fabric from Coromandel, at very little profit but in exchange for buckskin (much in demand in Japan) and pewter from Ligot, in which it had exclusive buying rights and which it sold in India and Europe 'at some profit'. And so on. In the eighteenth century, in order to obtain in Italy the 'piastres and sequins [necessary for] their Levant trade', the Dutch[12] carried to Genoa or Leghorn goods from as it might be India, China, Russia, or Silesia; coffee from Martinique and cloth from Languedoc loaded at Marseilles. I quote these examples to suggest what might lie behind the simple formula of 'the return journey'.

Circuits and bills of exchange

Closing the circuit, rarely a simple matter, could not always be effected with goods for goods, or even with goods for coin; so merchants were regularly obliged to resort to bills of exchange. Initially a form of compensation, they also became, in Christian countries where interest on loans was forbidden by the Church, the most frequent form of credit. Credit and compensation were thus closely linked, as will quickly be understood from one or two minor examples – usually abnormal cases since the documents tend to mention the exception rather than the rule, the deal that went wrong rather than the success.

I have described elsewhere in some detail[13] apropos of credit how Simón Ruiz, a merchant of Medina del Campo, managed in his later years, after 1590, to make money at no risk and with little difficulty, by the practice of 'merchant usury' – which was in fact perfectly lawful. This old fox would buy at Medina bills of exchange from the Spanish wool producers sending their fleeces to Italy, who wanted to avoid the usual delays of transport and payment. They were in a hurry for their money. Simón Ruiz would advance it to them against a bill of exchange usually drawn on the purchaser of the wool and payable in three months' time. If possible, he would buy the bill at less than its face value and send it to his friend, commission agent and compatriot, Baltasar Suárez in Florence. Suárez would collect the money from the nominee, use it to buy another bill of exchange this time drawable on Medina del Campo, which Simón Ruiz would cash three months later. This final operation, at the end of the six months, represented the closing by Simón Ruiz of the circuit opened by the transaction between the wool producers and their customers in Florence. It was because the parties concerned either would not or could not tolerate the usual delays of the export trade, that Simón Ruiz handled it for them, making a clear profit of 5% in return for credit over six months.

But deals could always go wrong. In any given money market, paper and specie operated in a certain relationship, in order to fix the rate for bills of

A letter from the heirs of Lodovico Benedito Bonbisi & Co. Lyons, 23 March 1575, to Francisco de la Pressa and the heirs of Victor Ruys at Medina del Campo (received 13 April) concerning settlements of bills of exchange (the sums at the bottom of the page show the calculations made). At the end of the letter, just above the signature, the rates of exchange in various cities are quoted. (Simón Ruiz Archive, Valladolid.)

exchange at higher or lower cash prices. If specie was abundant, paper appreciated, and vice versa. The operation of the direct return with a regular profit on the second bill was sometimes difficult or even impossible, if bills were quoted at Florence at too high a rate. Baltasar Suárez would then be obliged to draw on his own account (or rather on the account opened in his name by Simón Ruiz) or to 'launder' the money via Antwerp or Besançon. Thus the money would make a triangular trip, taking another three months. This was still acceptable – but Simón Ruiz would be furious if at the end of the day he found that he had not made the interest he was counting on. He wanted to play the market – but only on a safe bet. As he wrote in 1584, he preferred to '*guardar el dinero en caxa que arisgar en cambios y perder del principal, o no gagnar nada*',[14] 'keep his money in a chest rather than risk losing some of his principal on the exchanges, or forego all profit'. But while Simón Ruiz might feel hard done by, the circuit had been completed normally for all the other parties concerned.

No closure, no deal

If in certain circumstances a trade circuit could not be closed at all, it was clearly doomed to disappear. Wars, frequent as they were, were not usually sufficient to do this, but it sometimes happened. Let us take an example.

Azure, a dyestuff of mineral origin based on cobalt (always mixed, especially when of poor quality, with sparkling sand) was used in the manufacture of china and porcelain to give blue glazes; it was also used to bleach canvas. We find a merchant in Caen (12 May 1784) complaining to his stockist about the latest batch: 'I did not find this azure as dark as usual and it seems to contain much more sand.'[15] The correspondence of an azure supplier, Bensa Brothers of Frankfurt-am-Main with a stockist in Rouen, who worked on commission, Dugard Fils, reflects a series of transactions so unchanging over thirty years that the surviving letters repeat themselves word for word, year after year. The only differences, apart from the dates, are the names of the captains of the boats who took on board, usually in Amsterdam, sometimes in Rotterdam and occasionally in Bremen, the kegs of azure which Bensa manufactured and sent to Dugard Fils. Hitches were rare; a boat might be late, another run aground in the river near Rouen (but this was a real exception);[16] or a competitor might appear on the horizon. The kegs regularly piled up in the warehouse of Dugard Fils, who sent them off day by day to Dieppe, Elbeuf, Bernay, Louviers, Bolbec, Fontainebleau or Caen. The French firm sold to its clients on credit and recovered its money in the form of bills of exchange, discounts, or direct dispatches of cash.

As for the return payment from the French stockist to Bensa Brothers, this could have taken the form of merchandise, since Dugard handled anything and everything: fabrics, gum from Senegal, madder, books, Burgundy wines (in cask or bottle), scythes, whalebone, indigo, Smyrna cotton. But in fact the bill was always paid in money, by draft and discount, following a procedure insisted upon by the German supplier. One example will serve to illustrate it. On 31 October 1775,[17] Rémy Bensa was adding up the goods he had sent to Rouen from Frankfurt: 'I estimate them with the usual deduction of 15% extinctive[18] expenses, at 4470 l[*ivres*] 19 s[*ols*], 2/3 of which I am taking the liberty of drawing on you as of today, viz. 2980 l[*ivres*] in three instalments, payable to my account in Paris.' The instalments (*usances*) corresponded to delays in payment, each probably of two weeks. So by the named date, Dugard would have to pay 2980 *livres* to a Paris banker, always the same one, who would send the money to Frankfurt. The settling of accounts, of which this was the first stage, was completed at the end of the year; all outstanding payments were made and the books balanced in good faith on both sides, between Dugard who seems from his letters to have been courteous, good-humoured and obliging, and the correspondents at the Frankfurt end who are inclined to grumble and lay down the law. The final settlement in fact depended on the smooth passage of bills of exchange between Paris and Frankfurt. If this line of communication was interrupted, the peaceful operations of thirty years would be disturbed. And of course this is precisely what happened at the beginning of the French Revolution.

By March 1793, Bensa could no longer be under any illusion: all trade was forbidden between Holland and France, and the people of Frankfurt did not even know exactly what their position was faced with the wave of belligerence gradually invading Europe. 'I do not know, Monsieur,' he writes to Dugard Fils, 'if the inhabitants of our country are accounted enemies, although we are not such, but if that should be the case, I should be most distressed, since our business would have to stop forthwith'.[19] And indeed it was about to stop, very abruptly, for 'paper drawn on Paris is constantly falling here, and it is to be presumed that it will fall further', as one of the last letters says. In other words, the return journey was now compromised beyond all rescue.

On the problems of the return journey

For bills of exchange, which were the everyday solution to the problem of returns, the security of the financial circuit was of course essential. This security depended on the possibility of effective communication as much as on the personal credit of the correspondents. No merchant was completely safe from nasty surprises; all the same one was better off in Amsterdam than in say Saint-Malo.

In 1747, Picot de Saint-Bucq, an important merchant in Saint-Malo, who had invested money in the cargo of the vessel *Le Lis*, sailing to Peru, was anxious to recover what was owed him from the return trip, when the ship reached Spain. So he wrote on 3 July to MM. Jolif & Co. in Cadiz: '... when you are in a position to reimburse me, please make it in completely reliable bills of exchange, and above all, may I recommend that you do not take out any on the French Indies Company nor on any of its agents, whoever they may be, on any account

...'[20] It is not surprising to find that there were agents of the *Compagnie française des Indes* in Cadiz: like those of other companies, they came there to collect silver piastres (the old 'pieces of eight') which were indispensable for the Far East trade. The company was prepared, if a French merchant offered it piastres, to give him immediately in return a bill of exchange payable in Paris. Why did Picot de Saint-Bucq refuse to accept this? Perhaps because he already had dealings with the company and did not want to confuse two separate deals? Perhaps because the company and the Saint-Malo merchants had crossed swords in the past? Or perhaps because the enormous company was known for its bad habits regarding prompt payment? Whatever the reason, Picot was in any case dependent upon the choice made by his correspondent: in the first place, and this mattered, as he himself says in another letter, 'Saint-Malo as you know does not have a money market.'[21] A valuable piece of information when one is aware of the predilection Saint-Malo's merchants always had for cash in their commercial dealings.

It was always advantageous for a firm to have direct links with one of the major financial centres. Pellet Brothers of Bordeaux successfully established one such when in 1728 Pierre Pellet married Jeanne Nairac, whose brother Guillaume was soon to be their correspondent in Amsterdam, then the leading centre in Europe.[22] Here it was easy both to find outlets for merchandise and to place cash which could be more fruitfully invested here than anywhere else; and one could borrow money at the lowest rates in Europe. From this super-efficient centre, in touch with all the others, it was easy to do good turns to one's own firm or to others, even to rich Dutch merchants.

For the same reasons, the firm of Marc Fraissinet of Sète had its branch Fraissinet Fils in Amsterdam in 1778. This was why when the Dutch vessel *Jacobus Catharina*, owned by Cornelis van Castricum of Amsterdam, arrived in Sète in November 1778, her master, Captain Gerkel had been recommended to the local firm of Fraissinet.[23] He was carrying 644 'baskets' of tobacco for the National Monopoly, which paid for the cargo (16,353 *livres*) on the spot. The service requested by the Dutch shipowner was a simple one: that the money from

Bill of exchange to the order of the Bordeaux merchant Jean Pellet (1719). (Departmental Archives of the Gironde.)

the deal should reach him 'promptly'. But as bad luck would have it, (a) Captain Gerkel had entrusted the Tobacco Monopoly's 'money order' to Fraissinet, who had promptly cashed it; (b) the Fraissinet Fils firm in Amsterdam went bankrupt at the end of 1778, and drew the Sète headquarters down with it. And poor Captain Gerkel was immediately embroiled in legal proceedings: at first with some success, later less so. He had run into the obvious bad faith of Marc Fraissinet and equally into the demands of the creditors of the bankrupt firm. Everyone combined against the foreign creditor who had blundered into a hornet's nest. In the end the return payment was made, but after a long delay and on disastrous terms.

On long-distance runs – to the West Indies or the Indian Ocean – the most profitable business of the time – the return trip often raised problems. Merchants had to be prepared to improvise and take risks.

With a clear view to speculation, the merchant Louis Greffulhe had established his brother in the island of Saint-Eustatius, one of the smaller West Indian islands under Dutch rule. The operation was beneficial in more ways than one; but it was risky and finally ended dramatically. After April 1776, with the war between England and the American colonies, international communications were disturbed and trade with America became difficult and suspect. How was Greffulhe to repatriate his funds? The brother in the West Indies, in some despair, sent his partner Du Moulin (Louis' brother-in-law) to Martinique 'to obtain discount bills', payable in France of course, which was still at peace with England, and via France in Amsterdam. What nonsense, stormed the older brother in Amsterdam.

> What will come of this? Either he will not find any negotiable ones and that will mean more delay; or if he does manage to obtain paper payable in Bordeaux or Paris, even if the signatory is the soundest inhabitant of Martinique it is almost always challenged in Europe and God knows when one will catch up with one's money. If he sends us a bill from there, God grant that this will not be the case.[24]

The bill of exchange was indeed an excellent instrument for 'settling accounts': but it had to be accessible, sound and easily negotiable.

In October 1729 (after he had given up the profession of sailor in the service of the French *Compagnie des Indes* for that of a merchant adventurer) Mahé de la Bourdonnais was in Pondicherry.[25] He was thinking of setting up a new company with friends from Saint-Malo who had already agreed to share the costs. They would advance funds and merchandise to be used for trading within the Far East, in Mocha, Batavia, Manila, even China. For sending back the profits as well as the capital investments, Mahé had plenty of ideas. There was the straightforward solution of bills on the *Compagnie des Indes*; or returns in the form of merchandise (he had just sent 700 cotton shirts from India to one of the partners who wanted his money back immediately: these 'run no risk of confiscation', Mahé pointed out, unlike printed calicoes, which were forbidden to enter France at this time). Another solution was to send gold with a cooperative captain returning to France (this meant avoiding paying freight charges, a saving of 2.5%, and making an extra 20% profit). Mahé was not on the other hand very keen on sending back diamonds, a method used by the English and other Europeans in India. For 'I confess quite frankly,' he writes, 'that I do not know enough about them to trust my own judgment ... nor am I so gullible as to place my trust blindly in the professional valuers'. If the new company did not work out, Mahé was to bring back the goods and the money to France in person: but he would take a Portuguese boat if possible so as to call in Brazil where certain goods from the Indies could be sold profitably. This tells us, incidentally, that Mahé de la Bourdonnais had friends and business connections on the Brazilian coast where he had stayed before. For long-distance travellers like him, the world was already becoming a global village, with familiar faces in every port.

The French publication *Manuel de commerce des Indes orientales et de la Chine* (*Trading manual for the East Indies and China*) by Captain Pierre Blancard, which appeared belatedly in 1806, describes the profitable arrangements formerly enjoyed by French merchants in the *'île de France'*, now Mauritius. They had frequently enriched themselves, by rendering services (certainly not disinterested) to English settlers in India who wished to repatriate discreetly the fortunes they had made, more or less lawfully, abroad. The French merchants gave the English 'drafts on Paris payable in six months at an exchange rate of 9 francs to the starred pagoda, which meant 2 francs fifty centimes to the rupee'.[26] (The use of the words *francs* and *centimes* tells us that Blancard, writing in the time of Napoleon, was translating the financial operations of the previous century into contemporary currency.) The drafts were not of course drawn on empty accounts, but on the profits of the French trade with the Indies, which were regularly repatriated to Parisian bankers – the same ones who would later honour the drafts held by the English. So in order for this circuit to be completed profitably for the French in Mauritius, the following conditions were necessary: the English had to be unable to use their own system of repatriating funds; the trade in printed calicoes from India handled by the French had to be well established; and both in commercial dealings and currency exchange, the conversion of rupees into *livres* had to be in their favour. We may be confident, I think, that the French saw that these conditions were fulfilled.

Collaboration between merchants

The networks of trade encircled the world. At every halt or crossroads we can assume that there was a merchant, either settled or passing through. The role he played was determined by his position on the map: 'Tell me *where* you are and I will tell you *who* you are.' The hazard of birth, inheritance or any other twist of fate might land him in, say, Judenburg in Upper Styria like Clemens Körbler (*florebat* 1526–1548): in that case he would handle Styrian iron or steel from

Leoben, and would have to attend the Linz fairs.²⁷ If he was a wholesaler in, say, Marseilles, he would have the choice of the three or four local possibilities – a choice generally dictated by the circumstances of the day. If the wholesaler, before the nineteenth century, always dealt in several commodities, was this dictated simply by prudence – to avoid putting all his eggs in the same basket? Or, to change the metaphor, was he obliged to seize at the flood the tide of trade (which he did not create) whenever it flowed past his door? To stake everything on one commodity alone would not bring him the desired living standard. If the latter explanation is true, the 'polyvalence' of the merchant was the result of outside pressures, of the inadequate volume of trade. Certainly the wholesaler in a busy commercial city, who had access to the major currents of trade, was consistently less specialized than the retailer.

Any commercial network brought together a certain number of individuals or agents, whether belonging to the same firm or not, located at different points on a circuit or a group of circuits. Trade thrived on these communications, on the cooperation and connections which automatically flowered with the increasing prosperity of the interested parties.

A good example, perhaps a little too good to be true, is provided by the career of Jean Pellet (1694-1764): born in the Rouergue, he became a merchant at Bordeaux after a difficult start as a humble retailer in Martinique where, as his brother reminded him when they had made their fortune, he used to eat 'mildewed manioc flour and bitter wine, with warmed-up beef'.²⁸ In 1718²⁹ he returned to Bordeaux and set up in business with his brother Pierre, two years his elder, who went to Martinique. This was a firm with very little capital, exclusively handling trade between the island and Bordeaux. Each brother held one end of the rope, which was no bad thing when Law's system collapsed. 'You will remark', wrote Pierre from the West Indies, 'that we are very fortunate to have survived this year without loss; all the traders are operating on credit now' (8 July 1721).³⁰ A month later, 9 August, he wrote, 'I view with the same astonishment as you the desolation of France and the risk of losing one's fortune very rapidly; luckily we are in a position to be able to survive this better than most, because of the outlets we have here [in Martinique]. Make sure you do not hang on to any money or bills' – in other words stick to commodities. The brothers remained in partnership until 1730, after which date they maintained commercial links with each other. Each had been launched on his career by the enormous profits they had amassed and which they concealed with greater or lesser resourcefulness. We shall follow the affairs of the more adventurous brother Jean after 1730: by 1733, he was sufficiently rich, operating now through a number of commission agents or 'captain-managers' of the ships he owned, not to need a formal partnership any longer. The range of his business connections and the number of his business interests is quite staggering: he was ship-owner, wholesaler, occasional financier, landed proprietor, wine producer and merchant, and investor; he had connections in Martinique, Saint Domingue,

Caracas, Cadiz, Biscay, Bayonne, Toulouse, Marseilles, Nantes, Rouen, Dieppe, London, Amsterdam, Middelburg, Hamburg, Ireland (for purchases of salt beef), Brittany (for purchases of linen cloth) and more places besides. And of course he was in touch with bankers in Paris, Geneva and Rouen.

It is worth noting that the double Pellet fortune (Pierre, although more prudent and reluctant to take risks than his younger brother, also made his millions, confining himself entirely to ship-owning and the colonial trade) was founded on a family partnership. And Guillaume Nairac, the brother of the bride Pierre married in 1728, became the two brothers' correspondent in Amsterdam.[31] Since the merchant profession could not do without a network of reliable go-betweens and associates, the family offered the most natural and sought-after solution. The history of the great merchant families is therefore every bit as valuable as the history of princely dynasties in the study of political fluctuations, as the works of Louis Dermigny, Herbert Lüthy and Hermann Kellenbenz eloquently demonstrate. Romuald Szramkiewicz's study of the list of the regents of the *Banque de France* under the Consulate and Empire is another good example.[32] Even more fascinating, to my mind, would be the pre-history of the *Banque de France*, of the families who founded it, who all, or almost all, seem to have had connections with the silver of Spanish America.

The family firm was not the only answer of course. In the sixteenth century, the Fuggers made use of factors, who were merely employees in their service. This was the authoritarian model. The Affaitadi,[33] a firm originally from Cremona, preferred to run subsidiaries, sometimes associated with local firms. Before them, the Medici had set up a system of branches,[34] which it could declare independent at any moment simply by rearranging the accounts if economic circumstances warranted it (a way of avoiding a local bankruptcy having repercussions on the whole firm). By the end of the sixteenth century, the commission system, more flexible, less costly and more time-saving, was tending to become general. All merchants – in Italy or in Amsterdam for instance – worked on commission for other merchants, who did the same for them. They took a small percentage on deals negotiated for other people and expected the same commission to be subtracted from their own accounts for a similar arrangement. We are not talking about partnerships, simply of reciprocal services. Another practice gaining currency at the time was the informal association known as participation, in which the interested parties went into partnership but only for one operation: the performance could be repeated the next time. More of this later.

Whatever the form of agreement or cooperation between merchants, it required loyalty, personal confidence, scrupulousness and respect for instructions. There was quite a strict code of behaviour among merchants. Hebenstreit and Son, an Amsterdam firm, had agreed a fifty-fifty contract with Dugard Fils of Rouen. On 6 January 1766,[35] they wrote a stiff letter to the French firm, because it had sold 'very cheaply', 'without any necessity and even against our express instructions', the Senegal gum they had dispatched to Rouen. The

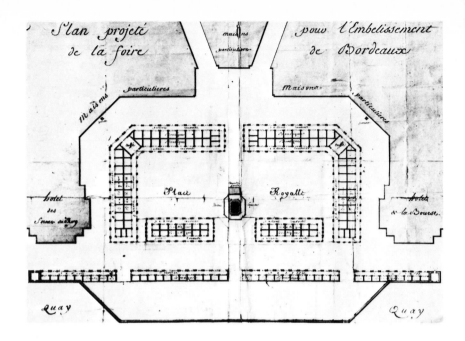

Bordeaux, plans for the Place Royale by J. Gabriel (1733). (Departmental Archives of the Gironde.) Below, the present-day Place de la Bourse. The oblique section on the right was allocated to Jean Pellet in 1743, alongside the site acquired by the banker Pierre Policard. (Photo B. Beaujard.)

conclusion is plain: 'We insist that you replace our half-share[36] yourself, at the same price you have sold it for so inopportunely.' At least they are proposing an amicable settlement, 'so that we do not have to appeal to a third party', evidence that in an affair like this, merchant solidarity, even in Rouen, would have operated in favour of an Amsterdam supplier.

One had to have confidence in one's agents then, and instructions had to be obeyed. In 1564, the merchant Simón Ruiz had an agent in Seville called Gerónimo de Valladolid, a young man, and probably a Castilian like himself.[37] One day, Simón Ruiz lost his temper with his agent and accused him, rightly or wrongly, of some mistake or malpractice. The presence of a second agent (who had seized the opportunity to inform his master) did not of course help matters. Gerónimo promptly disappeared, since the Seville police were after him. But before long he turned up at Medina del Campo, where he flung himself at his master's feet to beg his pardon. When by chance I was reading some papers dating from 1570, I came across the name of Gerónimo de Valladolid again. Six years after the above incident, he had become a merchant specializing in cotton and woollen cloth in Seville. Had he made good? Although the details of this little story are unknown, it throws some light on the vital question of the reliability that a merchant expected, and had a right to expect from his agent, his partner or his employee. And it also reveals a little about the relations between master and servant, superior and inferior, which seem to be rather 'feudal'. A French agent in the early eighteenth century is still talking about the 'yoke' and the 'domination' of the masters from whom he is glad to have recently escaped.[38]

To trust one's agents, whatever happened, was indeed the only way an outsider could penetrate the bewildering world of Seville; and a little later, in Cadiz, an equally bewildering city for the same reasons, it was the only way to have a share in the vital trade with the Americas, in theory confined to Spanish nationals. Seville and Cadiz, the bridgeheads to America, were very special ports, where fraud and chaos flourished, and where local authorities and regulations were regularly flouted – sometimes with official complicity. But within this atmosphere of corruption, there was a sort of 'professional code', just as there was an understanding between the wrongdoers and the *alguazils* in the suburb of Triana or in the port of San Lucar de Barrameda, two notorious haunts of the Spanish underworld. For if you were a foreign merchant in Spain and your trusted agent let you down, you would, as a foreigner, naturally be considered in the wrong and prosecuted with the full rigour of the law. And yet this only happened extremely rarely. The Dutch were, from the late sixteenth century, regularly and with impunity using go-betweens as front men for placing their cargoes on board the Spanish fleets and bringing back the counterpart from America. Everyone in Cadiz knew the *metedores* (smugglers and runners), often gentlemen fallen on hard times who specialized in the fraudulent conveyance of bullion or precious goods, sometimes mere tobacco, from overseas, and who made no secret of their trade. Taking risks and living flamboyant lives, they were looked down on by respectable society, but were whole-hearted participants in a system of solidarities which was the very backbone of this trading city. Even more important were the *cargadores*,[39] Spaniards by birth or naturalization, who went on board with the cargoes entrusted to them for the Indies fleet. The foreigner was completely dependent on their good faith.

Networks, conquests, trading empires

Solidarity between merchants was in some ways solidarity within a class, though it did not of course rule out business rivalries between individuals, between cities and between 'nations' as a national group of merchants was called. Sixteenth-century Lyons was not dominated by 'Italians', as is commonly said, but by colonies of Lucchese, Florentine and Genoese merchants[40] (before the problems of 1528 which removed them), that is by organized rival groups, each living as a 'nation'. The Italian cities somehow contrived to hate each other, to quarrel with each other and yet to support each other against outsiders. We must imagine these groups with their kinship systems and friendships, their servants, correspondents, accounts and ledger clerks. As early as the thirteenth century, when the Gianfigliazzi settled in the south of France, they arrived there, Armando Sapori tells us, *'con una vera folla di altri Italiani, altri mercatores nostri'*.[41]

Their presence meant the establishment of empires, networks, and colonies in certain areas. Trade circuits and communications were regularly dominated by powerful groups who appropriated them and might forbid other groups to use them. Such groups are easy to find once one starts looking for them, in Europe and even outside Europe. The merchants and bankers of Shansi province went all over China, from the Yellow River to the Canton River. Another Chinese network originated on the south coast (especially in Fukien) and reached to Japan and the East Indies, building up a Chinese overseas economy which for many years resembled a form of colonial expansion. The merchants of Osaka who were, after 1638, fully in control of the development of Japanese internal trade behind its protective barriers, represented the entire active economy of the archipelago. I have already mentioned the huge expansion of the Banyan network, throughout India and beyond: their bankers were present in large numbers in Isfahan according to Tavernier;[42] and they were also to be found in Istanbul, Astrakhan, and even in Moscow. In 1723[43] the widow of an Indian merchant in Moscow asked permission to be burned alive alongside her husband on his funeral pyre. Her request was refused. At once, 'all the Indian factors, disgusted by this act, decided to leave Russia, taking their wealth with them'. Faced with this threat, the authorities gave in. The incident was repeated in 1767.[43] Better known and more spectacular is the spread of the 'Gentile' ('Gentoo') or Muslim Indian merchants across the Indian Ocean to the shores of the East Indies. The networks they established stood up to the surprise attacks of the Portuguese and the brutalities of the Dutch.

In Europe and in the Mediterranean, in East and West, there were always of course the Italians. What better prize than the Byzantine Empire, before and even more after the Fall of Constantinople in 1204?[44] The wave of Italian merchants had soon reached the shores of the Black Sea: Italian shopkeepers, sailors and notaries were soon quite at home there. Even more extraordinary was their conquest of the West, achieved slowly over many centuries. There were Italians at the Ypres fairs in 1127.[45] 'By the second half of the thirteenth century, their powerful firms, which were only branches of the great merchant companies of Florence, Piacenza, Milan, Rome and Venice, were established throughout France. They were in Brittany by 1272-1273, in Guingamp, Dinan, Quimper, Quimperlé, Rennes and Nantes ... [as well as] in Bordeaux, Agen and Cahors.'[46] They brought new life by turn to the fairs of Champagne, to Bruges, later to the fairs of Geneva and later still to the brilliant fairs of Lyons; they created the early prosperity of Seville and Lisbon; they were present at the beginning of Antwerp's career, and later at that of Frankfurt; and finally they controlled the Genoese fairs known as the Besançon fairs.[47] Intelligent, lively, extremely irritating to everyone else, detested as much as they were envied, they were everywhere. In the northern seas, at Bruges, Southampton, London, sailors from the huge merchantmen of the Mediterranean invaded the quaysides and the harbour taverns, just as the Italian merchants invaded the cities. Was it an accident that the Atlantic became the great battlefield between Protestants and Catholics? The long history of hostility between northern sailors and southern sailors might explain many persistent quarrels.

Other merchant networks can be identified too: the long-lasting Hanseatic connection for instance, or the High German network which surpassed itself during what was known as the 'Age of the Fuggers'[48] (only a few decades in fact, but very spectacular ones). And then there were the Dutch, the English, the Armenians, the Jews, the Portuguese in Spanish America. There was on the other hand no major French network apart from the Marseillais in the Mediterranean and the Levant, unless one counts the conquest of the market of the Iberian peninsula, which was shared with the Basques and the Catalans in the eighteenth century.[49] This limited French success is significant: failure to impose one's rule on others meant being dominated by them.

Armenians and Jews

Plenty of information is available about the Armenian and Jewish merchants, but not enough to make it easy to reduce the mass of details and monographs to a few clear features.

Armenian merchants had colonized the whole of Persia. Indeed it was from their base in Julfa, the vast and busy suburb of Isfahan where Shah Abbas the Great had confined them, that they set out to conquer the world. Very early, they had made their way right across India – notably if report is accurate, from

The official reception of Domenico Trevisiano, Venetian ambassador to Cairo, 1512, painting by Gentile Bellini. (Paris, Louvre, Photo Giraudon.)

the Indus to the Ganges and the Bay of Bengal.[50] But they were also to be found in the south, in Portuguese Goa, where, like the French and Spanish merchants, in 1750 or so, they borrowed money from 'the convent of the Poor Clares'.[51] Armenian traders also crossed the Himalayas and reached Lhasa, trading from here to the Chinese frontier almost a thousand miles away.[52] But they virtually never crossed it. Oddly enough, China and Japan seem to have been closed to them.[53] But the Armenian merchant was a familiar figure, from very early on, in the Spanish Philippines;[54] and an ubiquitous one in the great Turkish Empire, where he turned out to be a pugnacious rival for Jewish and other merchants. On the European side, the Armenians had reached Muscovy, where they were well placed to develop companies handling raw silk from Iran, which changed hands many times as it crossed the length and breadth of Russia, to Archangel (1676) and to neighbouring countries. Armenians settled permanently in Muscovy and travelled its interminable roads as far as Sweden, which they had also reached with their merchandise by way of Amsterdam.[55] They had prospected the whole of Poland and even more Germany, where they were prominent at the Leipzig fairs.[56] They turned up in the Netherlands, in England and in France. They were comfortably settled in Italy by the seventeenth century, starting with Venice, as a part of the relentless invasion by eastern merchants which was so characteristic of the late sixteenth century.[57] They were in Malta even earlier than this: the documents call them *'poveri christiani armeni'* – *poveri* perhaps, but they were there *'per alcuni suoi negotii'* (1552, 1553).[58] Needless to say, they were not always welcomed with open arms. In July 1623, the consuls of Marseilles wrote to the king complaining of an invasion of Armenians with bales of silk. This was a threat to the city's trade, 'since there is', said the consuls, 'no nation in the world as greedy [as this]; although they have plenty of opportunity to sell these silks in great markets like Aleppo and Smyrna and other places and make an honest profit, nevertheless to make even more money, they come running to the other end of the world [i.e. Marseilles] and they have a way of life so swinish [*si porque*] that most of the time they only eat *herbes*' – that is vegetables.[59] But the Armenians were not so easily got rid of, since twenty-five years later, an English vessel captured by the French squadron under the *Chevalier* Pol off Malta in January 1649, was carrying from Smyrna to Leghorn and Toulon 'about 400 bales of silk, mostly for the 64 Armenians on board'.[60] Armenian merchants were also settled in Portugal, in Seville, and in Cadiz, at the gateway to America. In 1601, an Armenian, Jorge da Cruz arrived in Cadiz, claiming to have travelled there straight from Goa.[61]

In short, they made their presence felt practically throughout the trading world. Their triumph is revealed by the trading manual written by one of themselves, Lucas Vanantesti, in their own language, and printed in Amsterdam in 1699.[62] Designed for the use of 'you my merchant brothers, who belong to our nation', the book had been written with the encouragement of a wealthy patron, one Bedros, who came, we are not very surprised to learn, from Julfa. The book opens by quoting the Gospel: 'Do unto others ...', and its first concern is to inform the reader about the weights, measures and currencies used in the chief commercial centres. Which are these? All the ones in the West of course, but also some in Hungary, as well as Istanbul, Cracow, Vienna, Astrakhan, Novgorod, Hyderabad, Manila, Baghdad, Basra, Aleppo, Smyrna. The section on markets and merchandise describes trade centres in India, Ceylon, Java, Amboyna, Macassar and Manila. Within this mass of information, which really calls for close and detailed analysis, one of the more curious chapters compares the cost of staying in different cities in Europe, and another, although full of gaps and mysteries, offers a description of Africa, from Egypt to Angola, Monomotapa and Zanzibar. But this little book, which reflects the trading world of the Armenians does not provide the key to their fabulous success. On commercial techniques, it confines itself to extolling the merits of the *rule of three* (can this really have worked for everything?). The book does not tackle the problem of book-keeping, and above all, does not reveal whatever was the compelling commercial or capitalist motive behind this trading network. How were these long-distance connections set up and related to each other? Were they all linked by the huge headquarters at Julfa and by this alone? Or were there, as I believe, subsidiary centres? In Lwow in Poland, on the border between East and West, a little Armenian colony – the 'Persians' as they were called – with its own rules, its printing-houses and its many trading connections, dominated the huge carrying-trade towards the Ottoman Empire. The master of these wagon-trains the *caravan bacha*, was always an Armenian. Was it by the transport trade that the two mighty pitches colonized by the merchants of Julfa – no less than the eastern and the western worlds respectively – were locked to each other? In Lwow, perhaps significantly, the Armenians were known for their 'noisy and insolent luxury'.[63]

The networks of Jewish merchants also stretched all over the world. Their success story was even more ancient than that of the Armenians: from Roman antiquity, the Syri, whether Jewish or Gentile, were present everywhere: in the ninth century A.D., using the communications opened up by the Muslim conquest, Jews from Narbonne 'were travelling to Canton by way of the Red Sea and the Persian Gulf';[64] the Geniza documents[65] show an overwhelming preponderance of trading links operating for the benefit of Jewish merchants from 'Ifriqya': from Kairwan to Egypt, Ethiopia and the Indian sub-continent. In the tenth to twelfth centuries, in Egypt (and in Iran and Iraq) certain very rich Jewish families were engaged in long-distance trade, banking, tax-collecting – sometimes for entire provinces.[66]

Jewish merchants were thus perpetuating a tradition stretching over many centuries, far surpassing the long Italian supremacy we have already admired. But while they might hold the record for duration, they also hold the record for brilliant success followed by mighty downfalls. Unlike the Armenians, who had their headquarters in Julfa, the secret homeland of their money and their affections, the Jews lived dispersed and uprooted, and this was the source of their dramatic fortunes; these were also the result of their dogged determination not to mingle with other people. Not that we should be too ready to see only the catastrophes which brutally punctuate this eventful history, destroying long-standing acclimatizations or healthy trade networks. There were also solid successes – in thirteenth-century France for example;[67] and outstanding achievements in fifteenth-century Poland, in various regions of Italy, in medieval Spain and elsewhere.

Expelled from Spain and Sicily in 1492, and from Naples in 1541,[68] the Jewish exiles divided in two directions: to Mediterranean Islam and to the Atlantic seaboard. Jewish merchants were to make huge fortunes from the sixteenth century in Turkey – in Salonica, Bursa, Istanbul, and Adrianople, as business men or tax-farmers.[69] Portugal where they were tolerated for a while after 1492, was the point of departure for another large dispersion. Amsterdam and Hamburg were chosen destinations for merchants who were either already rich or

ARCHANGEL

LIBAU
NARVA
LIVONIA
MITAU
COURLAND
DUBENAH
NOVGOROD
LITHUANIA
VITEBSK
SMOLENSK
MOSCOW
NIJNI–NOVGOROD
MUSCOVY

LWOW
KAMENETZ
KIEV
HAYAKAGHAK
RUTHENIA
ELISABETHPOL
SUCEAVA
MOLDAVIA
VOLGA

WALLACHIA
AZOV
CRIMEA
ASTRAKHAN
RUMELIA
THEODOSIUS

C.
B.
GALATIA
TREBIZOND
GEORGIA
E.
S.
S.
LESSER
PONTIA
Ani
(ruins)
AGHORANIA
D.
RHODES
CARAMANIA
C.
ARMENIA
A.
K.
ARMENIA
N.
C.
S.
CILICIA
GREATER
E.
M.
MOKS
B.
A.
V.
ARAXE
E.
A.
O.
T.
CYPRUS
RASHT
TRIPOLI
LAHIDJAN
GILAN
MAZANDARAN
ALEXANDRIA
JERUSALEM

BAGHDAD
KASHAN
ISPAHAN
New Julfa
BASRA

SHIRAZ
FARS
BANDAR–
ABBAS
LAR

0   500km

who would rapidly become so once more. They undoubtedly contributed to Holland's increased trade with the Iberian peninsula – whether to Lisbon or Seville, Cadiz or Madrid; as well as to its trade with Italy, where active Jewish colonies survived for many years in Piedmont, Venice, Mantua and Ferrara; and it was thanks to them that Leghorn was launched on its prosperous new career in the seventeenth century. Undoubtedly too, they were among the architects of the first colonial fortunes of America, in particular with the spread of sugar cane and the Brazilian and Caribbean sugar trade. In the eighteenth century, they were equally to be found in Bordeaux, Marseilles, in England (from which they had been banished in 1290, and to which they returned under Cromwell between 1654 and 1656). This boom in the fortunes of the Sephardic Jews, the Jews of the Mediterranean, has found its historian in Hermann Kellenbenz.[70] The fact that their fortunes waned with the decline in American silver production, which was felt earlier in some places than others, raises some odd problems. If the general economic situation provoked their downfall (but did it?) it must mean that they were less vigorous than has been supposed.

The eclipse of the Sephardic Jews ushered in a period if not of total silence at least of relative decline for Jewish merchants everywhere. The next Jewish success would take time to become established, based as it was on the travelling merchants of central Europe. This was to be the age of the Ashkenazim, the Jews of central European origin whose first achievement was the triumph of the 'Court Jews' in the German principalities of the eighteenth century.[71] This was not, despite what one might read in hagiographic literature[72] a *spontaneous* rise of exceptional individual entrepreneurs. In a Germany which had lost most of its capitalist merchants with the Thirty Years' War, a vacuum had been created, which was filled by Jewish traders at the end of the seventeenth century, their rise being visible quite early, at the Leipzig fairs for example. But the real age of the Ashkenazim was to be the nineteenth century, with the spectacular international fortune of the Rothschild family.

That said, let me add in contradiction to Sombart[73] that the Jews certainly did not invent capitalism (supposing, which I do not, that capitalism ever was invented at a certain time in a certain place by certain identifiable individuals). If the Jews had invented or re-invented it, it could only have been in collaboration

11   ITINERARIES OF ARMENIAN MERCHANTS IN IRAN, TURKEY AND MUSCOVY IN THE SEVENTEENTH CENTURY

This map shows only a section of the routes covered by the Armenian network: links with the Ottoman Empire – Aleppo, Smyrna and Istanbul – and with Russia, via the Caspian Sea and the Volga. From Moscow, there were three trade routes to Libau, Narva and Archangel. The new Julfa, to which Abbas the Great deported the Armenians between 1603 and 1605, became the centre of Armenian activity throughout the world. The old Julfa in Armenia, on the Araks, provided most of the population of the new town. Note that to be styled 'a merchant of New Julfa' signified that one was a wealthy merchant or businessman. Map drawn by Keram Kevonian, 'Marchands arméniens au XVIIe siècle' in *Cahiers du monde russe et soviétique*, 1975.

with many other people. The fact that Jewish merchants were to be found in all the key centres of capitalism does not mean to say that they created them. There are outstanding Jewish scientists all over the world today; are we therefore to describe nuclear physics as a Jewish invention? In Amsterdam, they certainly *became* leading practitioners of speculation in the forward market of stocks and shares, but such manipulations had originated with non-Jewish speculators like Isaac Le Maire.

As for Sombart's argument that the capitalist mentality coincides with the principal tenets of the Jewish religion, this is to re-echo Max Weber's theory about Protestantism, for which there are the same good and bad arguments. One might just as well say the same of Islam; 'it has been suggested that Islamic law and the Islamic ideal of society shaped themselves from the very first in accordance with the ideas and aims of a rising merchant class', but 'this tendency [should not be] linked ... specifically with the religion of Islam' itself.[74]

The Portuguese in Spanish America: 1580–1640

The role of the Portuguese merchants in the huge area covered by Spanish America, has been illuminated in a number of recent studies.[75]

From 1580 to 1640, the crowns of Portugal and Castile were united under the same monarch. This union of the two countries, which was more theoretical than real (with Portugal retaining the fairly broad autonomy of a sort of 'dominion') did however contribute to erase the also rather theoretical frontier between the great expanse of Brazil, which the Portuguese controlled from a few key points on its Atlantic seaboard, and the distant Spanish realm of Potosi, in the Andes. In any case, since it was virtually virgin territory for trade, Spanish America was wide open to foreign merchants trying their luck, and Portuguese seamen and merchants had long been clandestine visitors to Spanish territory. For every one we know about, there were scores who went unrecorded. I will quote as evidence an isolated report of 1558 about the island of Santa Margarita, in the Caribbean, the 'island of pearls' which was eyed with much envy. In that year there arrived 'several caravels and other vessels from the kingdom of Portugal, with Portuguese crewmen and passengers aboard'. They were supposedly travelling to Brazil, but storms and chance had driven them towards the island. 'It seems to us that rather a lot of people arrive like this', comments our informant, 'and we are afraid that it may be with harmful intent,' *maliciosamente*.[76] The presence of the Portuguese increased, not surprisingly, afterwards to the point of penetrating all of Spanish America and in particular its capital cities: (Mexico City, Lima), and its important ports: (Santo Domingo, Cartagena in the Indies, Panama and Buenos Aires).

The last-named city, founded for the first time in 150 and destroyed by series of misfortunes, was re-founded in 1580 thanks to a decisive contribution by Portuguese merchants.[77] From Brazil to the Rio de la Plata (River Plate), constant stream of little ships of about forty tons ferried clandestine cargoes of sugar, rice, fabrics, black slaves and perhaps gold. They returned *carregados de reaes de prata*, laden with silver reals. Similarly, merchants would come from Peru down the River Plate, bringing coins to buy merchandise in Pernambuco, Bahia or Rio de Janeiro. The profits from this illegal traffic according to one merchant, Francisco Soares, (1597) could be anywhere between 100% and 500% – and even, if this is to be believed, 1000%. 'If the merchants ... knew about this traffic', he adds, 'they would not risk so many of their goods through Cartagena [in present-day Colombia]. This is why the Rio [de la Plata] is a great commercial waterway, the quickest and easiest way to get to Peru.'[78] And indeed for a small group of well-informed Portuguese merchants, the River Plate was indeed, until about 1622, a clandestine way out for silver from Potosi. In 1605, this contraband was estimated at 500,000 *cruzados* a year.[79] Only the setting up of the internal customs control, the *Aduana seca* of Cordoba (7 February 1622) *appears* to have put an end to it.[80]

Portuguese penetration was not however confined to the Atlantic seaboard of the Spanish possessions. In 1590, a Portuguese merchant from Macao, João da Gama,[81] crossed the Pacific and landed at Acapulco (not that it did him any good as it happened). Meanwhile, the Portuguese were opening, in Mexico City and in Lima, general stores where everything was sold, 'from diamonds to mere cumin, from the cheapest black slave to the costliest pearls'[82] not to mention those luxuries in colonial outposts, goods from home: wine, oil, wheat flour, fine cloth, and the spices and silks of the East which were brought in by long-haul trade from Europe or the Philippines; and here too there was a major contraband traffic in Peruvian silver, which was the real inspiration of all these activities.[83] Even in a town of still only moderate size, like Santiago in Chile (perhaps 10,000 inhabitants in the seventeenth century) one could find a Portuguese merchant, Sebastian Duarte who had previously been in Guinea in Africa and who travelled with his partner Juan Bautista Perez between 1626 and 1633 as far as Panama and Cartagena in the Indies, buying black slaves, precious woods and all kinds of merchandise, sometimes purchasing as much as 13,000 pesos' worth on credit.[84]

But these fortunes were short-lived. The Portuguese shopkeepers, who doubled up as usurers, made their money too quickly. The townspeople were easily roused against them – in Potosi in 1634 for instance.[85] Public opinion accused them of being 'new Christians' – which was often true – and of secretly practising Judaism, which may have been the case. The Inquisition eventually got wind of them and an epidemic of trials and *auto-da-fés* put an end to this overnight prosperity. The last-mentioned events are well-known – the Mexico City trials of 1646, 1647 and 1648, or the *auto-da-fé* of 11 April 1649 in which several rich merchants of Portuguese origin figured prominently.[86] But that is another story.

Centred on Lisbon, extending to both the African and the American sides of

Foodstuffs displayed outside a shop in Mexico City in the eighteenth
century; the customers are European.
(Mexico City, National Historical Museum. Photo Giraudon.)

the Atlantic, with connections in the Pacific and the Far East, the Portuguese
trading system was a huge network which spread throughout the New World in
a matter of ten to twenty years. This rapid expansion was inevitably an event of
international importance. Without it, Portugal might not have reasserted herself
in 1640, that is regained her independence from Spain. To explain Portugal's
new-found independence simply in terms of Brazilian sugar as people often have,
will not do. And who is to say that the Brazilian sugar 'cycle'[87] itself was not
connected to this trading prosperity? It may well also be that the latter played
some role in the short-lived triumph of the Sephardic Jews in Amsterdam, Lisbon
and Madrid. In this way, the clandestine silver shipments from Potosi might,
thanks to the Portuguese new Christians – who lent money to Philip IV, the

'Planet King' – have joined up with the official stream of silver which was regularly landed on the quaysides of Seville. But this huge and fragile system lasted in all only a few decades.

Conflicting networks and networks in decline

These trade networks could complement each other, work together and assist each other or they could compete. Competing did not automatically mean destroying each other. There were 'complementary enemies' and forms of un-peaceful coexistence which were destined to last. Christian merchants and merchants from Syria and Egypt faced each other in competition for centuries it is true, but the balance between these necessary adversaries never leaned too far to one side. The Europeans rarely went beyond the cities at the edge of the desert: Aleppo, Damascus, Cairo. After that the world of caravans was the special preserve of the Jewish and Muslim traders. Islam did however lose control of the huge commercial zone of the Mediterranean, at the time of the Crusades.

Similarly, the Venetians or Ragusans who bought up goats-hair camlets, and whom the documents show to have been settled in Bursa or Ankara, were only a discreet presence in the Turkish Empire. The most serious infiltration of westerners into Turkish territory was that of the Ragusans, but on the whole this did not extend beyond the Balkan peninsula. The Black Sea even became, or rather became once more, in the sixteenth century, Istanbul's private property and only opened once again to Christian traders at the end of the eighteenth century, after the capture of the Crimea by the Russians (1783). The anti-western reaction inside the Turkish Empire worked to the advantage of Jewish, Armenian or Greek merchants.

Similar forms of resistance were encountered elsewhere. In Canton, after 1720, the Co-Hong of the Chinese merchants was a sort of 'anti-Indies Company'.[88] In India itself, the Banyan network was, incredibly, to survive the British occupation.

Hostility and hatred were the natural companions of such resistance and competition. The strongest was always an obvious target. When Mandelslo was staying in Surat in 1638[89] he noted: 'To be proud and insolent, [the Muslims who were often merchants themselves] treat the *Benjans* [Banyans] almost as slaves, with great scorn, in the same way as the Jews are treated (where they are tolerated) in Europe.' The same attitude could be found in another age and another place, in western Europe in the sixteenth century vis-à-vis the Genoese, who were waiting 'to swallow everything up', according to Simón Ruiz and his friends,[90] and who were always in league to manipulate others. Similar attitudes are found towards the Dutch in the seventeenth century and the British after that.

All networks, even the most solid, sooner or later encountered difficulty or misfortune. And any failing at the centre of a network sent out ripples that affected all its outposts, perhaps most of all those on its periphery. This was what happened throughout Europe with what is known, vaguely and rather misleadingly as the 'decadence of Italy'. Decadence is not perhaps quite the right word, but by the end of the sixteenth century, the Italian network was running into difficulties and complications: it was losing its former positions in Germany, England and the Levant. A similar process occurred in the Baltic in the eighteenth century as Holland was eclipsed by the growing influence of England.

But wherever the dominant merchants were being eclipsed, substitute structures gradually emerged. 'French Tuscany' – in other words the Italian merchants who had settled in France – began to look shaky in about 1661, or even earlier with the financial crisis of 1648; the well-established Dutch network in France was running into problems by the early eighteenth century. And as if by accident, it is in approximately 1720,[91] that an increased number of French *négociants* appear, promoting the spectacular fortunes of the French ports and laying the foundations of large-scale French capitalist enterprises. The rise of the French merchant was effected partly by 'indigenous' Frenchmen, but also oddly enough with the aid of returning Protestants who had earlier left France. The same phenomenon of substitution can be glimpsed in Germany, where the beneficiaries were the Court Jews; and in Spain with the rise of the Catalan and Basque merchants, as well as that of the Madrid merchants of the *Cinco Gremios Mayores*, now promoted moneylenders to the state.[92]

Such new fortunes were only possible of course when there was an upturn in the economy. It was French, German or Spanish prosperity which made possible the new crop of local or rather national successes in the eighteenth century. But if the domination of foreign traders in France, Germany and Spain had not been interrupted at an earlier date the expansion of the eighteenth century would have taken a rather different course – perhaps with more initial difficulties.

However an active network once frustrated always has a tendency to compensate for its losses. Driven out of one region, it may press its capital and the advantages it offers upon another. This seems at any rate to have been the rule whenever a really vigorous and accumulative form of capitalism was concerned. Such was the case of the Genoese merchants of the Black Sea in the fifteenth century. A quarter of a century after the fall of Constantinople (1453), when the Turks occupied their trading-posts in the Crimea, notably the important commercial centre of Kaffa (1479), the Genoese did not immediately give up all their positions in the Levant: they were still in Chios for example in 1566. But most of their energies now went into reinforcing and developing the already existent business network in the West, in Spain and Morocco, and before long in Antwerp and Lyons. One empire was lost to them in the East, so they built another in the West. In the same way, the Portuguese Empire, contested throughout the Indian Ocean and the East Indies and mortally wounded on the scene of its former exploits, fell back in the last years of the sixteenth century and the first of the seventeenth, on Brazil and Spanish America. So too in the early seventeenth

century, despite the spectacular losses of the big Florentine firms, it was in
Central Europe, in an area bounded by the routes fanning out from Venice, that
Italian merchants found modest but steady compensation for the hard times
brought by the economic downturn after 1600.[93] It was not entirely by accident
that Bartolomeo Viatis,[94] a native of Bergamo and thus a Venetian subject,
became one of the richest merchants (and perhaps even the richest) in Nuremberg, his adoptive city; or that Italians were actively engaged in trade in Leipzig,
Nuremberg, Frankfurt, Amsterdam and Hamburg; that Italian goods and
fashions continued to reach Vienna and particularly Poland, through the busy
relay points of Cracow and Lwow. Correspondence preserved in the Polish
archives[95] shows that there were Italian merchants in the cities and fairs of
Poland in the seventeenth century, in sufficient numbers to be noticed by the man
in the street, as can be seen from the following anecdote: in 1643, a Spanish
soldier was sent from the Netherlands to take to the queen of Poland in Warsaw
gifts of lace and a doll dressed in the French fashion which she had requested,
'so that the tailors in her service could make her clothes in this fashion, since
Polish styles cramped her and did not suit her'. When the courier arrived, he was
treated like an ambassador. 'Knowing Latin helped me quite a lot', he admitted,
'for otherwise I could not have understood a single word of their language ...
and they know only enough of ours to greet one, *dar señoria*, in the Italian way,
for there are many Italian merchants in that country'. On the way back, he
stopped at Cracow, the city 'where the kings of Poland are crowned', and here
too he noted 'many Italian merchants who traffic above all in silks' in this great
trading centre. A little story, but a telling one.[96]

Controlling minorities

The previous examples show that successful merchants who controlled trade
circuits and networks often belonged to foreign minorities, whether by nation-
ality (the Italians in the France of Philip the Fair or François I, and in Philip II's
Spain) or by religion – the Jews, the Armenians, the Banyans, the Parsees, the
Raskolniki in Russia or the Christian Copts in Muslim Egypt. Why should this
have been? Clearly any minority will have a tendency to stick together, for
mutual aid and self-defence: when abroad, a Genoese merchant would back up
his fellow-citizen, an Armenian a fellow-Armenian. Charles Wilson[97] has recently demonstrated with some amusement the extraordinary incursion into the
London business world of the exiled French Huguenots. Historians have usually
chosen to emphasize their skills as craftsmen. But it seems that they always
formed, and do so still today, a compact group in the English capital and one
very jealous of its own identity. Secondly, a minority may easily feel oppressed
or discriminated against by the majority and this may in turn dispense it from
being over-scrupulous in its dealings with the majority in question. Was this how
to become the perfect 'capitalist'? Gabriel Ardant writes: '*Homo oeconomicus*

Bruges, Place de la Bourse: the building is flanked by the Genoese House on one side and the Florentine House on the other, tangible evidence of the strength and influence of the Italian merchants. (A.C.L., Brussels.)

[i.e. one who has completely assimilated the capitalist system] has no feeling of affection for his fellow man. He wishes to see in front of him only other economic agents, purchasers, vendors, borrowers, creditors, with whom he has in theory a purely economic relationship.' In similar vein, Sombart attributes the superiority of the Jews in the formation of the 'capitalist spirit' to the fact that their religious rules allowed them to act towards Gentiles in a manner forbidden towards their co-religionists.

But this explanation contains its own contradictions. In a society which operates certain prohibitions, which regards as unlawful usury and even money-handling – the source of so many fortunes not only in trade – it is surely the social machinery itself which reserves to 'outsiders' such unpleasant but socially essential tasks. If we are to believe Alexander Gerschenkron[98] this was what happened in Russia to the orthodox heretics the Raskolniki, who played a role comparable to that of the Jews or the Armenians. If they had not existed, it would surely have been necessary to invent them. 'Jews are as necessary in a country as bakers', declared the Venetian patrician Marino Sanudo, indignant at the idea of prohibitive measures against them.[99]

In this debate, it is preferable to talk about society rather than about the 'capitalist spirit'. The political quarrels and religious passions of medieval and modern Europe excluded from their communities of origin many individuals who then formed minorities in the foreign countries to which they were exiled. The cities of Italy, like those of Greece in classical times, were hornets' nests of conflict: there were the citizens *intra muros* and the exiles – such a frequently encountered social category that they were given the generic name of the *fuorisciti*. To maintain their wealth and their business connections in the very heart of the city which had expelled them and might one day receive them back was characteristic of the majority of these families – Genoese, Florentine, Lucchese. Such *fuorisciti*, if they were merchants, were in fact thus launched on the road to success. The most profitable business was long-distance trade – and they were condemned to practise it. In exile, they prospered by their very distance from home. In 1339 for instance, a group of Genoese nobles refused to accept a new popular government which ruled by so-called perpetual doges, and left the city.[100] The exiles became known as the *nobili vecchi*, while those who remained in Genoa under the new dispensation were called the *nobili nuovi* – and the distinction survived even after the return of the exiles. It so happened that the *nobili vecchi* became by far the most important handlers of foreign trade.

Other notable exiles were the Spanish and Portuguese *marranos*, who reverted to Judaism in Amsterdam; or the French Protestants. The Revocation of the Edict of Nantes, in 1685, did not create *ex nihilo* the Protestant Bank which was subsequently to hold the purse strings of the French economy, but it undoubtedly helped to launch it. These *fuorisciti* of a new kind had kept their connections inside the kingdom and its capital, Paris. They succeeded more than once in transferring abroad a substantial share of the capital they had left behind. And like the *nobili vecchi*, they would return one day in force.

A minority in other words was a solid and ready-made network. The Italian merchant who arrived empty-handed in Lyons needed only a table and a sheet of paper to start work, which astonished the French. But this was because he could find on the spot his natural associates and informants, fellow-countrymen who would vouch for him and who were in touch with all the other commercial centres in Europe – in short everything that goes to make up a merchant's credit and which might otherwise take years and years to acquire. Similarly in Leipzig and Vienna – cities on the outskirts of the densely-populated part of Europe which were borne along on the tide of expansion of the eighteenth century – one cannot fail to be struck by the fortunes made by foreign merchants, exiles from the Netherlands, French refugees after the Revocation of the Edict of Nantes (the first of whom arrived in Leipzig in 1688), Italians, Savoyards, Tyroleans. There were virtually no exceptions – the foreigner was smiled on by fortune. His origin linked him to cities, business centres and distant countries which drew him willy-nilly into the world of foreign trade, the big business of the day. Would it really be an exaggeration to say that this was an ill wind that blew everyone good?

Trading profits, supply and demand

Networks and circuits combined to make up a system: like a railway system with rails, power-cables, rolling stock and personnel. Everything was conceived with a view to movement. But movement could itself pose problems.

Trading profits

When goods travelled, they naturally increased in price the farther they went. This was what I shall call the 'trading profit'. Can this be described as a universal rule? With near certainty. At the end of the sixteenth century, a Spanish piece of eight was worth 320 *reis* in Portugal, 480 in India.[101] At the end of the seventeenth century, a bolt of muslin cost 3 reals in the mill at Le Mans, 6 in Spain and 12 in America.[102] And so on. So in any given place, rare goods from far away might cost astronomical prices. In Germany in about 1500, a pound of saffron (from either Italy or Spain) cost as much as a horse, and a pound of sugar as much as three sucking-pigs.[103] In Panama in 1519, a horse was worth $24\frac{1}{2}$ pesos, an Indian slave 30 pesos and a skin of wine 100 pesos.[104] In Marseilles in 1248, 30 metres of Flanders cloth was from two to four times the price of a Saracen slave.[105] But even in Ancient Rome, Pliny the Elder reported that Indian products like pepper and spices were sold at a hundred times their original price.[106] It is clear that on a journey of this kind, profits had to be made to prime the pump so to speak, to induce merchants to pay the expenses of transport. For to the purchasing price of a product had to be added the cost of carriage and in the past this could be very high indeed. The cost of carriage for six consignments of cloth bought at the Champagne fairs in 1318 and 1319 and taken to Florence (including taxes, packing and other expenses) amounted respectively to: 11.80; 12; 12.53; 15.96; 16.05; 19.21; and 20.34% of the purchasing price, the *primo costo*.[107] The merchandise was the same in every case and the journey identical – but the cost of transport could be almost twice as much for one consignment as for another. And these are fairly low rates: cloth was expensive to buy, but not heavy to transport. Heavy goods that cost less – grain, salt, wood, wine – did not as a rule travel overland for long distances except in cases of absolute necessity – and the necessity meant paying over the odds for transport. Chianti (which was already known by this name in 1398) was a cheap wine ('*povero*') costing one florin a hectolitre (whereas malmsey cost 10 or 12). If it was transported from Greve to Florence – a distance of 27 kilometres – its price went up between 25 and 40%; if taken on to Milan, it tripled in price.[108] In about 1600, the transport of a keg of wine from Vera Cruz to Mexico City cost as much as the keg had been bought for in Seville.[109] Later still, in Cantillon's time, 'the carriage of wines from Burgundy to Paris often costs more than the wine itself does on the spot'.[110]

In the first volume of this book, I emphasized the obstacles presented by a transport system that was invariably expensive and lacked flexibility. Federigo Melis[111] has shown how an enormous effort was nevertheless made in the fourteenth and fifteenth centuries to improve sea transport, with the increased size of hulls and therefore of holds, and the establishment of progressive tariffs related to value: thus expensive commodities paid part of the costs for ordinary goods. But the practice took a long time to become general. In Lyons in the sixteenth century, the price of transport overland was calculated according to the weight of the goods.[112]

In any case, the merchant's problem remained the same: at the end of the day, the goods travelling towards him, in sailing ship, cart or pack-saddle, had to fetch a price which would not only cover incidental expenses, purchasing price and transport costs, but also the profit the merchant hoped to obtain from the whole operation. If not, what was the point of risking one's money and peace of mind? Some goods were safer than others. For 'royal merchandise' – Simon Ruiz's expression for pepper, spices, cochineal (and I would add pieces of eight) – there was no problem; the voyage was long but profits were assured. If the selling price was disappointing, the merchant had only to wait: with a little patience things worked out in the end, since the demand was virtually always there. Every country and every period had its own 'royal merchandise' which promised higher profits than any other goods.

The journeys of Giambattista Gemelli Careri, which are fascinating to read in many respects, admirably illustrate the rule. This Neapolitan, who decided to travel round the world in 1694, more for pleasure than for profit, found an answer to the problem of travelling expenses on his long voyage: he would buy in one place goods he knew to be particularly highly valued in the next place on his route. In Bandar Abbas on the Persian Gulf for instance, the traveller should, he says, buy up 'dates, wine, spirits, and all the fruits of Persia which one carries to India either dried or pickled in vinegar [and] on which one makes a good profit';[113] when taking the Manila galleon for New Spain, the best thing to take is Chinese quicksilver: 'three hundred per cent profit', he confides.[114] And so on. Travelling with its owner, merchandise thus became a kind of capital which appreciated at every move, paid the traveller's expenses and even, on his return to Naples, afforded him a handsome profit. Francesco Carletti[115] who had also embarked on a voyage round the world a century earlier, in 1591, had chosen for the first leg of his journey black slaves, 'royal merchandise' on any reckoning, whom he bought in the island of Sao Tomé and sold again at Cartagena on the Caribbean.

Things were not so easy where ordinary goods were concerned of course. The operation could yield a profit but only if a number of precautions were taken. In theory, it was all quite simple, at least for an economist like Condillac:[116] the golden rule of long-distance trade was to establish communication between a market where a given merchandise was plentiful and another where the same merchandise was rare. In practice, to master these conditions, one had

Saffron and spices arriving in Nuremberg, between 1640 and 1650. From left to right, the goods are delivered, registered, weighed, examined, and dispatched elsewhere. (National Museum, Nuremberg. Photo by the Museum.)

to be both prudent and well-informed, as merchants' correspondence abundantly proves.

The month is April 1681, and we are in Leghorn in Giambattista Sardi's shop.[117] Leghorn (Livorno), the major port of Tuscany, had connections throughout the Mediterranean and the whole of Europe, at least as far as Amsterdam. In the latter city, Benjamin Burlamacchi, a native of Lucca, runs a trading firm which handles goods from the Baltic, Russia, India and elsewhere. When the correspondence between our two merchants opens, a fleet belonging to the Dutch East India Company has just arrived and forced down the price of cinnamon. The Leghorn merchant, thinking of doing a deal in this 'royal merchandise', writes a letter full of plans to Burlamacchi, explaining that he wants this to be 'on his own account', that is without going shares with his correspondent. In the end the venture comes to nothing and Sardi, this time ready to cooperate with Burlamacchi, can only see one product worth bringing from Amsterdam to Leghorn – *vacchette*, that is Russian hides which would soon be flooding the Italian market. By 1681 they are already regularly being quoted at Leghorn, where they sometimes arrive directly from Archangel. If the hides are 'of a good colour, both inside and outside, broad, thin and not over 9 or 10 pounds Florence weight', then Burlamacchi is to load a certain number on to two ships (thus spreading the risk), '*de buona difesa, che venghino con buon convoglio*' and to be sure to do so before the winter closure of northern shipping. The hides which are selling in Amsterdam at 12 units, are quoted at $26\frac{1}{2}$ or 28 in Leghorn, that is at over twice the price. Cost price on delivery at Leghorn must not be more than 24, writes Sardi, who thus hopes for a profit of 10%. Six bales of hides will be embarked at Texel, and Burlamacchi will be reimbursed for half the purchasing price by drawing a bill of exchange on a Venetian banker, on Sardi's instructions. So all the sums had been done. And yet in the end, the deal did not turn out very well. Several other large consignments of hides arrived in Leghorn and brought down the price to 23 in May 1682; Sardi's hides, which turned out to be of poor quality, did not sell well: on 12 October of the same year there were still some left in stock. Not that this greatly mattered to the Sardi firm, which was handling a multitude of operations in 1681 and 1682, notably the export of oil and lemons from the Genoese Riviera, and which had many dealings with Amsterdam and England, sometimes chartering entire ships for its own purposes. But the interesting thing about this deal is that it shows how difficult it was to predict and arrange profits over a distance.

The merchant was condemned to perpetual calculation, running the whole operation over in his mind many times before trying it. When a methodical merchant in Amsterdam[118] was contemplating a deal in France, he wrote to Dugard Fils, the commission agent in Rouen, asking him 'to quote me in your reply the prices of the commonest articles where you are, and also to send me a hypothetical statement of sale [i.e. an estimate of all the costs]. Above all, please quote me the price of whalebone, red whale oil, madder, fine and peeled, Smyrna cotton, yellow wood, steel wires ... and green tea.' Similarly, a French merchant[119] would ask for information from Amsterdam: 'Since I do not know how much these spirits sell for with you, you would oblige me by telling me how much 30 *veltes* would be in French currency, after which I will do my sums and then, if I think it is worth while, I may decide to send you some.'

That trading profit provided the necessary motive for all commercial exchange is so obvious that it may seem absurd to labour the point. But it also explains a certain number of less obvious things. In particular, is it not the case that it automatically favoured countries supposedly the victims of a high cost of living? These became beacons, exerting a magnetic appeal. Merchandise was attracted by high prices. Venice, having long held the Mediterranean in fee, had always been an expensive city and still was in the eighteenth century.[120] Holland had become a country of high prices and therefore of low living standards, especially among the poor, but among the not-so-poor as well.[121] Spain, from the time of Charles V, had become a terribly expensive country.[122] 'I learnt a proverb here,' said a French traveller in 1603, 'everything is dear in Spain, except silver.'[123] And it was the same story in the eighteenth century. But England was soon to break all records: it was the country where one had to pay the highest daily expenses: renting a house or a carriage, eating or staying in a hotel was ruinous for foreigners.[124] Was this rise in the cost of living, visible even before the 1688 revolution, a price that had to be paid, a sign or condition of the British trade supremacy which was being established? Was it indeed the price of any supremacy? Fynes Moryson, Lord Mountjoy's secretary in Ireland from 1599 to 1606, a seasoned traveller who had visited France, Italy, the Netherlands, Germany and Poland between 1591 and 1597, and who was a careful observer, makes this extraordinary remark:

> My selfe having in Poland and Ireland, found a strange cheapenesse of all such necessaries, in respect they want, and so more esteeme Silver, this observation makes me of an opinion much contrary to the vulgar, that there is no more certaine signe of a flourishing and rich commonwealth, than the deere price of these things...[125]

Pinto draws the same conclusion. And Quesnay pronounced the famous paradox: 'Abundance plus high prices equals wealth'.[126] Passing through Bordeaux in 1787, Arthur Young noted:

> The rent of houses and lodgings rises every day as it has done since the peace [of 1783] considerably, at the same time that so many new houses have been and are erecting, unites with the advance in the prices of everything: they complain that the expences of living have risen in ten years full 30 per cent – there can hardly be a clearer proof of an advance in prosperity.[127]

And the young Abbé Galiani had said the same twenty years earlier in 1751 in his book on money: 'The high prices of goods are a sure guide to where the greatest wealth is to be found.'[128] This is reminiscent of writers like Léon Dupriez on the present day: advanced countries have wage levels and prices 'substantially higher than those of countries whose development lags behind'.[129] But we shall have more to say later about the reasons for these differences in level. It is easy to talk of superior structures or organization. But one really has to consider the structure of the whole world.[130]

It is clearly tempting to relate the exceptional career of Britain to this reality. High prices and wages both helped and hindered the island's economy. The cloth industry, advantaged by the exceptionally low costs of basic woollen production, managed to weather the storm. But was the same true of other industrial activity? The machine revolution of the late eighteenth century was, it must be admitted, a providential way out.

Supply and demand: which came first?

The principal stimulus to trade comes of course from supply and demand, various supplies and various demands: these may be familiar old friends in economics, but that does not make them any easier to define and discern. There are hundreds and thousands of different kinds of supply and demand. They form chains end to end, and provide the current for trade circuits. Classical economics explains everything else in terms of these two concepts and also draws us into endless debates on the respective roles of supply and demand as prime movers – debates which have gone on down to the present day and still play a part in the inspiration of economic policies.

Conventional wisdom has always been that there is no supply without

Seventeenth-century vignette, illustrating advice given to a young German merchant on his departure abroad. (National Museum, Nuremberg. Photo by the Museum.)

demand and vice versa: both arise from the exchange that they create, and which creates them. The same could be said of sale and purchase, of the merchant's outgoings and incomings, of gift and counter-gift, even of labour and capital, consumption and production – consumption being to demand what production is to supply. Turgot argues that if I offer something I possess, it is because I want something else; and I shall simultaneously request whatever it is I do not have at present. If I ask for something I do not possess, that is because I am determined, or at least willing to provide the counterpart, to offer some good or service or sum of money. Thus, Turgot concludes, we have four elements. 'Two things possessed, two things desired.'[131] It goes without saying, a present-day economist has written, 'that every supply and every demand supposes a counterpart'.[132]

We should not be too ready to shrug off such remarks as truisms or naïvetés. They help us to avoid artificial distinctions and affirmations, and they incline to prudence anyone wondering whether supply or demand is the more important, or what amounts to the same thing, which of the two plays the role of *primum mobile* – a question to which there is really no answer, but which takes us to the heart of the problems of exchange.

I have often found my mind going back to the example so thoroughly studied by Pierre Chaunu,[133] of the *Carrera de Indias*. After 1550, the picture is quite clear, its outlines and mechanisms visible on a large scale: there was a sort of

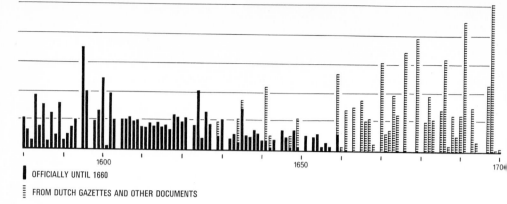

12 SHIPMENTS OF AMERICAN SILVER TO EUROPE

Michel Morineau (*Anuario de historia economica y social*, 1969, pp. 257–359) has reconstructed, from a critical reading of the sources in Dutch gazettes and of the reports of foreign ambassadors in Madrid, the graph of imports of precious metals in the seventeenth century. The standstill, then falling-off of shipments after 1620 and the substantial revival after 1660 are clearly visible on this table. (Scale: 10, 20, 30 million pesos.)

clockwise conveyor belt running from Seville to the Canaries, to the ports of America, through the Bahama straits south of Florida, then to the Azores and back to Seville. Shipping was the concrete evidence of a working circuit. Pierre Chaunu is quite positive that in the sixteenth century, the real impetus, came from the 'outward movement' of shipping from Spain to America. He goes on: 'Waiting for the European products bound for the Indies was one of the principal preoccupations of the merchants of Seville when the ships were due to sail'[134]: mercury from Idria, copper from Hungary, building materials from the northern countries and whole boatloads of woollen or canvas cloth in bales. At first, there were even products from Spain itself – oil, flour and wine. Spain was not the only source of the great transatlantic traffic then; the rest of Europe also made its contribution and asked for its share of the precious manna brought back by the fleets. The French thought that the system would be unable to function without their shipments. And the Genoese[135] who had financed the lengthy and time-consuming trade operations with the New World on credit from the early days until 1568, were also indispensable; there were others too. The necessary flow of goods towards Seville before the departure of the fleet thus represented the mobilization of many forces within the western world; it was a flow largely replenished by sources outside Spain, drawing on the money of Genoese businessmen, the mines of Idria, the looms of Flanders and the score or so of village markets where Breton sailcloth was sold. Proof *a contrario* is that everything came to a halt at Seville (and later in Cadiz) to suit the 'foreigners'. And this rule was to last: in February 1730,[136] 'the departure of the galleons has been held up once more', reported a gazette, 'until the beginning of March, to give the foreigners time to load a large quantity of merchandise which has not yet arrived in Cadiz because of contrary winds'.

But does that necessarily mean that we have here the initial stimulus the *primum mobile*? In theory a conveyor belt, to keep this image, can be set in motion at any point on its travels – set in motion or by the same token halted. And it does appear that the first prolonged slowdown, in about 1610 to 1620, was caused by a fall in production in the American silver mines, possibly because of the 'law' of diminishing returns, and undoubtedly by the demographic collapse of the population which had provided the essential labour force for the mines. And when in about 1660, things got under way again in Potosi as well as in the silver mines of New Spain – while Europe still seemed to be embedded in persistent stagnation – the impetus came from America, from native miners using their traditional *braseros* once more[137] even before the great 'modern' mining equipment was reactivated. In short, on at least two occasions, the initiative (first a negative, then a positive one) came from the other side of the Atlantic, in America.

But this was by no means a rule. When after 1713, using both the privilege of the *asiento* and contraband, the British penetrated the Spanish American market, they soon swamped it with their own goods, particularly cloth, advanced in large quantities on credit to retailers in New Spain and elsewhere. The returns were naturally in silver. This time, powerful British pressure was the driving force, on this side of the Atlantic. Defoe explained candidly apropos the same process in Portugal that it was to 'force a vend abroad' to force one's supply on foreigners.[138] Even so, it was important that cloth did not remain too long unsold in the New World.

But how is one to distinguish supply and demand here without recourse to Turgot's quadruple schema? The masses of goods which piled up in the holds of the departing fleet in Seville, and which the merchants had only been able to amass by exhausting their own reserves of money and credit, or by drawing, in desperate cases, bills of exchange on foreign payers (between the eve of one fleet's departure and the return of another, not a maravedi could be borrowed locally!), the supply in other words promoted by the many-sided and various production of the western world, was accompanied by an underlying demand, clearly and imperiously enunciated and by no means discreet: the financial centre and the merchants who had invested their capital in exports expected to be paid by returns in silver bullion. The same was true in Vera Cruz, Cartagena or Nombre de Dios (later Porto Belo) where the demand for goods from Europe, whether agricultural or industrial, at very high prices, was balanced by a visible supply of silver. In 1637, 'the heaps of silver wedges lay like heaps of stones in the street' in Porto Belo.[139] Without this 'thing desired', the wheels of trade would not of course have turned. Here too, supply and demand were at work simultaneously.

Should we therefore conclude that the two supplies – that is the two kinds of production which stood face to face across the ocean – were more important than the two demands, the desires for 'what-I-do-not-have'? Would it not be more accurate to say that they only come into existence through their connection with *foreseeable* and *foreseen* demand?

In any case, the problem does not only arise in these economic terms (although supply and demand are far from being 'purely' economic concepts but that is another story). It must also clearly be posed in terms of power. A command structure ran from Madrid to Seville and thence to the New World. It is commonplace to ridicule the laws of the Indies, the *leyes de Indias*, that is the illusion that the Catholic Kings exerted any real authority on the other side of the Atlantic. I agree that they did not invariably get their way in these far-flung countries. But the royal will did achieve certain objectives and it found material expression so to speak in the cohorts of royal officials – who were not entirely concerned with feathering their own nests. The quint was after all regularly levied in the name of the king, and the documents always record his share of the return shipments, alongside that of the merchants. On the *earliest* voyages, the royal share was by far the greater: the ships returned virtually with their ballast – which already consisted of silver bars. And colonization had not yet progressed far enough to be demanding much merchandise from Europe in the other direction. This was exploitation rather than exchange, a form of exploitation which neither stopped nor declined in later years. A French report of 1703 says that 'the Spaniards had been in the habit [before the War of the Spanish Succession which broke out in 1701] of shipping out 40 millions *livres tournois*' worth of goods, and bringing back 150 million in gold, silver and other goods' – and this every five years or so.[140] These figures only represent the gross volume of exchange. But whatever calculation one makes to estimate the volume of true profit, allowing for the expenses of the return journey, this is a clear example of unequal exchange, with all the economic and political implications such an imbalance supposes.

It was not of course necessary for a king or a state to be involved for exploitation, that is unequal or forced exchange, to take place. The Manila galleon was an exceptionally good way of closing a circuit from a commercial point of view, but there is no doubt that it represented a form of domination to the advantage of the merchants of Mexico City.[141] Making their hasty visits to the Acapulco fairs, they held the whip hand, from a distance of months and years, over the merchants of Manila (who took it out on the merchants of China), just as Dutch merchants for so long kept the whip hand over their commission agents in Leghorn. When there was a balance of power of this kind, what exactly did the terms supply and demand mean?

Demand in isolation

That said, it is now perhaps legitimate to isolate demand for a moment from its surrounding context. I am encouraged to do so by the writings of present-day economists on under-developed countries. Ragnar Nurske[142] for instance is quite positive that the right string to pull to start the engine is demand. Merely to increase production would lead to imbalances. I am well aware that what is true of the Third World today is not necessarily true of the societies and economies of the *ancien régime*. But the comparison may provoke thought in both directions. Is the following observation made by Quesnay in 1766 really true only of the past? There will never be any shortage 'of consumers who cannot consume as much as they would like: people who only eat black bread and drink water would like to eat wheaten bread and drink wine; people who never have eaten meat would like to do so; people with poor clothes would like better ones; people without wood to warm themselves by would like to buy it, and so on'.[143] What is more, this mass of consumers is constantly increasing. *Mutatis mutandis* then, one could argue that there is always a potential consumer society. Only the size of its income, of which it regularly and easily devours nine-tenths, places a limit on its appetite. But to the vast majority of mankind, this limit makes itself relentlessly felt. French economists in the eighteenth century were as conscious of this limit as are the development economists of today; they were always looking for recipes to increase income and consumption, 'the ruin of which', as Boisguilbert was already pointing out, 'is the ruin of income'.[144] In short, they wanted to increase demand.

There was of course demand and demand. Quesnay was hostile to the demand for 'luxury of decoration', and favoured 'subsistence consumption',[145] that is an increase in everyday demand by the 'productive class'. And he was not mistaken: this demand was essential because it was *durable*, massive, capable of maintaining its pressure and its requirements over a long period of time, and therefore of acting as a reliable guide for supply. Any increase of this demand was crucial to growth.

Such fundamental demands originated of course in choices made in the far-distant past (between grain, rice and maize for instance) which had multiple consequences and unforeseen effects;[146] and they corresponded to basic human requirements: salt, wood, cloth. It is alongside such primordial needs whose history has so rarely been recorded, that we should judge the massive scale of essential demands, and the almost superhuman achievements which went towards meeting them. Achievements such as the transport of rice, salt and wood from the southern provinces of China all the way along the Imperial Canal in the north and as far as Peking; the transport by sea of rice from Bengal to all parts of India, or the overland carriage of rice and grain by caravans consisting of thousands of oxen; the transport throughout the West of grain, salt and wood. Salt from Peccais in Languedoc travelled all the way up the Rhône to Seyssel;[147]

salt from Cadiz, Setubal, and the bay of Bourgneuf travelled from the Atlantic to the North Sea and the Baltic. The United Provinces could have been brought to their knees if their supplies of salt had been blocked at the end of the sixteenth century. Spain did no more than dream of this.[148]

As for wood, which was used on a massive scale, as we saw in the first volume of this book, one is simply amazed at the vast quantities that must have travelled along all the rivers of Europe and China: rafts, log-trains, floating tree-trunks, boats demolished on arrival (at the mouth of the Loire and many other waterways), sea-going vessels laden with planks and beams, or even specially built to bring to the West and South the unbeatable masts grown in northern forests. It would take a century of successive adaptation before wood was replaced by coal, oil, and electricity. As for wine, which was a basic component of European civilization, it was transported uninterruptedly. Pierre Chaunu is only slightly exaggerating when he says that the wine fleets were to the economies of the *ancien régime* what the transport of coal was to the eighteenth and even more the nineteenth century.[149] Wheat, a heavy and comparatively cheap commodity, travelled as little as possible, in the sense that it was grown everywhere. But if a bad harvest meant that it was in short supply for any length of time, it might be sent on very long journeys.

Alongside these massive and bulky traffics, luxury goods might be lightweight, but they were spectacular and much talked of. Money flowed towards them and obeyed their dictates. There was thus a sort of *super-demand* with its own circuits and changes of humour. Fickle desires, quick changes in fashion created artificial but imperative 'needs' which might vanish overnight only to make way for other apparently equally frivolous passions: sugar, alcohol, tobacco, coffee, tea. And although many people still spun and wove at home for their everyday needs, it was fashion and the luxury trade which increasingly dictated demand for textiles in the most advanced and commercialized sectors.

At the end of the fifteenth century, the rich forsook gold and silver fabrics for silk, which as it spread and became available to more people, was to emerge as the symbol of social mobility and to bring a last wave of prosperity to Italy for about a hundred years, before silk manufacture developed all over Europe. The pattern shifted again as English cloth became fashionable with the last decades of the seventeenth century. The next century saw the sudden appearance of 'painted cottons' that is printed calicoes, first imported from India, then imitated in Europe. In France, the authorities desperately tried to protect national manufacturers from this invasion of light fabrics, but in vain. Nothing worked, supervision, inspections, confiscation, imprisonment, fines, not even the imaginative flights of fancy of would-be advisers like Brillon de Jouy, a merchant in the rue des Bourdonnais in Paris, who proposed to pay anyone 500 *livres* 'to strip ... in the street, any woman wearing Indian fabrics', or if people thought this too extreme a measure, to 'dress up streetwalkers in Indian fabrics' in order to strip them publicly as a salutary example.[150] A report to the controller-general

Chinese silk fabric (*lampas*) in the age of Louis XV. Lyons, Musée Historique des tissus. (Photo Giraudon.)

Desmaretz in 1710, expressed serious anxiety over such campaigns: when food was so dear, money scarce and government bonds so inconvenient and difficult to use, were people to be forced to change their wardrobes? In any case, how could one fight fashion?[151] At most one could mock it, as Defoe did in an article in *The Weekly Review* in 1708:

> Such is the power of a mode as we saw our persons of quality dressed in Indian carpets, which but a few years before their chambermaids would have thought too ordinary for them; the chints were advanced from lying upon their floors to their backs, from the footcloth to the petticoat; and even the Queen herself at this time was pleased to appear in China and Japan, I mean China silks and calico. Nor was this all, but it crept into our houses and bedchambers; curtains, cushions, chairs and at last beds themselves were nothing but calicoes or Indian stuffs.

Ridiculous or not, fashion provided an insistent, many-sided and disconcerting demand, which always had its way. In France, over thirty-five judgments did not succeed in 'curing people of this obstinate contraband [in Indian cottons]; even though, besides the confiscation of goods and a fine of one thousand *écus* on those who buy and sell them, it was deemed necessary by the edict of 15 December 1717 to add to these even harsher punishments, among others sentencing to the galleys for life, and even worse if the case called for it ...'[152] The ban was finally lifted in 1759 and cotton industries were established in France which were soon competing with those of England, the Swiss cantons, Holland – and even India itself.[152]

Supply in isolation

Economists interested in the pre-industrial world are agreed on one point: supply was not a significant factor. It lacked elasticity; it was unable to respond quickly to any demand.[153] One should however distinguish between agricultural supply and industrial supply.

What mattered most in the economy of this period was agricultural activity. It is true that in some parts of the globe, particularly in England, agricultural production and productivity rose so quickly as to constitute a 'revolution' thanks to the combined effects of certain technical and social factors. But even in this case, historians have often pointed out that it was the fortunate series of good harvests between 1730 and 1750[154] that substantially contributed to the economic take-off of Great Britain. As a rule, agricultural production was an area where little changed.

There were on the other hand two areas, industry and commerce, where some progress soon became evident, although before machines revolutionized the former, and as long as the latter was curbed by the large proportion of the population remaining in the near self-sufficiency of the small-holding, there were external and internal limitations on any burst of activity. I am prepared to suggest however on the basis of some rather doubtful indications relating only to an order of magnitude, that industrial production multiplied at least five times, in Europe, between 1600 and 1800. I also believe that circulation expanded and improved its range. The barriers between economies were breaking down and the number of exchanges increased. In the large area covered by France, which is a very good field of observation in this respect, this collapse of trade barriers is the most striking phenomenon of the eighteenth century in the eyes of historians.[155]

The nature of supply by the end of the eighteenth century then, and this is the point I want to make, was not as modest and inadequate in response to the monster of consumption as one might have supposed. And it was of course to gain strength with the advance of the industrial revolution. By 1820, it had become a weighty factor. So economists naturally started to take notice of it and to admire the role it was playing. Supply became even more prominent with the formulation and diffusion of what became known as 'Say's law' (Jean-Baptiste Say, 1767–1832).[156]

This admirable popularizer (not a genius, protested Marx) was no more the inventor of his 'law' than Gresham was of the more famous law which bears his name. But he was the most prominent of the economists of his time, and the label seems to have stuck. In fact there are elements of the law in Adam Smith and even more in James Stewart (1712–1780). One could even argue that Turgot was working along the same lines when he attributed to Josiah Child the 'incontestable maxim that one man's labour provides labour for another'.[157] In itself, the law is simply stated: goods supplied on the market will regularly stimulate the demand for them. But since apparent simplicity as usual conceals a fundamental complexity, every economist has interpreted this statement to suit himself. For John Stuart Mill (1806–1873), 'Every increase of production, if distributed without miscalculation among all kinds of produce in the proportion which private interest would dictate, creates, or rather constitutes, its own demand.'[158] A rather obscure statement, though claiming to clarify. And the unwary reader might be equally puzzled by Charles Gide (1847–1932): 'A product will find more markets', he explains, 'where there is a greater variety and abundance of other products',[159] in other words, a supply will create its own demand more easily if there are plenty of other forms of supply. 'Both hands are held out', writes Henri Guitton (1952), 'one to give and the other to receive ... Supply and demand are two sides of the same coin.'[160] Quite true. Another, more logical way to put the same thing is that the production of any good which will sooner or later be *in supply* on the market, has already led, in the very process, to a distribution of money: the raw materials have had to be paid for, the costs of transport found, and the workers given their wages. Once this money has been distributed, its normal function is to reappear, sooner or later in the form of a demand or if one prefers, a purchase. Supply makes an appointment with itself.

Say's law was the guiding principle of several generations of economists who, with very few exceptions did not question it until about 1930. But the laws or so-called laws of economics probably last only as long as the desires and realities of the period they reflect or interpret more or less faithfully. A new age brings its own 'laws'. And in the 1930s, Keynes had little difficulty in standing Say's law on its head. Among other things, he argued that the beneficiaries of the supply as it was being produced would not necessarily appear immediately on the market-place as purchasers. Money offers its possessor a choice: he can keep it, spend it or invest it. But I am not here concerned to develop Keynes's critique of Say, fruitful and realistic as it undoubtedly was in its time. We are not here concerned with whether Keynes was right or not in 1930, nor indeed whether Say was right or not in 1820. But was Say right (that is, does Say s law apply retrospectively) about the period *before* the industrial revolution? This is the only question we have to answer – but it is unlikely that we shall be able to do so to our entire satisfaction.

Before the industrial revolution, the economy we are contemplating had frequent breakdowns; its different sectors were poorly related to each other and often out of step, whatever the overall situation. One might have a burst of prosperity, but it did not necessarily take the others with it. And every single sector could act in turn as a bottleneck: progress was never smooth. We know of course that merchants complained constantly at the time, and that they tended to exaggerate. But they were not systematically lying, nor inventing their problems, the ups and downs of the economy, the collapses, breakdowns and bankruptcies, which could occur even at the very highest financial levels of wealth. The sector of 'industrial' production – of which Say was thinking – could not, in these circumstances, expect that what it supplied would automatically find a reliable and *permanent* market. The money that the production process had distributed had been shared unequally between the suppliers of tools and raw materials, the transporters and the workers. The latter represented the largest single bill. But they were rather special economic 'agents'. Among the workers, money went straight 'from hand to mouth', as the saying has it. This was why as Isaac de Pinto explained the 'circulation of coin speeds up when it passes through the hands of the subordinate classes'[161] and small change circulated faster than anything else. The German cameralist F. W. Schrötter[162] called for the development of manufacturing activity as a means of developing the circulation of money (1686). To distribute money to artisans meant losing it only briefly: it would come hurtling back into general circulation. We may believe him since Ricardo in 1817 still considered that the 'natural wage' of the workman, around which the 'market wage' fluctuated, was the one that provided him with his subsistence and the means to reproduce his species.[163] Since he earned only a bare minimum, he devoted it primarily to food. He was therefore responding primarily to agricultural supply, and indeed it was the price of foodstuffs which determined his wage-level. He was not therefore the source of a demand for the manufactured objects he produced, often luxury goods.[164] And in this case the supply in question had created at best only an indirect demand for such goods. As for agricultural production, its irregular surpluses were not such that the sale of foodstuffs led the share-cropper, the day-labourer or the small farmer to make a very substantial indirect demand for manufactured goods.

In short it is in this heavily-weighted context that we must try to understand the thought of the physiocrats, which we so easily dismiss today. Was it really so mistaken to place prime importance on agricultural production and wealth, in an age when the supply of agricultural foodstuffs always found difficulty in meeting demand and keeping up with population increases? By contrast, were the frequent breakdowns in industrial production not the result of weakness of demand, either from the rural population or from the artisans and workmen of the towns? F. J. Fisher's distinction between agriculture (limited by supply) and industry (limited by demand) is a formula which seems to me to sum up quite forcefully the *ancien régime* economy.[165]

In the circumstances then, I fear that Say's law is much less applicable to the centuries before the Revolution than it is to the twentieth century. And in any case, eighteenth-century manufacturers only launched their large-scale enterprises with subsidies, interest-free loans and *previously-guaranteed* monopolies. They were not really entrepreneurs at all, it might be argued. And yet even with these ideal conditions, they did not always succeed. The days of constantly-growing supply, able to create new needs out of nothing, were still in the future; this was the breakthrough that would come with the machine age. No one has described better than Michelet how the industrial revolution was in the end a revolution in demand, a transformation of 'desires' to use Turgot's word, which might please some of today's philosophers. In 1842, Michelet writes, 'the cotton mills were in crisis. They were choking to death, as the warehouses were overflowing and there were no buyers. The panic-stricken mill-owners dared neither to work nor to stop work with their all-devouring machines ... Prices fell, but that accomplished nothing; they fell yet again, until cotton was selling at six *sous* ... Then something unexpected happened. The sound of *six sous* seemed to act as a trigger. Millions of buyers, poor people, who had never bought [textiles] before, began to stir. And it could then be seen how powerful and immense a consumer the people can be when it is aroused. The warehouses were emptied in a flash. The machines went frantically back to work ... And the result was a major, though little remarked revolution in France, a revolution in cleanliness and the suddenly improved appearance of the poor home: people had bed linen, body linen, linen for the table and the windows: it was now possessed by whole classes who had never had any since the world began.'[166]

Markets and their geography

The individual merchant has been absent from the foregoing paragraphs, which looked only at the role played by economic constraints and rules. He will remain absent from the next section, which considers markets *per se*: the area they occupied, their weight and volume – in short a retrospective geography of markets. For every form of exchange occupied an area and no area was neutral, that is untouched and unorganized by human agencies.

Historically speaking, it is therefore useful to map out the changing area dominated by a firm, a trading city or a nation – or the area occupied by a given trade – grain, salt, sugar, pepper or precious metals. This is one way to bring to light the impact the market economy made over a given area, including the many gaps and insufficiencies, but also the lasting dynamic stimulus it could contribute.

Firms and their catchment areas

A merchant would always be in touch with buyers, suppliers, lenders and creditors. If the addresses of these agents are plotted on a map, they reveal a catchment area which governed the very life of the merchant. The larger the area the more likely, in theory and almost always in practice, the merchant in question was to be an important one.

The catchment area of the firm of Gianfigliazzi,[167] Florentine merchants who had settled in France during the second half of the thirteenth century, covered the Alps, especially the Dauphiné and the Rhône valley; to the west, they had dealings as far afield as Montpellier and Carcassonne. Three centuries later, in about 1559, the Capponi of Antwerp[167] – a branch of the world-famous Tuscan family – were, according to their letters and order-books, operating within a long narrow strip running from the North Sea to the Mediterranean, to Pisa and Florence, where the firm had several branches. The same geographical area or very nearly, from the Netherlands to Italy, was the stamping-ground of the Salviati of Pisa, whose monumental archives are still virtually unexplored. In the seventeenth century, the Italian networks were tending to spread all over the Mediterranean, while losing their monopoly in the north. A register of *commessioni e ordini* (1652–1658) of the Tuscan firm of Saminiati[168] centred on Leghorn, reveals an essentially Mediterranean network: Venice, Smyrna, Tripoli in Syria, Tripoli in Barbary, Messina, Genoa, Marseilles are the most frequently mentioned places, while Constantinople, Alexandretta, Palermo and Algiers also appear quite often. The key cities for communication with the north were Lyons and above all Amsterdam. The boats used were often Dutch or English. But Leghorn was rather a special city, and the Saminiati records mention two ships taking on cargoes of red Russian leather in Archangel – the exception that proves the rule.

If hundreds or thousands of registers like this were available for us to consult,

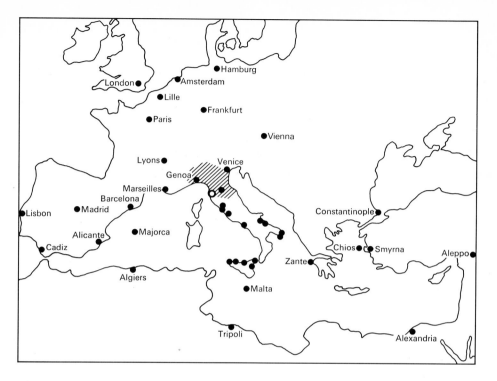

13   THE TRADING LINKS OF THE SAMINIATI FIRM IN THE SEVENTEENTH CENTURY

The Saminiati firm was established in Florence and Leghorn. Its many documents were saved *in extremis* by Armando Sapori and are preserved at the Bocconi, Milan. The shaded zone (central and northern Italy) corresponds to the area where most of the firm's transactions took place. It had representatives throughout the Mediterranean, in Cadiz, Lisbon, and also in the north (Paris, Frankfurt, Lille, London, Amsterdam, Hamburg and Vienna). Map drawn by Mlle M.C. Lapeyre.

they would automatically yield an invaluable typology of trade catchment areas. This would make it possible to contrast the sales area with the purchasing area, to explain one in terms of the other, and to distinguish between centripetal and centrifugal market forces; it would make it possible to distinguish too between the long, narrow catchment area, virtually linear in shape, which seems to reflect a decision to operate along a vital axis, and a broad circle corresponding to periods of expansion and unhampered trade. After considering two or three examples, it would no doubt be clear that a merchant prospered – and it goes without saying that he did – when he was firmly incorporated into the catchment area of a large city. As Cotrugli, a sixteenth-century Ragusan put it: 'The fattest fish are caught in the biggest lakes.'[169] I also like the story told by Eric Maschke[170] of the merchant and chronicler of Augsburg whose beginnings were so difficult and who only began to break even the day he reached Venice. The two crucial dates in the fortunes of the Fugger family were September 1367, when Hans Fugger left his native village of Graben for nearby Augsburg and settled there with his wife and children as a weaver of *Barchent* (fustian); and 1442, when his heirs became merchants trading over long distances, in touch with the nearest large cities and with Venice.[171] The story is a familiar one, repeated countless times. Federigo Melis quotes the example of the Borromei, natives of the *contado* of Pisa, '*che alla fine del secolo XV si milanesizzarono*', who 'Milanized themselves' and as a result made their fortune.[172]

The merchant's catchment area was a section of one or several national territories at any given period. In a period of growth, the merchant's trading surface might quickly expand, especially if he had access to the big business of the time – bills of exchange, currency, precious metals, 'royal merchandise' (like pepper, spices and silk) or fashionable goods, for instance the Syrian cotton necessary for the fustian weavers. From a very incomplete examination of the archives of Francesco Datini of Prato, I derived the impression that the really big business of about 1400 was the circulation of bills of exchange from Florence to Genoa, Montpellier, Barcelona, Bruges and Venice. Was the financial trading area more developed and extensive than any other, in the late fourteenth century and early fifteenth?

If sixteenth-century expansion was the reason as I have suggested, for the very active superstructure of fairs and commercial centres, it is easier to understand the sudden enlargement of the zone covered by the many dealings of the Fuggers and Welsers of Augsburg. By the standards of the time, these were massive concerns, alarming other merchants and public opinion by their very size. The Welsers of Augsburg were present throughout Europe, in the Mediterranean and in the New World: in 1528 they appeared in Venezuela, where Spanish ill-will and terrible local atrocities brought about their failure. But then the Welsers seemed to take a delight in going wherever there were risks to be taken, fortunes to be won or lost. The less adventurous Fuggers represented an even more spectacular success story and a more solid one. They controlled the largest mining enterprises of central Europe, in Hungary, Bohemia and the Alps. They were solidly established, through third parties in Venice. They dominated Antwerp, which in the early sixteenth century was the beating heart of the world. They appeared very early in Lisbon, and in Spain where they became allied to the Emperor Charles V. They had a branch in Chile in 1531, but moved out again quite soon in 1535.[173] In 1559, they opened in Fiume (Rijeka) and Dubrovnik,[174] their personal windows on to the Mediterranean. At the end of the sixteenth century, when they were facing great difficulties they briefly participated in the international pepper consortium in Lisbon. And they were represented in India by their compatriot Ferdinand Cron, who arrived there in 1587 at the age of twenty-eight, and who was to act for both the Fuggers and Welsers first in Cochin then in Goa. He stayed there until 1619, during which time he amassed a large personal fortune and performed many services for his far-off masters in

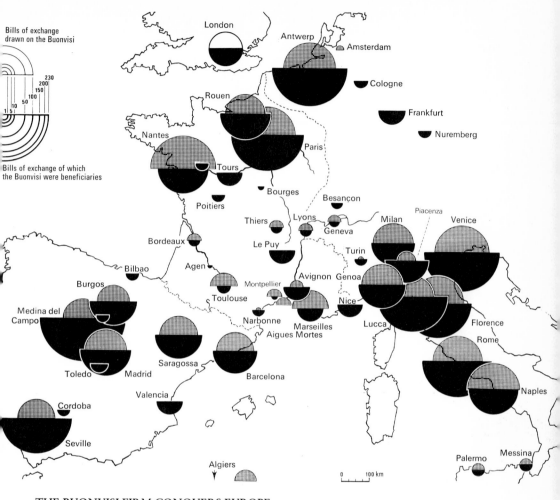

Bills of exchange
drawn on the Buonvisi

230
200
150
100
50
10
1 5

Bills of exchange of which
the Buonvisi were beneficiaries

14 THE BUONVISI FIRM CONQUERS EUROPE

From 1575 to 1610, the European trade area was covered with the network of firms owned by the Buonvisi family, merchants originally from Lucca who had settled in Lyons and who were represented by relatives or correspondents in every important trade centre. Bills of exchange wove a web joining a wide range of affairs. This diagram shows only the number of bills exchanged, not their value; so we should not perhaps take entirely for granted the impression given here that the position was favourable to the Buonvisi firm everywhere except in Nantes and Toulouse. It would be interesting to know more about the small number of bills drawn in Lyons on Lyons and about the abnormally large number of bills exchanged with Lucca, the Buonvisi's native town. (Map adapted from diagram by Françoise Bayard, 'Les Buonvisi, marchands banquiers de Lyon, 1575-1629' in *Annales E.S.C.*, 1971, pp. 1242-3.)

Spain, as well as for his Portuguese masters on the spot, whose black ingratitude he was to taste after 1619 in the form of injustice and prison.[175] In short, the empire of this huge firm was vaster than the mighty empire of Charles V and Philip II, on which as we know the sun never set . . .

But these huge figures of the contemporary stage are not necessarily the most significant. It would be more interesting to find out about the averages, that is firms of various sizes, and their overall fortunes. In the seventeenth century, the average size of firm appears to decline. Then in the eighteenth, there is expansion once more as finance spreads to the outer frontiers of Europe and then the world. The rich men's club was more firmly established than ever. But to test whether this hypothetical scheme is correct many more examples and comparisons are needed; a great deal of detailed research remains to be done.

The catchment area of town or city

A town or city lies at the centre of a number of interlocking catchment areas: there is the circle from which it obtains supplies; the circle in which its currency, weights and measures are used; the circle from which its craftsmen and new bourgeois come; the circle of credit (the widest one); the circle of its sales and the circle of its purchases; and the successive circles through which news reaching or leaving the town travels. Like the merchant's shop or warehouse, the town occupies an economic area assigned it by its situation, its wealth and its long-term context. It is defined at all times by these surrounding circles. But their message has to be interpreted.

Take for instance the city of Nuremberg in about 1558, the year of publication of a *Handelsbuch* by one of its citizens, Lorenz Meder. In this trading manual, which has recently been re-edited with a commentary by Hermann Kellenbenz,[176] Lorenz Meder set out to provide his fellow-citizens with practical information – not to solve our retrospective problem of plotting and interpreting the respective circles of which Nuremberg was the centre. But the facts he gives, completed by Hermann Kellenbenz's comments, make it possible to draw the map reproduced in Figure 15, which is rich in data and speaks for itself. Nuremberg, one of Europe's leading industrial, commercial and financial cities, was still, in the latter half of the sixteenth century, riding the wave which had a few decades earlier made Germany one of the powerhouses of European economic activity. Nuremberg was therefore connected to a long-distance economy, and its products, passed on from place to place, reached the Middle East, India, Africa and the New World. The city's *activities* however remained circumscribed within Europe. The central zone for its trade was effectively Germany, where it had short- and medium-range connections. The outer ring – Venice, Lyons, Medina del Campo, Lisbon, Antwerp, Cracow, Breslau, Poznan and Warsaw – marked both the furthest extent of its direct links and the points where it handed over to others so to speak.

Johannes Müller[177] has shown that Nuremberg was virtually the geometric centre of the economic life of Europe during the early sixteenth century. And this is no excess of local patriotism. But why should it have been so? Part of the answer must have been the increased volume of overland transport. Another reason could be Nuremberg's position, halfway between Venice and Antwerp, between the ancient trading zone of the Mediterranean and the new theatre of Europe's economic fortunes, the Atlantic (and its dependent seas). The Venice–Antwerp axis probably remained throughout the sixteenth century the most active of all the European 'isthmuses'. The Alps cut it in half, it is true but Alpine passes were the scene of constant miracles in the transport world – as if sheer difficulty had created a communications system superior to all others. So we should not be too surprised to find that pepper was arriving in Nuremberg at the end of the sixteenth century by way of both Antwerp and Venice. Pepper from the south and pepper from the north were in fact on such an equal footing that this merchandise could travel directly from Antwerp to Venice or from Venice to Antwerp (by land or by sea).

This reflected the situation of the German economy at a given period, of course. Over the long term, a pendulum movement operated to the advantage of the eastern, continental half of Germany. This rise of the East found concrete expression in the sixteenth century, particularly after the 1570 bankruptcies in Nuremberg and Augsburg, in the new prominence of Leipzig and its fairs. Leipzig succeeded in capturing the mines of Germany, in attracting the most important market in *Kuxen* (mining shares) to the city, and in setting up direct links with Hamburg and the Baltic, which was weaned away from its previous way-station of Magdeburg. But it also remained firmly attached to Venice, as 'Venice goods' propped up an entire sector of its activity. Leipzig also became *par excellence* the transit station for goods travelling between East and West. With the years the city's prominence became confirmed. In 1710, it could be argued that the Leipzig fairs were *'weit importanter und considerabler'* than those of Frankfurt, at least for commodities, for the city on the Main was still, at this period, a financial centre of much greater importance than Leipzig.[178] The money market still conferred lasting privileges.

The reader will have gathered that such urban catchment areas are hard to interpret, particularly since the documents rarely answer the kind of question we are asking. Even Jean-Claude Perrot's recent and extremely rich study of Caen in Normandy, *Genèse d'une ville moderne, Caen au XVIIIe siècle* (1975), cannot resolve all the problems he examines with exemplary care and intelligence. It is not altogether surprising that Von Thünen's schema applies to Caen: it is easy to identify the first circle, surrounding the town, fitting it like a garment and even encroaching inside the walls: 'a belt of market gardens and dairy producers'. Beyond it came a cereal-growing zone and a grazing zone.[179] But it is already more difficult to distinguish the areas penetrated by the industrial goods made in the town, or the markets and fairs which distributed such goods. Perhaps the most interesting aspect of the question is the double organization of the local catchment area and the international arena which the town had to handle: here were two different kinds of circulation, the first along a network of capillaries where the flow was continuous but within a small radius; the other

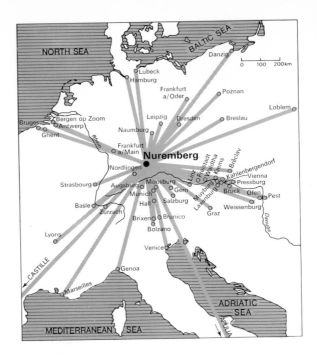

15　A CITY'S CATCHMENT AREA:
THE COMMUNICATIONS OF NUREMBERG IN ABOUT 1550
From *Das Meder'sche Handelsbuch*, ed. Hermann Kellenbenz, 1974.

more intermittent, but in times of food crisis capable of activating water-transport along the Seine, or shipping from London or Amsterdam. The two systems can be seen as complementary, contrasting, combined or alternating. The manner in which international trade affected a town could sometimes exert more influence on it than its everyday connections with nearby places. Local history might be swallowed up in a broader history.

The market in primary commodities: sugar

It would not be too difficult to write a history of the major commodity markets between the fifteenth and the eighteenth centuries, on the lines of Fernand Maurette's classic textbook about the 1920s.[180] And if we prudently confine ourselves to significant examples, there is plenty of choice: any goods produced on a large scale could provide us with evidence, and although what they tell us might vary considerably, it would agree on at least one point: like the most active cities or the most important merchants, the most profitable commodity trades operated over enormous distances. Distance is a constant indicator of wealth and success. The 'spice' trade – the word 'covers an amazing variety of products' from those used to 'improve the taste of a dish ... to medicinal products and dyestuffs for fabric'[181] – is so well known and such a classic example that one hesitates to suggest it as a model. The advantage of taking it would be that this trade is an instance of sustained expansion over a long period, with various inter-related episodes, followed by a visible decline in the seventeenth century.[182] But I have already discussed it elsewhere.[183] Sugar on the other hand is a comparatively recent product, which constantly extended both its consumption and its area of distribution at a rapid rate between the fifteenth and twentieth centuries. With a few minor exceptions (like corn or maple syrup) this precious commodity was obtained (until the Continental Blockade and the cultivation of sugar-beet) from sugar-cane. This plant, as we have seen,[184] spread from India to the Mediterranean and the Atlantic (Madeira, the Canaries, the Azores, Saõ Tomé, 'Prince's Island', then to the tropical coasts of America, the West Indies and Brazil). The invasion was the more remarkable in that it demanded what was for the time very heavy investment.

Consequently sugar, which continued as in the past to figure on the apothecary's shelves, was increasingly to be found in kitchens and on tables. In the fifteenth and sixteenth centuries, it was still a luxury, presented as a gift by one prince to another. On 18 October 1513, the king of Portugal offered the Pope a lifesize sugar effigy of himself, surrounded by twelve cardinals and three hundred candles, one and a half metres high – all made by a long-suffering confectioner.[185] But even then, although it had not yet become an everyday foodstuff, sugar was increasingly being eaten. In 1544, there was a German saying '*Zucker verderbt keine Speis*', sugar spoils no dish.[186] Brazil had begun its shipments: an average of 1600 tons a year in the sixteenth century. In 1676, 400 ships, each carrying on average 180 tons of sugar (total 72,000 tons) left Jamaica.[187] In the eighteenth century, Saint Domingue was to produce as much if not more.[188]

But we should not therefore imagine that the European market was flooded with sugar from the Atlantic; nor that the great sugar boom was the original cause of the Atlantic shipping boom and indirectly of the increased modernity of Europe. Such elementary determinism is not difficult to stand on its head: one could well argue that it was the European boom, aided by newly-stimulated appetites, which led to the boom first in sugar and later in coffee.

There is no room here to describe how the elements of the great story of sugar were put into place, piece after piece: the black slaves, the planters, the production techniques, the refining of raw sugar, the cheap food supplies for the plantations which were unable to feed themselves; the shipping routes, the warehouses and the retailers in Europe. In about 1760, when the whole operation was in working order, different kinds of sugar were on offer on the Paris market or elsewhere:

> Muscovado, cassonade, seven-pound sugar-loaves, royal sugar, semi-royal sugar, candy sugar and red or Cyprus sugar. A good muscovado should be fairly white, with as little moisture as possible and hardly tasting of caramel at all. Cassonade, which was known as the Sugar of the Islands, should be choice, white, dry,

A Brazilian sugar mill. Drawing attributed to F. Post, c. 1640. Note in the foreground a typical Brazilian ox-cart with solid wheels, and the yoked animals working the machines. (Atlas van Stolk Foundation.)

fine-grained and violet-scented. The best comes from Brazil but trade in this has almost fallen away; Cayenne is second best and then the Islands. Confectioners use a great deal of cassonade from Brazil and the Islands in their preserves and even prize it more highly than refined sugar, they say the preserves made with it are better and less likely to crystallize.[189]

It is clear that by this time, sugar had lost its rarity value: it had become an item in grocers' and confectioners' shops.

But what interests us most here is rather the significance the sugar trade had for the merchant: we know at least some details about this. In the first place, sugar was spoken of, from the beginning of its career in the Mediterranean, as an excellent commodity investment. In this connection, the example of Venice and the sugar of Cyprus is particularly clear, since it was in the hands of the Cornaro or Cornero family, sugar kings who (as their name suggests) had an unshaken monopoly in it. In 1479, when Venice occupied Cyprus, she won a sugar war.

We do not know a great deal about the Cornero sugar business. But other documented cases leave one with the impression (hardly surprising perhaps), that in the sequence of operations in the sugar trade, *production* was never the sector in which fortunes were made. In fifteenth- and sixteenth-century Sicily, the sugar mills financed by Genoese capital turned out to be mediocre or downright unprofitable ventures. Similarly, the sugar boom in the Atlantic islands in the early sixteenth century might have been expected to produce considerable profits; but when the great capitalist firm of Welser bought up land in the Canaries in 1509 and established sugar plantations there, they found the affair did not pay and abandoned it in 1520.[190] The same was true in the sixteenth century even on the Brazilian plantations: they provided a living for the planter, the *senhor de engenho*, but not a very rich one. One has much the same impression in Saint Domingue despite its record production. Was it for this imperative reason that production was relegated to the low status work of slave labour? Was this the only way in which outlay could be covered?

But this observation takes us even further. Any capitalist market has a series of links in a chain, and somewhere near the middle there is a point higher and more remunerative than the rest. In the pepper trade for instance, this high point was for many years the *Fondaco dei Tedeschi*: Venetian pepper piled up here before being dispatched to the big German buyers. In the seventeenth century, the real centre of the pepper trade lay in the great warehouses of the *Oost Indische Companie*. As for sugar, which was entirely oriented towards the European market, the links are more complicated, since one had to control production in order to benefit from the highest point of the commercial enterprise. Atlantic sugar did not become really important until the latter half of the seventeenth century, with the successive fortunes of the various Caribbean islands. When the Dutch lost the Brazilian Nordeste, in 1654, they suffered a setback which the English and French-controlled production would only aggravate. In short, there was a division of production, followed by a division of refining, and finally a sharing of the market.

There were only a few sketchy attempts to set up a single dominant sugar market: in Antwerp, where in 1550 there were 19 sugar refineries; in Holland after the decline of the Antwerp market in 1585. After 1614 Amsterdam had to forbid the use of coal in the refineries, since it was polluting the atmosphere – but that did not prevent the number of refineries from increasing: 40 in 1650, 61 in 1661. But in this the century of mercantilism, national economies defended themselves and succeeded in keeping their own markets for themselves. In France for instance, where Colbert protected the national market by the tariffs of 1665, refineries began to prosper in Dunkerque, Nantes, Bordeaux, La Rochelle, Marseilles, Orleans. As a result, after 1670, no sugar refined abroad was entering France; on the contrary, refined sugar was being exported, thanks to a sort of export subsidy which worked by retrospective refunds of the customs duties paid on raw sugar entering the country, if it was exported as refined sugar.[191] French exports were also helped by low domestic consumption (1/10 of colonial production as against 9/10 in England) and by the plantations receiving food supplies from France at lower costs (because of the lower price levels in France) than did those of Jamaica, which were chiefly supplied from England, with some help from North America. 'Before the War' [The Seven Years' War, as it was to be] writes the *Journal du Commerce*,[192] 'sugar from the English colonies was up to 70% more expensive in London than sugar from the French colonies in French ports, quality for quality. This excessive price can have no other explanation than the excessive cost of the foodstuffs England sends to its colonies; and at these prices, what can England do with her sugar surpluses?' She had to eat them of course – since the English domestic market was, it must be remembered, already capable of absorbing them.

In spite of exports and reselling by the larger producing countries, national control of sugar markets, by means of the purchase of raw sugar and the installation of refineries, was in any case spreading throughout Europe. From 1672, taking advantage of Holland's difficulties, Hamburg developed its own refineries and perfected new techniques which it tried to keep secret. And refineries were created even in Prussia, Austria and Russia where they were state monopolies. In order to have an exact picture of the movements of sugar markets and of the really profitable stage of the operation then, we should have to reconstruct the complicated network of communications between the producing areas, the money markets which dominated production, and the refineries which were a means of at least partly controlling wholesale distribution. After these 'factories' came the countless retail shops which bring us back to the ordinary level of the market with modest profit margins governed strictly by straight-forward competition.

At what point or points in the entire process would one find the real profits being made? If the example of London is anything to go by, they occurred at the wholesale market stage, somewhere near the warehouses in which cases and barrels of sugar piled up, before going on to the purchasers who bought white or brown sugar or molasses according to whether they were refiners, confectioners or ordinary retailers. The manufacture of the white sugar originally reserved for the refineries in the home country, eventually became established in the planta-tion islands, despite the original prohibitions. But was this industrial venture not a sign precisely of the difficulties these islands were experiencing? The key position on the wholesale market lay, in my opinion, at the state *after* refining; refining itself does not *seem* to have attracted big businessmen. To be sure of this, one would have to have more information about relations between whole-salers and refiners.

Precious metals

Let us now leave the subject of sugar, to which we shall return later. We have an even better example to consider: precious metals. They travelled world wide, they bring us to the highest level of exchange, and they are an indicator, if indeed any is needed, of the ever-changing construction of hierarchies in economic life which was constantly achieving new peaks and records at its upper levels. Supply or demand for this ubiquitous commodity, which was coveted by all and travelled all over the world, always matched each other.

But the very expression 'precious metals', which comes so easily to the pen, is not as simple as it looks. It may denote different objects:

A Genoese chest, with complicated locks, of the kind used to transport silver bars or coins from Spain to Genoa. (Genoa, Savings Bank, Photo Armand Colin.)

1 metallic ores, as they emerged straight from the mines or from the sandy river-beds of the gold-panners;

2 semi-processed products, ingots, bars or pigs (pigs, masses of the irregular metal, light and porous, as it was left after the evaporation of the mercury used in the amalgam process, were in theory recast into bars and ingots before being distributed on the market);

3 processed products, coins which were in fact forever being re-minted. In India, the rupee, though of constant weight and nominal value was actually valued according to the date of issue; previous coinages were worth less than the current year's.

In these different forms, precious metal moved about constantly and quickly. As Boisguilbert was already saying, silver was only useful so long as it was 'in perpetual motion'.[193] And indeed money moved without cease. 'Nothing is transported so easily and with less loss', remarked Cantillon[194] who was (according to Schumpeter at least) the first economist to write about the velocity of circulation of coin.[195] It sometimes moved at such speed that it disturbed the order of the successive operations between the ingot and the minting of coin. This was happening by mid-sixteenth century and later even more so: off the coast of Peru in the early eighteenth century, vessels from Saint-Malo were clandestinely loading, not only pieces of eight but also 'unquinted' pigs of silver, (that is contraband silver which had not paid the royal quint or fifth). In any case, pigs were always contraband. Legal silver, as yet unminted, was transported in ingots or bars which often circulated in Europe.

But money moved even faster. Trade brought it 'cascading' in and smuggling helped it to overcome all barriers. For money, there were indeed 'no Pyrenees', as Louis Dermigny put it.[196] In 1614, 400 different currencies were circulating in the Netherlands; in France at the same time there were 82.[197] There was no known region of Europe, even the very poorest, where the most unlikely currency might not find itself trapped – the Alpine wilderness of Embrunois in the fourteenth century for example[198] or the backward and isolated Gévaudan in the fourteenth and fifteenth.[199] Paper offered its services – from very early times – in vain: specie, 'cash in hand' kept its prerogatives. In central Europe, the battlefield on which the west European powers had adopted the convenient habit of settling, or trying to settle, their own conflicts, the strength of the competing adversaries – France or England – could be measured by their distributions of coin. In 1742, Venetian dispatches reported that the English fleet had brought huge sums destined for Maria Theresa 'the Queen of Hungary'.[200] The price of the alliance with Frederick II in 1756, paid out by mighty Britannia consisted of thirty-four wagon loads of silver coin, trundling towards Berlin.[201] As soon as peace approached in the spring of 1762, her favours were transferred to Russia: 'the mail of the 9th of March from London', writes a diplomat, 'brought for Amsterdam and Rotterdam bills of exchange for more than 150,000 pieces of eight, in order that this amount should be passed on to the Court of Russia'.[202] In February 1799, 'five million' in English money passed through Leipzig in ingots and coin; dispatched from Hamburg, this money was on its way to Austria.[203]

That said, the real problem is simply to try to distinguish as far as possible the causes, or at least the mechanisms of this circulation which penetrated all the leading economies the world over. Both causes and mechanisms will be better understood, I believe, if we distinguish the three visible stages of production, transmission and accumulation. There certainly were countries that produced raw metal, others which regularly exported specie, and others again which were receptacles from which neither coin nor metal ever emerged. But there were also cases – the most informative – which combined more than one function, and these included China and Europe, which were both importers and exporters.

Countries producing gold and silver were almost always primitive, even savage places whether Borneo, Sumatra, the island of Hainan, the Sudan, Tibet, the Celebes, or the mining areas of Central Europe in the eleventh to thirteenth centuries, (and again from 1470 to 1540 when they flourished once more). Gold panning went on – until the eighteenth century and even later – in European rivers, but its contribution was scanty, almost negligible. In the fifteenth and sixteenth centuries, there were mining camps in the howling wastes of the Alps, the Carpathians or in the Erz Gebirge. It was a hard life for those who worked there – but at least these miners were free men.

In Africa, by contrast, in the Bambuk, the gold-mining heart of the Sudan, the 'mines' were ruled by the village chiefs. Here there was semi-slavery, to put it mildly.[204] There is less ambiguity about the New World, where the Europeans re-created the slavery of ancient times on a grand scale for the extraction of precious metals. What were the Indians of the Mita (the mine-belt) or the black gold-washers of Central Brazil in the eighteenth century if not slaves? Strange towns sprang up, the strangest of all being Potosi, 4000 metres up in the High Andes, a colossal mining-camp and an urban eyesore where more than 100,000 human beings huddled together.[205] The cost of living here was ridiculous even for the rich: a hen could cost eight reals, an egg two, a pound of wax from Castile 10 pesos, and so on.[206] What can this mean, except that here money was useless? Neither the miner, nor even the mine-owner could earn a living here, only the merchant who advanced minted coin, rations, and the mercury the mines needed – and who quietly collected his due in metal. It was the same story, in gold-producing Brazil in the eighteenth century. Along the waterways and portages went the flotillas known as the *monções*[207] from São Paolo, to supply both masters and slaves in the gold-washing centres of Minas Gerais and Goyaz. Only the merchants made any money. The miners often lost whatever they might have earned, gambling when they returned briefly to the city. Mexico City was an notorious gaming centre. At the end of the day, gold and silver weighed less on the profit scales than manioc flour, maize, and the sun-dried beef, *a carne do sol*, eaten in Brazil.

How could things have been otherwise? In the division of labour, *on a world scale*, the trade of miner was the lot of the most wretched and deprived of men. The stakes were too high for the mighty of the world, whoever and wherever they might be, not to make their presence heavily felt. For the same reasons they did not let prospecting for diamonds and precious stones out of their clutches either. Tavernier[208] paid a visit as a buyer in 1652 to the famous diamond mine 'known as Raolkonda ... five days' journey from Golconda'. Everything was admirably organized for the benefit of the prince and the merchants, and even for the convenience of the customers. But the miners were wretched, naked, ill-treated and suspected – not without reason – of constant attempts at theft. The

Brazilian *garimpeiros*,[209] the diamond-seekers, of the eighteenth century were adventurers whose fantastic voyages are impossible to follow – but the profits of their exploits went into the pockets of the merchants, the king in Lisbon, and the diamond-sales farmers. If a mining enterprise was set up with any degree of independence (as in medieval Europe) one could be sure that it would be taken over sooner or later by some ring of merchants. The mining world foreshadowed the industrial world with its proletariat.

A second category is that of the 'receptacle-countries' – above all in Asia, where the monetary economy was only irregularly functioning, and where precious metals circulated less freely than in Europe. Here, there was consequently a tendency to hoard precious metals and under-employ them. These countries were like sponges or as they were called at the time 'graveyards' for precious metals.

The two biggest reservoirs were China and India, countries rather different from each other. India welcomed almost equally gold and silver, whether the gold dust of the Contracosta (Monomotapa to be more precise) or the silver of Europe and later Japan. According to Indian historians, the influx of silver from America even created a price rise there, about twenty years after the European price 'revolution' of the sixteenth century. This is one more indication that imported silver stayed put, an indication too that even the fabulous treasure of the Great Mogul could not neutralize all the consignments of silver, since prices went up.[210] It was American silver after all that fed the countless mintings and re-mintings of coins in India.

We probably know rather less about what went on in China. One original feature is that China did not give a monetary value to gold, but exported it to anyone who wanted to exchange it for silver at exceptionally low rates. The Portuguese in the sixteenth century, were the first Europeans to realize and take advantage of this extraordinary preference of the Chinese for silver. In 1633, a Portuguese writer was still confidently saying '*Como os chinos sentirao prata, em montoes trouxerao fazenda*', when the Chinese smell silver, they will bring mountains of merchandise.[211] But we will not believe Antonio de Ulloa, a Spaniard who claimed in 1787 that 'the Chinese labour continually to acquire silver which is not to be found in their country', whereas theirs is 'one of the nations that needs it least'.[212] On the contrary, silver currency was widely used in Chinese trade for higher denominations (it was cut into thin slices to settle bills) alongside the base coinage of *caixas* or *sapekes* made of alloyed copper and lead.

A recent historian of China[213] thinks that at least half the silver mined in America between 1527 and 1821 found its way to China, which was a destination of no return. Pierre Chaunu[214] suggests a figure of one-third, including the direct exports from New Spain to the Philippines across the Pacific, and even this would be enormous. Neither calculation can be vouched for, but there are several reasons why they are quite plausible. In the first place, there were the profits (which remained high for a long time, at least until the late eighteenth century) from the operation of exchanging silver for gold in China.[215] This trade was carried on even from India and the East Indies. Secondly, American silver found a new outlet in 1572, crossing the Pacific in the Manila galleon[216] which sailed between the Mexican port of Acapulco and the capital of the Philippines, carrying silver in exchange for silks, Chinese porcelain, luxury cottons from India, precious stones and pearls. This trade route had its ups and downs, but lasted right through the eighteenth century and beyond. The last galleon returned to Acapulco in 1811.[217] But the whole of South-East Asia was probably engaged in this traffic, as an anecdote will illustrate, if it does not entirely explain it. The *Hindostan*, a large sailing vessel carrying the ambassador Macartney to China, took on board a Cochinchinese pilot in 1793. The old man was ill at ease. 'But when a few Spanish dollars were put into his hands, he shewed he had a knowledge of their value, by carefully wrapping them up in a corner of his tattered clothing.'[218]

Between the producing countries and the accumulating countries, Islam and Europe stood in a singular position: they served as intermediate, transit zones.

There is no need to dwell long on the role of Islam, which reproduced the situation of Europe in this respect. But it is worth pausing to consider the case of the huge Turkish Empire. It has too often been regarded as an economically neutral zone, through which European trade passed as it pleased with impunity: in the sixteenth century this was through Egypt and the Red Sea, or by way of Syria using the caravans that travelled to Persia or the Persian Gulf; in the seventeenth, it went through Smyrna and Asia Minor. It was assumed that all these trade routes through the Levant were neutral, that is that the flow of silver travelled along them without having any significant effect, hardly stopping even, but hastening on towards the silks of Persia and the calicoes of India. The more so since the Ottoman Empire had been and would remain predominantly a gold zone – the gold, originally from Africa, from the Sudan and Abyssinia, being brought in through Egypt and North Africa. In fact, the price rise (broadly covering the sixteenth century) brought to light by the research of Omer Lutfi Barkan and his pupils[219] proves that the Empire shared in the silver inflation which was very largely responsible for the crisis of the asper, the small silver coin so crucial to the economy since it was used in everyday transactions and for the pay of the janissaries. The Empire may have been an intermediary, but it was not untouched.

Its role was, however, modest compared to that played by Europe, on a world scale. Before the discovery of America, Europe had somehow managed to extract from her own territories the silver and gold necessary to meet the deficit of her trading balance in the Levant. With the mines of the New World, Europe became confirmed and anchored in this role of distributor of precious metals.

To some economic historians, this one-way traffic in metal appears as a disadvantage, a loss of substance for Europe. Surely this is to argue from mercantilist prejudices. Metaphor for metaphor, I would prefer to think of Europe as bombarding, with her gold (and above all silver) currencies the countries whose gates would otherwise have been firmly closed to her, or would have been opened only with difficulty. And does not any victorious monetary economy tend to replace other currencies with its own – doubtless by a kind of inevitability, without any deliberate manœuvre on its part? In the fifteenth century for instance, the Venetian ducat (a real currency at the time) was replacing the Egyptian gold dinar, and the Levant was soon overrun by silver coins minted in the Zecca in Venice, until in the last decades of the sixteenth century it was flooded with Spanish pieces of eight, later known as piastres, or 'dollars', the European economy's long-distance weapon against the Far East. Mahé de La Bourdonnais[220] (October 1729) asked Closrivière, his friend and associate in Saint-Malo, to collect funds and send them to him in Pondicherry in piastres, so that he could use them for the various possibilities of Far East internal trade. If his associates sent him large sums of money, he explained, he would be able to attempt a trip to China, which required a great deal of silver and which the English governors of Madras liked to keep for themselves as a sure way of making a fortune. It seems clear that in such circumstances, ownership of a mass of silver coin was the secret of opening a trade route and forcing entry. In any case, adds La Bourdonnais, 'it is always advantageous to handle large sums, because that makes you a master of trade, for streams will always run into a river'.

Similar forced entries, it would appear, were made to the Regency of Tunis, where in the seventeenth century the Spanish piece of eight had become the standard currency;[221] and to Russia, where the balance of payments drew in a large injection of Dutch and then English currencies. In fact without this monetary transfusion, the huge Russian market would have been neither willing nor able to reply to western demand. In the eighteenth century, the successes of the English merchants came from the advances they made to Muscovite merchants, who collected or acted as middlemen for the products England wanted. The first steps taken by the British East India Company on the other hand were difficult, as long as the company insisted on sending out cloth, and being very sparing with the cash it allowed its desperate factors, who were forced to borrow money locally.

Europe was therefore obliged to export an important proportion of her stocks of silver and sometimes, though much less lavishly, her gold coin. This was in a way her structural position: she found herself thus placed by the twelfth century and remained so for many hundreds of years. So it is rather amusing to see the efforts of the first territorial states to prevent the outflow of precious metals. 'To find ways of keeping [inside the state] all gold and silver, without letting any out', was for Eon in 1646 the maxim of all 'major policy'. The trouble is, he adds, that 'all the gold and silver that is brought in [to France] seems to be thrown into a bottomless bag, and France is nothing but a canal through which the water flows without stopping'.[222] Contraband and clandestine trade of course were the agents undertaking this necessary function. But they could handle only small amounts. Wherever trade was a predominant activity, sooner or later the gates had to be flung open wide and coin had to be free to circulate briskly like a commodity.

Fifteenth-century Italy recognized this obligation. In Venice, a liberal decision on the outflow of currency had been taken by at least 1396;[223] it was renewed in 1397,[224] and on 10 May 1407, by a measure passed by the *Pregadi*[225] which carried only one restriction: any merchant who wished to take out money (silver undoubtedly for the Levant) must have imported it first and was to deposit one quarter of the total in the Zecca, the Venetian Mint. After that, he was free to take the rest *'per qualunque luogo'* ('wherever he pleased'). Indeed, Venice was so accustomed to its role as an exporter of silver to the Levant or North Africa that the Signoria always over-valued gold, making it, if such a thing is possible, a 'bad money', plentiful locally and therefore chasing out the 'good' money, silver. This was the point after all. One could also demonstrate how Ragusa or Marseilles arranged such necessary and profitable silver exports. Marseilles, which was jealously watched over by the royal authorities, always met harassment and incomprehension from them. If the free movement of piastres is forbidden in the city, as well as their export to the Levant, the city tried to explain in 1699, and if it is made compulsory to melt them down in the mints, they will simply go straight to Genoa or Leghorn instead. The wisest course would be to allow them to be exported not only from Marseilles but also from maritime towns 'like Toulon, Antibes or others, where the navy is paid'.[226]

There were no such problems in Holland, where trade swept all before it: gold and silver coins could come and go as they pleased. And the same freedom eventually prevailed in England, now on its way up. In spite of discussions which remained passionate until the end of the seventeenth century, the gates were opening wider and wider to let coin out. The livelihood of the India Company depended upon it. The act passed by the English Parliament in 1663, after pressure precisely from the company contains a revealing preamble: 'It is found by experience that they [i.e. coins] are carried in greatest abundance ... to such places as give free liberty for exporting the same'.[227] And the influential Sir George Downing remarked that 'money that in former time was only used as the measure to value all commodities by is become now itself a commodity'.[228] From then on, precious metals circulated quite openly. By the eighteenth century, all resistance was at an end. On 16 January 1721 for instance, the gazettes announced after a customs declaration in London, the dispatch of 2315 ounces of gold to Holland; on 6 March 288 ounces to the same destination and 2656 to the East Indies; on 20 March, 1607 ounces left for France and 138 for Holland, etc.[229] It was no longer possible to turn back the clock, even during the acute financial crisis which flared up after the conclusion of the treaty of Paris in 1763. London would have liked to restrain somewhat 'the excessive flow of gold and silver

Venetian coin of 1471: the lire of the Doge Niccolò Tron, the only doge whose head appeared on a minted coin. (Photo B. N., Paris.)

which has gone out to Holland and France in a short time', but 'to place obstacles in its way would mean striking a mortal blow at public credit which must at all times be maintained inviolate'.[230]

But this was not, as we know, the attitude of all European governments. The open door policy was not universally adopted overnight and it took time for notions to come up to date. France was certainly no pioneer in this respect. A French emigré, the comte d'Espinchal, arriving in Genoa in December 1789, felt it necessary to comment on the fact that 'gold and silver [are] commodities in the State of Genoa'[231] as if this was a curiosity. Though doomed in the long run, mercantilism died hard.

But we should not go away with the impression that Europe was blindly emptying itself of precious metals. Matters were more complicated. For one thing, we should bear in mind the constant duel between gold and silver, to which F. C. Spooner long ago drew attention.[232] Europe let silver out all over the world. But it over-valued gold: this was one way of holding on to it, hoarding it and keeping it handy for the internal servicing of the 'world-economy' of Europe, for all important settlements within Europe, between merchants or between nations. It was also a way of attracting it in from China, the Sudan, Peru. In its own way the Turkish Empire – European in this respect – had the same policy: hold on to the gold and let the silver flow through. One might stretch a point and reformulate Gresham's Law – bad money drives out good – to explain the process. In fact one currency drove out another whenever its value was over-estimated in relation to the level of a given economy. France in the eighteenth century over-valued silver until the reform of 30 October 1785 'which changed the gold-silver relation from 1: 14.4 to 1: 15.5.'[233] As a result, eighteenth-century France was like China in miniature: silver was attracted there. Venice, Italy, Portugal, England, Holland and even Spain[234] put a high price on gold. Indeed minimal differences in the exchange rate were sufficient to draw gold towards these high-rate countries: it thus became the 'bad money' driving out silver and forcing it to travel the world.

The massive outflow of silver nevertheless caused frequent crises within the European economy. But by so doing, it encouraged the rise of paper-money, which was used as a stop-gap; it stimulated prospecting for precious metals in foreign places; and it encouraged trade to look for substitutes for coin – to send cloth to the Levant, Indian cotton and opium to China. While Asia struggled to pay for silver with textiles, but also with vegetable products, spices, drugs and

Golden guinea from the reign of Charles II, 1678. (Photo B. N., Paris.)

tea, Europe redoubled her mining and industrial enterprises in order to balance her trade bill. In the long run could it not be argued that Europe rose to this challenge and turned it to her advantage? It is at any rate apparent that one should not refer, as many people do, to the outflow of silver as a harmful haemorrhage – as if Europe was paying for the luxury of spices and chinoiserie with her own life-blood!

National economies and the balance of trade

We shall not at this point be studying the national market in the classic sense of the term: this developed rather slowly and unevenly depending on the country. We shall return in Volume III to the importance of this gradual formation process, still unfinished in the eighteenth century, which laid the foundation of the modern state.

Here I intend only to show how the circulation of goods brought face to face the different national economies (let us for the moment avoid the term national market) whether backward or precocious; how it set them against each other and how it ranked them in order. Equal and unequal exchange, balance and imbalance of trade, domination and subjection serve to draw a general map of the commercial world. The balance of trade helps us to trace a preliminary outline of this map; not that it is the best or the only way of tackling the problem, but because in practice rudimentary and incomplete as they are, these are the only figures we possess.

The 'balance of trade'

The trade balance of a given economy is something like the balance sheet a merchant draws up at the end of a year: he has either made money or lost it. In the *Discourse of the Common Weal of this Realm of England* (1549), (now attributed to Sir Thomas Smith) one reads the following: 'We must always take heed that we buy no more from strangers than we sell them, for so we should impoverish ourselves and enrich them'[235] – a sentence which sums up all we need know about the trade balance and perhaps all anyone has ever known. For this wisdom was not new. Well before 1549, English merchants were obliged by their government to repatriate to England the proceeds of their surplus sales abroad in the form of minted coin. And foreign merchants had to use the proceeds from their sales in England to purchase English goods before they were allowed to leave the country. Thomas Mun's *Discourse of trade*, written in 1621 offers a theory of the trade balance which is realistic and which clearly corresponds to a growing awareness. His contemporary Edward Misselden was able to write in 1623: 'Wee felt it before in sense; but now wee know it by science.'[236] This was of course an elementary theory, far removed from modern conceptions of the problem which embrace a series of simultaneous balances (of trade, of labour, of capital and of payments). The trade balance in the early period simply meant the balance of the value of goods exchanged between two countries, the sum total of reciprocal imports and exports or rather the reciprocal debts. For example, if 'France owes Spain 100,000 *pistoles* and Spain owes France 1,500,000 *livres*,' since the *pistole* is worth 15 *livres*, the debt is cancelled out. 'As such equality is rare, it becomes necessary for the nation which owes the most to convey metal to cover that part of the debt which has not been compensated for.'[237] The deficit might be temporarily accounted for by bills of exchange, that is postponed. But if it persisted, there had of necessity to be a transfer of precious metals. It is this transfer which, when we can observe it, is for historians the sought-for indicator: it clearly states the problem of the relations between our two economic units, one obliged by the other to surrender part of its reserves in coin or bullion whether it wants to or not.

The whole of mercantilist policy was directed towards at least breaking even on this balance. The outflow of precious metals was to be avoided by all possible means. In January–February 1703 then, if instead of buying locally rations for the English troops fighting in Holland, the government were to send 'grain, manufactured products and other goods' from England, the corresponding sums of silver 'could remain' in the kingdom. Such an idea could only occur to a government obsessed by the fear of losing its metal reserves. In August of the same year, when England was due to pay a subsidy in cash as promised to Portugal, following the Methuen treaty, she proposed settling it by exports of wheat and cereals 'so as both to acquit herself of her obligations and to allay anxiety about letting specie out of the kingdom'.[238]

'To achieve a balance',[239] to have approximate equality between exports and imports, was only a minimum requirement. Best of all would be to achieve a favourable balance – the dream of all the mercantilist governments who identified national wealth with monetary reserves. All these ideas emerged, as one might expect, at the same time as the territorial states: hardly had they appeared than they were defending themselves and indeed they had to. As early as 1462, Louis XI was taking steps to control and limit the export to Rome 'of gold and silver, in coin or otherwise which might be extracted, carried and transported from this our kingdom'.[240]

Interpreting the figures

Shifts in the trade balance – even when we know about them – are not always easy to interpret. And there are no rules that can be applied confidently to every case. One would not for example say that Spanish America had a deficit in her trade balance on account of the massive exports of bullion extracted from her. Father Mercado (1564) was clear-sighted on this point: in these circumstances, he said 'gold and silver ingots are held to be a kind of commodity in all these

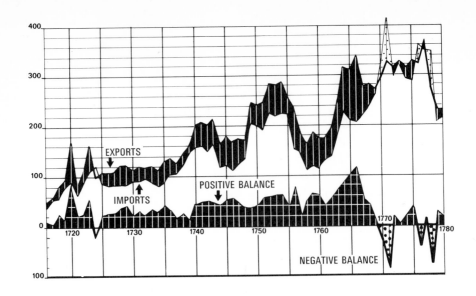

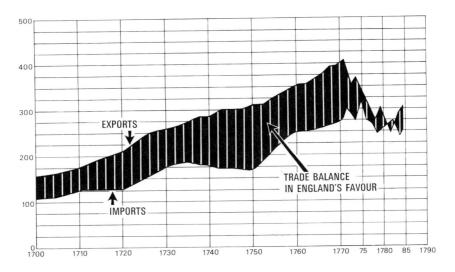

16 THE TRADE BALANCES OF FRANCE AND ENGLAND IN
    THE EIGHTEENTH CENTURY

As their trading balances show, England and France lived comfortably at the expense of the rest of the world until about the 1770s, when poor or even negative balances began to show up. Was this because of the general climate, a decline in commercial capitalism, or, more probably because of the disturbances caused by the War of American Independence? French figures from Ruggiero Romano, 'Documenti e prime considerazioni intorno alla "balance du commerce" della Francia 1716-1780' in *Studi in onore di Armando Sapori*, 1957, pp. 1268-1279. The unpublished sources of this research are indicated p. 1268, note 2. For England, since I wished to show only a general picture of English trade, I have used William Playfair's *The Exports and Imports and General Trade of England, the National Debt . . . 1786.*

regions of America: their value may rise and fall for the same reasons as that of ordinary commodities'.[241] Of Spain, Turgot explained: 'Silver is a foodstuff there: and since it cannot be exchanged for money, it is exchanged for foodstuffs.'[242] Nor would one say without measuring one's words that the trade balance between Russia and England in 1786 favoured the former rather than the latter, merely because Russia usually sold more to England than she bought from her. On the other hand, one would not argue the contrary, as John Newman tried to do in October 1786. Newman was the Russian consul in Hull, the large seaport where English ships heavily laden with Russian goods, would put in, after setting a direct course from the Skagerrak. He saw, or thought he saw the problem at first hand. He took the public figures, with which there was no argument: in 1785, £1,300,000 worth of goods passed through the Russian customs bound for England; in the other direction went £500,000 worth. The trade benefit to Catherine II's Empire was £800,000 sterling. 'But notwithstanding this apparent pecuniary profit for Russia', he writes, 'I have always maintained and I maintain still that it is not Russia but Great-Britain which is the *sole* beneficiary [this is where he exaggerates] of this trade.' Think about the consequences of the trade, he explains: the freighting of about 400 English ships 'each of 300 tons' cargo, almost 7000 to 8000 seamen', the rise in price of the Russian goods as soon as they land on English soil (about 15%), and everything that these cargoes contribute to industry and to the re-exports from England.[243] Clearly John Newman suspected that the balance between two countries could only be appreciated if a whole series of factors was included in the calculation. What he says shows an intuitive premonition of modern theories of the trade balance. When Thomas Mun (1621) argued that money shipped out to India would yield five times its value in the end, he was saying something similar, but something else as well.[244]

Moreover a particular bilateral trade balance is significant only when placed within the whole trade context, when all the balances of a given economy are added together. The simple figure for the England–India or England–Russia balance would not give us the whole picture: we need to know all the trade balances of Russia, of England or of India. Every national economy today reckons the balance of its external trade as a total.

The trouble is that for the past we only have bilateral figures, as between two countries. Some are classic, others deserve to be: in the fifteenth century, the balance favoured England, a wool exporter, as against Italy; Italy in return had a favourable balance with Flanders; France long had a favourable balance vis-à-vis Germany, but the advantage shifted to the latter if not immediately after the first blockade decreed by the Reichstag in 1676, at any rate with the arrival of the French Protestants after the Revocation of the Edict of Nantes (1685). France had a positive balance with the Netherlands for much longer, and with Spain her trade was always in surplus. Do not let us create difficulties for the Spanish in our ports, says an official French document in 1700;[245] 'the particular and the general good' are at stake since 'the advantage of trade between Spain and France is all on the French side'. And in the previous century (1635) the French were described crudely but accurately, as the 'lice gnawing away at Spain'.[246]

Here and there the trade balance shifted and was even reversed. We may note, though these examples cannot be regarded as representative, that trade between France and Piedmont favoured the former in 1693; that trade between Sicily and Genoa in 1724 favoured the former; and that in 1808, according to the brief impression of a French traveller, the trade of Persia 'with the Indies is [at present] advantageous'.[247]

Only one trade balance seems to have been stuck in the same position, from the Roman Empire to the nineteenth century: trade with the Levant always left Europe with a negative balance.

France and England before and after 1700

Let us stop for a moment to look at the classic case (though is it really as well-known as people have claimed?) of Anglo-French trade. Over the last quarter of the seventeenth century and the early years of the eighteenth, it was frequently and forcefully claimed that the balance was in France's favour. France was apparently making an annual profit, taking the good years with the bad, of a million and a half pounds sterling out of her trade with England.

That at any rate is what was said in the House of Commons in October 1675, and repeated in letters from Carlo Ottone the Genoese agent in London in September 1676 and January 1678.[248] He even claims to quote figures from a conversation he had with the ambassador of the United Provinces, who cannot be suspected of undue preference for the French. One of the reasons advanced for this surplus in France's favour was the sale of her manufactured goods, 'which are sold in this island much more cheaply than those produced locally, for the French artisan is content with modest earnings'. This is odd, because French manufactured goods were in fact banned by the English government and had to be smuggled in clandestinely. This only made the English the more anxious '*di bilanciare questo commerci*' as our Genoese correspondent succinctly puts it – and to this end to oblige the French to use more English broadcloth.[249]

Against this background, when war was declared, it was seen as a good opportunity to put an end to the detestable and detested invasion of French goods. De Tallard,[250] ambassador extraordinary in London, wrote to Pontchartrain on 18 March 1699:

What the English were buying from France before the last war was declared [that is the War of the Augsburg League 1689-1697] was, according to them, worth far greater sums of money than what was sent from England to us. They are so strong in this belief, and so persuaded that our wealth comes from them, that as soon as the war began, they made it capital [*sic* – for of capital importance?] to prevent any French wine or merchandise from entering their country directly or indirectly.

To understand this text, one has to remember that at the time war did not automatically interrupt commercial relations between the belligerents. So this absolute prohibition in itself ran counter to international custom.

Some years went by. War broke out once more over the Spanish succession (1701). When the hostilities were over, the question arose of restoring commercial links between the two crowns which this time had been seriously disturbed. So in the summer of 1713, two 'experts', Anisson, representative for Lyons to the French Council of Trade, and de Fenellon, the Paris representative, were on their way to London. As the talks took time to get started and then dragged on, Anisson had time to look over the Commons debates and the English customs declarations. What was his amazement to find that everything that had been said about the trade balance between the two countries was quite simply wrong. 'For over fifty years, English exports have been superior to those of France by several millions' [millions of *livres tournois* that is],[251] is his stark and unexpected conclusion. Can we really believe him? Believe, that is that official hypocrisy could so systematically have concealed figures revealing beyond a shadow of doubt that the trade balance favoured Britain? A careful study of the archives in both Paris and London would clearly be valuable – but it is not certain that even this would provide the last word on the subject. Interpreting official figures inevitably brings mistakes. Merchants and officials spent all day telling lies to the government, and governments spent all day deceiving themselves. I know that what was true in 1713 was not necessarily true in 1786 and vice versa. All the same, just after the Eden treaty (signed between France and England in 1786), a Russian correspondent in London (10 April 1787) who does no more than reproduce common report, indicates that the figures 'give only a very imperfect idea of the nature and extent of this trade [Anglo-French] since it is known from certain sources that legitimate commerce between the two kingdoms forms at most a third of the whole, and two-thirds is effected by contraband, which will be remedied by this commercial treaty, to the advantage of both governments'.[252] If this really was the case, what is the point of discussing the official figures at all? We need to know the balance of contraband as well.

The long-drawn-out trade talks between France and England in 1713 shed no light on this point. But the echo they aroused in British public opinion is nonetheless revealing about the nationalist passions that underlay mercantilism. When on 18 June 1713, the project was rejected by the House of Commons by 194 votes to 185, the explosion of popular rejoicing was much more spontaneous than on the occasion of the announcement of peace. There were fireworks, illuminations and many festivities in London. In Coventry, the weavers held a long procession headed by a fleece and a quart-bottle, mounted on poles, with the inscription 'No English wool for French wine'. All this, running quite

The Lord Mayor's Show in London, by Canaletto, about 1750. The traditional water-procession covered the Thames with boats. Alongside those of the merchant companies of the City were a number of small craft (perhaps the same that a French visitor to London in 1728 called 'gondolas', cf. Chapter I, note 84, because they were used as water-taxis much as in Venice). (Prague, National Gallery. Photo Giraudon.)

contrary to economic arguments, was inspired by national sentiment and poor reasoning,[253] since it would obviously have been in the interests of both nations to open their doors to the other. Forty years later, David Hume noted with some irony that 'there are few Englishmen who would not think their country absolutely ruined, were French wines sold in England so cheap and in such abundance as to supplant in some measure all ale and home brewed liquors'. And yet, 'we transferred the commerce of wine to Spain and Portugal, where we buy worse liquor at a higher price'.

England and Portugal[254]

When eighteenth-century Portugal is mentioned, most historians will rightly respond with the name of John Methuen, the man who in 1702, just before what turned out to be the lengthy War of the Spanish Succession, sought out an alliance with little Portugal the better to encircle Spain which was loyal to the Duke of Anjou, Philip V, and the French. The alliance made much stir, but nobody thought fit to remark upon the trade agreement which accompanied it as a mere routine clause. After all, similar treaties had been signed between London and Lisbon in 1642, 1654 and 1661. And the French, Dutch and Swedish, at different dates and in different conditions had obtained the same advantages. The history of Anglo-Portuguese relations does not therefore begin with this celebrated treaty. It was the outcome of certain economic processes which eventually closed on Portugal like a trap.

As the eighteenth century opened, Portugal had practically abandoned the Indian Ocean. Now and again she would send out a boatload of convicts, Goa being to Portugal what Cayenne was to France or Australia to England. The old association only had any commercial interest for Portugal when the great powers were at war. Then two or three Portuguese vessels, chartered by other nations it is true, would sail round the Cape of Good Hope. On the return journey, the foreigners who had engaged in this dangerous game often burned their fingers. The Portuguese were too experienced to be anything but prudent.

They lavished daily attention on the other hand on the huge territory of Brazil, the growth of which was vigilantly watched and exploited. The masters of Brazil were the merchants of Portugal, in the first place the king, then the businessmen of Lisbon and Oporto and their trading colonies established in Recife, Parahyba, Bahia (the old Brazilian capital) and Rio de Janeiro (which became the new capital in 1763). The Brazilians dreamed of getting the better of these detested Portuguese merchants – who wore heavy rings on their fingers and dined off silver platters – but rarely managed it. Every time Brazil launched a new product – sugar, then gold, diamonds, later coffee – it was always the merchant aristocracy of Portugal who reaped the benefit and lived in even greater ease than before. Up the Tagus floated untold wealth: hides, sugar, cassonade, whale-oil, brazil-wood, cotton, tobacco, gold dust, caskets full of diamonds. The king of Portugal was said to be the richest sovereign in Europe: his castles and palaces yielded in nothing to Versailles – except perhaps in simplicity. The huge city of Lisbon expanded like a parasitic plant: shanty towns grew up where once there had been fields on the city outskirts. The rich became excessively rich, and the poor wretched. Yet the high wages there attracted to Portugal 'a prodigious number of men from the province of Galicia [in Spain] whom we call here *galegos*, who work in the capital and the principal cities of Portugal as porters, labourers and servants, as the Savoyards do in Paris and other cities in France'.[255] As the century drew to a close, under slightly worsening conditions, the atmosphere deteriorated: attacks on people and houses after dark, murders and thefts committed even by honourable townsmen, became daily occurrences. Lisbon and Portugal accepted quite casually the economic climate from the Atlantic: when it was fair, everyone took advantage; when it was bad, things slowly fell apart.

Into the lazy prosperity of this little country, came the English and pressed home their advantage. They shaped Portugal to suit their own ends, developing the vineyards in the north, creating the fortunes of port wines; becoming sole providers of Lisbon's grain and codfish supplies; introducing enough bales of English cloth to clothe every peasant in Portugal and to flood the distant market in Brazil. It was all paid for in gold and diamonds, Brazilian gold which after landing in Lisbon made its way north. Things might have been different; Portugal might have protected her own market and built up her own industry: that was what Pombal later thought. But the English solution was the easy one. Even the terms of trade favoured Portugal: while the price of English cloth fell, that of Portuguese export goods rose. So the English gradually consolidated their hold on the market. The Brazil trade, the key to Portugal's fortunes, demanded capital which then became immobilized in a long circuit. The English played in Lisbon the same role as the Dutch had earlier in Seville: they provided goods for sending to Brazil, and they provided them *on credit*. The absence of a commercial centre in France of the dimensions of London or Amsterdam 'may well have been the most serious factor handicapping French merchants'[256] who nevertheless also formed quite a large colony in Lisbon. But it is not easy to understand why the Dutch were so reticent on this market.

In any case, English control was a *fait accompli* by the time the eighteenth century really got into its stride. In 1730 even, a Frenchman could write:[256] 'The trade carried on by the English in Lisbon is the most considerable of all; many people think it is as much as all the other Nations put together.' This triumph can be attributed to British tenacity as much as to Portuguese indolence. In 1759, Malouet[257] a future member of the French Constituent Assembly of 1789, travelled through Portugal, in his eyes 'an English colony'. 'All the gold of Brazil went to England', he explained, 'which kept Portugal under a yoke. I will quote only one example to condemn the Marquis de Pombal's administration: port wines, the only really important export of the country, were bought up wholesale by an English company, to which every vineyard-owner was obliged to sell at prices fixed by English commissioners.' I think Malouet was right. When a foreign power has access to the first-hand market, at the point of production, that is indeed commercial colonization.

In 1770–1772 however, when the great age of Brazilian gold seemed to be over – although ships were still arriving carrying gold and diamonds – and when the general economic situation in Europe was taking a downward turn, the Anglo-Portuguese trade balance began to shift a little. Was it about to be reversed? Not immediately. In 1772, if only to further attempts to open up trade

Lisbon in the sixteenth century. (Photo Giraudon.)

with Morocco, Lisbon tried to loosen the English grip, 'to stop as far as possible the export of gold to London',[258] without much success. But ten years later, a possible solution appeared. The Portuguese government decided to 'mint many coins in silver and very few in gold', much to the irritation of the English, who 'find no advantage in [repatriating] silver but plenty in gold. This is a little war which Portugal is slyly waging against them,' concluded the Russian consul in Lisbon.[259] But another ten years were to pass, according to the same consul (one Borchers, a German in the service of Catherine II) before he witnessed the amazing sight of an English vessel putting in at Lisbon without loading any gold! 'The frigate *Pegasus*', he wrote in December 1791[260] 'is perhaps the first ship, since trade relations have existed between the two countries, to have returned home without taking any gold.' In fact, the current had been reversed. 'Every packet or warship coming from England' took back to Lisbon, 'some of the Portuguese specie ... which had been imported [to England] over the previous century' (estimated by historians at no less than 25 million pounds sterling between 1700 and 1760).[261] A single packet in the same month of December 1790 had just unloaded £18,000 sterling.[262] The whole problem of Anglo-Portuguese relations has yet to be fully discussed, or rather replaced within a general context which was soon to become tragic with the outbreak of war between England and revolutionary France; and that is another story.

East Europe, West Europe[263]

So far we have looked at fairly clear examples. There are more difficult cases. Western Europe taken as whole had an unfavourable balance with the Baltic, that northern Mediterranean uniting hostile nations with similar economies: Sweden, Muscovy, Poland, Germany beyond the Elbe, and Denmark. And this balance raises several tricky questions.

This is because it appears from S. A. Nilsson's sensational article – written in 1944 but only recently brought to the knowledge of most western historians – and also from other research (notably Arthur Attmann's book which was translated into English in 1973) that the money the West owed for eastern goods was only partly covered by direct dispatches of specie.[264] In other words, the quantities of silver that ended up in the cities of the Baltic and the volume of which can be estimated by historians (in the Narva for instance) are less than the quantity required to balance the western deficits. Not enough silver was sent, and it is hard to see what else in the circumstances could have balanced the books. Historians are still looking for the elusive explanation.

The only possible course is to follow S. A. Nilsson and to situate the Nordic balance within the whole complex of trade and exchange in the eastern part of Europe. He thought that part of the surplus of the Baltic trade must have reached Europe by series of linked exchanges between eastern, central and western Europe, but in this case overland through Poland and Germany. While the western balance was in deficit with the northern ports, it may have been partially compensated by a favourable balance in overland traffic – the payments being effected, as the Swedish historian's seductive hypothesis suggests, by way of the Leipzig fairs. Miroslaw Hroch[265] has argued however that these fairs were not frequented with any assiduity by eastern European merchants (notably the growing numbers of Polish-Jewish merchants) until the early eighteenth century. Therefore to claim that the balance was settled at Leipzig is to mistake the period. According to M. Hroch, the most that could be claimed is that some trade went via Poznan and Wroclaw, where there seems to have been an unfavourable balance for the east – but these were no more than trickles.

But Nilsson's hypothesis may not be incorrect; perhaps it simply needs broadening a little. We know for instance[266] that Hungary, a silver-producing country was constantly seeing her better currency, heavy silver coin, disappear abroad – that is in part to the West. And the gap was filled by small Polish coins of silver alloy, which accounted for virtually all the money in circulation inside Hungary.

What is more, alongside the flow of merchandise there were bills of exchange. We know that they existed in eastern Europe by the sixteenth century and

Jewish merchants in Warsaw in the second half of the eighteenth century. Detail of a painting by Canaletto, *Wiodowa Street*. (Photo Alexandra Skarzynska.)

became more numerous in the seventeenth. In that case, the presence or absence, or poor attendance of eastern European merchants at the Leipzig fairs is hardly a compelling argument. We might note in passing that, contrary to M. Hroch's view, Polish Jews were in fact quite numerous at the Leipzig fairs in the seventeenth century.[267] But even without attending the fairs in person, Marc'aurelio Federico,[268] an Italian mercer settled in Cracow, was in 1683–1685 drawing bills of exchange on friends of his in Leipzig. And the bill of exchange, when it travelled straight from the Baltic to Amsterdam or vice versa, was usually the consequence of a loan, an advance on goods. Could it not be said that these advance payments, which carried interest charges, were a levy on the surplus in precious metals which the East had acquired or was about to acquire? The reader is referred to what I shall later have to say about Holland and the 'acceptance' trade.[269] And he or she should also bear in mind that the Baltic was a region dominated and exploited by western Europe. There was a close correlation between the prices in Amsterdam and in Danzig, but it was Amsterdam that fixed the prices, called the tune and chose its own terms.

To conclude then, the classic Baltic trade can no longer be considered as a self-contained circuit. There were several partners in a trade which was responsible for movements of merchandise, money and credit. The paths of credit were constantly proliferating. To understand them properly would require journeys to Leipzig, Wroclaw, Poznan – and also to Nuremberg, Frankfurt and even, if I am not mistaken, to Istanbul and Venice. Did the Baltic as an economic unit have feelers stretching to the Black Sea or the Adriatic?[270] There was at any rate a correlation between the Baltic traffic and the economy of eastern Europe. The score was written for two, three or four parts. After 1581 when the Russians lost Narva[271] the Baltic seaboard lost trade to the overland routes by which Muscovy goods were then dispatched. With the outbreak of the Thirty Years' War, the roads through deepest central Europe were cut – and the Baltic traffic increased once more.

Overall balances

Let us move on now from these bilateral links – England–France, Portugal–England, Russia–England, East Europe–West Europe. It is more important to consider economic units in the whole context of their external relations – as the representatives of the 'West' (i.e. the Atlantic ports) were already arguing in 1701 in the French Council of Trade, against the representatives from Lyons. 'Their principle in relation to the trade balance', was not to 'calculate a particular balance, nation to nation, but a general balance as between the trade of France and all other states' – which in their view must have a bearing on trade policy.[272]

To tell the truth, whenever we have the data on overall balances, they tend to confirm previous expectations. They indicate how modest the volume of external trade was in relation to overall national income – even if, against all the rules, external trade is defined as the *seum* of imports and exports, whereas these two headings should really be set against each other. But if only the balance itself is considered, positive or negative, it is a small fraction of national income and hardly seems capable of affecting it one way or the other. This is how I would interpret the remark made by Nicholas Barbon (1690), one of the many authors of the pamphlets by which the science of economics was born in England, when he writes, 'the Stock of a Nation [is] Infinite and can never be consumed'.[273]

But the problem is more interesting and more complicated than it might at first appear. I will not dwell on the clear-cut cases of the overall trade balances of France and England in the eighteenth century (see the graphs in Figure 16). I prefer to look at the case of France in mid-sixteenth century, not because the data for that period is superior, nor even because the overall figures provide a rough outline of the hesitant emergence of a national market, but simply because the observable pattern applicable to both England and France in the eighteenth century is already visible two hundred years before the statistics of the Age of Enlightenment.

Henri II's France probably had a positive balance with all its neighbours –

except one. Portugal, Spain, England, the Netherlands and Germany all bought more from France than they sold to her. Thanks to these exports, France picked up gold and silver coins in exchange for her grain, wines, fabrics and woollen cloth not to mention the money sent back by the stream of emigrants to Spain. But these advantages were countered by a perennial deficit with Italy: most of the money flowed out through Lyons, which was both a financial centre and a site of fairs. Aristocratic France was too fond of costly silks and velvets, pepper and other spices, and marble; she called rather too often on the services – never unpaid – of Italian artists, and of the businessmen from beyond the Alps who controlled the wholesale trade and the traffic in bills of exchange. The Lyons fairs were a very effective vacuum pump operated by Italian capitalism, as the Geneva fairs had been in the previous century and as the ancient Champagne fairs had largely been too in all probability. The entire benefits of the favourable trade balances were thus added together and handed over, to all intents and purposes, to the profitable speculations of the Italians. In 1494, when Charles VIII was preparing to cross the Alps, he had to obtain the complicity or the blessing of the Italian businessmen established in France, who had ties with the merchant dynasties of their homeland.[274] The latter, being warned in good time, hastened to Court and acquiesced without too much difficulty, but 'obtained in return the restoration of the four annual fairs of Lyons' – proof in itself that the fairs served them well, and proof too that Lyons, a link in a foreign-controlled superstructure, was already a capital apart, an ambiguous centre of French wealth.

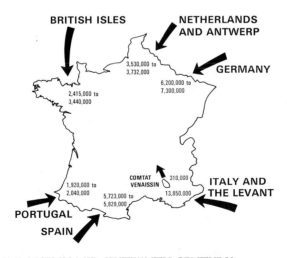

BRITISH ISLES

NETHERLANDS AND ANTWERP

3,530,000 to 3,732,000

GERMANY

6,200,000 to 7,300,000

2,415,000 to 3,440,000

COMTAT VENAISSIN 310,000

ITALY AND THE LEVANT

13,850,000

1,920,000 to 2,040,000

5,723,000 to 5,829,000

PORTUGAL

SPAIN

17   FRENCH IMPORTS IN MID-SIXTEENTH CENTURY

From manuscripts 2085 and 2086 in the Bibliothèque Nationale, Paris. ('Le commerce d'importation en France au milieu du XVIe siècle' by Albert Chamberland, in *Revue de géographie*, 1892–1893.)

An exceptional document, unfortunately incomplete, has come down to us: it gives details of French imports in about 1556,[275] but the accompanying 'book', detailing the exports, has disappeared. The graph in Figure 17 summarizes the figures we have. The total is somewhere between 35 and 36 million *livres tournois*; and as the economically active France of the period certainly had a trade surplus, exports must have been several points higher than the 36 million figure. Exports and imports together must have totalled 75 million *livres*, an enormous sum. Even if they balance out in the end, these twin currents, running alongside each other, crossing from side to side, creating backflows or whirlpools, represent thousands of transactions and exchanges replenished from never-failing sources. But even the busy picture this conjures up does not, I must repeat, represent the whole of France's economic activity – what would today be called her *national income* and which of course cannot be calculated, only imagined.

Using calculations which the reader will encounter more than once in this work, I have estimated the per capita income of the Venetians in about 1600 at 37 ducats; that of the Signoria's subjects in the mainland territory dependent on Venice at about 10. These are tentative figures of course and probably underestimate income in the city of Venice itself. But they do at least register the huge gap between incomes in a dominant city and those in the territory dependent on it. That said, if I allow per capita French income in 1556 to be somewhere in the region of that of the Venetian mainland (10 ducats, that is 23 or 24 *livres tournois*), the total income of the twenty million Frenchmen would be 460 million *livres* – a huge sum, but not one that could be mobilized since we are setting a money value on production which was *to a large extent not commercialized*. I could equally have begun with the receipts of the royal exchequer in order to calculate national income. These amounted to some 15 or 16 million *livres*.[276] If we take this to be one twentieth of national income, the total would be between 300 and 320 million *livres*. This is lower than our first estimate, but well above the volume of external trade, and brings us once more up against the much-discussed problem of the respective weight of national production (mostly agricultural) which was enormous and the comparatively small figure for foreign trade – which is not necessarily less important economically, as far as I am concerned.

In any case, every time we have to deal with a *comparatively* advanced economy, its trade balance is in surplus as a general rule. This was undoubtedly the case with the leading cities of the past – Genoa and Venice; and it was also true of Gdansk (Danzig) from the fifteenth century.[277] Looking at the English and French trade balances in the eighteenth century one sees that they were in surplus for virtually the entire century. And we should not be surprised to find that in 1764, when the Swedish economist Anders Chydenius[278] estimated Swedish foreign trade, this too was in surplus: Sweden which saw tremendous expansion of her fleet at this time, exported 72 million *dalers*' worth of goods and imported 66 million (the *daler* was a copper currency). So the 'nation' made a profit of over 5 million *dalers*.

Not everyone was successful at this game of course. 'No one can win without someone else losing', was Montchrestien's commonsense observation. Someone else did indeed lose: the colonies which were bled white; and the dependent territories.

Even 'developed' and apparently invulnerable states might find themselves in trouble. I imagine this was the case when Spain in the seventeenth century was exposed, by her governments and by the force of circumstances, to the devastating inflation of copper. And it was France's fate during the Revolution too; as a Russian agent in Italy said, 'she is fighting this war with her capital, while her enemies are using only their income'.[279] These examples would repay closer study, for by maintaining her political importance at the price of the copper inflation and of the deficit caused by her foreign payments in silver, Spain was destroying herself from within. And the external collapse of revolutionary France, even before the dramatic events of 1792–1793, weighed very heavy upon her destiny. The French exchange rate tumbled in London[280] between 1789 and spring 1791, and this movement was accompanied by a large-scale flight of capital. In both cases, it looks as though a catastrophic deficit in the balance of trade and the balance of payments led to the destruction, or at least decline of the economy from within.

India and China

Even when the situation was not so dramatic, if deficit became a permanent feature it spelled certain structural deterioration of the economy sooner or later. And this was precisely what happened in India after 1760 and in China after about 1820–1840.

The successive waves of Europeans arriving in the Far East had not brought immediate disorganization. They did not at once endanger the structures of Asian trade. For long ages – centuries before the Europeans sailed round the Cape of Good Hope – there had been an immense network of trade covering the Indian Ocean and the seas bordering the Pacific. Neither the occupation of Malacca, (captured by force in 1511) nor the settling of the Portuguese in Goa, nor the establishment of European merchants in Macao, upset the ancient equilibrium. The early depredations of the new arrivals enabled them to seize cargoes without paying for them, but the general rules of trading were quickly restored, like fine weather after a storm.

The long-standing rule had been that spices and other Asian goods had to be paid for in silver; sometimes, though less often, with copper, which was widely used for coin in India and China. The European presence changed nothing in this respect. The Portuguese, Dutch, English and French traders all borrowed from Muslims, from Banyans or from the moneylenders of Kyoto, the silver

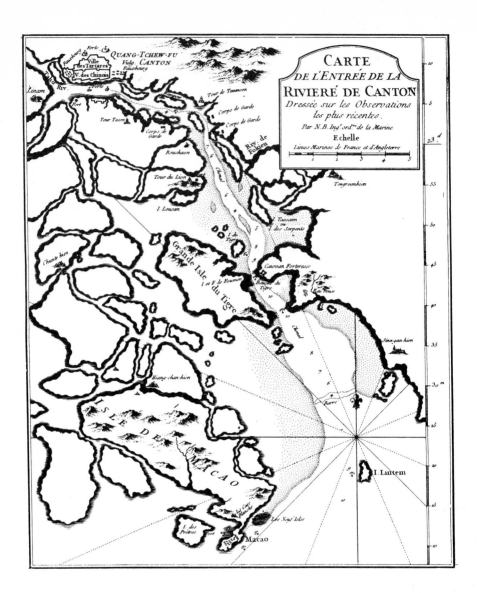

The Canton delta (10,000 km²). Three rivers, flowing from the east, the north and the west (the Si Kiang) mingle their water, mud and sand in this huge bay dotted with mountainous islands. The whole area was produced, like the *rias* in Brittany, by sea-flooding long ago. There was a channel (depth marked here in fathoms: 1 fathom = 1m 949, and distance marked here in leagues: 1 league = 5 km 4 or 3 English sea-miles) which allowed the large ships of the time to sail right up to Canton (3 metres draught). But there were the river shallows, sandbanks and tides to watch out for. Canton, on the River of Pearls, was really two cities: the Tartar and the Chinese. Macao, held by the Portuguese, was perched on the end of a large island (16 km²). It would only have taken a little pressure to drive them into the sea.

without which no transaction was possible from Nagasaki to Surat. It was to resolve this insoluble problem that first the Portuguese, then the great India companies sent silver coin out from Europe, but the price of spices went up at the point of production. The Europeans, whether the Portuguese in Macao or the Dutch, tried to get a foothold in the Chinese market, and were forced to look on helplessly at the piles of goods out of their reach. 'Until now', writes a Dutch trader in 1632, 'we have not failed to find goods . . . but we have failed to produce the money to pay for them.'[281] The solution eventually adopted by Europeans was to embark upon local trading, to devote themselves entirely to the coasting trade known as trade 'from Indie to Indie' [i.e. entirely within the Far East]. The Portuguese made substantial profits from it when they reached China and Japan. Following in their footsteps with more success than anyone else, the Dutch too adapted themselves to this system.

None of this would have been possible without an enormous effort of colonization. Already the Portuguese had too few men and maintained their fortress with some difficulty. For the 'Indies to Indies' trade, they had to build ships on the spot and recruit crews too – the lascars from Goa, 'who are in the habit of bringing their wives with them'. The Dutch also had to establish settlements in Java where they founded Batavia in 1619, and even on Formosa, where they did not manage to stay. They had to adapt to conquer – but conquer is too strong a word. Very often, they were not even able to trade on equal terms. One has only to look at the modest way the English lived on their island of Bombay, a gift from Portugal to Charles II's wife, the Portuguese princess Catherine of Braganza (1662); or the equally modest style of their behaviour in the few villages around Madras which they were conceded in 1640,[282] or in the first lowly establishments in Bengal (1686).[283] When one of the directors of the East India Company presented himself before the Great Mogul, how did he introduce himself: 'The most humble dust, John Russell, Director of the said company' did not hesitate to 'prostrate himself upon the ground'.[284] Or consider the defeat of the combined English and Portuguese forces in 1722 against Kanoji Angria,[284] or the pitiful rout of the Dutch in 1739 when they tried to land in the kingdom of Travancore.[284] 'It would have been impossible in 1750', the Indian historian K. M. Panikaar rightly points out, 'to predict that in another fifty years, one European power, England, would have conquered a third of India and would be preparing to snatch from the Mahrattas hegemony over the rest of the country.'[284]

And yet, after about 1730, the trading balance of India had begun to shift. European shipping had increased the number of its voyages, and the size of its cargoes of goods and of silver. An energetic intruder, it stimulated and developed its own trading networks and hastened the end of the mighty structure of the Great Mogul's Empire which was no more than a shadow after the death of Aurangzeb (1707). It had placed active agents in the courts of the Indian princes. This momentous shift dated from before mid-century[285] although it was little remarked in the years when the centre of the stage was occupied by the noisy confrontations between the French and English India Companies, in the age of Dupleix, Bussy, Godeheu, Lally-Tollendal and Clive.

In fact the Indian economy was slowly rotting away. The battle of Plassey (23 June 1757) hastened its collapse. William Bolts, the adventurer who was Clive's enemy and his victim, was to remark that the English company did not have much trouble taking Bengal; it took advantage of certain favourable circumstances and the artillery did the rest.[286] A dismissive and not very convincing judgment, since the company did not merely take Bengal, it stayed there, not without consequences. How can one estimate the importance of the free 'primitive accumulation' that the plundering of Bengal meant to the English (£38 million sterling transferred to London between 1757 and 1780, it has been said).[287] The first new rich, the 'nabobs' (who had not yet received this name) repatriated their fortunes in silver, gold, precious stones and diamonds. 'We are assured', said a gazette on 13 March 1763, 'that the value of the gold, silver and precious stones which have been brought back from the East Indies to England, independently of merchandise, since the year 1759, amounts to £600,000.'[288]

This may be a figure tossed in the air, but it bears witness to a trade balance by now heavily in England's favour, in the first place, and perhaps even in favour of Europe as a whole: even the profits of the French India Company between 1722 and 1754[289] show that the times had become easier. But England more than any other stood to gain from these advantages. No observer could fail to see 'the immense fortunes that various private individuals and all the envoys of the India Company are making in this country. These Asiatic sponges *per fas et nefas*' explained Isaac de Pinto, 'periodically bring home part of the treasures of the Indies'. In March 1764, news of disturbances in Bengal reached Amsterdam. They were commented on unsympathetically, as being the natural response, it was said, to a series of misappropriations leading to the amassing of fabulous fortunes. The wealth of the governor of Bengal was quite simply 'monstrous'. His friends, who were not presumably inclined to exaggerate it, thought it at least £1,200,000.[290] And to what lengths did the younger sons of English families not go, when they were sent off to India for the company, and corrupted unintentionally and even unconsciously, as they were taken in hand by their colleagues or even more likely by the Banyans as soon as they arrived. Unlike the Dutch company, the English company allowed its employees to trade on their own account, on condition it was within the Indies. This was opening the door to all kinds of malpractice – as long as it was only at the expense of the natives. So one is sympathetic to Sir George Saville who in April 1777 spoke out against the India company and its Asian possessions, against the tea trade and the 'public thefts to which he did not wish in any way to be a party'.[291] But when do the just ever prevail? Las Casas had after all failed to save the American Indians and in his way he had contributed to the setting up of the black slave trade.

From now on, India was enmeshed in the relentless destiny which would demote her from the proud ranks of the great producing and trading countries to the status of a colony, buying English products – even textiles! – and providing raw materials; and this for almost two hundred years.

This cautionary tale foreshadowed the future fate of China, which was slower to take shape since China was further away from Europe, more self-contained and better-protected. The 'China trade' was however beginning to bite deeply into the country by the eighteenth century. The soaring demand from Europe was forever increasing the areas given over to tea-planting, often at the expense of cotton fields. Cotton would soon be in short supply: in the nineteenth century it had to be brought in from India, which provided an opportunity for the latter (that is for the English in fact) to readjust the balance with China. The last straw (so to speak) after the 1780s, was the arrival of Indian opium.[292] China was now literally being paid in smoke (and what smoke!). In about 1820, the trade balance swung the other way, just at the moment (1812–1817) when the world economy was also entering upon a decline which would last until mid-nineteenth century. The so-called opium war (1839–1842) set the seal on this development and opened the disastrous era of 'unequal treaties' which was to last a good hundred years.

China's fate in the nineteenth century, then, echoes that of India in the eighteenth. Here too internal weaknesses played a part. The Manchu dynasty was confronted by various conflicts which were partly responsible for China's vulnerable position just as the slow dismembering of the Mogul Empire was for India's. In both cases, an external shock was magnified by weakness and disorder within. But was the opposite not also true? If these internal troubles had developed without external pressure from Europe, they would surely have followed a different pattern. The economic consequences would have been different. Without wishing to venture too far into the area of moral responsibility it is clear that Europe upset for its own ends the systems of exchange and the ancient balances obtaining in the Far East.

Locating the market

By way of conclusion to these two chapters, is it possible to 'locate' the market in its proper place? This is not as easy as it might look, because the word 'market' is itself equivocal. On one hand it is used, in a very loose sense, of all types of exchange that go beyond self-sufficiency, of all the wheels of trade, large and small, that we have described, of all the categories relating to trading areas (urban market, national market) or to a given product (the market in sugar, precious metals, spices etc.). In this sense the word is the equivalent of exchange, circulation, distribution. On the other hand, the word 'market' is often applied to a rather large broad form of exchange, also known as the *market economy*, that is, to a system.

The difficulty is first, that the market complex can only be understood when it is replaced within the context of an economic life and no less a *social* life that changes over the years; and secondly that this complex is itself constantly evolving and changing; it never has the same meaning or significance from one minute to the next.

To try to grasp this notion in its concrete reality, I intend to approach it in three ways: through the simplifying theories of economists; through the evidence of history in the broad sense, that is over the long term; and through the tangled but possibly helpful lessons of the present-day world.

The self-regulating market

Economists have laid great importance on the market. Adam Smith considered the market as the regulator of the division of labour. Its volume determines the level that will be attained by this division, which is the process that accelerates production. More than this, the market represents the 'hidden hand', bringing together supply and demand, seeing that they automatically match each other by means of the price mechanism. Oskar Lange put it even more strikingly: the market was the first computer mankind ever had, a self-regulating machine which would itself ensure the equilibrium of economic activities. D'Avenel[293] expressed himself in the language of his times, that of self-satisfied liberalism: 'Even if nothing else were free in a state, the price of things would be, and it would never let itself be subjugated by anyone. The price of silver, of land, of labour, of all foodstuffs and merchandise has never been other than free: no legal constraint, no private agreement has ever succeeded in enslaving them.'

Such views implicitly accept that the market, which is controlled by no one, is the motor mechanism of the entire economy. The growth of Europe and even of the world in this view represented that of a market economy constantly enlarging its domain, and drawing into its rational order more and more people, more and more kinds of traffic, local or distant, the combination of which turned the world into an economic unit. Exchange invariably stimulated both supply and demand, guiding production, leading to the specialization of huge economic regions which therefore became committed to exchange, as a necessity to ensure their own survival. Examples? Wine-growing in Aquitaine, tea in China, cereals in Poland or Sicily or the Ukraine, the successive economic adaptations of colonial Brazil (dye-woods, sugar, gold, coffee). In short, exchange binds economies together. It is both an enclosing circle and a turning hinge. The price is the matchmaker between buyer and seller. If the price goes up or down on the London Stock Exchange, it may transform the bears into bulls or vice versa (bears in Stock Exchange slang bid down, bulls bid up).

On the margins and even in the heartlands of active economies, there may still be pockets, large and small, virtually untouched by the movement of the market. Only a few signs, (money, the arrival of some rare foreign produce) show that these little worlds are not entirely cut off. Such pockets of inertia and immobility were still to be found in the England of the Georges or in the hyperactive France of Louis XVI. But economic growth meant precisely the reduction of such isolated zones, as they were progressively called upon to share in overall production and consumption – as the industrial revolution finally generalized the market mechanism.

The self-regulating market – all-conquering and rationalizing the entire economy – is in this view essentially what is meant by the history of growth. Carl Brinkmann[294] once wrote that economic history was the study of the origins, the development and the latter-day decomposition of the market economy. Such a simplification accords with the teachings of generations of economists. But it cannot satisfy the historian, who does not view the market as a simply endogenous phenomenon. Nor is it merely the sum of various economic activities, nor even a precise stage in their development.

The market through the ages

Since exchange is as old as human history, a *historical* study of the market should extend to cover all the known ages through which man has lived, and should seek assistance from the other social sciences: it should consider the possible explanations they offer, without which it would be impossible to grasp long-term developments and structures, and the combinations that created new life. But if we accept such an enlargement of the field, we are precipitated into a huge venture without beginning or end. All markets can tell us something: the first that spring to mind are those archaic scenes of exchange still visible here and there, which are shadows of ancient realities, like species which still survive from the antediluvian world. I must own to a weakness for the markets of present-day Kabylia, which spring up regularly in some empty spot below the villages perched up on the hills around;[295] or for the brightly-coloured markets of Dahomey, which are also held outside the villages;[296] or the elementary markets on the delta of the Red River, which Pierre Courou has minutely observed.[297] There are so many others too – in the quite recent past in the hinterland of Bahia there were markets attended by shepherds from the interior with their semi-wild flocks;[298] Even more archaic were the ceremonial exchanges in the Trobriand Islands, south-east of New Guinea, watched by Malinowski.[299] In such markets, the ancient past and the present join hands: history and pre-history, field-studies in anthropology, retrospective sociology, and the economy of long ago.

Karl Polanyi,[300] his pupils and his disciples have responded to the challenge provided by this mass of different evidence. They have gone through it as best they could, seeking to suggest an explanation, almost a theory: the economy is

Traditional market in Dahomey today – in the country outside the villages. (Photo A.A.A., Picou.)

only a 'sub-division'[301] of *social life*, one which is enveloped in the networks and constraints of social reality and has only disentangled itself recently (sometimes not even then) from these multiple threads. If we are to believe Polanyi, it was not really until capitalism burst fully on the world in the nineteenth century that the 'great transformation' took place, that the 'self-regulating' market achieved its true dimensions and subjugated the social factors hitherto dominant. Before this change, only controlled or false markets, or non-markets, could be said to exist.

As examples of exchange which do not conform to 'economic' behaviour, Polanyi cites ceremonial exchange governed by the principle of *reciprocity*; or the *redistribution* of goods by a primitive state which confiscates all production; or the '*ports of trade*', neutral exchange points where the merchant did not dictate terms and of which the best examples are the havens of Phœnicean colonization along the coasts of the Mediterranean where trade was carried on within a determined area. In short, a distinction must be made between trade (commerce, exchange) and the market (the self-regulating price mechanism) the appearance of which in the last century constituted a social upheaval of the first magnitude.

The trouble with this theory is that it is entirely based on a distinction based (if it can be said to be based at all) on a number of heterogeneous samples. There is no law against introducing into a discussion of the 'great transformation' of the nineteenth century such phenomena as the *potlatch* or *kula* (rather than say the very diversified trading organization of the seventeenth and eighteenth centuries). But it is rather like drawing on Levi-Strauss's explanation of kinship ties to elucidate the rules governing marriage in Victorian England. Not the slightest effort has been made to tackle the concrete and diverse reality of history and use that as a starting-point: no mention of Ernest Labrousse or Wilhem Abel, or the classic and very numerous studies of price history. The question of the market in the 'mercantilist' period is dismissed in twenty lines.[302] Sociologists and economists in the past and anthropologists today have unfortunately accustomed us to their almost total indifference to history. It does of course simplify their task.

Moreover, the motion of the 'self-regulating market'[303] proposed in this research – which 'is' this or that, 'is not' the other, 'cannot accommodate' such and such a deformation – seems to be the product of an almost theological taste for definition. This market, in which the only elements are 'demand, the cost of supply and prices, which result from a reciprocal agreement'[304] is a figment of the imagination. It is too easy to call one form of exchange economic and another social. In real life, all types are both economic and social. For centuries on end, there have been a whole variety of socio-economic types of exchange which have coexisted in spite of – or because of – their diversity. Reciprocity and redistribution are economic types of exchange too (D. C. North[305] is quite right on this point) and the market where money changes hands, which appears very early on, is also both a social and an economic reality. Exchange is always a dialogue and the price is always subject to change. It may be influenced by pressures (from the ruler, the city or the capitalist etc.) but it must also obey the dictates of supply, which may be plentiful or scarce, and demand. Price control, which is used as a key argument to deny the appearance of the 'true' self-regulating market before the nineteenth century, has always existed and still exists today. But when we are talking of the pre-industrial world, it would be a mistake to think that the price-lists of the markets suppressed the role of supply and demand. In theory, severe control over the market was meant to protect the consumer, that is competition. One might go so far as to say that it was the 'free' market, such as the 'private marketing' phenomenon in England, that tended to do away with both control and competition.

Historically, one can speak of a market economy, in my view, when prices in the markets of a given area fluctuate in unison, a phenomenon the more characteristic since it may occur over a number of different jurisdictions or sovereignties. In this sense, there was a market economy well before the nineteenth and twentieth centuries – the first in all history, according to Polanyi's colleague W. C. Neale,[306] to experience the self-regulating economy. Prices have fluctuated since ancient times; by the twelfth century they were fluctuating in unison throughout Europe. Later on, this concord became more precise within ever stricter limits. Even the tiny villages of the Faucigny in eighteenth-century Savoy, a high mountain region where communication is difficult, saw prices go up and down, from one week to the next, on all the markets in the area according to harvests and needs, in other words supply and demand.

That said, I would not claim that this market economy, reasonably approximating to fair competition, covered the entire economy, far from it. Nor does it do so today any more than yesterday, although the scale is now different, and quite other reasons are responsible. The incomplete nature of the market economy may have to do with the size of the autarkic sector, with the intervention of the state which may take a proportion of production out of normal circulation; or equally and sometimes even more, simply with the money supply which can artificially intervene in price determination in a thousand ways. The market economy then can be sapped from below or from above, in both backward or very advanced economies.

What is certain is that alongside the 'non-markets' beloved of Polanyi, there always have been exchanges exclusively in return for money, however little. In rather minimal form perhaps, markets nevertheless existed in very ancient times within a single village or group of villages – the market being a sort of itinerant village, as the fair was a sort of travelling town. But the decisive step in this long history was taken when the *town* appropriated these hitherto modest little markets. It absorbed them and inflated them to its own dimensions, in return having to accept the demands they made on it. The important development was surely the launching on to economic circuits of the towns as *heavy units*. The *urban* market may have been invented by the Phœnicians.[307] Certainly the Greek city-states of about the same period all had a market on the *agora*, the central square;[308] they also invented or at any rate propagated money, which clearly furthered the career of the market, if it was not the *sine qua non* of its existence.

The Greek city even had experience of the large-scale urban market, drawing in supplies from a wide radius. Indeed how could it have managed without one? A city, once it reached a certain size was unable to live off the immediate neighbourhood, usually dry, stony and infertile. It became necessary to look further afield, as the Italian city-states were already doing by the twelfth century, and even earlier. Who was to feed Venice, since the city had never had more than a few poor gardens reclaimed from the sands? Later, in order to master the large circuits of long-distance trade, the merchant cities of Italy went beyond the stage of the large market and created a new and effective mechanism, the almost daily meetings of wealthy merchants. Athens and Rome had after all already invented the upper layer of banking, and the formula of the merchant's meeting – an embryo Stock Exchange.

To sum up then, it would be more accurate to think of the market economy as being built up step by step. As Marcel Mauss used to say, 'it was the societies of the Western world that turned man into an economic animal, in very recent times'.[309] Not everyone is yet agreed of course on the exact sense of 'very recent'.

Can the present teach us anything?

Market development did not come to an end in the last century, in the palmy days of the self-regulating market. Over enormous stretches of the planet inhabited by millions of people, socialist economic systems with authoritarian price control have put an end to the market economy. Where it still survives in such countries, it has had to compromise and confine itself to small-scale activities. These experiences provide at any rate one conclusion, not the only possible one, to the curve projected by Carl Brinkmann. Not the only one, because in the view of some economists today, the 'free' world is undergoing a singular transformation. The increased potential of production, the fact that the people of certain large nations – not all of course – have now progressed beyond the stage of scarcity and hardship and do not have serious difficulty in ensuring their everyday subsistence, the mushroom growth of huge, often multinational firms – all these transformations have overturned the old order of the all-powerful market, the power of the customer and the market economy. The laws of the market no longer apply to huge firms which can influence demand by their very effective advertising, and which can fix prices arbitrarily. J. K. Galbraith has described in very clear terms what he calls the 'industrial system'.[310] French economists are more inclined to speak of 'organization'. In an article in *Le Monde* (29 March 1975) François Perroux even refers to 'the organization, a model far more important than the market'. But the market survives all the same. I can walk into a shop, go to an ordinary street market, to test my modest power as customer and consumer. And for the small manufacturer – if one takes say the classic example of the dressmaking trade – operating of necessity in a very competitive world – the laws of the market still apply. In the book referred to, Galbraith talks about 'the two parts of the economy', the world of the 'thousands of small and traditional proprietors', (the market system) and that of the 'few hundred ... highly organized corporations' (the industrial system).[311] Lenin wrote in very similar terms about the coexistence of what he called 'imperialism' (or the new monopoly capitalism of the early twentieth century) and ordinary capitalism, based on competition, which had, he thought, its uses.[312]

I agree with both Galbraith and Lenin on this, with the difference that the distinction of sectors between what I have called the 'economy' (or the market economy) and 'capitalism' does not seem to me to be anything new, but rather a constant in Europe since the Middle Ages. There is another difference too: I would argue that a third sector should be added to the pre-industrial model – that lowest stratum of the non-economy, the soil into which capitalism thrusts its roots but which it can never really penetrate. This lowest layer remains an enormous one. Above it, comes the favoured terrain of the market economy, with its many horizontal communications between the different markets: here a degree of automatic coordination usually links supply, demand and prices. Then alongside, or rather above this layer, comes the zone of the anti-market, where the great predators roam and the law of the jungle operates. This – today as in the past, before and after the industrial revolution – is the real home of capitalism.

3

Production: or Capitalism Away from Home

WHETHER THROUGH CAUTION, or negligence, or because my subject matter did not seem to require it, I have only used the word *capitalism* five or six times so far, and even then I could have avoided it. 'Why didn't you!' may be the reaction of all those who would like to ban this 'fighting word'[1] for good. Ambiguous, hardly scientific, and usually indiscriminately applied,[2] it is – above all – a word that cannot be used of the ages before the industrial period without being accused of anachronism.

Personally, after a long struggle, I gave up trying to get rid of this troublesome intruder. I decided in the end that there was nothing to be gained by throwing out along with the word the controversies it arouses, which have some pertinence to the present-day world. To the historian, understanding the past and understanding the present are the same thing. A passion for history can hardly be expected to stop short at a respectful distance from the present day, pleading that it is unseemly, or even dangerous, to take another step. In any case, such precautions are delusive: if capitalism is thrown out of the door, it comes in through the window. For whether one likes it or not, there was, even in the pre-industrial era, a form of economic activity irresistibly evocative of this word and of no other. While such activity may not yet have been employing the industrial 'mode of production' (which I do not myself consider the be-all and end-all of capitalism) it cannot in any case be confused with classic market transactions. I shall try to define this activity in Chapter 4.

Since the word is so controversial, let us begin with a study in vocabulary, by tracing the historical development of the words *capital, capitalist, capitalism*, three terms that are linked and indeed inseparable. This may help to eliminate some ambiguities from the outset.

Capitalism, having been identified as the realm of investment and of a high rate of capital formation, must next be related to economic life, with which it was not entirely coterminous. There are thus two zones in which it can be located: its native soil so to speak, the sector in which it was completely at home; and another sector which it entered only obliquely, insinuating itself into this zone without ever completely dominating it. Until the industrial revolution of the nineteenth century, when capital moved into industrial production, now newly-promoted to the rank of large profit-maker, it was in the sphere of circulation, trade and marketing that capitalism was most at home; even if it sometimes made more than fleeting incursions on to other territory; and even if it was not concerned with the whole of circulation, since it only controlled, or sought to control, certain channels of trade.

In short, in this chapter we shall be studying the different sectors of production as territories on to which capitalism occasionally ventured – before tackling in the next chapter those preferred areas where it was truly at home.

Capital, capitalist, capitalism

First of all, let us turn to the dictionary. The advice of Henri Berr and Lucien Febvre[3] was that the key words of the vocabulary of history should only be used after asking a number of questions. Where do they come from? How have they come down to us? Are they likely to mislead us? I have tried to heed this warning apropos the words *capital*, *capitalist* and *capitalism* – three words which first appeared in the order given here. A slightly tedious procedure, I admit, but an unavoidable one.

The reader should be warned that this is a complicated area of research to which the following summary can do only minimal justice.[4] Every civilization – Babylon, Greece, Rome and any other which had to grapple with the necessities and disputes of exchange, production and consumption – was obliged to create special vocabularies, the meanings of which were constantly deformed with the passing of time. Our three words are no exception. Even the word *capital*, the oldest of the three, did not take on the meaning we now associate with it (from the writings of Richard Jones, Ricardo, Sismondi, Rodbertus and above all Marx), indeed did not even begin to have this sense, until about 1770, with the work of Turgot, the greatest French economist of the eighteenth century.

The word 'capital'

Capitale (a Late Latin word based on *caput* = head) emerged in the twelfth to thirteenth centuries in the sense of funds, stock of merchandise, sum of money, or money carrying interest. It was not at first defined with any rigour, as the discussions of the time centred primarily on interest and usury (to which scholastics, moralists and jurists eventually opened the door in good conscience, because, they said, of the risk run by the moneylender). Italy, the forerunner of modernity in this respect, was at the centre of such discussions. It was here that the word was first coined, made familiar and to some extent matured. It appears incontestably in 1211 and is found from 1283 in the sense of the capital assets of a trading firm. In the fourteenth century, it is to be found practically everywhere:

in Giovanni Villani, in Boccaccio, in Donato Velluti. On 20 February 1399, Francesco di Marco Datini wrote from Prato to one of his correspondents: 'Of course, if you buy velvet or woollen cloth, I want you to take out an insurance on the capital (*il chapitale*) and on the profit [to be made]; after that, do as you please.'[5] The word, and the reality it stood for appear in the sermons of St Bernardino of Siena (1380-1444) '... *quamdam seminalem rationem lucrosi quam communiter capitale vocamus*', 'that prolific cause of wealth we commonly call capital'.[6]

The word gradually came to mean the *money* capital of a firm or of a merchant, something which was in Italy often called *il corpo*, in Lyons, even in the sixteenth century, *le corps*.[7] But the image of head finally overcame that of body, after a long period of uncertain usage throughout Europe. Perhaps the word came from Italy and spread through Germany and the Netherlands. It eventually reached France where it came up against other derivatives of *caput*: *chatel, cheptel, cabal*,[8] the last of which appears in Rabelais.[9]

The word *capital* certainly figures in the *Thrésor de la langue françoise* (1606) by Jean Nicot. But we should not conclude that its meaning was settled from now on. In both English and French, it was surrounded by a cluster of rivals – wealth, money, funds, goods, principal, assets, property, patrimony – which were frequently used where we would expect to find it.

The word *fonds*, funds, led the field for a long time: a ship from Marseilles puts in to Genoa to pick up its '*fonds*' in piastres to sail to the Levant[10] (1713); a merchant wanting to wind up an affair has only to 'bring home his '*fonds*'. (1726).[11] On the other hand, when Véron de Forbonnais writes in 1757 'Only those funds (*fonds*) which have the present advantage of bringing in income seem to merit the name of *richesses*',[12] where the word *richesses* (literally riches) is used instead of capital (as the rest of the text makes clear), it seems incongruous to twentieth century readers. Other expressions are surprising too: a document concerning England (1696)[13] estimates that 'this nation still has the intrinsic value of six hundred million [*livres tournois*: roughly the figure advanced by Gregory King] in land and *fonds* of all kinds'. Turgot, in 1757, where we would automatically use the terms 'variable' or 'circulating' *capital*, talks of 'advances (*avances*) circulating in enterprises of all kinds'.[14] The word '*avances*' tends to mean investment in his vocabulary: he is in fact using the modern concept of Savary's *Dictionnaire* apropos of merchant companies, the mention of 'capital funds' (*fonds capitaux*).[15] The word has now become an adjective. Savary did not of course invent the term. Some forty years earlier, 'the capital funds of the [French India] Company amount to 143 million *livres*', reported a paper from the *Conseil supérieur de Commerce* (the Board of Trade).[16] But at almost the same date, (1722) a letter from Van Robais the elder,[17] the Abbeville manufacturer, complains after the shipwreck of his vessel, the *Charles de Lorraine*, that the damages amount to 'more than half the capital' (*plus de moitié du capital*).

Capital did not triumph over its rivals until they had been slowly eroded, a process which must have meant the emergence of new concepts, 'an epistemological break' as Michel Foucault would say. Condillac in 1782 put it more simply: 'Every science requires a special language because every science has its own ideas. It seems that one ought to begin by composing this language, but people begin by speaking and writing and the language remains to be composed.'[18] The spontaneously-used language of the classical economists was indeed still being spoken long after their death. J. B. Say admitted (1828) that the word *richesse* (wealth) was 'still poorly defined' in his day,[19] but he went on using it. Sismondi speaks readily of 'territorial wealth' (i.e. real estate), of national wealth, commercial wealth – *richesse* in every case – and he even used the last expression as the title of his first essay.[20]

Meanwhile the word *capital* was gradually ousting its rivals. It is already to be found in Forbonnais who speaks of 'productive capital';[21] and in Quesnay who states: 'All capital is an instrument of production'.[22] And it was already in colloquial use, in all probability, since we find it used as an image: 'Monsieur de Voltaire has been living, since he has arrived in Paris, on the capital of his strength'; his friends ought to wish 'that he would only live on the income' – a correct diagnosis by Dr Tronchin in February 1778, a few months before the celebrated writer died.[23] Twenty years later, at the time of Bonaparte's Italian campaign, a Russian consul, reflecting on the exceptional situation of revolutionary France, made the remark I have already quoted once: France was fighting the war 'with her capital', her enemies only 'with their income'! In this clear-sighted observation, capital is used in the sense of patrimony, wealth, of a nation. It is no longer the traditional word meaning a sum of money, the total amount of a debt or loan, or a merchant's funds, meanings found in Crespin's *Thrésor des trois langues* (1627), in Furetière's *Dictionnaire universel*, (1690) in the *Encyclopédie* of 1751 and the *Dictionnaire de l'Académie française* in 1786. But the older meaning was surely linked to the notion of monetary value, so long accepted unquestioningly. The notion of productive money and the labour theory of value would take some time to replace it. And yet one does find this more modern meaning in Forbonnais and Quesnay whom I have already quoted; in Morellet (1764) who made a distinction between 'idle capital' and 'active capital' (*capitaux oisifs* and *capitaux agissants*)[24]; and more clearly in Turgot, for whom capital no longer exclusively refers to money. Only a few finishing touches were needed to arrive at the 'meaning which Marx explicitly (and exclusively) gave to the word: that of a means of production'.[25] Let us stop at this still rather uncertain borderline, to which we shall have to return.

Capitalist and capitalists

The word *capitalist* probably dates from mid-seventeenth century. The *Hollandische Mercurius* uses it once in 1633, and again in 1654.[26] In 1699, a French

Commerce, fifteenth century tapestry. (Paris, Musée de Cluny, photo Roger-Viollet.)

memorandum notes that a new tax levied by the States-General of the United Provinces distinguishes between 'capitalists', who will pay 3 florins, and other people who will pay 30 sols.[27] So the word had already been in use for some time before Jean-Jacques Rousseau wrote to one of his friends in 1759: 'I am not a great lord nor a capitalist; I am poor and happy.'[28] But the word only appears as an adjective in the *Encyclopédie*. The noun did have many competitors, it is true. There were plenty of ways to describe the rich: men of means, millionaires, *nouveaux riches*, moneybags, *fortunés* (a word disliked by purists), etc. In Queen Anne's day in England, the Whigs, who were invariably rich, were described as 'moneyed men'. And all these terms had a pejorative tone: Quesnay in 1759 spoke of those 'holders of pecuniary fortunes' who 'know neither king nor country'.[29] Morellet thought of the capitalists as forming a group or category, almost a class apart in society.[30]

The owners of 'pecuniary fortunes': this was the narrow sense of the word *capitalist* in the latter part of the eighteenth century, when it was used to describe the possessors of 'public bonds', of stocks and shares, or liquid money for investing. In 1768, a shipping firm, largely financed from Paris, set up its head-quarters in the French capital, in the rue 'coqueron' (Coq-Héron) because, as they explained to interested parties in Honfleur, 'the capitalists who live in Paris are glad to be within reach of their investments and to keep constant watch on their progress'.[31] A Neapolitan agent in the Hague wrote (in French) to his government in February 1769: 'The capitalists of this country will be very unwilling to expose their money to the uncertainties of the consequences of this war',[32] (that is the war just beginning between Russia and Turkey). Recalling, in 1775, the foun-dation by the Dutch of the colony of Surinam, in Guiana, the Frenchman Malouet distinguished between *entrepreneurs* and *capitalists*: the former de-signed plantations and drainage-schemes on the spot; 'then they applied to European capitalists for funds, associating them with their enterprises'.[33] *Capi-talists* was coming more and more to mean handlers of money, providers of investment. A French pamphlet written in 1776 had the title: *Un mot aux capitalistes sur la dette d'Angleterre*[34] – was not the national debt *a priori* a concern of capitalists? In July 1783, there was talk in France of granting ordinary merchants leave to become wholesalers. On the intervention of Sartine, lieuten-ant of police, Paris was exempted from the measure. If it had not been, it was argued, the city would have been exposed to the 'avidity of a large number of capitalists [who] would have hoarded foodstuffs and would create excessive problems for the police chief supervising the city's food supply'.[35] Here the word, which already seems to have a bad reputation, clearly refers to people who already own money and are prepared to use it in order to obtain even more. A little booklet, published in Milan in 1799, distinguished between landed pro-prietors and *possessori di ricchezze mobili, ossia i capitalisti*.[36] In 1789, some of the *cahiers de doléances* (complaints registers) in the Draguignan area, com-plained about capitalists, defined as those 'who have fortunes in their wallets'[37] and who therefore escaped taxation. As a result, 'the great landowners of this province sell their patrimony to acquire capital and to protect themselves against the exorbitant levies to which landed property is subjected, freely investing their money at 5%'.[38] It was the other way round in Lorraine in 1790: 'The most considerable estates [in this area]', writes an eye-witness, 'are owned by people who live in Paris: several have been bought up recently by capitalists: they have directed their speculation towards this province because it is the one where land is the cheapest in proportion to its income.'[39]

The word is never, the reader will have noticed, used in a friendly sense. Marat, who had already adopted a violent tone in 1774, even writes: 'Among the trading nations, the capitalists and rentiers almost all [cast] their lot with the tax-farmers, financiers and speculators.'[40] With the Revolution, the tone became fiercer still. On 25 November 1790, the comte de Custine fulminated from the rostrum of the National Assembly: 'Will this Assembly, which has destroyed all kinds of aristocracy, flinch before the aristocracy of capitalists, these cosmo-politans whose only fatherland is the one in which they can pile up their riches?'[41] Cambon, speaking to the Convention on 24 August 1793, was even more cate-gorical: 'There is at the present time a struggle to the death between all the money merchants and the strengthening of the Republic. These associations destructive of public credit must be killed if we wish to establish the regime of liberty.'[42] If the word capitalist does not actually appear here, it is no doubt because Cambon wanted to use the even more scornful epithet 'money mer-chants', (*marchands d'argent*). It is well known that high finance which encour-aged the first revolutionary movements, only to be taken by surprise by the Revolution, eventually emerged unscathed. Hence the bitterness of Rivarol who unhesitatingly wrote in his exile: 'Sixty thousand capitalists and the anthill of speculators decided the course of the Revolution.'[43] Rather a hasty explanation of 1789 perhaps. But capitalist did not yet mean investor, entrepreneur. The word, like its partner *capital*, remained attached to the idea of money, of wealth for its own sake.

Capitalism: a very recent word

Capitalism, the most exciting of the three words for us, but the least real (would it even exist without the other two?) has been pursued relentlessly by historians and lexicologists. According to Dauzat,[44] it is to be found in the *Encyclopédie* in 1753, but with a very particular meaning: 'The state of one who is rich'. Unfortunately, this statement seems to be inaccurate; the text quoted cannot be traced. In 1842, the word occurs in the *Enrichissements de la langue française* by J.-B. Richard.[45] But it was probably Louis Blanc, in his polemic with Bastiat, who gave it its new meaning when in 1850 he wrote: '. . . What I call "capitalism" [and he used quotation marks] that is to say the appropriation of capital by some to the exclusion of others.'[46] But the word still occurred only rarely. Proudhon occasionally uses it, correctly: 'Land is still the fortress of capitalism', he writes – and indeed this was one of his major theses. And he defines it very well: 'Economic and social regime in which capital, the source of income, does not generally belong to those who make it work through their labour.'[47] Six years later however, in 1867, the word was still unknown to Marx.[48]

  In fact, it was not until the beginning of this century that it fully burst upon political debate as the natural opposite of socialism. It was to be launched in academic circles by Werner Sombart's explosive book *Der moderne Kapitalismus* (1st edition 1902). Not unnaturally, this word which Marx never used was incorporated into the Marxist model, so much so that the terms *slavery*, *feudal-ism* and *capitalism* are commonly used to refer to the three major stages of development defined by the author of *Capital*.

  It is a political word then; hence perhaps the ambiguous side of its career. It

was long banned by the economists of the first years of the century – Charles
Gide, Canwas, Marshall, Seligman, Cassel – and only appeared in the *Dictionnaire des sciences politiques* after the First World War. It did not receive an
article in the *Encyclopedia Britannica* until the 1926 edition; and appeared in the
Dictionnaire de l'Académie française only in 1936 and then with this ludicrous
definition: 'Capitalism: sum total of capitalists' (*Capitalisme: ensemble des
capitalistes*). The new definition of 1958 is not much better: 'Economic regime in
which the goods of production (*les biens de production*) belong to private
individuals or firms' – what is wrong with 'means of production' (*les moyens de
production*)?

In fact this word, which has become loaded with meaning since the beginning
of the century and in particular since the Russian Revolution of 1917, clearly
causes many people embarrassment. A reputable historian, Herbert Heaton, has
suggested simply abolishing it: '[Of all] the "isms" ... the greatest noisemaker
has been capitalism. That word unfortunately has acquired such a motley of
meanings and definitions that one may justly plead that capitalism, like imperialism, is a term that should be cut out of the vocabulary of every self-respecting
scholar'.[49] Lucien Febvre himself felt it could be dropped, since it had been
over-used.[50] But if we were to listen to this not unreasonable advice, we should
start missing the absentee immediately. As Andrew Shonfield says, 'one ...
justification for the continued use of the word "capitalism" is that no one, not
even its severest critics, has proposed a better word to put in its place'.[51]

Historians were perhaps most tempted of all by the new word, in the days
when it did not yet have a whiff of brimstone about it. Blithely disregarding
anachronism, they opened up the entire field of historical prospecting to it, from
ancient Babylon to Hellenistic Greece, ancient China, Rome, the European
Middle Ages, India. All the great names of yesterday's historiography, from
Theodore Mommsen to Henri Pirenne, dabbled in this sport, which later occasioned a virtual witch-hunt. The imprudent were rebuked, Mommsen first of all
and by no less an authority than Marx himself. And rightly so perhaps: capital
cannot simply be used as a synonym for money. But the mere mention of the
word seems to have been enough reason for Paul Veyne[52] to berate Michel
Rostovtsef – the outstanding expert on the ancient economy. J. C. Van Leur
insisted on seeing only 'pedlars' in the economy of South-East Asia. Karl Polanyi
is full of scorn for historians who have dared to refer to Assyrian 'merchants' –
and yet we have thousands of tablets bearing their correspondence; and so on. In
many cases, the aim of the assault is to reduce everything to a post-Marxian
orthodoxy: we are not allowed to talk about capitalism before the end of the
eighteenth century, in other words before the industrial mode of production.

Well this is really a question of terminology. I need hardly point out that no
historian of *ancien régime* societies, *a fortiori* of ancient civilizations, would ever,
when using the term *capitalism*, have in mind the definition Alexander Gerschenkron calmly gives us: 'Capitalism, that is the modern industrial system'.[53]

I have already indicated that capitalism in the past (as distinct from capitalism today) only occupied a narrow platform of economic life. How could one possibly take it to mean a 'system' extending over the whole of society? It was nevertheless a world apart, different from and indeed foreign to the social and economic context surrounding it. And it is in relation to this context that it is defined as 'capitalism', not merely in relation to new capitalist forms which were to emerge later in time. In fact capitalism was what it was in relation to a *non-capitalism* of immense proportions. And to refuse to admit this dichotomy within the economy of the past, on the pretext that 'true' capitalism dates only from the nineteenth century, means abandoning the effort to understand the significance – crucial to the analysis of that economy – of what might be termed the former topology of capitalism. If there were certain areas where it elected residence – by no means inadvertently – that is because these were *the only areas which favoured the reproduction of capital.*

Capital: the reality

If we now move on beyond the preceding discussion, it is important to shed some light on the change that occurred in the meaning of the word *capital* (and the two other words accompanying it) between Turgot and Marx, to discover whether the new content of the word really has no application at all to an earlier phenomenon, whether, that is, capitalism in its true sense really sprang to life fully armed at the same time as the industrial revolution. British historians are now inclined to date the origins of the industrial revolution at least as far back as 1750, if not a century earlier. Marx placed the beginnings of the 'industrial era' in the sixteenth century – but admitted that 'the first attempts at capitalist *production*' (not merely capital accumulation, it should be noted) appeared precociously in the Italian city-states in the Middle Ages.[54] Any emerging organism, even if it is still far from having developed all its final characteristics, bears within it the potential for such development and can already be assigned a name. All things considered then, the new notion of capital can be regarded as an indispensable theoretical concept for the understanding of the centuries covered by this book.

Fifty years ago, capital was described as being a sum of *capital goods* (*biens capitaux*) – an expression which is going out of fashion now, but which has some advantages. A capital good can after all be grasped, touched, and unequivocally defined. It is in the first place 'the result of some previous labour'; in fact it is 'accumulated labour'. It might be the field within the village boundaries that was cleared of stones far back in time; the millwheel built too long ago for anyone to remember; or the stony country lanes, lined with blackthorn, which may date back to primitive Gaul, according to Gaston Roupnel.[55] Such capital goods are inherited; they are more or less durable human constructions. Secondly, capital goods are necessarily reabsorbed into the process of production: and they can

Forests as a capital good. In the forest of Tronçais in the *département* of the Allier in France,
there are still standing oak trees which Colbert had planted in 1670 with a view to providing
solid masts for the French fleet from the nineteenth century on. Colbert had thought of
everything except the steamship. (Photo Héraudet.)

only be defined as such precisely on condition that they contribute to further human labour, which they may stimulate or at least facilitate.

Their contribution enables them to be regenerated, rebuilt and improved and to produce an income. For production is constantly absorbing and reshaping capital. The grain I sow is a capital good: it will germinate. The coal thrown into Newcomen's steam-engine is a capital good; the energy it provides will produce results. But the grain I eat in the form of bread, or the coal I burn in the fireplace are immediately taken out of the production process, as directly consumed goods. Similarly a forest that is not made use of by man, or the money hoarded by a miser are outside production and cannot be considered capital goods. But money that passes from hand to hand, stimulating commerce, or is used to pay rents, incomes, profits and wages – money that is in other words launched on to trade circuits, forcing open doors and dictating the speed of flow, is a capital good. It leaves its point of departure only to return to it. David Hume was right to say that money was 'nothing but the representation of labour and commodity'.[56] As early as 1564, Villalón was already saying that some merchants made money with money.[57]

So it becomes something of an academic puzzle to find out whether a given object or property was, or was not, a capital good. A ship was one *ipso facto*. The first ship to arrive in St Petersburg in 1701, a Dutch vessel, received from Peter the Great the privilege of paying no customs duties for the rest of its physical life – a concession which had the effect of prolonging the ship's life for almost a century, three or four times the normal span.[58] A very useful capital good!

The same might be said of the forests in the Harz mountains[59] between Seesen, Bad Harzburg, Goslar and Zellerfeld, which were known as the *Kommunionharz* between 1635 and 1788, when they were the undivided property of the princely houses of Hanover and Wolfenbüttel. Indispensable for the charcoal which fuelled the furnaces of the region, these reserves of energy were organized at a very early date in order to prevent haphazard and unplanned use of the wood by the local peasants. The first known forestry agreement dates from 1576, when the whole area was divided into sections according to the variable rate of growth of the different species of trees. The forest was mapped out and plans were devised for floating tree-trunks downriver, for guarding the wood and for inspection on horseback, thus preserving the forest zone and providing for the rational organization of production for the market: a good example of the conservation and improvement of a capital good.

Wood was used for so many purposes at this time that the Harz example is by no means unique. Buffon took great care of his woods in Montbard in Burgundy. In France, rational forestry can be detected as early as the twelfth century; so it was already an ancient tradition which did not begin – though it was certainly accentuated – under Colbert. Whenever West Europeans reached the huge forest belts of Norway, Poland and the New World, such forests, if they were accessible by sea or river that is, immediately joined the category of capital goods. In 1783, England made her treaty with Spain conditional on free access to the dye-woods of the tropical forests of the Campeachy region of Mexico. She eventually obtained three hundred leagues of wooded coastline: 'If we manage this area wisely', remarked a diplomat, 'there ought to be enough wood for eternity.'[60]

To list further examples is unnecessary: they all lead us directly and without mystery to the known opinions of economists on the nature of capital.

Fixed capital, circulating capital

Capital or capital goods, which come to the same thing, can be divided into two categories: fixed capital which has a long or fairly long *physical* life and provides the infrastructure for human labour: roads, bridges, canals, aqueducts, boats, implements or machines; and variable, working, or circulating capital ('rolling' capital as it used to be called) which is absorbed and swallowed up in the production process: seed-corn, raw materials, semi-finished products, the money for all the various settlements of accounts (incomes, profits, rents, wages), and above all wages and labour. All economists make this distinction, Adam Smith, Turgot (who talked about 'original advances' and 'annual advances') and Marx (who referred to constant capital and variable capital).

In about 1820, the economist Heinrich van Storch[61] explained the difference to his young pupils, the Grand-Dukes Nicholas and Michael, at the court of Saint Petersburg.

> Let us suppose, [their tutor began] that there is a nation which has been extremely rich and which has consequently *fixed* [my italics] a huge amount of capital in improving the land, building houses, erecting factories and workshops and making tools. Let us then suppose that there is an invasion by barbarians who descend immediately after the harvest and carry off all the circulating capital, all rations, materials and manufactured goods, but who leave untouched the houses and workshops; all industrial (that is to say all human) labour would cease forthwith. For in order to work the land, one needs horses and oxen for ploughing, grain for sowing, and above all bread for the workers to eat until the next harvest. In order for the factories to work there must be grain for the mill, metal and coal for the forge; the craftsmen will need raw materials and everywhere the workers will need food. It will be impossible to work, not by reason of the area of fields, the number of factories and workshops or of workers, but by reason of the very small amount of circulating capital left behind by the barbarians. Happy the people that is able, after such a disaster, to dig up treasure which was buried out of fear. For while precious metals and fine jewels cannot replace true circulating wealth [*richesse*, i.e. capital] any more than fixed capital can, they can be used, that is exported in their entirety to buy from abroad the circulating capital that is needed. To seek to prevent such exports would be to condemn the population to inactivity and the famine that would result.

The text is interesting in itself, for its vocabulary and for the archaic character of Russian economic life it indicates (horses, oxen, craftsmen, famine, buried treasure). The 'barbarians' act in a textbook manner, leaving fixed capital intact while carrying off circulating capital in order to demonstrate the irreplaceable nature of the latter. But if the barbarians had had a different programme of vandalism and chosen to destroy the fixed capital instead of the circulating capital, it would have been equally difficult for economic life to begin again in a nation that had been conquered, pillaged and then liberated.

The production process is a kind of two-speed engine: circulating capital is destroyed quickly only to be reproduced and even increased. As for fixed capital, it may take more or less long to do so, but it wears out in the end: the road deteriorates, the bridge collapses, the sailing ship or galley is one day good for nothing but firewood for some Venetian monastery,[62] the wooden gears of the machinery wear down, the ploughshare breaks. This equipment has to be replaced: the deterioration of fixed capital is a pernicious economic ill from which there is no respite.

Trying to calculate capital in the past

These days, capital is most accurately estimated in national accounting, which measures everything: variations in the national product (gross or net), per capita income, savings, the rate of capital reproduction, demographic change, etc. – all collected with the aim of measuring economic growth. The historian clearly does not have the means of applying this statistical framework to the *ancien régime* economy. But even if we are short of figures, the very attempt to envisage the past through the theoretical categories of the present inevitably alters our ways of seeing and explaining it.

Such an altered perspective is apparent in the few attempts at quantification and retrospective calculation which have been undertaken – more often by economists than by historians. Alice Hanson Jones, for example, in a recent article and book,[63] has succeeded in calculating fairly convincingly the private wealth, or if one prefers, the amount of capital owned in 1774 in New Jersey, Pennsylvania and Delaware. She began by collecting wills and studying the wealth they revealed, then estimated inherited property where no wills survived. The results were rather curious: the sum of capital goods (C) was three or four times national income (I) – indicating that this economy had behind it immediately available reserves roughly equivalent to three or four years' income put together. Now it so happens that Keynes in his calculations for the 1930s always used the basic equation $C = 4I$: which seems to indicate a certain correspondence between past and present. It is true that the 'American' economy of the early days of independence gives the impression of already being exceptional, if only by the high productivity of labour and by an average living standard (per capita income) probably higher than that in Europe, even in England.

This unexpected coincidence is also compatible with the calculations and reflections of Simon Kuznets, the American economist, who has made a special study of the growth of national economies between the end of the nineteenth century and the present day.[64] He was tempted, and fortunately for us he gave into the temptation, to look back beyond the nineteenth century, working out or estimating the possible developments of the eighteenth, using the substantial graphs on English growth provided by Phyllis Deane and W. A. Cole;[65] and from there he was able to work back as far as 1500 and even earlier. I do not here intend to go into details of method or the conditions in which this exploration of the past was undertaken – with the aim it must be said of identifying problems and suggesting research programmes and useful comparisons for today's Third World countries, rather than with that of providing hard and fast solutions to a historical question.

But the fact that this historical journey was undertaken by a leading economist, convinced of the explanatory value of the long term in economics, was of course a development after my own heart. His conclusions constitute a challenge to all previous approaches to the *ancien régime* economy. Of the broad picture before us, we shall concentrate on capital – but this single factor lies at the heart of the debate, where we shall follow it.

Simon Kuznets is convinced that present-day correlations (whose movements and developments over the eight to ten well-documented decades since the end of the last century he has studied in about ten countries) make it possible, *mutatis mutandis*, to work backwards through history: evidence that in his eyes at least there are similarities, connections and continuities between the distant past and the present – though there are also breaks and discontinuities from one period to another. In particular, he does not believe that there was a sudden change in the rate of savings which A. Lewis and W. W. Rostow have suggested as the origin of modern growth. Kuznets draws attention to the ceiling on savings, that upper limit which the savings rate never seems to exceed even in very high income countries:

> Whatever the reason, the essential point is that even the richest countries of the world today, with a wealth and capacity far beyond the imagination of our forebears even in the late eighteenth or early nineteenth century, raise the capital formation proportions to only moderate levels – indeed to levels that, on the net savings side, many earlier societies might have found not impossible and perhaps not even too difficult, to attain.[66]

Whether one calls it savings or capital formation, it is the same debate. If consumption amounts to 85% of production, 15% must be regarded as savings and thus potentially as the formation of reproducible capital. (These are hypothetical figures.) With a little exaggeration, it might be argued that no society ever saves more than 20% of production, or does so only briefly, under conditions of effective coercion which were not typical of past societies.

That said, Marx's pronouncement that 'no society can manage without producing and consuming' should be expanded to include 'and saving'. This underground structural task depends on the number of individuals in the society in question, its level of technical progress, its living standards – and equally on the social hierarchy which determines the distribution of income within the society. A hypothetical model imagined by Simon Kuznets, based on England in 1688 or on the social hierarchies of German towns in the fifteenth and sixteenth centuries, would have an elite consisting of 5% of the population (probably a maximum) disposing of 25% of national income. That would leave the vast majority of the population (95%) with only 75% of the national income and thus 'on a per capita income ... well below the countrywide average'. This majority is thus condemned by the exploitation of the privileged to what is evidently a restrictive regime (as Alfred Sauvy[67] long ago demonstrated in a book that has not yet been surpassed). In short, savings can only be accumulated by the privileged section of society. Let us suppose that consumption on the part of the privileged is about three to five times that of ordinary people: their savings would thus amount to 13% of national income in the first case, 5% in the second. It *was* possible then to save in the societies of the past, despite their low per capita income, and they did indeed save; the social hierarchy did not prevent this, indeed after a fashion it contributed to it.

There are two essential variables in this calculation: the size of the population and its living standard. Between 1500 and 1750, over the whole of Europe, the population growth rate can be estimated at 0.17% per year (compared with 0.95% from 1750 to the present). In the long run, the growth of per capita output would have settled at about 0.2% or 0.3%.

These are of course conjectural figures. It is quite clear however that the rate of capital reproduction in pre-1750 Europe remained at very modest levels. But it did so with one peculiarity which seems to me to touch the root of the problem. Every year, society produced a certain amount of capital, gross capital that is, part of which had to go towards replacing worn-out fixed capital which was being used up in the processes of active economic life. Net capital is, thus, broadly speaking, gross capital minus the amount taken out for maintenance. Kuznets's hypothesis, namely that the difference between gross capital formation and net capital formation was much greater in ancient societies than in modern ones, seems to me to be a fundamental and incontrovertible point, even if the abundant documentation supporting it is more qualitative than quantitative. Quite clearly, the economies of the past produced a considerable quantity of gross capital, but in some sectors this gross capital just melted away. There was in other words a congenital weakness in the basic equipment of production, giving rise to various shortcomings which had to be met by a greater outlay of labour. Land itself was a very fragile kind of capital. Its fertility was reduced from year to year: hence crop rotation, continually going round and round on the spot; hence the need for fertilizers (but how could enough ever be produced?);

German ship with square rig and centre-line rudder. Woodcut from *Peregrinationes*, by Brendenbach, Mainz, 1486. From about this period, a ship was a capital good of which shares were sold and divided among several part-owners. (Photo Giraudon.)

hence the determination of the peasant to plough the land over and over – five or six ploughings in some areas and even, in Provence according to Quiqueran de Beaujeu[68] fourteen; hence the very high percentage of the population obliged to work in the fields – a factor which we already know to operate against economic growth. Houses, ships, bridges, irrigation canals, tools and all the machines man had already invented to ease his work and to harness the forms of energy available to him – all were subject to deterioration. The apparently insignificant fact that the city gate of Bruges was repaired in 1337–1338, rebuilt in 1367–1368, modified in 1385, 1392 and 1433, only to be rebuilt again in 1615, does not seem to me to be entirely negligible: these trivial little details took up the whole of everyday life and structured it.[69] The correspondence of the *intendant* of Bonneville in Savoy in the eighteenth century is monotonously full of mentions of the dykes which have to be rebuilt, the bridges that have to be mended, the roads that have become impassable. If one reads the gazettes of the time, one finds an endless succession of towns and villages going up in flames: Troyes in 1547, London in 1666, Nijni Novgorod in 1701,[70] Constantinople on 28 and 29 September 1755 – where the fire left 'an empty space in the *çarsi* or business quarter of more than two leagues around';[71] a few examples among thousands.

In short, I think Simon Kuznets is absolutely right when he says:

> At the danger of exaggeration, one may ask whether there was *any* fixed, durable capital formation, except for the 'monuments' in pre-modern times, whether there was any significant accumulation of capital goods with a long physical life that did not require current maintenance (or replacement) amounting to a high proportion of the original full value. If most equipment lasted no more than five or six years, if most land improvement had to be maintained by continuous rebuilding amounting to something like a fifth of the total value per year, and if most buildings were destroyed at a rate cumulating to fairly complete destruction over a period from 25 to 50 years, then there was little that could be classified as durable capital ... the whole concept of fixed capital may be a unique product of the modern economic epoch and of modern technology.[72]

This amounts to saying, with a little exaggeration, that the industrial revolution was above all a transformation of *fixed* capital: from now on, it would be more costly but more durable: its quality would be improved and it would radically alter rates of productivity.

The value of sector analysis

The things we have been talking about affected the entire economy of course. But it is sufficient to have strolled round the *Germanisches Museum* in Munich for instance and looked at the reconstructed (sometimes working) models of the many wooden machines which were the only energy-driven motors as lately as two hundred years ago, with their extraordinarily complicated and ingenious interlocking gears used for transmitting the energy of water, wind or animal traction – to understand which sector was more vulnerable than any other to the wear and tear of equipment: production, especially where it could in any sense be described as 'industrial'. In this case, it was not only the social hierarchy which confined high incomes and the possibility of saving to the privileged 5% previously mentioned; it was the economic and technical structure that condemned certain sectors – especially 'industrial' and agricultural production – to slow capital formation. Is it then surprising that the capitalism of the past is essentially found in the commercial sector, that its greatest efforts and investments went into the 'sphere of circulation'? The approach outlined at the beginning of this chapter – an analysis by sector of economic life – unequivocally explains both the choice made by capitalism and the reasons for that choice.

It also explains an apparent contradiction in the economy of the past, namely that in countries visibly under-developed, net capital, which was easily amassed in the protected and privileged sectors of the economy, was sometimes over-plentiful and could not all be usefully invested. There was always a strong tradition of hoarding. Money lay idle and stagnated: capital was under-employed. I shall quote at a later stage some curious documents relating to France in the early eighteenth century in this connection. It would perhaps be teasingly paradoxical to say that whatever else was in short supply, money certainly was not. But what *was* lacking, for a whole number of reasons, was the opportunity to invest it in a really profitable enterprise. This was the case in Italy which was still on brilliant form at the end of the sixteenth century. After a period of great activity, Italy was suffering from an over-abundance of specie, a *largezzo* of silver which was in its way destructive, as if the country had overshot the quantity of capital goods and money that her economy could consume. So this was an age when poor land was bought up and magnificent country residences built, great monuments erected and cultural extravagance financed. If this explanation is valid, perhaps it might contribute to resolve the contradiction pointed out by Roberto Lopez and H. A. Miskimin[73] between the depressed economic climate and the splendours of Florence under Lorenzo the Magnificent?

The key problem is to find out why that sector of the society of the past which I would not hesitate to call capitalist, should have lived as if in a bell-jar, cut off from the rest; why was it not able to expand and conquer the whole of society? Perhaps in fact this was the condition of its survival, since in yesterday's societies a significant rate of capital formation was possible only in certain sectors and not in the whole market economy of the time. Capital which was adventurously invested outside this favoured zone bore little fruit, when it was not simply swallowed without trace.

To find out precisely where capitalism took up residence in the past thus offers a certain interest to the historian, since the topology of capital provides us with a reverse topology of the weaknesses and unprofitable sectors of former societies. But before trying to identify capitalism in those sectors where it was really at home, we shall first examine those sectors which it penetrated only obliquely and above all to a very limited extent: agriculture, industry and transport. Capitalism often made incursions on to these foreign territories, but often withdrew quickly as well, and in every case the withdrawal was significant. Why did the cities of Castile for instance give up investing in the agriculture of the nearby countryside after the middle of the sixteenth century,[74] while the merchant capitalism of Venice, fifty years later, was on the contrary moving into the country, and the enterprising landlords of South Bohemia were at the same time drowning their estates under huge ponds to farm carp instead of rye?[75] Why did the French bourgeois stop advancing money to peasants after 1550, preferring to lend it to nobles or to the king?[76] Why did the big merchant firms withdraw from almost all the mining enterprises of central Europe even before the end of the sixteenth century, leaving them to be forcibly taken over by the state which ran them and took full responsibility? In all these apparently contradictory cases as well as in many others, one finds that the abandoned enterprise had ceased to be sufficiently profitable or safe, and that it had become advisable to invest elsewhere. As a merchant put it, 'better to stand idle than to labour in vain'.[77] The hunt for and maximization of profits were already implicit rules of capitalism, even then.

Land and money

The intrusion of capitalism, or rather of urban money (from both nobles and bourgeois) into the countryside had begun very early. There was not a town in Europe whose money did not spill out on to the neighbouring land. And the more important the town, the wider the radius of urban-owned property outside the walls, driving all before it. Indeed property was acquired outside the immediate vicinity, sometimes very long distances away: in the sixteenth century, Genoese merchants bought up estates in the far-off kingdom of Naples. In eighteenth-century France, the land market stretched to the very boundaries of the national market. Breton *seigneuries*[78] and Lorraine estates[79] were bought in Paris.

Purchases like this often stemmed from social pretensions. '*Chi ha danari compra feudi ed è barone*' said a Neapolitan proverb (he who has money buys himself a fief and becomes a baron). Land did not instantly confer titles of nobility, but it was a step in the right direction, a means of social promotion. Economic reasons, though certainly not the only ones, did however play some part. I might buy an estate near my home town simply to ensure a food supply for my household – acting as a provident *paterfamilias*. Or it could be a way of investing money safely: land never tells lies, as they used to say and as merchants well knew. Luca del Sera wrote from Florence on 23 April 1408 to Francesco Datini, the merchant of Prato: 'I advised you to buy some estates and I do so again even more pressingly if possible. Land has at least the virtue of not being exposed to the risk of the sea, or an unscrupulous factor, or a merchant company or a bankruptcy. Therefore I urge and request you all the more to do so ('*più ve no conforto e pregho*').'[80] The trouble for the merchant was that an estate could all the same not be bought and sold as easily as a share on the Stock Exchange. When the Tiepolo Pisani bank failed in Venice in 1584, the estates which had stood guarantee for it were sold only slowly and at a loss.[81] In the eighteenth century, it is true, the merchants of La Rochelle were quite willing to place their capital in vineyards[82] or part-shares in vineyards, since they considered that money thus invested could be recovered without too much difficulty or loss when required. But these were vineyards in a region which exported its wines in large quantities: land of such a special nature was as good as a bank! The same was

Fire, the dreaded scourge of city life. This illustration from Diebold Schilling's *Chronicle of Berne* shows women, children and priests fleeing the city with their possessions. The only means of fighting the fire seem to be ladders and wooden buckets filled from the town moat. Berne was almost completely destroyed; according to the chronicle the fire spread throughout the town in a quarter-of-an-hour. (Burgerbibliothek, Berne, photo G. Howald.)

probably true of the land that the Antwerp merchants bought up around the city in the sixteenth century. They were able to borrow money on the strength of it, to increase their credit; and the income it brought in was not negligible.[83]

That said, whatever its origins, urban-owned property (which usually belonged to the bourgeoisie) was not automatically capitalist property, particularly since very often, and increasingly after the sixteenth century, it was not farmed directly by its owner. The latter might in fact be an authentic capitalist and money-handler, but that made no difference in this respect. The Fuggers, the fabulously rich merchants of Augsburg, towards the end of their spectacular career bought up numbers of feudal estates and principalities in Swabia and Franconia. They administered them of course according to good housekeeping methods, but they did not alter their structure. These manors remained manors, with all their feudal dues and peasant quit-rents.[84] Nor did the Italian merchants of Lyons, or the Genoese businessmen in Naples, who bought titles along with their estates, become agricultural entrepreneurs.

And yet there were occasions when capitalism took over land and effectively subjected it to its own rules, completely reshaping its organization. We shall presently examine some such examples of capitalist agriculture: there are plenty of them, some rather doubtful, others indisputable, but compared to the examples of traditional management and farming patterns, they were always in the minority, so much so indeed as almost to be, at least in the eighteenth century, the exception that proves the rule.

The pre-conditions of capitalism

The countryside of Western Europe was inhabited by both landlord and peasant. Consequently it was far from being easy to manipulate. The seigniorial regime died hard everywhere. For a capitalist system of management and economic rationalization of the land to come into being, many pre-conditions would have been necessary: the seigniorial regime would have had to be if not abolished, certainly reduced or modified (sometimes from within in which case it was the lord himself, or an enriched peasant, the local cock of the walk, who played the capitalist); peasant liberties would have had to be if not suppressed, at least contained and outmanœuvred (the sensitive question of common lands came under this heading); the whole undertaking would have to be connected to an active long-distance commodity trade: export grain, wool, woad,[85] madder, wine, sugar; some form of 'rational' management would have to be introduced, governed by a careful policy of crop yields and land enrichment; tried and tested techniques would have to govern investment and the installation of fixed capital; and lastly, the system would have to be based on a wage-earning proletariat.

Unless all these conditions were fulfilled, the enterprise might be on the way to being capitalist, but it was not capitalist in the proper sense. And these

Almoshof: two anonymous paintings in the Nuremberg Museum, illustrating the extension of a country house in the seventeenth century. The first (above) shows the property in the sixteenth century; the second shows what it looked like by the seventeenth, inside the same perimeter walls ...

conditions, whether negative or positive, were hard to realize. Why were they so elusive, nine times out of ten? The answer must be that one could not simply walk into the countryside and do as one pleased; the feudal superstructure was a living, resistant reality; and above all the peasant world was always ready to oppose innovation.

A French consul observed in 1816 the 'alarming state of neglect and poverty' of Sardinia; and yet this lay 'in the heart of European civilization'.[86] The crucial obstacle to 'enlightened' efforts at improvement came from the world of back-ward peasants, subjected to the triple yoke of Church, state and 'feudalism', a world of 'savage' peasants who 'guard their flocks or plough their fields with a dagger at their side and a gun over their shoulder', their lives bedevilled by feuds between families and clans. It was not easy for anything to penetrate this archaic world, not even potato-growing, which had been tried successfully but which had 'not passed into common practice' despite the usefulness of this 'famine root'. 'The attempts to grow potatoes', notes the consul, 'were mocked and ridiculed; the attempt to grow sugar cane [tried by a Sardinian nobleman who was an enthusiastic agronomist] were the object of jealousy, and either ignor-ance or ill-will punished them as a crime; the workmen who had been brought in at great expense were assassinated one by one.' A visitor from Marseilles marvelled at the orange-groves of the Ogliastra region, trees 'full of health and vigour whose blossom falls to make a thick carpet, and the inhabitants of this region ... derive not the slightest benefit from them'. With a few of his fellow-countrymen, he installed a distillery and worked for a whole season. Alas, the following year when the team of workers, who had meantime returned to France, came back to start work again, they found the work-shops ransacked, the tools and utensils stolen. The whole scheme had to be abandoned.

Elsewhere no doubt, there were peasant societies living under different rules and more open to change. Sardinia is a very extreme example, one that even today is regarded as an archaic society. But what about the Genoese merchant of the Spinelli family, who acquired the noble estate of Castrovillani in the kingdom of Naples: when he announced that he would himself fix the arrival date and the hiring period of the *bracciali* (seasonal workers, who were also called *fatigatori* in that part of the world), he immediately had the whole village community, the *università*, up in arms, and had to give way. Do not ask too much of the *fatigatori*, the villagers explained, or they will refuse to come and work in our vineyards as usual.[87]

It was no accident then that new farming ventures were so often launched on waste marsh or woodland. It was better not to upset existing land systems and customs. In 1782, an innovating farmer called Delporte chose for his experiment in sheepbreeding 'English style', part of the forest of Boulogne-sur-Mer which

... Part of the old, quite modest house which belonged to the landowner has now been made over into a house for the steward or lodgekeeper; part of it has been levelled off to form a terrace. The proprietor's new house, a huge turreted affair, is built in the style of a castle.

he had himself cleared and enriched with marl.[88] Incidentally he had to protect his flock from wolves – but at least it was safe from human interference!

The peasant masses: numbers, inertia, productivity

The peasantry represented immense numbers of people, the vast majority of human beings. Standing shoulder to shoulder they could offer considerable active or passive resistance. But numbers were also a sign of insufficient productivity. If the land produced only a poor yield, which was generally the case, larger surfaces had to be put under the plough, more efforts made by the workers, in the attempt to compensate for under-production by extra labour. Frasso and Arpaia were two poor villages behind Naples, not far from a third, Montesarchio, which was comparatively prosperous. In the two poor villages, productivity was so low that in order to produce the same amount as Montesarchio, three times the surface area had to be cultivated. Consequently the poor villages had and tolerated a higher birth rate and a lower age of marriage, since they had to produce a comparatively greater labour force.[89] Hence the constant paradox of so many *ancien régime* economies whose country districts were relatively over-populated and living on the borderline of penury and famine, yet which had regularly to call in large numbers of seasonal workers for the grain harvest, grape-picking and winter threshing, and labourers to dig ditches with pickaxes – all from the destitute world of outcasts and the great reservoir of the unemployed. In the *généralité* of Orléans in 1698, statistical records show that there were 23,812 peasants with ploughs, 21,840 winegrowers, 2121 millers, 539 gardeners, 3160 shepherds, 38,444 day-labourers, 13,696 servant-girls, 15,000 menservants. And even these figures do not represent the whole of the peasant population, since apart from the servant-girls, women were not included, nor indeed were children. Out of an active population of almost 120,000 people, if one adds together farmhands, servants and daylabourers, there were over 67,000 wage-earners.[90]

Paradoxically this surplus population was an obstacle to increased productivity: a peasant population as large as this, living very nearly at subsistence level, obliged to labour endlessly in order to compensate for the blows dealt by frequent bad harvests or to pay its many dues, was imprisoned within its everyday tasks and preoccupations and hardly able to move outside them. This was not the kind of milieu in which technical progress made much headway or in which risks could be taken with new crops or new markets. The chief impression it gives is of routine-bound, even slumbering masses – but not necessarily calm and docile ones. The masses could be aroused to outbursts of unexpected brutality. In 1368, the foreign domination of the Mongols in China was overthrown, in favour of the Mings, by a peasant revolt of tidal wave proportions. And although peasant uprisings were rarely on this scale in Europe, they were regular happenings everywhere.

It is true that these rebellions flared up only to die down one after another: the *jacquerie* of the Ile-de-France in 1358, the Peasants' Revolt of 1381 in England, the Hungarian peasant war led by Dosza in 1514[91] which ended with thousands of hangings, the German peasant uprising of 1525, or the widespread rural rebellion in the kingdom of Naples in 1647. The landowning class, the social superstructure of the rural world, always succeeded in winning back the advantage, with the aid of the prince or the more or less conscious complicity of the town-dwellers who needed peasant labour. But while he regularly lost battles, the peasant never gave up. Undeclared war alternated with open hostilities. According to Georg Grüll,[92] who has written about the Austrian peasants, even the mighty defeat which ended the *Bauernkrieg* of 1525 did not put an end to the latent social war which continued uninterrupted until 1650 or later. Peasant war was a structural kind of warfare without end – going on far longer than the Hundred Years' War.

Poverty and survival

Maxim Gorky is supposed to have said 'Peasants are the same everywhere.'[93] Was he right?

Peasants everywhere shared more or less constant poverty, almost unlimited patience, an extraordinary capacity for resistance by bowing to circumstances, a slowness to act despite outbursts of rage during revolts, a maddening habit, brought to a fine art, of rejecting any *'nouvelletez'*,[94] and an unparalleled perseverance in snatching an always precarious existence from the soil. Their living standards were invariably low, though there were a few exceptions: such as the grazing area of the Dithmarschen in southern Jutland in the sixteenth century;[95] or the 'islands of peasant prosperity' in the Black Forest, in parts of Bavaria, Hesse and Thuringia;[96] or a little later the Dutch countryside in general, because of its proximity to the large urban markets; the west of the region round Le Mans;[97] a considerable area of England; and winegrowers almost everywhere – to give only a few examples. But if one were to draw a complete picture, the black areas would overshadow all the rest: they are the great majority.

We should not however exaggerate these very real hardships. The peasant survived, managed to pull through, and this was true everywhere. But it was usually thanks to plying a hundred extra trades:[98] crafts, the wine-making 'industry' as it should be termed, haulage. We are not surprised to find the peasants of Sweden or England also working as miners, quarrymen or iron workers; or the peasants of Skåne becoming sailors and carrying on an active coasting trade in the Baltic or the North Sea; or that all peasants spent at least some of their time weaving, or occasionally worked as carters. When, in the late sixteenth century, a latter-day wave of serfdom descended on Istria, many of the peasants escaped to become pedlars and carriers travelling to the Adriatic ports, and some set up an elementary iron-working industry with blast furnaces in country districts.[99] In the kingdom of Naples, we are told in a serious report by the *Sommaria*, 'there are many *bracciali* who do not live only by their work as day-labourers, but who every year sow six *tomola* [unit of land measurement] of wheat or barley ... grow vegetables and take them to market, cut and sell timber and use their animals to transport goods; then they have the gall to pay tax only as *bracciali*'.[100] A recent study has also shown that they were, in addition, both borrowers and lenders of money, small-time usurers and careful herdsmen.

Long-term stability does not mean absence of change

These examples in themselves show that Gorky was not altogether right. There were a thousand ways of being a peasant and a thousand ways of being poor. Lucien Febvre used to say, thinking of her different provinces, 'France spells variety.' But the whole world spells variety too. There was the nature of the soil, the climate, the crops, the 'drift' of history, the choices made long ago. There was also the question of land tenure and rank: peasants could be slaves, serfs, freeholders, share-croppers or tenants; they might have as their overlords the Church, the king, great noblemen, gentry of higher and lesser degree, or rich tenant-farmers: every distinction made a difference to their personal status.

Nobody would dispute this diversity over space. But within any given system, modern historians of peasant life tend to see a fairly unchanging pattern over time, one that is endlessly repeated. Elio Conti, the eminent historian of rural Tuscany, considers that the region can only be explained in terms of consistent observations going back over a millennium.[101] Another historian has said of the countryside round Paris that 'its rural structures hardly changed between the time of Philip the Fair and the eighteenth century'.[102] Continuity is the dominant feature. Werner Sombart long ago remarked that European agriculture did not change between Charlemagne and Napoleon: he was probably out to shock certain historians of his time: today hardly an eyebrow would be raised at the statement. Otto Brünner, the historian of rural society in Austria goes much further: 'From its formation in Neolithic times, right down to the nineteenth century,' he coolly remarks, 'the peasantry has constituted the foundation stone of the structure of European society and throughout all these millennia it has hardly been touched in substance by structural changes in the political forms of that society's upper layers.'[103]

We should not unthinkingly assume however that peasant history is one of total immobility. Yes, it is true that the landscape of this or that village has not changed since the days of Louis XIV; the aged cousins of one historian of the Forez 'are still today so similar, so close to the spirit of the writers of wills in the fourteenth century';[104] and the livestock of the region does not seem to have been 'very different in 1914 from the livestock of 1340'.[105] Houses, fields, animals, people, forms of speech and proverbs may indeed have remained the same. But how many things have been constantly changing over that time! In Mitschdorf, a little village in northern Alsace, spelt, an ancient cereal, was finally abandoned in about 1760–1770, in favour of wheat;[106] is that so negligible? The same village between 1705 and 1816 (probably in about 1765) went over from a triennial to a biennial rotation system,[107] and that was not negligible either. These were small changes, the reader might answer, but there were big ones too. Any long-standing situation crumbles sooner or later, though never all at once: cracks will appear gradually. A vital breach was opened when in the age of Blanche of Castile and Saint Louis, the peasantry around Paris, composed both of serfs (identifiable by the three burdens of poll-tax, the ban on outside marriages and mainmorte) and of free men, won its liberty from the nobles as manumissions and enfranchisements became frequent – since the free man living among serfs was always liable to be confused with them. Another serious crack appeared when the peasants combined in Orly, Sucy-en-Brie, Boissy and elsewhere to buy their freedom from seigniorial dues: the economic climate was in their favour and the movement was to become widespread.[108] It was equally significant that peasant enfranchisement should have travelled through some parts of Europe like an epidemic, affecting active regions most, but sometimes, through proximity, reaching less privileged areas. The kingdom of Naples was affected and even Calabria, which is most unlikely to have been a pioneering region in this respect; but the last fugitive peasants claimed in 1432 by the Count of Sinopoli were claimed in vain.[109] Peasant serfdom, and the attachment to the 'glebe' had disappeared. The old words (*adscripti, villani, censiles, redditici*) dropped out of the Calabrian vocabulary which now referred only to *vassalli*.[110] It was also significant that the liberated peasant of the Austrian mountains was able to sport a red cap as a sign of his enfranchisement.[111] Or that the *triage* – the dividing up of common lands between peasants and landlords – largely failed in France in the eighteenth century, whereas it had resulted in the enclosures in England. A significant development in the opposite direction occurred when the 'second serfdom' in Poland shackled once more a peasant who already had some direct experience of the town market or even of foreign merchants.[112] All these developments were important: each one might profoundly alter the situation of thousands of people.

It seems then that Marc Bloch[113] was right when he disagreed with Ferdinand Lot's description of the French peasantry as 'such a closely-cemented system that cracks in it were impossible'. There were indeed cracks, breaches, erosions and backward collapses. Such breaches were occasioned not only by landlord-peasant relations but also by the coexistence of town and countryside which by automatically developing a market economy, upset the rural balance.

The market was not the only factor. Towns often sent craftsmen into the countryside to escape the grip of the guilds within their walls – only to fetch them back when the situation demanded it. Peasants were always moving into the towns, drawn by the high wages. And noblemen built their town houses or palaces there. Italy, ahead of the rest of Europe, was the first country to witness this *inurbamento*. When they came to town, nobles brought with them their close-knit clan of rural dependants who in turn had an impact on the economy and the life of the city.[114] And the town was of course the home of the men of law who wrote letters for the illiterate – and who were often false friends, masters of chicanery, or usurers who made the peasant sign IOUs, who charged high interest and seized goods left as security. Even in the fourteenth century, the Lombard's *casana* was a trap for the unwary peasant borrower. He began by pledging his kitchen utensils, his wine-jars and his farm implements – and ended up signing away his livestock and land.[115] Usury reached fantastic rates as soon as there were economic difficulties. In November 1682, the *intendant* of Alsace denounced the intolerable usury of which the peasants were the victims: 'The townspeople have forced them to sign agreements of up to 30% interest'; some lenders even insisted that their land should stand security, with as interest 'half the crop yield . . . which comes in a year to as much as the principal of the loan' – in other words, money was being lent at 100%.[116]

In West Europe, the seigniorial regime was not dead

The seigniorial regime, deeply penetrating peasant life and intermingling with it, was both protective and oppressive. Traces of it can still be seen today throughout the whole West European landscape. I know two modest villages, between the Barrois and Champagne, which were both in the past part of the same small *seigneurie*. The château is still there, near one of the villages, probably looking much as it did after being restored and improved in the eighteenth century, with its park, its trees, its lakes and even a grotto. The landlord owned the mills (they no longer work but they are still standing) and the fishponds (which were still there quite recently). As for the peasants, they had their own gardens, hemp-patches, orchards, plots and fields, around the houses which huddled together in the village. In the very recent past, the fields were still divided into three *soles* (wheat, oats and fallow) which rotated every year. The lord himself had exclusive rights over the nearest woodland, on the hills, and over two *réserves*, one in each village. One of these blocks of land had bequeathed its name to a hamlet, *La Corvée* (the old name for compulsory labour); the other has now become a large farm of compact shape which looks odd alongside the tiny plots of the villagers. Only the further woods were available for the villagers to use. The whole gives an impression of a self-contained little world, with its artisan-peasants (blacksmith, cartwright, shoemaker, cooper, joiner) intent on producing all its needs, even its own wine. Over the horizon lie other villages, similarly clustering together; other manors which the villagers would hardly have known and which they would have mocked from a distance. Folklore is full of these ancient rivalries.

The picture needs filling out: who was the landlord? What dues, in money, kind or labour (*corvées*) were exacted? In the little example I have quoted, the

A château with gilded roof-tiles in the Burgundian style, dominating the village: la Rochepot, on the road up to Arnay-le-Duc in the Côte-d'Or. (Photo Rapho-Goursat.)

dues payable in 1789 were quite light and the *corvées* not many (two or three days a year in ploughing or carting); the only disputes of any consequence were over the use of the woods.

But things could vary from one place to another. One has to take several journeys: to Neubourg in Normandy with André Plaisse;[117] to Montesarchio in the kingdom of Naples with Gérard Delille;[118] to Gémeaux in Burgundy with Yvonne Bézard;[119] and we shall shortly be guided through Montaldeo by Giorgio

Doria. There is no substitute for the direct and precise picture one almost always finds in a village monograph, many of which are excellent.

But this will not entirely answer our questions. We have to ask, on a general level, why it was that the seigniorial regime, going back a thousand years or more, at least as far as the great estates of the Late Roman Empire, managed to survive until early modern times.

It was certainly not without its problems. The landlord was enmeshed in the toils of the feudal system from above – and these toils were not notional; they meant the payment of feudal rents which were not always trifling, and the taking of the feudal oath which sometimes led to disputes; there were also the 'casual offerings' and the feudal dues which had to be paid to the prince, and these could be heavy. Jean Meyer thinks that in the eighteenth century, nobles (though he is talking about the Breton nobility which was a special case) would have seen 10 to 15% of their income deducted annually.[120] Vauban was already saying in his time that 'if the question were properly investigated, one would find that gentlemen were no less encumbered with dues' than peasants, which is putting it rather strongly.[121]

As for the rents and dues the nobles could themselves collect from their peasants, these had an unfortunate tendency to be whittled away. Dues fixed in money terms in the thirteenth century had become derisory. *Corvées* in West Europe were usually bought back. The income from the lord's bread-oven was a mere few handfuls of the dough that the peasants brought in for baking once a week. Some payments in kind had become symbolic: the subdivisions of quit-rent meant that certain peasants owed a quarter, an eighth or a sixteenth of a capon![122] Seigniorial justice might be expeditious in minor cases, but it was hardly enough to bring in a living for the judges appointed by the landlord: in Gémeaux in Burgundy in about 1750, out of a total revenue of 8156 *livres*, fines and the administration of justice accounted for only 132 *livres*.[123] This trend was likely to be confirmed since the richer landowners, those who might have effectively defended their local rights, rarely lived on their estates any more.

Another factor working against the noble landowner was the growing luxury of modern life; he had to try to keep up appearances. Like the peasant, the landlord was putty in the hands of the bourgeois money-lender. The noble family of Saulx-Tavannes in Burgundy was able, thanks to the immense size of their estates, to weather bad times without suffering too much. But the prosperity of the latter part of the eighteenth century caused them unexpected problems. Their revenues were going up – but they were spending money like water and consequently heading for a fall: a quite common story.[124]

Even more effectively, political and economic crises wiped out great tracts of the feudal world. In the days of Charles VIII, Louis XII, François I or Henri II, it was still possible – just – to spend the summer campaigning in Italy with the king and to return to one's estates in winter. But after 1562, the Wars of Religion opened up a bottomless pit; and the economic recession of the 1590s brought the crisis to a head. In France, but in Spain and Italy too, many noble families, sometimes with the most gilded of escutcheons, tumbled through this yawning trapdoor. And to all this must be added the rages and discontents of the peasants; when a revolt had been put down, concessions often had to be made.

Riddled with weaknesses and surrounded by hostile forces, the institution nevertheless survived: for many reasons. Ruined noblemen gave way to other landlords, often rich bourgeois who nonetheless maintained the system intact. There were revolts and shows of force by the peasants, but there were just as many movements of reaction by the aristocracy – as in France on the eve of the Revolution. If the peasant was not so easily parted from his rights, neither was the landlord from his privileges – or rather if he lost some, he managed to keep or acquire others.

So the landlord was not at a total disadvantage. Before 1789 in France, the nobility probably controlled 20% of the landed property in the kingdom.[125] Taxes on *lods et ventes* (alienation) stayed high (up to 16 or 20% of the proceeds of sales at Neubourg in Normandy). The landlord did not simply live off his rents, he also owned outright a great deal of land: the nearby home farm, a large proportion of the best land, which he could either work directly himself or put under a farmer. He owned much of the forest land and '*haies*', uncultivated or marshy soil. In Neubourg, the barony derived 54% of its income, which was not small, from its woods.[126] As for the uncultivated areas, if parts of these were cleared, they might be conceded to peasants and would yield the *champart*, a kind of tithe. Last, but certainly not least, the landlord could put in a bid every time a holding came up for sale, since he had the right of pre-emption (the *retrait féodal*). If a peasant gave up his *censive* (tied holding) or if it fell vacant for some other reason, the lord of the manor could either rent it out to a tenant-farmer or sharecropper or let it out again under the feudal arrangement. He could even in certain circumstances impose the *retrait féodal*. He also had the right to levy a tax on the markets, fairs and tolls on his estate. When a census was taken in France, in the eighteenth century, of all the tolls in the country, with a view to buying them up to ease the passage of goods, the authorities realized that many of them were recent creations, having been arbitrarily set up by landowners.

Feudal law then left quite a lot of room for manœuvre. The lords of the Gâtine in Poitou in the sixteenth century[127] somehow managed, by rearranging various holdings, to establish a new series of share-cropper farms with planted hedges which changed the landscape. This was a decisive transformation. The feudal nobles of the kingdom of Naples, upon whom fortune always smiled, were equally successful in absorbing peasant holdings into their own home farms, the *scarze*.

In conclusion, although it is an essential feature of the time, one should not have too many illusions about the economic effects of peasant liberty. To be liberated from serfdom meant being able to sell one's holding and go where one pleased. But note that a preacher in Austria in 1676, talking of the advantages of the age, said 'God be praised, there are no more serfs here, and every man today *can* and *must* serve where he *will*.'[128] (The *must* reinforces the *can* and detracts rather from the *will*!) The peasant was free, but he still had to serve, to cultivate the land which was always controlled by a feudal overlord. He was free, but everywhere the state demanded taxes from him, the Church tithes, and the landlord feudal dues. The result is not hard to guess: in the Beauvaisis in the seventeenth century, peasant income was docked about 30 to 40% by these various levies,[129] and similar rates have been recorded elsewhere. The dominant society was everywhere alive to the possibility of mobilizing and increasing for its own benefit the mass of agricultural surpluses. To think that the peasant was unaware of this would be an illusion. The *Nu-pieds* (literally 'barefoot') rebels of Normandy (1639) denounced in their manifestos the tax-farmers, 'those people who have enriched themselves ... and wear velvets and satins at our expense', that 'pack of thieves who eat the bread out of our mouths'.[130] In 1788, according to their peasants, the canons of Saint-Maurice near Grenoble 'hold feasts and only think of fattening themselves like pigs to be killed at Easter'.[131] But what could the country people expect from a society in which, as the Neopolitan economist Galanti wrote, 'the peasant is a beast of burden who is left with just enough to be able to carry his load',[132] that is to survive, to reproduce and to continue doing his work? In a world living under constant threat of famine, the nobles had the easy part: along with their privileges, they were defending the security and equilibrium of a certain society. Double-edged as this could be, it was there to support them and back them up, assuming, with Richelieu that peasants were like 'mules, which being accustomed to carry burdens, are harmed more by a long rest than by working'.[133] There were plenty of reasons then why feudal society, though constantly battered, shaken or undermined, was nevertheless able to maintain itself in being, to reshape itself for centuries on end, and to put obstacles in the path of any new development that challenged it in the countryside.

Montaldeo

Let me open a parenthesis at this point and take the reader to a little village in Italy, whose story has been beautifully told by Giorgio Doria, a historian who has inherited the papers of the great Genoese family, and is a descendant of the one-time lord and master of Montaldeo.[134]

Montaldeo was a poor village (300-odd inhabitants and a little under 500 hectares of land), lying on the border between the Milanese and the territory of the republic of Genoa, between the Lombardy plains and the Apennines. The tiny area it occupied in the hills was a fief directly dependent on the emperor. In 1569, the Doria family bought it from the Grimaldis. Both Dorias and Grimaldis belonged to the business aristocracy of Genoa, families who were not averse to acquiring a few feudal titles while at the same time investing their capital safely and providing themselves with a refuge outside the gates of the city (a sensible precaution, since Genoese politics were violent). But they administered their estate like careful merchants, neither prodigally nor as entrepreneurs or innovators.

The reciprocal positions of the peasants and the landlord emerge in life-like detail from Giorgio Doria's book. The peasants were free to go where they pleased and marry whomever they liked – but how poor they were! The author's estimated *minimal* consumption for a family of four, of 9.5 quintals of cereals and chestnuts and 560 litres of wine a year, was reached or exceeded by only 8 households out of 54. All the others must have been living in conditions of chronic malnutrition. In their wattle and daub cabins, the families increased in size, even in bad times 'for these seemed to encourage procreation' but when a family was reduced to one hectare of poor soil, it had to seek its pittance elsewhere, by labouring on the landlord's fields, or on those of the three or four rich peasants who had acquired land locally; or the family could go down to the plain as hired hands at harvest time. Sometimes a nasty shock could await migrant workers: the harvester, who had to provide his own rations, could spend more on food than his employer paid him – as was the case in 1695, 1735 and 1756. Sometimes they reached the plain only to find that there was no work, and had to go further afield: in 1734, some workers even went to Corsica.

To these hardships were added the excesses of the feudal overlord and his agents, in particular the factor (*fattore*). There was not much the village community with its consuls (*consoli*) could do about these. Everyone had to pay his dues, discharge his lease, and accept that the master would buy up the harvest cheaply and sell at a profit, that the master also had the monopoly of money-lending at interest and of the proceeds of the administration of justice. Fines were constantly increasing: the trick was to impose a heavier penalty on minor offences, which were the most frequent. Compared to the fines charged in 1459, those of 1700, allowing for monetary devaluation, had multiplied twelve times for causing bodily harm; 73 times for insulting behaviour; 94 times for gambling (which was an offence); 157 for poaching; and 180 for grazing animals on someone else's land. Here seigniorial justice was obviously quite a profitable activity.

The little village followed the major developments of the economy with a certain time-lag. But it did experience some of the dispossessions and alienations of peasant property in the seventeenth century. Then came the progress of the age of enlightenment, which broke down the barriers separating the village from the outside world: trade now became the rule, favouring the transporters with their mule-trains. The glimmering of a village bourgeoisie began to appear; and with it a certain spirit of independence if not of open revolt. But if one of these poor devils stepped out of line, it was regarded as an act of indecency by the gentry from the height of their prerogatives. And if he dared to be insolent, there was outright scandal. In Montaldeo, a certain Bettoldo, a *huomo nuovo*, drew down upon himself the wrath of the marquis Giorgio Doria. He was one of the muleteers who had made a small fortune (this was in 1782) transporting the village's wine to Genoa; no doubt he was known for the violent behaviour often attributed to muleteers. 'The insolence of the said Bettoldo much worries me,' the marquis wrote to his factor, 'as does the facility with which he blasphemes ... He must be punished, since he is incorrigible ... In any case, he must be deprived of any employment from us; perhaps hunger will improve him.'

This was hardly likely, since blasphemy, insults and mockery were as much a need as a temptation. When a man was humiliated, what a relief it was to be able to mutter, even under one's breath, the Lombardy motto of the period: '*Pane di mostrue, acqua di fosso, lavora ti Patron, che io non posso*' ('Mouldy old bread, ditchwater to sup, do the work yourself boss, with me it's all up!'). A few years later it had become commonplace to say of Giorgio Doria, *E marchese del fatto suo e non di più* (He's a marquis when it suits him and no further). In counterpoint to such revolutionary sentiments, the priest of Montaldeo, who deplored the new age, wrote to the marquis in 1780: 'for some years imposture, vendetta, usury and fraud have been making great strides'. Similar remarks could be heard all over Italy at the time, even from a liberal economist like Genovesi. Appalled by the state of mind of the Neopolitan workers, he could envisage only one remedy in 1758: military discipline and the stick, '*bastonate, ma bastonate all'uso militare!*'[135] From then on things went from bad to worse in the kingdom of Naples where social disobedience was growing to near-epidemic proportions. Day-labourers on the land were insisting on being paid double the wages of previous years, whereas food prices had fallen, commented shocked landowners: they were prolonging their midday break to go to the *bettole* and lose their money drinking and gambling in these taverns.[136]

Overcoming the barriers

In certain circumstances, capitalism might overcome or circumvent the barriers put up by lord and peasant. The initiative for such structural changes sometimes came from within the seigniorial system, sometimes from without.

Examples of an impetus from within might be the capitalism which the *seigneur* himself practised, imitated or tried to invent; or a form of capitalism of peasant origin, based on the successes of rich tenant-farmers.

But the most significant initiatives came from outside. There was an uninterrupted flow of money from town to countryside – to be half-squandered if it was poured into purchases for the sake of social advancement or luxury. But sometimes such money altered and transformed everything, even if it did not immediately bring about a model form of capitalist farming. The magic touch was always the connection of agricultural production to the wider economy. It was to meet the demand of a profitable outside market that Genoese businessmen introduced sugar cane and the sugar mill (*trapeto*) to Sicily in the fifteenth century; that the merchants of Toulouse encouraged the growth of woad in industrial quantities in their region; and that the vineyards of Bordeaux and Burgundy were developed in the following century into larger properties, making solid fortunes for the presidents and counsellors of the *parlements* of Bordeaux and Dijon. The result was a division of tasks and roles, and the establishment of a capitalist chain of administration very clear to see in the case of Bordeaux:[137] the *régisseur* was in charge of the whole enterprise, the *homme d'affaires* managed the wine-growing sector, assisted by the *maître valet* who organized the ploughing and the *maître vigneron* who cared for the vines and saw to the wine-making, and who had workers with clearly-defined skills working under him. In Burgundy[138] the structures were less developed: the best vineyards and the choice wines of the Côte d'Or were still, in the seventeenth century, ecclesiastical property. But when the *parlement* of Dijon proposed an advantageous price, the holy fathers of Cîteaux were prepared to part with their Corton – one example among many. The new owners knew how to launch and market the products of their '*clos*'. They even came to live in person in these little villages that nestled halfway up the *côte* (the ridge of winegrowing slopes), with their narrow lanes, their tumbledown cottages, their primitive wine-cellars and, at the foot of their main street, a few stores and artisans' workshops. The new masters built themselves grand houses: little villages like Brochon or Gevrey could soon boast 36 (the former) or 47 (the latter). This was a kind of colonization, the direct supervision and guardianship of a type of product that was easy to sell and which was sure of a good profit.

From the margins to the heart of Europe

In the search for early agrarian capitalism, it would be easy to lose ourselves in hundreds of particular cases. Let us rather try to pick out a few significant examples. We shall always of course remain within the European experience, whether in Europe proper, on its eastern margins, or in its western outposts, in the extraordinary laboratory provided by European settlement in America. These different contexts will provide an opportunity to see how far capitalism was able to penetrate systems structurally very foreign to it, either by head-on assault, or by dominating production from a distance merely by controlling it at the bottleneck of distribution.

Capitalism and the 'second serfdom'

This heading does not arise from a taste for paradox. The 'second serfdom' was the fate in store for the peasantries of East Europe who were still free in the fifteenth century but saw their lot altered in the sixteenth. After this, huge areas moved back into the age of serfdom: from the Baltic to the Black Sea, the Balkans, the kingdom of Naples, and Sicily, and from Muscovy (a very special

The Beaujolais vineyards (near Belleville-sur-Saône) photographed by Henri Cartier-Bresson.
(Photo Cartier–Bresson–Magnum.)

case) by way of Poland and Central Europe as far as a line running approximately from Hamburg to Vienna and Venice.

What role did capitalism play in these areas? None at all, apparently, since it is usual in this case to speak of 'refeudalization', as both regime and system. And Witold Kula's admirable study, which analyses step by step what the 'economic calculations' of the serf-peasants and their masters might have been in Poland between the sixteenth and the eighteenth centuries, spells out why the landlords were not 'real' capitalists and would not be before the nineteenth century.[139]

An economic conjuncture with multiple effects was pushing East Europe back, in the early sixteenth century, towards a *colonial* destiny as a producer of raw materials, a development of which the second serfdom was only the most visible sign. Everywhere, though with variations according to time and place, the peasant was being ever more firmly attached to the land; he was losing his mobility, both in theory and in practice, losing his right to marry whom he pleased, and losing his right to free himself, by cash payment, from dues fixed in kind or compulsory labour. The latter in particular was becoming a crushing burden. In Poland,[140] in about 1500, compulsory labour was insignificant; the statutes of 1519 and 1520 fixed it at one day a week, that is 52 days a year; in 1550 or so, it was increased to three days a week and in 1600 to six days. The same thing was happening in Hungary: one day a week in 1514, then two, three days, presently one week in two, and finally all regulations were suspended and compulsory labour was to be determined entirely by the good will and pleasure of the lord.[141] In Transylvania, it was four days a week; the peasants had two days a week, apart from Sundays, to call their own. But in 1589-1590, in Livonia,[142] '*jeder gesinde [arbeitet] mitt Ochsen oder Pferd alle Dage*', every liable peasant worked with a team of oxen or horses *every day*. Two hundred years later (1798) in Lower Silesia, it was officially reported that 'compulsory labour by the peasants is unlimited'.[143] In Saxony, there was a form of conscription for young men, who had to work for two or three years in the service of the lord.[144] In Russia, it was the indebtedness of the peasantry which made it possible for the nobles to draw up contracts for their tenants pinning them down to one estate, in a sort of 'voluntary enserfment' as it has been described, which was later legalized.[145]

In short, although it might be organized differently or mitigated here and there, the rule of six days a week unpaid labour was tending to become established everywhere without exception. Perhaps one should set aside the peasants on princely estates or on the narrow territories surrounding the cities. Perhaps too there was a less oppressive regime in Bohemia or East Prussia. In fact it is impossible to find statistics and therefore to draw up any maps of the question, as this labour was invariably adapted to features of the local society and to peasant work-habits. Ploughing teams were provided by the peasants who had the most land and who therefore maintained extra draft animals with a son or

Grain arriving at Gdansk down the Vistula, heaped up in boats or even light skiffs, sometimes on rafts made of tree-trunks. Bottom left, the prow of a boat and the hauliers on the towpath. (Photo Henryk Romanowski.)

a farmhand detailed to look after them. But serving with a team, *Spanndienste* or *Spannwerke* as it was called in Germany, did not dispense one from manual labour, *Handwerke*, and since in all feudal villages there were some smallholders and some landless labourers, there was a whole series of different systems and rotas. And this unpaid labour covered everything: domestic chores, tasks in the stables, barns or cowsheds, ploughing, haymaking, harvesting, haulage, navvying, woodcutting. It amounted to a huge-scale mobilization, which came to seem quite natural, of the entire rural labour force. An extra turn of the screw was always possible: one merely had to change the rota, keep a ploughing team on longer, increase the burdens to be transported, lengthen the journeys to be travelled – and, if need be, use threats.

There were both internal and external reasons for this general increase in compulsory labour in the countries of East Europe. From outside there was the massive demand of West Europe which needed food and raw materials. Hence the strong pull exerted on exportable products. As for internal reasons, in the constant tug-of-war between state, cities and nobles, the latter were almost always the dominant group (except in Russia). The decline of the cities and the urban markets and the weakness of the state corresponded to the takeover of the labour force (and also of the best land) which formed the drive behind the success of the feudal lords. Compulsory labour was an enormous machine harnessed to serve what German historians call *Gutsherrschaft* (estate-ownership) as opposd to *Grundherrschaft* (landlordship), traditional feudalism. In eighteenth-century Silesia, statistics for a single year show that 373,621 compulsory days were worked with teams of two horses, 495,127 with oxen. Corresponding figures for Moravia are respectively 4,282,000 and 1,409,114.[146]

This oppressive regime was not established overnight: it came gradually, through custom, and there were some violent episodes. In Hungary, it was immediately after the defeat of the Dosza uprising (1514)[147] that the Werbocz Code proclaimed the *perpetua rusticitas*, that is the perpetual serfdom of the peasant. It was proclaimed once more, a century later, in the State Assembly of 1608, after the revolt of the Haiduks, peasants who had taken flight and lived by marauding and pillaging the Turks.

The peasant's weapon against a repressive master was indeed flight. How did one catch the man who crept away at nightfall, taking his wife and children, with the family belongings piled up on a cart and their cows following behind? A few turns of the wheels and he would be receiving help along the road from his brothers in misery before eventually finding a welcome either on another estate or among the ranks of the outlaws. In Lausitz after the Thirty Years' War, there were many angry complaints by deserted landlords to the Landtag.[148] At the very least, they demanded, those who shelter and help the fugitives should be punished; any recaptured runaway should have his ears or nose cut off, or be branded on the forehead. Will the elector of Saxony in Dresden not give out a *Reskript*? But the number of such *Reskripte* or edicts, forbidding the free movement of serfs (in Moravia in 1638, 1658, 1687, 1699, 1712; and in Silesia in 1699, 1709, 1714, and 1720) proves how powerless legislation was in this respect.

On the other hand, the landlords had succeeded in integrating the peasantry into closed economic units, sometimes very large ones: one thinks of the Czerny family in Bohemia, the Radziwills or Czartoriskis in Poland, of the magnates of Hungary who traded in wine and livestock. These economic units were self-contained. The peasant had virtually no access any longer to the urban markets which were in any case much reduced. When he did come to town, it was only for small-scale transactions, to get together the little money he needed to pay certain dues, or to drink a glass or beer or spirits in the local inn – which was also the property of his overlord.

But in the end these economic units cannot be called autarkic, since they were open to the rest of the world at the top end. The noble, who owned serfs and land like his forefathers, now produced grain, wood, livestock, wine, and later on saffron and tobacco, to meet the demands of a distant customer. A regular river of grain from these noble estates flowed down the Vistula to Gdansk. From Hungary, the chief exports were wine and livestock on the hoof; from the Danube provinces, grain and sheep to satisfy the insatiable appetite of Istanbul. Throughout the zone of the second serfdom, the manorial economy dominated everything, including the towns which it had subjugated – a strange form of rural revenge.

In addition, it was often the case that noblemen's estates had their own home villages, which served as a base for industrial enterprises: brickworks, alcohol distilleries, breweries, mills, potteries and blast furnaces (in Silesia for instance). Such manufacture used compulsory labour and very often paid nothing for its raw materials either, so these could not properly be entered into a strict balance-sheet. During the latter half of the seventeenth century in Austria, the nobles participated in the establishment of textile manufacture. They were remarkably active and alive to the possibilities available to them; they relentlessly pursued the *Arrondierung* ('rounding-off') of their domains, usurped forest land or the jurisdiction of the prince, introduced new crops like tobacco, and subjugated any small towns within reach, taking advantage of any tolls established there.[149]

But to return to our original question, what, among all the many aspects of the second serfdom, had anything to do with capitalism? Nothing at all, replies Witold Kula in his book, and his arguments are undoubtedly relevant. If one takes the traditional image of the capitalist, the identikit portrait – rationalization, calculation, investment, profit maximization – the Hungarian magnate and the Polish noblemen are certainly not capitalists. Everything was too easy for them, from the money they received to the natural economy which they trod underfoot. They had no need to calculate because the machine worked on its own. They did not strive to reduce the costs of production, they took little interest in improving or even in maintaining the productivity of the soil although it constituted their capital, they shrank from any real investment, and as far as possible they were content to employ serfs, an unpaid labour force. Whatever the state of the harvest, it was all profit to them; they sold it in Danzig exchanging it automatically for manufactured products from the West, usually luxuries. By about 1820 however[150] (though I cannot pinpoint the exact nature of the change) the situation had completely altered: a fair number of proprietors now considered their land as capital which it was vital to preserve and improve whatever the cost; they were getting rid as fast as possible of their serfs who represented too many mouths to feed in return for little effective work: they preferred wage-labourers. Their 'economic calculation' was no longer the same: rather late in the day they were now observing the rules of a kind of management that anxiously compared investment, cost price and net profit. This contrast is in itself a powerful argument for classifying the Polish noblemen of the eighteenth century as feudal landowners rather than as entrepreneurs.

I would not of course wish to contest this argument. But it does seem to me that the second serfdom was the counterpart of a merchant capitalism which discovered in the structures of Eastern Europe certain advantages and even in some cases its *raison d'être*. The great landowner was not a capitalist, but he was a tool and a collaborator in the service of capitalism in Amsterdam and else-where. *He was part of the system.* The mightiest landowner in Poland received advance payments from the merchant of Gdansk and through him from the Dutch merchant. In a sense he was in precisely the same position as the sheep-breeder of Segovia in the sixteenth century, who sold the fleeces of his flocks to the merchants of Genoa long before shearing time; or the cereal-growers, needy or otherwise, who were always looking for advance payment and who in all periods and throughout Europe, sold their standing grain to merchants of every kind, great and small, to whom such deals promised illicit profits and a way of escaping the rules and prices of the market. Should we not rather say then, that our Polish noblemen were among the victims, rather than actors and participants, of a form of capitalism which operated at long distance, via intermediaries, and which maintained at its beck and call any and everything that could be mobilized by sea passages, inland waterways and the limited possibilities of overland traffic?

Yes and no. There was a difference between the sheep-breeder in Segovia or the cereal-grower, who were both under a usurer's thumb, when all was said and done, and the Polish lord, who might be at a disadvantage on the market place of Gdansk but who ruled the roost *at home*. He used his undisputed power to organize production in such a way as to meet capitalist demand – which only interested him in so far as it balanced his own demand for luxury goods. A letter sent to the Queen Regent of the Netherlands in 1534 says: 'All the great lords and masters of Poland and Prussia discovered about twenty-five years ago how to send their grain down certain rivers to Danzwick [sic] and there to sell them to the townspeople of that city. And for this reason, the kingdom of Poland and the great nobles have become very rich.'[151] If we were to take this letter literally, we might imagine these people as gentlemen-farmers, entrepreneurs à la Schumpeter. Not at all: it was the western entrepreneur who had first come knocking at their door. But it was the Polish noble who had the power – as he amply demonstrated – to set all the peasants and a good number of the towns to work for him, to dominate agriculture and even manufacture, virtually the whole of production in other words. When he mobilized all this power in the service of foreign capitalism, he was himself becoming an active participant in the system. If it had not been for him, there would have been no second serfdom; and without serfdom, the volume of *exportable* cereals produced would have been infinitely smaller. The peasants would have preferred to eat their own grain, or to exchange it on the marketplace for other goods, if the nobleman had not taken over all the *means of production* and if, by the same token, he had not nipped in the bud an already lively market economy, thus keeping for himself all the *means of exchange* as well. This was not a feudal system since, far from being a self-sufficient economy, this was a system in which as Kula himself says, the noble was seeking, by every traditional means, a way of increasing the quantity of grain for marketing. Nor was it, by any means, a modern capitalist agriculture on the English model. This was a monopoly economy: there was monopoly of production, monopoly of distribution, and all in the service of an international system itself thoroughly and indisputably capitalist.[152]

Capitalism and the American plantations

Europe had a fresh start in America: an immense opportunity. Here she could make a new beginning superimposing her own diversity on the diversity of the new continent.

The results yielded a whole crop of experiences. In French Canada, a seigniorial regime instituted from above failed from the start. Of the English colonies, the north was a free country like England – and the distant future lay with these states. But the south was slave-owning: all the plantations worked with slave labour, particularly the sugar plantations in the Caribbean and along the endless coastline of Brazil. Seigniorial regimes flourished spontaneously in grazing regions like Venezuela and the Brazilian interior. Feudal regimes collapsed throughout Spanish America with its large indigenous population. Indian peasants were indeed ceded to Spanish nobles but the *encomiendas*, granted only for life, were actually *benefices* rather than *fiefs*; the Spanish government did not wish to transform the restive world of the *encomenderos* into a feudal system; it always kept them firmly in hand.

Of these experiences, it is the plantations alone that will concern us here. More straightforwardly than the regions of second serfdom, these were capitalist creations *par excellence*: money, credit, trade and exchange tied them to the east side of the Atlantic. Everything was remote-controlled from Seville, Cadiz, Bordeaux, Nantes, Rouen, Amsterdam, Bristol and Liverpool.

To create the plantations, everything had to be brought over from the old continent: the masters – white settlers; the labour force – black Africans (since the Indians of the coastal regions did not long survive the shock of the conquest); the plants themselves, except for tobacco. Along with the sugar cane, the techniques of sugar production had to be imported: these had already been introduced by the Portuguese to Madeira and the far-flung islands in the Gulf of Guinea, Principe and São Tomé; these island experiments were thus prototypes for America and Brazil. When in 1555, French sailors encountered sugar cane in Rio Bay (where they had been sent by Admiral Coligny's dreams of glory) their ignorance of it is very revealing: they steeped it in water to make a kind of vinegar.[153]

It was on the coast of the Brazilian Nordeste, and further south on the island of São Vicente, that the first American sugar-plantations were set up, in about 1550, with their sugar-mills or 'engines', the *enghenos de assucar*. The first sugar-growing landscapes were all the same: the waterlogged shallows, the boats carrying cane along the coastal rivers, and the *carros de boi* with their creaking axles, rolling along the cart-track. Then came the eternal trinity – still to be seen standing in quite recent times in Recife or São Salvador (Bahia): the master's house (the *casa grande*); the slaves' cabins (the *senzalas*) and the sugar mill. The master would patrol on horseback; he reigned over his family – an abnormally large family because of a freedom of morals uninhibited by the colour of his slaves' skin – distributing to his people a summary justice from which there was no appeal: the modern equivalent of Sparta or Rome under the Tarquins.[154]

Since detailed accounts have survived, we are able to say straight away that the Brazilian *engheno de assucar* was not in itself a very good investment. A fairly realistic estimate of the profits was about 4 or 5%.[155] And things could always go wrong. In this archaic institution, only the *senhor de engheno* had anything to do with the market economy: he had bought his slaves, he had borrowed money to build his mill, he sold his own crop and sometimes the crop of the small-scale *enghenos* living in his shadow. But he was himself dependent on the merchants in down-town São Salvador or in Recife, lying at the foot of the seigniorial town of Olinda. Through them, he was connected to the export merchants of Lisbon who advanced money and goods, as those of Bordeaux and Nantes were to do to the planters in St Domingue (Haiti), Martinique and Guadeloupe. It was European trade that commanded production and output overseas.

Cane-growing and the sugar industry had probably been introduced to the West Indies by the Portuguese *marranos* when they were expelled from the Brazilian Nordeste after the Dutch left in 1654.[156] But it was not until 1680 that sugar spread into the western half of the island of St Domingue which had been

A plantation in Pernambuco province: dwelling-house and sugar mill (note the hydraulic mill and grind-stones, cartload of cane, boilers). In the background the *casa grande* and in the distance the *senzalas*. Cartouche from map drawn by C. Barlaeus, *Rerum per octennium in Brasilia et alibi gestarum ... historia*, Amsterdam, 1647. (Photo B.N.)

French since the middle of the century (though this was only ratified legally by the peace of Ryswick in 1697).

Gabriel Debien[157] has described in detail one of the plantations on the island, certainly not one of the best, lying between Léogane in the west and Port-au-Prince in the east, some distance from the sea which was visible from the little hill where the principal buildings stood. Nicolas Galbaut du Fort had come into possession of this run-down sugar plantation in 1735. Arriving on the spot to get it going again, he restored the buildings, relocated the mills and the boilers, increased the establishment of black slaves and planted fresh patches of cane. A rather imprecise plan drawn in 1753, reproduced in Figure 18, will give the reader some idea of what the plantation was like, though the boundaries are not very clear, the relief is hardly visible and the scale is inaccurate. Water was provided by a stream, the Court-Bouillon, which could sometimes be dangerous, but which dried up almost completely during droughts. The master's house was not a *casa grande*: three rooms, whitewashed brick walls, an entrance made of canes and a huge kitchen. Nearby was the storehouse. A little further off were the cabin of the steward, overseer and accountant, whose pen and figures were indispensable for the running of the whole estate, the garden, the sugar-mill, the flour-mills, the forge and the *guildiverie* (distillery).[158] This plantation had not been 'set up in white', that is it produced only raw sugar not refined white sugar – but it distilled scums and syrups in the *guildiverie*; the *tafia* manufactured here was sold on the spot: it brought in quicker returns than exporting it to France.

The plan also shows the shed for the *cabrouets* (carts used for transporting the cut cane), the bell that called the slaves to prayer or more frequently to work, the cookhouse, the hospital, the cabins of the slaves (about a hundred), the square plots a little over a hectare in size planted with sugar cane; and the areas set aside for food plants (potatoes, bananas, rice, millet, manioc, yams), crops which were sometimes left to the slaves who sold some of the produce to the plantation. In the savannahs around the hillocks – to be used eventually perhaps for further sugar-planting – oxen, mules and horses grazed as best they could.

During his second visit to Léogane (1762–1767) when he came to rescue the plantation once more from decline, Nicolas du Fort tried to introduce some novelties: better forage for the animals, intensive cultivation with much more manuring than usual – a recipe that was in any case debatable. But the opposite course would have been equally open to criticism: expanding the plantation which would inevitably have meant finding more slaves. And slaves were expensive. Moreover, when the planter put in his place a manager or '*procureur*' who automatically received a percentage of the crop, these men would seek to increase output without worrying about costs: they grew rich while the owner was ruined.

The planter, whether his 'habitation' was in sugar, coffee, indigo, or cotton, was not usually a rich man. It is true that colonial products sold at high prices in Europe. But there was only one harvest a year; it took time to market it and recover the price – whereas expenses had to be paid every day and could be very heavy. Whatever the planter bought for his personal use or for his estate came by sea; its cost was increased by the price of transport and above all by the profits fixed by merchants and retailers to their own advantage. Since the '*Exclusif*' forbade any of the islands to trade with foreign powers, they were delivered hand and foot to the metropolitan monopoly. The settlers readily resorted to contraband, which meant cheap deliveries and advantageous exchanges in kind. But smuggling was neither easy nor adequate. In 1727, a French squadron arrived unexpectedly to combat it. 'The inhabitants are greatly mortified [at this]' wrote a merchant from Martinique; 'on the other hand it pleases the importers, since it could be said that their interests are totally incompatible.'[159] How in any case could the islanders escape the stratagems of the shipowners? The latter knew (indeed Savary spelt it out for them) in which month they should arrive to find sugar cheap, or when the tropical heat would probably have turned the wine so that if one turned up with a boatload of casks, 'it would be possible to sell them for any amount of money'.[160] And prices simply rose of their own accord with the expansion of the eighteenth century. Goods were unbelievably expensive in the islands at this period: food, household goods, the copper vats for boiling the sugar, Bordeaux wines, textiles and last but not least slaves. 'I am spending nothing', writes Nicolas du Fort in 1763. And the next year, 'my supper consists of a little bread with preserves'.[161] The situation went from bad to worse. On 13 May 1782 a young settler writes: 'Since the war [i.e. the American War of Independence] our shoemakers charge for one pair of

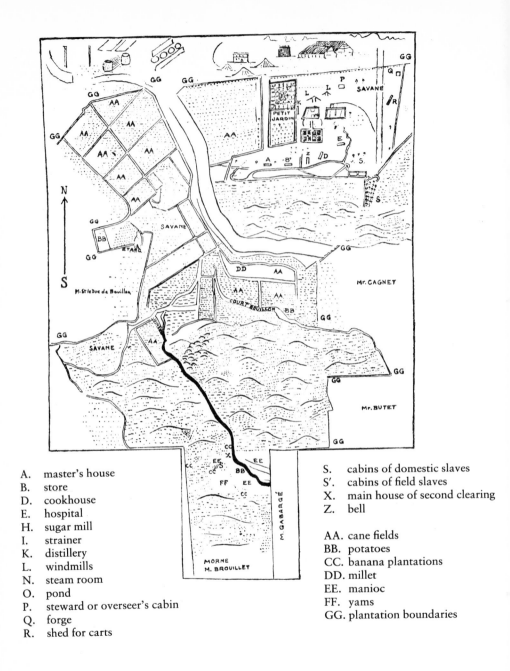

A. master's house
B. store
D. cookhouse
E. hospital
H. sugar mill
I. strainer
K. distillery
L. windmills
N. steam room
O. pond
P. steward or overseer's cabin
Q. forge
R. shed for carts

S. cabins of domestic slaves
S'. cabins of field slaves
X. main house of second clearing
Z. bell

AA. cane fields
BB. potatoes
CC. banana plantations
DD. millet
EE. manioc
FF. yams
GG. plantation boundaries

18   A SUGAR PLANTATION IN THE FRENCH COLONY OF SAINT-DOMINGUE
(HAITI)

The plan of the Galbaud du Fort plantation is not very clear. It has to be examined with a
magnifying glass and patience to discover the details referred to in the key and which are also
discussed in the text on pp. 274–5. But it is worth making the effort.

shoes 3 [piastres] *gourdes* which comes to 24 *livres* 15 *sols*, and I need a new pair every month ... hose of the coarsest weave are sold at 9 l. a pair. Coarse canvas for working smocks costs 6 l. That is 12 l. 10 *sols* made up. A passable and by no means magnificent hat costs 16 l. 10 *sols* ... Tailors charge 60 l. for making a coat, 15 for a jacket and the same again for the breeches. As for food ... we have paid up to ... 330 l. for a keg of flour, 600 or 700 l. for a keg of wine, 150 l. for a barrel of beef, 75 l. for ham, and 4 l. 10 *sols* for a pound of candles.'[162] This was in wartime of course, but then war and privateering were not uncommon occurrences in American waters.

When trying to market his products, the planter suffered if he sold locally from seasonal fluctuations which might make prices fall 12, 15 or 18% at times when sugar was being made in abundance. If he entrusted sales to a commission agent in France, he might have to wait months or even years to be paid because of the slow pace of communications. As for the price he could expect, the market in colonial commodities in European ports like Bordeaux was one of the most speculative in existence. The merchants were in the habit of bidding up and down, and for a stockist this was a good excuse for saying that the goods must wait in the warehouse until the price improved. Hence the long delays which often meant that the planter ran out of money and was obliged to borrow. If in addition he had indebted himself at the start to buy all or part of his plantation and his slaves, thinking he was going to make his fortune, he would soon be at the mercy of his creditors.

The wholesalers, commissioners and shippers of Bordeaux, who obliged the islanders to use the services of their boats, their captains (who often had instructions to sell cargoes for them) their warehouses and their life-saving advance payments, were thus the masters of the machine that turned out the riches of the colonies. Whenever we can follow the day-to-day correspondence of a settler, he says so in so many words. The Raby and Dolle families, who were partners notably in farming the huge plantation of Vazes in one of the best regions of St Domingue, were thus obliged to deliver themselves hand and foot in 1787 to the big firm of Frederick Romberg and Sons of Brussels, whose Bordeaux branch was (wrongly) considered the cornerstone of the entire commercial life of the port.[163]

Now all this hardly seems to correspond to the overall statistics for colonial trade. In Bordeaux, where half of all French trade with the colonies was carried on, exports only amounted to a third, later a quarter, later still back to a third, of the imports to Bordeaux of products from St Domingue, Guadeloupe and Martinique.[164] And there is a similar imbalance in the figures for Marseilles.[165] Is there not a contradiction somewhere? If the balance of trade really benefited the islands as much as this, they should have been rolling in money. And cash would have had to be exported from France in compensation. And yet St Domingue, to take only one example, was constantly drained of her piastres: they were smuggled in from nearby Spanish America and did no more than pass through the island. The extraordinary truth was that they went straight to Bordeaux – in huge quantities after 1783.[166] Is this apparent paradox not explained by the fact that the trade balance was calculated in the French ports in local prices? If the same calculation had been made in the islands, the volume of French products being sold there would have represented a much greater sum of money than it did in Bordeaux, whereas colonial exports were worth less before being shipped to France, where transport costs, commissions etc. were added on to the purchasing price. So the distance between the two figures could be reduced by these considerations. One should also mention the artificial difference in the moneys of account: the colonial *livre* was depreciated by 33% by comparison with the French mainland *livre*. And lastly the dispatch of money by settlers to their families who had remained in France, as well as to absentee landlords, also affected the balance of payments. However the most important heading from this point of view was still of course a financial one, the repayment of interest and of loans.

In short, the planters were caught up in a system of exchange which barred them from making any large-scale profits. Already in the fifteenth century, the Sicilian sugar-works, in spite or because of the intervention of Genoese capitalism, were money-losing ventures oddly enough, according to Carmelo Trassi. One can feel some pity in retrospect for the castles in the air built by so many purchasers of sugar plantations, who were sometimes well-off merchants. 'Well, I have emptied my purse my dear friend', writes Marc Dolle, a Grenoble merchant, to his brother, 'to send you this sum of money and I have no more spare funds ... I am sure that by advancing you your share in the purchase of a huge plantation, I shall have made your fortune and increased my own' (10 February 1785).[167] Disillusion followed. It was not as planters but as merchants – small shopkeepers at first, later importers and exporters – that the Pellet brothers made their fortune from their beginnings in Martinique. They had chosen the right side of the fence, returning to Bordeaux and its dominant position in good time, whereas the money-lenders of Amsterdam who had thought they could not lose by advancing money to Dutch or English planters in the West Indies, just as they would have done to merchants at home, woke up one morning to the disagreeable surprise of finding themselves proprietors of plantations that had been named as security.[168]

The plantations in Jamaica

The case of English Jamaica matches what we know about St Domingue. Here too would be the *casa grande* or master's house, the black slaves (nine or ten to every white man), the omnipresent sugar canes, exploitation by merchants and sea-captains, a colonial pound with a lower value than the pound sterling (£1 sterling equalled £1.4 Jamaican), piracy and pillage of which on this occasion the English were the victims since the aggressors were French (though nobody could ever be said to have the last word in the Caribbean). Here too were the difficulties and dangers of runaway slaves, the 'maroons' who fled to the mountains of the island, sometimes from neighbouring coasts or islands. The general situation was most critical during the 'Maroon War' of 1730 to 1739.[169]

Jamaica was a large island, vast by the standards of the time, and very big estates were developed there, especially after the years 1740–1760, which saw the beginnings of the expansion of the island's sugar economy.[170] As happened in the French islands, the families of the early settlers, who often worked with their own hands on small plantations of tobacco, cotton or indigo, began to be eclipsed. Sugar cane required large-scale investment. It meant the coming of owners of capital and large properties. From the statistics, one has the impression of larger-scale property, with more slaves, richer too perhaps than St Domingue. It was however a fact that this island, which was supplied with salt meat and flour from England and the English colonies in America, and which had to provide a good half of England's sugar supply, did so at higher prices than were charged by St Domingue and the other French possessions.

In any case, Jamaica, like the other sugar islands, was a wealth-creating machine, a capitalist machine serving the rich.[171] The same causes produced the same effects and the pattern was much the same as in St Domingue, that is most of the wealth produced in the colony went to swell the coffers of rich men in the home country. The planters made a profit of 8 to 10% at the very most.[172] The 'whole of the import and export trade' (not to mention the profits of the slave trade which was organized exclusively from England) 'revolves and circulates in this kingdom ... and is, so far as it regards our profit, in the nature of a home trade, as much as if, the several countries of America and Ireland were all pieced on to Cornwall,' words written by Burke,[173] who argued the usefulness of the West Indies to the English economy and who vigorously pointed out how deceptive the trade balance figures were in practice.

In fact the balance of *trade* for Jamaica, even calculated in colonial pounds, works out at a slight advantage for the island (£1,336,000 to £1,335,000) but at least half of the total for imports and exports made its way invisibly back to England (in freight charges, insurance, commissions, interest on debts, and transfers of money to absentee landlords). All in all, the net benefit for England in the year 1773 was getting on for £1,500,000. In London as in Bordeaux, the proceeds of colonial trade were transformed into trading-houses, banks and state bonds. They made the fortunes of certain powerful families whose most active representatives were to be found in the House of Lords as well as in the Commons. There were however a few, very rich settler families, but it so happened that these were never exclusively planters: they played bankers to other planters in debt; they had family connections with London merchants, when it was not one of their own sons who went there himself to handle the marketing of the plantation's crop, to make purchases and act as commission agent for other Jamaican settlers. Such families were in fact combining the

English traders in the West Indies, packing up their goods. Vignette from map of the West Indies in Herman Moll's *Atlas royal*, 1700. (Photothèque Armandèque Colin.)

profits of sugar production, of the import and export trade, selling on commission and banking. So it is not surprising if, having settled in London, either managing their plantations from a distance or selling them, they were able to invest very largely in England not only in the commodity trade but also in advanced agriculture or in various infant industries.[174] Like the Pellet brothers, these planters had realized that one had to be back in the Old Country to make money out of the colonies!

Wherever one turns for examples – tobacco in Virginia, livestock in Cuba, or the cocoa plantations of Venezuela with the creation in 1728 of the Caracas Company[175] – one finds the same mechanisms everywhere at work. If we want to escape from this monotonous pattern, we must turn to places far from the interested vigilance of European merchants, where wild American settlements grew up on their own, each with its own adventurous history: in Brazil, around São Paulo, the starting point for the *bandeiras*, expeditions to the interior in search of gold or slaves; in the hinterland of Bahia, along the São Francisco valley, *o rio dos currais*, the river of corrals, into which huge herds of cattle were driven; in the Argentinian pampas, in the early days of its 'European' period; or in southern Venezuela, in the *llanos* of the Orinoco basin where the *señores* of Spanish origin, the huge flocks of sheep and the horseback shepherds (Indians and half-breeds) created an old fashioned seigniorial society with powerful ruling families. This was an ancient not to say primitive kind of 'capitalism' (where livestock equalled money) the kind of thing to delight Max Weber, who did indeed briefly take an interest in it.

Back to the heart of Europe

What I call 'the heart of Europe' is in fact the western extremity of the continent, west of the line from Hamburg to Venice. This favoured part of Europe was too available for exploitation by cities, bourgeoisies, rich merchants or enterprising nobles, for capitalism not to have been introduced in a hundred ways to the activities and structures of the very old rural areas of the west.

Would it help for the sake of clarity to proceed as in mathematics and assume the answer to the problem? In the Europe of lord and peasant, capitalism appeared as a new order, not winning every battle, far from it, but winning in certain specified areas. Let us start with those areas where the experiment was successful, since the problem whose solution we are after was solved here.

England is the first place that springs to mind. I shall not spend long on it here though, since I shall be returning to it at greater length later. Reduced to its main features, the English model will serve at this point only as a reference grid on which to locate certain other specific cases. The English revolution did not of course extend to the whole of Great Britain, which contained backward areas far away from the major currents of trade, some of them very archaic indeed, even in 1779 and even in counties as developed as Essex and Suffolk.[176]

So let us take as an example a region where innovation incontestably won the day, Norfolk in East Anglia. In the article *'culture'* (i.e. agriculture) in the *Encyclopédie*, Véron de Forbonnais[177] describes – precisely in a Norfolk setting – the marvels of an agricultural economy which he proposed as a model. The features that most caught his eye were: liming and marling the land, 'paring' – that is taking off the topsoil by slow burning – the introduction of forage crops, extension of artificial meadows (i.e. in rotation), the development of drainage systems, intensive manuring of the fields, more attention to selective breeding, the development of enclosures and consequently the enlargement of estates, and the planting of hedges all round the fields to give the typical patchwork pattern of the English countryside. Other features to consider were: plentiful farming implements of good quality, the benevolence of the landed gentry, the longstanding presence of large tenant-farms, the early establishment of capitalist management methods, credit facilities, and a sympathetic government, less concerned with the supervision and regulation of markets than with yields and the towns' food supply, one which had introduced a sliding scale to encourage and subsidize the export of cereals.

In this development, the criteria which carried most consequences were:

1 the disappearance from the most advanced areas of the English countryside of a feudal system which had begun to fade quite early, as Marx emphatically noted:

> Under the Stuart Restoration [he wrote], landed proprietors ... abolished the feudal constitution of the land, that is they released it from the burdens previously imposed on it, compensating the State with taxes to be levied on the peasants and the rest of the people, claiming as private property in the modern sense, what had previously been their feudal possessions.[178] In other words, traditional life was being swept away.

2 the leasing of rural property to capitalist tenant-farmers who assumed responsibility for it themselves;

3 the employment of wage-earning labourers who were forming a proletariat: they had nothing to sell their employers but their labour power;

4 the vertical division of labour: the landowner leased out the land and received his rent; the tenant acted as entrepreneur; and the wage-labourer brought up the rear.

If we bear these criteria in mind, we shall discover, in the history of Europe, examples more or less close to the English model – proving incidentally that the agricultural revolution was a European phenomenon, just as much as the industrial revolution which accompanied it.

The order in which I have taken these examples: seventeenth-century Brie, eighteenth-century Venetia, the Roman Campagna in the early nineteenth century and Tuscany in the fifteenth and sixteenth century, has no particular significance. Nor do I intend to study these different cases for their intrinsic interest or to attempt to draw up an exhaustive list of European examples. I am here concerned simply to outline an argument.

The outskirts of Paris: Brie in the days of Louis XIV

In the country around Paris, property owned by town-dwellers had for centuries been encroaching on land owned by noble or peasant.[179] To possess a country house, and thus to have a source of regular supplies of grain, of wood for the winter, of poultry or fruit, and not to have to pay the toll on entering the city (for this was the rule when a declaration of ownership was duly registered) – all conformed to the tradition of the manuals of perfect housekeeping which flourished everywhere, particularly in Germany where the *Hausväterliteratur* was very abundant, but in France too. *L'Agriculture et la maison rustique* by Charles d'Estienne, which was first published in 1564, then revised by his son-in-law Jean Liébaut, went into 103 editions between 1570 and 1702.[180] Land bought up by the bourgeoisie, whether small plots, orchards, kitchen gardens and pastures, or regular country properties, could be found outside any big city.

But just outside Paris, on the clayey plateau of Brie, the phenomenon had a different significance. Urban-owned properties here were *large* estates, whether noble or bourgeois, and they were being bought up before the beginning of the eighteenth century.[181] The Duc de Villars 'who under the Regency lived in his château at Vaux-le Vicomte, personally farmed only 50 *arpents* of the 220 he owned … the title holder to the *fief de la Commune* [in the parish of Ecrennes] a resident bourgeois, owned 332 *arpents* but had reserved for himself only 21 *arpents* of pasture'.[182] So these estates were hardly worked at all by their proprietors: they were left in the hands of rich tenant-farmers who usually amassed land belonging to *several* owners – five, six, sometimes even eight. In the centre of their farms stood the large farmhouses still visible today 'sheltering behind their high walls, a reminder of troubled times … [with their] buildings arranged round the main courtyard ... Around them cluster a few tumbledown cottages, which are themselves surrounded by gardens and small plots of land; here live the labourers who hire themselves out to the farmer.'[183]

All the signs indicate a 'capitalist' organization, such as the English revolution had instituted: the landowner, the rich tenant and the agricultural labourers. With the difference, and it is an important one, that here nothing changed in the shape of *technology* until the ninteenth century.[184] There was the other difference that the imperfect organization of these production units, their specialization in cereal-growing, the high percentage of consumption on the spot and the high cost of leases, made them extremely sensitive to grain prices. If these fell two or three points on the Melun market, some farmers would be in difficulties, and might even go bankrupt if poor harvests or years of low grain prices followed too closely one upon another.[185] All the same, this tenant-farmer was a new feature of the landscape, the owner of a slowly accumulating capital which was already turning him into an entrepreneur.

At all events, the rebels of the Flour Wars of 1775 were certainly in no doubt about the enemy: it was at the rich tenant-farmer that they directed their wrath, around Paris and elsewhere.[186] There were at least two reasons for this: for one thing, a large farm, the object of envy, had almost always been built up by a tenant farmer; secondly, he was the real ruler of the village world, quite as much as the resident nobleman, and perhaps even more effectively since he was closer to the peasant way of life. He was at one and the same time grain-hoarder, work-provider, money-lender or usurer – and was often entrusted by the land-owner with 'the collecting of quit-rents, *champarts* (payments in kind on certain land), *banalités* (charges for using the communal oven or mill), or even tithes ... Throughout the Paris region, [these tenant farmers] eagerly bought up the land of their former masters at the Revolution'.[187] This was undoubtedly a form of capitalism trying its strength from inside. Before long its efforts were to be crowned with success.

We should have a clearer picture if we knew more about the everyday life of these tenant-farmers, if we could see how they really behaved towards their servants, their grooms, their farmhands and carters. A glimpse of this life is revealed, but the page is quickly turned, at the beginning of the memoirs of Captain Coignet.[188] He was born in 1776 in Druyes-les-Belles-Fontaines in the present-day *département* of the Yonne, but found himself just before or during the early days of the Revolution working for a rich horse-dealer in Coulommiers, who would soon be contacted by the remount department of the revolutionary army. This livestock merchant had pastures, ploughed fields and tenants, but the memoirs do not enable us to place him exactly. Was he primarily a merchant, a working farmer or a rentier who leased out his land? Probably all three at once. And he had probably risen from the ranks of the well-off peasantry. His paternal, even affectionate attitude to his retainers, as they all sat round the big table with the master and mistress at the top, and 'the snow-white bread' they ate are very suggestive. The young Coignet visited one of the large farms in the district, and went into ecstasies at the dairy, ('taps everywhere') the refectory where everything was sparkling clean; the rows of pans and the polished table and benches. 'Every two weeks', the mistress of the house told him, 'I sell a cartload of cheeses; I have 80 cows ...' Unfortunately these images are too brief and the old soldier who wrote the lines was setting down his memories in some haste.

Venice and the Terraferma

With the conquest of its territories on the mainland, Venice became a great agricultural power in the early fifteenth century. Even before this, some patricians had owned land, 'beyond the Brenta' in the rich plain of Padua. But at the end of the sixteenth century and in particular after the crisis of the first decades of the seventeenth, the wealth of the Venetian patriciate did a radical about-turn, abandoning trade to throw all its weight into farming.

The patrician had often acquired his land from peasant holdings – the old story – so that in the sixteenth century and after, agrarian crimes committed against the landowner, his family or his possessions were frequent. He had also taken advantage, during the conquest of the Terraferma, of the confiscations carried out by the Signoria and the land sales that followed. And increasingly, new land was being created by hydraulic works which made it possible, with canals and locks, to drain waterlogged ground. These land improvements with the collaboration or supervision of the state and the not always notional participation of the village communities, were typically capitalist undertakings.[189] It is not surprising then that after many years of this experience, in the age of enlightenment, the grass lands of Venetia became the scene of a determined agricultural revolution, firmly directed towards livestock and meat production.[190]

Facing Rovigo across the Adige, near the village of Anguillara, the Trons, an old patrician family, possessed a piece of land of 500 hectares. In 1750, 360 people worked on it (177 of them were permanently on the payroll, 183 were hired temporarily as *salariati*) in teams of 15 men or more. It was in fact a capitalist undertaking. The word, says Jean Georgelin 'is not an anachronism. It was in common usage in eighteenth-century Venetia (and Piedmont). The mayors of the Bergamask, who were barely literate – as their writing shows – replied yes, unhesitatingly, on being asked in an enquiry carried out by the *podesta* of Bergamo: "*Vi sono capitalisti qui?*" And by "capitalist" they meant the man who came from outside to make the peasants work with his own capital.'[191]

Anguillara was a sort of agricultural factory. Everything was done under the watchful eye of the steward. The foremen never let the labourers out of their sight: they had the right only to one hour's rest a day: the supervisor checked them off '*orologio alla mano*'. Everything was carried out with method and

The Excursion, Venetian painting by G. Tiepolo, eighteenth century. (Photo O. Boehm.)

discipline: ditching, care of the dovecotes, planting out mulberry trees, distilling fruits, fish-farming, the planting in 1765 of potatoes, a new crop, the building of dykes to protect against the dangerous waters of the Adige, or even to reclaim land from the river. The estate was 'a beehive, constantly buzzing even in winter':[192] cultivation was with hoes, picks and ploughshares with mould boards, but there was also deep ploughing and airing of the soil. The crops were wheat (with a yield of 10 to 14 quintals per hectare), maize, and above all hemp; and there was intensive rearing of cattle and sheep. Yields were high, and so therefore were profits, though they varied naturally from year to year. In 1750, a very poor year, profits (not counting the paying off of capital) came to 28.29%. But in 1763, which was an excellent year, they were 130%! By comparison, on the best lands in Brie between 1656 and 1729, the gain in a good year was hardly more than 12% if the available calculations are right.[193]

These recently established facts oblige us to review our ideas about Venice. The return of patrician capital to the mulberry trees, rice, wheatfields and hemp-patches of the mainland cannot be entirely described as a flight towards security and away from trade which had become more risky and difficult in the late sixteenth century, among other reasons because of a revival in piracy in the Mediterranean. Indeed, Venice, thanks to foreign shipping, remained a very busy port, perhaps the busiest in the whole sea in the seventeenth century. So business had not collapsed overnight. It was the rise of agricultural prices and profits that drove Venetian capital towards the land. And here land was not in fact a passport to nobility: it was more a matter of investment and income.

Taste came into it too no doubt. If the rich families of Venice in Goldoni's time forsook their city palaces for villas which were in effect country palaces, it was partly a question of fashion. At the beginning of autumn, fashionable Venice would be deserted as 'country holidays, outdoor banquets and village dances were pursued with application and success'. There are so many descriptions of this kind of thing that we must take their word for it: everything was 'artificial' in these over-elaborate country mansions with their decorated rooms, their rich tables, their concerts and theatrical performances, their gardens, mazes, clipped hedges, walks bordered with statues and their throngs of servants – perfect material for a film. The grand lady in Tiepolo's painting, returning home at nightfall from a visit to friends, accompanied by her dog and her servants, 'leaning on the arm of her confessor who lights the way with a lantern'[194] would make a suitable final shot. But there was more to these houses than show. They had barns, wine-presses, cellars; they were the centres of farming activity, the vantage point from which the estate was supervised. In 1651, a book was published in Venice with the revealing title *L'Economia del cittadino in villa* (The economy of the city-dweller in his country house). The author, a doctor, Vincenzo Tanara, had produced one of the best books on rural economy ever written. He gives plenty of sensible advice to the new landowner taking posses-sion of his estate: he should take care in choosing the site of his villa, with due attention to climatic conditions and water supplies. He should consider digging a pond for breeding tench, perch and barbel – the best way of feeding his family cheaply and of providing an inexpensive *companatico* (food to accompany bread) for his farmhands. For in the countryside he would above all be making others work for him.

So there was a certain amount of illusion in the rather curious letter young Andrea Tron sent to his friend Andrea Quirini on 22 October 1743. The patrician letter-writer had spent much time in Holland and England.

> I tell you ... that they [the men in the Venetian government, patricians like himself] can issue all the decrees they like, they will never achieve anything in the way of commerce in this country ... There is no commerce useful to the State in any country where the richest men do not engage in trade. In Venice, we must persuade the nobility to put their money into trade ... something of which it is impossible to persuade them at present. The Dutch are all merchants and that is the chief reason why their trade flourishes. If only this spirit could be introduced into our country, then one would soon see a great trade revival here.[195]

But why should the patricians give up a peaceful and agreeable activity which brought them in a comfortable income, to embark upon some maritime venture of which the profits would probably be less substantial and less secure, since now all the best positions were occupied? It would have been difficult for them to recapture the Levant trade, now firmly controlled by foreigners, or by Jewish merchants and the bourgeoisie, the *cittadini*, of Venice. And yet the young Andrea Tron was not entirely mistaken: to abandon to those who were not 'the richest men' in the city all dealings in trade, imports, exports and money-handling, meant abdicating from the great international scene where Venice had once played a leading role. If the lot of Venice is compared to that of Genoa, *in the long run*, the city of Saint Mark did not make the best capitalist choice.

The deviant case of the Roman Campagna in the early nineteenth century

Over the centuries, the vast Roman Campagna changed its appearance several times. Why was this? Perhaps because there was nothing there to start with? Sismonde de Sismondi[196] saw it in 1819 and described it as an admirable example of the division of labour.

A few shepherds on horseback, clad in sheepskins and rags, some flocks of sheep, a few mares and their foals, and the occasional large farm, isolated and set a long distance from any other – these were the only signs of life to be seen as a rule, in a countryside rolling away as far as the eye could see. There were no crops, no villages; brambles, broom and tangles of wild, sweetsmelling vegetation were always reinvading any open ground and slowly but surely killing the grazing land. To try to combat this relentless plant life, the farmer had to clear land at regular intervals and sow it with wheat. It was one way of restoring the pastures for another few years. But since this was a region without peasants, how could the heavy work required in these exceptional years, from land-clearing to harvest, be effected?

The solution was to bring in outside workers: more than

ten classes of different workers, whose names [cannot be] rendered in any language . . . [For certain tasks] there are day-labourers who come down from the Sabine mountains; [for others] workers from the Marches and Tuscany; for the bulk of the work, men from the Abruzzi; finally, for building the ricks, idlers from the public squares of Rome (*piazzauoli di Roma*) who are good for nothing else, are employed. This division of labour makes it possible to adopt the most thorough agricultural processes; the wheat is hoed at least twice and sometimes more often; since every man is assigned a particular task, he does it all the more promptly and precisely. Almost all this labour is carried out at a fixed rate, under the supervision of a large number of factors and under-factors; but the farmer always provides the food, for it would be impossible for the labourer to find any in this desert. He owes each man a measure of wine, the equivalent of 40 *baiocs* of bread a week and three pounds of some other nutritive substance such as salt meat or cheese. During the winter season, the workers return at night to sleep in the *casale*, a huge unfurnished building in the centre of an immense farm. In summer . . . they sleep near their work, usually in the open air.

This is of course an incomplete picture, merely the impression of a traveller. Surprised by the highly picturesque sight before him, Sismondi did not see the dark shadows on the scene, not even the malaria which was so deadly in this marshy and little-cultivated region. He did not ask himself any serious questions about the system of land tenure, which was in fact a curious one. The problems it raises indeed go beyond the *agro romano* itself. The land around Rome was owned by great feudal nobles and by about a hundred religious establishments. These estates were often huge properties belonging to men like Prince Borghese, Duke Sforza or the Marquis Patrizi.[197] But neither the nobles nor the religious houses farmed their land directly. It had all been taken over by a few large tenant-farmers, known curiously as *negozianti* (or *mercanti*) *di campagna*. There were barely a dozen of them and they formed an association which was still in existence in the nineteenth century. Of very diverse social origin – merchants, lawyers, brokers, tax-collectors, estate managers – they were not really like the English tenant-farmers, for while they often kept the best land to work themselves, they usually sub-contracted land to many small tenants, or even shepherds or foreign peasants from outside. In their desire to have a free hand, they had systematically expelled all the peasants from the original holdings.[198]

What was clearly happening was a capitalist invasion, which became more definite in mid-eighteenth century, and of which the Roman Campagna was one of several Italian examples. The phenomenon is also found in some parts of Tuscany, in Lombardy and Piedmont, which was undergoing a complete transformation in the eighteenth century. These *appaltatori* (capitalist tenant-farmers) had a bad reputation both with landowners and peasants, and with the state. They were regarded as keen-toothed speculators, anxious to make as much money as possible, as quickly as possible, out of the land, and taking little trouble to protect its yields. But they were the shape of things to come: these were the origins of the large agricultural estates in nineteenth-century Italy. They were also, discreetly, the inspiration of agrarian reforms, some beneficial, others harmful, at the end of the eighteenth century. Their concern was to rid themselves of the old conditions of tenure, the entailments and mainmortes, to be forearmed both against the nobility and the peasant, and against the state which kept rather too watchful an eye on marketing. When the 'French period' came and the properties of the former privileged families were thrown on to the market, the *appaltatori* were first in the queue to buy them up.[199]

The interest of Sismondi's account is that it shows an exemplary case in the Roman Campagna of an authentic and undeniable division of agricultural labour, a topic on which little has been written. Adam Smith passed rather quickly over this question:[200] the division of labour operates in industry, he says, but not in agriculture where the same hand ploughs and scatters. In fact, farming under the *ancien régime* covered a multitude of different tasks and even in very backward areas, the peasants were obliged to share out the activities of the village economy among themselves, thus creating specialization. Every village needed a blacksmith, a wheelwright, a cooper, a joiner and the inevitable and indispensable shoemaker. It was not necessarily the same hand that always sowed the corn, ploughed the fields, guarded the flocks, trimmed the vine or cut wood. The peasant who felled trees, sawed up the timber and made faggots of sticks tended to be a man apart. Every year, at grain harvest, threshing or grape-picking, reinforcements of more or less specialized workers came flocking. The 'manager of the wine-harvest' had under him 'cutters, hod-carriers and tramplers.' For land-clearing operations in Languedoc for instance, Olivier de Serres[201] watched the workers divide themselves into separate teams: woodcutters, burners, ploughmen with their ploughs and powerful ox-teams, and the 'tampers' who 'reduced to dust humps that were resistant and too hard'. And finally, the great division of labour in the countryside has always been that between crops and livestock, arable and animal, Cain and Abel, two worlds, two different peoples, always hostile and ready to quarrel. Shepherds were almost always untouchables. Folklore has kept traces of this down to the present day. In the Abruzzi, a song tells a country girl in love with a shepherd: '*Nenna mia, muta pensiere ... 'nnanze pigghiate nu cafani caè ommi de società*', change your mind little girl, take a peasant who is a 'man of society', a civilized man, not one of these cursed shepherds who 'do not even know how to eat off a plate'.[202]

The poderi *of Tuscany*

Slowly, under the impact of the fortune of the Florentine merchants, the Tuscan countryside was deeply altered. The old villages, the subdivided plots of poor peasants, only survived in the hills or a few remote areas. In the lowlands and on

Detail from the map of the Roman Campagna by Eufrosino delle Volpaia (1547). This is a comparatively well-cultivated area north-west of Rome. It shows a few ploughed fields, and a yoked team, but also a vast amount of waste space, dotted with Roman ruins and bushes.

the foothills, well before 1400, a sharecropping regime had been established (*podere a mezzadria* or *podere* for short). The *podere* was all in one piece, though the size might vary according to the quality of the land, and the rule was that it had to be farmed by one sharecropper and his family. In the middle would stand the peasant dwelling with its barn and cowshed, its bread-oven and threshing-floor; close at hand the arable land, the vines, the willow-stumps with their crown of pale twigs, the olive trees and the land *a pascolo* and *a bosco* (pasture and wood). The size of holding was calculated to bring in twice the amount needed to keep the peasant and his family, since half the total output went to the *oste*, the landowner, and half to the *mezzadro*, the sharecropper. The *oste* sometimes possessed his own villa near the peasant's house, not necessarily a luxurious one. In his *Ricordi*, written between 1393 and 1421, Giovanni di Pagolo Morelli[203] advises his sons: 'You must realize that you yourselves will have to go to the villa, and go over the whole property field by field with the *mezzadro*, pick him up over any poor work, estimate the harvest in wheat, wine, oil, cereals, fruits and the rest, and compare previous years' figures with the present crop.' Was this painstaking supervision an early example of 'capitalist rationalization'? It was certainly an attempt to maximize production. On his side, the *mezzadro* besieged the owner with demands and recriminations, forcing him to invest and repair, and chivvying him on every occasion. Donatello refused the *podere* he was offered, which would have enabled him to live 'comfortably'. Was he wise or foolish? He simply did not wish to have a *contadino* bothering him three days a week.[204]

In this system, the peasant, who did all the same have some independence, was doomed to keep up productivity, to use the soil as profitably as possible and to choose the most marketable products, like oil and wine. And it has been said that the competitive nature of the *podere* was responsible for its triumph over older forms of agriculture. Possibly so, but this success is also explained by the fact that Florence had the means to buy grain from Sicily, and was able to reserve her own land for more rewarding crops. Sicilian grain played its part in the success of the bourgeois *poderi*.

That the *podere* was also in a way, as Elio Conti put it, 'a work of art, an expression of the same spirit of rationality which pervaded so many aspects of Florentine economics, politics and culture in the time of the Republic',[205] most people would agree. The Tuscan landscape, today alas disappearing fast, was once the most beautiful in the world. In it could be seen, if not the triumph of capitalism, which would be putting it rather strongly, at least the triumph of money well spent by merchants who were awake to profits and who calculated in terms of return on investment. But the *oste* was not dealing with a peasant deprived of his means of production; the *mezzadro* was not a wage-labourer. He had direct contact with land he knew well, of which he took excellent care and which was passed on from father to son for centuries; he was generally a peasant of means, well-nourished, living in a comfortable if not luxurious house, with

The classic Tuscan landscape: vines, olive trees and wheat. From the fresco *Buon Governo* which decorates the *Palazzo Civico* of Siena.

plenty of linen and clothes woven and made up at home. There are many reports of this rather rare equilibrium between landowner and farmer, money and labour. But there are some discordant notes too and certain Italian historians have even suggested that sharecropping remained something close to serfdom.[206] Indeed it does seem that the system deteriorated in the course of the first half of the eighteenth century, for reasons to do with general circumstances, higher taxation and grain speculation.

The Tuscan experience draws attention to another obvious point. Wherever there was crop specialization (oil and wine in Tuscany, rice, irrigated grassland and mulberries in Lombardy, raisins in the Venetian islands, even in a way wheat grown for export) agriculture had a tendency to move in the direction of capitalist 'enterprise', because these were essentially cash crops, dependent on a large home or foreign market, and productivity was sooner or later bound to become a preoccupation. Another example, identical despite the obvious differences, is that of the Hungarian cattle breeders: in the seventeenth century, when they realized the profits to be made by exporting cattle to west Europe, and the potential size of this market, they stopped intensive cultivation of their arable land and no longer produced their own grain but bought it.[207] They were already making a capitalist choice. The same was true of the Dutch dairy farmers who specialized (perhaps without much choice) in dairy products and the large-scale export of cheese.

Advanced areas: the minority

So there were some advanced areas which prefigured the capitalist future. But in Europe, areas which were backward, if that is the right word, or immobile, were in the vast majority. The bulk of the peasant world remained rather a long way from capitalism with its order, its progress and the demands it made. There is no shortage of examples if we want to find regions still embedded in a past which maintained its grip.

If one had gone to southern Italy after the savage repression of Masaniello in 1647 and the long and violent peasant troubles which accompanied it, one would have found a ruthless restoration of feudalism.[208] Things were much the same in the first decades of the eighteenth century, according to a contemporary witness, Paolo Mattia Doria, who attacked not the feudal system, but its abuses: 'The baron has the power to impoverish or ruin his vassal, to imprison him without letting the governor or the village magistrate intervene; having power of life and death, he has anyone he wants murdered and pardons assassins ... He abuses his power both against his vassals' property and their honour ... To prove a baron guilty of a crime is impossible ... The government itself ... has only indulgence for a powerful baron ... These abuses show that some barons are like sovereigns on their own estates.'[209] Statistics confirm this extraordinary power since even in the age of enlightenment, almost everywhere in the kingdom of Naples, over 50% of the population were subject to feudal justice, and the figure was 70, 80 and even 88% in certain provinces.[210]

In Sicily, this second serfdom was well and truly *in situ* even in 1789, when G. M. Galanti's book, *Nuova descrizione storica e geografica della Sicilia* appeared. In the years before the French Revolution, reforming viceroys (Caracciolo and Caramanico) only succeeded in achieving minor reforms.[211] Another region of serfdom or near-serfdom was Aragon, at least until the eighteenth century, so much so indeed that German historians have used the term *Gutsherrschaft* to describe it, that is the word for the kind of seigniorial system which had introduced the second serfdom beyond the Elbe. The south of Spain too, where the Christian conquest had introduced a system of large estates, was still deep in the past. And there were backward areas too, of course, in the Highlands of Scotland and in Ireland.

In short it was generally on the *periphery* of western Europe that backwardness most clearly persisted, if one excepts the example of Aragon (and even then it should be remembered that in the complex world of the Iberian peninsula, Aragon was a marginal, peripheral region for many centuries). In any case, if one imagines a map showing the advanced areas – few and small – and the backward areas, on the periphery, one would also have to find a colour to indicate the zones that marked time, or developed only slowly, under both the seigniorial and the feudal system; they were often behind the times, but in some respects were undergoing change. In Europe taken as a whole, the role played by agrarian capitalism was in the end rather small.

The case of France

France provides a fairly good summary of the European experience, with its combinations and contradictions. Anything that happened anywhere else can usually be found in one of the French regions. So asking questions about France can be relevant to her neighbours. Eighteenth-century France was marked by agricultural capitalism for instance, less so than England, of course, but more than Germany between the Rhine and the Elbe. France had regions comparable – though only just – to the modern areas of Italy, which were sometimes more advanced than their French counterparts, but she lagged less far behind than the Iberian peninsula, with the exception of Catalonia (which was undergoing drastic transformation during the eighteenth century although the seigniorial regime still kept its strongholds there).[212]

But if France can be seen as exemplary, it is above all during the latter half of the eighteenth century, by virtue of her progressive development, and of the acute character and transformation of the conflicts that broke out there. France was at this time the scene of demographic increase (the population rose from 20 million in the age of Louis XIV to perhaps 26 million under Louis XVI).[213] And agricultural income undoubtedly rose. That landowners in general, and the noble landowner in particular, should want their share of it was hardly surprising. After the long years of penitence, from 1660 to 1730, the landed aristocracy wanted to make up for its past privations, the 'days in the wilderness'.[214] Hence a period of seigniorial reaction, perhaps the most spectacular in France in modern times. Everything was grist to this mill: licit actions such as increasing or doubling the cost of a lease; or illicit moves, such as reviving ancient claims to a property, reinterpreting doubtful points in law (there was never any shortage of these) moving the boundaries, trying to divide up common land, picking quarrels to such a point that the peasant in his exasperation could see nothing but 'feudal' barriers being put up against him on every side. He did not always realize the development, which would have fateful consequences for him, underlying this offensive by landed proprietors.

For the seigniorial reaction was determined not so much by a return to tradition as by the spirit of the times, the climate, new to France, of financial racketeering, stock exchange speculation and investment bubbles, as the aristocracy began to take an interest in overseas trade or mining, in short, what I would describe as a capitalist temptation as much as a mentality. For true rural capitalism and modern management on the English pattern were still rare in France – but they were coming. People had begun to put their trust in land as a source of profit and to believe in the efficacity of modern methods of management. In 1762, Despommiers's *L'Art de s'enrichir promptement par agriculture* (How to get rich quick in farming) was a best-seller; it was followed in 1784 by another, *L'Art d'augmenter et de conserver son bien, ou régles générales pour l'adminstration d'une terre* (How to increase and preserve your property, or the rules of estate management) by Arnould. Many estates were bought and sold. Landed property was touched by the general mania for speculation. An interesting article by Eberhard Weiss (1970)[215] analyses the situation in France, which the author sees as a capitalist reaction as much as a seigniorial one. A sustained effort was made by both tenant-farmers and proprietors to restructure large estates, beginning with the *domaine direct*, the *seigneur*'s home farm. This aroused panic and resentment among the peasants, a development which Eberhard Weiss compares and contrasts with the situation of the German peasants in the regions of *Grundsherrschaft*, i.e. the classic seigniorial system between Rhine and Elbe. The German landlords did not try to use their own home farm or adjoining territory as a base for taking in hand the style of farming throughout their estates. They were content simply to live off their rural rents and made up for it by entering the service of princes, the Duke-Elector of Bavaria for instance. The home farm was therefore divided up and leased to peasants who were thus spared the anxieties and frustrations of their French counterparts. And indeed the language of the French Revolution, the denunciation of noble privileges, did not find in Germany the echo one might have expected. Once more, we must be grateful to a foreign historian (German in this case) who has followed in the footsteps of the innovating Russian historians Lutchinsky and Porchnev, and come along to shake up some of the received ideas of French historiography.

Emmanuel Le Roy Ladurie has, in a recent article,[216] added a few qualifications to Weiss's hypothesis, with the aid of some excellent monographs, including his own on the Languedoc. He has tried to discover precisely which were the regions where the seigniorial reaction in France had a modern flavour. We already knew that rich tenant-farmers and modernizing nobles existed. Now we have overwhelming proof of this in Pierre de Saint-Jacob's excellent book on Upper Burgundy. He cites the example – verging on a caricature perhaps – of one Varenne de Lonvoy,[217] a nobleman who was relentless in his amalgamation of fields, putting them end to end, driving off the peasants and seizing common

A rich tenant receiving his landlord. Rétif, *Monument du costume*, engraving, after Moreau the Younger, 1789. Here there is no sign of the noble-peasant contrast – the scene could be taking place in England. (Photo Bulloz.)

lands – but who also introduced novelties like irrigation and 'artificial' pastures. But we should remember that for every bustling modernizer, there were ten or twenty unconcerned noble squires, drawing their rents sometimes in complete indifference.

Can the scale of this subterranean capitalist movement be measured and judged by the discontents, claims and agitation of the peasants? We know that such agitation was virtually continuous. But in the seventeenth century, it was directed more at taxes than at landlords, and took place mostly in western France. In the eighteenth century, the revolts were increasingly directed against the *seigneur* and indicated a new geography of dissidence: the north-east and east of the kingdom, that is the great cereal-growing plains, where farming was advanced (horse teams were used for ploughing here)[218] and where there was overpopulation. The Revolution was to demonstrate even more clearly that these were the rural areas where feelings ran highest. Might it not be thought that it was at least partly because the language of capitalism had not found the vocabulary to handle a new and surprising situation, that the French peasant reverted to the familiar old language of anti-feudalism? For it is this language exclusively that bursts out in the *cahiers de doléance* (complaints registers) of 1789.

There is still a need to clarify some rather contradictory evidence, and to nuance our perhaps over-simple contrast between seventeenth and eighteenth centuries. What lies behind the anti-seigniorial movements in Provence for instance, which quite often seem to have stirred up peasant revolts?[219] One thing is certain: vast areas of France (Aquitaine, the Massif Central, Brittany) were peaceful at the end of the *ancien régime*, whether because peasant freedoms still survived here; because the advantages of peasant property were still a reality; or because, in the case of Brittany, the peasantry had already been reduced to near-poverty and obedience. One can of course ask oneself what would have happened to French agriculture if the Revolution had not taken place. Pierre Channu thinks that peasant-holdings, at the time of the reaction under Louis XVI had been reduced to 40 to 50% of the land holdings overall.[220] If France had continued to develop along these lines, would she soon have seen an English-style evolution, encouraging the establishment of agrarian capitalism? That is the kind of question that must for ever remain unanswered.

Capitalism and pre-industry

Industry: the word emerged with some difficulty from its old meaning: work, activity, diligence – to acquire more or less in the eighteenth century, and not always then, the specific sense in which it is used today, in an area where words like (handi)craft, manufacture, were for some time its rivals.[221] When it eventually triumphed in the nineteenth century, the word tended to refer to 'large-scale industry'. So we shall often have occasion in these pages to use the word *pre-industry* (although it is not particularly elegant). But this need not stop us here and there using the word *industry* itself without feeling too guilty, or referring to *industrial* rather than *pre-industrial* activities. No possible confusion can occur, since we shall always be talking about the days before the steam engine, before

Newcomen or Watt, Cugnot, Jouffroy or Fulton, and before the nineteenth century since when 'large-scale industry has surrounded us on all sides'.

A fourfold classification

As luck would have it, we need not build our own model for the first stage of exposition. A model was designed some time ago now, in 1924, by Hubert Bourgin, and has been so little used that it still has the bloom of youth. Bourgin[222] classified all industrial activities between the fifteenth and eighteenth centuries into four categories which he distinguished *a priori*:

Category A: The tiny family workshops, countless in number and grouped in 'clusters', each with a master-tradesman, two or three journeymen and one or two apprentices, a family in itself. Such would be the cutler, the nail-maker, the village blacksmith (who has survived almost to the present day and still indeed exists in Africa and India, working in the open air with his assistants). The cobbler or shoemaker would come into this category, as would the goldsmith's workshop, full of precision tools and rare materials, the locksmith's shop with its cluttered shelves, or the upstairs room where the lacemaker worked when she was not sitting at her open door. Into this category too would come the 'horde of little establishments, where family craftworking was carried on', in the Dauphiné in the eighteenth century: after the harvest or grape-picking, 'everyone sets to work ... some families weave, others spin'.[223] In each of these 'monocellular' elementary units, 'the tasks were undifferentiated and continuous', so that there was often no division of labour. Their family structure placed them half outside the market economy and the usual profit norms.

I would also place in this category activities that are sometimes a little hastily classified as non-artisanal: the baker delivering bread, the miller grinding flour, the cheesemakers, the distillers of *eau-de-vie* or *marc*, the butchers who worked from 'raw material' to produce meat in a form that could be consumed. What a number of skills they must have, an English document says in 1791: 'They must not only know how to kill, cut up and dress their meat to advantage, but how to buy a bullock, sheep or calf, standing.'[224]

The essential feature of this artisanal pre-industry was its size: it represented the vast majority and, remaining true to itself, resisted all capitalist innovations (whereas these sometimes gathered round a wholly specialized craft until it fell like a ripe plum into the hands of wealthy entrepreneurs). It would require a long study to discover all the traditional arts and crafts which survived, often into the nineteenth or even the twentieth century. In 1838, the old *telaio da velluto*, the velvet loom, was still to be found in the Genoese countryside.[225] In France, craft industry long remained predominant and only began to yield to modern industry in about the 1860s.[226]

Category B: workshops which were scattered, but connected to each other.

The cutler's family workshop, from the *Codex* by Balthasar Behem.
(Photo Morch Rortwonrski.)

Hubert Bourgin describes these as '*fabriques disséminées*', dispersed factories, a felicitous term borrowed from G. Volpe (I confess that I would slightly prefer to say 'dispersed manufactories', *manufactures*, but that is a quibble: see below for a discussion of these terms). Whether we are talking about the manufacture of *étamines* (fine woollens) in the Le Mans district in the eighteenth century, or about the Florentine *Arte della lana* in about 1350, in the time of Villani (60,000 people scattered over a radius of fifty kilometres around Florence as well as in the city)[227] we are referring to a number of individual units spread over a wide area but interconnected. The coordinator, or go-between, or director of the work was the merchant entrepreneur who advanced the raw material, saw that it went from spinner to weaver, to fuller, to dyer, to shearer, who took care of the finishing processes and the payment of wages, and at the end of the day, pocketed the profits from sales at home or abroad.

This dispersed manufacture was established as early as the Middle Ages, not only for textiles but also 'from very early on for cutlery, nail-making and iron-working, which have retained until our own time, in certain regions like Normandy and Champagne, some signs of their origins'.[228] The same could be said of metal-working near Cologne from the fifteenth century, in Lyons in the sixteenth, or in the Brescia region, from the Val Camonica where the ironworks were, to the armourers' shops in the town.[229] The pattern in every case was a sequence of manufacturing operations, culminating in the appearance of the finished product and its marketing.

Category C: 'concentrated manufacture', which appeared later, at different dates depending on the industry and the country. The water-operated forges of the fourteenth century were an early example of concentrated manufacture: several operations were brought together in one spot. The same was true of breweries, tanneries and glassworks. Even more obviously in this category were the manu-factories (*manufactures*)[230] established both by the state and by private individuals. They made all kinds of goods, but mostly textiles, and spread throughout Europe, particularly during the latter half of the eighteenth century. Their characteristic feature was the bringing together under one roof, usually in a large building, of the labour force; this made possible supervision of the work, an advanced division of labour – in short increased productivity and an improvement in the quality of products.

Category D: factories (*fabriques*) equipped with machinery, using the additional energy sources of running water and steam. In Marx's vocabulary, these were quite simply 'factories'. In fact the terms factory and manufactory (*fabrique* and *manufacture*) were commonly interchangeable in the eighteenth century,[231] but we may feel it is worth preserving the distinction for our present purpose. For the sake of clarity, let me make it plain that mechanized manufacture falls outside the chronology of this book and would be introducing us to a nineteenth-century reality by way of the industrial revolution. But I would regard

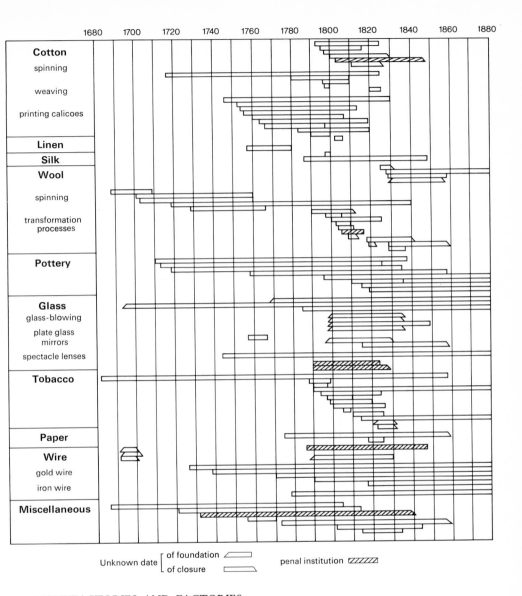

	1680	1700	1720	1740	1760	1780	1800	1820	1840	1860	1880

Cotton
spinning

weaving

printing calicoes

Linen

Silk

Wool
spinning

transformation processes

Pottery

Glass
glass-blowing

plate glass mirrors

spectacle lenses

Tobacco

Paper

Wire
gold wire

iron wire

Miscellaneous

Unknown date ⎡ of foundation ◿▱   penal institution ▨▨▨
⎣ of closure ▱

19 MANUFACTORIES AND FACTORIES

The principalities of Ansbach and Bayreuth were very small, but very densely-populated territories in 'Franconian' Germany, attached to Bavaria in 1806–1810. A survey of almost a hundred manufacturing establishments covers a fair sample and helps to clarify the Marx-Sombart controversy as to whether manufactories did (Marx) or did not (Sombart) become factories in the modern sense. About twenty of these factories survived in 1850, that is about one in five. As usual, the truth is somewhere between the two. Graph by O. Reuter in *Die Manufaktur im Frankischen Raum*, 1961, p. 8.

the typical *modern* mine of the sixteenth century for instance, such as existed in central Europe and which can be seen in the illustrations to Agricola's *De re metallica* (1555) as an example, and an important one, of mechanization, even if steam was only introduced two hundred years later and then only very slowly and grudgingly. Similarly in the Cantabrian region, 'in the early sixteenth century, the use of water as motive power had produced a veritable industrial revolution'.[232] Other examples are the naval yards of Saardam near Amsterdam in the seventeenth century, with their mechanical saws, their cranes, their mast-erecting machines; and so many little 'factories' using hydraulic wheels: paper-mills, fulling mills, saw-mills or the sword-works in Vienne in the Dauphiné, where the grindstones and bellows were mechanically operated.[233]

So there are the four categories, four types of production in roughly chronological order, although 'while they followed one upon the other, these different structures did not immediately replace each other'.[234] Above all – Sombart was for once right against Marx[235] – there certainly was no natural and logical transition from the manufactory to the factory. The table I have borrowed from Ortulf Reuter[236] on the manufactories and factories in the principalities of Ansbach and Bayreuth from 1680 to 1880, shows that there were some overlaps in the move from one to the other – but no logical and natural succession.

Is Bourgin's classification valid outside Europe?

This classification can easily be extended to any densely-settled societies in the world.

Outside Europe, the first two categories predominated – that is the individual workshop and the chain of workshops linked to each other; more concentrated forms of manufacture were exceptional.

Black Africa, with its blacksmiths (who had much in common with witch doctors) its primitive weavers and potters, fitted entirely into Category A. Colonial America was perhaps a little worse provided for at this elementary level. But wherever American Indian society had survived, craftworkers were still active: spinners, weavers, potters and workmen capable of building the churches and convents – colossal structures even to our eyes – of colonial Mexico and Peru. The occupiers even took advantage of them to instal *obrajes*, workshops where forced labour processed wool, cotton, linen and silk. At the top of the scale, there were also the huge silver, copper and mercury mines, and before long in the Brazilian interior, the vast rather disorganized sites where black slaves were employed at gold-panning. Still in Brazil, and in the islands and the tropical belt of Spanish America, there were the sugar mills which were in fact manufactories, concentrations of labour, of hydraulic or animal power, with workshops producing the various kinds of sugar as well as rum or tafia.

But colonial America was subject to the bans imposed by the metropolitan monopolies – there were so many rules and prohibitions. The various layers of 'industry' were not harmoniously developed there. What was missing was the craft base, that rich and plentiful community of artisans present in Europe, who had such a high reputation for workmanship. A traveller in the second half of the seventeenth century remarked as much:[237] 'In the Indies', he writes, 'there are only inferior craftsmen [and no engineers at all we might add] for everything to do with war, and even for many other things. For instance there is no one who can make good surgical instruments; and the manufacture of mathematical and navigational instruments is totally unknown.' This was surely true of more everyday articles. All the nails, and the copper or iron boilers for the sugar mills, to take only these examples, came from overseas. If there was not the same thriving craft base here as in Europe, the overall population figure was no doubt to blame and equally the extraordinary poverty of the natives. As late as 1820 when Kotzebue, a naval officer in the service of the Tsar (and the son of the poet killed in 1819 by the German student Karl Sand) arrived in Rio, he found Brazil, Portugal's gold and diamond mine, 'in itself a poor, oppressed country, thinly inhabited and inaccessible to all culture of the mind'.[238]

In China and India on the other hand, there was a very rich craft base with plenty of highly-skilled artisans, in both town and village. The textile industry of Gujerat or Bengal was a sort of constellation of 'disseminated manufactories' or a milky way of individual workshops. And the third category of manufacture was present in both countries. North of Peking, the coal-mining region already foreshadowed a clear form of concentration, despite control by the state and the small amount of capital investment.[239] Cotton-working in China was primarily a peasant and family occupation, but by the end of the seventeenth century, the cotton works of Songjiang south of Shanghai were permanently employing over 200,000 workers, not counting tailoring and dressmaking.[240] Su-Chu, the capital of Kiang-Su, had between 3000 and 4000 silk-looms.[241] It is another Lyons, remarked one recent historian, or perhaps Tours, or 'better still, Lucca'.[242] Similarly 'Kin-te-chin' had in 1793 'three thousand furnaces for baking porcelain ... lighted at a time, which gave to the place, at night, the appearance of a town on fire'.[243]

The amazing thing is that in China as in India, this extraordinarily skilled and ingenious workforce did not produce the high quality of tools with which we are familiar in European history. This was even more true of India than of China. A traveller through India in 1782 noted: 'Indian crafts look simple to us, because in general they employ few machines using only their hands and two or three tools to work with, where we would use over a hundred.'[244] Similarly, the European could not but be astonished at the Chinese blacksmith

who carries his tools, forge and furnace everywhere with him and works wherever he is asked to. He sets up his forge in front of the house of the man who summons him; he crumbles earth to make a little wall and places his hearth in front of it; behind the wall are two leather bellows which an apprentice works by pressing them alternately; in this way he kindles the fire; a stone serves as an anvil and his only tools are pincers, hammer, sledgehammer, and file.[245]

He was equally amazed by the sight of a weaver – probably in the countryside since there were some magnificent Chinese looms in the towns:

> he puts up his loom under a tree outside his house in the morning, and takes it down at sunset. The loom is very simple: it consists of two cylinders supported by four stakes hammered into the ground. Two rods, running across the warp and held attached at each end, one by two strings tied to the tree and the other by two strings tied to the workman's feet ... enable him to part the threads of the warp to pass the shuttle through.[245]

This was the elementary horizontal loom still used today for making coverings by certain nomads in North Africa.

Why this imperfect equipment which could only operate at the cost of much human labour? Was it because such human labour was only too plentiful, poverty-stricken and therefore cheap, in India and China? There is after all a correlation between equipment and labour force. The workers became aware of this when the machines arrived, but long before the outbursts of the Luddites, some authorities and intellectuals had already realized what was happening. When he was informed of the invention of a fabulous mechanical saw, Guy Patin advised the inventor not to make himself known to the workmen if he valued his life.[246] Montesquieu deplored the building of mills – for him all machines reduced the number of men required and were 'pernicious'.[247] The same idea, but the other way round appears in an odd passage in the *Encyclopédie* noticed by Marc Bloch:[248] 'Wherever labour is dear, it must be supplemented by machines; this is the only way to compete with those countries where it is cheap. The English have been telling Europe this for a long time.' Such remarks are not after all surprising. More surprising, but still leaving our curiosity unsatisfied, is an incident from a hundred years earlier, briefly described in two letters from the Genoese consul in London in August 1675: 10,000 silk-workers in the capital had risen up against the introduction of French ribbon-looms, with which a single worker could weave 10 or 12 ribbons at a time; the new looms were burnt and had it not been for the intervention of the soldiers and the patrol of guards, worse might have happened.[249]

No gulf between agriculture and pre-industry

Hubert Bourgin's model puts the accent on technology; it is therefore somewhat simplified and incomplete. We shall have to introduce the complications.

My first remark is self-evident: pre-industry, despite its original character, was not a sector with clearly-defined frontiers. Before the eighteenth century, it was barely distinguishable from the omnipresent agricultural life which ran alongside it and sometimes submerged it. There was even a grass-roots peasant industry at the level of practical exchange, working strictly for the family or the

Dyeing in Venice, seventeenth century. (Museo Correr, Viollet Collection.)

village. I recall as a child watching the wheelwright making cartwheels in a village in the Meuse: an iron hoop, expanded to red heat, was fitted round the wooden wheel which immediately began to smoulder: the whole thing was thrown into the village pond and as the iron cooled with a hiss it clamped on to the wood. The entire village turned out to watch. But one could go on for ever listing the things that were made in every country home in the past, even among the rich,[250] but especially among the poor: they made their own cloth, smocks of coarse linen, furniture, harnesses of vegetable fibre, ropes out of lime-tree bark, wicker baskets, wooden handles for tools and for ploughs. In less developed countries in East Europe, like the West Ukraine or Lithuania, such self-sufficiency was even more pronounced than in western Europe.[251] For in the West, alongside home-made articles, there was also a cottage industry, *but this time intended for the market.*

This cottage industry is familiar: all over Europe, in village, hamlet and farm when winter came, widespread 'industrial' activity replaced farm work, even in very isolated settlements, like the thirty or so villages 'of difficult access' in the Norman *bocage* in 1723; or the villages of the Saintonge which in 1727 put on the market products which did not conform to guild rules.[252] Should they be disciplined? The manufacturing inspectors thought it would be better to go out there to explain 'the manufacturing regulations' to people who were certainly ignorant of them 'in the back of beyond'. Near Osnabrück in 1780, 'linen industry' meant the peasant, his wife, children and farmhands. The output of this complementary work was incidental. It was winter: 'The farmhand has to be fed whether he works or not.'[253] So he might as well work for his living! It was the 'calendar' as Giuseppe Palomba says, the rhythm of the seasons which dictated all these activities. In the sixteenth century, even the coalminers of Liège left the pits every August at harvest-time.[254] Whatever the trade there are hardly any exceptions to the rule. A merchant's letter from Florence on 1 June 1601 for example says: 'Wool sales are slower now, which is hardly surprising: little work is being done because there are no workmen; they are all out in the fields.'[255] In Lodève or Beauvais or Antwerp, in any 'industrial' town, once summer came, farm work took priority. With the return of winter, cottage industry took over again, by candlelight indeed, in spite of fear of fire.

There are of course examples that indicate the opposite, or at any rate some variations. There were some attempts to establish uninterrupted craft-working. In Rouen in 1723, 'the country workers [who] used to leave their looms to get in the harvest . . . [do so] no more, since they find it pays better to carry on making cloth and other fabrics'. As a consequence, the wheat was in danger of sprouting 'on the stalk for want of workers to fetch it in'. The *Parlement* proposed forbidding all work in manufacturing 'during the season of harvesting wheat and other cereals'![256] Was work really continuous or not? We might bear in mind Vauban's calculation that the artisan worked 120 days per annum: holidays (there were plenty of these) and seasonal tasks swallowed up the rest of the year.

So the distinction emerged irregularly and belatedly. Goudar[257] is probably wrong to talk of a geographical split between industry and agriculture. Nor am I over-impressed by Roger Dion's idea of a line 'from Laval to Rouen, Cambrai and Fourmies'[258] separating the two Frances: the north, home of the traditional crafts, and the wine-growing south. After all, wine-producing Languedoc had 450,000 textile workers in 1680 according to the *intendant* Basville.[259] And in a wine-growing region like Orleans, the 1689 census records 21,840 peasants who owned vineyards and '12,171 artisans scattered among the villages and hamlets'. It is true on the other hand that cottage industry was not much practised among wine-growers' families who were usually quite well-to-do. Around Arbois, in another wine district, no textile industry could become established for lack of workers.[260] The woollen trade of Leyden, so vigorous in the seventeenth century, was unable to put work out to its rural areas, because they were too prosperous.

When in the eighteenth century, the trade absolutely had to find out-workers, it had to look to poor rural districts, *further away*. And these curiously enough were to become the great textile centres of modern Holland.[261]

Industry: providential refuge from poverty

Industry can in fact only be explained by a multiplicity of factors and motives. Lucca, the silk-centre, had by the thirteenth century become 'for lack of land [around the city and belonging to it] ... so industrious that it is proverbially known as the Republic of Ants', claims Ortensio Landi in one of his *Paradossi* (1543).[262] An industry in coloured woollen stockings appeared unexpectedly on the coast of Norfolk in the sixteenth century. It was no accident. Along this coast ran a string of little fishing ports, with nets hung out along the quaysides. The men, when they were not on the Iceland run, were in the North Sea catching herring, mackerel and sprats. The considerable female workforce employed to salt the fish in the salthouses found itself with nothing to do outside the fishing season. And it was this semi-employed workforce that tempted merchant entrepreneurs, so a new industry was set up.[263]

Thus poverty often took pre-industry by the hand. Textbooks talk of Colbert as if he persuaded a reluctant and undisciplined France to go to work, whereas the economic situation and increased taxation alone would have been sufficient to push the kingdom into industrial activity. Modest though such industry might be, was it not a life-raft, a 'second providence'? Savary des Bruslons, who was given to sententiousness, declares: 'It has always been noted that the prodigies of industry [note that he uses the word unhesitatingly] spring from the heart of necessity.' This remark is worth remembering. In Russia, the poorest land fell to the 'black' peasantry – free peasants who sometimes had to import grain to survive. And it was among them that craft industry tended to develop.[264] The mountain dwellers around Lake Constance, in the Swabian Jura or in the Silesian hills, were linen-workers from the fifteenth century on, to compensate for the poverty of their agriculture.[265] And in the Scottish Highlands, the crofters who could not make a living from their meagre crops, survived either by working as weavers or as coal-miners.[266] The market towns where the villagers of north-west England brought their cloth, woven at home and still greasy, provided a large proportion of the products collected by the London merchants who undertook to finish them before selling them in the Cloth Hall.[267]

An unsettled workforce

The less closely-attached to the land, the more likely craft-working was to be urban and consequently unsettled. After the traditional rural craftsmen (who also moved about, especially in poor regions) came artisans *stricto sensu*, and they were the most mobile sector of the population. This is explained by the very nature of pre-industrial production which consisted of a series of sudden expansions followed by vertical plunges, as the graphs reproduced in Figure 21 help to show. Business would boom for a while; then it would be time to move on. A sketch-map showing the waves of artisan immigration which gradually created pre-industry in England would illustrate this admirably. Artisans, always poorly paid, and obliged to pass under the Caudine Forks of the market for their daily food, were sensitive to any shift in wages and fall in demand. Since they were never the gainers, they were perpetual migrants, 'a precarious and shifting community which could uproot itself at the least event'.[268] The workers 'will vote with their feet to go abroad' if the manufactories should close, came a warning from Marseilles in 1715.[269] The fragile nature of industry, explained the 'Friend of Mankind', Mirabeau, comes from its 'being entirely rooted in the dexterity of the workmen, who are always ready to emigrate in pursuit of genuine abundance', and who remain essentially 'rootless men'.[270] 'Can we answer for the constancy of our artists [artisans] as we can for the immobility of our fields?' Of course not, says Dupont de Nemours,[271] and Forbonnais goes even further: 'The arts [i.e. trades] are incontrovertibly perambulant.'[272]

Artisans were mobile by tradition (the old journeyman system); and they became so by necessity, whenever their miserable living conditions grew insupportable. 'They only live from day to day so to speak', wrote a bourgeois of Reims who did not care for them, in his *Journal* (1658). Five years later, when times were bad, he wrote: 'The people ... find markets for their work, but at very poor prices so only the shrewdest can subsist'; the others were reduced to the almshouses or to begging or 'rascalling' in the street. In the following year, 1664, the workers were leaving off their trades and 'becoming labourers or returning to the villages'.[273] London seemed to be little better-off. A French gazette of 2 Januáry 1730, reporting that bread had gone down two 'sols' (about 9%) adds: 'So the workers are at present able to live off their wages.'[274] In about 1773, according to a report by the inspector of manufactories, many of the weavers of Languedoc, 'without bread and without the means of obtaining any' (since there was no work) were obliged 'to go abroad in order to survive'.[275]

An unexpected accident or blow could precipitate the movement. There was of course a rush to escape from France after the Revocation of the Edict of Nantes (1685). And the same happened in New Spain in 1749 and even more so in 1785–1786, when famine struck the northern mines, with the interruption of the maize supply. There was a flight towards the south and Mexico City, a veritable Gomorrah, '*lupanar de infamias y disoluciones, cueva de picaros, infierno de caballeros, purgatorio de hombres de bien ...*' Somebody seriously proposed in 1786 walling up the gates of the city to keep out the new multitude.[276]

On the other hand, any industry wishing to develop had no difficulty in seducing from other cities, even from distant and foreign countries, the skilled labour it required, and all sought energetically to do so. As early as the fourteenth century, the towns of Flanders were trying to counter the policy of the king of

England who was luring away their journeymen weavers by promising them 'good beer, good beef, good beds and even better bedfellows, since English girls are the most renowned for their beauty'.[277] In the sixteenth and even the seventeenth century, migration by the labour force often corresponded to collapse, to the total disorganization of the international division of labour. Consequently draconian measures were sometimes taken to prevent workers emigrating – turning them back at the frontiers or along the road and forcibly bringing them home, or negotiating for their extradition from foreign cities.

In 1757, this policy was judged out of date in France. Orders went out from Paris to the *maréchaussées* of Lyons, the Dauphiné, Roussillon and the Bourbonnais to abandon all pursuit of runaway workers: it was regarded as a waste of public money.[278] Times had indeed changed. By the eighteenth century, industrial activity was widespread, virtually ubiquitous, and trading links had proliferated. There was not a town or city, no market town in particular, no village even, without its own looms, forges, brick or tile works, or sawmill. State policy (contrary to everything suggested by the word *mercantilism*) was industrialization, which sprang up of its own accord and was already breeding its social evils. Huge concentrations of workers were coming into being: 30,000 people employed by the coal industry in Newcastle;[279] 450,000 weavers in Languedoc by 1680, as we have already seen; 1,500,000 textile workers in 1795 in the five provinces of Hainaut, Flanders, Artois, Cambrésis and Picardy, according to Paires, a representative of the people sent there on a mission. Industry and trade were reaching truly colossal proportions.[280]

With the economic expansion of the eighteenth century, industrial activity became general. In the sixteenth, it had essentially been concentrated in the Netherlands and Italy; now it developed all over Europe as far as the Urals. These were times that saw many hopeful ventures, mushroom enterprises and ambitious plans, inventions that were not always brand-new and, already, a thick scum of fraud and intrigue.

From country to town and back again

Seen *en bloc*, the migrations of artisans were not haphazard: they were the surface sign of massive undercurrents. When the silk industry for instance was transferred almost in a single sweep from the south to the north of Italy in the seventeenth century; or when major industrial activities (and with them the corresponding trade) withdrew from the Mediterranean countries in the late sixteenth century, to find a new home in France, Holland, England and Germany – these were powerful pendulum movements, heavy with consequences.

But there were other quite regular movements to and fro. J. A. Van Houtte's study[281] draws attention to the way in which industry moved between cities, market towns and villages in the Netherlands, from the Middle Ages until the eighteenth or even mid-nineteenth century. At the beginning of this long period, industry was scattered throughout the countryside: hence the impression that it was something at the same time *sui generis*, spontaneous and ineradicable. But in the thirteenth and fourteenth centuries, pre-industry very largely moved into the towns. This urban phase was followed by a powerful turn of the tide after the long depression between 1350 and 1450: the countryside was once more invaded by handicrafts, particularly as labour in the towns was imprisoned in the straightjacket of the guilds, difficult to manipulate, and above all expensive. The town regained its industrial activities to some extent in the sixteenth century, only to see the countryside take its revenge once more in the seventeenth, before beginning to lose some of its industry again in the eighteenth.

This simplified outline conveys the fundamental point that there were two possible sounding-boards for pre-industry: town and countryside, throughout Europe and perhaps throughout the world. There was thus in yesterday's economy a choice, and therefore a certain flexibility, a possible freedom of manœuvre for entrepreneurial merchants or for the state. Is J. A. Van Houtte right when he argues that the fiscal systems of rulers, depending on whether they applied only to the cities or also to the surrounding countryside, contributed to create these varying patterns, these alternating waves of growth and decline? Only a detailed study could answer this question with any certainty. But one thing is beyond question: wages and prices must have played some part.

Did not a very similar process drive Italy's industry out into the second-rank and small towns, villages and hamlets in the late sixteenth and early seventeenth century? The most dramatic problem faced by Italian industry between 1590 and 1630 was competition from the low-priced products of northern industry. According to Domenico Sella in his work on Venice,[282] where wages had risen prohibitively high, there were three possible solutions: to put industry out into the country; to specialize in luxury goods; or to make up for the shortage of labour by using hydraulically-powered machines. In this state of emergency, all three were used. The trouble was that the first-mentioned, the quasi-natural return to cottage industry, was not and could never be an unqualified success: the Venetian countryside needed every able-bodied worker it could get. In the seventeenth century, it was turning to new crops – mulberry trees and maize, and arable farming was becoming particularly profitable. Venetian exports of rice to the Balkans and Holland were regularly increasing. Exports of both raw and spun silk quadrupled between 1600 and 1800.[283] The second solution, luxury goods, and the third, mechanization, did develop, because of the labour shortage. Some useful observations have recently been offered on mechanization by Carlo Poni.[284] Seventeenth-century Italy thus appears (once again) much less lethargic than general histories would lead one to believe.

It might also be argued that Spanish industry, still so flourishing in mid-sixteenth century, yet so badly deteriorated by the end of the century, was caught in a similar trap. The peasant community was unable to act as a fallback labour force when, in about 1558, industry was beginning to spill out of the towns and

The linen-bleaching industry in the Haarlem countryside in the seventeenth century. Until the use of chlorine bleach, linen used to be soaked several times in butter-milk, then washed with soft soap and spread out to dry in the fields. (Copyright Rijksmuseum, Amsterdam.)

into the countryside. This shows up by contrast the strength of the English position, where the rural sector reliably provided a labour force tied, from a very early date, to wool production through the major industry of cloth making.

Were there key industries?

We have now reached the stage of our argument where we can dimly perceive the complicated outlines of pre-industry. One question now arises – an awkward and possibly premature question insidiously suggested by the present-day world. Were there or not key industries in the *ancien régime*, the kind of industries that today, and perhaps in the past too, attract capital, profits and labour; industries whose take-off may theoretically have a galvanizing effect on neighbouring sectors drawing them along in its wake – notice that I say only '*may*'. For the economy of the past had little coherence, and was indeed often dislocated, as it can be in under-developed countries today. Consequently what happened in one sector did not necessarily have a knock-on effect. So at first glance, one would not expect the pre-industrial world to have the zig-zag profile of industry today with its immense disparities and its advanced sectors.

One could go further and say that pre-industry in the mass, comparatively significant as it was, did not exert any great pull on the rest of the economy. Until the industrial revolution indeed, far from being a leading factor in growth, pre-industry was in fact dominated by the uncertain progress of growth, and by the overall movement of the economy, subject to halts and breakdowns: this explains the hesitant development and uneven swings of pre-industry. What is at issue here is the entire problem, of the value of production as a cradle of change. It may be easier to form a judgment if we single out the really 'dominant' industries before the nineteenth century – and they are of course primarily located, as has many times been pointed out, in the vast and varied domain of textiles.

Such concentration may surprise us today. But past societies set a very high store by fabrics, costumes and ceremonial dress. And then too household interiors were full of fabrics, with their curtains, hangings, tapestries, and their linen cupboards piled high with sheets and fine linens. Social vanity was at its height here and fashion ruled the world. Nicholas Barbon was delighted that it should be so (1690): 'Fashion or the alteration of Dress', he wrote, is a great promoter of trade, 'because it urges people to spend money on new clothes before the old ones are worn out: it is the life and soul of commerce; it ... keeps the whole merchant body in movement; it is an invention which makes man live in perpetual springtime, without ever seeing the autumn of his clothes.'[285] Long live textiles then, was the motto of trade: they represented so much work and even had the advantage of travelling easily, since they were light in relation to their value.

But can one go as far as Georges Marçais (1930) and say that the textiles of the past were, *mutatis mutandis*, the equivalent of the steel industry today, an opinion shared by William Rapp (1975)?[286] The difference is that textiles in so far as they were an *industrial* product, were still predominantly luxury articles. Even when the quality was only moderate, cloth was still an expensive item, which poor people often preferred to make for themselves; it was certainly something they bought only sparingly, failing to follow Nicholas Barbon's advice to renew their wardrobes often. It was not really until the English textile explosion and particularly the cotton revolution of the late eighteenth century that the clientele for textiles acquired a popular character. Now the definition of a truly dominant industry implies the existence of a substantial demand. So we should read the history of textiles with caution. In any case, the successive waves of prosperity recorded do not necessarily correspond to changes in fashion: they also reflect shifts and reorganizations of production at the upper levels of trade. Various rivals were constantly competing for supremacy in the textile world.

In the thirteenth century, the wool trade was synonymous with the Netherlands and Italy;[287] in the following century, Italy predominated: 'The Italian renaissance is really all about wool!' as Gino Barbieri told a recent conference. Then silk took most of the limelight and Italy owed her last years of industrial prosperity, in the sixteenth century, to this precious fabric. But silk soon reached the north, the Swiss Cantons (Zurich), Germany (Cologne), Holland after the

Revocation of the Edict of Nantes, England and above all Lyons, which was about to embark on the career it has pursued to the present time as a great silk centre. But then came a new change in the seventeenth century, as fine English-style woollens made a breakthrough at the expense of silk, in about 1660 if French mercers are to be believed,[288] and this vogue even reached Egypt.[289] Last on the scene, and the new favourite, was 'King Cotton'. There had been cotton in Europe for a long time.[290] But with the stimulus of calicoes, which were printed and dyed by techniques unknown in Europe, and which quickly became all the rage,[291] cotton was soon the leading textile.[292] Would Indian cottons now flood the European market? All barriers were swept aside by the newcomer. So Europe had to set about imitating India, weaving and printing cotton herself. By 1759, there were no obstacles in the way of calico manufacture in France.[293] Shipments of raw cotton to Marseilles in 1788 totalled 115,000 quintals, ten times as much as in 1700.[294]

It is true that in the latter half of the eighteenth century, the generally thriving state of the economy led to a widespread increase in production in all branches of the textile industry. The old manufactories were swept by a fever of novelty and technical ingenuity. Every day, new processes and new fabrics appeared. In France alone, where there was a profusion of craft-shops, '*mignonettes, grisettes, férandines* and *burats* are made in Toulouse, Nîmes, Castres and other towns and localities' in Languedoc;[295] '*espagnolettes*' were seized in Champagne because they did not conform to the norms of width and length; they seem to have come from Chalons;[296] new-style light woollens were made in Le Mans (white warp and brown woof);[297] and there was embossed gauze, *gaze soufflée*, a very light silk fabric on which patterns were printed by sticking on with a fixative a 'powder made of chopped linen thread and starch'. This caused serious customs problems: should it be classified as linen or silk – since the latter only amounted to one-sixth of the weight?[298] In Caen a mixture of linen and cotton known as '*grenade*' was made, and it sold well in Holland.[299] 'Roman serge' was manufactured in Amiens,[300] and there were the clerical cloths of Normandy.[301] This bewildering variety of names was not without significance. Nor should one overlook the outburst of inventiveness in silk manufacture in Lyons, or the new machines appearing one after another in England. One can sympathize with Johann Beckmann[302] one of the first historians of technology who was delighted to find D'Alembert writing: 'Has anything ever been imagined, in any domain at all, more ingenious than the process of weaving striped velvet?'

All the same, the leading place of textiles in pre-industrial life does seem slightly paradoxical to us. This was the 'retrograde' primacy of an activity which had been 'carried on since the depths of the Middle Ages'.[303] And yet the evidence is there. To judge from its volume and its circulation, the textile sector would bear comparison with coal mining, a much more modern industry, or even with French steel-making which was actually in decline, as the enquiries of 1772 and 1778 reveal.[304] Finally, there is the decisive argument, hardly requiring emphasis,

FV FATTO LANNO 1517 SOTTO MISIER ZACHARIA DANTONIO GASTALDO DE MARANGONI DNAVE D'
FV RINOVATO D'LANNO 1753 SOTTO LA GASTALDIA DI FRANCESCO ZANOTTO GASTALDOECO

The sign of the carpenters' guild attached to the Venice Arsenal, seventeenth century. The 'gastaldo' was the leader of a group of craftsmen. Museum of Venetian History, Venice. (Photo Scala.)

that cotton, whether as prime mover or not, played a leading role in the beginnings of the industrial revolution in England.

Merchants and guilds

We have located industrial activities in their various contexts. We have now to decide what part capitalism played in them, and this is not an easy question. The capitalism of the time was that of the urban merchants. But these merchants, both as import-exporters and as entrepreneurs, had been introduced from the start into the guild system created by towns as the means of organization of all craft activity. Merchants and artisans were both caught in the toils of a net from which they never entirely escaped; hence ambiguity and conflict.

The guilds (*corps de métiers* in France – the term *corporations* did not appear there until the Le Chapelier law of 1791 which abolished them) developed between the twelfth and fifteenth centuries throughout Europe, at different dates depending on the region. The last formed were in Spain: the dates traditionally quoted are Barcelona (1301), Valencia (1332) and Toledo (1426). But nowhere were these bodies (French *corps de metiers*, German *Zünfte*, Italian *Arti*, English guilds, Spanish *gremios*) able to have it all their own way. Some towns were controlled by them, others were 'free'. And there might even be separate jurisdictions within the same conurbation – in Paris and London for instance. Their great days were over in the West by the fifteenth century. But in some places they stubbornly survived – particularly in Germany: where the museums today are full of relics of the *Meister* of the *Zünfte*. In France, the expansion of the *corps de metier* in the seventeenth century primarily corresponded to the desires of the monarchy, which was concerned to impose unity, control and in particular taxation. All the guilds went into debt to meet fiscal demands.[305]

In the heyday of the guilds, they controlled the bulk of trade, labour and production. When economic life and the market developed, and the division of labour required new creations and distinctions to be made, there were of course many demarcation disputes. But the number of guilds nevertheless increased, in order to keep up with developments. There were 101 in Paris in 1260, under the strict supervision of the Provost of merchants, and the fact that there were a hundred trades indicates that there was already a high degree of specialization. New sub-divisions later appeared. In Nuremberg, which was ruled by a strict and vigilant aristocracy, the metal-working guilds – the *Metallgewerbe* – had divided as early as the thirteenth century, into several *dozen* independent professions and trades.[306] The same process occurred in Ghent, Strasbourg, Frankfurt and Florence, where the woollen industry as elsewhere, became a collection of trades. In fact it would be true to say that the boom of the thirteenth century arose out of this newly-created division of labour as it proliferated. But the economic upturn it brought was soon to threaten the very structure of the guilds, now endangered by the triumph of the merchants. From this violent opposition there naturally emerged a civil war for control of power within the city. German historians refer to the *Zunftrevolution*, with guilds rebelling against patricians. Behind this rather simplified schema, it is easy to recognize the struggle between merchant and artisan, punctuated by alliances and quarrels – a long class struggle waged to and fro over the years. But the age of violent clashes was comparatively short and in the undeclared war that was to follow, the merchant eventually emerged victor. Collaboration between merchant and guild could never be conducted on a completely equal footing, since what was at stake here was the conquest of the labour market and economic domination by the merchant, not to say by capitalism.

The purpose of the guilds was to bring together the members of a single trade which they defended against all others, in quarrels that were often petty but which had an impact on everyday life. The eagle eye of the guilds was trained above all on the town's market, of which every trade wanted its fair share. This meant security of employment and profit and 'liberties' in the sense of privileges.

But money, the money economy and external trade – in other words the merchant – were now beginning to intervene in a process that was never simple. At the end of the twelfth century, woollen cloth from Provins, one of the little towns around which the Champagne fairs revolved, was being exported to distant Naples, Sicily, Cyprus, Majorca, Spain and even Constantinople.[307] Spires (Speyer), a very modest town at the time, which did not even possess a bridge over the nearby Rhine, was in the same period producing a rather ordinary woollen cloth, black, grey or 'white' (i.e. natural or unbleached). And yet this somewhat inferior product was being marketed as far away as Saint-Gall, Zurich, Vienna and even Transylvania.[308] And at the same time the towns were being invaded by money. The Paris *taille* (tax register) for 1292 tells us that there were quite a number of well-off citizens (paying over 4 *livres* of a tax levied at one-fiftieth) and a few extremely rich people (over 20 *livres*), the top score of 114 *livres* being achieved if that is quite the word by a 'Lombard'. There were clear distinctions between different trades, between rich and poor within a given trade, and also between 'mean streets' often wretchedly poor, and certain others unusually privileged. Above the mass rose the profile of a whole community of money-lenders and merchants, Milanese, Venetian, Genoese and Florentine. The evidence is so uncertain that one could hardly claim that this combination of merchants and shopkeeping tradesmen (shoemakers, grocers, mercers, drapers, upholsterers, coopers etc.) was already producing some form of micro-capitalism at its upper levels, but this seems quite probable.[309]

The money was certainly there at any rate, showing that it could be accumulated, and that once accumulated it could play its role. The unequal struggle had begun: some guilds were to become rich; others, the majority, remained modest. In Florence, they were openly distinguished: the *Arti maggiori* and the *Arti minori* – already there was *il popolo grasso* and *il popolo magro*. Everywhere differences and disparities became more marked. The *Arti maggiori* progressively fell into the hands of the wealthy merchants, as the *Arti* system became no more than a way of controlling the labour market. The organization it concealed was the system known to historians as the *Verlaggsystem* or putting-out system. A new age had dawned.

The Verlagssystem

The *Verlagssystem* or *Verlagswesen* became established all over Europe: these two approximately equivalent terms coined by German historians have unintentionally become part of the *lingua franca* of other nations' historians, although the English expressions 'domestic' or 'putting out system', do exist; the nearest French equivalents are *le travail à domicile* (cottage industry) or *à façon* (hand made).

In this system, there is a *Verleger*, a merchant who 'puts out' work: he provides the artisan with the raw materials and a part-wage, the remainder being paid on delivery of the finished product. The system appeared very early – much earlier than is usually reckoned and certainly by the time of the thirteenth-century boom. How else can one interpret the decision of the Provost of merchants in Paris in June 1275[310] 'forbidding the spinsters of silk to pawn the silk the mercers give them to work, or to sell or exchange it, under pain of banishment'? With the passing of time, there are more indicative documents; in the modern period, the system became widespread: there is a wealth of examples to choose from. In Lucca, on 31 January 1400, two silk merchants, Paolo Balbani and Pietro Gentili, set up a company. The partnership agreement makes it quite clear that '*il trafficho loro serà per la maggiore parte in fare lavorare draperie di seta*', 'that their principal activity will be to have silk sheets made'.[311] 'Fare lavorare' is a direct translation of the Latin expression still current at the time for the function of the entrepreneurs *qui faciunt laborare* who 'have work done'. Contracts signed with the weavers were often witnessed by a notary and their conditions could vary. Sometimes there were disputes after the event: in 1582, a Genoese employer wanted a silk-spinner to recognize that he owed his money and called a witness, who said he knew what had happened, because he was a journeyman of Agostino Costa's and had seen the employer Battista Montorio in the former's shop '*quale li portava sete per manifaturar et prendeva della manifatturrate*', who brought him silk to manufacture and took it away manufactured.[312] This is as clear a picture as one could ask: Montorio was obviously a *Verleger*, a putter-out. So too, in the little town of Le Puy-en-Velay in 1740, was the merchant who had lace made at home by women workers: he provided them with 'a certain weight' of Holland thread 'and took the same weight back in lace'.[313] In Uzès at about the same time, 25 manufacturers had 60 looms working for them in the neighbouring towns and villages, weaving serge.[314] Diego de Colmenares, the historian of Segovia, was already referring to the 'cloth manufacturers' in the time of Philip II, 'who are improperly described as merchants; they are really the heads of great families, for in their own houses and outside they provide a livelihood for a great many persons [some 200, others 300] employing other men's hands to manufacture all kinds of magnificent cloth'.[315] Other examples of *Verleger* are the merchant-cutlers of Solingen, known curiously as *Fertigmacher* (finishers) or the company of hatters in London.[316]

In the putting-out system, the master of a guild was often himself a wage-earner too. He was dependent on the merchant who provided raw materials, often imported from abroad, and who would afterwards handle the sale and export of the cloth, fustians, or silks he had woven. In this way, all the sectors of craft life were touched, and the guild system was gradually being destroyed, although outward appearances were maintained. By obliging the craftsmen to accept his services, the merchant was imposing his choice of activity, whether in iron-work, textiles or ship building.

In fifteenth-century Venice, in the private shipyards (that is outside the huge state Arsenal) the masters of the *Arte dei Carpentieri* and the *Arti dei Calafati* came with their assistants (one or two *fanti* each) to work for the shipping magnates, those who owned shares in the boat to be built. They were thus in the shoes of the ordinary wage-earner.[317] Business was bad in Brescia in 1600. How could the armour trade be stimulated? By appealing to a certain number of *mercanti* in the town who could offer work to both master-craftsmen and journeyman.[318] Once again, capitalism was appearing in a different context. A merchant might also contract with a whole guild, the linen-makers of Bohemia and Silesia for instance, in a system known as the *Zunftkauf*.[319]

All these developments encountered occasional sympathy from within the urban guilds, but more often came up against their determined opposition. The system met with little or no resistance in the countryside though, and the merchant took full advantage of this bonus. He was not only the middleman between the producer of raw materials and the artisan, between the artisan and the purchaser of the finished product, and between his local town and foreign markets, but also had one foot in the town and the other in the country. To combat the ill will or high wages of the town, he could if necessary call extensively on cottage industry. The Florentine wool trade was a combination of activities in both town and country. Similarly in the countryside surrounding Le Mans (which had 14,000 inhabitants in the eighteenth century) there was a whole industry built upon *étamines* (luxury light-weight woollens).[320] Paper-making around Vire is another example.[321]

In the month of June 1775, an observant traveller crossing the Erzgebirge from Freyberg to Augustusberg, journeyed through the string of mountain villages where cotton was spun and lace made (black, white and 'blond', that is combining linen, gold and silk threads). Since it was summertime, all the women were sitting outside on their doorsteps; under a lime tree, a circle of girls sat round an old grenadier. And everyone, including the old soldier, was hard at work. It was a matter of life and death: the lacemaker's fingers only stopped for a moment to pick up a piece of bread or a boiled potato sprinkled with salt. At the end of the week, she would take her work either to the local market (but that was the exception) or more probably to the *Spitzenherr*, the 'lord of the lace', who had provided her with thread and patterns from Holland and France, and who had placed an advance order for her work. Then she would be able to buy her rations: oil, a little meat and rice for Sunday.[322]

Cottage industry was thus responsible for whole networks of family or guild workshops, linked by the marketing organization which both gave them employment and dominated them. As one historian puts it; 'The dispersal of the artisans was only apparent: it is as if the cottage industries were caught up in an invisible financial spider's web, its threads controlled by a few merchants.'[323]

But the spider's web did not catch everything in its toils. There were large regions where production remained beyond the direct reach of the merchant. Wool manufacture in many parts of England is probably one such case; the

The weaver's repose, by A. van Ostade (1610–1685). A typical example of cottage industry. The loom takes up much of the space in the communal room.
(Brussels, Musées Royaux des Beaux-Arts. Copyright A.C.L.)

thriving population of nail-makers around Bédarieux in the Languedoc is possibly another; and this is undoubtedly true of linen-manufacture in Troyes, which was not controlled by a *Verleger* even in the eighteenth century. There were many other such regions, even in the nineteenth century. Such free production was only possible if raw materials were easily available on the nearby market, where the finished goods were also usually sold. In the sixteenth century, at the end of winter, the weavers would come to the Spanish fairs, to sell their woollen cloth as many villagers still did in eighteenth-century England.

And there were no putters-out in the Gévaudan, a particularly poor part of the Massif Central in about 1740. In this inhospitable countryside, some 5000 peasants would settle down at their looms every year when they were 'chased indoors by the ice and snow which would cover the land and the hamlets for six months'. Whenever they finished a length, they would 'carry it to the nearest market ... so that there are as many vendors as lengths; the price is always paid in cash' and this was no doubt what attracted these poverty-stricken peasants. Their cloth, although made with fairly good local wools, was 'of mediocre value, since they are only sold at between 10 or 11 and 20 sols, if one excepts the heavy serges known as *escots*. The buyers are usually merchants from the province of the Gévaudan, scattered in the seven or eight small towns where there are fulling mills, such as Marvéjol, Langogne, La Canourgue, Saint-Chély, Saugues and above all Mandes' (i.e. Mende). The sales took place in the fairs or markets. 'In two or three hours, everything is sold, the buyer makes his choice and decides the price in the front of the booth where he is offered the lengths' and where, once the deal is done, he will check the length with his measure. The sales were noted on a register, with the name of the workman and the price paid.[324]

It was probably at about this time that an entrepreneur by the name of Colson tried to introduce to the primitive Gévaudan the putting-out system, together with the manufacture of the cloth known in England as 'corduroy' and in France as 'Marlborough'. He described in a memorandum addressed to the Estates of Languedoc,[325] the steps he had taken, the degree of success achieved and the need for a subsidy if they wanted him to persevere in his attempt. Colson was a *Verleger* as well as an entrepreneur, who did his best to introduce to the area his special looms, his vats and procedures (in particular a machine of his own invention 'to burn the fluff off the material ... with an alcohol-based flame'). But the chief purpose of the enterprise was to set up an efficient network of cottage industry and to train the spinsters in particular to 'produce, eventually, a thread that is fine, clean and even'. All this cost money, especially since 'everything is paid for in cash in the Gévaudan, and both spinners and weavers are paid half the money in advance, and the poverty of the inhabitants of the region will not induce them to change this custom for a long time'. There is not a word about the level of pay, but we may be sure that it was low. Otherwise why would Colson have gone to all this trouble in a backward area!

The Verlagssystem in Germany

Although it was first detected, christened, analysed and explained by German historians in their own country, the putting-out system was not in fact invented there, spreading only later to other countries. If one had to plump for its country of origin, one might hesitate between the Netherlands (Ghent and Ypres) and industrial Italy (Florence and Milan). But the system which soon spread all over Europe was very widely distributed throughout the regions of Germany, which are therefore from the point of view of historical research, a rich field of observation. An as yet unpublished article by Hermann Kellenbenz, which I shall summarize here, offers us a detailed, varied and convincing picture of the system at work. These putting-out networks are the first hard evidence of a merchant capitalism which was intended to dominate though not to transform craft production. What interested these merchants was undoubtedly marketing. Thus conceived, the *Verlagssystem* might concern itself with any branch of production as soon as a merchant could see any benefit to himself in controlling it. Everything favoured this expansion: the general advance in techniques, the increased speed of transport, the increase in accumulated capital, now handled by expert hands, and finally, the prosperity of the German mines after the 1470s.

The buoyancy of the German economy was visible from many signs, if only the precocious price-rise, or the way its centre of gravity moved from one city to another: in the early fifteenth century, Ratisbon (Regensburg) on the Danube was still the hub of the economy; then Nuremberg took over; the great days of Augsburg and its merchant financiers came later in the sixteenth century: it was as if Germany was constantly pulling after her a Europe which both surrounded and adapted to the German experience – and as if Germany was also changing to conform to her new destiny. The *Verlagssystem* benefited from these favourable circumstances in Germany. If one were to draw a map of the communications it set up, the whole of Germany would be criss-crossed with a network of tiny threads. One after another, the different trades were caught in these webs. In Lübeck the woollen workshops of the fourteenth century were an early example; in Wismar it was brewing with its *Bräuknechte* and *Bräumägde* – already wage-earners; in Rostock, milling and malting. But in the fifteenth century, the vast sector of textiles became the favoured terrain of the system, from the Netherlands, where the concentrations were much greater than in Germany, to the Swiss cantons (linen in Basle and Saint-Gall). The manufacture of fustian – a mixture of linen and cotton – which depended upon the importing of Syrian cotton via Venice, was by its very nature a branch in which the merchant who provided raw materials from abroad played an important role, whether in Ulm or in Augsburg where cottage industry helped *Barchent*'s fortunes.[326] Elsewhere the system was applied to cooperage, paper-making (the first paper-mill in Nuremberg, 1304), printing, and even the manufacture of rosaries.

Mining and industrial capitalism

With mining, in Germany or rather Central Europe in the broad sense, including Poland, Hungary and the Scandinavian countries, capitalism entered upon a new and decisive stage. For here the merchant system took control of production and reorganized it. The real innovation in this respect dates from the end of the fifteenth century: this key period did not actually invent mining or the occupation of miner, but it was a turning point for both technical and working conditions

The miner's trade was an ancient one. Throughout Central Europe groups of artisans, journeymen miners – *Gewerkschaften, Knappschaften*[327] are attested as early as the twelfth century, and the rules of their associations became generalized in the thirteenth and fourteenth centuries, as many German miners moved into the eastern countries. All went well for these tiny mining teams as long as the minerals lay close to the surface and could easily be reached. But when mining had to plunge deeper into the earth serious problems arose: long galleries had to be dug and strengthened with props; winding-gear to bring men and loads out of the pits had to be built, and the ever-present water had to be drained. This was not so much a technical problem (new methods often arise spontaneously to meet a challenge from inside an industry) as a financial one. From now on, mining would require the installation and maintenance of equipment huge by the standards of the time. The changeover, at the end of the fifteenth century, opened the door to rich merchants. From their position of strength as owners of capital they were able to take over the mines and associated industrial enterprises from a distance.

This development occurred almost everywhere at about the same time: in the silver mines of the Harz mountains and Bohemia; in the Tyrolean Alps where there had long been copper mines; and in the gold and silver mines of Hungary from Königsberg to Neusohl along the steep-sided little valley of the Gran.[328] As a consequence the free workers of the *Gewerkschaften* everywhere became wage-labourers, dependent workers. And indeed this was when the word *Arbeiter*, worker, first appeared.

Capital investment resulted in spectacular advances in production, not only in Germany. At Wielicza, near Cracow, the peasant trade of extraction of rock salt by evaporating salt water in shallow iron containers had seen its last days. Galleries and shafts were now dug to a depth of 300 metres, and enormous winches powered by teams of horses brought blocks of salt to the surface. At its peak, production stood at 40,000 tons a year, and the mines employed 3000 workers. By 1368, the cooperation of the Polish state had been obtained.[329] Also near Cracow, but in Upper Silesia, the lead mines near Olkusz which had been producing 300 to 500 tons a year at the end of the fifteenth century, were bringing out 1000 to 3000 tons by the sixteenth and seventeenth centuries. Here the problem was not so much depth (a mere 50 to 80 metres) but too much water. Long tunnels had to be built with wooden supports, sloping downwards so that the water would drain away by gravity, a number of pumping machines operated by horse power had to be installed, and more labour employed – particularly since the rock was so hard that a worker could only advance a tunnel by 5 cm in eight hours' work. It all required capital and automatically placed the mines in the hands of those who possessed it: a fifth of the pits thus fell to the rentier king of Poland, Sigismund Augustus; a fifth to the nobility, the office-holders and the prosperous inhabitants of the new towns nearby; and three-fifths to the merchants of Cracow, who controlled Polish lead just as the merchants of Augsburg had been able, from a much greater distance, to seize control of the gold, silver and copper of Bohemia, Slovakia Hungary and the Tyrol.[330]

It was tempting for such businessmen to *monopolize* the sources of such rich incomes. But they were sometimes biting off more than they could chew: even the Fuggers failed, though only just, to establish a monopoly in copper; the Hochstetters ruined themselves through persisting in trying to set up a mercury cartel in 1529. The size of the investment required usually deterred any single merchant from handling even the whole of one mine. It is true that the Fuggers for many years had sole charge of the mercury mines at Almaden in Spain, but then the Fuggers were a special case. Normally, just as ships were divided into shares or *carats*, the stock of a mine was divided into *Kuxen*, usually 64, sometimes 128. This division made it possible by the granting of a few honorary shares, to associate the prince himself with the enterprise – and indeed he retained effective rights over the sub-soil. In 1580, Augustus I of Saxony owned 2822 *Kuxen*.[331] Thus the state was always present in mining enterprises.

But this glorious, that is to say untroubled phase in the history of mining did not last long. The law of diminishing returns inexorably made itself felt: the mines first prospered then declined. The repeated strikes by miners in Hungary from about 1525–1526, were probably a sign of the changing times. Ten years later, there were increasing indications of a progressive collapse. It is sometimes said that competition from the American mines was responsible, along with the economic recession which for a while interrupted the expansion of the sixteenth century. In any case, merchant capitalism which had been eager to intervene at the end of the fifteenth century, quickly became more prudent and began to pull out of what was no longer a money-making affair. Now the removal of investment is as characteristic of capital as investment: one kind of economic climate sees money put in, another sees it being taken out. Some famous mines were abandoned to the state – an early example of nationalization of unprofitable concerns. If the Fuggers remained in Schwaz in the Tyrol, it was only because the simultaneous occurrence in the ore mined there of both copper and silver still enabled mining to show a considerable profit. In the copper mines of Hungary, other Augsburg firms took their place: the Langnauers, the Haugs, the Links, the Weiss, the Pallers, the Stainigers and lastly the Henckel von Donnersmarks and the Rehlingers. They were in turn to sell out to Italians. Such a quick turnover hints that the mines were making losses or at best only modest profits which their backers one day no longer thought worth the candle.

If however they left most of the mines to the princes, the merchants continued to handle the less risky business of distributing the products of mining and metallurgy. So we no longer look at the history of mining, and beyond it at the history of capitalism itself, through the same optic as Jacob Strieder, sharp though his vision was.[332] If the explanation outlined here is correct – and we

The market in silver ore at Kutna-Hora (Bohemia) in the fifteenth century. Sales took place under the supervision of the mining official who represented the king. The buyers are seated round a table on which the miners spread out the ore. Detail of the Kuttenberger *Gradual*. (Vienna, Österreischische Nationalbibliothek, photo by the Library.)

need to be sure of this – the capitalists who had invested or who were investing funds in mining only pulled out of the insecure and exposed positions in the primary sector: they fell back on the manufacture of part-finished articles, on blast furnaces, foundries and forges or better still on distribution alone. They had retreated to a safe distance.

It would certainly be useful to have a decent number of first-hand accounts of these moves into and out of mining. But for us, the essential problem lies elsewhere. As these powerful mining networks were set up, can we not see emerging a genuine working-class proletariat, a labour force in its plainest form, ('the workers shorn of all but their labour power', according to the classic definition of capitalism, the second element which leads to its existence)? The mines brought together what were for the time huge concentrations of labour. In 1550, in the mines of Schwaz and Falkenstein (Tyrol) there were over 12,000 professional workers; 500 to 600 labourers were solely employed pumping out the water that threatened the tunnels. In this crowd, it is true that there were pockets of non-wage earners: a few small transport entrepreneurs or tiny teams of independent miners. But all or almost all of them depended for their food supply on the large employers: the *Trucksystem*, an extra means of exploiting the workers, provided them, at prices favouring the merchant, with grain, flour, fat, clothes and other *Pfennwert* (cheap goods). This trade provoked frequent protests among the miners, who were often violent by nature and also quick to take to the road. But for all that a labouring world was being built and taking shape. In the seventeenth century, workers' houses appeared around the iron foundries of Hunsrück. As a rule, foundries were capitalist, but iron-mining remained under free enterprise. Lastly, everywhere a labour hierarchy appeared with levels of command: at the top the *Werkmeister* or the mining supervisor, representing the merchant and below him the *Gegenmeister*, the foremen. How many of these emerging patterns foreshadow things to come!

Mining in the New World

The partial but visible withdrawal of capitalism from mining after mid-sixteenth century remains a significant event. Europe, because of her very expansion, was acting as if she had decided to delegate the trouble of handling the mining and metallurgy industries to dependent regions on her periphery. In the heart of Europe, not only were falling yields limiting profits, but the 'fiery furnaces' were destroying forestland, and the price of wood and coal was becoming prohibitive, so that the blast furnaces could only operate part of the time, thus immobilizing fixed capital to no purpose. Meanwhile wages were going up. Small wonder then that the European economy as a whole applied to Sweden for iron and copper; to Norway for copper; before long to distant Russia for iron; to America for gold and silver; to Siam for tin (in addition to the output of the Cornish tin mines); to China for gold; and to Japan for silver and copper.

The Potosi *Cerro* in the background. Men and pack-trains are climbing up the slopes. In the foreground is the *patio* where the silver ore was treated: a hydraulic wheel helped to crush it and hammers reduced it to powder or 'flour' which was then cold-mixed with mercury in paved enclosures: the paste was trodden by Indians. The canal leading to the wheel was fed by the melting snow from the mountain and rainwater from the reservoirs (*lagunas*). Towards the *Cerro* can be seen the cabins ('*rancherias*) of the Indians; on the other side, in front of the *patio*, but not shown here was the town with its long straight streets, often depicted in eighteenth-century drawings. From Marie Helmer, 'Potosi à la fin du XVIIIe siècle' in *Journal des Américanistes*, 1951, p. 40. (Library of the Hispanic Society of America, New York.)

But alternatives were not always available. Mercury, essential for the American silver mines, was an example. Discovered in 1564 and made operational only slowly, the quicksilver mines of Huancavelica[333] in Peru were insufficient, and supplies still had to be brought from the European mines of Idria and Almaden. Significantly enough, these mines were precisely the ones capital did not desert. Almaden remained under the exclusive control of the Fuggers until 1645.[334] As for Idria, where the mines were first discovered in 1497 and first worked from 1508-1510, the merchants were constantly challenging the monopoly held by the Austrian state which had taken them all over in 1580.[335]

Did capitalism commit itself wholeheartedly in these far-off mines to the production from which it was gradually withdrawing in Europe? Yes, up to a point in Sweden and Norway; no, if we look at Japan, China, Siam or America itself.

In America, gold, which was still produced by artisanal techniques near Quito in Peru or in the gold-panning wastes of the Brazilian interior, formed a contrast with silver which was already being produced by a modern technique, the amalgam process imported from Europe and used in New Spain from 1545, and in Peru from 1572. At the foot of the *Cerro* of Potosi, the huge hydraulic wheels crushed the ore and prepared it for the amalgam. This mining required both expensive equipment and expensive supplies of raw materials. It is possible that some kind of capitalism may have been introduced here: we know that in Potosi and New Spain some lucky miners made fortunes overnight. But they were the exceptions. The rule, here as elsewhere was that the profits went to the merchants.

They went in the first place to the local merchant. As in Europe, or rather more than in Europe, the mining population pitched camp in a desert – whether the north of Mexico or the bleak heart of the Andes in Peru. So supplies became a vital question, as they had already been in Europe, where the entrepreneur provided the miners with food, making substantial profits by so doing. In America, supplies dominated everything; in the gold-panning areas of Brazil; in Mexico where the northern mines required the dispatch of enormous supply trains from the south. In 1733, Zacatecas consumed 85,000 *fanegas* of maize (one *fanega* = 15 kg); Guanajuato was consuming 200,000 in 1746 and 350,000 in 1785.[336] But here it was not the *minero* (the mine-owner) who saw to his own supplies. The merchant advanced him rations, textiles, tools and mercury against silver and gold, thus imprisoning him within a system either of barter or of limited partnership. The local merchant thus indirectly controlled the mines, discreetly or openly; but he did not ultimately control the chain of trade links handling these supplies, with representatives in Lima, Panama, in the fairs at Nombre de Dios or Porto Belo, in Cartagena in the Indies and finally in Seville or Cadiz, the terminus of another distribution network in Europe. Another chain led from Mexico City to Vera Cruz, Havana and Seville. And it was along these trading-chains with their ample opportunities for fraud that the real profits were made – not so much at the stage of extraction itself.

Salt, iron and coal

Some activities did however remain in Europe: the extraction of salt, iron and coal for example. No salt mine was ever abandoned and the scale of the equipment needed put these mines in the hands of merchants from very early days. Salt-marshes on the other hand, were exploited by artisanal methods: the merchants took control only of transport and marketing, both in Setubal in Portugal and in Peccais in Languedoc. Salt-marketing was probably quite big business along the Atlantic seaboard or the Rhône valley.

As for iron, the mines, blast furnaces and ironworks long remained production units of limited scope. *Merchant* capital rarely intervened directly. In 1785, in Upper Silesia, out of 243 *Werke* (blast furnaces) 191 belonged to rich landowners (*Gutsbesitzer*), 20 to the king of Prussia, 14 to various principalities, two to foundations and only two to merchants in Breslau.[337] This was because the iron industry tended to be built up vertically and at the beginning the owners of mining sites and the vital forest land had played a crucial role. In England the gentry and nobility often invested in iron mines, blast furnaces and ironworks located on their own property. But these long continued to be individually-mounted enterprises, with uncertain outlets, rudimentary techniques and fixed plant that had cost little. The major items of expenditure were the necessary flow of raw materials, fuel and wages. Credit was the answer. But not until the eighteenth century would large-scale production become possible or technical progress and investment follow the expansion of the market. Ambrose Crowley's giant blast furnace in 1729 was a much less important enterprise than a large brewery of the time.[338]

Coal-mining too was for a very long time in the hands of small or medium-sized concerns. In sixteenth-century France, only certain peasants extracted coal open-cast, for their own use or for a little easy export, along the Loire for instance, or from Givors to Marseilles. Similarly the great fortune of Newcastle did not destroy an ancient and well-entrenched guild organization. In the seventeenth century, in the whole of England, 'for every pit sunk deep [with modern equipment] there were a dozen shallow shafts worked with little expense ... [and with] a few simple tools'.[339] If there were innovations, profits and participation by merchants, these lay in the increasingly widespread distribution of coal. In 1731, the South Sea Company considered sending its ships, recently returned from whaling, to load coal from Newcastle and other ports on Tyneside.[340]

But this was in the eighteenth century when things had already changed. Even in France which lagged behind Britain, the *Conseil de commerce* and other competent authorities were inundated with requests for mining concessions – apparently there was hardly a region of France which did not hold reserves of coal or possibly peat. It is true that the use of coal was spreading, albeit at a slower rate than in England. It was used in the new glass-works in Languedoc, in the breweries in northern France, in Arras or Béthune[341] for instance, and even in the ironworks in Alès. This rekindled the interest of merchants and capital-owners, particularly since the authorities realized that amateurs could not handle undertakings on this scale, as the *intendant* of Soissons wrote to an applicant in March 1760: 'companies like those of Beaurin and M. de Renausan' should be called in, as only these were capable of 'finding the necessary funds to pay for proper mining extraction which can only be done by people who know the job'.[342] Such were the beginnings of the Anzin mines, whose later fame need not concern us here. They would soon take the place of Saint-Gobain as the second-largest enterprise in France after the *Compagnie des Indes*; they may even have had 'fire-operated pumps', that is steam-engines like Newcomen's in 1750;[343] but we need not venture over the threshold of what is already the industrial revolution.

Manufactories and factories

The bulk of pre-industry took the form of the many elementary units of craft production, or the *Verlagssystem*. But above these dispersed workshops, there were already emerging enterprises of a frankly capitalist nature, the *manufactories* and the *factories* (also known as mills or works).

The two words are regularly used interchangeably in the eighteenth century. Historians have on the whole followed Marx and applied the word 'manufactory' (*manufacture*) to concentrations of labour of an artisanal type, using manual labour (particularly in textiles) and the word factory (*fabrique*) to enterprises using machinery such as was already to be found in mines, in metallurgy and in shipyards. We find the French consul in Genoa however writing about the creation in Turin of an establishment employing a thousand weavers of silk with thread of gold or silver, 'this factory (*fabrique*) ... will in time considerably damage the *manufactures* in France'.[344] The two words are evidently synonymous as far as he is concerned. In French, the word '*usine*' which is usually associated with the larger factories of the nineteenth century, already existed in the eighteenth: in 1738, permission was sought to create an '*usine*' near Essonne, 'to manufacture all sorts of copper wire for the coppersmith's trade'.[345] It is true that the same factory was referred to as a 'copper manufactory' in 1772! And in 1768, the smiths and scissors-moulders of the Sedan region asked if they could establish near the mill at Illi[346] 'the factory (*usine*) necessary to them for the manufacture of their *forces*' (*forces* were huge shears for cutting cloth). In 1788, the baron de Dietrich hoped that the ban on 'the establishment of too many *usines*' (i.e. furnaces, foundries, tilt-hammers, glassworks and hammers) would not be applied to him.[347] So the words factory and *usine* can perfectly legitimately be used of the eighteenth century. I have also found an example of the word '*entrepreneur*' dating from 1709[348] although it was still very rare. And according to the Dauzat dictionary, '*industriel*' ('industrialist') in the sense of head of an enterprise, appears in 1770 from the pen of the Abbé Galiani. But it only became current after 1823 with the writings of Saint-Simon.[349]

That said, let us maintain the traditional distinction between manufactory and factory. In both cases since I am here concerned to follow the progress of concentration, I shall not be referring to very *small* units (the word manufactory was sometimes applied to very tiny outfits indeed: in Sainte-Menehould a 'manufactory of serges' employed 5 people in 1690;[350] in Joinville a 'manufactory of druggets' had twelve workmen[351]). In the principality of Ansbach and Bayreuth in the eighteenth century, according to O. Reuter's study, which is something of a survey,[352] the first category of manufactories had between 12 and 24 workers only. In Marseilles in 1760, 38 soap-works employed about a thousand people between them. If such establishments literally correspond to the definition of a manufactory given by Savary des Bruslons in his *Dictionnaire* (1761): ('place in which several workmen or craftsmen are assembled to work on the same kind of material')[353] they are so small that they would take us back to artisan manufacture.

There clearly were manufactories much bigger than this, although in a general way these large units were not necessarily concentrated in one place. They were principally housed in a central building, it is true. As early as 1685, an English book with the promising title *The Discovered Gold Mine*[354] describes how 'the manufacturers, at great cost, build whole great houses wherein the wool sorters, combers, spinners, weavers, pressers and even dyers work together'. The gold mine, as the reader will have gathered, was a woollen manufactory. But, and this was a rule virtually without exceptions, manufactories always employed, besides their concentrated labour-force, out-workers in the town or the nearby countryside, all working at home. So they were really at the same time a centre for the putting-out system. The Van Robais manufactory of fine woollen cloth in Abbeville employed almost 3000 workers, but it is hard to say how many of these worked at home, in the neighbourhood.[355] A stocking manufactory in Orleans in 1789 had 800 persons working under one roof but double the number outside.[356] The woollen manufactory founded by Maria Theresa, in Linz, employed no less than 15,600 workers (26,000 by 1775) – and there is no misprint in this colossal number; it was indeed in Central Europe where industry had some leeway to make up, that the highest concentrations were to be found. But of this total, about two-thirds were spinners and weavers working at home.[357] Manufactories in Central Europe often recruited their workers from the ranks of peasant serfs – proving incidentally once again that a technical innovation is quite indifferent to the social context it encounters. And slave labour or something very like it was also to be found in the West, since some manufactories used the inmates of the workhouses, the indigent, the out-of-work, the criminal or orphans. Not that this prevented them from putting out work as well, like other manufactories.

It might be thought that manufactories spread outwards from a centre as they grew larger. But the opposite seems to have been the case if one considers the actual origins of the manufactory. It was often the focal point of a network of cottage industry, the place where the production process was eventually finished. And the finishing process, as Daniel Defoe tells us in the case of wool,

Glass-working, an illustration from the *Voyages de Jean de Mandeville* about 1420.
(British Library.)

could be almost half the entire work.[358] So a certain number of *final* operations
took place in the central building which later increased in size. The woollen
industry in Tuscany in the thirteenth and fourteenth centuries in fact amounted
to an enormous *Verlagssystem*. The *Compagnia dell' Arte della lana* which
Francesco Datini founded on his return to Prato in February 1383 consisted of a

dozen people working in a small shop, with a thousand others scattered over an area of more than 500 km² around Prato working for him too. But gradually certain processes tended to be concentrated in one place (weaving and combing) and a manufactory began to take shape although at an extremely slow pace.[359]

But why were so many manufactories content to do only the finishing? And why were so many others, although they handled almost the complete cycle of production, prepared to employ all these out-workers? In the first place, the finishing processes – fulling, dyeing etc. – were the most technically delicate and required comparatively large amounts of equipment. Logically they took manufacturing beyond the artisanal phase and called for capital investment. In addition, for the merchant, taking responsibility for the finishing processes meant controlling what interested him most, the marketing of the product. Price differences between urban and rural products may also have contributed something. London for instance had every reason to go on buying cloth in its unfinished form from provincial markets, where prices were low, and then see to the finishing and dyeing which counted for a great deal in the value of a fabric. Finally, and most important, using out-workers meant having the freedom to adjust production to a very variable demand without throwing out of work the skilled labour of the manufactory. When demand fluctuated, one simply put more or less work out. But it is also clear that the profits of the manufactory must have been fairly low, and its future relatively insecure, for it not to have become self-sufficient, preferring to remain semi-imprisoned in the *Verlagssystem*. This was probably through necessity rather than choice – in short through weakness.

And in any case, manufacturing industry remained a very minority activity. All the records tell the same story. Friedrich Lütge writes that 'all the manufactories put together placed a much less prominent role in production than one might think from the frequency with which they are cited'.[360] There were in Germany perhaps a thousand manufactories, of all sizes. When attempts are made, as in the case of Bavaria[361] to estimate how they compared with the national produces as a whole, the answer is less than 1%. More statistics are needed but we may be sure that the same pessimistic conclusion would be reached.

The manufactories were nevertheless models and instruments of technical progress. And the modest place occupied by manufacturing production at least proves one thing: the great difficulties encountered by pre-industry in the contexts in which it developed. It was to help break this circle that the mercantilist state so often intervened; and that it financed and initiated a national policy of industrialization. Except perhaps for Holland any European state would serve as an example, including England, where industry originally developed behind a wall of highly protective tariffs.

In France, state intervention goes back at least as far as the installation by Louix XI of a silk loom at Tours: the problem was already perceived as a need to produce goods at home instead of buying them abroad, in order to reduce the outflow of precious metals.[362] The mercantilist and already 'nationalist' state was intrinsically 'bullionist'. It could have taken its motto from Antoine de Montchrestien, the 'father' of political economy: 'the country should provide for the country'.[363] Louis XI's successors followed his lead whenever they could, Henri IV with special attention: by 1610, the year of his death he had set up 40 of the 47 existing manufactories. Colbert did the same. And his creations, as Claude Pris[364] has remarked, also corresponded to the desire to combat a difficult economic climate. Did their artificial character explain why most of them disappeared fairly quickly? The only ones to survive were those either administered or granted far-reaching privileges by the state – Beauvais, Aubusson, the Savonnerie, the Gobelins and, among the so-called *manufactures royales*, the Van Robais woollen centre in Abbeville (founded in 1665 and surviving until 1789); the mirror manufactory founded in the same year, partly established at Saint-Gobain in 1695 – which is still there today; or the royal manufactories in Languedoc, one of which in Villeneuve was still active in 1712 with its 3000 workers, evidence that the Levant trade was still providing it with outlets.[365]

The economic expansion of the eighteenth century brought a whole string of manufacturing projects into being. The individuals responsible outlined their intentions to the *Conseil de commerce* and unfailingly applied for privileges which they claimed were in the public interest. Their ambitions regularly went beyond the local scene: the national market was what they were after – proof that it was at least beginning to exist. A factory in Berry making 'iron and tempered steel'[366] asked straight out for a privilege covering the whole of France. But the biggest difficulty for the new manufactories or those about to be set up was how to capture the coveted Paris market, access to which was staunchly defended by the six *Corps* which formed the elite of the guilds and themselves represented large capitalist interests.

The papers of the *Conseil de commerce* between 1692 and 1789, though incomplete and out of order, record many applications either from existing manufactories seeking to obtain some privilege or renewal, or from people wishing to start one up. A sample of the industries mentioned shows the growing diversity of this sector: 1692, lacemaking in Tonnerre and Chastillon; 1695, tin in Beaumont-en-Ferrière; 1698, red and black morocco leather 'Levant fashion', and calf-skin 'English fashion' in Lyons; 1701, porcelain and pottery in Saint-Cloud; bleaching of fine thread in Anthony on the Bièvre; 1708, serge at Saint-Florentin; starch in Tours; 1712, cloth (England and Holland style) at Pont-de-l'Arche; 1715, wax and candles at Anthony, *moquette* in Abbeville; soft soap in Givet; cloth in Châlons; 1719, pottery in Saint-Nicolas, a suburb of Montereau; cloth in Pau; 1723, cloth in Marseilles, a sugar refinery and soap-works in Sète; 1724, pottery and porcelain in Lille; 1726, cast iron and steel in Cosne; wax, household and church candles in Jagonville, a suburb of Le Havre; 1756, silk in Le Puy-du-Velay; 1762, wire and scythes in Forges in Burgundy; 1763, tallow candles imitating wax in Saint-Mamet near Moret; 1772, copper at the Gilat mill near Essonnes; wax candles in Tours; 1777, tiles and pottery in Gex; 1779, paper-making at Saint-Cergues near Langres; bottles and windowpanes in Lille; 1780, coal-working in Marseilles (three years later the manufactory claimed to have 300 workers); iron cut 'round, square and in flakes in the German fashion' in Sarrelouis; paper-making in Bitche; 1782, velvet and cotton sheets in Neuville; 1788, cotton calicoes in Saint-Veron; 1786, handkerchiefs 'English fashion' in Tours; 1789, cast iron in Marseilles.

The appeals of the manufacturers and the considerations of the commissioners of the Council explaining their decisions give us some precious glimpses of the way manufactories were organized. We learn that Carcassonne was in 1723 'the best-supplied town' in France 'for woollen manufactories', 'the manufacturing centre of Languedoc'. When fifty years earlier, Colbert had established royal manufactories in Languedoc so that Marseilles could follow the English example and export cloth to the Levant instead of sending money, the enterprise had got off to a difficult start in spite of considerable aid from the provincial estates. But the industry had subsequently prospered to such a degree that manufacturers who did not benefit from privileges came and settled or remained in Languedoc, especially in Carcassonne. These manufacturers alone accounted for four-fifths of production, and after 1711 they were even paid a small allowance on every length of cloth made, 'so that there shall not be too great a disparity between them and the entrepreneurs of the royal manufactories'. The latter did indeed continue to receive an annual subsidy, not to mention the advantage of being exempt from inspection; by the sworn custodians of the guilds who checked whether the fabric met the standards required by the profession. It is true that the royal manufactories did receive visits from the inspectors of manufacture, but at very long intervals, and that they were bound to manufacture every year the quantity of material specified in their contract, whereas other enterprises were 'free to stop working when they are making no profit because of the high price of wool, in times of war or for any other reason'. Nevertheless there was a great outcry among 'the community of manufacturers and the communities of weavers, dressers, shearers and dyers' etc. when one of the Carcassonne manufacturers pulled strings to get his business registered as one of the royal manufactories, and briefly succeeded. The decision was referred to the *Conseil de commerce* and finally went against him. We learn incidentally that the *Conseil de commerce* saw no advantage 'at the present time in multiplying the number of royal manufactories', especially in towns, where as the experience in Paris had shown, they were the source of many conflicts and much fraud. What would have happened if De Saintaigne – the applicant – had succeeded? His business would have become a rendezvous for unskilled workers who would have been able, thanks to the royal privilege, to work on their own account. So he would have drained off workers towards him.[367] It is clear then that there was opposition between the workshops subject to the usual rules and those with royal dispensation who could set up a unit of production outside the jurisdiction of the law – rather like the privileged shipping companies which also operated outside the law and for even bigger stakes.

The Van Robais enterprise in Abbeville[368]

The royal cloth manufactory founded in Abbeville in 1665 on Colbert's initiative by the Dutchman Josse Van Robais, was apparently a sound enterprise: it did not close its doors until 1804. Originally, Van Robais had brought about fifty workers with him from Holland, but apart from these early arrivals, the workforce (3000 in 1708) was recruited entirely from local people.

For a long time, the enterprise consisted of several large workshops dispersed around the town. It was not until quite late, 1709–1713, that a large building known as *Les Rames* (the *rames* were 'long wooden stretchers . . . on which the cloth was spread to dry') was erected outside the town to house it. There was a central hall for the masters and two wings for the weavers and cloth-shearers. Surrounded by hedges and moats, and backing on to the town walls, Les Rames was a little world in itself: at all the doors were stationed 'Swiss guards' in royal livery (red, white and blue). This made it easier to enforce supervision, discipline and respect of the rules (the workers were forbidden among other things to bring in spirits). From his office, the master 'could keep an eye on most of the workers'. However even this enormous building (it cost 300,000 *livres*) could not contain the stores, wash-houses, stables, the forge or the grindstones where the *forces* (shears) were sharpened. The spinsters were scattered around various workshops in town. And there were also considerable numbers of outworkers, since eight spinners were required to feed each of the hundred 'flying looms' in the manufactory. A fulling mill for the de-greasing of the cloth was built far outside town, by the clear waters of the Bresle.

So while concentration was quite advanced, it was not perfect. But the organization here was resolutely modern. Division of labour was the rule: the manufacture of fine cloth, the chief activity of the enterprise, 'passed through 52 different processes'. And the business provided its own supplies, whether of fuller's earth (brought from Ostend in little boats called *bellandres*) or of fine wool from Segovia, the best in Spain, which was loaded in Bayonne or Bilbao aboard the *Charles-de-Lorraine* (and after this ship was wrecked, aboard the *Toison d'Or*, the *Golden Fleece*). Both these vessels appear to have sailed up the Somme as far as Abbeville.

It all ought to have worked perfectly; in fact the Van Robais fortunes seem to have gone up and down. There were some sordid quarrels inside the Van Robais family which need not concern us. But there were always the nagging demands of the balance sheet. Between 1740 and 1745, the business sold on average 1272 lengths at 500 *livres* each, a total of 636,000 *livres*. This sum represented circulating capital (wages, materials and costs) plus profit. The

Manufactory of printed cottons in Orange (section of a mural in a private house in the town, painted by J. C. Rossetti in 1746). In the printing-hall stands the founder of the business, the Swiss Jean-Rodolphe Wetter, and his wife; nearby an employee is showing one of the printing plates to a Swiss friend of Wetter's. To the left and right are other workshops. There was a large workforce – 600 in 1762. But the manufactory did not prosper to the same extent as the one in Jouy-en-Josas near Versailles. After several reorganizations, it closed its doors in 1802. (Photo N. D. Roger-Viollet.)

major problem was to pay out the 120,000 to 200,000 *livres* of the wage-bill and at the same time pay off a capital investment which must have been a million or more and which had periodically to be renewed or serviced. There were difficult moments and tensions and usually the easy answer was to lay off workers. The first protest by the workers dates from 1686; and there was a tumultuous strike in 1716. In fact these workers were almost perpetually semi-unemployed, since in hard times the manufactory kept on only an elite – foremen and skilled workers. Indeed the characteristic development of new enterprises was a move towards an ever larger scale of pay differentials and work-rôles.

The 1716 strikers did not give in until the arrival of a small detachment of armed troops. The ringleaders, of whom there were a few, were arrested then pardoned. The *subdélégué* of Abbeville clearly had no sympathy with the rebels, people who 'in time of plenty give themselves up to licentiousness instead of saving up for hard times' and 'who do not seem to realize that the manufactory is not there for them, but that they are there for the manufactory'. Order was firmly restored apparently, if we are to go by the remarks of a traveller who passed through Abbeville a few years later in 1728 and admired everything about the manufactory: its buildings 'in the Dutch style', the '3500 workers and 400 girls' working there, the 'exercises executed to the sound of the drum', the 'girls who are supervised by mistresses and work separately'. He concluded that he had seen 'nothing better-ordered or more cleanly kept'.[369]

In fact, without the generosity of the government, the enterprise would not have lasted as long as it did – particularly since it had the misfortune to be located in an industrial and 'guild-ruled' town, where it stuck out like a sore thumb. The hostility towards it was inventive and competitive. Here there was no peaceful coexistence between past and present.[370]

The finances of capitalist enterprise

What we really need is to be able to follow the financial operations of large-scale industrial enterprises in the seventeenth and eighteenth centuries. But with the exception of the glass manufactory at Saint Gobain, we must be content with the occasional reference. The growing part played by capital – both fixed and circulating – is however beyond doubt. The initial investment was sometimes great. According to F. L. Nussbaum, a minimum of between £500 and £1000 was required for a printworks employing 40 workers in London in 1700;[371] between $5000 and $25,000 for a sugar refinery where the number of workers was only ten or twelve;[372] 'not less than £2000' for a distillery, with the promise of profits which were usually substantial.[373] In 1681, a 'cloth manufactory was founded at New Mills, Haddingtonshire, with a capital of £5000'.[374] Breweries, which had long been small-scale undertakings, expanded, attaining the capacity to brew huge quantities of beer at the cost of heavy expenditure on equipment. £20,000 was spent on 'fixed plant' by Whitbreads, 'to satisfy the thirst of three-

Printed cotton, designed by J. B. Huet, the artistic partner of the founder of the manufactory of Jouy-en-Josas, Oberkampf, showing the manufactory's buildings during this time of prosperity and the new machines that had been invented one after another since its foundation in 1760. These particularly concerned the scouring of the woven fabric, and printing from copperplates instead of from wooden blocks. (Viollet Collection.)

quarters of a million Londoners' in the 1740s'.[375] This costly equipment had to be renewed periodically. How often? Much more evidence is needed before an answer can be given. And major problems could crop up, depending on the industry, either from fixed or circulating capital. The latter was more often a problem. Large manufacturers were always finding themselves short of money. In January 1712, the royal manufactory of Villeneuve in Languedoc, founded by Colbert, and confirmed in its privileges for ten years from 1709, ran into difficulties.[376] In order to continue delivering its Holland and English style cloth, it asked for an advance of £50,000 *livres tournois*: 'This sum ... is necessary for the upkeep of my workers who are over three thousand in number' – it was what would today be called a cash-flow crisis.[377]

In January 1721, another royal cloth manufactory, run by the brothers Pierre and Geoffroy Daras, found itself on the brink of ruin. It had been established in Chalons for over thirty years, and had already asked for help from the *Conseil de commerce* which had allocated it on 24 July 1717 the sum of 36,000 *livres*, payable within eighteen months and repayable in ten years without interest. Although the instalments were not paid regularly, the Daras brothers had received most of it by October 1719. But then everything went wrong: first of all there was the 'extraordinarily high cost' of wool. Then, after putting 'all their funds' into making cloth and 'having sold it to retail merchants, following the usual commercial practice, with six months' and a year's credit, these retailers, taking advantage of the discrediting of bank notes, had paid them in this money just before it was devalued'. So they were victims of John Law, having had to sell these notes 'at rock-bottom prices' in order to pay their workers 'every day'. And since troubles never come singly, they had been thrown out of the house they had leased thirty years earlier and converted into a manufactory at a cost of 50,000 *livres*. In the new building which they had bought for 10,000 *livres* (of which 7000 were borrowed) they had had to spend 8000 *livres* to instal the looms, dyeing vats and other 'utensils necessary for manufacturing'. So they asked for, and received, more time to repay the royal advance.[378]

Another example dates from 1786, a very poor year it is true. The royal manufacture of Sedan (proprietors: Madame *Veuve* Laurent Husson and Carret brothers), an establishment of longstanding reputation which had remained in the same family for ninety years, found itself owing 60,000 *livres*. Its difficulties were the result of a fire, and of the death of Laurent Husson which had obliged the manufactory (because of inheritance claims I imagine) to give up part of its premises and build new ones; and lastly there had been an ill-advised investment in exports to New England – that is to the American insurgents just after their Declaration of Independence – funds 'which have not yet returned'.[379]

The case of Saint-Gobain on the other hand[380] can be considered a success, after about 1725–1727. This mirror manufactory, founded in Colbert's time in 1665, had its privileges renewed right down to the Revolution, in spite of violent protests, in 1757 for example, from the partisans of free enterprise. In 1702, poor

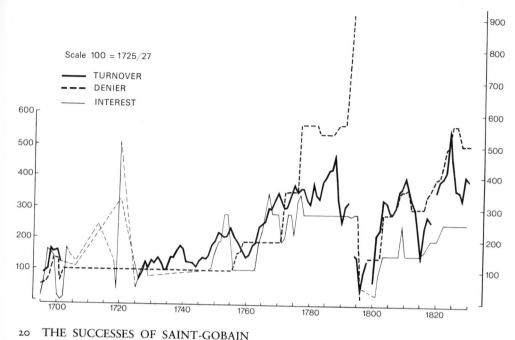

Scale 100 = 1725/27

—— TURNOVER
--- DENIER
— INTEREST

20   THE SUCCESSES OF SAINT-GOBAIN

For details see pp. 340-1, notably concerning the *denier*. This graph is taken from Claude Pris's unpublished thesis, *La Manufacture royale de Saint-Gobain, 1665-1830*, 1297 pp., which deserves to be published.

management led to a bankruptcy, which was a major setback, but the enterprise was put back on its feet with a new management and new shareholders. Thanks to the exclusive monopoly it held of making mirrors for the French market and for export, thanks too to the general expansion of the eighteenth century, sales took off after 1725-1727. The graph in Figure 20 shows the general fortunes of the enterprise, the interest paid to shareholders and the movement of the price of the *denier* (which was not be confused with an ordinary share, the price of which would be quoted on the Stock Exchange). Nor did the enterprise enjoy the freedom of manœuvre of an English Joint Stock Company of the time, or of the firms created in France after the *Code du commerce* of 1807.

The manufactory had been set back on its feet in 1702 thanks to certain Parisian tax-farmers (*traitants*), in other words bankers and financiers who were at the time looking for a safe place to invest their money, whether in land or in shares. The capital stock of the company was divided at this time into 24 *sols*, and each *sol* sub-divided into 12 *deniers*: so there was a total of 288 *deniers*, unequally distributed among the 13 shareholders of the rescue operation. These part-shares as they may be termed fell into the hands of successive owners, through inheritance or occasionally transfer. In 1830, Saint-Gobain had 204 shareholders, some of whom owned tiny fractions (eighths or sixteenths) of a *denier*. The price of whole *deniers* (valued when they formed part of an inheritance) enables us to reconstruct the upward curve over time.

Evidently the capital of the company had multiplied. But perhaps this can be explained in part by the behaviour of the shareholders. In 1702, these were businessmen; but by 1720, the shares were passing into the hands of the great noble families into which the daughters of the original financiers had married. Thus Mademoiselle Geoffrin, the daughter of the treasurer of the manufactory, and of Madame Geoffrin whose salon became famous, married the Marquis de La Ferté-Imbault. The manufactory thus gradually came under the control of noble rentiers rather than true businesssmen. The rentiers were content with regular modest dividends instead of demanding their full share of profits. Perhaps this was one way of increasing and safeguarding the company's capital.

On the profits from industry

It would obviously be rash to risk an overall judgment on the question of industrial profits. This difficulty, or rather near-impossibility, is a major obstacle to our *historical* understanding of the economic life of the past and in particular of capitalism. We need more figures, reliable figures and series of them. If historical research, which has in the past come up with a wealth of data on prices and wages, could today present us with a documented record of rates of profit, the results could be analysed to provide valid explanations: we should better understand why it was that capital hesitated to regard agriculture as anything more than a source of rent; why the shifting world of pre-industry looked to the capitalist like a trap or a quagmire; and why he felt he did better to stay on the sidelines of this diverse field of activity.

What is clear is that the choice made by capitalists could only widen the gap between industry and commerce. Since commerce, commanding the market, was all-powerful, industrial gains were regularly dwarfed by trading profits. This is plain to see in centres where a modern industry could easily have prospered: in machine-made bonnets for instance or lace-making. The latter consisted in eighteenth-century Caen of nothing more or less than the establishment of a number of training-schools, using child labour, followed by the setting up of workshops and manufactories, thus preparing the ground for the group discipline without which the industrial revolution would never have succeeded so quickly in operating its 'painful grafts'. And yet the Caen lace industry collapsed, and one firm for instance was only set on its feet again by an enterprising young man in the wholesale trade – in which he included his own lace production. So when the business was once more prosperous, it is impossible to estimate how much of this was accounted for by manufacturing.

It is of course a simple matter to explain why our measurements are so inadequate. Profit rates are not an easily ascertainable figure; and above all they do not have the comparative regularity of interest rates[381] of which we can take samples so to speak. Profits were variable, unreliable and hard to pinpoint. Jean-Claude Perrot's study which breaks so much new ground, has however demonstrated that the search is not entirely futile, that one can dimly perceive the quarry – and that one can even select as a unit of reference if not the individual enterprise (and even this is not always impossible) either the town or the province. As for the national economy, well that is perhaps better left alone!

In short, the attempt is worthwhile, although the path is strewn with obstacles. Profit was the approximate[382] point of intersection of innumerable lines: so we have to discover, trace, reconstruct and sometimes simply imagine these lines. There are many variables, but J.-C. Perrot has shown that it is possible to bring them together and to associate them in comparatively simple relationships. There are, there must be, approximate coefficients of correlation which can be worked out: if I know x I can have some idea of the size of y. Industrial profits came, as we already know, at the point where the price of labour met the price of raw materials, the price of capital and the point of entry to the market. J.-C. Perrot is able to show that the profits of the all-powerful merchant were constantly eating away at industrial 'capitalism'.

In short, what historical research really needs in this area is a methodical model, the *model* of a *model*. If it had not been for François Simiand and above all Ernest Labrousse, historians would never have set to work as willingly as they did on the study of wages and prices. We need a new impetus. So let me list, if not the precise stages of the future method, at least the requirements it will have to satisfy:

1 The first task will be to *collect* all the profit rates, known or indicated (even if they come in limited sequences or as isolated pieces of data (the good evidence can be sorted out from the bad at a later stage). Thus we know for instance:

– that a steel factory 'under feudal monopoly' dependent on the bishop of Cracow and located outside this city, made profits of 150% in 1746, but that these dropped in subsequent years to 25%;[383]

– that in Mulhouse[384] in about 1770, profits on calicoes were about 23% to 25%, but that they were nearer 8.5% in 1784;

– that there is a series of records for the paper mill at Vidalon-lès-Annonay,[385] running from 1772 to 1826, with a marked contrast between the period before 1800 (profit rates of below 10% except in 1772, 1793 and 1796) and the period after 1800, when there was a sharp rise;

– that substantial profits are recorded in Germany for the same period, where von Schüle, the Augsburg cotton king, was making an annual profit of 15.4% between 1769 and 1781; where a silk manufactory in Crefeld had profits varying over five years (1793–1797) between 2.5% and 17.25%; where the tobacco manufactories of the Bolongaro brothers, founded in Frankfurt and Hochst in 1734–1735, possessed two million *thalers* in 1779;[386]

– that the coal-mines of Littry in Normandy, not far from Bayeux, for an investment of 700,000 *livres* made a profit from 1748 to 1791 of between 160,000 and 195,000 *livres*.[387]

I will stop the list here: it is merely indicative. After transferring figures like these to a graph, I would then mark *in red ink* the 10% level which might provisionally be regarded as the crucial borderline. Anything over 10% would be considered very good indeed; success would be represented by scores in the region of or just below 10%, and outright failure by zero or below zero scores. The first point to be made, and it need not necessarily surprise us, is that there are some very wide and unanticipated variations among these figures.

2 Secondly a *classification* will have to be made which distinguishes between new and old industries, regions and, above all, differing economic circumstances, bearing in mind that these circumstances could vary greatly: industries did not prosper or decline simultaneously.

3 Thirdly an effort will have to be made to get a *historical perspective*, by looking back as far as possible, to the sixteenth, fifteenth and even fourteenth centuries, that is *to escape from the extraordinary statistical monopoly of the late eighteenth century*, in order to locate the problem in the long term – in other words, to repeat in this domain the brilliant successes achieved in price history. Is this possible? I am sure that it would be possible to calculate the profit made by an entrepreneur cloth manufacturer in Venice in 1600. In Schwaz in the Tyrol, the Fugger's *Eisen und Umschlitthandel* 'business' (which combined industry and trade) made a profit of 23% in 1547.[388] And the historian A. H. de Oliveira Marques[389] has gone one better and produced a quite detailed analysis of craft working in Portugal in the late fourteenth century. He has managed to distinguish in a given product the proportion accounted for respectively by labour (L) and raw materials (M). For shoes, M = 68% to 78%; L = 32% to 22%; the same equation works for horseshoes and articles of saddlery (M = 79 to 91%) etc. The surplus (*ganho e cabedal* – profit and capital) reserved for the master has to be extracted from the labour costs (L): this percentage – the profit – varies between a half, a quarter, a sixth or an eighteenth of the wages for labour, i.e. between 50 and 5.5%. Once the cost of materials is included in the calculation, the profit margin is reduced to very little.

Walter G. Hoffmann's law (1955)[390]

In short we must start with production. In this immense and hardly-explored area, are there any rules to light our way?

In my work with Frank Spooner published in 1967,[391] I showed that the curves for industrial production we know about in the sixteenth century regularly take the form of a parabola. The examples of the American mines, of cloth production in Leyden, *sayette* (worsted) production in Hondschoote, or woollen cloth in Venice, are quite telling in themselves. It is of course out of the question

Combing cotton in Venice, seventeenth century. (Museo Correr, Viollet collection.)

to generalize from such slender evidence: we have plenty of price curves, but very few production curves. All the same, the typical pattern of a sharp rise followed by an abrupt fall can very easily be imagined as the probable profile, in the pre-industrial economy, reflecting the brief hour of glory of some city's industry, or a passing boom in exports, over almost as quickly as last year's fashions; or competing industries of which one regularly ousts the other; or the perpetual migration of industries which seem to rise from their ashes when they leave their place of origin.

Jean-Claude Perrot's study of Caen in the eighteenth century extends and confirms these observations apropos four different industries which he has studied minutely in the context of the economic life of the Normandy town where they flourished in succession: the cloth trade, both luxury and ordinary; bonnet-making; calicoes; and finally the 'exemplary' case of the lace industry. Broadly, the story is of very short-term success, that is a series of parabolas. External influences naturally played their part: the rise of the *étamines* industry of Le Mans did much damage to textiles in Caen. But one feature of *local* significance stands out: as one industry declined it seems to have helped another to rise, and vice versa. Thus 'the manufacture of woven hose [was to be] the successful rival of the cloth industry, which was abandoned when it was bringing in hardly anything'.[392] 'The prosperity of bonnet-making and the decline in woollen fabrics are ... exactly simultaneous between 1700 and 1760.'[393] In turn, bonnet-making gradually made way for cotton fabrics. Then calicoes were eclipsed by the lace industry which also expanded and then declined in a perfect parabola, as if the rule admitted of no exception. In fact it seems as though in Caen each rising industry prospered at the expense of a declining industry, as though the town's capacity, not so much for investment as for outlets for finished goods and access both to raw materials and above all labour, was too limited for several industrial activities to be able to flourish simultaneously. Under such conditions, the choice fell in turn on the most viable of the possible industries.

All this seems quite natural in a period when economies consisted of sectors still somewhat disconnected from each other. What is surprising, on the other hand, is that in Walter G. Hoffmann's book *British Industry 1700–1950*, one finds, backed up by a wealth of statistical evidence, the same kind of parabola presented as a sort of general law to be applied to the very well-developed world of the nineteenth and twentieth centuries. For Hoffmann, any given industry (and the exceptions merely prove the rule) will pass through three stages: expansion, plateau, decline, or to be more precise: '(i) the stage of industrial expansion which is characterised by a rising rate of growth of output; (ii) the stage of industrial development, when the rate of growth is declining; and (iii) the stage ... when there is an absolute decline of output'. In the eighteenth, nineteenth and twentieth centuries, the only exceptions Hoffmann encountered were four 'non-typical' industries: tin, paper, tobacco and hempen goods. But perhaps, he suggests, there were industries with a longer rhythm than the others (rhythm being the chronological distance between the beginning and end of the parabola, a distance which could vary with the product and no doubt with the period. Oddly enough, Frank Spooner and I had noticed that even in the sixteenth century, tin did not conform to the rule.

This must all mean something, but that is not to say we have found the explanation. The really difficult task is to detect the link between the particular industry studied and the *economic context surrounding it* upon which its own career depends.

That context might be a town, a region, a nation, or a group of nations. The same industry could disappear in Marseilles and expand in Lyons. When, in the early seventeenth century, the thick cloth, made of unbleached wool, which England had previously exported in large quantities to the whole of Europe and the Levant, suddenly went out of fashion in the West and became too dear in the East, there was a crisis of overproduction and unemployment, particularly in Wiltshire, but elsewhere as well. There was a move over to lighter cloth, dyed on the spot, which made it necessary not only to change weaving practices in the countryside, but also the equipment in the centres where the cloth was finished. This conversion occurred *unevenly* according to region, so that after the intro-

Average price of wheat
in Europe

Fabric production
| Lengths of fabric

Leyden

100 000

Hondeschoote

10 000

Venice

2 000

Silver production   Potosi mines, Peru (in pesos)

3 000

Tin production   Tin mines in Devon
and Cornwall (in kg)

1 000

Scale of fabric production

Scale of
metal production

10
9
8
7
6
5
4
3
2
1

1440   1500   1600   4   1700   1760

21 DO INDUSTRIAL PRODUCTION CURVES ALWAYS TAKE THE FORM OF PARABOLAS?

The curves of industrial production for the sixteenth century are
already showing parabolas comparable to the graphs calculated by
W. G. Hoffmann (*British Industry 1700-1950*, 1955) for a much later
period. Note the aberrant curve for Devon tin; in Leyden there were
two parabolas. Graph by F. C. Spooner, *Cambridge Economic History
of Europe*, IV, p. 484.

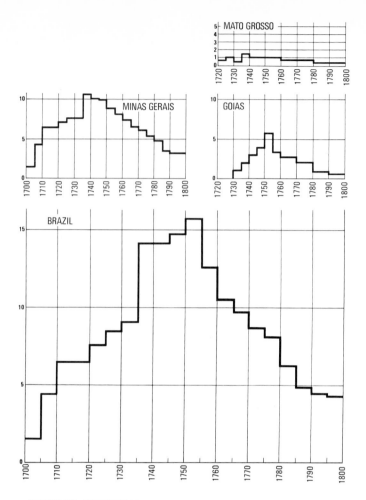

22 GOLD PRODUCTION IN EIGHTEENTH-CENTURY BRAZIL
In tons. After Virgilio Noya Pinto, *O ouro brasileiro e o comercio anglo-portugues*, 1972, p. 123. Here too, we find a series of parabolas.

duction of the 'new draperies' *regional* cloth production was no longer on the same footing everywhere: there were new successes and some failures beyond repair – in short the map of English national production had to be redrawn.[394]

But the context could sometimes be wider even than the nation. When in 1600, Italy saw much of her industrial production wither away, and Spain at about the same time also witnessed the disappearance of much of her craft-working in Seville, Toledo, Cordoba, Segovia and Cuenca,[395] – and when the Italian and Spanish losses coincided with a corresponding rise in activity in the United Provinces, France and England, what better evidence could there be that the European economy was a coherent whole and thus in its own way explanatory? And that this order was one of circulation, structure formation and hierarchical ordering of the world economy, as successes and failures counterbalanced one another in a fairly coherent system of interdependence? Pierre Goubert[396] has considered classifying individual fortunes and wealth according to their age – the young, the mature and the old or long-standing. This is thinking in parabolas. One could see industries too as young, mature or old: the young ones are on the way up while the old ones are sliding downhill.

All the same, did not the life expectancy of industries, like that of human beings, improve with time? If for the period of the fifteenth to the eighteenth century we had a large number of graphs like Hoffmann's, we should probably note an important difference: rhythms of progress would have been much shorter and more abrupt, with much sharper rises and falls than today's. Any industrial production in the old days of the economy ran the risk of meeting a bottleneck very soon, whether in raw materials, labour, credit, technology, energy, or the home or foreign market. This is an experience familiar today in the countries of the Third World.

Transport and capitalist enterprise

Means of transport that are as old as the world itself have a tendency to carry on in the same way for century after century. In the first volume of this work, I described the archaic infrastructure with its many unspectacular means of transport: rowing-boats, sailing-ships, carts, horse-teams, pack animals, processions of bell-horses (which carried Staffordshire pottery or bales of wool from the provinces to London), mule trains in the Sicilian fashion (each beast attached to the tail of the one in front),[397] or the 400,000 *burlaki*, the hauliers who pulled or propelled boats along the Volga in about 1815.[398]

Transport is the necessary finishing process of production: the faster it goes, the better it is for business. Simon Vorontsov, Catherine II's ambassador in London, described the rise of England's prosperity as the multiplying by five in fifty years of the speed of circulation.[399] The economic take-off of the eighteenth century in fact coincided with the peak achieved by traditional methods of circulation, without the introduction of any really revolutionary new techniques – though some new problems were created. Even before the royal highways had been built in France, Cantillon pointed to a new dilemma:[400] if improved traffic meant more horses, they would have to be fed – to the detriment of human mouths.

Transport was an industry in itself, as Montchrestien, Defoe, Petty and the Abbé Galiani all remarked. 'Transport', wrote the latter, '... is a species of manufacture.'[401] But it was an ancient kind of manufacture to which the capitalist did not wholeheartedly commit himself. And one can see why: only traffic along trunk routes really 'paid'. Everything else, the ordinary, everyday, unspectacular traffic was left to anyone who was prepared to countenance the very modest reward it brought. So an estimate of capital investment in transport gives us an estimate of the modernity or archaism, or rather the 'return' of the various branches of transport: capital investment in overland transport was low and in inland waterways it was of limited significance; maritime transport aroused a little more interest but even here money was very selective and made no effort to take over everything.

Overland transport

Overland transport is usually represented as inefficient. For centuries, roads remained more or less in a state of nature. But this was only comparative inefficiency: the traffic of the past corresponded to the economy of the past. Vehicles, beasts of burden, couriers, messengers and post-horses all played their part in relation to a specific demand. And when all is said and done, not enough importance has been given to Werner Sombart's now-forgotten argument[402] establishing that, contrary to commonsense assumptions, overland transport carried more goods than inland waterways.

Sombart's rather ingenious calculation fixes an order of magnitude for Germany in the late eighteenth century. The number of horses used for transport is estimated at 40,000: so one can calculate at about 500 million 'kilometre tons' the volume of goods carried in a year by carts or pack animals (incidentally the figure for rail transport over the same area in 1913 is 130 times as great, striking evidence of the way railways opened up the country). The figure for waterways, obtained by taking the number of boats and multiplying it by their average capacity and number of trips, works out at between 80 and 90 million 'kilometre tons'. So over the whole of Germany in the late eighteenth and early nineteenth centuries – in spite of the substantial river traffic along the Rhine, the Elbe and the Oder – overland transport carried 5 times as many goods as waterways. Moreover, the figure of 40,000 horses only covers horses classified as transport animals, and does not include the many farm horses (there were 1,200,000 of these in France in Lavoisier's time). And these farm animals were used for transporting many things more or less regularly or seasonally. So Sombart in fact rather under-estimated overland transport, though it is also true that he left out of the calculation for waterways the considerable floating down of timber.

Can one generalize from the German example? Certainly not in Holland, where most goods travelled by water. And probably not in England where there were many small navigable rivers and canals and where Sombart estimates that the two kinds of transport ran neck and neck. But the rest of Europe was if anything worse off than Germany for inland waterways. A French document even puts it with some exaggeration in 1778: 'Transport almost all goes overland because of the difficulty of the rivers.'[403] It is curious to note that Dutens, in

The Ludlow mail. Painting by J.-L. Agasse (1767–1849). This shows traditional road transport at the peak of its development: a good road surface and a reinforced team. Compare the old roads so often painted by Brueghel. (Basle, Oeffentliche Kunstsammlung, photo by the Museum.)

1828[404] estimated that of 46 million tons of goods in circulation, 4.8 million went by water and the rest by land (30.9 in small haulage enterprises, 10.9 in long-distance haulage): a ratio of 1 to 10. It is true that between 1800 and 1840, the number of haulage vehicles doubled.[405]

This huge volume of road transport is partly explained by the large number of short-haul trips, for over a short distance a cart cost no more than a boat: thus in 1708, the cost of carrying grain to Paris from Orleans was the same on the king's highway as along the Orleans canal – two modern routes.[406] Moreover, since the waterway network was incomplete, there were connections, sometimes diffficult ones, to be made between systems – the equivalent of the portages in Siberia or North America. Between Lyons and Roanne that is between the Rhône and the Loire, 400 to 500 ox-teams were permanently employed.

But the fundamental reason was the permanent and plentiful supply of peasant transport paid for, like all *sidelines*, at less than its true cost price. And this source was freely used by all. Certain rural regions – Hunsbruck in the Rhineland, Hesse, Thuringia[407] – certain villages like Rembercourt-aux-Pots in the Barrois whose carters ('*charretons*') went as far as Antwerp in the sixteenth century,[408] or all the Alpine villages which passed goods along from one to another – specialized in transport.[409] But alongside these professionals, the bulk of transporters were simple peasants who carried goods from time to time. 'The trade of haulage should be absolutely free,' says a French edict in 1782: 'it should have no restriction but the privileges of the *messageries* [i.e. the regular mails carrying passengers, and packets not exceeding a certain weight] ... Nothing must therefore be done to alter in the least degree this liberty so essential to trade; the peasant-farmer who has temporarily turned carrier in order to employ and maintain his horses must be able to take up or leave off this trade without any formality whatever.'[410]

The only trouble about peasant labour was that it was seasonal. But people learnt to put up with that. Salt from Peccais in Languedoc for instance was sent up the Rhône in convoys of boatloads, under the control of important merchants; when it was unloaded at Seyssel, it had to travel overland to the little village of Regonfle near Geneva where it rejoined the waterway. The merchant Nicolas Burlamachi wrote on 10 July 1650 from Geneva: '... and if it were not that harvest is beginning, we should receive the salt in a few days'; on 14th July: 'Our salt is on the way and we receive some every day, and if the harvest does not hold us up, I hope to have it all here within a fortnight ... We received about 750 cartloads from this convoy.' 18 September: 'the rest is arriving from day to day, although at the moment the cartloads are less frequent because of the autumn sowing. But once everything is sown, we shall get it all at once.'[411]

A century later, 22 July 1771, in Bonneville in the Faucigny, there is a grain shortage and the *intendant* wants rye transported urgently: 'When one is hungry, one does not argue about the kind of bread to eat.' The trouble is, he writes to the syndic of Sallanches, 'that we are at the height of harvest, and without seriously hindering it, we cannot have as many local carts as we would like'.[412] And we even find the factor of a steelmaster (23 Ventôse, Year VI) gloomily reflecting that 'the ploughs [i.e. the ploughing season] have completely prevented the carters from working'.[413]

Between this labour force which offered its services whenever the 'farming calendar' permitted, and the regular system of mails and deliveries with fixed timetables which was gradually installed from an early date in almost every state, there was also a specialized transport trade, with a degree of organization, although nine times out of ten this was elementary. These were the small carriers, whose business consisted of a few horses and carters. A register from Hanover in 1833 indicates that the small carrier was still the rule for land transport. Germany was still cross-crossed from north to south, as in the sixteenth century, by 'free' and unregulated transport (*Strackfuhrbetrieb* as this was known in the Swiss Cantons), in the hands of carters who set off looking for custom, 'navigating like boatmen' far from home for months on end – sometimes because they were simply stranded high and dry. This trade was at its peak in the eighteenth century but it was still there in the nineteenth. And these carters seem to have been their own masters.[414]

Every kind of transport relied on the inns as halts – as could already be seen in sixteenth-century Venetia,[415] and even more clearly in seventeenth-century England, where the inn was becoming a hub of commercial activity quite different from the inn of today. In 1686, Salisbury in Wiltshire, then a small town, could accommodate 548 travellers and 865 horses in its inns.[416] In France, the innkeeper was in fact a commission agent for the transporters. So much so indeed that in 1705, the government which tried to create the office of 'commissioner for transporters' and which succeeded in doing so only briefly in Paris, waxed indignant, accusing innkeepers of every crime:

> All the hauliers in the Kingdom complain that for several years now, the hoteliers and inkeepers in Paris and other towns, have become the masters of all haulage, so that they are obliged to pass through their hands, that they no longer know the people who send the freight and only receive the price it pleases the said innkeepers and hoteliers to give them for it; and the said innkeepers make them use up their money in expenses by unnecessary stays which they are obliged to make, so that they spend all the money their carts have earned and can no longer maintain themselves.[417]

The same document indicates that in Paris, about fifty or sixty inns operated as terminuses for the haulage trade. Jacques Savary in *Le Parfait Négociant* (1712) describes innkeepers as virtually 'commission agents for hauliers';[418] they also handled the various taxes, tolls and customs and collected from the merchants the fees which they then advanced to the hauliers. The picture is very much the same as above, less critical perhaps but not necessarily more accurate.

It is consequently easier to understand why so many provincial inns seemed opulent places. An Italian traveller in 1606 was very taken with the refinements offered by an inn in Troyes: the hostess and her daughters 'of noble bearing' and 'as beautiful as Greek ladies'; the tables laid with massive silver, the bed-curtains fit for a cardinal, the delicate fare, the unexpected taste of walnut oil with fish, and 'a white ... Burgundy, rather cloudy like a Corsican wine, and which they said was natural and better-tasting than the red'. The traveller remarked incidentally that there were forty draft horses and more in the stables – probably not realizing that one thing explained the other.[419]

There was in fact more conflict and rivalry between private and public transport than between hauliers and innkeepers. 'The official transporters' of the royal *messageries* (mails) in France who delivered passengers and small packets, wanted to have the monopoly of all transport. But the edicts in their favour were never put into effect, since the merchants put up such vigorous opposition. It was not so much the freedom as the price of transport that was at issue. 'The recent lifting of price controls is so ... important for trade', reports Savary des Bruslons, 'that the Six Merchant Guilds in Paris in a memorandum of 1701 call it the Right Hand of Trade, and are not afraid to say that where it used to cost them 25 or 30 *livres* to have goods carried by the *Messagers* in the official coaches and carriages, it only costs them 6 *liv.* with the Hauliers (*Rouliers*) because of the fixed price which the official *Voituriers Fermiers* would never drop, whereas the others would negotiate a price of which the merchants might be as much the masters as the hauliers themselves.'[420] We should re-read these lines to appreciate their piquancy and significance: now we know what protected and perpetuated the free enterprise of haulage by small contractors and carriers. If I have correctly interpreted a short passage in Sully's *Memoirs*, he applied to small contractors to bring to Lyons the bullets needed by the royal artillery in the war of Savoy: 'I had the pleasure', he writes, 'of seeing all this arriving in Lyons in sixteen days; whereas by the usual channels it would have taken two or three months and cost the earth'.[421]

It was also true though, that along the major routes of national and international traffic – from Antwerp or Hamburg to Northern Italy for instance – large transport firms were already appearing: Lederer, Cleinhaus,[422] Annone and Zollner.[423] In 1665, there are some brief reports on a transport firm operating on this route or part of it, Fieschi & Co. About twenty years later, applying for some concessions, the firm sang its own praises, pointing out that it spent 300,000 *livres* in France every year, 'which money is distributed and scattered along the roads, whether to agents posted in towns on the way to handle transit, to hoteliers, blacksmiths, wheelwrights, coopers and other subjects of the king'.[424] Most of the bigger firms were based in the Swiss Cantons or in Southern Germany where haulage played a crucial role, since this was the zone where traffic between places north and south of the Alps had to be relayed across. The towns concerned were places like Ratisbon, Ulm, Augsburg, Coire and particularly perhaps Basle where every route met: overland traffic, the Rhine, the mule-trains from the mountains. Indeed one transport firm had a thousand mules

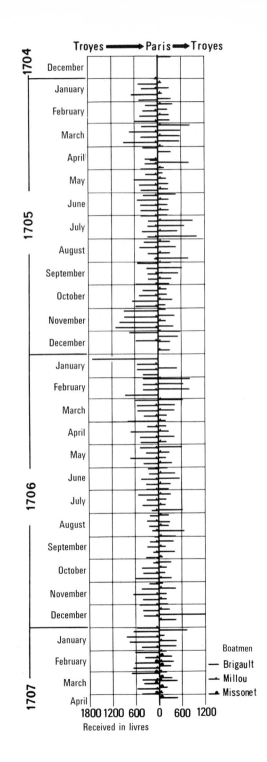

23 FROM PARIS TO TROYES AND BACK BY HORSE-DRAWN BARGE

Jacques Bertin's graph shows that the trips to Paris were more profitable than outward journeys to Troyes, if the takings are added up. There were 108 trips downstream and 111 upstream – virtually the same. This works out at about 4 trips a month each way, or approximately one a week. One or two journeys aborted in December 1705 which explains the sudden jump in takings for the first journey of January 1706. From documents in the Archives Nationales, 2209.

Troyes ➡ Paris ➡ Troyes

1704
December
January
February
March
April
May
1705
June
July
August
September
October
November
December
January
February
March
April
May
June
1706
July
August
September
October
November
December
January
February
1707
March
April

1800 1200 600 0 600 1200
Received in livres

Boatmen
— Brigault
⊢ Millou
▲ Missonet

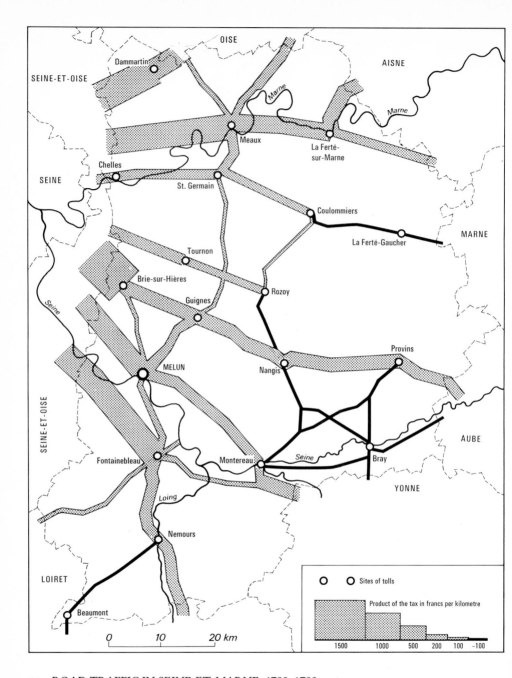

OISE
AISNE
SEINE-ET-OISE
Dammartin
Marne
Marne
Meaux
La Ferté-
sur-Marne
SEINE
Chelles
St. Germain
Coulommiers
La Ferté-Gaucher
MARNE
Tournon
Brie-sur-Hières
Guignes
Rozoy
Seine
Provins
MELUN
Nangis
AUBE
Fontainebleau
Montereau
Seine
Bray
YONNE
Loing
Nemours
SEINE-ET-OISE
LOIRET
Sites of tolls
Product of the tax in francs per kilometre
Beaumont
0   10   20 km
1500   1000   500   200   100   −100

24   ROAD TRAFFIC IN SEINE-ET-MARNE: 1798–1799

From the receipts of the road maintenance tax between 1 Frimaire and 30 Prairia, Year VII. Map by Guy Arbellot, 'Les barrières de l'An VII' in *Annales, E.S.C.*, July–August 1975, p. 760.

in the town.[425] In Amsterdam, needless to say, there was already a modern organization: 'We have here', writes Ricard *fils*,[426] 'some very rich and prosperous people called *Expediteurs* (dispatchers) whom the merchants have only to ask whenever they have some merchandise to send overland. These dispatchers have carters and carriers in their service who work only for them.' In London there were similar facilities, whereas in the rest of England, specialized haulage contractors were probably slow to appear in the world of travelling merchants and manufacturers who thronged the roads of Britain in the seventeenth and eighteenth centuries.[427] In Germany, even in the early nineteenth century, merchants were still arriving at the Leipzig fairs with their own transport and merchandise.[428] And transport did not develop very quickly in France either: 'It was not until after 1789 that the large haulage firms were created. There were about 50 in 1801 and 75 in 1843.'[429]

Faced with this traditional but ubiquitous organization, the merchant simply swam with the current. Why should he trouble to organize (or 'rationalize') in capitalist fashion a system where abundant competition operated to his advantage and where, as the *Six Corps* 'were not afraid to say ... the merchants might be as much the masters as the hauliers themselves' of the asking price?

River traffic

Much has been made of inland waterways: how they carried big boats and little boats, barges, rafts, tree-trunks roped together – and how they stood for easy transport and low prices. But this was true only to a rather limited extent.

The most frequent complaint about river traffic was that it was slow. With the current, one could of course take the horse-drawn barge from Lyons to Avignon in 24 hours.[430] But when a convoy of boats, attached to one another, had to go up the Loire from Nantes to Orleans, the *intendant* of the latter town (2 June 1709) had 'done a deal with the boatmen to bring the wheat [from Brittany] come wind or high weather [i.e. without stopping], because otherwise you will not have it for three months'.[431] This is a far cry from the 12 kilometres a day Werner Sombart estimates as the distance travelled on German rivers. Lyons in 1694 suffered a food shortage verging on famine and was waiting for the boats bringing grain up from Provence: the *intendant* feared that they would not arrive for six weeks (16 February 1694).[432] Apart from its naturally slow pace, river traffic was subject to the 'caprices of the rivers', high or low water, wind and ice. In Roanne, whenever the boatman was held up by high water, it was agreed that he should make a statement in front of a notary.[433] And there were so many obstacles too: abandoned wrecks, fishing-weirs, mill races, markers that disappeared, sandbanks and rocks which could not always be avoided. Then there were the countless river tolls where everyone had to stop: there were dozens of these on the Loire and the Rhine, as if to discourage shipping. In France in the eighteenth century there was a systematic attempt to eliminate

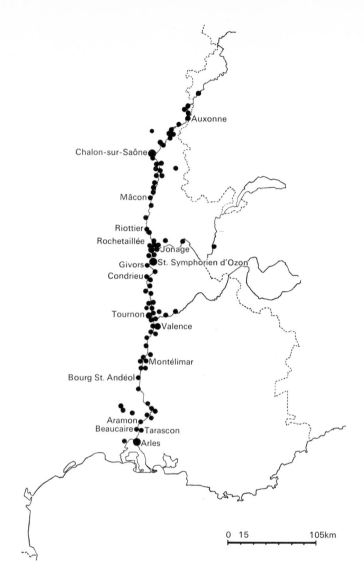

Auxonne

Chalon-sur-Saône

Mâcon

Riottier
Rochetaillée
Jonage
Givors St. Symphorien d'Ozon
Condrieu

Tournon
Valence

Montélimar

Bourg St. Andéol

Aramon
Beaucaire Tarascon
Arles

0 15   105km

25 TOLLS AND CUSTOMS ALONG THE SAÔNE AND RHÔNE IN MID-SIXTEENTH
    CENTURY
Charles Carrière argues that the tolls on the Rhône (in the eighteenth century that is) were not the
terrible obstacle described by contemporaries and historians. All the same for everyday transport
what a number of halts and complications they must have caused! Sketchmap from Richard
Gascon's book, *Grand commerce et vie urbaine au XVIIe siècle, Lyon et ses marchands*, 1971, I,
p. 152, fig. 20-21.

those tolls which had been installed recently and arbitrarily; the monarchy hesitated about suppressing the others because of the compensation it would have to pay.[434]

Canals were the rational modern solution: but here the slowdown took the form of locks. The Orleans canal had 30 locks in 18 leagues; the Briare canal 41 locks in 12 leagues.[435] The canal from Lübeck to Hamburg had so many that according to a traveller in 1701, 'it sometimes takes nearly three weeks to get to Lübeck from Hamburg by this route; [and yet] there are always a good number of boats coming and going along the canal'.[436]

Last but not least, there were the boatmen themselves – independent characters, who formed groups and backed each other up. They were a race apart, still visible in all their individuality in the nineteenth century. The state everywhere attempted to control this unruly community. The towns subjected them to rules and censuses. In Paris, there was a list of boatman according to the 'ports' on the banks of the Seine. Even the ferrymen who conveyed passengers and goods from one bank to the other were subject to the rules of a quasi-association set up by the town in 1672.[437]

The state also busied itself creating regular 'water-coach' services, leaving on set days, or conceded them to individuals: the Duc de la Feuillade received the right of installing these *coches d'eau* 'on the river of the Loire' (March 1673);[438] the Duc de Gesvres (1728) was granted the 'privilege of water-coaches on the Rhône' – which he later sold for 200,000 *livres* – a fortune.[439] Rules and regulations sprang up setting tariffs, carrying conditions ashore and afloat, for water-coaches (which were horse-drawn barges) and other vessels, and fixed towing-rates. A number of offices of master-*voiturier* (10,000 *livres* each) were created along the Seine from Rouen to Paris, producing a monopoly in their favour.[440] Thousands of disputes arose between carriers and passengers, water-coaches and other vessels, merchants and boatmen.

There was a sharp conflict for instance between the boatmen of the Seine and the merchants of Amiens, Abbeville and Saint-Valéry in 1723 and 1724.[441] The boatmen were known as *gribaniers* from the name of their boats, *gribanes*, which were not supposed to be more than 18 or 20 tons according to the rules then in force. They complained about the low tariffs, fixed fifty years earlier in 1672. Given the price increases since these far-off days, they wanted to double the rate. Chauvelin, the *intendant* of Picardy, preferred to abolish any fixed tariff and to allow supply and demand to find their own level, as we should say between boatmen and merchants, the latter having 'freedom to send their goods with whomever they pleased and at a price agreed with the carriers'. The *gribaniers* stood to lose a corporative advantage in this free-for-all: the practice by which boatmen had to take their cargoes on board in strict order of precedence on the quayside.

This dispute tells us several useful things about the rules of the trade. For instance, any misappropriation or damage of goods in transit meant corporal punishment for those responsible. A boatman loading goods at Saint-Valéry for Amiens did not have the right to drop anchor 'for more than one night at Abbeville, under pain of being responsible for damages and interests that might result, for which the *gribane* ... will be preferentially distrained to the creditors whoever they may be, *even from its owner*' – the last four words suggest that there was a separate owner of the *gribane*: the boat was a 'means of production' operated by a non-owner.[442]

The problem can be seen even more clearly in a case like Roanne.[443] Situated at the point where the Loire becomes navigable, Roanne also had overland links with Lyons, that is with the Rhône, and thus occupied a key position on the axis which linked the capital with the Mediterranean, via Lyons, the Loire and the Briare canal. Roanne derived from the *sapinières* which took goods downstream (and were demolished on arrival) and from its oak-built boats with a cabin for wealthy passengers, at least half the direct and indirect livelihood of its population of merchants, carriers, carpenters, boatmen, oarsmen and labourers. A distinction quickly appeared between the master-boatmen who worked with their own boats, alongside their journeymen and apprentices, and the merchant carriers, small-time capitalists who owned boats but had them operated by factors and boatmen. Here again we find a separation between the worker and his means of working. The master-boatmen, who lived in comfortable houses and married their daughters off to each other, formed an elite, living off the painful labour of others – for it was hard work going down the Loire, especially after about 1704, when the fast-flowing river was opened up to a heroic and hazardous fleet of small craft from Saint-Rambert, a little port upstream from Roanne which was the outlet for coal from the Saint-Etienne mines. River traffic on the Loire was immediately transformed by the transport of this coal downstream to Paris (and in particular to the Sèvres glass-works) and also by the traffic in casks of Beaujolais wine, which were brought by road to Roanne and the down-river ports, and were also destined for Paris. This double traffic, centred on Roanne, Decize and Digoin, brought great profits to the merchant-carriers. Some of them now headed what were virtually transport firms. The Berry Labarre concern for instance, the largest, had its own boat-builder's yard. Its major coup was to obtain a near-monopoly in the carriage of coal. So when on 25 September 1752, the master-boatmen in Roanne seized the boats filled with coal belonging to Berry Labarre and proposed to sail them to Paris themselves, this tells us something about a social conflict which did not subside after the incident. Yes, there was some kind of capitalism at work here, but traditions and innumerable restrictive practices – from both administration and guilds – did not give it much room for manœuvre.

England, by contrast, looked even more free than it really was. Arranging for transport was a simple matter for an innkeeper, merchant or go-between. Coal, which was taxed only when carried by sea, could travel without hindrance along any road or river in England, and even from one river to another via the

The water-coach, by Ruysdael. There was dense shipping along the waterways of Holland, dykes, rivers and canals. A typical 'coach' was pulled by a horse but there were more luxurious ones than this, with cabins and overnight passengers. (The Hague, Marcel Wolf collection, photo Giraudon.)

Humber estuary. If coal increased in price in the course of the voyage, it was entirely because of the costs of transport and trans-shipping – which were not light incidentally: coal from Newcastle cost at least five times as much in London as it did at the pithead. When it was sent on from the capital to the provinces on other boats, its cost on arrival might have multiplied by ten.[444] In Holland, the ease and freedom of canal transport were even more obvious. The 'water-coaches' here were quite small vessels with 60 passengers, two steersmen and one horse[445] which left every town from hour to hour. They even sailed at night and cabins could be hired aboard. One could leave Amsterdam in the evening and arrive in The Hague the next morning.

At sea

At sea, stakes and investments were much greater. The sea was the gateway to wealth. And yet even here, transport was not entirely controlled by capital. Everywhere, there was a thriving population of small cargo-carriers – little ships, sometimes even open boats, which sailed in their hundreds, carrying anything and everything, from Naples to Leghorn or Genoa, from Cape Corse to Leghorn,

from the Canaries to the West Indies, Brittany to Portugal, London to Dunkerque; fleets of Dutch or English coasters; or light *tartanes* which sailed up the
rivers of Genoa or Provence and offered the attraction of a quick trip to travellers
who were in a hurry and not afraid of the sea.

This small-time sea traffic was the counterpart of the small hauliers on land.
It was primarily engaged in local trade. Country areas were often closely tied to
the sea in a primitive alliance. If one were to travel along the coastal strip of
Sweden, Finland, the Baltic countries, Schleswig Holstein, Denmark, along the
Hamburg coast to the Gulf of Dollard where the little port of Emden was the
scene of constant, if changing activity, and then up the many inlets of the
Norwegian coast, as far as say the Lofoten islands – one would be looking at
regions that were almost without exception far from urbanized in the sixteenth
century. And all these coastlines were live with fishing boats, usually small and
simply constructed, which carried everything under the sun (*multa non multum*):
wheat, rye, wood (laths, beams, planks, rafters, barrel-staves), tar, iron, salt,
spices, tobacco, textiles. Strings of them sailed out of the Norwegian fjords near
Oslo, mostly carrying wood bound for England, Scotland or nearby Lübeck.[446]
When Sweden took control of the straits, establishing a bridgehead in the
province of Halland (the peace of Brömsebro 1645) she inherited an active peasant
shipping fleet which sailed abroad carrying stone for building and wood, and
sometimes bringing back cargoes of tobacco unless the boats had spent the
summer calling in at ports from Norway to the Baltic, in which case they
returned before the winter storms with their rewards in ready cash. These
'Schuten' played their part in the Scanian War (1675–1679) and it was they who
transported Charles XII's army to the nearby island of Seeland in 1700.[447]

The documents also afford us glimpses of the peasant sailors of Finland,
small traders who frequented Revel and later Helsingfors (which was only
founded in 1554); or the peasants of the island of Rügen and the fishing villages at
the mouth of the Oder, who were attracted by Danzig; or the small cargo-vessels
of Hobsum, at the neck of Jutland, which took grain, and local ham and bacon
to Amsterdam.[448]

All the examples quoted, and many more besides – including the Aegean of
course – give a picture of an archaic kind of shipping, where the men who built
the boats themselves loaded goods on board and put to sea with them, thus
handling all the tasks and functions occasioned by maritime trade.

This is abundantly clear in medieval Europe. To judge by the laws of Bergen
(1274) the sea-laws of Oleron (1152) or the ancient *coutume* of Olonne, it appears
that the merchant vessel originally sailed *communiter* – that is 'as a joint
venture'.[449] It was the property of a small group of users: as the Oleron sea-laws
put it 'the ship belongs to several companions'. Each one would have an allotted
place on board where he would load his own merchandise – the system known
as *per loca*. The little community would decide on the voyage and the sailing
date, each member being responsible for stowing his own goods, helping or

JE *François Ledos* ——————— demeurant à *Cherbourg* ————
Maître après Dieu du Navire nommé *La Marie Joseph* ——————— – du port
de *Cinquante* Tonneaux ou environ , étant de préfent à Cherbourg , pour du premier tems
qu'il plaira à Dieu envoyer , aller à droite route à *Rouen* ————————————
reconnois & confeffe avoir reçu & chargé dans le bord de mondit Navire , fous le franc-Tillac
d'icelui , de vous Meffieurs POTEL , Freres *La Quantité De Vingt huit* —
Tonneaux foudes De Vareg, allant En Paffedebout p. *Pav Verrerie*

, Pour Compte & Rifques Des Cui Il appartiendra

le tout fec & bien conditionné & marqué de la marque en marge ; lefquelles Marchandifes je
promets & m'oblige porter & conduire dans mondit Navire , fauf les périls & rifques de la Mer ,
audit lieu de *Rouen* ———— & là les délivrer à M *cff: Le Borgne et Comp.*
en me payant pour mon Fret , la fomme de *Douze Livres pav tonneau, pour*
toutes Chofes ————————————
avec les avaries felon les Us & Coutumes de la Mer. Et pour ce tenir & accomplir , je m'oblige
corps & biens avec mondit Navire , Fret & Apparaux d'icelui. En témoignage de vérité , j'ai figné
trois Connoiffemens d'une même teneur , dont l'un accompli , les autres de nulle valeur.
FAIT à Cherbourg , ce *Deuxième* jour de *feptembre* mil fept cent *foixante*
et Quinze frs *qui Dit être François Ledos*

Loading papers of a ship's master at Cherbourg, Archives Nationales, 62. AQ 33. See for
comparison, Savary's *Dictionnaire*, II, pp. 171-2.

being helped by his neighbour. On board too, everyone took his turn, whether
in navigation, watching or chores, although in fact as a rule each had a paid
'valet' who lived 'on the bread and wine' of his master, and carried out his duties
on board, in particular relieving the master when the boat arrived in port, so
that he could go off to 'carry out his negotiations'. The actual sailing was handled
by three officers, the pilot, the *nocher* (navigator) and the mate, all paid a wage
by the group of proprietors and placed under the command of the master who
was chosen from among the co-owners and was certainly not able to play God
the Father on board: as a partner himself, he had to consult his fellows and only
received a few token gifts in exchange for his temporary command: a hat, a pair
of hose, a flask of wine. So the cargo vessel was a miniature republic, an ideal
one provided that the co-owners remained on friendly terms as custom recommended. It was not unlike the mining companionships before the capitalist
takeover. There was no long-drawn-out wrangling and calculation among the
merchant-owner-shippers: there were no freight charges, since each man had
paid in kind or rather in service; as for the overheads – provisions for the journey,
initial outlay etc. – these were provided out of a kitty (known as a 'joint account'
in Marseilles, and the 'great purse' in Olonne, etc.) 'No book-keeping was
required from start to finish' as Louis-A. Boiteux[450] puts it with perfect clarity.

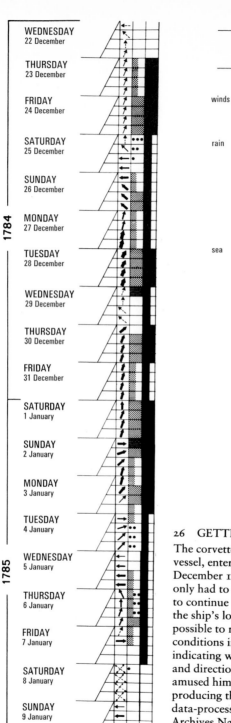

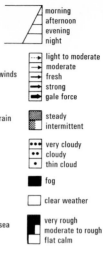

morning
afternoon
evening
night

winds

-→ light to moderate
→ moderate
➔ fresh
⇒ strong
▬ gale force

rain

▦ steady
▤ intermittent

∴ very cloudy
∶ cloudy
• thin cloud

■ fog

☐ clear weather

sea

■ very rough
▨ moderate to rough
☐ flat calm

26   GETTING OUT OF PORT

The corvette *La Levrette*, a French vessel, entered Cadiz Bay on 22 December 1784; she was lucky and only had to wait until 9 January 1785 to continue her journey. The entries in the ship's log kept on board make it possible to reconstruct the weather conditions in the Atlantic. The arrows indicating wind also give their force and direction. Jacques Bertin has amused himself by ingeniously producing this little masterpiece of data-processing. Documents from Archives Nationales, A.N., A.E., Bi, 292.

But even before the fifteenth century, the size of hull of some ships had increased out of all proportion. Building, maintaining and sailing these ships now became technically impossible tasks for the old merchant venturers. Instead of being divided *per loca*, the vessel was now divided *per partes*, into part-shares so to speak, usually into 24 *carats* (although this was not a universal practice: one ship in Marseilles, according to a contract dated 5 March 1507, was 'divided into elevenths, which were themselves subdivided into halves or three-quarters of an eleventh'). The owner of a part-share (*parsonier*) would receive his share of the profits every year. He did not of course sail with the ship himself. And he would appeal to the authority of a magistrate if there were any difficulty in obtaining what we would call the dividend of his carat. We have a perfect example of this system of ownership in the large Ragusan merchantmen of the sixteenth century, some of which approached or even (occasionally) exceeded a thousand tons; their co-owners were sometimes scattered throughout the Christian ports of the Mediterranean. Whenever one of these vessels arrived in port – in Genoa or Leghorn – carat-owners would try to obtain their share of its profits, amicably or with threats: the captain had to have his accounts ready to justify himself.

This is a good indication of a development which would be repeated throughout the merchant fleets of the North, those of England and the United Provinces. Its consequences were in fact two- or three-fold.

For one thing, the links between the ship and the owners of capital were multiplied. We know of owners of shares (like the rich Englishman in the seventeenth century who had shares in 67 vessels)[451] and victuallers who, as in the case of cod-fishing, provided the ship with rations and equipment, on condition they received a third or some other percentage of the profits.

Secondly, besides participation, which was really a commercial operation whereby the risks and profits were shared out in certain proportions – it had become frequent practice to advance 'multi-purpose loans' (*à la grosse aventure*), which gradually became almost independent of the actual affair of the moment, the voyage the ship was making, and tended to become a completely financial form of speculation. The *Compagnon ordinaire du marchand* (The Merchant's Companion)[452] written in 1698 gives an enlightening explanation of what a contract *à la grosse aventure* might mean. This was a maritime loan (and it was sometimes known, one might note, as *usura marina*). The best course for an investor was to lend money on a voyage at 30, 40 or 50% depending on the length of the trip (if the ship went to the Indies the round trip could last three years or more). Once the loan had been made, he should immediately insure his money – that is the capital loaned plus the agreed interest – a properly constituted insurance with a premium of say 4, 5 or 6%. If the ship was lost at sea, or captured by pirates, then he would recover his initial loan and the expected benefit, less the insurance premium. So he would still come out ahead. 'There are these days people so wily', says our anonymous guide, 'that not only do they

Shipyard in Amsterdam. Engraving by L. Backuysen (1631-1708). (Amsterdam, Rijksmuseum, photo by the Museum.)

want ships to be mortgaged to them, but they also look for a good merchant to stand caution for their money.' Those who, even more astutely, had borrowed the money to lend in the first place, in Holland for instance where interest rates were two or three points lower than English ones, would make a profit if all went well, without even having to deprive themselves of their capital. This was a sort of transfer to the shipping business of the Stock Exchange practices of the time, where the last word in sophistication was to speculate with money one did not actually possess.

Meanwhile yet another development was also emerging alongside such practices. As maritime transport increased, it was divided into separate branches – by the Dutch at first, later by the British. The first distinction was that shipbuilding yards were hived off as an autonomous industry. In Saardam and Rotterdam,[453] independent entrepreneurs took orders from merchants or states and were able to meet them without delay although the shipbuilding industry was still very largely artisanal. And even in the seventeenth century, Amsterdam was not only a market for new ships, or for orders to build them, but had also become a huge market for the resale of secondhand vessels. Now too, brokers had begun to specialize in handling freight: they procured merchandise for transporters or ships for merchants. And there were insurers, now no longer simply merchants who handled insurance as a sideline. Insurance was spreading, although not all shippers or merchants necessarily used it, even in England where, as I have already mentioned, Lloyd's had embarked on their successful career as insurers.

So there was undeniably capital being mobilized and much activity taking place in the seventeenth and especially the eighteenth century in the overseas shipping sector. The providers of funds, the shipowners or *armateurs* (this word was still rare in the seventeenth century) were indispensable for the initial outlay on long-haul trips that lasted several years. Even the state insisted on taking an interest, though this was not in itself new: the *galere da mercato* of the fifteenth and sixteenth centuries were boats built by the Venetian government and placed at the disposal of patrician merchants for long voyages; similarly, the Portuguese carracks, the giants of the sea in the sixteenth century, or the large ships of the Indies Companies (of which more later) were so to speak both capitalist and state-sponsored.

Unfortunately not a great deal is known in detail about this ship-fitting and the undoubtedly very diverse origins of the capital invested in it. Hence the interest of the few cases I shall quote, not on the face of it very good examples since they were failures. But history is dependent on documents, and failures followed by lawsuits leave more traces than successful voyages.

In December 1781, two Parisian bankers still did not know how the affair of the *Carnate* would end: she was a vessel which had been fitted by Bérard Brothers & Co. of Lorient, twelve years earlier in 1776, with a view to a voyage to the Ile de France (Mauritius) and the Ile de Bourbon (Réunion) and then on to Pondicherry, Madras and China. The bankers had advanced a multi-purpose loan 'on the body and cargo of the said vessel of 180,000 *livres* at 28% of the maritime profits' over a period of thirty months. They had prudently insured themselves with friends in London. But the *Carnate* never reached China. She had sprung a leak going round the Cape of Good Hope. After repairs, she limped on nevertheless from Mauritius to Pondicherry where the leak reappeared. She then left the open harbour of Pondicherry and sailed up the Ganges to Chandernagor where she was repaired again and where she passed the winter monsoon (25 September to 30 December 1777). Then having taken on merchandise in Bengal, she called in at Pondicherry again and made her way back to Europe without incident – only to be captured by English privateers off the Spanish coast in October 1778. It would have been nice to make the London insurers pay up, (this often happened) but counsel for the insurers at the King's Bench maintained that the *Carnate* had been deliberately re-routed after Mauritius and they won their case. The bankers then turned to the shipfitters: if there had been a change of route, it was their fault. And a new lawsuit loomed.[454]

Another case concerned the bankruptcy of the house of Harelos, Menkenhauser & Co. of Nantes (1771) an affair which was still not resolved in September

1778.[455] Among the creditors was a certain Wilhelmy 'a foreigner' (which is all we know about him) who had taken out a participation of 9/64 (almost 61,300 *livres*) in five of the firm's ships already at sea. As usual, the creditors had been divided into *privilégiés* (who took priority) and '*chirographaires*' (second rank) who took second place). Good arguments were apparently found for classifying Wilhelmy among the latter – as confirmed by the *Conseil de Commerce* (25 September 1788) quashing a decision by the Breton *parlement* (13 August 1783). Wilhelmy probably never saw his money again. Was he insured? We don't know. But the moral of the story is that one could still lose in court, however good one's case, once the lawyers began unrolling their imperturbable logic. (I confess I found these cases very entertaining to read.)

So even loans *à la grosse aventure*, covered by insurance, were subject to risk, but only within limits and the deal was usually worth it, since interest rates were always high in the long-distance shipping sector which required huge advances, meant long delays and brought substantial profits. It is hardly surprising that the multi-purpose loan, a sophisticated and speculative operation, intimately linked to trading profits rather than to the transporter's profit, was almost the only way in which large-scale capital intervened in shipping. Routine short-haul trips (on routes which might have looked alarming in the age of Saint-Louis but had become familiar) were left to small-time moneylenders. Competition here was very effective in cutting down freight charges to the merchant's advantage; exactly the same situation as that of overland transport.

In 1725 for instance, small English ships literally flocked to load any available freight in Amsterdam and other ports of the United Provinces.[456] They offered their services, for trips as far as the Mediterranean, at rates so far below the usual tariff that the normal ships on this route, Dutch or French vessels of high tonnage carrying large crews and cannon to defend themselves against Barbary pirates, found themselves virtually unemployed, evidence if any is needed that large vessels did not automatically take precedence over smaller ones. Indeed the opposite is rather more probable in a trade where the profit margin, when this can be estimated, was slender. A Belgian historian, Wilfrid Brulez, has written to me on this subject: 'The accounts for thirteen voyages by Dutch ships during the last years of the sixteenth century, mostly between the Iberian peninsula and the Baltic, with one trip to Genoa and Leghorn, show a total net profit of 6%. Some voyages made more money of course, but others incurred losses for the shipping firm, while others again only managed to break even.' This explains the failure in Amsterdam in 1629 and again in 1634, of plans to set up a company with a monopoly of maritime insurance. The merchants were against it and one of their arguments was that the proposed premiums would come to more than the predicted profits, or would at the very least seriously reduce them. This is in the early seventeenth century, it is true. But there were still even in later times a large number of small boats working for small entrepreneurs, as can be seen from the fact that they were often the property of a single owner, instead of several 'part-owners'. This was certainly true of the great majority of Dutch boats handling the Baltic trade or participating in the *beurts* (Dutch *beurt* = turn), that is the journeys to nearby ports such as Rouen, Saint-Valéry, London, Hamburg and Bremen where each boat took its turn to load cargo. And it was also true of most of the Hamburg shipping in the eighteenth century.

Working out costs: capital and labour

As in the case of industrial activity, in order to calculate profits with any accuracy, we ought to be able to see how things worked from the inside, and establish a model of shipping finance. But model-building means setting aside the incidental, atypical or accidental. And in the shipping of the past, accidents and incidents were common coin. They made an incalculable difference to cost prices, and conceal the rule, if any rule there be. The list of possibilities gives added piquancy to the expression 'worse things happen at sea': there were wars, pirates, reprisals, requisitions and sequestrations; there were the vagaries of the winds which might keep a ship imprisoned in port for days, or blow it far off course; there were running repairs (leaks, broken masts or rudders); there were shipwrecks, on the coast or at sea, with or without the possibility of saving the cargo, and storms which sometimes made it necessary to jettison cargoes to save the ship; there were fires – a ship could become a floating torch, burning even below the waterline. Calamity could even strike within sight of home: how many ships of the *Carrera de Indias* were lost crossing the bar at San Lucar de Barrameda, a few hours from the calm waters of Seville! Historians have sometimes suggested that the life expectancy of a wooden ship was about twenty to twenty-five years. I would say that was an absolute maximum, if luck was on her side.

So instead of model-building, it would perhaps be more sensible to stick to concrete examples, to follow boats over their entire careers. But the accounts have little regard for the long-term yield of a merchant vessel. They read more like a set of balance-sheets for the return trip and the figures are not always clearly distributed under the various headings of expenditure. But the accounts of an expedition to the Pacific coast by seven ships from Saint-Malo in 1706 do give us some data.[457] Let us take one of them, the *Maurepas* as a case study: overall, the initial outlay (known as the *mise-hors*) amounted to 235,315 *livres*; expenses on the voyage to 51,710; and on the return trip to 89,386: a total expenditure of 376,411. If these figures are broken down into fixed capital (the price of the ship, refitting, equipment and overheads – the latter very small) and circulating capital (rations, pay for the crew) the result is 251,236 *livres* of circulating capital as against 125,175 of fixed capital, that is 2 to 1. The graph in Figure 27 shows figures for the other six vessels as well: they all tell the same story. Without attaching too much importance to the coincidence, we might note that the available detailed records of a Japanese boat which sailed to China

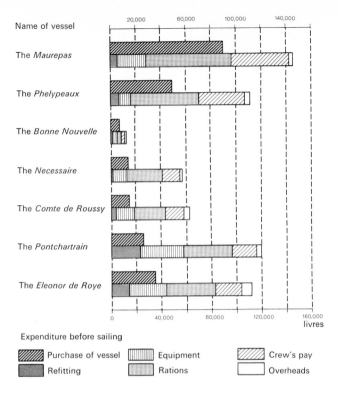

Name of vessel

20,000   60,000   100,000   140,000

The *Maurepas*

The *Phelypeaux*

The *Bonne Nouvelle*

The *Necessaire*

The *Comte de Roussy*

The *Pontchartrain*

The *Eleonor de Roye*

0   40,000   80,000   120,000   160,000
                                        livres

Expenditure before sailing

Purchase of vessel   Equipment   Crew's pay

Refitting   Rations   Overheads

27   THE EXPENSES OF SEVEN SHIPS FROM SAINT-MALO

These ships sailed to the South Seas and the accounts were worked out when they returned to France in 1707. This figure shows the sums expended on both fixed and circulating capital before leaving Saint-Malo on the outward trip. When the expenses of the voyage are added (see p. 369) it is clear that circulating capital (rations and the crew's pay) amounted to about double fixed capital (price of the ships, refitting etc.). Documents from Archives Nationales, A.N., Colonies, F² A 16, Graph by Jeannine Field-Recurat.

in 1465,[458] on a long-distance merchant voyage, shows a very similar breakdown: the hull and rigging together cost 400 *kwan-mon*; the crew's rations for the estimated twelve months of the voyage came to 340; and their pay to 490. Again the fixed/circulating ratio is 1 to 2.

Until the eighteenth century then, in shipping as in most manufacture, circulating capital expenses were much greater than fixed capital. One has only to think of the length of voyage and what this meant – slow circulation of the money and capital invested, many months of paying wages and feeding the crew – to see that this was only to be expected. But as in manufacturing, it seems that the ratio of fixed to circulating capital (F/C) was tending to be reversed in the course of the eighteenth century. Take for instance the complete accounts for the voyages made by three ships from Nantes in the latter part of the century: the *Deux Nottons* (1764), the *Margueritte* (1776 to Saint-Domingue), the *Bailli de Suffren* (1787, to the Caribbean). Over these three voyages the C/F ratio was respectively 47,781 *livres* to 111,517; 46,194 to 115,574; 28,075 to 69,827 (these were of course shorter voyages than the Saint-Malo boat's trip to the coast of Peru).[459] In all three cases, the figures give an approximate equation $2C = F$. That is, the situation indicated by the 1706 figures had been turned on its head.

These samples are too imperfect and too small to resolve the problem. But they help to pose it. The proportion of fixed capital had greatly increased. Labour was no longer the major item of expenditure. Machines – since a ship was a sort of machine – were now costing more. If this as yet rather unsubstantiated proposition could be proved true, it would have far-reaching consequences and might be compared with the observations of Ralph Davis, Douglas North and Gary M. Walton who have noted that there was an increase in productivity in North Atlantic shipping of 50% (or 0.8% per annum) between 1675 and 1775.[460] But to what can the new ratio between fixed and circulating capital be attributed? Undoubtedly shipbuilding became more sophisticated (copper-lined hulls for instance) and the price of ships went up. But in order to estimate this precisely, it should be related to the general price rise of the eighteenth century; and one should also find out whether the life of a hull varied and whether the initial investment was thus written off more quickly or not. Looking at the labour side, had not ships' crews' pay fallen in real terms, along with the cost and quality of the rations on board? Or had their number perhaps declined in relation to the tonnage, along with an improved adaptation to their task by officers (captain, chief officers, pilot, scrivener) and crew, who were often, even at the beginning of the eighteenth century, a proletariat of unskilled workers. And what is the reality concealed behind the obvious deterioration of the 'press-gang' system, which although applied only to recruitment of seamen in time of war, tells us something about conditions for all sailors? There are as yet no satisfactory answers to these questions.

But the productivity of a vessel was of course related to the volume, value and fate of its cargo. What we have so far calculated is only the cost of transport. If the shipowner was simply a professional transporter, his problem was merely to collect the freight charges to offset expenses and to give him his profit. This was what the big cargo vessels of Ragusa did in the Mediterranean generally for short-haul voyages. So too did hundreds and thousands of boats of small and medium tonnage in the Mediterranean and elsewhere. But this was a difficult, risky trade, and brought small or only moderate rewards. In the examples I have quoted here, there is never any mention of freight charges. The merchants themselves fitted the ship in order to send their goods in it and the vessel was thus itself part of a trading operation which went beyond or rather totally encompassed it. In fact, and this is something to which we shall return, the risks and the cost price relative to the cargoes transported were so great in long-distance shipping that they made transporting as a simple freight industry virtually unthinkable. Normally, long distance transport was organized within the context of a trading operation in which it represented one heading among others of the merchant's expenditure and risks.

A rather negative balance sheet

This long chapter can be summed up in a few words. It sets out to describe the sectors of production in order to try and discover the inroads made by capitalism into this area where it was not usually very firmly, if at all, integrated. And quite clearly, in the areas we have looked at, the balance sheet of pre-industrial capitalism is pretty negative.

With a few exceptions, the capitalist, that is in this period the 'important merchant' with many undifferentiated activities, did not commit himself whole-heartedly to production. He was practically never a farming landowner with feet firmly planted in the soil; while he was often a rentier owning land, his real profits and concerns lay elsewhere. Nor was he the master of a craft workshop wedded to his trade, nor a transport entrepreneur. Whenever one of these businessmen owned a boat or shares in a boat, whenever he controlled a putting-out system, it was always as a corollary of what he really was: a man of the market, the Stock Exchange, of the networks and long chains of commerce. Above all a man in distribution, marketing – the sector in which real profits were made.

The Pellet brothers for instance, whom we have already met, possessed their own boat, but for these Bordeaux merchants with a thriving trade with the West Indies, this was simply a secondary asset, a way of saving on freight. Owning one's own boat meant being able to choose the sailing date, arriving at the right time and sometimes even being able to arrive alone; it meant having in the ship's captain an agent who could carry out various assignments or adapt them to local circumstances. It meant stacking all the best trading cards in one's hand. Similarly the merchants of Saint-Malo who bought and fitted the ships already described, were interested above all in the merchandise they had aboard, bound for the coasts of Chile and Peru, and in the return cargo. In order to undertake this risky operation, in war time, which required secrecy and promised extremely good profits (a promise that was kept incidentally) one had to be the master of one's own ship. Transport was here once again a secondary consideration, one of a series of operations that stretched far beyond it. And when on Colbert's death, the great mercers of Paris, who were very rich merchants indeed, invested in cloth manufacture, what they wanted above all was the privilege of *selling* this cloth both in France and outside – a privilege they vigorously defended when it was challenged.[461]

In short, these ventures by capitalism outside its favoured sector were rarely justified in themselves. It only took an interest in production when necessity or trading profits made it advisable. Capitalism did not invade the production sector until the industrial revolution, when machines had so transformed the conditions of production that industry had become a profit-making sector. Capitalism would then be profoundly modified and above all extended. It did not however abandon its habit of oscillating according to the circumstances of the day, for over the years other options besides industry became open to it, in the nineteenth and twentieth centuries. Capitalism, even in the industrial era, was not exclusively attached to the world of industrial production, far from it.

4

Capitalism on Home Ground

WHILE CAPITALISM was most at home in the sphere of commerce, it did not occupy the whole of this sector, but elected residence only on routes and in places where trade was most lively. In everyday, traditional exchange or the very local market economy, capitalism took little interest. Even in the most developed regions, there were some tasks it willingly handled, others it shared, and others again which it would not accept, leaving them firmly alone. Decisions of this kind might be aided and abetted, or alternatively obstructed, by the state – the only obstructive agency that could at times take capitalism's place, drive it out or, on the contrary, force upon it a role it would not have chosen of its own accord.

The great merchants of the past found it quite easy, on the other hand, to delegate to shopkeepers and retailers certain everyday tasks, such as the collecting, storing and retailing of goods, or taking regular supplies to the market – minor operations that were either too insignificant, or too routine-bound and traditionally supervised to allow much room for manœuvre.

Capitalism was thus invariably borne along by a general context greater than itself, on whose shoulders it was carried upward and onward. This commanding position at the pinnacle of the trading community was probably the major feature of capitalism in view of the benefits it conferred: legal or actual monopoly and the possibility of price manipulation. It is at any rate from this commanding height that we can most conveniently view and appreciate the panorama described in the present chapter, the better to understand its logical development.

At the top of the world of trade

Wherever it was being modernized, the world of trade was subject to a far-reaching division of labour. Not that the latter was a self-propelled force. It received both its impetus and its dimensions, as Adam Smith diagnosed, from the increased size of the market and the volume of trade. The real motive force

374

'Merchant banker negotiating in a foreign land', a 1688 engraving. (Photo B.N., Paris.)

was the expansion of economic life which, by allowing certain people to take the initiative in progress, leaving subordinate tasks to others, tended to create considerable inequalities in the world of trade.

The trade hierarchy

Indeed there has probably never been a country, in any period of history, where the merchants were all on the same footing, equal to each other and interchangeable so to speak. Even the laws of the Visigoths refer to *negociatiores transmarini*[1] – special merchants who traded overseas in the luxury products of the Levant, probably the *Syrii* who were to be found in the West by the end of the Roman Empire.

In Europe, such inequalities became increasingly apparent after the economic revival of the eleventh century. As the Italian cities began to take part once more in the Levant trade, they witnessed the rise of a class of wealthy merchants, who quickly secured the leadership of the urban patriciates. And this tendency towards hierarchy became more pronounced during the prosperity of the following centuries. High finance could probably be described as the ultimate development in this direction. And already, by the time of the Champagne fairs, the Buonsignori of Siena were running the *Magna Tavola*, a large firm exclusively devoted to banking: they were, as Mario Chiaudano called his book about them, the *Rothschild del Duecento*, the Rothschilds of the thirteenth century.[2] The Italian example was followed throughout the West. In France for instance, great merchants were already visibly in business in Bayonne, Bordeaux, La Rochelle, Nantes and Rouen in the thirteenth century. In Paris, the names of Arrode, Popin, Barbette, Piz d'Oe, Passy and Bourdon were well known as wealthy merchant families, and in the *taille* (tax register) for 1292, Guillaume Bourdon figures as one of the most heavily-taxed commoners in Paris.[3] In Germany, Friedrich Lütge tells us,[4] the distinction between wholesalers and retailers was already appearing by the fourteenth century, because of the geographical expansion of trade, the need to handle different currencies, the new division of labour (agents, factors, warehousekeepers), and the new book-keeping made necessary by the everyday use of credit. Until then, even an important merchant still had his retail shop; he lived on a par with his servants and apprentices, like a master-craftsman with his journeymen. Now the split was beginning to appear. Not all at once perhaps: for a long time, and practically everywhere, even in Florence or Cologne, wholesale merchants continued to engage in the retail trade.[5] But the profile of big business was beginning to stand out – on both the social and the economic plane – from ordinary small shopkeeping. And this was what mattered.

All trading communities sooner or later produced such hierarchies, identifiable in everyday vocabulary. The *tayir* in Islam was the wealthy import-export merchant who sat in his counting-house and directed brokers and commission agents. He had nothing in common with the *hawanti*, the shopkeeper in the souk.[6] In Agra in India – still a huge city when Maestre Manrique travelled through it in about 1640 – the name of *Sodagor* was given to 'a man we should describe in Spain as a *mercader*, but some of them call themselves by the special name of *Katari*, the grandest title for those who practise the mercantile arts in these countries, which denotes a very rich merchant with excellent credit'.[7] Western vocabularies contain similar distinctions. The French equivalent of the *Katari* was the *négociant*, the wholesale merchant, the aristocrat of trade. This word first appeared in the seventeenth century, without entirely replacing the existing terms *marchand de gros, marchand grossier* (wholesale merchant), *magasinier* (warehouse keeper), or in Lyons, *marchand bourgeois*. In Italy, there was a wide gap between the *mercante a taglio* and the *negoziante*; as there was in England between *tradesman* and *merchant* – the latter handling foreign trade in the English ports. In Germany, the *Krämer* (salesman) was a very different man from the *Kaufherr* or *Kaufmann*. Already in 1456, Cotrugli regarded the practice of *mercatura* – the art of trade – as separated by a great divide from *mercanzia* – mere shopkeeping.[8]

The difference was not simply a matter of words: there were manifest social distinctions from which men either suffered or drew comfort. At the top of the pyramid were the proud ranks of those who 'understood finance'.[9] So the Genoese, money-lenders to Philip II in Madrid, had nothing but scorn for all commodity trade, which was according to them a profession *de bezariote* [stall-holders] *et de gente più bassa*, the *mercanti* and other small-timers. And the French *négociant* looked down on the shopkeeper: 'Do not call me a retailer', protests Charles Lion, a rich merchant of Honfleur, (1679): 'I am no fishmonger but a commission agent', selling on commission, therefore in the wholesale trade.[10] From the other side of the divide came envy bordering on anger. A bitter man, whose affairs had not entirely succeeded one guesses, was the Venetian who wrote from Antwerp in 1539, complaining of the 'men of the great merchant companies, who are cordially detested by the Court and even more by ordinary people', and who 'take pleasure in flaunting their wealth'. It is commonly said, he reports, 'that these great bankers gobble up the poor and humble' (*questi grandi banchieri mangiano li picoli e poveri*) – including small traders of course.[11] But the latter in turn looked down on the artisan-shopkeepers who worked with their hands.

Specialization: at ground level only

At the lower levels of the hierarchy there swarmed a multitude of pedlars, street-criers, 'travelling market folks as we call them',[12] hawkers, 'higlers' (Defoe), shopkeepers, *blattiers* and *regrattiers* (corn-chandlers and 'regraters', cheap victuallers). There is an assortment of names in every language for the different categories of this trading proletariat. And to these can be added all the professions created by the trading community and very largely dependent on it: cashiers, book-keepers, factors, commissioners, brokers of all kinds, carters, sailors, errand-boys, packers, porters, heavy-goods men, etc. Whenever a barge arrived in Paris, before it had even touched the quayside, a horde of porters would have swarmed off the ferryboats and practically taken it by storm.[13] They were all inhabitants of the world of trade, which had its own logic, its own contradictions, its chains of dependence running from the regrater who travelled into remote country districts looking for cheap sacks of grain, to the keepers of shops, whether shabby store or fashionable boutique, to the warehouse-keepers of the towns, the bourgeois merchants of the ports who equipped fishing expeditions, the wholesalers of Paris and the powerful *négociants* of Bordeaux. All were united in the world of trade. And alongside it there was always to be seen that detested but indispensable fellow-traveller, the usurer, from the great financier who lent money to the crowned heads of Europe, to the humble pawn-broker. According to Turgot, the most outrageous usury was

> what is known in Paris as lending money *à la petite semaine* [short-term and at high interest]; people have been known to charge 2 *sous* a week on an *écu* of three *livres*; that is the equivalent of $173\frac{1}{3}$ *livres* for a hundred in a year. And it is on this truly enormous usury that the *retail trade* [my italics] is conducted in the Halles and markets of Paris. The borrowers do not complain about the conditions of the loan without which they would not be able to carry on the trade which is their living; and the lenders do not enrich themselves thereby, since the exorbitant price no more than compensates the risk run by their capital. Only one borrower has to default to wipe out the profit the lender makes from thirty.[14]

There was thus a trading community within the larger community of society. And it is important to see this as a whole and not to lose sight of it. Felipe Ruiz Martín[15] is justifiably fascinated by the nature of this community and its peculiar form of hierarchy, without which capitalism cannot be properly understood. After the discovery of America, Spain was presented with an unprecedented opportunity, but international capitalism successfully captured it from her. A three-tier pyramid came into being: the bottom tier consisted of peasants, shepherds, silk-producers, artisans, *regatores* (who were pedlars and small-time moneylenders); above them came the capitalists of Castile who controlled these small fry; and finally, orchestrating everything from above, were the factors for the Fuggers, and before long the Genoese, flaunting their new power.

This pyramid of trade, always identifiable, a society within a society, can be found anywhere in the West, and in any period. It had its own laws of motion. Specialization and division of labour usually operated from the bottom up. If modernization or rationalization consists of the process whereby different tasks are distinguished and functions subdivided, such modernization began *in the bottom layer of the economy*. Every boom in trade led to increased specialization of shops and the appearance of new professions among the many hangers-on of trade.

Curiously enough, the wholesaler did not in fact observe this rule, and only specialized very occasionally. Even a shopkeeper who made his fortune, and became a merchant, immediately moved out of specialization into non-specialization. In eighteenth-century Barcelona, a *botiguer* who went up in the world would begin handling all manner of goods.[16] In 1777, André, a lace-manufacturer in Caen took over the family firm which was on the verge of ruin: he restored its fortunes by extending the area of sales and purchases, and to this effect visited towns as distant as Rennes, Lorient, Rotterdam – and New York. He had become a merchant: and lo and behold, he was now handling not only lace, but muslins, spices and foodstuffs, and furs,[17] obeying the rules of trade at its upper levels. To become and above all to remain a wholesaler meant having not only the right but the duty to handle, if not everything, at any rate as much as possible. I have already said that in my view, this many-sidedness cannot be explained, as it sometimes is, by prudence on the part of the wholesaler, a desire to spread the risk (why should small traders not have been prudent too?). This phenomenon is surely too regular not to require a broader explanation. Capitalism in our own times is after all equally versatile. Could not one of our large merchant banks of today stand comparison, *mutatis mutandis*, with the big Milan firm Antonio Greppi on the eve of the French Revolution? Although it was in theory a bank, Greppi's also handled the state tobacco and salt monopoly in Lombardy, and bought mercury from Idria in Vienna, for the king of Spain – in enormous quantities. But it did not invest at all in industry. Similarly, its numerous branches in Italy, in Cadiz, Amsterdam and even Buenos Aires, dabbled in many enterprises, but always on the marketing side, from Swedish copper (for the bottoms of Spanish ships) to grain speculation in Tangier, sales on commission of linen, silk and silk fabrics from Italy, or the countless commodities quoted on the Amsterdam Exchange; not to mention the systematic use Greppi's made (for trading in bills of exchange) of all the contacts the great financial centre of Milan had with similar centres all over the world. One might even add to the list what was frankly a smuggling operation, in ingots of American silver fraudulently loaded at Cadiz.[18] Another example was the Dutch firm of Tripp in the seventeenth century: it was forever shifting the focus of its affairs from one place to another and extending its range of activities. It tended to play one monopoly off against another, one alliance against another, and rarely hesitated to attack any rival foolish enough to tread on its toes. It did consistently prefer certain commodities: the arms trade, tar, copper, gunpowder (and consequently saltpetre from Poland, the Indies or even Africa); it played a considerable part in the affairs of the *Oost Indische Compagnie* and provided that mighty enterprise with several of its directors; it also owned ships, made loans, and had some interests in ironworks, foundries and other industrial concerns; it exploited peat-bogs in Friesia and Groningen, had substantial interests in Sweden where it owned a

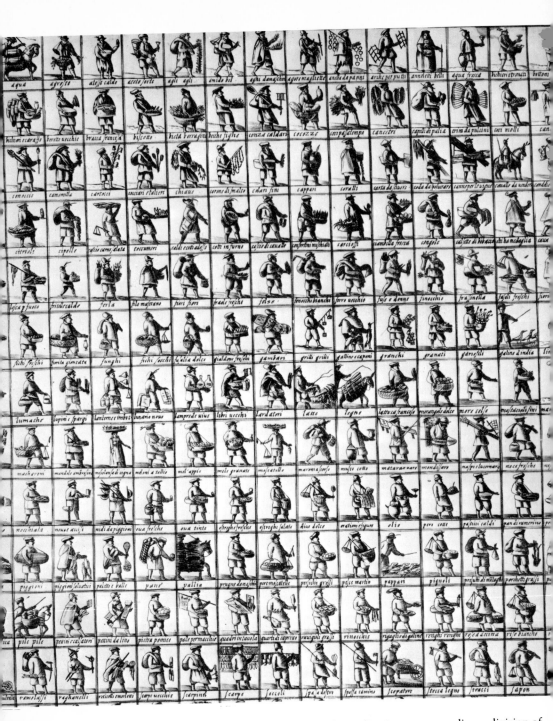

The street cries of Rome: at least 192 specialized trades, indicating an extraordinary division of labour at grass-roots level. There were vendors of every kind of agricultural produce, including straw; of forest products (from mushrooms to charcoal); of fish; of handmade goods (soap, brooms, clogs, wicker baskets). There were pedlars (of herrings, paper, needles, glass, spirits, secondhand clothes) and those who sold their services (knife-grinders, wood-choppers, tooth-pullers, travelling cooks). (Photo Oscar Savio.)

number of huge estates, did business with Guinea in Africa, Angola and both Americas.[18] When, in the nineteenth century, capitalism moved so spectacularly into the new world of industry, it did of course give the impression of specializing, and historians in general have tended to regard industry as the final flowering which gave capitalism its 'true' identity. But can we be so sure? It seems to me rather that after the initial boom of mechanization, the most advanced kind of capitalism reverted to eclecticism, to an indivisibility of interests so to speak, as if the characteristic advantage of standing at the commanding heights of the economy, today just as much as in the days of Jacques Coeur (the fourteenth-century tycoon) consisted precisely of *not* having to confine oneself to a single choice, of being able, as today's businessmen would put it, to keep one's options open.

The rational division of labour thus operated at a level lower than that of the wholesale merchant; the profusion of middlemen and intermediary tiers listed for late seventeenth-century London in R.B. Westerfield's study[19] – the factors, commission agents, brokers, cashiers, insurers, hauliers, and the armateurs (shipfitters) who were by the late seventeenth century, in La Rochelle and elsewhere too no doubt, putting up the *mise-hors* (initial outlay) for a ship's voyage – all these people were effectively specialized auxiliaries offering their services to the merchant. Even the specialized banker (not the 'financier' of course) was at the merchant's command – and the latter did not hesitate, if the occasion looked promising, to discharge the functions of insurer, armateur, banker or commission agent himself. And of course he always stood to gain the most. In Marseilles, although it was one of the busiest trading places in the eighteenth century, bankers were by no means top people, according to Charles Carrière.[20]

In short, as the trading community constantly renewed its structures, there seems to have been one position virtually unassailable, and which by virtue of its very impregnability was strengthened and confirmed, as divisions and subdivisions multiplied at lower levels: that of the wholesale merchant with many interests. In London, and in all the active ports in England, he was becoming a leading figure by the seventeenth century – indeed his was the only success story in these rather difficult times. In 1720, Defoe noted that London merchants were acquiring more and more servants, that they even wanted footmen, like the gentry: hence 'the infinite number of blue liveries, which are become so common now that they are called "the tradesmen's liveries" and few gentlemen care to give blue to their servants for that very reason'.[21] The entire life-style, the amusements of the rich merchant were changing. The export-import merchant, enriched by trade with the whole world, was becoming a great man, in quite a different class from 'traders of the middling sort', who were content with the home market and who 'though highly useful in their station, are by no means entitled to the honours of higher rank'.[22]

In France too, by at least 1622, the merchants were putting on airs. 'Clad in silk costume and cloak of plush', they left all tedious chores to their chief clerks. 'They can be seen at "Change" in the mornings ... one would not know them to be merchants; or on the Pont-Neuf, discussing business on the mall'[23] (in Paris the mall or pell-mell was on the Quai des Ormes, near the Celestins, and 'Change' was in the present-day law courts, the Palais de Justice). This was a far cry from the shopkeeper's baize apron. What was more, an ordinance of 1627 permitted nobles to participate in maritime trade without losing rank. This was one way of improving the status of merchants in a society that still tended to look down on them. That French merchants still did not feel entirely at home in society can be seen from the curious petition they presented in 1702 to the *Conseil de commerce*. This requested neither more nor less than a purge of the profession, distinguishing once and for all between the merchant and any *manual* worker - apothecary, goldsmith, furrier, bonnet-maker, wine-seller, stocking-knitter, second-hand clothes dealer, 'and also a thousand other trades [practised by men who are] *workers* (*ouvriers*) and yet have the status of merchants'. In a word, the 'status of merchant' should only be granted to those 'who sell merchandise without either making it themselves or adding anything of their own to it'.[24]

So the eighteenth century saw the heyday of the wealthy merchant all over Europe. Let me emphasize once more that it was thanks to the spontaneous expansion of the economy, at the grass roots, that such businessmen were able to further their careers. They were carried along on the current. Even if there is a grain of truth in Schumpeter's theory of the spirit of enterprise, empirical observation nine times out of ten shows that the innovator was borne along on a rising tide. What then was the secret of his success? In other words, how did a merchant become one of the elect?

Success in trade

One condition towered above all the others: a good start in life. Men who rose from rags to riches were as rare in the past as they are today. And the recipe given by Claude Carrière, writing about fifteenth-century Barcelona - 'The best way to make money in big business ... [was] to have some to start with'[25] - applies to every period in history. In 1698, just after the Peace of Ryswick (which brought only a short respite) Antoine Hogguer, a very young man from a merchant family in Saint-Gall, received a sum of 100,000 *écus* from his father 'to see what sort of stuff he's made of'. He 'managed so well' in Bordeaux, 'that within a month, he had tripled his money'. Over the next five years, he amassed considerable sums of money in England, Holland and Spain.[26] In 1788, Gabriel-Julien Ouvrard (later to be 'the great' Ouvrard) was only eighteen. With money received from his father (a well-to-do stationer of Entiers in the Vendée) he had already made handsome profits from trade in Nantes. At the beginning of the Revolution, he speculated in paper, of which he stocked huge quantities; and this paid off too. Next he moved to Bordeaux where he continued to prosper.[27]

Frontispiece of *Le Parfait Négociant* by Jacques Savary, 1675. (Viollet Collection.)

For a beginner, having some launching capital was worth all the letters of recommendation in the world. Remy Bensa in Frankfurt was on the point of engaging a commission agent in Rouen: the candidate had references from three merchants but Bensa was still hesitating: 'I favour M. Dugard', he writes, 'because he is a young man who is not afraid of work and who keeps his books pretty well. The trouble is, he has no property, at least I know of none.'[28]

Another advantage for a beginner was to make his debut during a favourable phase in the economy. But success was not assured even then. The climate of trade was changeable. When it seemed set fair, a whole flotilla of novice businessmen would regularly put to sea. The winds and tide were favourable, so they were confident and even inclined to boast. Surprised by stormy weather, they went down with all hands. Only the shrewdest, the most fortunate, or those who had had reserves to start with, escaped this massacre of the innocents. The conclusion we are approaching is clear: the successful merchant was someone who could cross these stormy waters without mishap. If he pulled through, it was of course because he had certain advantages and knew how to use them; at worst, he had the means to beat for the shore and shelter until the weather improved. M. G. Buist, who has compared the turnover figures of six large firms in Amsterdam from their *banking* records, concludes that they all survived the sudden crisis of 1763 (with one exception, which in fact recovered quite quickly).[29] And yet this *capitalist* crisis of 1763, just after the Hundred Years' War, had brought havoc to the economic heart of Europe, and had been marked by a whole string of failures and bankruptcies, from Amsterdam to Hamburg, London and Paris. Only the princes of trade weathered the storm.

To say that capitalist success depended on having money is of course a truism if one is only referring to the capital indispensable for any enterprise. But money meant other things besides the ability to invest. It meant social prestige and thus a whole range of guarantees, privileges, connections, patronages. It meant being able to choose between the available affairs or opportunities – and having a choice was both a temptation and a privilege – being able to break into a resistant circuit, to defend a threatened advantage, to make good one's losses, to ward off rivals; it meant being in a position to wait for returns which were slow, but promising, and even to obtain the favours and indulgence of princes. Last but not least, it meant the freedom to obtain even more – since only the rich could borrow large sums of money. And credit was increasingly becoming the indispensable tool of the merchant's trade. His own capital, the 'principal', was rarely sufficient for his needs. 'There is no commercial centre on earth', wrote Turgot, 'where business does not run on borrowed money: there is perhaps not a single businessman who is not obliged to call on other men's purses.'[30] And an anonymous writer in the *Journal de commerce* (1759)[31] exclaims: 'What method, what a head for figures, what a wealth of ideas and what courage are demanded by the occupation of a man at the head of a trading-house managing a turnover of several million *livres* every year with a capital of a mere 200 to 300 thousand *livres*!'

And yet, if we are to believe Defoe, the entire hierarchy of trade, from top to bottom, operated on the same principle. From the small shopkeeper to the businessman, from the artisan to the manufacturer, everyone lived on credit, that is on forward sales and purchases ('at time' as Defoe calls it), which made it possible to have an annual turnover of £30,000 with a stock of £5000.[32] Even the time given for repayment, which everyone allowed and received in turn ('it is borrowing as it were'[33] – Defoe) could be extended: 'Not one man in twenty keeps to his time: and so easy are tradesmen to one another that in general it is not much expected.'[34] On every merchant's books, alongside the stock of goods, there regularly figured his assets (credit) and liabilities (debts). The wise trader sought to maintain a balance, but never abandoned these forms of credit which in the end amounted to a huge mass, multiplying the volume of trade by four or five.[35] The entire commercial system depended on it. If credit arrangements broke down, the economy would grind to a halt. The important point is that this was a kind of credit inherent in the commercial system, generated by it – an internal form of credit *which was interest-free.* The particularly vigorous form it took in England seemed to Defoe to explain the secret of English prosperity, *overtrading*[36] as he calls it, which also enabled British trade to make conquests abroad.

The wealthy merchant could also take advantage, and enable his clients to take advantage of this *internal* facility. But he had recourse fairly regularly to another form of credit, calling on the money of financiers and moneylenders *outside* the system. These were cash loans which regularly carried interest – a crucial difference since a trading operation mounted on this basis had at the end of the day to show a rate of profit well above interest rates. Such was not the case in everyday trading in Defoe's opinion: 'interest of money is a canker-worm upon the tradesman's profit', capable even at the 'lawful' rate of 5%, of wiping out his gains altogether.[37] *A fortiori*, recourse to usury would be suicidal. So if the great merchant could regularly borrow money 'from other men's purses', calling on *external* credit, it must mean that his normal profit margins were very much greater than those of the ordinary run of merchants. This takes us to the crucial dividing line separating off a particular and privileged sector of the world of trade.

In a book from which I have greatly benefited, K.N. Chaudhuri[38] asks why the prestigious Indies Companies stopped short at the point of distribution; why they auctioned their goods at the warehouse door, on advertised dates. Was it not simply because they received cash from such sales? It was a way of avoiding the rules and practices of the wholesale trade, with its long delays in payment, a way of recovering capital so as to redeploy it as quickly as possibly in the profitable Far East trade – in short a way of saving time.

Who put up the money?

'Accumulate, accumulate! This is the golden rule' of the capitalist economy, wrote Marx.[39] Just as golden a rule would be 'Borrow, borrow!' Every society accumulates capital which is then at its disposal, either to be saved and hoarded unproductively, or to replenish the channels of the active economy, which in the past chiefly meant the merchant economy. If the flow was not strong enough to open all the sluice-gates, capital was almost inevitably immobilized, its true nature as it were unrealized. Capitalism cannot fully be said to have arrived until accumulated capital is being used to maximum capacity – though the 100% level is of course never reached.

This injection of capital into economic life governed variations in the interest rate, one of the major indicators of the well-being of trade and the economy. And if interest rates fell almost continuously in Europe between the fifteenth and eighteenth centuries; if they were ridiculously low in Genoa in about 1600; if they dropped spectacularly in Holland and subsequently in London in the seventeenth century; it was above all because accumulation had increased the mass of capital. This was now so abundant that its price, that is the interest rate, fell, and the turnover of trade, although growing, was unable to keep pace with capital formation. Another reason was that in these highly-animated centres of the international economy, the demand for loans was sufficiently brisk and persistent to have brought about an early meeting between capitalist and investor, thus creating an accessible money market. It was also easier and cheaper for a merchant to raise money in Marseilles or Cadiz for example, than in Paris.[40]

When surveying the world of those who provided funds, we should not forget the multitude (soon to grow even larger) of small savers. This was the money of the innocent. There had always been, in the Hanseatic or Italian ports, and still were in sixteenth-century Seville, a number of small investors – people prepared to take modest risks, to send a few goods on a departing ship for instance. When it returned, they were good people to do business with, since they needed their money immediately. The great *party* (loan) of Lyons in 1557 attracted a considerable number of small subscribers, 'micro-investors'. The savings of many humble folk were included in the capital raised by the Höchstetters of Augsburg, who failed to obtain the monopoly of mercury extraction and went bankrupt in 1529. It is not without significance that in the early eighteenth century, we find 'the valet of J.B. Bruny [a wealthy merchant of Marseilles] putting 300 *livres* into the outfitting of the *Saint-Jean Baptiste*, or Marguerite Truphème, a domestic servant of R. Bruny [ditto], putting 100 *livres* into the *Marianne* – whereas her annual wages came to 60 *livres*'.[41] And a woman-servant in Paris had 1000 *écus* in the *Cinq Grosses Fermes* (the state tax farms), according to a register of 1705 – not that this is necessarily to be taken literally.[42]

There were middling investors as well as small savers. The Genoese mer-

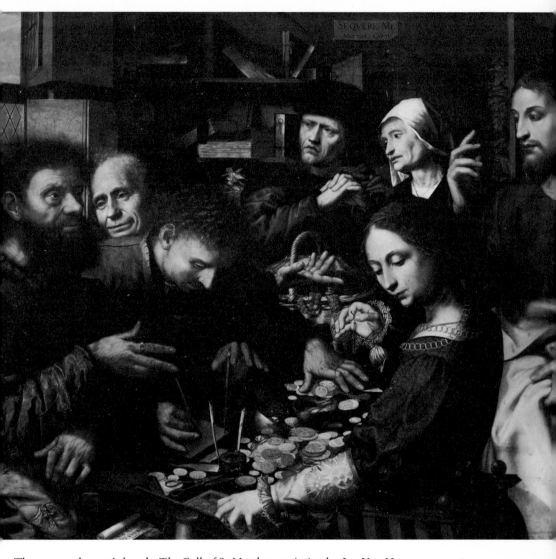

The money-changer's booth. *The Call of St Matthew*, painting by Jan Van Hemessen, 1536. (Bayerische Staatsgemäldesammlungen, photo by the Museum.)

chants who arranged Philip II's short-term loans drew in turn on Italian and Spanish investors, who were contacted by intermediaries. The king ceded to his Genoese financiers Spanish state bonds, *juros*, against the money which was or would be advanced to him. These bonds, which were handed over blank, were then offered on the open market. The Genoese banker-financier paid out the interest on them, but he would already have received the whole sum lent to the king – thus himself incurring a low-interest loan. When he was eventually paid by the king, he would give him back *juros* of the same face-value and interest as the ones originally received as security. It might be possible to find in the archives at Simancas the lists of subscribers who took up the Genoese offer. I was once lucky enough to lay hands on one such – but not knowing at the time the significance of my find, unlucky enough not to have noted the reference number.

It would certainly be interesting to know how many there were of these not-very-adventurous lenders of money, how much they lent and what their social status was. The extension of the subscribing public was a major phenomenon of the nineteenth century. But one has a suspicion that it was already quite large in England and Holland in the eighteenth century, and other things being equal, even earlier in Venice, Genoa and Florence. One historian has suggested that there may have been as many as 500,000 subscribers – mostly Parisians – to Louis XVI's loans just before 1789.[43] This is not an impossible figure, though it has yet to be substantiated. It is in any case clear that the investments of modest savers went more readily into government bonds than into trade.

The middle-rank investor often had the same reflexes, since he was caught between a desire for gain and a fear of insecurity – and the latter very often gained the upper hand. Do not expect to find in the 'investment guide', *Il Dottor vulgare* (1673),[44] much evidence of audaciousness and risk-taking. It does, it is true, say, 'Nowadays, no one boasts of having his money lying idle and unproductive [at home]. ... There are always ample opportunities to invest, especially since the recent more frequent introduction and spread of ... public bonds or annuities ... known in Rome as *luoghi de monti*', – but one should not be misled: the author is really recommending gilt-edged securities.

The really big lenders, those who counted, were usually men of substance known by the end of the seventeenth century by the specific title 'capitalists'. Lookers-on at the business world, they sometimes joined in on an impulse (anything *could* happen after all) seduced by the skilful pleading of a would-be borrower (according to Defoe, a shopkeeper who had made his fortune and retired often threw caution to the winds) – but more often their decision was a calculated one. Almost any rich man sooner or later fell into the category of financial backer, *bailleur de fonds*: office-holders of the French *noblesse de robe* for whom the *traitants*, or tax-farmers,[45] were often only front-men; magistrates and regents of the Dutch towns; patricians of Venice, who as a sixteenth-century register shows, could be *piezarie* (underwriters) giving backing to the small-time farmers of taxes and dues for the Signoria;[46] their backing was not – needless to say – disinterested. In La Rochelle, merchants and shipowners had 'regular teams of financial backers'.[47] In Genoa, the entire upper class of businessmen, that thin stratum of *nobili vecchi* (old nobility), was composed of financiers whose activities we shall consider later. Even in Amsterdam, where a lending-bank, supported by the Bank of Amsterdam, had existed since 1614, this only advanced loans for trade for a limited period. In about 1640, it became a sort of safe deposit institution, and left trade to private capital.[48] Holland's triumph mean the triumph of easy credit, even for foreign merchants. In seventeenth-century London, the money-market was not so forthcoming.[49] But cash was so scarce that credit developed out of necessity among 'bill-brokers [who] were largely concerned with bills of exchange ... scriveners who specialized in land transfers and mortgages' and above all goldsmiths who were already virtually acting as bankers, being the accredited organizers of subscriptions to Crown bonds, which as Isaac de Pinto emphatically points out, were soon to become substitute money.[50]

There was nothing comparable in mid-eighteenth-century France, which had not yet begun to catch up with Holland or England in business matters. Credit seems to have been poorly and almost clandestinely organized there. The social climate was not particularly encouraging. The financier, either because of his position (as royal office-holder, say) or his noble status (for fear of losing rank) was anxious to observe the greatest discretion over lending money. And the borrower was equally afraid of publicity which might damage his credit-worthiness. In certain business circles, a firm that borrowed money was regarded with some suspicion.

In 1749,[51] a wealthy Rouen merchant, Robert Dugard, was engaged in founding at Darnetal, a suburb of the town, a linen-manufactory and dye works, employing certain technical secrets (acquired not entirely by fair means, but that is another story). To launch his enterprise, he needed money; and this would have to be borrowed, anticipating on the future proceeds of the works. One of Dugard's partners, Louvet the younger, took on this difficult assignment. He set off for Paris, where he raced from door to door, trying to persuade backers to accept bills or drafts in exchange for cash. The point of the operation was to repay them on the due date and start again. His progress can be traced from his correspondence. He dashes about, pleading his case, is either overjoyed or downcast, but always returns to the same addresses as a petitioner – and if possible as a friend. 'Just hold on', he writes to Dugard who was getting impatient, 'everything takes time, especially in this kind of business where one cannot be too careful. Someone less cautious and more talented than I might get what he wanted the first time, but I am afraid of having doors closed to me, and once they are closed, one has to pass them by.'[52] So he tried every kind of inducement. Instead of bills (some left blank) and drafts, 'we have had an idea', writes Louvet: 'We would offer them [i.e. reluctant backers] a sort of share, which we would pay back after five years, with an annual dividend increasing every year.' These particular backers were related to another partner, d'Haristoy, of whom Louvet tells us: 'Mr d'Haristoy has gone to dine with his relations; I have given him a prod and sent him off with fire in his belly.' Here is a final example of his contortions, which one begins to understand only on third or fourth reading (28th January 1750): 'You may draw 20,000 *livres* on Mr Le Leu, for 20 February to 2 March, and 20,000 for 2 December, but it must be honoured: I have given him regular papers for all this. Or if you prefer, I will draw on him for you, and will send you the bills all signed and sealed; anyway, do as you please.' Louvet came to grief eventually, though this is by the way, and after giving up his partnership in the Darnetal works, which itself went bankrupt in 1761, had to flee to London in February 1755, where he was to be found 'at Mrs Steel's in Little Bell Alley, Coleman Street'. What does his story tell us? That he was a go-between with a sharp tongue, who was exasperated at having 'to go round ... with the begging bowl', at being obliged, in order to obtain paltry sums of money to make 'one call for courtesy, another call to dispose them in my favour and a third call to get down to business'; exasperated at being asked for impossible guarantees, at not being able to discount the best paper when he wanted to, because all the exchanges closed suddenly on account of some bank collapsing in Bordeaux or London – in short he was exasperated at being in a city where there were no arrangements for advancing normal credit to traders. And yet Robert Dugard was an important businessman, with interests in all kinds of affairs, including the Indies trade. He ought to have had no credit problems – particularly, and this is the paradox, since capital was not in short supply in Paris. The Le Couteulx bank, with branches in Paris, Rouen and Cadiz, refused to take deposits of money – 'we have too much money in stock as it is'; our 'capital is sitting in the vaults' – complaints repeated at intervals in 1734, 1754, 1758, and 1767.[53]

Credit and banking

In the medieval and early modern European context, banking was hardly a new invention. There had been banks and bankers in antiquity; and there had been Jewish moneylenders in Islam where, well before their appearance in the West, credit instruments such as the bill of exchange were being used by the tenth or eleventh century. In the Christian countries of the Mediterranean, the first bankers were the exchange-dealers, whether itinerant, travelling from fair to fair, or settled, in places like Barcelona, Genoa or Venice.[54] In Florence, according to Federigo Melis,[55] and in other towns in Tuscany no doubt, banks arose out of the services that merchant companies and other firms performed for one another. In this kind of operation, the vital partner was the 'active' firm, which asked for credit, thus obliging the other 'sleeping' partner which put up the money, to participate indirectly in a venture which was in principle quite separate from it.

The origins need not concern us here. Nor need we look closely at the general development of private banks, both before and after the creation of the public banks which was a crucial event: (the *Taula de Cambis* in Barcelona, 1401; the *Casa di San Giorgio* in Genoa, 1407 – which suspended activity between 1458 and 1596; the *Banco di Rialto*, 1587; the Bank of Amsterdam, 1609; the *Banco Giro* of Venice, 1619). Before the foundation of the Bank of England in 1694,

An Italian bank in the late fourteenth century.
Top: the strongroom and the desk where coins are being counted.
Bottom: deposits and transfers. (British Museum.)

public banks only handled deposits and transfers, not loans and advances, nor what we would today call share portfolios. But such activities very soon fell under the scope of the private banks, the Venetian *banchi di scritta* for instance, or the Neapolitan banks of the sixteenth century, many of whose registers have survived.

But our present purpose is not to dwell on individual histories: it is simply to find out how and when credit was tending to turn into an institution; how and when banking progressed towards the commanding positions of the economy. Broadly speaking, there were three occasions in the West when there was an expansion of banking and credit so abnormal as to be visible to the naked eye: in Florence before and after 1300; in Genoa in the latter part of the sixteenth century and the first two decades of the seventeenth; and in Amsterdam in the eighteenth century. Can any conclusions be drawn from the fact that three times a well-advanced development, which appeared to be leading in the medium or the long term towards the triumph of some form of financial capitalism, was blocked in mid-career? Not until the nineteenth century would this development be completed. Here then are three experiences, three substantial successes, which ended every time in failure or at any rate in some kind of withdrawal. I propose to delineate these three experiences in very general terms, in order to observe above all the curious amount they have in common.

In the Florence of the *Duecento* and *Trecento*, credit was something central not only to the entire history of the city, but to that of her rivals among the Italian towns, not to say the whole Mediterranean or the Western world. It is in the context of the revival of the European economy from at least the twelfth century that we must view the establishment of the great merchant banking houses of Florence. They were borne on the current which was to place Italy ahead of the rest of Europe for centuries on end: in the thirteenth century, Genoese boats were sailing the Caspian Sea, Italian travellers and merchants were reaching India and China, the Venetians and Genoese had occupied the vital points on the Black Sea; there were Italians looking for Sudanese gold in North African ports, while others had scattered to France, Spain, Portugal, the Netherlands and England. And wherever they went, Florentine merchants bought and sold spices, woollens, hardware, metals, cloth, silkstuffs – but most of all they trafficked in money. Their half-merchant, half-banking companies had, in their home town, a ready source of cash and *comparatively* cheap credit, hence the strength and efficiency of their networks. Compensatory payments, transfers of credit and money could easily be made between one branch and another, from Bruges to Venice, Aragon to Armenia, from the North Sea to the Black Sea; Chinese silks were sold in London for bales of wool. In good times after all, credit and paper were the ultimate form of money, flying indefatigably from place to place.

The greatest achievement of the Florentine firms was undoubtedly the conquest of and ascendancy over the far-off kingdom of England. In order to reach their position of influence here, they had to supplant the Jewish moneylenders, the merchants of the Hanseatic ports and the Low Countries, to overcome the stubborn resistance of native English traders, and they also had to shoulder aside some Italian competitors. The Florentines took the place of the pioneering Riccardi – the Lucchese merchants who had financed Edward I's conquest of Wales. A little later, it was the Frescobaldi of Florence who were lending Edward II money for his wars against Scotland; and the Bardi and Peruzzi subsequently acted as Edward III's backers in his moves against France in the opening stages of what was to be the Hundred Years' War. The triumph of the Florentines lay not only in holding the purse strings of the kings of England, but also in controlling sales of English wool which was vital to continental workshops and in particular to the *Arte della Lana* of Florence.

But the English venture ended in 1345 with the fall of the house of Bardi – 'a colossus with feet of clay' as it was called, but a colossus all the same. In that dramatic year, Edward III owed huge sums of money both to them and to the Peruzzi (900,000 florins to the Bardi and 600,000 to the Peruzzi) – a sum out of all proportion to the capital these firms actually owned, proof that they had made their gigantic loans with money from their own depositors – in a proportion of about 1 to 10. The crash when it came ('the most serious in the entire history of Florence' according to the chronicler Villani) was a heavy blow to the city because of the other disasters which accompanied it. As much as Edward III defaulting on his debts, the real villain was the recession which divided the fourteenth century in half, with the Black Death following on its heels.

Florence's fortune as a *banking* city now declined before the rising star of *trade* in both Genoa and Venice. And it was Venice, the queen of trade, which emerged triumphant after the Chioggia war in 1381. The Florentine experiment in what was evidently a forerunner of modern banking, did not survive the international economic crisis. Florence retained her trade and industry; and even revived her banking sector in the fifteenth century. But she never again played such a pioneering indeed world-leading role. The Medici were not the Bardi.

The second experiment in banking took place in Genoa. Between 1550 and 1560, at a time when the ebullient expansion of the earlier part of the century was slowing down, the European economy underwent a certain distortion. The flow of silver from the American mines had, on one hand, operated against the great German merchants who had previously controlled the silver production of Central Europe; and on the other, had put up the price of gold, which now became more scarce but was still the currency in which international transactions and bills of exchange were settled. The Genoese were the first to realize the new state of affairs. Offering to replace the merchants of High Germany as financial backers of the Spanish crown, they were able to lay hands on the treasure from America, and their city became the centre of the European economy, replacing Antwerp. There now developed a banking venture even more strange and modern than that of the fourteenth-century Florentines, that of credit based on negotiable bills of exchange, which were passed on from fair to fair or exchange to exchange. Bills of exchange were of course already known and made use of in Antwerp, Lyons or Augsburg, in Medina del Campo and elsewhere, and these money markets did not become deserted overnight. But under the Genoese, paper acquired a new importance. Indeed the Fuggers are supposed to have said that doing business with the Genoese meant playing with pieces of paper, *mit Papier*, whereas they themselves operated with real money, *Baargeld* – the typical reaction of traditional financiers failing to understand a new technique. For, by their loans to the Spanish crown, which were repaid in pieces of eight or silver bars when the American fleets returned, the Genoese were on the contrary turning their city into the leading market for silver. And through their bills of exchange or those they bought for silver currencies in Venice or Florence, they controlled the circulation of gold too. In fact they achieved the considerable feat of paying the king of Spain in gold, on the Antwerp money market (for his army, since soldiers were paid predominantly in gold coins) the sums they had received in silver from Spain.

The Genoese machinery really got going in 1579, with the Piacenza fairs which have already been mentioned.[56] These fairs centralized the many business transactions and international payments; they acted as a sort of clearing-house or *scontro* as it was called. Not until 1622 did this elaborately-constructed machinery begin to founder, bringing to an end shortly afterwards the exclusive reign of Genoese credit. What is the explanation of this collapse? The fall in shipments of silver from America was long considered to be the cause. But Michel Morineau's revolutionary studies have now stood the problem on its head.[57] There was no disastrous decrease in American treasure. Nor did chestfuls of pieces of eight stop arriving in Genoa. Proof to the contrary is now available. Genoa remained in contact with the flow of bullion. With the economic upturn at the end of the seventeenth century, the town was still absorbing 5 or 6 million *pezze da otto* – at least such sums were passing through the city, in 1687 for example.[58] In these circumstances, the problem of the comparative decline of Genoa becomes rather puzzling. According to Felipe Ruiz Martin, the Spanish purchasers of *juros* had stopped providing the capital necessary to the operations of the Genoese merchant-bankers as accredited moneylenders to the crown. Thrown back on their own resources, he argues, the latter repatriated their funds from Spain. This is possible, but I am tempted by another explanation. Dealing in paper, bills of exchange, was only worthwhile if the money-markets between which they circulated had different discount rates; a bill had to acquire value on its travels. In times of *'bestial larghezze'*[59] of specie – a contemporary's phrase – the bill of exchange stuck at the top of the high rates. If the flow of money was too strong, the mill-wheel would be submerged and no longer turn. And in 1590–1595, the money markets were certainly inundated with silver. Whether for this reason or some other, the Genoese paper mountain collapsed or at any rate lost its power to dictate the organization of credit. Once more, a sophisticated credit system, created at the topmost level of European affairs, was unable to maintain its position for more than a very short time – not even fifty years – as if these new experiences were beyond the capacities of *ancien régime* economies.

But the venture was to begin again in Amsterdam.

In the eighteenth century, effective banking supremacy was reconstituted in the quadrilateral Amsterdam-London-Paris-Geneva. The centre of the miracle this time was Amsterdam. Here various types of paper credit came to assume an unprecedented and extraordinary role. The entire commodity trade of Europe was governed, remote-controlled so to speak, by the rapid movement of credit and discounting. But just as in Genoa, the pivot of this delicate system was unable to hold out until the end of the century and the new prosperity it brought. The Dutch bank, having too much money on its hands, allowed itself to be caught in the treacherous toils of loans to European states. The bankruptcy of the French state in 1789 was a catastrophic blow to the precision-built Dutch mechanism. Once again, the reign of paper came to a bad end. And as on the other occasions, its failure raises more problems that we can answer. Perhaps it was simply too soon to create a steady and self-confident banking system, one in which the triple network of circulating commodities, circulating money and circulating credit could operate harmoniously and without incident. If so, the crisis, the intercyclical depression which began in 1778, was only a detonator, hastening a development that was virtually inevitable, written into the logic of events.

Money: in circulation or in hiding

The short-term rhythms of the economy are usually measured by wages, prices and production levels. Perhaps one ought also to pay some attention to another indicator, one which has so far been hardly measurable at all: the circulation of money-capital. It was by turns accumulated, used, then hidden away again. Sometimes it was locked up in strong-rooms: hoarding was an ever-present negative force in the economies of the past. It was often put into safe investments – land and real estate. But there were also times when the triple locks of the coffers were opened, when money circulated and was on offer to anyone who had a use for it. Indeed it was easier to borrow money in Holland in the 1750s than it is now in the 1980s. But in general, until the industrial revolution, productive investment was subject to many restrictions and depending on circumstances, these might be as much related to the difficulty of using what was available as to scarcity of capital.

There were times at any rate when money was abundant and times when it was quite unobtainable. Business either ran smoothly or ground to a halt without the apparent masters of the world being able to do much about it. Carlo M. Cipolla[60] has shown that the situation suddenly improved for Italy as a whole after the peace of Cateau-Cambrésis (1559) which mutilated the country politically, but provided a degree of peace and security. Similarly all over Europe, the successive peace-treaties of 1598, 1604 and 1609 were followed by times when money was in plentiful supply. It was not put to the same use everywhere, it is true. In Holland in the early seventeenth century, merchant capitalism was getting into full swing. In Venice at the same period, money originally made in commodity trading was being invested in capitalist agriculture. Elsewhere, money was being poured into cultural extravagance – an economically aberrant source of expenditure: the Spanish Golden Age, England under the Stuarts and the *style Henri IV*, better known as the *style Louis XIII*, in France, were undoubtedly drawing on nations' accumulated capital. In the eighteenth century, luxury and commercial or financial speculation developed hand in hand. Of England in his time, Isaac de Pinto[61] said that 'nobody puts money away in strong-boxes any more' and that even misers had realized that 'making one's property circulate; buying state stocks, or shares in companies or in the Bank of England, was more advantageous than having it lie idle – more advantageous even than putting it into bricks and mortar or land' (which had however been a profitable investment in sixteenth-century England). Defoe, singing the praises of investment in a business or even a small shop, in 1725, was already saying: 'An estate's a pond, but trade's a spring.'[62]

And yet even in the eighteenth century, there were reservoirs of money still untapped. There was sometimes good reason for hoarding. In France in the difficult year 1708, the government now in the throes of a war for which it was to mobilize all the nation's resources, printed bank notes: this bad money chased out the good, which went to earth, even in Brittany – or rather especially in Brittany, which was particularly rich in silver derived from profitable trade on the South Seas.

> Yesterday [reported an informant of the controller-general Desmarets, from Rennes on 6 March 1708], I was at the house of one of the leading bourgeois of the town, a man very conversant with trade, who has been and still is in business, on both land and sea, with the best known merchants of the province. He assured me he knew for a fact that there were more than thirty million piastres hidden away, and over sixty million in gold and silver, which will never see the light of day until the bank notes put into circulation by Louis XIV's government have been completely exhausted and hard money [the rates of which were in constant flux] has settled at a reasonable level, and trade to some extent been restored.[63]

The piastres in question were those the ships of Saint-Malo had brought back from Peru; as for the restoration of trade – which really meant the end of the War of the Spanish Succession dating from 1701 – this would not be achieved until the Treaties of Utrecht (1713) and Rastatt (1714).

Similar caution was observed by all businessmen. The Treaty of Utrecht was already several months old when the French consul in Genoa wrote: 'Lack of confidence keeps money in short supply; so those who usually do business on credit, which means most of the merchants in the city, are doing very little. The

Marseilles harbour in the eighteenth century (detail) by Joseph Vernet.
(Photothèque Armand Colin.)

best purses are shut.'[64] And they would not open again until the *Carrera de Indias*, on which they in fact depended, assumed once more its role as distributor of silver from Cadiz – for without silver or gold or dependable returns, the 'best purses' would not be giving, or indeed receiving anything. Genoa had already seen similar circumstances in 1627. The businessmen who lent money to the king of Spain had decided, after the bankruptcy of the Spanish crown, when no special measures had been taken to protect them from its consequences, not to lend Philip IV another penny. The governor of Milan and the Spanish ambassador besieged them with requests, exerted pressure and even issued threats, but to no avail. The city seemed to have completely run out of silver; all transactions ceased and there were not even any bills of exchange to be negotiated. The Venetian consul in Genoa describes the problems of the money market in several of his letters, but in the end he began to suspect that the *'stretezza'* (scarcity) was diplomatic, that it was being prolonged by the businessmen as an excuse for their refusal.[65] One is inclined to agree, if one calculates the number of *reals* that the Genoese in Spain were at the same period dispatching to their native city, to be piled up no doubt in coffers in the vaults of palaces.

From which they eventually emerged. For the money of merchants was only hoarded in expectation of better times. So in 1726, we find the following letter being written in Nantes, on the occasion of a proposal to withdraw the royal privilege from the French East India Company:

> We only discovered the strength and resources of our city on the occasion of the plan proposed by our merchants either to enter on their own account into the affairs of the king [the company] or to go into partnership for the same purpose with the merchants of Saint-Malo, who are very powerful. The latter suggestion was adopted so that the parties should not harm each other's interests, and the partnership will be known as the *Compagnie de Saint Malo*. It now appears that the subscriptions from our merchants amount to eighteen million [*livres*], whereas we thought that they would not be able to put up more than four million between them. . . . We hope that the large sums being offered at Court to withdraw the royal privilege from the *Compagnie des Indes*, which is ruining the kingdom, will succeed in making trade free everywhere.[66]

All this came to nothing, since the company's privilege in fact survived the tempests and the aftermath of the Law's system. However this is a good illustration of the general rule: as soon as peace and good opportunities return, 'the money which is in the Kingdom returns to trade'.[67]

But did it *all* return? I cannot avoid the impression that, even in the eighteenth century and if anything more so then, the money accumulated far exceeded the demand for capital; that England for instance certainly did not summon up all her reserves to finance her industrial revolution, and that much more effort and investment might have been forthcoming than actually appeared; that French monetary reserves, during the War of the Spanish Succession, were far greater than the 80 or 100 million notes issued by Louis XIV's government;[68] that

France's moveable wealth far exceeded the needs of industry before the industrial revolution, which explains why episodes such as Law's system occurred, or why the coal mines in the eighteenth century were able, without undue delay or difficulty, to find the fixed and circulating capital necessary to work them, when the occasion demanded it.[69] The correspondence of merchants[70] moreover abundantly proves that Louis XVI's France was full of unused capital, 'kicking its heels' as J. Gentil da Silva puts it, for want of employment. In Marseilles for example, in the latter part of the eighteenth century, owners of capital who offered merchants money at 5% found very few takers, and when they did find one, they thanked him 'for your kindness in keeping our funds' (1763). In fact, there was enough capital about for merchants to be able to operate with their own money or that of their partners who shared the risks, rather than with loans at interest. The same attitude prevailed in Cadiz. Businessmen refused loans, even at 4%, because they had 'enough and to spare of their own'. This was in 1759, in war time, but the same was true in 1754, in peace time.

It should not be concluded that businessmen never borrowed money at all in the latter part of the eighteenth century – this is quite untrue – or that money was being hawked about in vain everywhere. Robert Dugard's troubles in Paris are evidence to the contrary. Let us simply say that times when money was plentiful, indeed excessively so, and looking for a good investment, were more frequent than is usually thought. Nothing will reveal this so clearly as a visit to Milan just before the French Revolution. The city and the whole of Lombardy were at the time undergoing a complete overhaul of the fiscal and financial machinery, for the upturn of the economy had brought new prosperity to the state. In the face of the *Monti*, the banks, the great families, the religious institutions, the tax-farmers and powerful business groups, the Milanese state had actually become strong enough to undertake the reform of abuses so ancient that they had become quasi-structural, as the Milanese and Lombard nobility and bourgeoisie had gradually devoured the state, transforming into private revenues practically all the sections of the *regalia*, or public dues. There was only one remedy: to buy back all the revenues alienated by the state under various headings – which meant a truly enormous capital repayment. Since it was conducted at a fairly brisk pace, this policy unleashed a flood of cash into Lombardy and presented the former rentiers with a problem. What was to be done with this mass of capital suddenly placed in their laps? Although we do not know exactly what they did with it, we do know that comparatively little went into buying land or the bonds at 3.5% offered by the state, or into town properties, and that it did, through the good offices of bankers and exchange dealers, contribute in part to the current of international trade flowing through Milan, of which the house of Greppi is an example. But the point is that this manna did not benefit industrial investment, although there were textile manu-factories and metal-working enterprises in Lombardy. Those who disposed of funds on this scale simply did not regard these things as profitable investments

– betraying their reliance on ancient taboos and experiences. And yet the industrial revolution was already under way in England.[71]

So we must refrain from considering savings and accumulation as purely quantitative phenomena, as if a given savings rate or volume of accumulation were in some sense endowed with the power to generate creative investment and a new growth rate almost automatically. Things were more complicated. Every society has its own ways of saving and spending, its own prejudices and motivations and its own restraints on investment.

Policy also plays a part in capital formation and investment. Taxation for instance can block, redirect and redistribute, in more or less useful ways, the money it levies. In France, the fiscal system resulted in the arrival of huge sums of money in the hands of the *fermiers-généraux* and other financial office-holders. Recent studies[72] suggest that the latter redistributed very widely the wealth thus acquired, in constructive investments. Even in Colbert's time, and in the reign of Louis XV, it is said, many of them were putting money into commercial and even manufacturing enterprises, particularly into companies and manufactories with royal privileges. This may be so. But one must admit that, as Pierre Vilar says, the farming out of royal and seigniorial taxes in eighteenth-century Catalonia was a much more effective channel of redistribution than the French *ferme générale*, since the former 'were directed into the hands of traders and master-craftsmen and thus into the circuit of commercial and eventually industrial capital, and even into that of agricultural modernization'.[73] As for the English system, in which taxes became the security for servicing a consolidated national debt, giving the state unprecedented balance and strength, was this not another – and even more effective – way of reintroducing money derived from taxes into general circulation – even if contemporaries did not always realize it at the time?

Capitalist choices and strategies

Capitalism did not take up all the possibilities for investment and progress that economic life offered. It was constantly watching developments in order to intervene in certain preferred areas – in other words, it was both *sufficiently informed* and *materially able* to choose the sphere of its action. And more than the actual choices made – which might vary from century to century with changing circumstances – the very fact that it had the means to create its own strategy or to alter that strategy if necessary, defines capitalism as a superior force.

During the centuries that concern us, we shall see that the great merchants, although few in number, had acquired the keys to long-distance trade, the strategic position *par excellence*; that they had the inestimable advantage of a good communications network at a time when news travelled very slowly and at great cost; that they normally benefited from the acquiescence of state and

The seventeen governors of the Dutch East India Company. Engraving from *Histoire abrégée des Provinces-Unies des Pays-Bas*, Amsterdam, 1701. (Photo by the Atlas van Stolk Foundation.)

society, and were thus able regularly, quite naturally and without any qualms, to bend the rules of the market economy. What was binding on other people was not necessarily so for them. Turgot[74] thought that a merchant could never escape the rules of the market and its unpredictable price levels. But this was no more than half-true – if that.

The capitalist mentality

Does this mean that we must attribute to our capitalists a 'mentality', to be identified as the source of their superiority, characterizing them once and for all: a mentality made up of calculation, reason, cold logic, a lack of normal feelings, all subordinated to an unbridled appetite for gain? This explanation, once passionately held by Sombart, has lost much of its credibility, as have Schumpeter's widely-held views on the crucial role played by innovation and the spirit of enterprise. Could the capitalist really have united in his person so many attributes and qualities? In the explanation I prefer, the choice itself and the opportunity to choose, did not automatically confer an unerring perception of the right path or the wise decision. Our capitalist, we should not forget, stood at a certain level in social life and usually had before him the decisions, advice and wisdom of his peers. He judged things through this screen. His effectiveness depended not only on his innate qualities but also on the position in which he found himself, whether at the intersection or on the margins of the vital currents of trade, near to or far from the centres of decision-making – which had very precise locations in every period. Louis Dermigny[75] and Christof Glamman[76] have suggested good reasons for questioning the 'genius' of the *Heeren Zeven-tien*, the 'Seventeen Masters' who governed the Dutch East India Company. But did one really need to be a genius to succeed in business, if one had had the good fortune to be born a Dutchman in the seventeenth century and to have been placed among those who controlled the mighty machine of the *Oost Indische Compagnie*? 'There are … stupid men and I dare even say imbeciles', writes La Bruyère,[77] 'who find themselves good places and are able to die rich without one having any reason to suspect that they have contributed to this by their labour or the slightest industry; someone simply took them to the source of a river, or perhaps mere chance put them in its way; they were asked "Do you want water? Take it". And they took it.'

Nor should we believe that the *profit maximization* so frequently denounced entirely explains the behaviour of capitalist merchants. True, we have the much-quoted rejoinder made by Jakob Fugger 'the Rich' to someone who advised him to retire from business, 'that he intended to go on making money as long as he possibly could', until he dropped dead.[78] Even if this remark (which is probably as apocryphal as most historical quotations) were absolutely authentic, it would only tell us what one individual said at one moment in his life, not what a whole category of persons thought. Capitalists were human, and like other human beings, they behaved in various ways. Some were calculating, others ready to take risks, some were mean, others prodigal, some had a touch of genius, others were 'lucky' at best. A Catalan pamphlet of 1809[79] which states that 'the businessman only has regard and consideration for that which will multiply his capital by any means' could be confirmed a thousand times over by the correspondence between merchants which has survived. They were undoubtedly in business to make money. But to jump to the conclusion that the advent of modern capitalism is explained by a spirit of lucre, economy or rationality or by a taste for calculated risks is another matter. Jean Pellet, the merchant of Bordeaux, seems to illustrate his own eventful life when he writes: 'The biggest profits in trade come from speculation.'[80] Perhaps so, but this adventurous soul had a brother of much more conservative temperament, and they both made their fortunes at the same time, the prudent and the imprudent.

The 'idealist', single-factor explanation, seeing capitalism as the incarnation of a certain mentality was simply the way out adopted in desperation by Werner Sombart and Max Weber to escape the conclusions of Marx. We are in no sense obliged to follow them. Not that I believe that capitalism can, on the contrary, be entirely explained by material or social factors or by social relationships. But one thing seems to me to be beyond doubt: capitalism cannot have emerged from a single confined source: economics played a part, politics played a part, society played a part, and culture and civilization played a part. So too did history, which often decides in the last analysis who will win a trial of strength.

Long-distance trade: the real big business

Long-distance trade undoubtedly played a leading role in the genesis of merchant capitalism and was for a long time its backbone. This may seem a banal statement, but it has to be reaffirmed in the face of much opposition nowadays, since the consensus of modern historians is frequently hostile to it – for reasons both good and bad.

To take the good reasons first, it is clear that 'external trade' (*le commerce du dehors*, an expression already to be found in Montchrestien, who contrasts it with internal trade, *le commerce du dedans*) was a minority pursuit. No one will disagree with this. Jean Maillefer, a rich merchant of Reims, was bragging when he wrote to a correspondent in Holland in January 1674, 'Do not even suppose that the mines of Potosi are worth as much as the proceeds from the wines of our mountains [i.e. in Reims] and of Burgundy';[81] but Abbé Mably was being quite reasonable when he said, 'the grain trade is worth more than Peru'[82] – that is it weighed heavier in the balance, representing a greater volume of silver than was extracted in the New World. Jean-Baptiste Say, seeking to impress his readers in 1828, wrote that 'the shoemakers of France create more wealth than all the mines in the New World'.[83]

Historians have not found it difficult to illustrate this firmly-established truth from their own observations, but I do not always agree with their conclusions. Jacques Heers, writing about the Mediterranean in the fifteenth century, insists (1964) that the greatest traffic was in grain, wood and salt – that is in a large number of short-range trades, not in pepper and spices. Peter Matthias has established with statistics to prove it, that England's foreign trade on the eve of the industrial revolution was considerably smaller than her domestic trade.[84] And in a doctoral viva at the Sorbonne, Victor Magalhães Godinho readily conceded to Ernest Labrousse that the agricultural product of Portugal was greater than the value of the overseas trade in pepper and spices. In similar vein, Friedrich Lütge[85] who has always been concerned to minimize the *short-term* importance of the discovery of America has argued that inter-regional trade, within Europe, was a hundred times greater in the sixteenth century than the thin trickle of exchange that had begun between Seville and the New World. And he is of course quite right. I have myself written that sea-borne grain in the Mediterranean in the sixteenth century amounted to a million quintals at most, that is less than one per cent of what was consumed by its inhabitants, and therefore trifling in comparison with cereal production as a whole and local sales of grain.[86]

This selection alone is sufficient indication – hardly necessary perhaps – that today's historiography is concerned with the experience of the *majority*, of the millions forgotten by previous schools of history: it is more interested in the peasant than in the nobleman, in the 'twenty million Frenchmen' than in Louis XIV.[87] But this need not necessarily rob of all value the history of that minority which may often have been more influential than the great mass of people, goods and commodities – forces which were enormous but inert. Enrique Otto[88] is perfectly correct to say in a well-documented article, that the turnover of the Spanish merchants in the revitalized port of Seville, gateway to the Americas, was greater than that of the Genoese merchant bankers. But it was the latter who created a transatlantic credit system without which the trade circuit of the *Carrera de Indias* would hardly have been possible. By so doing, they found themselves strongly placed, free to act and intervene at will on the Seville market. The vital decisions in history were not taken in the past, any more than they are today, according to the reasonable rules of universal suffrage. There are plenty of reasons for arguing that the minority had a greater influence over the course of history than the majority.

In the first place, long-distance trade, known to German historians as *Fernhandel*, created groups of *Fernhändler* – import-export merchants who were always a category apart. Their native city was only one element in the system they operated. As Maurice Dobb[89] has shown, they introduced themselves into the circuit between the artisan and his distant raw materials – wool, silk, cotton. They also interposed themselves between the finished product and its marketing in distant places. The great *merciers* of Paris (i.e. general merchants who were in fact *Fernhändler*) spelled this out in 1684 in a long petition they addressed to the king against the *drapiers* (cloth-merchants) who wanted to exclude them from selling woollen cloth, a privilege they had been granted twenty years earlier as recompense for their part in the creation of the large new manufactories. The *merciers* explained that they 'maintain and keep in existence not only the manufactories of woollen cloth, but also all the other manufactories of fabrics [i.e. silks] in Tours, Lyons and other cities in the Kingdom'.[90] They argue moreover that by their initiative and marketing, they have brought into being manufactories of woollen cloth, England and Holland style, in Sedan, Carcasonne and Louviers. By marketing their products abroad and by acting as sole suppliers of Spanish wool and other materials, these merchants were in fact virtually supporting these enterprises. It could hardly be more plainly demonstrated that they controlled such industrial activity.

The products of far-off lands also found their way into the hands of the import-export merchant: silk from China and Persia, pepper from India and Sumatra, cinnamon from Ceylon, cloves from the Moluccas, sugar, tobacco, coffee from the islands, gold from Quito or the Brazilian interior, silver ingots, bars or coins from the New World. The *Fernhändler* was thus appropriating the surplus-value of the worker in the mines or plantations, or that of the primitive peasant on the Malabar Coast or the East Indies. Only on a minute volume of commodities, it will be argued. But when a historian[91] tells us that the 10,000 quintals of pepper and 10,000 of other spices consumed by Europe before the Great Discoveries cost 65,000 kilos of silver (about the equivalent of 300,000 tons of rye, enough to feed one and a half million people) we may wonder whether the economic significance of the luxury trade has not been a little hastily underestimated.

The same author moreover gives a very concrete idea of the profits of this trade: a kilo of pepper, worth one or two grammes of silver at the point of production in the Indies, would fetch 10 to 14 grammes in Alexandria, 14 to 18 in Venice, and 20 to 30 in the consumer countries of Europe. Long-distance trade certainly made super-profits: it was after all based on the price differences between two markets very far apart, with supply and demand in complete ignorance of each other and brought into contact only by the activities of the middleman. There could only have been a competitive market if there had been plenty of separate and independent middlemen. If, in the fullness of time competition did appear, if super-profits vanished from one line, it was always possible to find them again on another route with different commodities. If pepper became commonplace and declined in value, tea, coffee, or calicoes were waiting in the wings to take the place of the former prima donna. The risks of long-distance trade were out of the ordinary – but so were its profits. Many, many times, the gamble paid off handsomely, even in grain, which was not normally a 'royal' merchandise, worthy of the great merchant, but which could become one in certain circumstances – during famines needless to say. In 1591, serious food shortages in the Mediterranean brought hundreds of northern sailing-ships south, loaded to the gunwales with wheat or rye. Certain wealthy merchants not necessarily specialists in the grain trade had organized this spectacular operation with the aid of the Grand Duke of Tuscany. In order to divert the Baltic ships from their normal routes, they no doubt had to pay over the odds for their cargoes – but these were worth their weight in gold to the starving Italians. Envious tongues said that profits of 300% had been made by the Ximenes – the extremely rich Portuguese merchants of Antwerp who were soon operating in Italy.[92]

I have already mentioned the Portuguese merchants who made their way clandestinely to Potosi or Lima, travelling over the Brazilian wastes, or by the easier route from Buenos Aires. The profits they made were fantastic. Russian merchants in Siberia made immense amounts of money by selling furs to the Chinese, either through official channels, that is at the belatedly-created fair at Kiatka south of Irkutsk[93] (which made it possible to recover outlay fourfold in three years) or by clandestine trading, which was said to multiply their profits by four.[94] Perhaps this is an exaggeration? But after all, the English were able to pick up money by the shovelful when they realized that it was possible to effect, by the sea route, a similar meeting between Canadian furs and Chinese buyers.[95]

Another profitable rendezvous was Japan in the first decade of the seventeenth century – for a long time a Portuguese stamping-ground. Every year the Macao carrack – *a nao do trato* – brought to Nagasaki two hundred merchants who would stay in Japan for seven or eight months, spending their money freely – up to 250,000 or 300,000 *taels*, 'through which the populace profits greatly; and this is one of the reasons why they are still very friendly to them':[96] they picked up crumbs from the banquet. And I have already mentioned the annual voyage of the galleon from Acapulco to Manila. Here again, there were two disparate markets, whose products soared in price as they crossed the ocean in either direction, making the fortunes of the handful of men who were the only gainers from these huge price differences.

> The merchants of Mexico [wrote the Abbé de Béliardy, a contemporary of Choiseul], are the only people with an interest in preserving this trade [i.e. the galleon's annual trip] in order to sell the merchandise it brings from China, which enables them to double the money they spend on it every year. This trade is at present carried on in Manila by a very small number of merchants who order goods from China which they then send to Acapulco. in return for the piastres delivered to them.[97]

In 1695, a traveller reported that profits of 300% were to be made by taking Chinese quicksilver to New Spain.[98]

These examples – and the list could be prolonged indefinitely – show that distance alone, in an age of difficult and irregular communications, created ordinary everyday conditions for profiteering. As a Chinese document of 1618 puts it: 'Since that country [Sumatra] is a long way off, those who go there make double profits.'[99] When Giambattista Gemelli, on his voyage round the world, took from one port to another different merchandise, carefully selected on each occasion so as to make a profit on arrival that would generously defray his travelling expenses, he was of course merely following the example of the merchants he met on his way. In 1639, a European traveller was most indignant at the way the Javanese merchants made money:

> They go and look for rice in the towns of Macassar or Surabaya, which they buy for a *sata de caixas* per *gantans*; then sell it for twice the price. In Balambuam, they buy ... coconuts for a thousand *caixas* per hundred, then retail them in Bantam where they charge two hundred *caixas* for eight coconuts. They also buy oil from the same plant. They buy salt from Ioartam, Gerrici and Pati and Ivama at a hundred and fifty thousand *caixas* for eight hundred *gantans*, and in Bantam, three *gantans* cost a thousand *caixas*. They take quantities of salt to Sumatra.[100]

To appreciate this text, one does not need to know the exact size of the *gantans*, a measure of capacity. The reader will have recognized references to the *caixa*, the Chinese currency, widely used in the East Indies. A *sata* was probably a string of a thousand *caixas*. It would be more interesting to plot the sources of supply listed here and measure their distance from the Bantam market. Macassar for example was over 1200 kilometres from Bantam. However the differences between buying and selling prices were so great that even after deducting the cost of transport, the profit must have been considerable. And we should note that these were not the small lightweight goods which J.C. Van Leur describes as the typical long-haul merchandise of the Far East. These were basic foodstuffs which the spice islands needed to import continuously, even from far away.

Lastly, and this is perhaps the most telling argument: to say that grain was worth more commercially in Portugal than pepper or spices is not entirely correct. For the entire stock of pepper and spices went on to the market, whereas the historian has to reconstruct in imagination the value of the grain that was produced *but not sold*. Only a small proportion of grain production appeared on the market – the bulk was consumed on the spot. And what grain was marketed yielded only a very small profit to the peasants, landowners and retailers, profits moreover that were divided among many people, as Galiani had already pointed out.[101] There was little or no profit accumulation here, as Simón Ruiz[102] who for a while imported grain from Brittany to Portugal, bad-temperedly recalled. Most of the profit, he grumbled, went to the transporters who

The pharmacist at his accounts. Fresco in Issogna castle, late fifteenth century. (Photo Scala.)

were the real beneficiaries of this traffic. We might also bear in mind Defoe's remarks on English domestic trade, which he considered admirable because it passed through the hands of so many middlemen who all received a share of the manna (not a very large one though, to go by the examples Defoe himself quotes).[103] The indisputable superiority of *Fernhandel*, long-distance trading, lay in the *concentrations* it made possible, which meant it was an unrivalled machine for the rapid reproduction and increase of capital. In short, one is forced to agree with the German historians and with Maurice Dobb, who see long-distance trade as an essential factor in the creation of merchant capitalism, and in the creation of the merchant bourgeoisie.

Education and communication

Another precondition for merchant capitalism was some form of apprenticeship, previous instruction, and an acquaintance with methods which were far from primitive. Secular education had been organized in Florence from the fourteenth century.[104] According to Villani, 8000 to 10,000 children, boys and girls (at a time when the city's population was under 100,000), were learning to read in primary school (*a botteghuzza*). It was to the *botteghuzza* kept by the grammar-master Matteo, '*al piè del ponte a Santa Trinità*', that the young Niccolò Machiavelli was brought in May 1476 to learn to study in the abridged version of Donatus's grammar (known as the *Donatello*). Of these eight to ten thousand children, 1000 to 1200 went on to the high school, specially for merchant apprentices. Here a boy remained until his fifteenth year, studying arithmetic (*algorismo*) and accountancy (*abbaco*). After this 'technical' education, he was already able to keep the registers of accounts we can inspect today, which reliably recorded details of sales on credit, commission, compensatory payments between different centres, or the distribution of profits among the partners in companies. Serving as an apprentice in a shop came to be seen as a good way to round off the education of the future merchant. Some of the boys went on to higher education, notably to read law at the university of Bologna.

Moreover, this practical training sometimes went hand in hand with a background of real culture. In a Florence soon to be ruled by the Medici, no one will be surprised to learn that the merchants were friends of the humanists, that some of them were Latin scholars; that they wrote well and enjoyed writing; that they knew the *Divine Comedy* off by heart, quoting it readily in their letters; that they provided the readership of Boccaccio's *Cento Novelle*; that they appreciated the recondite work of Alberti, *Della Famiglia*; that they supported the new movement in art, taking the side of Brunelleschi against the medieval Ghiberti; in short that they carried on their shoulders an important part of the new civilization that is conjured up for us in the word Renaissance. These too were the benefits of money: one privilege led to others. Richard Ehrenberg[105] has said of Rome that wherever the bankers lived the artists would not be far away.

We should not imagine the whole of Europe in this image. But practical and technical studies were spreading everywhere. Jacques Coeur learnt his trade in his father's shop, and above all on the voyage aboard the Narbonne galley that took him to Egypt in 1432, which seems to have decided his career.[106] Jakob Fugger '*der Reiche*' (1455–1525) who was quite simply a business genius, had learnt in Venice the art of *partita doppia* (double-entry book-keeping) unknown in Germany at the time. In eighteenth-century England, a merchant's apprenticeship according to the statutes, lasted seven years. The sons of merchants, or the younger sons of great families destined for trade often served a term in the Levant, in Smyrna where they were made much of by the English consul and associated from the start with the profits of trading – rightly or wrongly reputed to be the highest in the world.[107] But even in the thirteenth century, the Hanseatic ports were sending their merchant apprentices to their overseas trading-posts.

In short, one should not underestimate the competence that had to be acquired: the young merchant had to be able to establish buying and selling prices, to calculate costs and exchange rates, to convert weights and measures, to work out simple and compound interest, to be able to cast up a 'simulated balance sheet' for an operation, and to handle the various instruments of credit. This was by no means child's play. Sometimes even experienced merchants felt the need to 'retrain' as we should say. And when one looks at the masterpieces of book-keeping that have survived in the great ledgers from the fourteenth century onwards, one is overcome with retrospective admiration. A generation of historians *today*, on a world scale, produces only two or three specialists able to find their way through these huge registers, and they have had to teach themselves how to read and interpret them. The manuals written for merchants of the time are a precious aid to understanding, from Pegolotti's (1340) which was not the first, to Jacques Savary's *Parfait Négociant*, which was not the last (1675). But even these are insufficient for this very special apprenticeship.

It is easier to make sense of the correspondence between merchants; many correspondences have been unearthed recently – once it occurred to people to look for them. After a few letters, still rather clumsy, dating from the thirteenth and fourteenth centuries in Venice, merchant correspondence quickly reaches a rather sophisticated level, which was maintained subsequently, since this sophistication was its *raison d'être*, the justification for the very *high cost* of this copious exchange of letters. To be well informed was even more important than to be well-trained and these letters were above all *informative*. The operations directly interesting the correspondents (orders sent and received, notes of dispatch or sale or purchase of goods, notices of payment etc.) only made up part of the contents. There inevitably followed messages to be passed on in confidence – political news, military news, news of the harvest or about expected merchandise. A letter-writer also punctiliously noted variations in the price of goods, of specie and of credit in his home-town. If it was relevant, he noted the movement of vessels in the harbour. And the letter unfailingly ended with a list of prices and exchange rates, usually as a post-script – there are thousands of examples of these. A rather special case was that of the *Fugger Zeitungen*, the newsletters which the Augsburg firm commissioned from a whole corps of correspondents abroad.[108]

The chief weakness of this information was the slow pace and uncertainty of the mails, even in the late eighteenth century. So any responsible merchant always took the precaution of sending with every letter a copy of the preceding one, if a letter carried an urgent order or an important message. *Subito habi il sensale*, 'have your broker come at once', was the advice of one merchant to another in 1360;[109] and it applied in all periods. A merchant had to be very quick on the ball. And the prime requirement was to send and receive large numbers of letters, to be included in as many as possible of the information networks which advised one where there was a promising opportunity, or on the contrary which should be avoided like the plague. The Comte d'Avaux, Louis XIV's ambassador in the United Provinces, kept a close eye on the Protestants who were still, in 1688, three years after the Revocation of the Edict of Nantes, flooding into the Netherlands. Among them a certain Monginot had just arrived, 'a great giant of a man, a Gascon I believe ... He has brought in about forty thousand *écus*. I spoke to him this morning. He is someone with a great deal of business, *he writes day and night*.'[110] The italics are mine: this last phrase is an unexpected detail, but it should not have been; it certainly fits Alberti's traditional image of the merchant 'with ink-stained fingers'.

The information received was not always reliable though. Circumstances could change, 'the coin could spin the other way'. An error of calculation, a delayed letter and the merchant found himself with a lost opportunity. But what good was it crying over the 'good deals we have missed', wrote Louis Greffulhe to his brother from Amsterdam on 30 August 1777. 'It is not back but forward that one must look in trade, and if people in this profession spent their time analysing the past, not one of them could say he had not had a hundred chances to make his fortune – or to ruin himself. If I were personally to make a list of all the good deals I have let slip, it would be enough to make a man hang himself.'[111]

The most advantageous information was something that no one else knew. In 1777, Louis Greffulhe wrote to a merchant in Bordeaux, his partner in an indigo deal: 'Remember that if word of this gets out, we are done for. This deal will be like everything else: once competitors get wind of it, there will be nothing left.'[112] In the same year, when the American War of Independence was turning into a generalized conflict, he wrote on 18 December: 'Consequently it is vital to go to any lengths to be more reliably and quickly informed than anyone else on what is likely to happen.'[113] To be more quickly informed than anyone else: 'if you receive a bundle of letters for yourself and other merchants', advises a *Trattato dei buoni costumi*, whose author was himself a merchant, 'open your own first. And take action. Once you have seen to your own affairs, it will be time to give the others their mail.'[114] This was in 1360. But in our own times, in the world of free enterprise, the same is true, as everyone knows: a prospectus produced in France in 1973 for the 'happy few' invited to take out an expensive subscription to a weekly bulletin containing a few typed sheets of exclusive information, opens with the words: 'You are well aware that once information becomes public it loses 90% of its value. Wouldn't you rather know things two or three weeks before everyone else?' Your actions would be 'considerably better-informed and more effective'. Our readers, it adds, 'will not quickly forget that they were the first to know of the imminent resignation of the Prime Minister and the approaching devaluation of the dollar'!

The Amsterdam speculators, whose decisions as we have seen were greatly influenced by items of news – true or false – had also devised a system for being the first to hear information. The evidence for this comes by chance from August 1779, during the brief panic caused by the entry of the French fleet to the Channel. Instead of using the regular packets, the Dutch speculators had chartered light vessels which made ultra-fast crossings between Holland and England. They left Katwijk near Scheveningen in Holland and landed at a small place near Harwich, 'where there is no harbour, only a sea front which does not hold them up long'. Record journey-times were as follows: London-Harwich 10 hours; Harwich-Katwijk 12 hours; Katwijk-The Hague 2 hours; The Hague-Paris 40 hours: that is, London-Paris in 72 hours.[115]

Apart from speculative news, merchants wanted to be the first to know what we would call the short-term market prospects, known at the time as *larghezza* and *strettezza*, from Italian merchants' jargon; in other words abundance or scarcity. Appropriate action would be dictated by the abundance or otherwise of commodities, cash or credit. The Buonvisi for instance, wrote from Antwerp on 4 June 1571, 'the abundance of specie persuades us to turn our attention to commodities'.[116] As we have seen Simón Ruiz did not take it so calmly fifteen years later, when the Italian money-market was suddenly flooded with specie: he flew into a rage and regarded it almost as a personal affront that the *larghezza* in Florence had upset his usual transactions in bills of exchange.

It is true that he did not really understand what was going on. By this time, merchants had acquired a certain amount of experience through observation: they knew how to be one jump ahead in the short term. But it took time for the elementary rules which we can now detect at work in past economies, to enter the collective consciousness, even that of merchants or historians. In 1669, Holland and the United-Provinces were suffering from a surplus of unsold stocks.[117] Prices fell, business dropped off, no ships were being freighted, the city warehouses were bursting at the seams. A few wealthy merchants kept on buying; it was the only way, they thought, to stop their goods depreciating too much, and they were sufficiently rich to be able to fight the downward trend. But as to the causes of this abnormal crisis which was gradually bringing business to a standstill, all the Dutch merchants, joined by the foreign ambassadors, were to spend months discussing the problem without making much headway. They did eventually realize that poor harvests in Poland and Germany had something to do with it – these had in fact precipitated what we would now regard as a typical *ancien régime* crisis – one where there were no buyers. But is this a sufficient explanation? Holland had so many strings to her bow besides German and Polish wheat and rye, that the problem must have been more general, possibly European in scale. Even today, this kind of knock-on crisis is never completely understood.

So we should not ask too much of men to whom even the economic theories of their own time were often quite foreign. They ventured on to such territory only when forced to do so – to find arguments to convince a prince or minister, when they were anxious to put off or repeal some decision or decree threatening their interests, or to defend a pet project, so useful to the general good that it deserved (of course) to be supported by privileges, monopoly or subsidy. And even on such occasions they hardly moved outside the narrow orbit of their everyday experience. In fact they evinced only indifference or irritation towards the earliest economists, their contemporaries. When *The Wealth of Nations* was published in 1776, Sir John Pringle declared 'that Dr Smith, who had never been in trade, could not be expected to write well on that subject any more than a lawyer upon physick',[118] an opinion which would no doubt have been echoed by many men of his time. The economists were a source of amusement, at least to men of letters (including Mably, the charming Sébastien Mercier and even Voltaire who mocked them in *L'Homme aux quarante écus*).

'Competition without competitors'[119]

Another source of irritation and delay to the merchant lay in the very detailed and cumbersome regulations governing public trading in general. The wholesaler was not the only one who wanted to shake off their tyranny. The system of 'private marketing' described by Alan Everitt,[120] was a widespread visible response to the demands of a market economy which was growing bigger, moving more quickly, changing, and calling for a spirit of enterprise at every level. But to the extent that the private system was often forbidden by law (it was not tolerated in France, for instance, anything like as much as in England), it remained confined to those active groups of merchants who, seeing advantages not only in price but also in the number and speed of transactions, were deliberately working to rid themselves of the administrative constraints and supervision which continued to apply to the traditional public market.

So there were two spheres of trading: the supervised market and the free market – or what passed for it. If these could be plotted on a map in different colours, we should see that they had separate identities, but also that they could coexist with or complement each other. The question to ask is which was the more important (at first, and even at later dates the old system); which was the fairer, the more truly competitive, and better-regulated; and whether one system

Eighteenth-century illustration showing the livestock market in Hoorn, northern Holland. (Photo Atlas van Stolk Foundation.)

was able to capture the other and take it prisoner. When one looks closely at them, one finds that the old trading regulations (details of which can be found in Delamarre's *Traité de la police* for instance) were aimed at preserving fair competition in the market and the interest of the urban consumer. If all goods are obliged by law to be put on sale in the public market-place, this becomes the occasion of a real-life confrontation between supply and demand, and the changing prices of the market are merely a way of maintaining genuine competition between producers, as well as between retailers. In the long run, such regulations which became cramping to the point of absurdity, were inevitably rendered obsolete by the increased volume of trade. But the purpose of the direct transactions of private marketing was not simply efficiency: they also tended to eliminate competition, to promote a sort of micro-capitalism at grass-roots level, which essentially observed the same pattern as capitalism at the highest levels of trade.

The usual procedure adopted by these micro-capitalists, who were making small fortunes, sometimes very fast, was in fact to stand outside the regular market price system, by means of advance payments and elementary forms of credit: they bought grain before it was harvested, wool before it was sheared, wine before the grapes were picked. And they controlled prices by hoarding foodstuffs; in the end they had the producer at their mercy.

However where everyday food supplies were concerned, it was difficult to go very far without incurring popular wrath and protests, without being denounced to the authorities – in France to the local police chief, the *intendant* or even to the *Conseil de commerce* in Paris. The deliberations of this body prove that even apparently trivial affairs were taken very seriously. It was reported to high places for instance 'that it is most dangerous' to take thoughtless measures 'touching grain', that it meant being exposed to popular frustration and possible chain reactions.[121] If some minor fraudulent, or at any rate unlawful practices succeeded for a while in escaping prying eyes and establishing a profitable monopoly, this generally meant that they went beyond the local market and were in the hands of well-organized groups provided with capital.

One quite sizeable affair, for example, was mounted by a consortium of merchants, in association with certain large butchers, with the aim of monopolizing Paris's meat supply. In league with them in Normandy, Brittany, Poitou, Limousin, Bourbonnais, the Auvergne and Charolais, were groups of fairground traders who arranged (by raising the prices) to divert to the fairs where they worked beasts who would otherwise have been sold at local markets, meanwhile dissuading the '*herbagers*' (graziers) from sending them straight to Paris, where, they were assured, butchers paid very badly. So the consortium was able to buy straight from the producers, 'which is of great consequence' explains a detailed report to the royal controller-general (June 1724), 'since having bought the beasts in a syndicate, and controlling half the market at Poissy, they charge any price they like, because people are obliged to buy from them'.[122] Only some indiscretion at the Paris end eventually brought to light the nature of this racket in which Paris was the headquarters of activities outwardly innocent and distributed among several grazing regions far removed from one another.

Another major fraud was reported to the *Conseil de commerce* in 1708:[123] the accused were the 'very numerous ... body' of 'merchants of butter, cheese and other foods ... commonly known as *graisseux* (fat-sellers) in Bordeaux'. Wholesalers and retailers had all joined a 'secret society' and on the outbreak of war in 1701, 'they had built up great stocks of these goods' for which they afterwards charged high prices. In order to counter them, the king granted passports to foreign traders willing to bring these foodstuffs to France despite the war. The reaction of the *graisseux* was to buy up 'all cargoes of this kind that arrive in the port'. And the prices remained high. They have ended up making a great deal of money 'out of this kind of monopoly' concludes the report, which proposes a rather complicated and unusual method of getting some of it back. All quite true, reads a comment in the margin of the report, but we must think twice before attacking these merchants, 'because it is thought that there are more than sixty of them, and very rich'.[124]

Such attempts were not infrequent, but since our sources are the administrative records, we only know about the ones that were found out. In 1723, in the Vendômois for instance, the wine-brokers hit on the idea of buying up all the casks in advance of the grape-harvest. The vinegrowers and local inhabitants complained and the brokers were forbidden to buy the casks.[125] In 1707 or 1708, the gentlemen-glassmakers of the Biesme valley were up in arms against 'three or four merchants who have completely monopolized the marketing of the *caraffons* [large glass bottles] which they transport to Paris and since they are rich [they] have taken the trade from the hauliers and other less well off persons'.[126] About sixty years later, the same idea occurred to a merchant in Sainte-Menehould and a notary in Clermont-en-Argonne. They went into business together and for ten months negotiated with 'the owners of all the glass-works in the Argonne valley,' in order to become the sole distributors of all the bottles made in their works for nine years, with an express clause that they could only be sold to [the firm in question] or on its behalf'. As a result, the Champagne winegrowers, who were the regular customers for the output of their nearest glass-works, suddenly found that the price of their bottles had gone up by a third. In spite of poor harvests and consequent low demand for three years running, the 'firm of millionaires who control the entire output of the glassworks does not want to lower the price it has seen fit to charge, and is even hoping that a good grape-harvest … will provide the opportunity to put the price up again'. Complaints in February 1770 from the mayor and aldermen of Epernay, backed up by the town of Reims, finally got the better of the 'millionaires' who beat a dignified but hasty retreat and cancelled their contracts.[127]

The monopolies, or so-called monopolies, of the iron-merchants, who sought to control all or most of the product of the nation's ironworks, were rather more serious affairs. One would like to know more about them, but the documents are too sparse. In about 1680, a memorandum denounces the 'cabal formed by all the merchants of Paris' who had bought iron abroad, in order to strengthen their hold over the French ironmasters. The conspirators met every week at the home of one of them in the Place Maubert, and made their purchases as a group, forcing more and more depressed prices upon the producers, while maintaining their selling-price at the same level.[128] Another attempt in 1724 concerned 'two rich merchants of Lyons'.[129] On both occasions, the guilty or presumed guilty parties protested their innocence, swore by all the saints that the charges were unfounded and brought forward authorities to testify in their favour. They did at all events escape a public outcry. Did this prove their innocence – or merely their strength? One wonders, when one reads, some sixty years later, in a report by the trade deputies in 1789, that iron was an important commodity on the Lyons market and that it was the 'merchants of Lyons', habitués of the Beaucaire fairs, who paid 'advances to the ironmasters of Franche-Comté and Burgundy'.[130]

There were undoubtedly plenty of comfortable little monopolies, inconspicuous, protected by local habit, and so much a part of normal practice that they caused little or no protest. The simple stratagem devised by the merchants of Dunkerque forces one's admiration: when a foreign ship entered the port to sell its cargo of grain (like the whole flotilla of very small English boats, of 15 to 30 tons, which arrived at the end of 1712, as trade was beginning to pick up just before the end of the War of the Spanish Succession), the rule was that no quantities smaller than 100 *razières* could be sold on the quayside. (The *razière* was a unit of capacity: and in this case the 'liquid *razière*' was used – one-eighth as much again as an ordinary *razière*).[131] So only wealthy merchants and a few local men of means could afford to buy grain on the dockside. Everyone else had to buy it in town, a few hundred yards away. But these few hundred yards represented an extraordinary rise in price! On 3 December 1712, the rates were respectively 21 on the quayside and 26-27 in town. And to the 25% profit which this represented, one should add the extra one-eighth accounted for by the difference between the liquid *razière* and the ordinary measure. One quite sees why the modest observer writing the reports for the *Contrôle général* protested, in veiled terms of course, against this monopoly of purchasing confined to the rich. 'The ordinary people have no joy of this', he writes, 'since they cannot buy such large quantities. If an order were to go out that every private citizen was entitled to buy 4 to 6 *razières*, that would relieve the public.'[132]

Monopolies on an international scale

Let us now move to the altogether different scale of the trade handled by big import-export merchants. The preceding examples will already have hinted at the even greater range of possibilities and the impunity allowed by overseas trade – which was beyond supervision, given the distances between the various points of sale and the individuals concerned in such exchanges – to those who wanted to evade the free market, to eliminate competition by holding a virtual or actual monopoly, and to keep supply and demand so effectively separated that the terms of trade were entirely dictated by the middleman, who alone knew the state of the market at either end of the long chain. The minimum qualifications for entry to these extremely profitable circuits were: to have sufficient capital and local sources of credit, to be well-informed and well-connected, and to have associates at strategic points along the trade route, who were a party to one's secrets. The *Parfait Négociant*, or even the *Dictionnaire de commerce* by Savary des Bruslons, spells out for us, in the context of international competition, a whole series of questionable commercial practices, rather upsetting if one believes in the virtues of free enterprise in achieving optimum economic conditions and an equilibrium in terms of price between supply and demand.

Father Mathias de Saint-Jean (1646) roundly condemned such practices, which he regarded as foreign pressures on the poor kingdom of France. The Dutch were great buyers of French wines and spirits. Nantes, the assembly point for 'the wines of Orleans, Bois-gency [Beaugency] Blois, Tours, Anjou and Brittany', had become one of their headquarters, to such an extent that wine-growing had spread, and cereal production in the Loire valley had dangerously declined. The wine surplus obliged producers to distil a good deal of it and 'put it into spirits', but this meant burning huge quantities of wood, so the neighbouring forests were being depleted and the price of fuel was rising. In this already difficult context, the Dutch merchants had little difficulty in buying up stocks before the harvest. They paid advances to the peasants, 'which is a kind of usury that the very laws of conscience do not allow'. They were on the other hand operating within the rules if they contented themselves with simply paying

The Nuremberg scales, sculpture by Adam Kraft, 1497. (Photothèque Armand Colin.)

a deposit, on the understanding that the wine would be paid for at the full market price after the harvest. But to make the price fall after the harvest was child's play. 'These foreign gentlemen', says our guide, 'are the absolute masters and arbiters of the value of their wines.' Another of their devices was to provide the winegrowers with casks – but casks 'in the German fashion, to make people in the countries to which they transport our wines think that they are Rhine wines' – which needless to say fetched higher prices.[133]

Another practice was deliberately to restrict supplies of a given commodity to the market – if that is, one could afford the waiting-period. In 1718, the English Levant Company (for trade with Turkey) decided to 'delay for ten months the departure of its ships for Turky [sic]; a delay which it since prolonged from time to time, and of which it openly and publickly declared the intention and the motive, "To be of raising the price of English manufactures in Turky and that of silk in England" '.[134] This way, profits could be made at both ends. Similarly, the Bordeaux merchants calculated the sailing dates and the size of cargoes bound for Martinique in such a way that European goods would be in sufficiently short supply there to send prices up, sometimes to a fantastic level, and that the sugar crop could be bought soon enough after the harvest to be at a still-advantageous price.

The most frequent temptation, and an easy way to make money in fact, was to contrive a monopoly in a widely-sold commodity. There have always of course been fraudulent monopolies, some hidden, some openly-flaunted, notorious and occasionally blessed with state approval. In the early fourteenth century, according to Henri Pirenne,[135] Robert de Cassel was accused at Bruges 'of seeking to institute an *enninghe* to buy up all the alum imported to Flanders and to govern its price'. And every firm tended to set up its own monopoly or monopolies. Even without explicitly seeking to, the *Magna Societas* which controlled half of Barcelona's external trade at the end of the fifteenth century was tending to monopolize it. It was at this time moreover that the definition of a monopoly gained currency. Konrad Peutinger, the historiographer of the city of Augsburg, a humanist and nevertheless a friend of merchants (it is true that he had married into the Welser family) said quite bluntly that to monopolize meant *'bona et merces omnes in manum unam deportare'*, to bring wealth and all merchandise into one hand.[136]

In fact the word monopoly became a real battle-cry in sixteenth-century Germany. It was applied indiscriminately to cartels, syndicates, hoarding and even usury. A few colossal firms – the Fuggers, Welsers, Höchstetters and others – impressed public opinion by the size of their networks, which extended throughout Germany and beyond. Small and medium-sized firms were afraid of going under and campaigned against the giant monopolists, one of which was swallowing all the mercury in sight, another the copper and silver. The Nuremberg Reichstag pronounced against the giant firms, but they were saved by two edicts in their favour issued by the Emperor Charles V on 10 March and 13 May 1525.[137] In the circumstances, it is rather odd that Ulrich von Hütten, who was a genuine revolutionary, should have directed his diatribes not at the exploitation of metals, in which the soil of Germany and neighbouring countries was rich, but at Asiatic spices, Italian and Spanish saffron and silks. 'Down with pepper, saffron and silk!' he cries, '... my dearest wish is that no man who cannot do without pepper should be cured of gout or the French disease'.[138] Was boycotting pepper in the struggle against capitalism a way of denouncing luxury or protesting at the power of long-distance trade?

Monopolies were the product of power, cunning and intelligence. The Dutch merchants of the seventeenth century were past masters of the art. We need not dwell on the well-known story of the two armaments kings – Louis de Geer, who had his cannon-foundries in Sweden, and his brother-in-law Elias Tripp who had the corner in Swedish copper; but there was certainly 'a ring of Amsterdamers who bought up whale products and forced up prices, ... an attempted corner in Italian silks, one in sugar, one in perfume ingredients, another in saltpetre, another in copper'.[139] Practical weapons for such monopolies were the great warehouses – bigger and more expensive than a large ship – which could hold enough grain to feed the United Provinces for ten or twelve years (1670),[140] as well as herrings and spices, English cloth and French wines, saltpetre from Poland or the East Indies, Swedish copper, tobacco from Maryland, cocoa from Venezuela, Russian furs and Spanish wool, hemp from the Baltic and silk from the Levant. The rule was always the same: buy goods directly from the producer for a low price, in return for cash or, better still, advance payments; then put them in store and wait for prices to rise (or give them a push). When war was in the air, which always meant that foreign goods became scarce and went up in price, the Amsterdam merchants crammed their five- or six-storey warehouses to bursting-point; on the eve of the War of the Spanish Succession, ships could not unload their cargoes for lack of storage space.

Dutch traders took advantage of their superiority even to exploit England in the early seventeenth century, just as they exploited the Loire region: buying directly from the producer, 'at the first hand and at the cheapest seasons of the year'[141] (which gives an extra twist to Alan Everitt's 'private marketing'), through English and Dutch agents who travelled round the towns and countryside, obtaining reductions on sales, made for cash or against advances, of textiles yet to be woven or fish that were still in the sea. As a result, English and French goods were sold abroad by the Dutch at prices equal to or below the cost of the same goods in England or France – a situation which never ceased to amaze French observers, who could think of no better explanation than low Dutch freight rates!

In the Baltic, similar practices gave the Dutch near-total control of the northern markets for a long period.

By 1675, when *Le Parfait Négociant* by Jacques Savary appeared, the English had managed to penetrate the Baltic, although this trade was still very unevenly shared between them and the Dutch. The French would have liked to gain a foothold there too, but obstacles sprang up in their path. One of the most serious was the difficulty of amassing the huge capital outlay required to break into the market. For goods taken to the Baltic were sold on credit, whereas all purchases made there had to be paid for in cash, in silver *rijksdaalder* 'which is the currency used throughout the north'. These *rijksdaalder* had to be bought in Amsterdam or Hamburg. And one had to have correspondents there to effect the transaction. Correspondents were also needed in the Baltic ports. And last but not least was obstruction from the English and particularly the Dutch. The latter

> do all they can ... to discourage and exhaust [the French] ... by selling their goods more cheaply, even if it means a heavy loss, and by buying local products more dearly, so that if the French find they are trading at a loss, they will not be anxious to try again ... There are countless examples of French merchants who have engaged in northern trade and been ruined by these Dutch malpractices, and have had to sell their goods at a considerable loss, otherwise they would not have sold them at all.[142]

The behaviour of the Dutch was obviously deliberate. In September 1670, when the French *Compagnie du nord* was being set up, J. de Wit (a cousin of the Grand Pensionary) was sent to Danzig to negotiate new privileges from Poland and Prussia, 'in order to pre-empt the trade which the French might introduce'.[143]

In the previous year, during the terrible sales slump I have already described, the reactions of the Dutch as reported by Pomponne are equally revealing. Eighteen vessels had docked or were about to dock from the Indies. What was to be done about this addition to the already-swollen stocks of the town? The company could only envisage one solution: to flood Europe 'with so much pepper and cotton fabric, at such cheap prices, that it will not be worth the while of other nations – especially the English – to go and look for such goods themselves. These are the weapons the people here have always used to combat their neighbours in trade. They may find them turned against themselves, if they are forced, in order to prevent other people making profits, to deprive themselves of profit too.'[144] In fact the Dutch were wealthy enough to carry off this or any other operation. The great quantity of merchandise brought by the Indies fleet was sold during the summer of 1669 – the Amsterdam merchants having bought it all up at good prices first, in order to support the value of the stocks they already held.[145]

But all the great trading cities – Venice and Genoa for instance – were in search of an international monopoly. Jacques Savary gives a detailed explanation of how Genoa controlled the valuable market in raw silk[146] which played a vital role in French industry. Raw silk from Messina was used notably for the manufacture of *ferrandines* and watered silk in Tours and Paris. But it was harder to get hold of than silk from the Levant, since it was eagerly coveted by the guilds and merchants of Florence, Lucca, Leghorn and Genoa. The French were virtually excluded from first-hand sales. The Sicilian silk market was firmly in the hands of the Genoese and everyone else had to go through them. Silk could however be bought locally from village producers – on condition the buyer paid cash. In theory then, there was a free market. In fact, when the Genoese, like so many other Italian merchants, had invested in land at the end of the sixteenth century, they had selected 'the best and most abundant silk-producing regions'. Consequently it was easy for them to buy *in advance* from the peasant producers. And if a good year threatened to bring down the price, they had only to buy up a few bales at high prices in fairs and markets to send it up again and see their previously accumulated stocks appreciate in value once more. Moreover, having citizenship rights in Messina, the Genoese were exempt from the duties foreigners had to pay. Hence the bitter disappointment of two silk merchants from Tours, who had a Sicilian contact and arrived in Messina with 400,000 *livres*, enough to break the Genoese monopoly, or so they thought. Their attempt failed, and the Genoese, who were as adept in these matters as the Dutch, taught them an immediate lesson by delivering silk to Lyons at a price below that which the unfortunate Frenchmen had been paying in Sicily. It is true that the Lyonnais, who often acted as factors for the Genoese during this period, were in league with the latter, if a report of 1701 is to be believed.[147] They took advantage of their position to damage the interests of rival manufacture in Tours, Paris, Rouen and Lille. Between 1680 and 1700, the number of silk-looms in Tours may have fallen from 12,000 to 1200.

The biggest monopolies of all were of course those enjoyed by the great merchant companies, especially the Indies Companies, not only in practice but with legal permission. This is however a rather different question, since such privileged companies were set up with the regular cooperation of the state. We shall be looking shortly at monopolies of this kind which combined economics and politics.

A monopoly venture that failed: the cochineal market in 1787

In case anyone should think I have overestimated the role of monopolies, let me tell the rather astonishing story of the speculation in cochineal attempted by the house of Hope and Co. in 1787, at a time when this was a huge firm handling the launching of large government loans, Russian and others, on the Amsterdam market.[148] Why did a great finance house venture into an affair like this? In the first place because the firm's directors considered that in the course of the crisis dating back at least to 1784 and the end of the 'Fourth War' with England, trade had been unduly neglected in favour of financial loans, and that this was perhaps a good moment to move back into commodities. Cochineal, which came from New Spain, was a luxury dyestuff for textiles and, an important detail, it kept well. From information he had received, Henry Hope was convinced that the new season's shipments would be modest, that existing stocks in Europe were low (a mere 1750 bales or seroons, he was assured, were lying in warehouses in Cadiz, London and Amsterdam), and that since prices had been falling for several years, buyers had been tending to purchase it as and when they needed it. His plan was quite simply to buy up, on all the European exchanges simultaneously (so as not to alert the market) at least three-quarters of existing stocks. Then he would force up prices and sell. The estimated cost of the operation would be 1.5 to 2 million guilders – an immense sum of money. Hope calculated that he could not lose, even if the huge profit he hoped for did not materialize. He obtained the collaboration of a firm in every major city: Baring and Co. of London even took a fourth-share in the speculation.

The operation was a fiasco. First because of the latent crisis: prices did not rise quickly enough. Secondly because of delays in the mails, which meant that instructions were not received or executed quickly enough. Last, and most important, it became clear as the firm proceeded with its purchases of stocks that these were much greater than had been reported. Hope persisted in his efforts to buy up everything in Marseilles, Rouen, Hamburg and even St Petersburg, not without some mishaps. He ended up with twice as much cochineal on his hands as he had originally anticipated. And he had terrible problems in getting rid of it, since sales slumped in the Levant because of the Russo-Turkish war, and in France because of the crisis in the textile industry.

Haarlem, unloading crane on the canal wharf. Painting by Gerrit Berckeyde (1638–1698). (Douai Museum, photo Giraudon.)

In short, the venture ended in substantial losses, which the extremely rich firm of Hope and Co. absorbed uncomplainingly, and without interrupting its fruitful speculation in foreign loans. But this episode and the copious correspondence on it in the firm's archives throw light on the entire climate of commercial life at the time.

Certainly in this case, one might question the relevance of the arguments advanced by P.W. Klein, the historian of the mighty Tripp firm.[149] He does not for a moment deny, indeed he quite accepts that all the big businesses in seventeenth-century Amsterdam had been built up on monopolies; some were more complete than others, but new ones were always appearing and were much sought after. He argues however that monopoly was justified because it was a condition of economic progress and indeed of growth. Monopoly, he explains, meant protection from the numerous risks that haunted the trader, it spelled security, and without security there would have been no steady investment, no constant expansion of the market, no research into new techniques. While morality might frown upon monopoly, the economy and indeed one might even say the general good benefited from it in the end.

In order to accept this thesis, one has first to be persuaded of the exceptional virtues of the entrepreneur – it is not surprising that Klein refers to Schumpeter. But did economic progress and the spirit of enterprise and technical innovation always come from the top? Was only large-scale capital capable of inspiring them? And if one comes back to the example of Hope and his pursuit of the cochineal monopoly, how can this be described as a search for security? Was it not rather a speculative gamble? And in what way was it innovatory or a contribution to the general good? A hundred years earlier, without any action by the Dutch, cochineal was already the 'queen of dyestuffs', a royal merchandise for all the importers of Seville. The stocks that Hope was pursuing all over Europe had been divided according to industrial needs and such needs dictated – or should have dictated – events. What possible advantage could European industry have derived from the concentration of all the stocks of cochineal in the hands of one firm, and the subsequent sharp price rise which was openly admitted to be the aim of the operation?

Klein does not in fact recognize that the position of Amsterdam as a whole constituted a monopoly in itself, and that monopoly was the pursuit not of security but of domination. His theory would be tenable only on the assumption that what was good for Amsterdam was good for the rest of the world, to paraphrase a much repeated formula.

Currency and its snares

There were other commercial advantages, other monopolies which were taken so much for granted that they were all but invisible to those who enjoyed them. The higher reaches of the economy, being peopled by the owners of capital, did in fact create routine structures operating to such men's advantage in everyday life, in ways they did not always fully realize. In matters of currency for instance, they found themselves in the same happy position as a possessor of a strong currency today travelling to a weak-currency country. For the rich were practically the only people who handled and kept beside them large quantities of gold and silver: poor people never came across anything but copper or copper-mixture coin. And these different coinages operated in relation to each other much as if a strong and a weak currency were to co-exist in the same economy with artificial attempts to maintain fixed parity – doomed to failure of course. There were constant shifts in value.

In the days of bi- or rather tri-metallism, there were in fact not one but several currencies. And they were as opposed to each other as affluence and poverty. Jacob van Klaveren, the economist and historian,[150] was mistaken in his view that money was money was money, in whatever shape it came, gold, silver, copper, or paper. And when the physiocrat Mercier de La Rivière wrote in the *Encyclopédie*: 'Money is a kind of river on which saleable goods are ferried', either we cannot agree, or the word 'river' should be in the plural.

Gold and silver were in competition. The ratio between the two metals was always provoking hurried movements from one country and economy to another. On 30 October 1785, it was decided in France to alter the gold-silver ratio from 1:14.5 to 1:15.3, to stop the flight of gold from the kingdom.[151] In Venice and Sicily, in the sixteenth century and later, as I have mentioned, the overvaluing of gold made it quite simply bad money, driving out the good as Gresham has it. Good money in this instance was silver, which was at the time essential for the Levant trade. The anomaly was realized in Turkey, and in 1603, quantities of *zecchini*, gold coins, began arriving in Venice to be changed at a profit, given the Venetian exchange rates. Monetary life in the West in the Middle Ages was completely dominated by the gold-silver relationship with its hiccups, about-turns and surprises which continued even in the modern period, though in a less extreme form.

It was not given to everyone to be able to benefit from these changes, to choose between metals according to the business in hand or to whether one was buying or selling: only to the privileged who had large amounts of coin or credit passing through their hands. Malestroit could write with little fear of contradiction in 1567 that money was 'a cabal understood by few'.[152] And naturally those who did understand stood to gain. So towards mid-century, there was a general re-assessment of fortunes when gold regained the supremacy it was now to hold over silver for a long time, as large amounts of the latter were shipped in from America. Until then, silver had been comparatively scarce and therefore safe to hold, a 'currency suited to hoarding, whereas gold was used as the currency for important transactions'. The situation was completely reversed between 1550 and 1560[153] and the Genoese merchants were the first to play gold against silver on the Antwerp money-market and to benefit from their shrewd judgment, a step ahead of everyone else.

A more general and less visible practice which had virtually passed into everyday life, was the conversion of base coinage – copper or billon (copper with an admixture of silver) – into high coinage, gold and silver. Carlo M. Cipolla's use of the simple term 'exchange rate' to describe this relationship annoyed Raymond de Roover because of the obvious ambiguities this implied.[154] But to say 'internal exchange rate' as the latter suggests, or 'vertical exchange rate' (J. Gentil da Silva) – as distinct from the 'horizontal' exchange rate between different currencies – does not get us much further forward. The simple term 'exchange rate' has survived, not unreasonably, since it refers to the purchasing power expressed in base coinage, of gold and silver pieces: an imposed relationship (though one that was not respected and therefore changeable) between coins

Girl weighing gold, painting by Jean Gossaert Mabuse, early sixteenth century.
(Viollet Collection.)

whose actual value did not correspond to the officially quoted rate. A twentieth-century parallel is the American dollar in post-war Europe: it was automatically over-valued in relation to local currencies. Either it changed hands above the official rate, on the black market, or quite legally, a purchase made in dollars benefited from a price reduction of 10 to 20%. This comparison helps to understand how those who held gold and silver could automatically drain wealth out of the rest of the economy.

In the first place, *all* small transactions in the retail trade were effected in base coinage (buying food from peasants on the market place for instance) and all wages of day labourers and artisans were paid in the same. As Montanari said in 1680,[155] base coinages were '*per uso della plebe che spende a minuto e vive a lavoro giornaliere*' for the common people who spend small sums and live by daily labour.

Secondly, base coinage was constantly depreciating in relation to gold and silver. Whatever the monetary situation on a national scale, ordinary people thus suffered the long-drawn out hardships of continuous devaluation. In Milan at the beginning of the seventeenth century for instance, the low denominations were small coins, *terline* and *sesine* which had originally been billon, but were by now simply small pieces of copper; *parpagliole*, containing a little silver were slightly more valuable. *Terline* and *sesine*, owing in part to state neglect, were in fact fiduciary currencies whose value was constantly falling.[156] The same was true in France, where d'Argenson noted in August 1738 in his *Journal*: 'This morning the 2-*sou* coin was devalued by 2 *liards*, a quarter of the total, which is a good deal.'[157]

All this had its consequences. In industrial towns with a proletariat and a sub-proletariat, money wages were dragged down in relation to prices which rose more readily. This was one of the causes of the revolts by the silk-workers of Lyons in 1516 and 1529. In the seventeenth century, these internal devaluations which had hitherto chiefly affected large towns, spread like the plague to the small towns and villages where industry and the mass of artisans had taken refuge. José Gentil da Silva, who pointed this important detail out to me, thinks that Lyons cast the web of its monetary exploitation over the surrounding countryside in the seventeenth century.[158] More evidence is needed to confirm this suggestion. But it has I think been sufficiently demonstrated that money was not the neutral liquid that economists still sometimes refer to. Money was indeed a miraculous agent of exchange, but it was also a confidence trick serving the privileged.

What merchants and other rich people did was quite simple: they returned any billon they received to circulation, keeping only the valuable coins whose purchasing power was very much greater than their official equivalent in base or 'black money' as it was called. Advice given to a cashier by a trading manual of 1638 was: 'In any payment he makes, let him reach out for the currency in lowest esteem at the time.'[159] And he should of course collect as much as possible of the higher coinage. This was the policy adopted by Venice, which regularly disposed of its billon, sending it by the ton to its islands in the Levant. The Spanish merchants of the sixteenth century operated a transparent strategem: they brought copper to be coined at the mint in Cuenca in New Castile and advanced this money to the master weavers of the town who needed it to buy the raw materials for their workshops; the merchants specified that repayment must be in silver coins, in the fairs and towns where the craftsmen went to sell their cloth.[160] In Lyons in 1574, brokers were forbidden not only to 'go in search of goods to corner them', but also to 'go round hostelries or private houses buying silver and gold coins at prices of their own choice'.[161] In Parma in 1601, attempts were made to put a stop to the activities of the money-changers, the *bancherotti*, who were accused of collecting gold pieces and removing them from circulation, exchanging them for base and low-quality coinage.[162] And foreign merchants, especially the Dutch, were said to proceed as follows in France in 1647: '... they send to their correspondents and commission agents specie from their own country, which is much debased or certainly of poorer metallic content than ours. And they use this money to buy our merchandise, keeping the best of our coins to send home.'[163]

In the money-changer's shop, woodcut, sixteenth century. (Viollet Collection.)

Nothing was simpler, but to succeed at this game, one had to be well placed to start with. This alerts one to the possible significance of the invasions by base coinage which regularly punctuate the history of money. These were not always spontaneous or innocent happenings. That said, quite what was in the mind of the sagacious Isaac de Pinto[164] when he gave the English, who were often short of specie, this serious but at first sight surprising advice: that they should 'multiply the supply of small coinage, like Portugal'? Was it perhaps a way of having more money to manoeuvre with at the upper levels of trade? Pinto was both Portuguese and a banker, and presumably knew what he was talking about.

Does this cover all the perverse problems money could create? Probably not. Arguably the most important factor of all was inflation, as Charles Mathon de La Cour put it with astonishing clarity in 1788:

> Gold and silver, which are ceaselessly drawn from the bowels of the earth, are spread every year throughout Europe and increase the amount of coin there. Nations do not thereby really become more wealthy, but their wealth becomes more voluminous: the price of foodstuffs and other things necessary to life increases by turn, one has to pay more and more gold and silver to buy a loaf of bread, a house, or a suit of clothes. Wages do not immediately rise to the same extent [and we know that they did indeed lag behind prices]. Men of feeling observe with sorrow that just when the poor man needs to earn more money to live, this very need sometimes makes wages fall or at any rate serves as a pretext to hold them for a long time at the old rate which no longer corresponds to the wage-earner's expenditure, and thus it is that the gold mines have provided weapons for the egotism of the rich, enabling them more and more to oppress and enslave the industrious classes.[165]

Putting aside the purely quantitative explanation of the price rise, who could fail to agree today with the author of these words that inflation certainly does not hurt everyone in the capitalist system?

Exceptional profits, exceptional delays

We have now surveyed most of the practices of capitalism, both conscious and unconscious. But probably the best way to appreciate the superior position of capitalists is to look at some figures for profits from trade and to compare them with the best achievements in agriculture, industry and transport. Going 'straight to the heart of economic results'[166] is perhaps the only way to put things in true perspective. In the eighteenth century, one can undoubtedly say that *almost* everywhere in Europe, *large-scale* profits from trade were superior to *large-scale* profits from industry or agriculture.

Unfortunately little research has been done on this question. The historian approaching it is like a journalist venturing into a classified area. He knows what ought to be going on there, but can rarely find any hard evidence. There is no lack of figures, but they are either incomplete, or invented, or both. Would they make any more sense to a businessman of today than to a mere historian? I doubt it. We have for instance an annual record of the capital investment and profits of the firm of Hope and Co. in Amsterdam, covering fifty years from 1762 to 1815, with notes of the sums paid out to different partners – apparently a first-class source of precise and precious information, including what seems a reasonable profit rate of 10%. But the historian of the Hope firm, M.G. Buist, warns us that 'it is clear ... that the Hope millions did not stem from profits on the firm's capital', which seem in fact to have been ploughed straight back into the firm. Each of the partners had his own private transactions and accounts, of which we have no record – and this is where 'the real profits' were made.[167]

Every document has to be checked and re-checked. The full accounts of an affair cannot be called complete until it has been carried through to a conclusion from A to Z. How can one be satisfied for instance with the presentation of the accounts of the French India Company, which simply says without further details that from 1725 to 1736, the difference between purchases in the Indies and sales in France showed an 'average profit of 96.12%'?[168] When a series of transactions is linked together like a multi-stage rocket, the last capsule cannot stand for the whole. The historian needs to know the initial outlay, the expenses of the voyage and of the laying-up of the ship, the value of the merchandise and cash taken on the outward leg, the series of deals and profits made in the Far East and so on. Only then would it be possible to calculate or even try to calculate the real profit.

Similarly, I doubt whether we shall ever get to the bottom of the accounts of the Genoese merchants who lent money to Philip II and his successors. They lent the Spanish Crown huge sums (mostly borrowed at low interest rates from other people, an initial stage which remains obscure); they derived profits from currency exchange in various places about which we know little; they also made money out of the *juros de resguardo* as I have already explained (but how much?); and finally, since they were generally paid in silver, the resale of these coins or ingots in Genoa itself usually brought them an extra 10% profit.[169] When the Genoese *hombres de negocios* discussed business with the officials of the Crown, they pointed out with reason that the interest rates on the loans were modest; the officials replied that the real profit was more like 30% – which was not entirely an exaggeration.[170]

Another point to remember is that the profit rate was not everything. One also has to bear in mind the volume of capital invested. If this was very large, thanks to borrowing (as in the case of the Genoese, the Hopes and in general large-scale moneylenders to states in the eighteenth century) the profit, even if interest charges were low, still represented a great deal of money. Compare this with the small-time moneylender quoted by Turgot or the village usurer: such men sometimes charged exorbitant interest rates, but they were lending their own money to small borrowers. They might amass a stockingful of gold coins, or acquire land from a defaulting peasant, but it would take generations to build up a real fortune.

Another point of some relevance is that profits could be links in chains of varying lengths. A boat leaves Nantes, let us say, and returns. Its expenses have not (as a rule) been settled in cash before its departure, but in bills over six or eighteen months. So if I were a merchant with a stake in the venture, I would have to pay only when the boat came in to be 'laid up'; the bills I would originally have given were a form of credit, usually obtained from Dutch moneylenders, local financial officials or some other backer. If the accounts were all in order, my speculative profit would be somewhere between the rate of interest on the borrowed money and the profit realized on the voyage overall. I would have been risking money that did not belong to me. There was of course an element of risk, as there was in speculation on the Stock Exchange. The *Saint-Hilaire*[171] sailed into Nantes on 31 December 1777. Bertrand *fils* had made a handsome profit (150,153 *livres* on an investment of 280,000 *livres*, that is 53%). But the return often opened the door to prevarications, there were delays in accounting, and 'chains' developed.[172] These delays were the bane of merchant's lives. Bertrand *fils* got his capital back immediately – but he had to wait twenty years before he received his profits in 1795!

This was an extreme case of course. But one has the impression that liquid money, attracted by investment, was always too tied up to settle current accounts – in France at any rate and no doubt elsewhere as well.

Lastly, the field of large-scale profits was not one from which the same harvest could be reliably reaped year after year. Profit rates varied all the time. An excellent commodity trade could go into decline. There was a tendency towards diminishing returns on any given line after a certain point, but large-scale capital almost always managed to remove elsewhere if this happened, and the profits began flowing again. The tobacco section of the French *Compagnie des Indes*, operating between America and France with royal privilege, experienced profit rates that were fabulous but declining: 500% in 1725 (before the distribution of dividends to shareholders); 300% in 1728-8; 206% in 1728-9.[173] According to the accounts of the *Assomption*, a ship from Saint-Malo which returned from the Pacific, investors received '2447 *livres* principal and profit on 1000 *livres*', that is a profit of 144.7%. On the *Saint-Jean-Baptiste*, the profit was 141%, on another ship 148%.[174] A voyage to Vera Cruz in Mexico, for which the accounts were settled in 1713, brought the same partnership 180% profit.[174] Just before the French Revolution, there was a decline in the profits from trade with the islands and the United States, and a standstill in the Levant trade, with a profit rate of only 10%; only trade with the Indian Ocean and China was prospering and it was here that large capital investment went, operating on the margins of the Indies companies. If the rate of profit is calculated in this sector *per month* of sailing time, on a voyage of 20 months (i.e. a slow boat) to the Malabar coast and back, it works out at $2\frac{1}{4}$%; on a voyage to China (where even better times had been known) at $2\frac{6}{7}$; Coromandel $3\frac{3}{4}$; and on the trade between India and the East Indies 6% (or 200% on a round trip of 33 months).[175] The last

A landlord arriving on his country estate, by Pietro Longhi (1702–1785). Compare this visit with the earlier French picture (chapter 3). Here the lord is not met by a prosperous tenant-farmer. He is one of the Venetian patricians who had reinvested their fortunes in land which they farmed themselves on capitalist lines, and he is being met by his hired hands who greet him with very respectful bows. (Photo André Held, Ziolo.)

was a record. In 1791, the *Illustre Suffren* which left Nantes for Mauritius and Réunion (expenditure 160,206 *livres*, profits 204,075) brought home a return of 120%, whereas in 1787, a similar ship, with a similar name (the *Bailli de Suffren*) which had also sailed from Nantes but to the West Indies (expenditure 97,922, profit 34,051), brought back only 28% profit.[176] And so on. The elements of the equation could change according to circumstances – anywhere in the world. In Gdansk for instance, purchases of rye from the Polish interior which were then sold to the Dutch brought in a large average profit of 29.7% between 1606 and 1650, but this average concealed wild fluctuations: a maximum in 1633 of 201.5%; and a minimum of −45.4% in 1621.[177] This naturally makes conclusions difficult.

What is clear though is that the really big profits were only attainable by capitalists who handled large sums of money – their own or other people's. The circulation of capital – another golden rule of merchant capitalism – played a crucial role. Money, ever more money was needed: to tide one over the long wait, the reverses, the shocks and delays from which no voyage was immune. The seven ships from Saint-Malo for instance which sailed to Peru in 1706[178] had required an immense outlay before departure: 1,681,363 *livres*. They only had 306,199 *livres* worth of goods on board. And these goods were the key to the whole venture, because ships never took money to Peru. The merchandise had to be sold in Peru and their equivalent brought back to France in such a way that their value multiplied by at least five – just to recover expenses. If the profit at the end of the day was in fact 145% – as it was in the case of a boat doing the same trip of which records survive – the original value of the goods, other things being equal, must have been multiplied 6.45 times. It is not surprising then to find Thomas Mun, the director of the English East India Company, explaining in 1621 that money sent out to India returned to England five-fold.[179] In short, in order to make a killing on such voyages, one had to be able to lay hands on the necessary capital before the ship set sail. If not, there was no point in going. Van Lindschoten, a Dutch traveller (and spy), went to Goa in 1584 and wrote from there: 'I should be much inclined to travel to China and Japan, which are the same distance from here as Portugal, that is, he who goes thither is three years on the road. If I only possessed two or three hundred ducats, they could easily be converted into 600 or 700. But to enter on such a thing with empty hands I thought folly. One must start tolerably provided to make profit.'[180]

One's impression then (since in view of the paucity of the evidence, impressions are all we have) is that there were always sectors in economic life where high profits could be made, *but that these sectors varied*. Every time one of these shifts occurred, under the pressure of economic developments, capital was quick to scent them out, to move into the new sector and prosper. Note that as a rule it had not precipitated such shifts. This differential geography of profit is a key to the short-term fluctuations of capitalism, as it veered between the Levant, America, the East Indies, China, the slave trade, etc., or between trade, banking, industry or land. For it did sometimes happen that a capitalist group (in sixteenth-century Venice for instance) left a leading position in trade to invest in industry (wool in this case) or more often in land and stockfarming; but this was because its dealings with the world of trade had ceased to bring in substantial returns. Venice is an example of another shift in the eighteenth century because she tried to move back into the Levant trade when it once more became profitable. But if she did not persist in the attempt, it was because land and agriculture were proving for the moment a gilt-edged investment. In about 1775, a sheep-farm 'in a good year' yielded 40% per annum of its original capital, a result likely to 'inspire the love of any capitalist', *'da inamorare ogni capitalista'*.[181] Such yields were not of course typical of the very varied agriculture of Venetia, but on the whole as the *Giornale Veneto* of 1773 reported, 'money employed in agricultural ventures always brings in more than any other kind of investment, including maritime ventures'.[182]

It is difficult then to establish a classification, valid once and for all, as between the profits from agriculture, industry and trade. Broadly speaking, the standard classification in descending order: trade, industry, agriculture, corresponds to a certain reality, but there were a number of exceptions which justified shifts from one sector to another.[183]

Let me emphasize the quality that seems to me to be an essential feature of the general history of capitalism: its unlimited flexibility, its capacity for change and *adaptation*. If there is, as I believe, a certain unity in capitalism, from thirteenth-century Italy to the present-day West, it is here above all that such unity must be located and observed. With only a few modifications, one could apply to the history of capitalism in its entirety the words of an American historian writing about his own country, 'whose history in the last century proves that the capitalist class has always been able to direct and control change in such a way as to preserve its hegemony'.[184] On a world scale, we should avoid the over-simple image often presented of capitalism passing through various stages of growth, from trade to finance to industry – with the 'mature' industrial phase seen as the only 'true' capitalism. In the so-called merchant or commercial capitalism phase, as in the so-called industrial phase (and both terms cover a multitude of forms) the essential characteristic of capitalism was its capacity to slip at a moment's notice from one form or sector to another, in times of crisis or of pronounced decline in profit rates.

Individual firms and merchant companies

Firms and companies are interesting not so much for themselves as for what they can tell us: through the evidence they offer, we can see beyond into the larger picture of economic life and capitalist practice.

In spite of their similarities and analogous functions, a distinction must be made between firms and big trading companies. The individual firm lies at the very heart of capitalism: the various forms it could take, and the successive importance of those forms, punctuate capitalist development; large trading companies on the other hand (such as the East India Companies) concerned both capital and the state. As the latter grew more important it intervened more forcefully; capitalists had to choose whether to submit, protest or as some did finally, pull out.

Individual firms: the beginning of a development

From the very earliest days, since the beginning (or the revival) of trade in the West, merchants had gone into partnership, worked together – how could they do otherwise? There had been trading firms in ancient Rome, and their activity had easily and logically extended to cover the Mediterranean. And commercial lawyers in the eighteenth century resorted to the precedents, vocabulary and sometimes even the spirit of Roman law, without doing too much violence to reality.

To discover the earliest forms taken by such firms in the West, one has to go back if not to ancient Rome, at least to the Mediterranean revival of the ninth and tenth centuries. Amalfi, Venice and other towns – all still very small places at the time – were just embarking on their careers. Money re-appeared. The renewal of trade with Byzantium and the cities of Islam presupposes both the ability to handle freight and the financial reserves needed for long-haul operations – which in turn imply strengthened trading units.

One of the first institutions was the *societas maris* or maritime firm (also known as the *societas vera*, or 'true' firm, 'which seems to suggest that this kind of organization was originally the only one').[185] It was also known as *collegantia* or *commenda*, with other variants. In theory this was a two-handed partnership between a *socius stans*, a partner who remained on the spot, and a *socius tractator*, who left in person on the ship. This would have been an example of an early division between capital and labour, as Marc Bloch and others before him thought, if the *tractator* (literally carrier; perhaps salesman is more accurate) had not also contributed (usually on a modest scale) his share of the finance. And unexpected combinations were possible, as we shall see later.[186] The *societas maris* was usually entered into for a single voyage; it was a short-term arrangement, although of course voyages across the Mediterranean lasted several months in those days. Mention of this kind of firm is found in the *Notularium* of the Genoese notary Giovanni Scriba (1155-1164) – over 400 references – or in the papers of a Marseilles notary of the thirteenth century, Amalric (360 references);[187] and it is also found in the Hanseatic seaports. This primitive version of the firm survived for a long time by virtue of its simplicity. It was still to be found in Marseilles or Ragusa in the sixteenth century, in Venice, of course, and elsewhere as well. As late as 1578 in Portugal, a *tractado* distinguishes between two types of partnership agreements: the second is immediately recognizable: it is signed by two persons '*quando hum põe o dinheiro e outro o trabalho*', when one puts in the money and the other the work.[188] I fancy I hear a distant echo of this partnership between capital and labour in the reflections which a Reims wholesaler confided to his journal in 1655: 'It is certain that you cannot enter a partnership with people who have no funds; for they share the profits and all the loss falls on you. And yet quite a few people make this arrangement, but I would never advise it.'[189]

IN-LADINGE
In een extraordinair wel - bezeylt
FLUYT-SCHIP
OP CADIX

En laet een ieghelijck weten, dat tot OOSTENDE par CADIX aen Ladinghe leght voor de tweede mael op die Vojagie , het extraordinair wel bezeylt Fluyt-Schip ghenaemt de *Jeff. Mary*, over dry weken ghearriveert van Cadix, Cartagena, Trypoly, en Trepana , daer voor Meester blyft op Cammanderen den Capiteyn ofte Schipper *Pieter Roelaud* van Amsterdam, voorsien met sijn Turckse Passen, de Vreghten zyn gereguleert de Canten tot Twee Realen de hondert guldens weerde, de Rauwe Lynwaten tot Twee Ducaten par Ballot van 12. tot 16. Stucken, en grooter naer advenante gelijck oock de Gaerens en ander Manufacturen, alles out gelt als voor de prematica : en dito Schip sal met Godt, weder ende wint dienende, zeylen op den 16. a 17. Mey 1715. goet ofte geen : die daer in gelieven te Laden sullen hun addresseren aen d'Heer *Thomas Ray*, of den boven-genoemden Capiteyn tot OOSTENDE.

Tract advertising the departures from Ostend for Cadiz of the 'extraordinarily good sailing-ship' the *Juffrouw Mary*, giving freight charges: 'for lace, two *reals* for one hundred florins' worth'; for unbleached linen, two ducats per bale of 12 to 16 lengths'. (A.N., Paris, G⁷ 1704, 67.) (Photo by the Archives.)

To return to the *societas maris*, Federigo Melis considers that it only makes sense in relation to a series of departing ships: the ship leaves and will eventually return. It creates both the opportunity and the obligation. For inland towns, the situation was different. And indeed they took time to become integrated to trade currents in Italy and the Mediterranean. In order to penetrate the networks of exchange, they had to overcome special difficulties and strains.

The *compagnia* was the product of these strains. This was a family firm – father, sons, brothers and other relatives – and as its name indicates (*cum* = with, *panis* = bread) it was a close association in which everything was shared – bread and risks, capital and labour. Later such a firm would be known as a joint liability enterprise, since all partners were jointly liable in theory *ad infinitum*, that is not only to the value of their holding but to the value of all their worldly goods. When we learn that the *compagnia* was soon admitting foreign partners (who contributed both capital and labour) and money from depositors (which, if one remembers the Florentine example, could run to ten times as much as the firm's own capital) we can understand how such firms were potent capitalist instruments. The Bardi, who had established themselves in the Levant and England, for a while held the whole of Christendom in fee. These powerful firms also lasted a surprisingly long time. On the death of the head of a firm, the *maggiore*, they would be reconvened and continue much as before. Almost all the agreements that have survived for us to read are contracts not of the foundation but of the renewal of a *compagnia*.[190] That is why we can use the names Bardi or Peruzzi as a shorthand for such firms.

In the end, the large firms of the inland Italian cities were far more important individually than those of the seaports, where firms were numerous but mostly small and short-lived. Away from the sea, some concentration was necessary. Federigo Melis contrasts the 12 individual enterprises of the Spinola family in Genoa for instance, with the 20 partners and 40 *dipendenti* of the single firm of Cerchi in Florence in about 1250.[191]

These large units were in fact both the means and the consequence of the entry of Lucca, Pistoia, Siena and lastly Florence, to the major currents of trade, where one would not originally have expected to find them. They virtually forced their way in and were presently vigorously excelling in the 'sectors' open to them: the secondary sector, industry; and the tertiary, services, commerce and banking. The *compagnia* was not, in short, an accidental discovery made by the landlocked towns, but a means of action developed as necessity arose.

In the preceding paragraphs, I have done no more than echo the ideas of André-E. Sayous,[192] who took Siena as his chief example and was thinking only of the towns of Italy; but I think the rule could be applied to trading firms in the continental interior, far from the Italian peninsula. Deep in Germany for instance was the *Magna Societas*, with headquarters in Ravensburg, a little town in Swabia, in the hilly region near Lake Constance, where flax was grown and linen woven. The *Grosse Ravensburger Gesellschaft*, a combination of three family firms[193] was to last a century and a half from 1380 to 1530. And yet it seems to have been reconstituted every six years. At the end of the fifteenth century, thanks to its 80 partners, it had a capital of 132,000 florins – a huge sum, halfway between the Welsers (66,000) and the Fuggers (213,000) at the same period.[194] Its main branches, apart from Ravensburg, were in Memmingen, Konstanz, Nuremberg, Lindau and Saint-Gall; and it had subsidiaries in Genoa, Milan, Berne, Geneva, Lyons, Bruges (and later Antwerp), Barcelona, Cologne, Vienna and Paris. Its representatives – a whole community of partners, commission agents, employees and merchant-apprentices, frequented the great fairs of Europe, in particular those of Frankfurt, to which they sometimes travelled on foot. The merchants associated in this firm were wholesalers who confined themselves to commodity trading (linen, woollen cloth, spices, saffron etc.), had little to do with finance, practically never gave credit and had retail shops only in Saragossa and Genoa – the extremely rare exceptions in a huge network ranging from inland traffic in the Rhône Valley to sea-borne trade from Genoa, Venice or Barcelona. The chance discovery of the firm's papers in 1909 enabled Aloys Schulte[195] to write his indispensable book on European trade between the fifteenth and sixteenth centuries, for the vast range of activities of these German merchants gives us a window on to the whole of commercial life, practically throughout Christendom.

That the *Magna Societas* did not follow the new trends dictated by the great discoveries – that it did not for instance hasten to open an office in Lisbon or Seville – seems to be characteristic. Should we regard it as immovably lodged in an old-fashioned system and thus incapable of breaking through to the powerful new flow of business which was to mark the beginning of modernity? Or was it impossible to distort a network which survived unaltered until 1530? The old methods were partly responsible. The number of partners fell; the directors, the *Regierer*, bought land and retired fom business.[196] But the typical, large and long-lived firm on the Florentine pattern did not die out with the *Magna Societas*. Some remained in business until the eighteenth century and beyond. These firms were concentrated and modelled on the family, they preserved the family fortunes and provided a living for the clan: this was the secret of their survival. A family firm was perpetually being dismantled and re-organized according to succession patterns. The Buonvisi, merchants originally from Lucca who had settled in Lyons in France, regularly changed the firm's name: from 1575 to 1577, it was called 'Heirs of Louis Buonvisi and Company'; from 1578 to 1584, 'Benoît, Bernardin Buonvisi and Company'; from 1584 to 1587, 'Benoît, Bernardin, Etienne, Antoine Buonvisi and Company'; from 1588 to 1597, 'Bernardin, Etienne, Antoine Buonvisi and Company'; from 1600 to 1607, 'Paul, Etienne, Antoine Buonvisi and Company'; the company was always the same yet always different.[197]

Such firms (known in the French ordinance of 1673 as *sociétés générales*) gradually came to be known as 'free' firms or 'joint liability' firms (*sociétés libres* or *à nom collectif*). It is worth insisting on the family or near-family atmosphere which characterized them (even when there was no actual family concerned), until a quite late date. Here is the text of a partnership agreement signed in Nantes on 23 April 1719 (between parties who were not in fact related):

> No money will be taken out of the firm except what is necessary for the livelihood and upkeep of each partner's family, so as not to diminish its capital; and for no other purpose, and whenever one partner takes out money, he must inform the other, who will take the same amount, so that no accounts will need to be kept under this heading.[198]

This 'interpenetration of private and commercial life was even more pronounced in small commercial and manufacturing firms'.[199]

Limited partnership

All such family firms were faced with the difficult problem of liability – and whether it should be total or limited. A solution emerged rather belatedly, the *commandite* or limited partnership agreement, which distinguished the liability of the firm's directors from that of those who only contributed their money and who wished to be liable for this amount and no more. This notion of limited liability was introduced more quickly in France than in England, where a limited partnership for a long time enjoyed the right to ask the *socii* for more contributions.[200] Federigo Melis[201] locates the first clear case of the limited partnership (*accomandita*) in Florence (though not before the sixteenth century since the first recorded contract dates from 8 May 1532); here it enabled Florentine capital, with its propensity for expansion, to participate in a whole series of operations similar to those of present-day holding companies. We can trace the volume, distribution and longevity of such agreements by the registrations of *accomandite*.

The limited partnership firm made its way through Europe, slowly replacing the family firm. It only really prospered to the extent that, by resolving new problems, it corresponded to the growing diversity of trade and to the increasingly frequent practice of long-distance partnership. It was also favoured by partners who wished their holding to be discreet. This system enabled an Irish merchant in Nantes to go into business in 1732 with an Irish merchant in Cork,[202] to 'get round ... the French legislation in force until the Revolution, forbidding non-French subjects to engage in [national] shipping enterprises'. It meant that a French merchant could be in league with the commanders of Portuguese trading posts on the African coast or with Spanish 'government officials' in America,[202] or with sea-captains who dabbled in trade; he might have a tame partner in Saint-Domingue or Messina or anywhere else. Not all the partners of firms registered in Paris, whether or not they were resident, were Parisians it seems. A firm was set up for instance on 12 June 1720 (it lasted only a year) 'for the purchase and sale of merchandise, between Joseph Souisse, former *juge-consul* of Bordeaux, living in rue Saint-Honoré, Paris, Jean and Pierre Nicolas, rue du Bouloi, François Imbert, Grand'rue du Faubourg Saint-Denis, and Jacques Ransson, merchant of Bilbao'.[203] In the winding-up agreement, Jacques Ransson described himself as French national representative and banker in Bilbao.

How, if the rather laconic documents do not make this clear, are we to distinguish between the limited partnership (*société en commandite*, or *conditionnée* or *de commodité*)[204] and the previous joint-liability family firm? Presumably when there is a restriction on the liability of any given partner. The French ordinance of 1673 clearly says: 'the parties to a limited partnership will be liable only to the equivalent of their shareholding'.[205] Here is an *écrite* or *scripte* (i.e. partnership agreement) signed in Marseilles on 29 March 1786: the partner, who was a woman, 'cannot be held in any way or in any eventuality responsible for the debts and commitments of the said firm beyond the sum of money she has put into it'.[206] This is an eminently clear example – but it is not always the case. Some parties to the *commandite* chose this type of association because it enabled them to remain in the background, even if they were in fact contributing a good deal of capital and sharing the risk. Since the 1673 ordinance (which made it compulsory for limited partnership agreements to be signed in front of a lawyer by the interested parties) only referred to 'partnerships between merchants and wholesalers', the current interpretation was that anyone 'not engaged in a mercantile profession' was not obliged to be listed among the partners on the agreement registered with the statutory authorities.[207] In this way, noblemen could be protected from loss of rank and royal officials could avoid revealing that they had commercial interests. This undoubtedly explains the success of the *commandite* system in France, where those who were 'in trade' were still not readily admitted to high society, even during the business explosion of the eighteenth century. Paris was not London or Amsterdam.

Joint stock companies

The limited partnerships were associations both of individuals and of capital. The joint stock companies or *sociétés par actions* as they were known in France, the last form to emerge, were associations of capital only. This capital or stock formed a single mass, identified with the firm itself. Partners or stockholders had holdings or shares in it.

Legal historians recognize as joint stock companies only those in which shares are not only transferable but *negotiable on the open market*. If one is not too particular about the last clause, one could say that Europe had some very early examples of the joint stock company, well before the creation in 1553–5 of the Muscovy Company, the first recorded English joint stock company, though others may have preceded it by a few years. Before the fifteenth century even, ships in the Mediterranean were often divided into shares – known as *partes* in

Venice, *luoghi* in Genoa, *caratti* in most other Italian towns, *quiratz* or *carats* in Marseilles. And these could be sold. The same was true of mines throughout Europe: as early as the thirteenth century, one could buy shares in a silver mine near Siena, and they were available from early days in salt mines or pans, in metal-works in Styria, or in a French copper mine in which Jacques Cœur had some holdings. With the expansion of the fifteenth century, the mines of Central Europe were taken over by merchants and princes, their stock was divided into shares known as *Kuxen*, and these were transferable and indeed the object of speculation.[208] Here and there, mills were owned in partnership, as in Douai, Cologne or Toulouse. In the latter town,[209] the mills were divided in the thirteenth century into shares, *'uchaux'*, which their holders (*'pariers'*) could sell like any other real estate. And indeed the structures of the mill-owning partnerships of Toulouse remained unchanged from the late Middle Ages until the nineteenth century; just before the Revolution the *pariers* were simply referred to in the firms' own documents as *'Messieurs les Actionnaires'* (the modern term for shareholders).[210]

In this search for antecedents, the place usually assigned to Genoa, special case though it was, may seem exaggerated. Because of its political needs and weakness, the Genoese Republic had allowed two sorts of company to develop, the *compere* and the *maone*. The *maone* were associations divided into shares which handled tasks properly those of the state: the attack on Ceuta for instance (when the first of the *maone* went into action) or the colonization of Chios in 1346: this operation was successfully undertaken by the Giustiniani and the island remained under their control until 1566, the year of its conquest by the Turks. The *compere* were state loans, divided into *loca* or *luoghi*, secured against the revenues of the *Dominante*. In 1407, *compere* and *maone* were brought together in the *Casa di San Giorgio*, which was in effect a state within the state, one of the keys to the secret and paradoxical history of the republic. But can these *compere* or *maone* really be described as joint stock companies? Scholars are still divided over this.[211]

In any case, if one excepts the big merchant companies with their privileges, the joint stock company did not spread very quickly. France is an example of a country where it did not catch on. The word *action* (share) itself took root only very late, and even when we do find it, it does not necessarily refer to easily transferable shares. The word was often there before the reality. Equally imprecise words for the same thing were *parts d'intérest* or *sols*, or *sols d'intérêts*. On 22 February 1765, a transfer or sale of shares of a 'firm in order to bring in receipts from its rents' concerned 'two *sols 6 deniers* of interest which ... belong [to the vendors], out of the 21 *sols* which make up the firm'.[212] Two years later, still in Paris, in 1767, the Beaurin company uses the word *actions* but describes its capital stocks of four million *livres* as follows: 4000 recognized 'simple interests' of 500 *livres*; 10,000 fifths of 'simple interests' of 100 *livres*; 1200 recognized 'rentier interests' of 500 *livres*; 4000 fifths of 'rentier interests' of 100 *livres*. '*Intérêts*

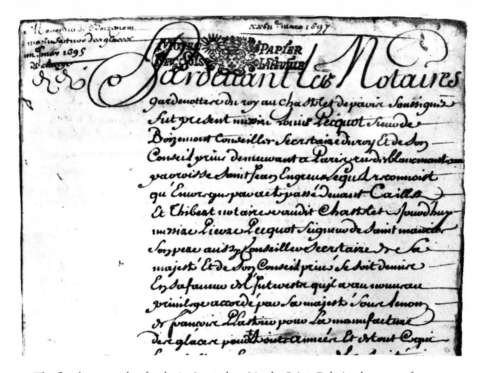

The first known sale of a *denier* [part-share] in the Saint-Gobain glass manufactory. (Photo Saint-Gobain.)

simples' were ordinary shares participating in both profits and losses; '*intérêts rentiers*' were what we would call debentures at 6%.[213]

The word *actionnaire* (shareholder in the modern sense) was also slow to catch on. In France at least, it had a pejorative tone, as did the word *banquier* (banker). Melon,[214] one of John Law's secretaries, wrote several years after the collapse of the famous system (1734):

> We do not claim that the Shareholder is any more useful to the state than the Rentier. These are odious partisan preferences from which we distance ourselves. The Shareholder receives his income as does the Rentier; neither works any more than the other, and the money paid by either to have a Share or a Contract [i.e. annuity] circulates equally well and is equally applicable to Trade or Agriculture. But the procedure for taking out these bonds is different. The Shareholder's Bond or Share is not subject to any formality and therefore circulates more easily, thus producing a greater abundance of value and a reliable resource in time of present or future need.

Whereas the '*contrat*' was only negotiable after lengthy procedures in front of a lawyer; it was what was known in France as a safe investment ('*de père de famille*'), one that was safe from 'under-age inheritors who often squandered their inheritance'.

In spite of the advantages of the ordinary share, the new type of company seems to have spread extremely slowly wherever records have been studied: in eighteenth-century Nantes or Marseilles for instance. It usually appeared in the modern or modernizing sector of insurance, and sometimes for the fitting of ships for privateering: what had already been the case in Elizabethan England was going on in 1730 in Saint-Malo. 'No one can be unaware', says a petition to the king, 'that according to the regular practice with regard to privateering vessels, any enterprise of this nature in Saint-Malo or any other port in the Kingdom is financed only by subscriptions, which being divided into shares of modest capital (*actions d'un capital modique*) make the profits from privateering flow into every corner of the Kingdom.'[215]

This is a significant document. The joint stock company was a way of reaching a much larger investing public, a way of extending both geographically and socially the zones from which money could be drawn. The Beaurin Company for instance was in contact with people prepared to collaborate and participate in Rouen, Le Havre, Morlaix, Honfleur, Dieppe, Lorient, Nantes, Pézenas, Yvetot, Stolberg (near Aachen), Lille, Bourg-en-Bresse.[216] With a little luck, the net could have been extended to the whole of France. The greatest activity was however in Paris, the business-crazy Paris of Louis XVI, where a number of companies were set up: the Marine Insurance Company (later made a General Company in 1753); the Anzin Mining Company, the Carmaux Mining Company, the Gisors Canal Company, the Briare Canal Company, the *Fermes générales* Company, the Water Company. Naturally shares in these were quoted, sold and circulated in Paris. Following an 'unprecedented upheaval', shares in the Water Company jumped from 2100 *livres* to 3200 and 3300 in April 1784.[217]

The list would be even longer of course if it included Holland and England – but this is hardly necessary.

A limited development

So we have the three generations of firms distinguished by the history of commercial law: the general or family firm; the limited partnership; and the joint stock company. The pattern of development is clear – at least in theory. In practice, setting aside a few exceptions, firms retained an old-fashioned and imperfect character chiefly as a result of their small size. Any attempt at a census – in what survives of the archives of the consular authorities in Paris for instance – finds a number of firms very ill-defined or defying definition. The very small ones are in the majority, as if there were safety in numbers.[218] One has to wade through ten contracts of tiny enterprises before coming across a sugar refinery, and twenty before one finds a bank. This is not to say that the wealthy did not go into partnership, on the contrary as the sharp-eyed Daniel Defoe noted of England in 1720: where were partnerships most frequent? Among the rich merchants, the mercers, linen-drapers, 'banking goldsmiths' and other 'considerable trades' as well as certain merchants in the overseas business.[219]

But 'considerable trades' were in the minority. And above all, even within this category, the firms, trading units, 'enterprises',[220] apart from a few privileged companies or large-scale manufactories were, for many years, of dimensions we should regard as derisory. A 'counting-house' in Amsterdam consisted of twenty or thirty people at most;[221] the biggest bank in Paris on the eve of the Revolution, Louis Greffulhe's, employed about thirty people.[222] A firm, however important, could easily be accommodated in a single house, usually the 'principal's'. And this long gave it a family, not to say patriarchal atmosphere. In Defoe's time, the servants lodged with the merchant, ate at his table, asked his permission to go out – and would certainly not be allowed to spend the night away. In a play put on in London in 1731, the merchant Thorowgood reprimands his apprentice Barnwell: 'Without a cause assigned or notice given, to absent yourself last night was a fault, young man.'[223] The same atmosphere is described in a novel by Gustav Freytag, *Soll und Haben* (1850) which is set in a German wholesale firm. Even under Queen Victoria, the masters and employers of big trading firms still lived in a sort of family community: 'In many business establishments, the day was begun by family prayers, in which the apprentices and assistants joined.'[224] So neither outward appearances, social realities nor mentalities changed very fast. Numerous small firms remained the rule. Size of firm only increased significantly when the state was concerned: the most colossal of modern enterprises, the state, helped others to grow as it increased in stature itself.

Forerunners of the great merchant companies

The great merchant companies were born of trade monopolies. On the whole, they date from the seventeenth century and are peculiar to north-west Europe. This point has been made many times, not without justification. Just as the cities of the Italian interior had created firms of the Florentine type (*compagnie*) and were thus able to break into the trade circuits of the Mediterranean and Europe, so the United Provinces and England are generally supposed to have used their companies to conquer the world.

Although this statement is not inaccurate, it is not entirely adequate to locate this astonishing phenomenon in a proper historical perspective. The monopolies established by the big companies have at least two, more properly three characteristics: they were the expression of high-intensity capitalist endeavour; they would have been unthinkable without the privilege granted by the state; and they appropriated for themselves whole sectors of overseas trade. One of the 'Companies' which preceded the *Oost Indische Compagnie* was entitled the *Compagnie Van Verre*, the 'Company of distant parts'. But neither long-distance trade, not state privileges, nor capital enterprise date from the early seventeenth century. In the world of *Fernhandel*, capitalism and the state were already in league well before the creation of the English Muscovy Company in 1553–1555. The whole of the Mediterranean and Europe, even the north, had become accessible to Venetian trade by the early fourteenth century: in 1314, Venetian galleys were sailing into Bruges. During the fourteenth century, faced with a growing general recession, the Venetian state organized the system of the *galere da mercato*. These big ships were built and fitted in the city arsenal (so that the initial outlay was all borne by the *Signoria*) and then hired out to patrician merchants to encourage trade. This led to 'dumping' on a grand scale, as did not escape the sharp eyes of Gino Luzzatto. The *galere da mercato* had their role to play until the first decades of the sixteenth century, as a weapon in Venice's struggle for hegemony.

Similar systems were established over an even wider area after the discovery of America and Vasco da Gama's voyage round the Cape. European capitalism found prodigious new opportunities here, but did not make any spectacular breakthrough. For the Spanish state had set up the *Consejo de Indias*, the *Casa de la Contratacion* and the *Carrera de Indias*. How could anyone evade this barrage of state constraints and surveillance? In Lisbon, there was a Merchant King, and what Nuñez Diaz[225] rightly calls the 'monarchical capitalism' of the *Casa de India*, with its state fleets, factors and monopoly. The independent merchants had to suffer it.

And these systems survived – the Portuguese until about 1615–1620 and the Spanish until 1784. So if the Iberian countries were long resistant to the establishment of big merchant companies, it was because the state had already provided facilities for merchants in Lisbon, Seville and Cadiz. The machine worked – and once it had started, who was to stop it? It is often remarked that the Spanish *Carrera de Indias* was imitated from the Venetian model, which is true; it is somewhat less accurate to say that Lisbon was imitating Genoa.[226] In Venice, the state was all; in Genoa, capital was all. And in Lisbon, where the modern state was securely in place, there was anything but the free-for-all typical of Genoa.

State and capital were two forces that could be yoked together for better or for worse. How did the arrangement work in the United Provinces and in England? This is the crucial question in the history of the great companies.

The rule of three

A company monopoly depended on the coming together of three things: first the state, which might or might not be effective, but which was never absent; then the world of trade, that is capital, banking, credit and customers – a world which might be hostile or cooperative – or both at once; lastly there was the trading zone to be exploited in some distant land and this could itself be a decisive factor in many ways.

The state was never absent: it distributed and guaranteed privileges on the

The *Oost Indische Compagnie*'s shipyard and entrepôt in Amsterdam. Engraving by J. Mulder, c. 1700. (Photo Atlas Van Stock Foundation.)

national market, which was an essential base for company operations. But such favours were not granted for nothing. Every company was part of a fiscal operation arising from the financial difficulties that were the perpetual bane of modern states. The companies paid for their monopolies many times over, and every renewal was preceded by long discussions. Even the apparently not-very-United Provinces could agree on taxing the tempting *Oost Indische Compagnie*, obliging it to advance money, to pay dues, and to suffer taxation on capital to hit its shareholders (at rates fixed according to the *real* value of shares as quoted on the Bourse – an aggravating detail). As someone who knew the company better than anyone else, the lawyer Pieter Van Damm remarked (and his comment can be applied to rival companies too): 'The state ought to rejoice at the existence of an association which pays it so much money every year that the country derives three times as much profit from trade and navigation in the Indies as the shareholders.'[227]

I need not labour this familiar point. But every state, by its choice of action, gave a particular character to its companies. They had more freedom of man-œuvre in England after the 1688 revolution than they did in Holland, where the weight of former success lay heavy. In France, the *Compagnie des Indes*, to take but one example, was established and re-established at the whim of the royal government which kept it in isolation from the rest of the economy as if suspended in mid-air, administered by a series of mediocre or incompetent men. No Frenchman could fail to note the difference. When a French correspondent wrote from London in July 1713, announcing the creation of an *Asiento* company (later to become the South Sea Company, which was immediately granted the privilege previously held by the French of providing Spanish America with black slaves), he remarked: 'The company which has been granted this provision is made up of private individuals: here the orders of the Court have no effect on the interests of private individuals . . .'[228] A slight exaggeration perhaps, but in 1713, there was already a big difference in the way business was conducted on either side of the English Channel.

In short, we must try to discover at what level and intensity relations between the state and the companies were established. The companies only developed if the state did *not* intervene in the French fashion. If on the contrary a certain degree of economic freedom was the rule, capitalism moved in firmly and adapted itself to all administrative quirks and difficulties. It must be admitted that the *Oost Indische Compagnie* – a few months junior to the English East India Company, but the first of the great companies to enjoy spectacular and fascinating success – had an extremely bizarre and complicated structure. It was divided into six independent 'chambers' (Holland, Zeeland, Delft, Rotterdam, Hoorn and Enkhuizen) over which sat the joint governing body of the 'Seventeen Masters' (*Heeren Zeventien*), eight of whom came from the Chamber of Holland. Through the chambers, the bourgeoisie of the regents of the towns had access to this huge and profitable undertaking. The directors of the local cham-bers (the *Gewindhebbers* who chose the *Heeren XVII*) in turn had access to the governing body of the company. We might note in passing the ripples caused by the different urban economies on the apparently smooth surface of the general economy of the United Provinces – not that this prevented the domination of Amsterdam – and also the permanent presence in the labyrinth of the *Oost Indische* of certain powerful family dynasties, such as the Bickers of Amsterdam and the Lampsins of Zeeland. It was not the state which promoted them but money and society. The same remark could be made of the English East India Company or South Sea Company, the Bank of England or, to take a small but quite glaring example, the Hudson's Bay Company. At the top of all these large enterprises were small ruling groups, obstinately attached to their privileges, thoroughly conservative and in no sense looking for change or innovation. They were too comfortably-off to have a taste for risk. And we may even hazard the disrespectful suggestion that they did not represent the brightest and best of business intelligence. It is too often argued that the *Oost Indische Compagnie* decayed from the bottom; it also decayed at the top. What preserved it so long was that it was attached to the most fruitful branches of exchange of the time.

The destinies of the companies were in fact partly governed by the commercial area over which they had the monopoly; geography accounts for a good deal. And in practice, the Asiatic trade proved the most solid basis for these mighty ventures. Neither the Atlantic – the African and American trades – nor the European seas, the Baltic, White Sea or even the great Mediterranean, offered operational areas that were so profitable for so long. In English history, compare the fate of the Muscovy Company, the Levant Company and the African Company or in Dutch history the eventual collapse of the West Indies Company. For these great trading companies, there was a definite and by no means fortuitous geography of success. Was this because the Asiatic trade lay exclusively in luxury products – pepper, spices, silk, calicoes, Chinese gold, Japanese silver and before long tea, coffee, lacquer, porcelains? As Europe made steady growth, her appetite for luxuries progressed. And the collapse of the Great Mogul's empire at the beginning of the eighteenth century delivered India up to the greed of Western merchants. But it was also the case that distance, the difficulties of the Asia trade and its sophisticated character confined it to large-scale capitalism which could alone pour into these circuits the enormous sums of cash they required. The huge outlay required at the start eliminated or at any rate reduced competition, by fixing the handicap at a certain level. An Englishman wrote in 1645, 'Private men cannot extend to making such long, adventurous and costly voyages.'[229] In fact this was a piece of special pleading for the companies, repeated many times both inside and outside England, and not entirely true: many 'private men' could have got together the necessary capital as we shall see. A final advantage of Asia was that the Europeans settled there could become self-supporting: the trade between different parts of the East was exceptionally profitable: it kept the Portuguese Empire going for one century, and the Dutch for two, until the British Empire swallowed up India.

But did it really swallow India? The local trade which formed the foundation for the European success, giving it regular structures to build on, was evidence of the vigour of a pre-existing economy, built to last. During the centuries of exploitation, the Europeans had the advantage of being faced with rich and developed civilizations, with agriculture and artisan manufacture already organized for export, with trading links and efficient intermediaries everywhere. In Java for instance, the Dutch depended on the Chinese for the collection of foodstuffs at the point of production and their assembly for sale. Instead of starting from scratch as they had to in America, the Europeans in the Far East exploited and diverted to their own ends a solidly-constructed trade system. Only their silver enabled them to force these doors. And it was only at the end of the period that military and political conquest, leaving Britain ruler of the East, seriously disturbed these ancient balances.

The English companies

The fortunes of English commerce did not get off to an early start. In about 1500, England was a 'backward' country, without a powerful navy, with a predominantly rural population and only two sources of wealth: huge wool production and a strong cloth industry (which developed to the point of absorbing the former). This largely rural industry produced stout broadcloth in the eastern and south-western counties, and fine soft kerseys in the West Riding of Yorkshire. This England, with its capital city of 75,000 inhabitants – not yet a monster but on the way there – its strong monarchy now that the Wars of the Roses were over, its powerful guilds and active fairs, remained a country with a traditional economy. But commerce was beginning to be distinguished from craftworking – a distinction broadly comparable to what happened in the Italian cities of the pre-Renaissance period.

It was of course in the sector of foreign trade that the first big English firms were created. The two largest of which records survive – the Merchants of the Staple, the wool exporters (the staple in question being Calais), and the Merchant Adventurers, cloth wholesalers – were still archaic in their organization. The Staplers represented English wool, but before long this was no longer being exported, so they are of limited interest to us. The Merchant Adventurers,[230] who had appropriated the rather loose term 'adventurers' (which in fact meant any merchant engaged in foreign trade) exported unbleached wool to the Low Countries under a series of agreements (1493–4 and 1505 for instance). Gradually the mercers and grocers of London began to assume a leading role among the mass of adventurers and sought to displace the rival group of provincial merchants from the north. From 1475, these London merchants were acting in unison, freighting the same boats for sending their goods, collaborating to pay customs duties and obtain privileges, under what soon appeared to be the dictatorship of the mercers. In 1497, the Crown intervened to force the company whose headquarters were in London, to accept merchants from outside the capital; but they were only admitted with inferior status.

The first thing that strikes one about the organization of the Merchant Adventurers is that their real operational base was outside England altogether, in Antwerp and Bergen-op-Zoom whose fairs competed for their custom. Being established in the Low Countries meant that the company could play these two towns off against each other and better preserve its privileges. Above all it was on the continental market that the vital transactions took place – the sale of cloth in exchange for spices or money. This was where English trade could communicate with the most thriving currents of the world economy. The older merchants who were afraid of travel and of these busy fairs remained in London; the younger men went to Antwerp. In 1542, the London residents complained to the Privy Council that 'the young men resident in Antwerp' paid no attention to the advice of their 'heads and masters' in London.[231]

But what interests us here is that the Merchant Adventurers Company remained a 'corporation'. The discipline to which the merchants were subject was similar to that exercised over its members by a guild, within a single town, as the articles granted to it by the state – the royal code of practice of 1608 for instance[232] – reveal in picturesque detail. Members of the company must be as 'brethren' for each other, and their wives as 'sisters'. The brethren must all attend together at religious services and funerals. They are forbidden to behave badly, to utter coarse words, to get drunk, to make an unseemly spectacle of themselves – for instance by entering the porter's lodge to collect their mail instead of waiting for it at the proper window, or by carrying heavy bales of goods on their own backs; disputes, insults and duels are also forbidden. The company was a moral entity and a legal personality with its own government (governor, deputies, judges and secretaries). It had a monopoly of trade and the privilege of perpetual succession (that is it could succeed to itself). All these characteristics are typical (to use the later vocabulary of Sir Josiah Child) of the *regulated company* – that is, something rather similar, *mutatis mutandis* to the guilds or to the *hanses* of the North Sea.

So there was nothing really new and original about all this. The Merchant Adventurers, whose origins undoubtedly go back beyond the fifteenth century, had not waited for the royal goodwill and pleasure to form their company. Its formation was probably, as Michael Postan suggests,[233] the consequence of a fall in cloth sales which made it necessary to band together to react effectively. But this was not a joint stock company. Its members (who each paid a membership fee on entry, unless they had inherited membership or served an apprenticeship with another member) all did business at their own risk. All in all it was an ancient organization which had gradually taken over a new function resulting from the development of the English economy – the transition from raw wool to woollen cloth – and it fulfilled its role admirably, as a sum of individual activities, coordinated but not combined. It would have been easy for it to become a large unified company with joint capital, a joint stock company. But the Merchant Adventurers, although in decline it is true, maintained their organization in its original form until 1809, when Napoleon took Hamburg (where the company had been firmly established since 1611)[234] and its career came to an end.

These details from the history of the Merchant Adventurers will have conveyed some idea of what the regulated company was like. The first joint stock companies which proliferated in England, with the burst of activity of the late sixteenth and early seventeenth century[235] did not immediately form the majority – far from it. They made their appearance among firms of the older type which performed the same services; sometimes the latter even seem to have gained the upper hand, since joint stock companies like the Muscovy Company (1555) or the Levant Company (1581) later became regulated companies, the first in 1622 and then in 1669, the second in 1605, and the Africa Company in 1750. Even the English East India Company, founded in 1599, and granted its privilege in 1600,

The Court Room of the Merchant Adventurers' Hall at York. (Photo *Country Life*.)

went through a curious crisis to say the least between 1698 and 1708, a period during which it became in part once more a regulated company.

And indeed during the first century of its existence, the English East India Company, which had been set up with much less capital than the Dutch company, was very far from being a joint stock company. Its capital was only constituted for one voyage at a time, and each merchant recovered his investment and profits on the ship's return. Shareholders for a long time had the right to withdraw their holding. Things were gradually modified. After 1612, accounts were reckoned not on the forthcoming voyage alone but on a series of projected voyages. And finally after 1658, the company's capital became intangible. By 1688, shares were negotiable on the London Stock Exchange, just as those of the Dutch company were on the Amsterdam Bourse. So the English companies did not immediately imitate the Dutch model – it took about a hundred years or so.

Companies and short-term economic fluctuations

The global success of the north-west European companies was in part a question of chronology and the short term economic climate. Amsterdam's fortune had its beginnings in about 1580–1585. In 1585, the recapture of Antwerp by Alexander Farnese had sealed the fate of the port on the Scheldt. Its destruction as a trade centre, although only partial, ensured the triumph of its rival. But in 1585, the creation of the *Oost Indische Compagnie* was still twenty years away (1602). So the company was born after the beginning of Amsterdam's fortune; it certainly did not create it, if it was in part created by it. Success at all events came almost immediately as it did to the English company set up a little earlier.

The failure of the French to set up trading companies must be dated between 1664 and 1682: the French East India Company, founded in 1664, 'was soon faced with financial difficulties' and its privilege was withdrawn in 1682; a Levant Company was formed in 1670, but was in trouble by 1672; the *Compagnie du Nord*, set up in July 1669, was a 'fiasco';[236] the West India Company, formed in 1664,[236] was closed down in 1674 – a series of failures which did little to compensate for the only partial success of the East India Company. Meanwhile the Dutch and the English companies thrived. Such a contrast requires some explanation. Factors hindering the French enterprises were distrust of the royal governments by the merchants, the comparative inadequacy of the means at their disposal and the immaturity of what might have been French capitalism. But undoubtedly it was also difficult to penetrate networks already organized: all the best positions were occupied, and would be defended to the death. Moreover, writes Jean Meuvret,[237] 'the foreign Companies, which had been created during the first half of the century had benefited from spectacular advantages which, because of the changed circumstances, never recurred'. The French had chosen the wrong moment: Colbert arrived on the scene too late. The half-century of unprecedented expansion had given the north, and in particular the Low Countries, a headstart which enabled them to withstand subsequent competition and even downturns in the economy.

Indeed the same economic causes could produce different results in different places. The turn of the century (1680–1720) was a difficult time all over Europe, but it was marked in England by a series of upheavals and crises which give an impression of general progress. Was this because in periods of recession or stagnation, some economies were better protected or less vulnerable than others? At any rate after the 1688 revolution, business picked up in England. Public credit facilities on the Dutch model were introduced; the Bank of England, successfully founded in a bold venture in 1694, stabilized the state bond market and gave an extra fillip to business – which was already improving: bills of exchange and cheques were playing an increasing role on the domestic market.[238] Foreign trade was expanding and diversifying: it was 'the impression of Davenant and Gregory King that foreign trade had come to be the fastest-expanding source of wealth'.[239] There was a 'promotion mania' for investment in joint stock companies, of which there were 24 (including Scottish ones) in 1688; between 1692 and 1695, 150 joint stock companies were founded, not all of which survived.[240] The recoinage of 1696 was a bitter blow, and did not only affect speculative affairs. Thousands of subscribers were also hit, hence the Act of 1697 which reduced the number of brokers and stock-jobbers to 100 with the aim of curbing the multitude of less than scrupulous canvassers.[241] But the investment boom picked up again until 1720, the year of the South Sea Bubble. All in all it was an unsettling period, but a fertile one for business, despite the large levies exacted by the governments of William III and Anne.

In this climate, the companies found it difficult to retain their privileges against competition from private enterprise. The monopolies of the Russian and Levant Companies were abolished. Was the East India Company also to founder now that its capital had considerably increased? In the new climate of freedom, a second company was set up and the struggle between the old and the new kept the Stock Exchange in suspense until 1708.

Without wishing to denigrate the aggressive form of capitalism which was appearing during these years, I will just mention one curious incident. In August 1698, the merchants of the old company considered giving up some of their establishments in the Indies either to merchants from the new company or – amazingly – to the French East India Company! Pontchartrain wrote to Tallard on 6 August 1698:[242] '*The Directors of the Compagnie des Indes have been advised that those of the old English company wished to sell their establishments in Masulipatam on the coast of Coromandel and that they might negotiate with them about this.* It is the intention of His Majesty that *you should try to discover discreetly if this is really true and if so, whether they have the right to give them up and what they want for them.*' (The passages in italics are in code in the original.) Tallard, who was still at Utrecht, replied to the minister on 21 August:[242] '*It is certain that the Directors of the old East India trading company of England wish to sell the establishments they have there, and the directors of the new company, in order to get them cheaper, are saying that* they do not want them and can do without them, *but I doubt whether the former,* who are rich London merchants with a great deal to lose would dare to sell them to foreigners.' Ten years later, the problem was resolved by the merging of the two English companies.

This episode can be compared to the attitude of certain Dutchmen who, irritated by the survival of monopolies which banned them from the East Indies trade, created or tried to create Indies companies in France, Denmark, Sweden, Tuscany, providing them with capital. It also explains the climate reigning at the end of the eighteenth century and beginning of the nineteenth in British India, where opposition by English merchants to the privileges of the East India Company (which were abolished only in 1865) was aided by the collusion not only of local agents of the company but also of a host of foreign traders of all nationalities actively engaged in smuggling particularly in the direction of China and the East Indies, and in the profitable traffic of clandestine imports of specie to Europe.

The companies and free trade

Peter Laslett[243] argues that the English East India Company and the Bank of England which 'had already set up the model for those institutional instruments which were to bring into being "business" as we know it', could only have had an 'infinitesimal' impact 'in relation to the whole of commercial and industrial activity'. Charles Boxer is even more positive on this score, without giving any detailed evidence to support his view[244] that the large trading companies were not paramount. W. R. Scott is more precise: he estimates that in 1703 (after a clear rise) the total capital amassed by the joint stock companies still stood at only £8 million, whereas in 1688, according to Gregory King, national income was £45 million and national wealth £600 million.[245]

These are familiar arguments: every time the volume of a leading sector is compared to the total volume of the whole economy, the larger picture reduces the exception to more modest or even insignificant proportions. I am not entirely convinced. The important things are those that have consequences and when these consequences amount to the modernizing of the economy, the 'business model' of the future, the accelerated pace of capital formation and the dawn of colonization, we should think more than once about them. The chorus of protests against the monopoly of the companies seems to suggest that the game was worth the candle.

Already before 1700, the world of trade had been grumbling about the monopolies. There had been complaints, anger, hopes and compromises. But if one does not over-interpret the evidence, it seems that while monopoly by a given company might have been borne without too much indignation in the seventeenth century, it was regarded as intolerable and scandalous in the following century. Descazeaux, a trade deputy from Nantes, says so bluntly in one of his reports (1701):[246] 'The privileges of the exclusive companies are prejudicial to trade', since there is today 'as much ability and emulation among our subjects as there was indifference and incapacity when the companies were founded.' Nowadays, he points out, merchants can themselves go to the East Indies, China, to Guinea for the slave trade, to Senegal for gold dust, leather, ivory and gum. Nicolas Mesnager, a deputy from Rouen thought the same (3 June 1704):[247] 'it is an incontestable principle in trade that all the exclusive companies are more likely to narrow it than to extend it, and it is much more advantageous for the state that its trade should be in the hands of all its subjects than that it should be restricted to a few'. According to an official report of 1699,[248] even those in favour of the companies thought that 'private individuals should not be deprived of the freedom to trade and then there should not be exclusive privileges in a state'. In England 'interlopers or adventurers are trading in the places where the English companies can do so'.[248] In fact in 1661, the company had abandoned internal trade within the East to private individuals. And after the 1688 revolution, which was a victory for the merchants, public opinion was running so high

Departure of a Dutch East Indiaman in about 1620. Painting by Adam Willaerts. (National Maritime Museum, Greenwich.)

that the privileges of the East India Company were suspended and the India trade was declared free. But everything returned to normal in 1698 or rather 1708, when the 'exclusive rights' became the rule once more.

There were similar vicissitudes in France. In 1681 (20 December) and 1682 (20 January) Colbert pronounced the Indies trade open to all, the company to retain only the monopoly of transport and warehousing.[249] The company itself sold off its privilege in 1712 to a company from Saint-Malo.[250] Could the India Company even be said to exist any more? 'Our companies of the French East Indies [sic] whose dilapidation dishonours the king's standard and the nation,' wrote Anisson from London on 20 May 1713.[251] But moribund institutions were a long time a-dying. The company survived the ups and downs of Law's System, and was reconstituted in 1722–3, with a capital of tangible assets but without a sufficient allowance of liquid cash. The struggle, and the profits, continued until the 1760s. In 1769, a powerful campaign organized by the 'economists' put an end to the monopoly and opened up to French trade, which quickly took advantage of them, the road to China and the Indies.[252] In 1785 Calonne, or rather the circle that gravitated round him, refloated the Indies Company, which was in fact now operating in the shadow of the English Company; after a number of speculative scandals, it was eventually suppressed by the Revolution in 1790.[253]

Back to a threefold division

Capitalism has therefore to be located in relation both to the different sectors of the economy and to the hierarchy of trade of which it occupies the summit. And this brings us back to the threefold division I outlined at the very beginning of this work:[254] the base, consisting of 'material life' – many-sided, self-sufficient and routine-bound; at the next level, 'economic life', more clearly defined and, as described here, tending to merge with the competitive market economy; and lastly, at the third level, the activities of capitalism. It would be all be so simple if this working distinction were clearly visible in real life, with demarcation lines discernible with the naked eye. Real life is not of course so simple.

In particular, it is very difficult to draw a line indicating what to my mind is the crucial distinction between capitalism and the economy. The economy, in the sense in which I wish to use the word, was a world of transparence and regularity, in which everyone could be sure in advance, with the benefit of common experience, how the processes of exchange would operate. This was always the case on the town market-place, for the transactions necessary for everyday life: goods were exchanged for money or vice versa and the deal was resolved on the spot, the moment these things changed hands. It was also the case in retail shops. And it was the case too, even if the distance was greater, for any *regular* trade of which the origins, conditions, routes and market were fixed: grain from Sicily, wines and raisins from the Levant, salt (when there was no state intervention), oil from Apulia, rye, wood, tar from the Baltic, etc. Such trade links were innumerable and usually long-established; their itinerary, calendar and price differentials were known by everyone – and as a result regularly open to free competition. It is true that the picture is complicated if a certain commodity for one reason or another became interesting to the speculator: in that case, it would be hoarded in a warehouse, then redistributed, usually over long distances and in large quantities. Cereals from the Baltic for instance normally came into the category of the open market: the purchasing price in Danzig regularly followed the curve of the selling price in Amsterdam.[255] But once it had been stored in the Amsterdam warehouses, this cereal changed its nature: it was now a counter in a complicated game which only rich merchants could play. They would send it to a variety of destinations – to places where famine had sent the price up out of all proportion to the original purchasing price; or to places where it could be exchanged for a certain desired commodity.

It is true that there were, at national level, possibilities of small-scale speculation, micro-capitalism, but these were swallowed up in the overall economy. The capitalist game only concerned the unusual, the very special, or the very long distance connection – sometimes lasting months or even years.

This being so, can we put the market economy – the transparent economy, to use this word one last time, in one category; and capitalism, speculation, in another? Is this merely a matter of words? Or are we here at a concrete frontier of which those concerned were to some extent conscious? When the Elector of Saxony wished to present Luther with four *Kuxen*, mining shares bringing in 300 *Gulden*, Luther retorted:[256] '*Ich will kein Kuks haben! Es is Spielgeld und will nicht wuddeln dasselbig Geld.*' 'I want no shares! This is speculative money and I will not make this kind of money multiply.' A significant, perhaps over-significant reaction (both Luther's father and brother were small entrepreneurs in the Mansfeld copper-mines and thus on the wrong side of the capitalist barrier). But one finds the same reticence in J. P. Ricard, a comparatively dispassionate observer of life in Amsterdam, where he witnessed many forms of speculation: 'The spirit of commerce reigns so completely in Amsterdam', he writes, that one absolutely has to do business in some form or another.'[257] It was, surely, another world. For Johann Georg Busch, the author of a history of trade in Hamburg, the stock exchange complications in Amsterdam and certain other financial centres[258] 'are not matters for a reasonable man, but for an inveterate gambler'. Once more we find a line being drawn. Standing on the other side of the frontier, Émile Zola in 1891 puts the following words in the mouth of a businessman about to launch a new banking firm: 'With the lawful and mediocre remuneration for one's labour, the prudent equilibrium of every-day transactions, existence is an unrelieved desert, a swamp where all forces slumber and stagnate ... But speculation is the temptation of life itself, the eternal desire that forces one to struggle and live ... Without speculation, no one would do any business at all.'[259]

Here an awareness of a difference between two economic worlds, two ways of living and working is expressed without ambiguity. Zola was 'only a novelist'? But listen to the Abbé Galiani (1728–1787) writing a good century earlier and describing though in quite different language the same economic gulf and human dividing line: In his *Dialogues on the grain trade* (1770)[260] he challenges the physiocrats with the sacrilegious notion that the grain trade cannot provide the wealth of a country. Grain, he argues is not only the foodstuff 'which is the lowest in value in proportion to its weight and the space it occupies', and therefore expensive to transport; not only is it perishable, easily destroyed by rats and insects and difficult to keep; not only does it 'decide to come into the world in the middle of summer' and thus have to be handled commercially 'in the most contrary season', when the seas are rough and the roads impassable; but worst of all 'wheat grows everywhere. There is not a kingdom without it'. And no kingdom has a monopoly in it either. Compare it with oil and wine, products of warm climates: 'Trade in these is steady, constant and regular. Provence will always be able to sell its wines and oils to Normandy ... Every year they will be requested on one side and delivered by the other; that will never change ... The real treasures of France, among the fruits of the earth, are wines and oils. The whole of the North needs them and the North cannot produce them. So a trade becomes established, carves itself a channel, ceases to be a speculation and becomes routine.' But when it comes to grain, no regularity can be taken for granted; one never knows where the demand will come from, who will be able to meet it, or whether one will arrive too late when someone else has already delivered the goods. The element of risk is large. That is why 'small merchants of modest means' can profitably engage in the oil or wine trade; 'indeed it is more lucrative if carried out on a small scale. Economy and probity make it prosper. . . . But for [large-scale] trade in grain, the most powerful hands and the longest arms must be sought out from the whole body of traders.' Only these powerful men are well-informed. Only they can afford the risk and 'since the glimpse of risk makes the crowd shrink' they become 'monopolists', with 'profits in proportion to the risk'. Such is the situation in the *foreign* grain trade'. On the home market, as between the different provinces of France for instance, the irregularities of harvests from place to place also allow a degree of speculation, but without the same profit. 'It is abandoned to the hauliers, the millers and the bakers who speculate on a very small scale on their own account. So [whereas] the external trade ... in grain is too vast and so ... risky and difficult that it engenders monopoly by its very nature, internal trade between neighbouring places is on the contrary too small.' It passes through too many hands leaving each man with only a small profit.

So even grain, a commodity present all over Europe, can be fitted without difficulty into our three-fold schema: it was consumed on the spot, staying at the lowest level of material life; it was marketed in a regular way over short distances, from the usual granaries to the nearby town, which had 'the advantage over them of situation'; it was the object of a less regular and occasionally speculative trade between provinces; and finally, during the frequently repeated famine crises, it was a highly speculative commodity, and its transport over long distances was big business. With every change, one moves up a rank in the hierarchy of trade, as new economic agents and participants take the stage.

5

Society: 'A Set of Sets'

To INTRODUCE social dimensions to this debate means going back over all the problems raised, and more or less adequately resolved, in the foregoing chapters. And it means compounding them with all the difficulties and complexities implied by society itself.

With its diffuse and all-embracing reality, of which we are sometimes as little aware of as the air we breathe, society wraps us round, penetrates and directs our entire lives. 'Society is thinking through me', wrote the young Marx.[1] Is not the historian too often misled by appearances, when he thinks he is dealing, retrospectively, only with individuals, whose responsibility he can weigh at his leisure? His real task surely, is not only to rediscover 'man', a much misused term, but also to identify past social groups of various sizes, all of them related to each other. Lucien Febvre[2] used to regret that philosophers, by inventing the word *sociology*, had stolen the only title appropriate to the kind of history he dearly wished to see. The birth of sociology, with the work of Emile Durkeim (1896),[3] was undoubtedly a sort of Copernican or Galilean revolution, a change of paradigm for social science as a whole; and its consequences are still being felt today. At the time, Henri Berr hailed it as a return, after years of heavy-handed positivism, to 'general ideas'.[4] 'It was', he said, 'putting the philosophy back into history.' Nowadays, historians may be inclined to think that sociology is rather too fond of general ideas, and that what it lacks is precisely a sense of history. Economics and history have been successfully united, but historical sociology does not yet exist.[5] And the reasons for the gap are only too obvious.

In the first place, sociology, unlike economics which is in a way a *science*, has not completely succeeded in defining its subject. What is society? The question is no longer even asked since the death in 1965 of Georges Gurvitch – and his definitions were even then unlikely to satisfy the historian entirely. '*La société globale*', total or overall society, as he described it seemed to be a kind of general integument surrounding all social life, a skin as transparent and fragile as a bell-jar. For the historian, who is bound so closely to the concrete world, total society can only be a sum of living realities, *whether or not* these are related to each other: to him it is not a single container, but several containers – and their contents.

It is with this in mind and for want of a better term, that I have come to think of society as a 'set of sets', the sum of all the things that historians encounter in the various branches of our research. I am borrowing from mathematics a concept so convenient that mathematicians themselves distrust it; and I am perhaps using rather a grand word (in French the word for *set* is *ensemble*, which also means 'whole') to underline the obvious truth that *everything* under the sun is, and cannot escape being, social. But the point of a definition is to provide an approach to a problem, to lay down some guidelines for preliminary observation. If it makes that observation easier, both at the beginning and in later stages, if it helps to produce an acceptable classification of the material and to develop the logic of the argument, then the definition is useful and has justified itself. If we use the expression 'set of sets' or *'ensemble des ensembles'*, does this not usefully remind us that any given social reality we may observe in isolation is itself contained in some greater set; that as a collection of variables, it requires and implies the existence of other collections of variables outside itself? Jean-François Melon, secretary to John Law, was already saying in 1734: 'There is such an intimate connection between the different parts of Society, that one cannot strike one part without its having repercussions on the others.'[6] Which is much the same as saying today, 'the social process is an indivisible whole'[7] or 'the only possible history is general history',[8] to quote only one or two of a hundred similar remarks.[9]

For practical purposes of course, this totality has to be split up into smaller sets for convenience of observation. Otherwise, how could such a mass of material be handled? 'With his classifying hand,' writes J. A. Schumpeter,[7] 'the researcher *artificially* extracts the economic facts from the great [unitary] mass of society.' A different scholar might choose to concentrate on political or cultural aspects. When he called his only too brilliant study: *English Social History*, G. M. Trevelyan intended the title to mean 'the history of the people with the politics left out',[10] as if it were really possible to separate the state, a social reality of the first order, from other kinds of reality. But there is no historian, economist or sociologist who does not proceed to make distinctions of this kind, however artificial they may be in the first instance, whether Marx's twofold division (infrastructure and superstructure) or the threefold division on which I have based the greater part of the preceding argument. Such procedures are never more than explanatory devices; what matters is whether or not they make it possible to grasp important problems effectively.

Every social science moreover has proceeded in similar fashion to define and divide its territory; by so doing it is carving up reality, in order to be systematic perhaps, but also because it cannot be avoided: which of us is not in some sense specialized from birth, by capacity or inclination, to explore one sector of human knowledge rather than another? The two social sciences most general by nature – history and sociology – have divided their territory into many specialized fields: thus we have economic and political sociology, the sociology of labour, of knowledge, etc.; and political history, economic and social history, the history of art, ideas, science, technology and so on.

So it is perfectly normal to divide up society as a whole, as I intend to, into a certain number of intermediate 'sets', whose nature is quite familiar: economic aspects are an obvious choice; the social hierarchy or framework is another (I prefer to keep the word *society* as the collective noun denoting 'the set of sets'); so too are politics and culture – each of these sets being broken down into sub-sets, and so on. In this classification, total history (or rather would-be total history, for it is an unattainable ideal) implies the study of at least four 'systems', both in themselves and in their mutual relationships, interdependence and en-croachment on each other's ground; numerous correlations are possible, and the variables proper to each group should not be sacrificed *a priori* to the *intervari-ables* and *vice versa*.[11]

Ideally – but this is impossible – one would try to present the whole panorama on the same plane and in a single movement. In practice, I can only recommend that when making our divisions we try to keep an overall vision in mind: this is bound to loom up here and there in the argument and will always tend to reintroduce unity, warning against false assumptions that society is a simple matter, and against the use of such familiar formulae as 'an ordered society', 'a class society', 'a consumer society', without first thinking of the overall analysis such expressions imply. It will help us to be on guard against facile equations such as merchants = bourgeois; or merchants = capitalists; or aristocrats = landowners;[12] and against talking about 'the bourgeoisie' or 'the nobility' as if these words referred unequivocally to clearly-defined entities, as if the border-lines between categories or classes were unmistakable, whereas such frontiers really have 'the fluidity of water'.[13]

It is equally important not to imagine *a priori* that a single sector may achieve permanent superiority over another, or over all the others. I do not for instance believe in the permanent and unchallenged superiority of political history and the sacrosanct primacy of the state. Sometimes the state is well-nigh all-impor-tant, at other times it has little or no influence. Paul Adam in an as yet unpub-lished history of France, advances the view that my book on the Mediterranean brings out the overwhelming importance of the political role of Philip II. But is he not imposing his own vision on a complicated picture? Sectors, groups and sets are in fact endlessly interacting in a hierarchy that remains fluid, within the overall society which may bind them more or less closely together but which never gives them perfect freedom.

In Europe, where these things are easier to observe than anywhere else, Europe which was so much ahead of the rest of the world, a rapidly-developing economy often seems to have dominated other sectors after about the eleventh or twelfth century, and even more markedly after the sixteenth. It obliged the other sectors to define themselves in relation to itself and this growing primacy of economic factors was undoubtedly one of the sources of the precocious modernity of the continent. But it would be misleading to imagine that before these centuries of economic growth the economy hardly counted at all, or that it would have been impossible for anyone to write, as a French pamphleteer did in 1622[14] that 'every city, republic or kingdom maintains itself principally by grain, wine, flesh and wood'. It would also be misleading to think that confronted with the mounting strength of the economy, productive as it was of so many revolutionary changes, the other sectors and society as a whole did not continue to play their part – sometimes (rarely however) as accelerators of change; more often as barriers, forces of resistance or drags on change, surviving and exerting their influence for centuries on end. Every society is shot through with currents, bristling with obstacles, with obstinate relics of the past that block the way, with long-lasting structures whose permanence is their most revealing feature for the historian. Such *historical* structures are visible, detectable, and to some extent measurable: their very duration is a form of measurement.

Speaking a rather different language, François Fourquet in a polemical and stimulating little book,[15] explains these confrontations by a conflict between 'desire' and authority: on one hand is the individual, not so much guided by needs as charged with desires, as a moving mass is charged with electricity; on the other, the repressive structures of authority – any authority – which maintains order in the name of preserving the equilibrium and productivity of society. I agree with Marx that needs are one explanation, with Fourquet that desires are an equally broad explanation (and cannot desires in any case include needs?) and that the apparatus of authority, both political and, no less, economic, is yet another explanation. But these are not the only social constants – there are others.

It is within this complex of conflicting forces that economic expansion took place between the Middle Ages and the eighteenth century, bringing with it capitalism, whose progress was faster or slower depending on the country and could take many forms. And the obstacles, the resistance that capitalism encountered will figure prominently in the argument of the following pages.

Social hierarchies

Whether in the singular or the plural, the term *social hierarchy* is here used to denote the ordinary, everyday but essential content of the word *society*, which for the sake of convenience of exposition I have promoted to a higher status. I prefer to talk about hierarchies than about social strata, or categories or even classes; although every society of a certain size does have its strata, categories, perhaps castes[16] and classes, whether the latter are externalized or not, that is, consciously perceived or not, in terms of permanent class struggle. This is true of *all societies*.[17] For once I do not agree with Georges Gurvitch when he argues that class struggle requires as a *sine qua non* a clear consciousness of struggle

The King's Bench in the time of Henry VI: judges, clerks and (bottom) prisoners. Illustration of a fifteenth-century English manuscript, Inner Temple Library. (Photo by the Library.)

and opposition, consciousness which in his view is not found before the coming of industrial society.[18] There is ample evidence to the contrary. And Alain Touraine is undoubtedly right when he says that 'any society of which a proportion of production is kept back from consumption and accumulated' must harbour *'a class conflict'*.[19] In other words, every society.

But to return to the word I prefer, *hierarchy*, it can readily be applied, without too much difficulty, to the entire history of densely-populated societies: none of these societies has ever developed horizontally, on a plane of complete equality. They are, invariably, openly hierarchical. Hence the astonishment of the Portuguese explorers who, in 1446, came across certain tiny Berber tribes engaged at the time in selling black slaves and gold dust on the Atlantic coast of the Sahara, near the Cabo de Rescate and elsewhere: 'They had no King!'[20] However on closer acquaintance, they did form clans, and the clans had chiefs. The Dutch were equally surprised by the primitive peoples of Formosa in 1630: 'They have neither King nor sovereign. They are always at war, that is one village against another.'[21] But even a village is a grouping, an ordering of some kind. Even Utopian societies, imagined as the opposite of existing societies, are usually hierarchical. Even the gods of Olympus had their hierarchy. We may conclude that there is no society totally without framework or structure.

Societies of our own time, whatever their political system, are hardly any more egalitarian than those of the past. At least today, privilege is so fiercely contested that it has lost something of its former naive self-satisfaction. In the past on the contrary, in any ordered society, maintaining one's rank was a form of dignity, a kind of virtue. Ridicule and condemnation were reserved only for those who flaunted the symbols of a social rank to which they were not entitled. In the early years of the eighteenth century, the following proposal was seriously suggested as a remedy for the evils of confusion of rank and excessive luxury which dissipated savings:[22] that the king of France should confer upon princes, dukes, high-ranking persons and their wives a blue ribbon, 'such as the Commanders of the Order of Malta and St Lazarus wear'; other noblemen should wear a red ribbon; all officers, sergeants and soldiers should always wear uniform; and livery should be compulsory for domestic servants, including valets and butlers, 'with no brocade, gold or silver trimmings on hats'. Would this not be the ideal solution? It would both inhibit sumptuary extravagance, and 'reduce the humble to the impossibility of being confused with the great'.

Such confusion was normally prevented more simply by the distribution of wealth – luxury on one side, poverty on the other; and power – command on one side, obedience on the other. 'One section of humanity', says an Italian text, 'is ill-treated to death so that the other can stuff itself to bursting-point.'

The pluralism of societies

The hierarchical order is never simple. All societies are diversified pluralities. They are divided against themselves and such division is probably intrinsic to their nature.

Let us take an example: so-called 'feudal' society, the essential pluralism of which has had to be admitted and explained by those Marxist or quasi-Marxist historians and economists who have subjected it to exhaustive definition.[23] May I just say before going any further that I share the allergy of Marc Bloch and Lucien Febvre to the word *feudalism* which is so frequently used. This neologism[24] derived from Low Latin (*feodum* = fief) should be applied, they said and I agree, only to the fief and things pertaining to it, and to nothing else. It is no more logical to use this word to describe Europe between the eleventh and the fifteenth century than it is to use *capitalism* of the same society between the sixteenth and the twentieth. But let us put aside such scruples and allow for the sake of argument that 'feudal society', to use another common formula, can be applied to a broad period in European social history, that this term can serve as a convenient label for what could after all be called 'Europe A', the next period being called 'Europe B'. The shift from A to B would in any case have to be located during what certain distinguished historians[25] have called the true Renaissance, between the tenth and the thirteenth centuries.

The best description of 'feudal society' is still to my mind Georges Gurvitch's brief sketch[26] (rapid and authoritarian as it undoubtedly is) based on a careful reading of Marc Bloch's marvellous study[27] but developing its conclusions in a very individual way. Shaped by centuries of sedimentation, destruction and germination, 'feudal' society was in fact a combination of at least five 'societies', five different hierarchies, existing side by side. The most ancient and fundamental of these, now dislocated, was seigniorial society, its origins lost in the mists of time, which bound together local landlord and peasants. Less ancient, but with historical origins in the Roman Empire and spiritual roots plunging even further back, was the theocratic society constructed by the Roman Church with fortitude and tenacity, for it had not only to conquer but also to keep and thus constantly control its faithful. A large share of the surpluses of early Europe went into this huge and far-flung enterprise: were cathedrals, churches, monasteries, church revenues an investment or a waste of capital? Thirdly, a younger society, pushing its way between the others and seeking a foothold, was taking shape around the territorial state. The latter had foundered with the last Carolingians, but the wreck as so often was not total. The fourth sub-sector was feudalism in the strict sense, a tenacious superstructure which insinuated itself into the upper reaches of society and the gaps vacated by the failure of the state: it united feudal lords in a long hierarchical chain and sought to control and manœuvre all society through this hierarchy. But the church was not entirely imprisoned within the net; the state would one day tear the mesh apart; and as for the peasant, he often lived on the margin of this agitation in high places. Finally, the fifth and last system, to us the most important of all, consisted of the towns. They appeared, or reappeared, from the tenth or eleventh century, as states apart, societies apart, civilizations apart, economies apart. They were daughters of a distant past – Rome often lived again in them. But they were also daughters of a present which helped them to blossom: they were new creations – the product in the first place of a colossal division of labour (between town and countryside), of consistently favourable economic circumstances, of the revival of trade and of a re-emergent money supply. Through money, a major multiplier, a sort of electric current was directed towards the West from Byzantium and Islam, across the great stretches of the Mediterranean. When the sea later went over to Christendom, this meant both revival and upheaval for early Europe.

This was not one society then but several, coexisting, resting on each other to a greater or lesser degree; not one system but several; not one hierarchy but several; not one order but several; not one mode of production but several, not one culture but several cultures, forms of consciousness, languages, ways of life. We must think of everything in the plural.

Georges Gurvitch, who did not fail to see this, is nevertheless perhaps too ready to argue that the five societies in question, making up feudal society as a whole, were antinomic, foreign to each other; that to leave one of them was to be cast out into darkness and despair. In fact these societies managed perfectly well to live together, mingled their elements, and called for a degree of cohesion. The city-states drew their citizens from the estates and manors in the surrounding countryside, annexing not only the peasants but also the nobles or rather the groups of nobles who had been born in the country but who came to live in town where they built up formidable clans with indissoluble links.[28] At the very heart of the Church, the Papacy was already in contact with the bankers of Siena in the thirteenth century, asking them to collect its taxes from the faithful. The English Crown under Edward I appealed to the moneylenders of Lucca and later Florence. Noblemen were from the early days selling their grain and livestock: merchants were obliged to buy them. As for the towns, we know that they were the prototypes of modern times, that when the modern state and national economy were born, city states served as the model; and that they remained – to the detriment of other societies – the scene *par excellence* of capital accumulation and wealth.

That said, any society, or sub-society, or social group – beginning with the family – has its own hierarchy: the Church does and so does the state; the merchant cities had their patriciates, and feudal society was intrinsically nothing but a hierarchy; in the seigniorial regime, the seigneur is at his castle and the peasant at the gate. If we could define a coherent *'société globale'*, would this not simply mean that one hierarchy had succeeded in asserting itself over society as a whole, without necessarily destroying the others?

All the same, among all the different societies that go to make up this *société globale*, one or more will tend to prevail, preparing the way for overall change – a change which always takes shape very slowly, and then becomes established – until such time as a new transformation challenges the former dominant pattern or patterns. This plurality is an essential factor both of movement and of resistance to movement. Any evolutionary schema, even Marx's, becomes more intelligible when viewed in this light.

Vertical elevation: the privileged few

However if one takes a vertical section through society as a whole, one is struck not by these sub-categories but by the fundamental inequality of both wealth and power dividing the mass from top to bottom. All observation reveals this deep-seated inequality which is a constant law of societies, a structural law that admits of no exception, as sociologists recognize. But how is such a law to be explained?

Conspicuous at the top of the pyramid is a handful of privileged people. Everything invariably falls into the lap of this tiny group: power, wealth, a large share of surplus production. This is the group that governs, administers, directs, takes decisions, sees to the continuity of investment and thus of production. To this group flow all goods, services, currencies. Below it ranges the multitude of economic agents, workers of every rank, the mass of the governed. And below everyone else, stretches that huge social scrapheap, the world of the unemployed.

Although it would not be true to say that one is dealt a hand for good, new deals are rare and bring little advancement. People struggle with all their might to climb the social ladder, but it often takes several generations to move up, and even after arriving it is an effort to keep one's footing. This social strife has been waged as long as there have been living societies with their stairways to honour and narrow doors to power. So we are already forewarned that nothing really counts – state, nobility, bourgeoisie, capitalism, culture – unless it has captured the commanding heights of society. In this rarefied air, all government, admin-istration, justice and indoctrination is carried on, all wealth and even thought is accumulated: it is at this altitude that brilliant cultures are constructed and reconstructed.

What is so surprising is that the privileged should *always* be so few. Since social advancement does exist, and since this tiny elite has always depended on the surplus provided by the labour of the non-privileged, whenever that surplus increased, the tiny elite at the top ought to have expanded too. But it never has – even in the twentieth century. The famous slogan of the Popular Front in 1936 was that France was governed by '200 families' – discreet but all-powerful. As a slogan, this was easy to ridicule. But a hundred years earlier, a man who was certainly no revolutionary, Adolphe Thiers, could write quite dispassionately: 'in a state like France, out of twelve million families ... we know that there are ... two or three hundred at most who can be called opulent'.[29] And a hundred years before that, Jean-François Melon, who was just as committed to the social order as Thiers,[30] had explained that 'the luxury of a Nation is confined to about a thousand men as against twenty million others, who are', he adds 'just as contented as the former, as long as a sound Police enables them to enjoy the fruits of their labour in peace'.

Are our present-day democracies so very different? We have at least one book, C. Wright Mills's *The Power Elite*,[31] which argues that all important decisions affecting the whole of the United States today are in the hands of an astonishingly small group of people. There too, the national elite is made up of a few ruling families, and these dynasties have changed little over the years. *Mutandis mutandis*, this is much what Claudio Tolemei, a Sienese writer was saying in a letter to Gabriele Cesano on 21 January 1531:[32]

> In every republic, even a great one, in every State, even a popular one, it is unusual for more than fifty citizens to rise to the posts of command. Neither in ancient Athens nor in Rome, neither in Venice nor in Lucca, are [or were] any citizens called to govern the State, *benché si reggano queste terre sotto nome di repubblica*, although these States govern themselves under the name of republic.

Is there not in short, whatever the society and whatever the period, an insidious law giving power to the few, an irritating law it must be said, since the reasons for it are not obvious. And yet this is a stubborn fact, taunting us at every turn. We cannot argue with it: all the evidence agrees.

In Venice, before the plague of 1575, the *Nobili* (men, women and children) numbered at most 10,000 persons, the highest figure in Venetian history: about 5% of the total population (of Venice plus the *Dogado*) which hovered around 200,000.[33] And from even this number must be deducted the impoverished nobles, who were often reduced to a sort of official beggary and who since they were exiled to the modest quarter of San Barnaba, were ironically referred to as the *Barnabotti*. Even after this deduction, the remaining patricians were by no means all rich merchants. After the plague of 1630, there were so few of these that only about 14 or 15 people capable of occupying the highest state positions survived.[34] In the archetypal capitalist city of Genoa, the nobility which con-trolled the Republic (by rank but also by wealth) consisted of 700 men at most (not counting their families) out of perhaps 80,000 inhabitants.[35]

And the percentages in Venice and Genoa are in fact among the highest. In Nuremberg,[36] power was by the fourteenth century in the hands of a restricted aristocracy (43 patrician families *by law*) or 150 to 200 people out of a total population of 20,000 in the town itself, plus another 20,000 in the district. These families had the exclusive right to appoint representatives to the Inner Council which in turn chose the Seven Elders (who in fact decided everything, governed, administered, rendered judgment and were answerable to nobody) from among the small number of ancient, historic and often wealthy families who dated back to the thirteenth century. This explains why the same names crop up over and

Pomp and circumstance attend the wife of the Lord Mayor of London. Sketch from the album of George Holzschuer who visited England between 1621 and 1625. (Photothèque Armand Colin.)

again in the annals of Nuremberg. The city survived, miraculously intact, the endless troubles in Germany in the fourteenth and fifteenth centuries. In 1525, the *Herren Älteren* made up their minds to rally to the Reformation. And that was that. In London in 1603, at the end of Elizabeth I's reign, business was entirely run by fewer than 200 wealthy merchants.[37] In the Netherlands in the seventeenth century, the ruling aristocracy, that of the Regents of the towns and the provincial office-holders, accounted for 10,000 out of a total population of two million.[38] In Lyons, an exceptional city both because of its liberties and its wealth, the ironical remonstrances of the clergy to the city councillors (8 November 1558) are unequivocal: they are addressed to 'You, *Messieurs les Conseillers* [who in fact held all power in the city], you who are almost all merchants ... There are barely thirty persons in the city who can hope to become councillors ...'[39] There was a similar oligarchy in sixteenth-century Antwerp, the 'Senators' or as the English called them the 'Lords' of the town.[40] In Seville in 1702, according to a French merchant, 'the consulate consists of four or five individuals who deal with commerce as it suits their own particular ends' and who alone grew rich, at the expense of other merchants. A memorandum penned in 1704 does not hesitate to condemn the 'fearful iniquities of the Consulate of Seville'.[41] In Le Mans in 1749, the manufacture and marketing of the fine woollens on which the town's prosperity depended were in the hands of eight or nine merchants, 'Messrs Cureau, Véron, des Granges, Montarou, Garnier, Nouet,

Fréart and Bodier'.[42] Dunkerque at the end of the *ancien régime*, prospering from its status as a free port, was a town of over 20,000 inhabitants dominated by a moneyed caste with no desire to be absorbed by a nobility which was, in any case, not present in the town itself. What point was there in chasing titles, when one lived in a free port where every citizen had the great advantage of being exempt from *taille, gabelle* and stamp tax? The tightly-knit Dunkerque bourgeoisie had closed ranks around a few 'veritable dynasties: the Faulconniers, Trescas, Coffyns, Lhermites and Spyns'.[43] The same was true of Marseilles. According to A. Chabaud,[44] 'the aldermen came, for a period of 150 years [before 1789], from a handful of families, ten at most, whose alliances, intermarriages and godparent ties before long made them a single family'. The businessmen of Marseilles in the eighteenth century, Charles Carrière tells us[45] amounted to 'not even 1% [of the population]; ... a tiny minority, but one that controlled all the wealth and

The patricians of Nuremberg dancing in the assembly room of the Town Hall. It is not exactly over-crowded. (Stadtbibliothek Nürnberg, photo A. Schmidt.)

dominated the activity of the city just as it monopolized its administration'. In Florence, the *benefiziati* numbered 3000 or more in the fifteenth century, but only 800 to 1000 in about 1760, so that the Habsburg-Lorraines, who had become grand-dukes of Tuscany in 1737 when the Medici family died out, were obliged to create new nobles.[46] In mid-eighteenth century, an ordinary little town like Piacenza (30,000 inhabitants) had 250 to 300 noble families, that is counting men, women and children, 1250 to 1500 privileged persons (about 4 or 5% of the total). But this comparatively high percentage includes 'nobles' of every category and means. And since the urban nobility was the only wealth-owning class in this rural region, one has to add to the population of Piacenza the 170,000 peasants of the surrounding countryside. The nobility as a proportion of this total falls to below 1%.[47]

This is by no means untypical. An estimate covering the whole of Lombardy in the eighteenth century puts the nobility as a percentage of the total population at about 1%, and this privileged minority possessed about half of all landed property.[48] In a smaller sample in the Cremona region in about 1626, of 1,600,000 *pertiche* of land, '18 feudal families alone owned 833,000', over half the total.[49]

Calculations made on a national scale tell a similar story. In estimates *very broadly* borne out by historical research, Gregory King in 1688[50] reckoned that there were about 36,000 families with an income exceeding £200 in England, at a time when the total English population was about 1,400,000 families (my round figures): something like 2.6%. And even to achieve this figure, one has to lump together lords, baronets, squires, gentlemen, royal 'officers' and wealthy merchants as well as over 10,000 men of the law on whom fortune was now smiling. It is also possible that the threshold chosen – £200 – yields a rather large elite in which considerable inequalities are concealed, since the highest incomes in the kingdom, those of the great landowners, are estimated as £2800 *on average*. The figures given by Massie[51] in 1760, on the accession of George III, suggest some redistribution of wealth, the merchant class having gained at the expense of the landed class. But if we want to find the really rich and powerful people in the kingdom, politically and socially, the experts tell us that they belonged to barely 150 families, 600 to 700 individuals.[52] In France in the same period, the old-established nobility numbered some 80,000 persons and the nobility as a whole 300,000, 'or 1 to 1.5% of the French population'.[53] And how are we to identify the bourgeoisie? It is easier to say what it was not than what it was, and figures are hard to come by. Perhaps 8.4% of the total, suggests Pierre Léon, but how many of these were '*grands bourgeois*'? The only convincing percentage is that of the Breton nobility (2%) but Brittany with its 40,000 nobles was well-known to be above the national average.[54]

To find a higher percentage established with any confidence, we have to go to Poland[55] where the nobility represented 8 to 10% of the population, 'the highest percentage in Europe'. But not all Polish aristocrats were magnates; many were indeed very poor and some were mere vagabonds, 'whose standard

Polish nobles and merchants discussing business at Gdansk (Danzig). Illustration from the Atlas by J. B. Haman, seventeenth century. (Photo Alexandra Skarżynska.)

of living hardly differed from that of the peasants'. And the rich merchant class was very small. Here as elsewhere then, the privileged stratum that really counted represented a minute proportion of the total population.

Even smaller proportionately, no doubt, were certain other minorities: Peter the Great's nobles, the mandarins in China, the *daimyos* in Japan, the rajahs and *omerahs* in India under the Great Mogul,[56] the handful of military adventurers who ruled and terrorized the primitive populations of the Regency of Algiers, or the scattering of landowners – not always rich – who established themselves against all the odds in the vastness of Spanish America. The importance of wealthy merchants in these countries varied enormously, but they were never numerous. We may conclude with Voltaire that in a well-organized country, the smaller number 'makes the greater number work for it, feed it and submit to its government'.

Is this really a conclusion though? We are once more stating a fact without entirely understanding it. To talk about the consequences of this 'concentration', visible as they are in the economic sphere and elsewhere, is to extend and relocate the problem. We are still no nearer explaining the concentration itself. And yet historians have brought all their efforts to bear on these upper reaches of society, 'choosing the easiest option' as Charles Carrière puts it.[57] But this is by no means sure after all, since the problem of the privileged minority is one to which there

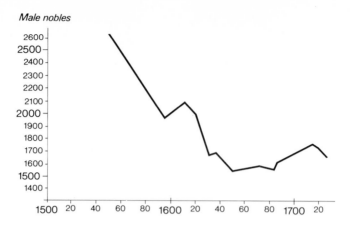

Male nobles

28 NOBLEMEN IN VENICE
Male nobles
A typical example: any aristocracy with highly restricted entry declines in number. New families were insufficient to fill the gap. The slight improvement after 1680 may correspond to better living conditions (?) From a table in J. Georgelin, *Venise au siècle Lumières*, 1978, p. 653, based on figures from James Davis, *The Decline of the Venetian Nobility as a Ruling Class*, 1962, p. 137.

are no easy answers. How did it maintain its position, even during revolutions? How did it compel the respect of the great masses fermenting below it? Why, in the struggle which the state sometimes engaged with the privileged, were the latter never entirely or permanently defeated? Perhaps after all Max Weber was not mistaken when, refusing to be mesmerized by the 'deep structures' of society, he insisted on the importance of the 'political qualifications of the dominant or rising classes'.[58] Is it not the nature of its elite (whether formed by blood ties or levels of wealth), which primarily characterizes an ancient society?

Social mobility

The rise of new classes, the ousting of elites, social mobility – these, the problems of *the bourgeoisie* (or *bourgeoisies*) and the so-called middle classes, classic though they may be, are no easier to resolve than the foregoing ones. The reconstitution and reproduction of elites is generally accomplished by shifts so slow and so slight that they cannot be measured or even properly observed, let alone analysed with any confidence. Lawrence Stone[59] thinks that improving economic conditions stimulated social advancement, which seems quite plausible. Hermann Kellenbenz[60] thinking even more generally along the same lines, notes that in trading cities on the coast where economic life was livelier than elsewhere, social mobility developed more freely than it did in inland towns. Here we meet once more the almost classic dichotomy between the sea-coasts and the continental interior. Social differences were less pronounced in Lübeck, Bremen or Hamburg than in reactionary Nuremberg – and the same fluidity is found in Marseilles or even Bordeaux. By the same token, economic decline is said to have closed the doors to promotion, reinforcing the status quo. Peter Laslett[61] has suggested that downward mobility was probably more widespread than upward mobility in preindustrial England – and he is not alone in this view in the wider context.[62] So if one could draw up a chart showing all arrivals in and departures from the top layer of society, would modernity be identified with the concentration of power and wealth, rather than with its extension? Reasonably detailed figures from Florence, Venice and Genoa show that the privileged families regularly declined in number and some died out altogether. In the County of Oldenbourg, of the 200 noble families recorded at the end of the Middle Ages, only 30 were left by about 1600.[63] As a result of the biological slide tending to reduce the small group at the top, inheritances and power were concentrated in a few hands, and critical thresholds were sometimes reached (as in Florence in 1737, in Venice in 1686, 1716 and 1775).[64] The doors had to be opened at all costs and fresh blood brought in; titles were granted for money, *'per denaro'* as the Venetians said.[65] Such crises, by precipitating the process of haemorrhage, accelerated the necessary transfusions, as if society were able to rouse itself to bind its wounds and make good its losses.

In certain circumstances, it is easier to see what was going on – when Peter the Great remodelled Russian society for instance; or even better, during the crisis caused in England by the Wars of the Roses. When the slaughter came to an end, Henry VII (1485-1509) and his son Henry VIII (1509-1547) found themselves facing only the remnants of the old aristocracy which had so stoutly resisted the Crown in the past. It had been devoured by the civil war: in 1485, only 29 of the former 50 lords were left. The age of the barons was over. The great families opposed to the Tudors – the de la Poles, the Staffords, the Courtenays – had all vanished in the turmoil. It was the minor gentry who stepped forward to take their place, along with bourgeois purchasers of land and even people of modest or obscure origin who had become royal favourites: they filled the social vacuum, in a major shift of English 'political geology' as it has been called. The phenomenon was not new in itself – but its scale was unprecedented. By about 1540, a new aristocracy had become established, and the newcomers had already achieved respectability.

Even before the death of Henry VIII, and subsequently during the eventful and threatened reigns of Edward VI (1547-1553) and Mary Tudor (1553-1558) the new aristocracy was already flexing its muscles and was soon standing up to the government. The Reformation, the sale of Church and Crown property and the increased activity of Parliament, all favoured it. During the apparently dazzling reign of Elizabeth (1558-1603) the aristocracy was consolidating and extending its advantages and privileges. Was it a sign of the times that the Crown which had until 1540 been building magnificent palaces, a sign of vitality, stopped doing so after this date? The reason cannot be the general economic situation, since the building went on – but now it was for the aristocracy. As the century drew to a close, country mansions of almost princely splendour went up all over England – Longleat, Wollaton, Worksop, Burghley House, Holdenby.[66] The rise of this nobility to power went hand in hand with the England's first age of maritime might, the rise in incomes from agriculture and the wave of expansion which John U. Nef has justifiably called the first industrial revolution. The aristocracy no longer greatly needed the Crown to further or consolidate its fortunes. And when in 1640 the Crown sought to re-establish its authority, it was too late. The aristocracy and the upper bourgeoisie – which was now following close on its heels – survived the difficult years of the civil war and came into their own with the Restoration of Charles II (1660–1685). 'After the ... imbroglio which took place in 1688–1689 ... the English Revolution [which had begun in 1640 or even by some reckonings earlier] had run its course.'[67] The English ruling class had been re-created.

The English example, which can be seen as a magnifying glass, is clear enough, not that that has prevented historians from arguing about it.[68] Elsewhere too, all over Europe, the bourgeois were being ennobled or marrying their daughters into the ranks of the aristocracy. But to follow all the movements of this process, further research is still necessary: if we are prepared to extend to the past Pierre Bourdieu's radical sociological theories, such research might usefully be guided by the assumption that the essential task of any society is to *reproduce* itself at its topmost level.[69] A further assumption, of which I approve, along with such historians as Dupâquier, Chaussinand-Nogaret, Jean Nicolas and no doubt others too, is that social change was itself often the determining factor: as one hierarchy or established order became worn out and eventually crumbled, new individuals came to the fore and nine times out of ten reproduced or closely imitated the former state of affairs. In Savoy, during the reign of Charles-Emmanuel I (1580–1630) amid calamities without number – plague, penury, bad harvests, wars – Jean Nicolas tells us, 'profiting from troubled times ... a new aristocracy, emerging from business, legal and administrative circles, was tending to supplant the old feudal nobility'.[70] The *nouveaux riches*, the newly-privileged were sliding into the seats of the old, while the impact that had shattered certain former privileges and made the new wave possible was inflicting serious damage, at lower levels, upon the living conditions of the peasantry. For there is always a price to pay, and someone has to pay it.

How can one detect change?

All this may seem very simple – too simple no doubt. And change was slow, much slower than we usually think. A social movement of this kind is hardly quantifiable of course, but some idea of the order of magnitude may be grasped if we make a rough estimate, in relation to the established nobility or patriciate, of the numbers of serious aspirants to social advancement, that is the wealthiest section of the bourgeoisie. Historians tend to make a rather schematic distinction

Burghley House at Stamford Baron in Lincolnshire, on the River Welland, built by William Cecil between 1577 and 1585. This is one of the few remaining examples (restored of course) of the many residences he built. (Photo British Travel Association.)

between the upper, middle and petty bourgeoisie. For once we must take them
at their word. We shall, that is, consider only the upper section, probably rather
less than one-third of the whole bourgeoisie. If we say for instance that the
French bourgeoisie in the eighteenth century represented about 8% of the whole
population of the country, the upper layer can hardly have accounted for more
than 2% – in other words it was roughly equivalent in size to the nobility. This
equivalence is merely a supposition – but take the case of Venice: here the
cittadini constituted a clearly defined upper bourgeoisie, often rich or at any rate
well-off, providing recruits for the government bureaux of the Signoria (since
minor offices were bought) even, after 1586, occupying positions as elevated as
those of Venetian consuls abroad, and also active in trade and industry: these
cittadini were numerically equivalent to the aristocracy.[71] And similar parity
also emerges from the well-documented and quantified case of the upper middle
class in Nuremberg where in about 1500, the patrician and rich merchant groups
were roughly the same size.[72]

Clearly social mobility took place essentially between the patriciate (or
nobility) and the rich merchant class immediately below it. In what proportions?
This is hard to estimate except in a few individual cases. Since the dominant
stratum only declined over the long term and therefore remained much the same
for long stretches, social advance can hardly have done more than fill gaps.
According to Hermann Kellenbenz,[73] this was what happened in sixteenth-
century Lübeck. The patrician class, that is the wealthy merchants, consisting of
about 150 or 200 families, lost about a fifth of its members in each generation;
they were replaced by a roughly equivalent number of newcomers. If we take a
generation to be twenty years and the number of families for the sake of
simplicity to be 200, two new families at most – in a city of 25,000 inhabitants
– can have crossed the fateful threshold every year to enter the ranks of the upper
class, joining a group a hundred times greater. Since this group had its own
hierarchy as well (12 families effectively held power at the top) how could the
newcomer possibly change the rules of the milieu he was entering? Isolated in
the establishment, he would quickly bow to its laws: tradition and custom would
soon claim him; he would change his way of life, perhaps his manner of dress,
and if necessary he would change his ideology.

That said, since real life is complex, it could also happen that a ruling class
itself altered its ideology or mentality, that it accepted or appeared to accept the
views of the newcomers or rather those which the socio-economic context
suggested; that it renounced, or appeared to renounce its former character. But
such abdication, when it occurred, was never simple nor complete, nor necessarily disastrous to the ruling class. For the economic wave which brought the
newcomers to power never left the establishment untouched. Alfons Dopsch[74]
has drawn attention to the precocious satires of the young Lucidarius, who
pokes fun at the lords of the late thirteenth century: they could talk about
nothing else at court he says but the price of grain, cheese, eggs, sucking pigs,

their cows' milk yield, or the size of the harvest. Can this nobility actually have become *embourgeoisé* by the thirteenth century? Later on, the aristocracy was to travel even further down the road of enterprise. In England, aristocracy and gentry were by the late sixteenth century enthusiastically participating in the new joint stock companies born of overseas trade.[75] Once the movement had begun, it was not to stop. In the eighteenth century, the nobilities of Hungary, Denmark, Poland and Italy all 'turned merchant'.[76] During the reign of Louis XVI, the French nobility was seized with a passion for business. According to one historian, it was the aristocracy which speculated the most and took the real risks; the bourgeoisie looked pusillanimous by comparison, timorously clinging to gilt-edged investments.[77] One should not perhaps be too surprised, for if the French nobility was only just beginning to dabble in private enterprise, it had been speculating boldly in another area of big business for some time, the royal finances and 'rentier' credit.

In short if the 'bourgeois mentality' was here and there gaining ground in high society, as has often been remarked, it was not so much because new recruits were joining its ranks (although there were more of them than usual towards the end of the eighteenth century) but rather because of the spirit of the times, and the beginning of the industrial revolution in France. This was the time when the higher nobility, 'the *noblesse d'épee* and the nobility of office-holders in royal and princely houses', was participating 'in all kinds of large lucrative enterprises, whether Atlantic trade, colonial plantations or mining projects'.[77] This business-loving aristocracy would from now on be found at all the growth points of the new economy: the mines of Anzin and Carmaux, the steelworks of Niederbronn and Le Creusot, the big capitalist firms which were proliferating at this time and promoting seaborne trade. So it is hardly surprising if this nobility which still commanded great wealth changed its outlook, underwent a conversion, and became *embourgeoisé*, if it seemed to renounce its past, moved towards liberalism, sought to curb royal power, and worked for a bloodless and painless revolution on the lines of the English Revolution of 1688. It was in for some unpleasant surprises of course. But we are concerned with the years before 1789, when it was the economy which was being transformed, and in the process transforming the structures and mentalities of French society, as had happened much earlier in England or Holland, and earlier still in the trading cities of Italy.

The synchronization of social change in Europe

No one will be surprised that the economy played some part in social mobility. What is more surprising is that despite the obvious time-lags between one country and another, social developments, like the familiar economic developments they coincided with or expressed, had a tendency to be synchronized throughout Europe.

The headiest days of the sixteenth century, for example, from as early as 1470 until say 1580, were, to my mind, an age of accelerated social promotion throughout Europe, almost like a spontaneous burst of biological growth. A bourgeoisie emerging from the background of trade was climbing by its own efforts to the highest place in contemporary society. The vigour of the economy created great trading fortunes, sometimes almost overnight, and the doorway to social advancement stood wide open. During the last years of the century by contrast, with the reversal of the secular trend, or at any rate a prolonged intercyclical depression, the societies of continental Europe put up the barriers once more. In France, Spain and Italy, one has the impression that after a period of substantial renewal of the establishment, with a series of newly-created titles as compensation for losses, the door to social advancement was in effect slammed shut, the ladder pulled up. This also seems to have happened in Burgundy;[78] in Rome;[78] and in Spain, where the *regidores* of the towns had rushed to fill gaps in the aristocracy; the same was true of Naples, where 'they have manufactured several dukes and princes whom we could have done without'.[79]

The process seems to have been general then; and it was twofold – in the course of this long century, a section of the nobility disappeared and was immediately replaced, but once the gaps had been made good, the door swung to behind the newcomers. So one is perhaps entitled to be sceptical when Pierre Goubert explains the obvious decline of the French nobility in terms of the Ligue and its fierce conflicts, arguing that 'the influence of economic conditions, particularly in the short term ... [must be] discounted'.[80] I would not of course rule the Ligue and its disasters out of the reckoning, though these were in a sense incorporated into the downturn at the end of the century and indeed are one of the forms the downturn took. It is perfectly normal that similar circumstances should take different forms in different European societies. George Huppert's analysis, to which I shall be referring later, is specific to France, but does nonetheless relate to the economic rise of a new class springing directly from fortunes made in trade. And the process took place all over Europe. Throughout the sixteenth century, the social and economic circumstances were the same, and they called the tune. The situation was similar in the eighteenth century, when social mobility was once more widespread in Europe. In Spain, satirists mocked the new noblemen who were so numerous that hardly a stream, village or field in the country did not have a noble title attached to it.[81]

Henri Pirenne's theory

Henri Pirenne's theory concerning the periodization of the social history of capitalism,[82] which is still worth some consideration, bypasses conjunctural explanations, suggesting rather a recurrent social pattern which can be confirmed in the context of individual or rather family behaviour.

The great Belgian historian, having studied pre-industrial capitalism, which he detected even in pre-Renaissance Europe, pointed out that merchant families do not appear to have survived long as such: two or three generations at most. After that, they abandoned trade, if they had prospered, for less risky and more prestigious operations, buying up office or more often feudal estates – or both. There was no such thing, Pirenne concludes, as a capitalist dynasty: one period had its capitalists and those of the next period would not be the same. Having reaped their benefits when the time was ripe, these businessmen made haste to forsake trade, if possible joining the ranks of the nobility – not out of social vanity alone, but because the spirit which had secured the success of their fathers would render them incapable of adapting to the kind of enterprise demanded by the new age.

This view has been widely accepted, since there is much evidence to support it. Hermann Kellenbenz[83] after studying the towns of northern Germany, found that merchant families appeared to have exhausted their creative energy after two or three generations and withdrew to a quiet life as rentiers, leaving their counting-houses for the country estates which helped them to acquire noble titles. The picture is accurate, particularly for the period in question, the sixteenth and seventeenth centuries. I would quarrel only with the term 'creative energy' and the entrepreneurial image it suggests.

Creative energy or not, these transfers and withdrawals took place in every period. In fifteenth-century Barcelona, the members of ancient merchant dynasties would sooner or later 'move into the *estament* of *honrats*', although a taste for rentierdom was by no means a dominant feature of the Barcelona milieu.[84] Even more impressive is the comparatively swift rate of extinction of 'all the big names of the sixteenth century' in southern Germany: 'the Fuggers, Welsers, Höchstetters, Paumgartners, Manlichs, Haugs and Hewarts of Augsburg; the Tuchers and Imhoffs of Nuremberg – and so many others'.[85] J. Hexter,[86] discussing what he calls 'the myth of the middle class in Tudor England' has pointed out that every historian considers the rise of the merchant bourgeoisie into the ranks of the gentry or nobility as a typical phenomenon of 'his' period (i.e. the one he studies) whereas it is a phenomenon of all periods, as Hexter has no difficulty in proving in the case of England. In France, 'did not Colbert, and a hundred years later Necker, both complain about the constant flight of moneyed men to the quiet life of the landed proprietor and gentleman?'[87] In eighteenth-century Rouen, merchant families also disappeared, either because they simply died out, or because they abandoned trade for the magistracy, like the Le Gendre family – locally reputed to be the richest merchants in Europe – or the Planteroses.[88] The same was true in Amsterdam: 'If one were to count up the best firms [in the city],' said an observer in 1778, 'one would find very few whose ancestors had been doing business at the time of the Revolution [1566–1648]. The old firms no longer exist; those which do most business today are newly-established firms founded only recently; thus it is that trade is constantly being transferred from one house to another, for it is naturally attracted to the most active and thrifty

Saying goodbye in the courtyard of a Dutch country house. Painting by de Hooch (circa 1675). (Photo Giraudon.)

of those who engage in it.'[89] These are a few examples among many. But how satisfying is the explanation?

If these regular eclipses of trading firms are attributable in some way to the wearing-out of the spirit of enterprise, must we conclude that the economic circumstances of the time are irrelevant? Further, to see this phenomenon as the crucial social aspect of capitalism – which would represent only a brief moment in the life of a family – is to confuse the merchant with the capitalist. If every great merchant was a capitalist, the opposite was not necessarily true. A capitalist might be an investor, a manufacturer, a financier, a banker, or a tax-farmer or manager of public funds. So it was possible to advance by stages *within* capitalism: a merchant could become a banker, a banker become a financier, and both become capitalist rentiers – thus surviving *as capitalists* for several generations. The Genoese merchant families who became bankers and financiers before the sixteenth century, survived the following centuries unscathed. What happened, in Amsterdam to those families who, according to our 1778 witness, were no longer in trade? Did they move into another branch of capitalist activity, which seems quite probable, given the Dutch context of the eighteenth century? And even when capital of this kind did leave trade for land or office, if we could trace its progress over a long period through society, we would not necessarily find that it had moved outside the capitalist orbit; there were movements back into commodity trading, banking, investment in real estate or moveable goods, even industry and mining, and sometimes into strange ventures, if only through marriages and dowries, which 'promoted the circulation of capital'.[90] A hundred years after the colossal bankruptcy of the house of Bardi, some of its direct descendants appear – surprisingly – among the partners of the Medici bank.[91]

A further problem is that in the various *stages of capitalism* studied by Henri Pirenne, what counts (even today) is not so much the individual family as the group to which it belongs, which supports and indeed nourishes it. If we consider not the Fuggers but all the big contemporary merchant firms of Augsburg as a group, not the fortunes of the Thélusson or Necker families but those of Protestant bankers in general, it is clear that one group was indeed periodically replaced by another, but that the duration of each episode was far superior to the two- or three-generation norm suggested by Pirenne; and above all, that the reasons for the eclipse and replacement are indeed at this level explained by economic change.

The only clear evidence (but it is quite telling) comes from Guy Chaussinand-Nogaret's study of the financiers of Languedoc,[92] men who not only combined the roles of entrepreneur, banker, ship-fitter, wholesale merchant and manufacturer, but were also financiers and financial office-holders. All or almost all of them had begun in trade, where they had enjoyed prudent and successful careers. And all were members of a tightly-interlocking local network of business and family connections. If we observe their history in one of the dioceses (the administrative unit) of Languedoc, we find that three groups reigned in succession, differing in their composition, their business links and their family connections. During transition periods from one to another, there was a break followed by a revival and new recruitment. The first group lasted from about 1520 to 1600, but did not survive the downturn of the late sixteenth century; the second, which took over from 1600 to 1670, lasted until the turning-point years of 1660–1680; and the third survived from 1670 to 1789, rather more than a hundred years. This lends broad support to Henri Pirenne's intuitive theory – but it is clear that these were not individual but collective movements, and that they were spread over the long term.

Advancing by stages within the world of capital was in the end only possible if society offered a choice: between shop, counting-house, royal office, land – or some other outlet. And society could simply say no and slam the door, as can be seen from the unusual but significant case of the Jewish capitalists and merchants. In the West, they had no choice as between money, land and office. We do not have to believe that the Jewish banking-house of Norsa actually lasted for six hundred years[93] but it probably did hold the world record for longevity. The merchant-bankers of India were similarly placed: their caste condemned them exclusively to handling money. And access to the nobility for the rich merchants of Osaka in Japan was extremely limited. As a consequence, they became even more wedded to their profession. The merchant dynasties of Cairo by contrast, as described in André Raymond's latest book,[94] were even shorter-lived than those observed by Pirenne: Muslim society may have devoured its capitalists young. Leipzig in the early years of its fortune as a trading city in the sixteenth and seventeenth centuries seems to have done the same: its rich men did not necessarily remain so all their lives, and their heirs literally decamped to the peace and tranquillity of country manors. But perhaps in this case the explanation is to be sought in the jerky rhythms of an economy in its infancy, rather than in society?

In France: gentry or noblesse de robe?

Any society viewed as a whole normally derives its complexity from its longevity. It may of course vary and certain of its sectors may be completely transformed, but it will obstinately maintain its major options and constructions, developing in an identifiable pattern. So if one seeks to understand it, one must realize that it embodies at one and the same time everything that it has been, is and will be in future; it is an accumulation over the long term of permanent features and successive inflections. A good example of extreme complexity – French high society in the sixteenth and seventeenth centuries – provides us with a perfectly valid test case in this respect. This is a unique example, illustrating a particular pattern of development, but it can serve in its way as evidence about other European societies. It also has the advantage of being well-documented in a voluminous literature, now vigorously reinterpreted by George Huppert in a book originally entitled *The French Gentry*.[95]

The word *gentry* is here used to describe that upper section of the French bourgeoisie, enriched by trade but having forsaken shop and business one or two generations back; having, that is, shed the stigma of being 'in trade', and sustained in its wealth and comfort by farming huge country estates, by continued financial dealings and by the purchase of royal office which had gradually become part of the heritage of these prudent, thrifty and conservative families. The term *gentry* will certainly cause a shudder among specialists in this period of French history. But this provocative word can stimulate a useful debate: it suggests the problem with which one must come to grips at the outset: the definition of a class, or group, or category making its way slowly towards nobility and traditional social success; a discreet and complicated class having nothing in common with the luxurious court aristocracy, or with the shabby gentility of the rural nobility – a class which was in short moving towards its own concept of nobility and a way of life peculiar to itself. This class or category requires a special word or expression in the historian's vocabulary, one which will immediately identify it among the range of social forms to be found between François I and the early reign of Louis XIV. If 'gentry' will not do, neither will '*haute bourgeoisie*'.

The word *bourgeoisie* has shared the fortunes of the word *bourgeois*: both were probably in use as early as the twelfth century. A bourgeois was a privileged citizen of a town. But depending on the region or the town in France, the word did not become really widespread until the late sixteenth or even the late seventeenth century. It was in the eighteenth century that it gained greatest currency, and the Revolution launched it for good. Where we would expect to find the word 'bourgeois' (and it is occasionally found) the usual expression was '*honorable homme*' a term which can serve as a kind of test: it unmistakably denotes the first rung on the ladder of social advancement, the difficult first step up from the 'condition of the earth', i.e. the peasantry, to that of the so-called liberal professions. These professions were primarily to do with the law – advocates, *procureurs* (prosecutors), notaries. Many of those who practised such professions had in fact received their training from an older colleague not through the university, and of those who had attended lectures many had studied only for form's sake. Among the professions were also numbered doctors and barber-surgeons – and of the latter, not many were 'surgeons of Saint Como or the long robe', i.e. graduates of medical school.[96] To these can be added the apothecaries who often, like the others, transmitted their skills 'within the family'.[97] But in the ranks of the *honorables hommes*, although not practising a liberal profession, merchants had their legitimate place ('merchants' preferably but not exclusively in the sense of wholesale merchants, *négociants*). In Châteaudun for instance there was, in appearance at least, a difference between the bourgeois merchant (the *négociant*) and the artisan merchant (the shopkeeper).[98]

But a profession alone was not sufficient to create *honorabilité*: the privileged person had to own a certain amount of wealth, to live in dignity and comparative prosperity, to have bought a few estates near the town and – a vital condition – to have a house with 'a gable on the street'. Even today the phrase *pignon sur rue* is evocative of a solid establishment. (Littré explains that the gable-end 'as in churches today, used to be the façade of the house', showing that the owner was a leading householder).

Such, in every little town of France, even the most unassuming in retrospect, is the handful of *honorables hommes* the historian invariably finds, above the mass of artisans, small shopkeepers, peasants and sons of toil. It is possible by consulting the notarial archives to reconstruct the worldly goods of the people on this the first rung of the privileged hierarchy. They are quite distinct of course from the group I have described as the gentry. To attain or even approximate to this, another rung had to be climbed before one could be numbered among the *nobles hommes*. It must be made plain that a *noble homme* was *not* a nobleman (*gentilhomme*); this was a title created out of both social vanity and social reality.

Even if the *noble homme* owned seigneuries, even if he 'lived nobly', that is without labouring or selling merchandise, he did not belong to the 'true nobility', but to an 'honorary, improper and imperfect nobility scornfully described as "town nobility", *Noblesse de ville*, which was in fact closer to the bourgeoisie'.[99] But if a *noble homme* succeeded in having himself referred to in a notarial document as an *écuyer* (squire) there was every chance that he would be recognized as belonging to the nobility.

But belonging was more of a *social* than a juridical phenomenon, that is it arose spontaneously out of current practice. Let me emphasize the ordinary conditions of entry to the nobility at this time. After 1520, such moves became easier and more frequent, visible and widespread. I am not referring to the granting of letters of nobility by the king, which was very rare, nor to the purchase of ennobling offices, nor to the exercise of aldermanic functions which conferred a kind of nobility (known disrespectfully as *noblesse de cloche*). The threshold of nobility was crossed most frequently by a judicial inquiry, after taking statements from witnesses who could testify that the applicant 'lived nobly', i.e. that he lived off his income without labouring, and that his parents and grand-parents had also 'lived nobly' in the sight of all. These ennoblements were only possible to the extent that the growing wealth of the privileged enabled them to live in 'gentlemanly style', that the rising classes enjoyed the sympathy of the judges who were often their kinsmen; and lastly that in the sixteenth century as we have seen, the aristocracy had not closed ranks. Peter Laslett's observation[100] that the demarcation line between noble and commoner was as clear as that between Christian and Infidel was certainly not true of France in this period. Rather there was a sort of no-man's-land where crossings could be made.

An extra complication was that this new nobility did not always feel the desire to merge into the ranks of the traditional nobility. If George Huppert is right – which seems more than likely – the *nobles hommes* of high rank bore no resemblance to Molière's *Bourgeois gentilhomme*. The first performance of this play took place in 1670, rather late in the day; a long time after the heady years of the sixteenth century; and the caricature was drawn to amuse the court aristocracy. Monsieur Jourdain is not a pure invention of course, but he corresponds to a very middle-class bourgeois, and it would be wrong to think of our new or would-be nobles of the sixteenth century pursuing noble rank with single-minded passion 'as if it were the elixir of life'.[101] That social vanity informed their behaviour there can be little doubt – but it did not drive them to share the tastes or prejudices of the *noblesse d'épee*, the nobility of the sword; they showed no enthusiasm for prowess in arms, hunting or duels; on the contrary, they expressed some scorn for the way of life of people whom they considered lacking in wisdom and culture, a scorn which they did not hesitate to put into writing.

Indeed the entire bourgeoisie, upper and middle, was of the same mind on this point. A late example is Oudard Coquault[102] a simple bourgeois of Reims, but quite a rich merchant. He writes in his journal on 31 August 1650:

> This is the state, life and condition of those gentlemen who say they are of high birth; and a great many of the nobility live hardly any better and are good only for berating and devouring the peasant in their village. There is no comparison: the honourable bourgeois of the towns and the good merchants are more noble than them all; for they are more gentlemanly, live better lives and set better examples, their family and household are better conducted; each according to his power does not cause anyone to murmur, pays every man who works for him, and above all would never commit an act of cowardice; and the majority of these little sword-bearers do the opposite. If there is ever a question of comparison, they consider themselves everything and think that the bourgeois should look at them through the same eyes as the peasant ... No man of honour has any regard for them. This is the present state of the world, and one should not expect to find virtue among the nobility.

These *grands bourgeois* who became nobles in fact carried on living, as before, sensible balanced lives, divided between their splendid town houses and their chateaux or country residences. Their pride and joy was their humanist culture; they took their greatest delight in their libraries, where the better part of their leisure was spent. The cultural frontier which marked them out and effectively identified them was their passion for Greek and Latin, law, ancient and national history. They were behind the founding of countless lay schools, in towns and even in villages. The only feature they had in common with the authentic nobility was their rejection of trade or labour, their taste for idleness or rather leisure, which was for them synonymous with reading and learned discussions with their peers. This way of life required a degree of affluence, and in general these nobles were more than comfortably off, possessing solid fortunes drawn from three chief sources: land, methodically farmed; usury, practised primarily at the expense of peasants and gentlemen; and lastly offices in the judiciary or in the royal finances, which had become hereditary and transmittable even before the establishment of the *paulette* (annual subscription) in 1604. But most of their fortunes were inherited rather than constructed: they consolidated and extended them, it is true, for money begat money and made social break-throughs and triumphs possible. But the launching of the dynasty was invariably the same: the gentry had sprung from trade, something it sought to hide from prying eyes and kept as dark as possible.

Not that anyone was taken in: L'Estoile's *Journal*[103] tells us, and indeed it was common knowledge at the time, that Nicolas de Neufville, seigneur of Villeroy (1542–1617), secretary of state, a man who held the reins of government practically all his life, fighting 'his battles with "paper parchment and pen"',[104] was the grandson of a fishmonger who had bought three seigneuries, then several offices, and had inherited by marriage the seigneurie of Villeroi near Corbeil. George Huppert quotes many similar examples. Obviously no one was deceived,

Pierre Séguier (1588–1672) was a member of the new 'nobility' which built up a solid fortune out of land, office and usury (see chapter 5). He himself had an outstanding political career as an unconditional servant of the crown. Chancellor by 1630, pitiless judge at the trial of Fouquet, he remained a man of culture – choosing to have himself painted in front of his magnificent library, which he bequeathed to the abbey of Saint-Germain-des-Prés. (Collection Viollet.)

but once more we should remember that in the sixteenth century, society did not put obstacles in the way of social mobility, but rather collaborated with it. And it is only in such a climate that one can comprehend the formation of a whole *class* of new nobles, merging awkwardly or not at all with the established nobility and deriving support from its own political power, its own network of connections within the group itself: an abnormal phenomenon this and one which was indeed not to last.

For in the seventeenth century, everything changed. Until then, the pseudo-nobility had experienced dramatic and testing times: the Reformation and the Wars of Religion – but it had lived through them, neither as Protestant or Leaguer, but as 'Gallican' and *politique*, steering a middle way where one was liable to be hit by missiles from both sides but where freedom of manoeuvre was preserved. After 1600, things were different – the social atmosphere, the economy, politics, culture. It was no longer possible to attain noble rank by means of a few witnesses testifying before a sympathetic judge: one had to produce genealogical tables and submit to searching investigations – and even rank already acquired was not safe from scrutiny. The social mobility which had brought so many recruits to the French gentry was now less a matter of course, and above all less widespread. Was this because the economy was less thriving than in the previous century? The monarchy, restored to strength by Henri IV, Richelieu and Louis XIV, became oppressive, showing it was determined to exact obedience from its officers, starting with the members of the *parlements*. Moreover the king had revived the court aristocracy, allowing it to thrive and prosper occupying the limelight around the Sun King – a 'player king' as one of his intimates described him[105] – but the theatre in which he appeared drew into a tight and visible circle all the means and possibilities of exercising power; it was more than greasepaint and footlights. This court nobility closed ranks against the *'noblesse de robe'*. The latter had to face not only this obstacle but also the monarchy which simultaneously conferred upon it both its powers and its limitations. The would-be nobles were in an equivocal situation both politically and socially. And as the last straw, the Counter-Reformation was unleashed in part against this class, against its ideas and its intellectual positions. Our 'gentry' foreshadowed the Enlightenment: it was informed by a certain rationalism, and on the point of inventing a 'scientific' form of history.[106] But everything started to go wrong for it: it was the target singled out for attack by the Jesuits. So its role was ambiguous and complex during the explosion of Jansenism and the Fronde. In the early months of 1649, until the Peace of Rueil (11 March) the *parlementaires* were masters of Paris, 'without daring to do anything with their victory'.[107]

It was in the course of these difficulties and this series of upheavals that the gentry gradually turned into what would be known as the *noblesse de robe*: that second-class nobility always contested by the first, and never merging fully with it. From now on, there would be a distinct hierarchy between the two nobilities, which the monarchy played off against each other the better to rule. It is surely no accident that the expression *noblesse de robe* appears only at the beginning of the seventeenth century – in 1603 at earliest according to recent research.[108] The linguistic evidence should not be dismissed lightly. One phase in the career of the gentry had come to an end. More clearly defined now, though less secure and certainly less arrogant than in the preceding century, it nevertheless continued to exert great pressure on the future destiny of France. To maintain its position, it used all the available hierarchies: the hierarchy of land (seigniorial), the hierarchy of money, the Church hierarchy, the hierarchy of state office, local, provincial or national (*bailliages*, *présidiaux*, *parlements*, the king's councils) as well as certain cultural hierarchies, which would pay off in the long run.

Progress was complicated, long-drawn-out and rather plodding: success came through perseverance. For George Huppert, the *noblesse de robe*, from its sixteenth-century origins to the Revolution, was central to France's destiny, 'creating its culture, managing its wealth and inventing both Nation and Enlightenment – in short inventing France'. So many famous names come to mind that it is tempting to agree. But I would make one important reservation: this fertile class, the expression of a certain French civilization, had been carried at arm's length by the rest of France which had underwritten its comfort and stability, even, dare one say, its intelligence. The *noblesse de robe* itself decided how to handle this material and cultural capital – whether for the good of the country is another question.

There was probably no country in Europe without some form or another of this jostling at the top of the hierarchy between two groups – one that had achieved greatness and the other seeking to achieve it. But George Huppert's book has the advantage of illuminating the peculiarities of the French example, pointing out the originality of the *noblesse de robe* both in its genesis and in its political role. By so doing, he usefully reminds us of the unique character of every social development. Causes are very similar everywhere, but solutions may vary.

From city to state: luxury and ostentation

There really are hardly any rules then about social mobility, or attitudes to the prestige conferred by money, birth, rank or power. From this point of view, societies do not have the same chronology, the same hierarchies or the same underlying mentalities.

In Europe, there was all the same a visible distinction between two broad categories: urban societies on one hand, that is the societies of the merchant cities of Italy, Holland and even Germany, with their precocious wealth; and the more extended societies of the territorial states, slowly emerging (not always completely) from a medieval past, and sometimes bearing the marks of their origins down to modern times. It is barely a century since Proudhon wrote: 'in the economic organism as in the real body politic, in the administration of justice and in education, feudalism is still stifling us'.[109]

That there were marked differences between these two worlds has been pointed out many times. One could produce a hundred versions, ancient and modern, of the remark made in a French memorandum of 1702: 'In monarchical States, the merchants cannot attain the same degree of consideration as in Republican States, where it is usually the men of business who rule.'[110] This will hardly surprise anyone, so let us move on from this obvious point and consider rather the behaviour of elites depending on whether they inhabited a city long accustomed to money and trade, or a large territorial state where the court (as in England and France) set the tone for the whole of society. 'The city [i.e. Paris] is said to ape the court.'[111] In short a city ruled by merchants will live very differently from a city ruled by a prince, as we are clearly informed by a Spanish *arbitrista* (that is a legal consultant, usually given to moralizing) Luis Ortiz, a contemporary of Philip II. The year was 1558 and Spain was in a state of anxiety. Philip II was absent from his kingdom, held up in the Netherlands by the pressures of war and international politics. In Valladolid, which was still for a short time to be the capital of Spain, luxury, ostentation, furs, silks and costly perfumes were the rule, despite the gravity of the hour and the high cost of living. And yet, our Spaniard reports, 'such luxury is not to be found in Florence, or Genoa, in the Netherlands, or even in neighbouring Portugal: '*En Portugal, ningun viste seda*', in Portugal no one wears silk.[112] But then Lisbon was a merchant city and set the tone for all Portugal.

In the Italian city-states which had been taken over early by the merchants (Milan in 1229, Florence in 1289, Venice in 1297 at latest), money was an effective and discreet cement of the social order, 'the strongest glue' as the Parisian printers used to say in the eighteenth century.[113] The patriciate did not need to dazzle and fascinate its subjects in order to rule – it simply controlled the purse-strings and that was enough. Not that luxury was unknown to the rulers, but they were discreet not to say secretive about it. In Venice, the nobleman wore a long black gown which was not even a sign of rank, since as Cesare Vecellio explains in the commentaries on his collection of '*habiti antichi et moderni di diverse parte del mundo*' (late sixteenth century), the gown was also worn by the '*cittadini, dottori, mercanti et altri*'. Young nobles, he adds, like to wear silken garments of delicate colours under their gowns, but they cover these bright fabrics up '*per una modestia propria di quella Repubblica*'. So the lack of ostentatiousness in dress of the Venetian patriciate was not involuntary. Similarly, the wearing of masks, which was not confined to Carnival and public holidays, was a way of losing oneself in the crowd, preserving one's anonymity and enjoying oneself without being conspicuous. Venetian ladies wore masks when they went to coffee-houses – public places forbidden in principle to persons of rank. 'What a convenient thing is a mask,' wrote Goldoni: 'under the mask, every man is equal and the principal magistrates can daily ... discover for themselves all the little things that concern the people ... Behind the mask, the doge himself may often be taking a walk.' In Venice, luxury was confined to public appearances, which were sometimes extravagant, or to strictly private life. In Genoa, the *nobili* dressed rather severely. Feasts were held discreetly in country houses or urban palaces, not on the streets or in public squares. I know that the luxury of carriages was introduced to seventeenth-century Florence – something unthinkable in Venice of course and impossible too in the narrow streets of Genoa – but the Florentine Republic had died with the return of Alexander de Medici in 1530, and the creation of the Grand Duchy of Tuscany in 1569. And yet even in this period, life in Florence seemed simple, almost bourgeois to a visiting Spaniard. What made Amsterdam the last *polis* of Europe was, among other things, the deliberate modesty of its wealthy citizens, which struck even Venetian visitors. Who could pick out the Grand Pensionary of Holland from any other bourgeois he might meet in an Amsterdam street?[114]

To move from Amsterdam or one of the long-established city-states of Italy to the capital of a modern state or a princely court, is to move into a completely different atmosphere. Here modesty and discretion were never the order of the day. The nobility of the front rank allowed itself to be dazzled by the magnificence of princes and wished to dazzle in its turn. It was obliged to parade and display itself. To shine at court meant standing out from the common run of mortals, to demonstrate in almost ritual fashion that one was of another race, and to keep others at a distance. Unlike the privilege conferred by money, which was self-evident and could be held in the hand, the privilege conferred by birth or rank was only of value when it was appreciated by other people. In eighteenth-century Poland, Prince Radziwill, who was capable of raising an army single-handed and equipping it with artillery (which he did in 1750), one day chose to distribute generous quantities of wine in his little town of Niewicz, 'with apparent indifference to the amount that was spilled and lost in the stream'; it was, says Witold Kula, a way of impressing observers (wine was a costly import to Poland), 'to make them think he had unlimited resources and to win their acquiescence to his will ... This wastage was therefore a rational act within a given social structure.'[115] Similar ostentation was to be found in Naples: in the time of Tommaso Campanella, the inspired revolutionary of *Città del sole* (1602): it used to be said of Fabrizio Carafa, prince della Roccella that he spent his money '*alla napoletana*', like a Neapolitan, '*cioè in vanità*' ('that is on vanities'). While their subjects were literally dying of hunger, the lords of Naples were spending fortunes on 'dogs, horses, clowns, cloth of gold *e puttane che è peggio*' ('or, what is worse, on whores').[116] Such spendthrifts (who might have 100,000 crowns a year, while their subjects were lucky to have three crowns to rub together) were certainly indulging themselves, but they were also under some obligation to provide a show. They were playing the role expected of them, one that the people were ready to admire as much as to envy, or later to hate. Affording a spectacle was, I must repeat, a way of ruling, a necessity. These

Neapolitan nobles were obliged to dance attendance at the court of the Spanish viceroy, winning his favour even if it meant ruining themselves in the process and returning penniless to their estates. And they would by then have acquired a taste for living in the capital city – one of the largest in Europe and inevitably an extravagant place. In 1547, the Bisignano family built their great palace of Chiaia; abandoning their Calabrian residences, they lived there like the other great nobles, holding court to a throng of artists, courtiers and men of letters, all maintained by the master of the house.[117]

Rational and 'profitable' as this public extravagance might be, it could often reach demented not to say psychotic proportions. Fénelon reports that 'Richelieu did not leave one door or window pane in the Sorbonne that did not bear his coat of arms'.[118] And in the little village of Richelieu which bears his name, 'where the paternal manor house stood, and which can still be seen today, between Tours and Loudun', the cardinal built a model town which remained half-empty.[119] This is strongly reminiscent of the princely fantasies of Vespasiano Gonzaga (†1591) of the family of the dukes of Mantua, who sought desperately to become an independent prince, and for want of a better way built the beautiful little town of Sabbioneta,[120] with its luxurious palace, its gallery of antique treasures, its *casino*, theatre (still a rarity in the sixteenth century), its church built specially to accommodate choirs and instrumental concerts, its modern fortifications – in short all the trappings of a capital city, whereas this little place near the River Po had no economic or administrative role and hardly any military importance – a fortress had once been built there. Vespasiano Gonzaga lived in Sabbioneta like a real prince with his little court, but after his death the town was abandoned and forgotten. It stands today like a deserted stage set, in the middle of the fields.

In short then, there were two ways of living and facing the world: display or discretion. Wherever a society based on money was slow appearing, ostentatious luxury, an old-fashioned policy, was forced upon the ruling class, since it could not rely too much on the silent support of money. Ostentation could of course creep in anywhere: it was never entirely absent wherever men had the time and the inclination to keep comparing themselves with others, to watch like hawks for the detail, the way of dressing or eating, of behaviour or speech that would give away respective social positions. And even merchant cities did not entirely lock their gates against display. However when they opened them a little too wide to it, it was a sign of disarray, of the approach of social or economic difficulties. Venice was too blinded by her wealth to appreciate her real situation after 1550; her decline had already begun. And luxury became more open, more visible and more varied in the city than ever before. Sumptuary laws multiplied: as usual they indicated but failed to prevent lavish spending: magnificent weddings and baptisms, ladies decked in pearls they said were false or wearing on their gowns '*zuboni et altre veste da homo de seda*'. A number of threats were directed at the 'tailors, embroiderers and designers' who were encouraging these

Masked women in Venice. Painting by Pietro Longhi (1702–1785). (Roger Viollet.)

evil ways. 'Weddings in rich families were probably a sort of public festivity ...
In the memoirs of the time, one reads of a constant procession of feasts,
tournaments, balls, descriptions of wedding costumes ...', evidence that the
Signoria was not seriously pursuing the matter. And the move from private to
public luxury is a point to note.[121]

It is tempting to say that the reverse was happening in England; but things
were more complicated. The seventeenth century was an age when luxury
glittered everywhere. There was the court and the extravagance of the nobility.
When Henry Berkeley, Lord Lieutenant of Gloucestershire, 'goes to London, he
takes 150 servants with him'.[122] In the eighteenth century, it is true, and especially
during the long reign of George III (1760–1820) the rich and powerful families of
England preferred luxury in the form of comfort to display. Simon Vorontsov,
Catherine II's ambassador to London,[123] who was used to the pomp and circum-

stance of the court of Saint Petersburg, relished the freedom of the English court, 'where one lives as one pleases and where there is no formality and etiquette in one's dealings'. But such remarks do not necessarily give a clear picture of the English social order. On close inspection this turns out to be complicated and diverse. The English nobility or rather the peerage, having on the whole reached the pinnacle of the social hierarchy since the Reformation, was of recent origin. But for a number of reasons, including self-interest, it gave itself the airs of an ancient landed aristocracy. A great English family had to have a great estate, and in the centre of the estate the symbol of success was a stately home, often of princely dimensions. This was an aristocracy 'both plutocratic and feudal'. As a feudal group, it was virtually obliged to do things on the grand scale, somewhat theatrically. When the new lords of the manor arrived in Abingdon in 1766, 'they offered a meal to several hundred gentlemen, farmers and local residents. A peal of bells was rung.' There was a horseback procession, preceded by fanfares, and fireworks at night.[124] There was nothing bourgeois about this display – display which was undoubtedly socially necessary if only to establish the indispensable local rule of the aristocracy. But such extravagance did not eliminate the taste for, or practice of business. Already in Elizabeth's reign it was the peerage, the highest in the realm, which was most readily investing in long-distance trade.[125]

A different picture emerged from Holland, where the Regents of the towns (who would have been known in France as *'nobles de cloche'*) reached the top of the hierarchy. They formed a bourgeois aristocracy.

In France, the picture is, as in England, rather complicated. The capital city, dominated by the court, developed rather differently from the big merchant cities which were just becoming aware of their growing strength and originality. Rich merchants in Toulouse, Lyons or Bordeaux made little display of their luxury, keeping it for the domestic interiors of their elegant town houses and even more for their 'country residences, pleasure houses scattered around the town at a radius of a day's ride'.[126] In Paris on the contrary, the plutocrats of the eighteenth century were bent on imitating and outdoing the luxury around them and copied the way of life of the highest aristocracy.

Revolutions and class struggles

The mass of society beneath this level was enclosed in the net of the established order. If the masses became too restive, the mesh was reinforced or tightened, or new ways of stretching it were devised. The state was there to preserve inequality, the cornerstone of the social order. Culture and its spokesmen were generally on hand to preach resignation to one's lot, obedience and good behaviour and the obligation to render unto to Caesar that which was Caesar's. The desirable solution was for the 'organic' mass of society to evolve peacefully, at its own pace, within limits that did not disturb the overall balance. There was no prohibition on moving from one low rung in the hierarchy to the low rung

England in the sixteenth century: the luxury and distractions of princes in a Renaissance court: Elizabeth and Leicester dancing. (Photo National Portrait Gallery, London.)

immediately above. Social mobility did not operate only at upper levels: it could mean the move from peasant to merchant-farmer and village leader; from village leader to local notable, to the 'purchasers of land rights, farmers in the English sense ... budding members of the bourgeoisie';[127] it could also mean the rise of the petty bourgeois to office and rentierdom. In Venice,[128] 'a man whose name did not figure on the registers of a *Scuola* (brotherhood) was regarded as the lowest of the low'. But there was nothing to stop him or one of his children from gaining entry to an *Arte* or guild, and thus attaining the bottom rung of the ladder.

All these little dramas of social climbing, the battles over *'el ser quien soy'*, about being who I am, as a character says in a Spanish picaresque novel of

1624,[129] can be seen as signs of a certain class consciousness. And in any case, the innumerable revolts[130] against the established order bear this out. Yves-Marie Bercé has found evidence of five hundred insurrections or would-be insurrections among the peasants of Aquitaine alone, between 1590 and 1715. Records relating to a hundred or so German towns from 1301 to 1550, reveal 200 clashes with authority, some accompanied by bloodshed. In Lyons, of the 357 years between 1173 and 1530, 126 were marked by disturbances (rather more than one year in three). We may call these clashes variously revolts, riots, tensions, class conflicts, incidents or disturbances – though some of them were so powerful and violent that only the word *revolution* really does justice to them. On a European scale, during the five centuries covered by this book, there were tens of thousands of incidents – not all of them yet classified properly and some still lying hidden in the archives. The research so far undertaken does however make it possible to draw some conclusions – with some confidence in the case of peasant revolts, but with much greater risk of error in the case of workers' risings, which were essentially an urban phenomenon.

A great deal of work has been done on peasant revolts in France, following Boris Porchnev's revolutionary book.[131] But it is obvious that France was not alone in this respect, even if the attention it has attracted from historians makes the French case exemplary. From the material so far assembled at any rate, an unmistakable picture emerges: the peasant community was in perpetual conflict with its oppressors: the state, the landlord, external circumstances, hard times, armed troops and anything that threatened or even impeded the village community which was the condition of its liberty. And in peasant eyes, all these foes were combined. When in 1530, a local nobleman sent his pigs to root in the common woodland, a little village in the Neapolitan county of Nolise rose up in defence of its grazing rights with the cry *'Viva il popolo et mora il signore'* ('Long live the people and death to the master!').[132] Hence the uninterrupted series of incidents revealing the traditional mentality and special conditions of peasant life, right down to the nineteenth century. If, as Ingomar Bog has remarked, one is looking for an illustration of 'the long term' with its repetitions, its revivals and monotonous patterns, the history of the peasants provides any amount of perfect examples.[133]

A first reading of this massive literature leaves one with the impression that all this agitation, while never dying down, rarely achieved anything. To rebel was 'to spit in the sky'[134]: the *jacquerie* of 1358 in the Ile-de-France; the English Peasants' Revolt of 1381; the *Bauernkrieg* of 1525; the salt-tax rebellion by the communes of the Guyenne in 1548; the violent Bolotnikov rising in Russia at the beginning of the seventeenth century; the Dosza insurrection in Hungary in 1614; the great peasant war which shook the kingdom of Naples in 1647 – all these furious outbursts regularly failed. So too did the minor rebellions which unwearingly relayed each other. The established order could not tolerate peasant disorder which, in view of the predominance of agriculture, might undermine the very foundations of society and the economy. State, nobles, bourgeois property-owners, even the Church and certainly the towns were almost constantly in league against the peasant. Flames were nonetheless smouldering under the ashes.

The failures were not however as complete as they appeared. The peasant was always rudely brought to heel it is true, but more than once progress was made as a result of rebellion. The 'Jacques' of 1358 did after all secure the liberty of the peasantry in the Paris region. The desertion, then repopulation, of this key region cannot entirely explain the process whereby this liberty was won, recaptured and maintained. Was the *Bauernkrieg* of 1525 a total failure? Not necessarily. The peasant rebels between Elbe and Rhine did not, like their brothers beyond the Elbe, become new serfs: they preserved their liberties and ancient rights. The Guyenne rising was crushed in 1548[135] – but the hated salt-tax was abolished. Through the *gabelle*, the Crown had been forcing the village community to open to the outside economy. It has been argued that the vast revolution in the countryside during the autumn and winter of 1789 also failed in a way: who got hold of the *biens nationaux* in the end? But the abolition of feudal privileges was by no means an insignificant gain.

We have even less information about workers' disturbances, particularly since the evidence is so dispersed, given the congenital instability of employment and the periodic collapse of 'industrial' activity. The working community was forever being regrouped and moved on, driven to new centres of employment, sometimes to new trades, and this robbed workers' protests of the solidarity born of stability which alone promised success. The early development of fustians in Lyons for instance had been very rapid, imitating the looms of the Milanese and Piedmont industry – employing up to 2000 masters and men. Then came a slump, and before long a collapse, at a time moreover when the cost of living was high. 'The workers of this trade, since they earn little, are no longer able to live in the town; some ... having removed to Forez and Beaujolais are working there,' but in such poor conditions that their output 'has lost its reputation'.[136] The fustian industry had in fact moved elsewhere, to new centres in Marseilles and Flanders. 'The decline of this manufacture,' concludes the 1698 memorandum I have been quoting, 'is the greater loss to Lyons since some of its workers are still to be seen here, all of them beggars and almost useless, a burden to the public purse.' If there had been a protest movement among the fustian weavers of Lyons (which we do not know) it would surely have collapsed of itself.

Another weakness was that labour concentration was imperfect, insofar as the workforce was generally split up into small units, even inside an industrial town; the journeyman was often itinerant (the *compagnon* system) or else he divided his time between town and country, being both peasant and wage-earner. As for the urban working community, it was everywhere divided against itself, partly imprisoned within the straitjacket of the guild system and the narrow and exclusive privilege of the masters. Free working existed quite widely, but this was far from possessing any coherence: at the top were the comparatively privileged 'wage-paying artisans' who worked for a master but in turn paid varying numbers of journeymen and domestics – acting in fact as subcontractors; below them came those who were of similar condition but employed only members of their own families; then came the great mass of wage-earners and, below them again, the unskilled day-labourers – porters, navvies, carriers, odd-job men, who were paid by the day if they were lucky and by the job if not.

In the circumstances it is hardly surprising that the history of workers' movements and protests should read like a succession of short and usually unconnected episodes, rarely forming a series. This is a history of isolated outbursts. But to conclude, as people often do, that class consciousness did not exist, is probably a mistake, to judge by the few episodes of which we do have details. The truth was that the entire world of labour was caught in a vice between low wages and the threat of incurable unemployment. It could only break out of this vice by violence, but it was in fact as powerless as workers are today in periods of high unemployment. Violence, anger and bitterness erupted, but for every success – or even semi-success, like the exceptional case of the paper-makers on the eve of the French Revolution[137] – there were a hundred failures. The city walls were not to be brought down so easily.

Workers' revolts: some examples

The first printing press was set up in Lyons in 1473.[138] By 1539, just before the first big printing strike (though not the first signs of agitation) there were about 100 presses in the town, which indicates a total workforce of about a thousand – apprentices, journeymen (compositors, pressmen, proof-readers) and master-printers – mostly from other provinces of France or from Germany, Italy or the Swiss Cantons, all newcomers therefore to the city. Most print-shops were small: a master-printer usually owned two presses; those who had done well might have as many as six. The equipment was always expensive to buy; and one had to have enough working capital to pay for wages, paper and type. However (and the workers themselves did not realize this) the master-printers did not really represent capital. They were in turn in the hands of the merchants, the 'publishers' who might be men of substance, some of them indeed sitting on the town governing body, the *Consulat*. Needless to say, the authorities backed the 'publishers', and the master-printers whether they liked it or not, had to curry favour with these powerful men on whom they depended. The only way they could make a living and increase their profits was in the end to reduce wages and increase working hours, and in this endeavour, the support of the municipal authorities was both valuable and indispensable.

There were several ways of going about this. The method of payment could be changed: if a master normally fed his workers, and food was going up in price,

Peasants attacking an isolated man-at-arms, Jean de Wavrin.
Chroniques d'Angleterre, fifteenth century. (Photo B.N., Paris.)

he could ban 'these greedyguts' from his table, paying them money instead and forcing them to eat with less satisfaction in the taverns – being forbidden the master's board could be a sore vexation. Another underhand solution was to take on extra apprentices, who were not paid, and have them if necessary handle the presses, something which was in theory forbidden. One could more straightforwardly depress the wage scale at the lower end: 8 sous a day for the compositors, $2\frac{1}{2}$ to 4 for the unskilled labour. Or the men could be forced to work endlessly long days: from two in the morning to ten at night with four hours break for meals (which hardly seems credible) each man being obliged to print

3000 pages a day. Small wonder then that some young workers protested, demanded better working conditions and denounced their masters' excessive profits. Small wonder either that they went on strike. To go on strike was to 'call *tric*' – the magic word[139] which the journeymen called as they walked out, when for instance an apprentice had been put to work on the press or some such incident. This was not all: the strikers beat up blacklegs (whom they called *fourfants*, from the Italian word *furfante*, a rascal or villain); they distributed leaflets and took their masters to court. They even went further and left the old printing confraternity which still united masters and men at the beginning of the sixteenth century, to form their own society known as the *Griffarins* (from an old French word meaning glutton). For propaganda purposes, in the regular feasts and comic processions in the streets of Lyons, they invented a grotesque creature whom all saluted and recognized when he passed, the *seigneur de la Coquille* (Printer's Devil – literally 'lord of misprints'). That they lost the battle in 1539, and again in 1572 after having held their own for a while, does not however come as a great surprise.

What is remarkable however about this miniature conflict, is its frankly modern character. It is true that the printing trade was a modern and capitalist sector and that everywhere – in Paris in the same years (1539 and 1572), in Geneva in 1560, and in Venice as early as 1504 in Aldo Manuzio's printing office – similar causes had similar effects and significant strikes and disturbances occurred.[140]

This example, although apparently ahead of its time, was not exceptional. From the very beginning, certainly earlier than is usually supposed, Labour must surely have felt itself to be fundamentally different from Capital. The precocious example of the textile industry, with its putting-out system and its abnormal concentrations of workers, was obvious territory for these early and repeated outbursts of class consciousness – as can be illustrated by the case of Leyden, a thriving manufacturing town of the seventeenth century, and indirectly by the case of Salisbury, the centre of the old woollen trade in Wiltshire.

The outstanding feature about Leyden[141] was not simply that it was the biggest cloth-making centre of Europe (in about 1670, its population was 70,000, of whom 45,000 worked in the cloth trade; in 1664, a peak year, it produced almost 150,000 lengths of cloth); nor even that it had drawn to its workshops thousands of workers from the southern Netherlands and northern France; but above all, that it handled, from start to finish, all the different processes needed to turn out cloth, *bayettes* and *sayettes* (light woollens). We should not imagine it on the pattern of Norwich or medieval Florence, dependent for weavers – or merely for spinners – on its outlying areas. The countryside round Leyden was too rich – it sent its agricultural produce to the insatiable and profitable market of Amsterdam. As we have seen, only poorer country districts accepted large amounts of outworking. So even in its heyday, in the mid-seventeenth century, this industrial town was obliged to handle everything itself – from washing, combing and spinning the wool, to weaving, fulling, shearing and finishing the cloth. It could do so only by employing a large workforce. The problem was to provide it with decent lodgings. There was not room for all the workers in the specially-built workers' housing. Many were crammed into rooms rented by the week or the month. Women and children formed a large part of the labour force. And since even all this was insufficient, machines made their appearance: fulling mills worked by horsepower or the wind, machines introduced into the great workshops for 'pressing, calendering and drying the cloth'. The comparatively advanced mechanization of an entirely urban industry is clearly visible in the paintings now in Leyden Museum, which once hung in the *Lakenhal* – the Cloth Hall.

The whole industry was governed by one imperative. While Amsterdam made luxury fabrics and Haarlem followed fashions, Leyden specialized in cheap textiles using wool of mediocre quality. Costs had constantly to be cut. So the guild system, though still surviving, allowed new enterprises to develop alongside it, workshops, manufactories and a domestic system where ruthless exploitation was gaining ground. Since the town had expanded rapidly (it had only had 12,000 inhabitants in 1581) it had not had time, in spite of the fortunes of certain entrepreneurs, to lay the foundations of its own capitalism. The entire activity of Leyden was dictated by the merchants of Amsterdam.

With such a concentrated workforce, clashes between Labour and Capital were only to be expected. The working population of Leyden was too numerous not to be restless and restive, the more so since the town's entrepreneurs did not have the option of turning in times of need to the more docile labour of the countryside. French agents, from the ambassador in The Hague and the consul in Amsterdam downwards, were on the lookout for these chronic outbursts of discontent, hoping, sometimes successfully, to tempt away a few workers to improve the French manufactories.[142] In short, if there was a truly 'industrial' town in Europe, and a truly urban concentration of labour, this was it.

It is no wonder then that strikes broke out in Leyden. But there are surprises on three counts: that strikes should have been so infrequent, according to Posthumus's careful record (1619, 1637, 1644, 1648, 1700 and 1701); that they should have been episodic, concerning only one trade at a time, weavers or fullers for instance, with the exception of the more general strike movements of 1644 and 1701; and lastly that historical research should be able to tell us so little about them – for lack of documents presumably.

So we must bow to the evidence: the working-class proletariat of Leyden was divided into functional categories – the fuller was not the spinner or the weaver. It was partly governed by guilds lacking any real solidity, partly organized as 'free' labour (a misnomer, as it was in fact closely supervised and controlled). In these conditions, it did not succeed in creating sufficient cohesion to further its own interests and threaten those who ruled and exploited it, the master manu-facturers in the first place, and beyond them the all-powerful merchants. And

An urban industry: mechanized spinning-wheels in Leyden. This painting by Isaac van Swanenburgh (1538–1614) is one in a series illustrating cloth manufacture commissioned for the Leyden Cloth Hall. A feature of all the paintings is the mechanization of the industry which was as advanced as the technology of the time allowed. (Photo A. Dingjan.)

yet there were regular assemblies of workers and a form of subscription to hardship funds.

But the dominant factor of textile organization in Leyden was undoubtedly the implacable force of the means of coercion employed: surveillance, repression, imprisonment and even execution were a constant menace. The regents of the town unrelentingly supported the privileged class. And the manufacturers were united in a kind of cartel covering the whole of Holland and even the whole of the United Provinces. They met every two years in a general 'synod' to eliminate any damaging competition, to fix prices and wages, and on occasion to decide what action was to be taken against workers' protests whether actual or potential. This modern organization led Posthumus to the conclusion that the class struggle was waged more consciously and aggressively by the employers than among the workers – but perhaps this is only the impression of a historian dependent on the documents. The workers may have left few records of their struggles and attitudes – but surely they thought the thoughts forced on them by their situation? Any workers' organization officially devoted to defending the interests of the labour force was prohibited. So workers could not speak out openly in their regular assemblies. But the employers' reaction alone proves that silence did not mean indifference, ignorance or acceptance.[143]

The last episode I intend to record is very different. It concerns a smaller industry and one whose structure conforms more closely to the norms of the time – so it is more representative in a sense than the gigantic industry of Leyden.

This takes us to Sarum in Wiltshire, not far from Bristol. Sarum (Salisbury) was the centre of an ancient wool-working region, controlled by the clothiers, who were merchants rather than manufacturers. A brief rising took place there in 1738 and some of the clothiers' property was ransacked. Retribution was swift: three ringleaders were hanged, and order was established. But this was not an inconsequential incident.

In the first place, south-west England, where the 1738 troubles took place, had been the scene of frequent social unrest since at least 1720. This was the region that produced the popular song 'The Clothier's Delight', quoted at length by Paul Mantoux in his classic study.[144] It probably dates back to the reign of William of Orange (1688–1702) and was therefore already quite an old song which had been sung many times in taverns over the years. In it, the clothiers are supposed to give a confidential account of their doings, their satisfactions and their apprehensions.

> And thus do we gain all our wealth and estate
> By many poor men that work early and late;
> If it were not for them that do labour full hard,
> We might go and hang ourselves without regard ...
> By these people's labour we fill up our purse.

It was easy to underpay for the work, or to 'find fault where there's no fault', to lower wages by making 'them believe that trading is bad':

> If trading grows dead, we will presently show it,
> But if it grows good, they shall never know it.

The cloth the workers produced was sold overseas, in distant countries far beyond their control. How could the poor men who toiled day and night know what prices were charged? And in any case they had only the choice between this work or no work: 'We bid them choose whether they will work at all'.

Another significant detail is that the 1738 incident gave rise, in 1739 and 1740, to the publication of pamphlets, not by the workers but by intermediaries trying to restore harmony. If there are troubles in the cloth trade, they say, does the fault not lie with foreign (notably French) competition? The employers should of course soften their attitude, but after all 'they can hardly be expected to ruin themselves as has been the misfortune of many of them these last years'. The incident becomes clearer: battle stations were drawn up on either side of the class barrier; and the barrier was firmly in position. It would be strengthened further with the increasing unrest of the eighteenth century.

Order and disorder

Such unrest was however local, confined to small areas. In the old days, in Ghent in 1280, or in Florence in 1378 at the time of the Ciompi rising, workers' revolts had been equally circumscribed, but then the city in which they occurred was a little world in itself. The issue would be resolved, one way or another, on the spot. The grievances of the Lyons printworkers in 1539 by contrast had to be referred to the Paris *Parlement*. Should we therefore conclude that the territorial state by its very extent and corresponding inertia, was able to isolate, circumscribe and even stifle these episodic outbursts and insurrections? It is certainly true that their dispersal both in time and space does complicate the task of analysing these numerous categories of events. They cannot easily be accommodated by general explanations which are more a matter of guesswork than of certainty.

I say guesswork, because disorder and the established order are part of the same set of problems and the debate has therefore inevitably to be widened. When we talk of established order, this means the state, the foundations of society, cultural reflexes and economic structure, plus the cumulative weight of the multiform development of the whole. Peter Laslett has suggested that a rapidly-developing society may call for a firmer order than in normal times. A. Vierkand argues that a diversified society leaves more freedom of movement to the individual and thus encourages protest.[145] I am rather sceptical about such generalizations: a strictly-controlled society cannot develop very freely; a diversified society may bring pressure to bear on the individual from ten directions at once; one obstacle may be bowled over, but the others remain.

Unquestionably however, any weakness in the state, whatever the cause, opens the door to social unrest. And the existence of unrest often in itself indicates a weakening of authority. In France, the years 1687–1689 and again 1696–1699 were years of much disturbance.[146] Under Louis XV and Louis XVI, 'when authority began to slide from the government's grasp', all the towns in France of any importance had their 'mutinies' and 'cabals', Paris leading the rest with over sixty riots. In Lyons in 1744 and 1786, the protest movements erupted into violence.[147] But it must be admitted that the nature of political or even economic leadership can only, in this case as in others, provide at most the beginning of an explanation. To convert into action what was originally emotion and social discontent required ideological leadership, a language, slogans and the intellectual backing of society, and this was rarely forthcoming.

The whole of the revolutionary ideology of the Enlightenment for example, was directed against the privileges of a leisured aristocratic class, defending by contrast, in the name of progress, the active population – including merchants, manufacturers and reforming landowners. In this debate, the privileges conferred by capital were somehow brushed aside. Underlying French political thought and social attitudes between the sixteenth and eighteenth centuries was a conflict of authority between monarchy, *noblesse d'épée* and the representatives of the *Parlements*. This surfaces in writings as diverse as those of Pasquier, Loyseau, Dubos, Boulainvilliers, Fontenelle, Montesquieu and the other philosophers of the Enlightenment. But the moneyed bourgeoisie, the rising force of these centuries, seems to be left out of the argument. Is it not extremely odd that in the *cahiers de dolèance*, the grievance registers of 1789, which provide a photograph of a collective mentality, one finds a merciless assault on the privileges of the nobility, but almost complete silence about both the Crown and capital?

If the privilege conferred by capital, well-established in practice (as anyone knows who has read the documents of the past through the eyes of the present) took so long to become visible – and on the whole this happened only with the industrial revolution – it was not merely because the 'revolutionaries' of the eighteenth century were themselves 'bourgeois'. It was also because capitalist privilege had benefited, during the eighteenth century, from other forms of consciousness, from revolutionary denunciation of other privileges. Attacks had been made on the mythology defending the nobility (such as Boulainvilliers' fantasies about the 'natural authority' of the *noblesse d'épée* as the descendants of the 'pure new blood' of the Frankish warriors 'reigning over a conquered land'); attacks had been made on the myth of a society of orders. Consequently the hierarchy of money – as opposed to the hierarchy of birth – was no longer singled out as an autonomous and unjust order. The idleness and uselessness of the high and mighty was compared to the industry and social usefulness of the active class. This was undoubtedly the source from which nineteenth-century capitalism, when it finally came into its own, drew its imperturbable self-satisfaction. It was here that the image of the model employer was first created – the engineer of the public good, representing healthy bourgeois morality, hard work and thrift, soon to be the dispenser of civilization and well-being to the colonized peoples; here too was born the myth of the economic advantages of laissez-faire, which would automatically engender social harmony and happiness. Even in our own time, these myths are still alive and well, although contradicted by the facts every day. Did not Marx himself identify capitalism with economic progress – until such time as its internal contradictions should manifest themselves?

A vagrant in the Flemish countryside. *The Prodigal Son* by H. Bosch, early sixteenth century. (Boymans-van Beuningen Museum, Rotterdam.)

Below subsistence level

A further brake on social unrest was the existence in all past societies – including those of Europe – of an enormous sub-proletariat. In India and China, this sub-proletariat bordered on endemic slavery, halfway between poverty and the receipt of charity. Slavery was to be found throughout Islam, in Russia, and still lingered on in southern Italy. It persisted in Spain and Portugal and spread across the Atlantic to the New World.

Europe was for the most part free of this evil, but vast areas even here were still given over to serfdom, a long-lasting phenomenon. Although the West was privileged, we should not imagine that everything was for the best in this best of 'free' worlds. With the exception of the rich and powerful, all men were harshly bound to their toiling condition. Was there always such a great difference between the serf in Poland and Russia and the sharecropper in so many parts of the West?[148] In Scotland, before 1775 and effectively until the 1799 Act, many coal-miners were bound by a life contract and 'were really serfs'.[149] And western society never looked kindly on the lower orders, the riff-raff, the 'men of nought'.[150] It had always with it its huge sub-proletariat of people without work, the lifelong unemployed, an ancient tribulation.

What appears to have happened in the West was that the great division of labour between town and countryside that took place in the eleventh and twelfth centuries, had left a permanent mass of unfortunates unprovided for, with nothing left to do. The fault lay in society no doubt and its usual evils, but it was perhaps even more to be found in the economy, which was powerless to create full employment. Many of the unemployed eked out a living somehow, finding a few hours of work here and there, a temporary shelter. But the others – the infirm, the old, those who had been born and bred on the road – had very little contact with normal working life. This particular hell had its own circles, labelled in contemporary vocabulary as pauperdom, beggary and vagrancy.

Potentially a pauper was the man who barely scraped a living from his work. If he lost his physical strength, if a marriage partner died, if there were too many children, if the price of bread was too high or the winter harsher than usual; if employers refused work, or wages fell – the victim would have to appeal for help to survive until better days. If urban charity provided for him, he was as good as saved. Pauperdom was still a condition in society. Every town had its paupers. In Venice if their numbers grew too high, they were rounded up and those found to have been born outside the city expelled; the others were given a paper or a disc, a *signo di San Marco* to distinguish them by.[151]

One step further into misfortune set one on the way to beggary and vagrancy – inferior conditions in which, contrary to received wisdom, one did not live 'free as air at others' expense'. I must stress the distinction one frequently encounters in contemporary documents between the pauper – wretched but not despised – and the beggar or vagrant, a ne'er-do-well who offended the eyes of respectable folk. Oudard Coquault, the bourgeois of Reims writes in his journal in February 1652 of the great number of the disinherited who had come to town, 'not seeking a living [that is looking for work, the worthy poor whom one should succour] but the unworthy poor, who eat bran, herbs, cabbage stumps, slugs, cats and dogs; to salt their soup, they take the water in which mussels have been soaked'.[152] Here is a pitiless distinction between the 'worthy poor', the 'true pauper'[153] and the miscreant, the 'beggar'. The good paupers were accepted, lined up and registered on the official list; they had a right to public charity and were sometimes allowed to solicit it outside churches in prosperous districts, when the congregation came out, or in market places, like a poor woman in Lille in 1788 who had devised a discreet way of begging: she went round to the stall holders with a flame, offering to light their pipes. Some of her brothers in poverty preferred to bang a drum outside certain houses in the town where they were in the habit of seeking alms.[154]

City archives then will usually tell us most about the 'good pauper', whose life, while on the borderline of serious hardship, was still just tolerable. In Lyons[155] where the profusion of documentation makes measurement and calculation possible for the sixteenth century, this borderline, the 'poverty threshold' can be worked out according to the relation between real wages and the cost of living, that is the price of bread. As a general rule, daily disposable income spent on food represented about half total income. So this sum had to exceed the cost of a family's daily bread consumption. Wage differentials at this time were marked: if a master's wage was 100, a journeyman's was 75, an unskilled 'jack of all trades' received 50, and a casual labourer 25. It was the latter two categories which verged on the poverty line and all too often slipped over it. Between 1475 and 1599, master-craftsmen and journeymen in Lyons kept their heads well above water; unskilled workmen found life difficult between 1525 and 1574 and ran into very hard times at the end of the century (1575–1599). As for the lowest category of workers, they were already in a poor way before the century began; their position went from bad to worse, and after 1550 they were in desperate straits. The table below sets this material out clearly, confirming the deteriorating price of the labour market in the sixteenth century, a time when progress was being made on all fronts, including prices, but when the cost of progress was, as usual, paid principally by the workers.

Below the poverty threshold, the documents can tell us little about the circles of hell inhabited by 'vagrants' and 'beggars'. When we read that in Stuart England a quarter or a half of the population lived near or below the poverty line,[156] it should be understood that we are still talking about the poor who received some kind of aid. This also applies to the figures given for eighteenth-century Cologne,[157] where the poor represented between 12,000 and 20,000 of a total population of 50,000, or Cracow where they formed 30% of the population.[158] In Lille in 1740, similarly, 'over 20,000 persons were permanently in receipt of aid from the Common Poor Fund and the Parish Charities, and on the

The poverty threshold in Lyons
(number of years in which the poverty threshold was crossed)

	Journeymen	Unskilled workers	Casual labourers
1475–1499	o	1	5
1500–1524	o	o	12
1525–1549	o	3	12
1550–1574	o	4	20
1575–1599	1	17	25

From Richard Gascon, 'Economie et pauvreté aux XVIe et XVIIe siècles à Lyon, ville exemplaire', in Michel Mollat, *Etudes sur l'histoire de la pauvreté*, II, 1974, p. 751; the poverty threshold was reached when 'daily disposable income was equal to expenditure on bread. It was crossed when income was inferior to the daily bread requirement'. (p. 749.)

capitation register, half the heads of families were exempted because of their low income'.[159] The same was true of the little towns in the Faucigny.[160] But all these records refer to the history of paupers, in town or 'in the fields'.[161]

When it comes to beggars and vagrants, it is a very different story, and different pictures meet the eye: crowds, mobs, processions, sometimes mass emigrations, 'along the country highways or the streets of the Towns and Villages', by beggars 'whom hunger and nakedness has driven from home' as Vauban notes.[162] There were sometimes brawls, always threats, occasionally fires, violent attacks and crimes. The towns dreaded these alarming visitors and drove them out as soon as they appeared on the horizon. But if shooed out at one door, they came in at another, in their vermin-ridden rags.[163]

In the old days, the beggar who knocked at the rich man's door was regarded as a messenger from God, and might even be Christ in disguise. But such feelings of respect and compassion were disappearing. Idle, good for nothing and dangerous, was the verdict passed on the destitute by a society terrified by the rising tide of mendicancy.[164] Measures were repeatedly passed against begging in public, and against vagrancy which was before long classed as an offence. The vagrant was arrested, and 'beaten over a wagon-end by the executioner';[165] his head was shaved; he was branded with a red-hot iron, and warned that if caught again he would be hanged 'without trial in any shape or form' or sent to the galleys, where many vagrants did in fact end up.[166] From time to time, able-bodied beggars were rounded up and set to work, perhaps in specially-created workshops; more often they were set to ditching, mending the town walls, or deported to the colonies.[167] In 1547, the English parliament decided that vagrants should simply be sent into slavery.[168] Two years later, the measure was revoked: parliament had been unable to agree who should receive these slaves and benefit from their labour, the state or private individuals! The idea was certainly in the air. Ogier Ghislain de Busbecq (1522–1572), the eminently civilized humanist

Beggars in the Netherlands, painting by Brueghel the Elder, 1568. These crippled beggars with their strange head-gear – a mitre, a paper hat, a red cylinder – and wearing chasubles, are celebrating Carnival and leading processions through the streets. (Photo Musées Nationaux.)

who was Charles V's ambassador to Suleiman the Magnificent, thought that 'if a just and mild form of slavery still existed, such as is prescribed by Roman law ... there would not perhaps be need of so many gallows and gibbets to restrain those who possess nothing but their life and liberty and whose want drives them to crime of every kind'.[169]

This was indeed the solution that prevailed in the seventeenth century – for what are imprisonment and forced labour but forms of slavery? Vagrants were put under lock and key everywhere, in the *alberghi dei poveri* in Italy, the workhouses in England, in the *Discipline* in Geneva, in the *Zuchthäuser* in Germany, and in the Parisian *maisons de force*: the Grand-Hôpital, built specially when the poor were 'enclosed' in 1662, the Bastille, the Château of Vincennes, Saint-Lazare, Bicêtre, Charenton, the Madeleine and Sainte-Pélagie.[170] Sickness and death lent the authorities a helping hand. When the weather was severe and rations were short, mortality ran high in the workhouses, even when there was no epidemic. In Genoa in 1710, the workhouse had to be closed because there were so many corpses inside: the survivors were transferred to the Lazaretto, the quarantine-hospital where there were fortunately no infected patients. 'The doctors say that these illnesses are merely the consequence of the want these poor people suffered last winter [i.e. the winter of 1709] and of the poor food they ate then.'[171]

But neither locked doors nor the steady death-toll could eliminate this scourge. The numbers of the down-and-out were constantly being replenished. In March 1545, there were 6000 or more of them at the same time in Venice; in the middle of July 1587, 17,000 presented themselves under the walls of Paris.[172] In Lisbon in mid-eighteenth century, there was a permanent population of '10,000 vagrants sleeping rough, marauding sailors, deserters, gypsies, pedlars, nomads, acrobats, cripples', beggars and villains of all shades.[173] On its outskirts, the town merged into a belt of gardens, wastelands and what we should call shanty-towns: it was dramatically unsafe at night. Intermittent police raids sent criminals and poor wretches alike off to Goa, Portugal's huge faraway penitentiary. In Paris at the same time, in the spring of 1776, according to Malesherbes, 'there are about ninety-one thousand persons without fixed abode, who go back at night to the special houses or shacks set aside for them and get up in the morning without knowing where their day's bread will come from'.[174]

In fact policing was powerless against this shifting mass which had allies everywhere, sometimes (though rarely) among the 'real underworld' – the organized rogues who had built up their little empires in the hearts of big cities, with their own hierarchies and their 'begging districts', their own forms of recruitment and their '*cours des miracles*'. San Lucar de Barrameda, near Seville, the rendezvous of all the ne'er-do-wells of Spain, was what we should call a no-go area, with a network of complicity extending even to the alguazils of the neighbouring city. Spanish literature and, later, writers from outside Spain painted a larger than life picture of the *picaro*, the classic rogue, hero of so many stories, who was able to throw respectable society into uproar single-handed, like a firebrand thrown on to an enemy ship. But this image of the romantic rebel should not be taken too literally. The *picaro* was not typical of the real-life down-and-out.

Despite economic expansion, and because of demographic expansion which worked in the opposite direction, the numbers of the destitute swelled even more in the eighteenth century. Was the reason, as J.-P. Gutton has suggested in the French case,[175] a crisis in rural areas dating back to the late seventeenth century with its strings of famines, shortages and the additional problems caused by the concentration of property, as a sort of undercover modernization went on in this traditional sector? Thousands of peasants were thrown on to the roads as had happened earlier in England, at the time of the Enclosures.

In the eighteenth century, all sorts and conditions were to be found in this human dross from which it seemed so difficult to shake oneself free: widows, orphans, cripples (like the legless veteran who used to exhibit himself in the streets of Paris in 1724),[176] journeymen who had broken their contracts, out-of-work labourers, homeless priests with no living, old men, fire victims (for insurance was barely in its infancy), war victims, deserters, discharged soldiers and even officers (the latter often proud and aggressive in their demands for alms), would-be vendors of useless articles, vagrant preachers with or without licences, 'pregnant servant-girls and unmarried mothers driven from home', children sent out 'to find bread or to maraud'; not to mention strolling players whose music was an alibi, 'instrumentalists whose teeth were as long as their viols and whose bellies were as hollow as their double-basses'.[177] Sometimes the ranks of marauders and brigands were swelled by the crews of ships who had been put ashore;[178] and there were always demobilized soldiers, like the little troop disbanded by the duke of Savoy in 1615. Where once they had looted the countryside, now they asked 'charity from the peasants whose poultry they had plucked the winter before ... they are soldiers without pay, and have become viol-players singing at doors, "*fanfara hélas, fanfara bourse plate!*"'[179] The army was the last refuge of the sub-proletariat: the rigours of 1709 gave Louis XIV the army that saved the country in 1712, at Denain. But the charms of war were limited and desertion was endemic. The roads were always thronged with fleeing soldiers. In June 1757, at the beginning of the Seven Years' War, 'the quantity of deserters passing through Ratisbon every day is quite incredible' writes an ambassador. 'These men are from every nation and most of them complain only of the strict discipline, or that they were enlisted by force.'[180] It was quite common to transfer from one army to another. In June 1767, Austrian soldiers, tired of the poor pay they received from the empress, 'to escape from their misery, joined the Prussians'.[181] Some French prisoners captured by Rossach fought among the troops of Frederick II, and the count de la Messelière was stupefied to see them appear from a thicket on the Moravian frontier, still 'dressed in the uniform of the Poitou regiment', surrounded by about twenty Russian, Swedish and Austrian uniforms – all deserters.[182] Almost forty years earlier in 1720, La Motte had been granted permission by the king to levy a regiment among the French deserters in Rome.[183]

Social instability on this scale was the most serious problem of these societies of the past. The sociologist Nina Assodorobraj[184] has considered the phenomenon in late eighteenth-century Poland, where the 'floating' population – runaway serfs, impoverished noblemen, indigent Jews, and urban paupers of every kind – attracted the attention of the earliest manufactories of the kingdom, as a potential workforce. But there was not enough work for all the undesirables and in any case the latter did not meekly allow themselves to be caught and domesticated. It became evident that they constituted a sort of anti-society. 'Once the individual becomes detached from his group of origin, he becomes a particularly unstable element, tied to no regular work, dwelling or master. One can even make the bold assertion that he deliberately avoids anything that might re-create fresh bonds of personal and stable dependence to replace those which have been broken.' This is a far-reaching remark. It might have been expected *a priori* that such a large body of unemployed men would exert heavy pressure on the labour market – and so it did of course in certain circumstances: for seasonal work in the fields, which was eagerly sought, or for the many menial jobs in the towns.

But it had less influence, proportionately, on the regular labour market and on wages than one might suppose, since this workforce was not reliably available. Condorcet in 1781, described the idle as 'cripples of a kind', unfit for work.[185] The *intendant* of Languedoc in 1775 went so far as to say: 'This high proportion of useless subjects ... is the cause of *dearer labour costs*, both in town and country, since it reduces the size of the workforce, and it becomes a burden on the people in taxes and communal works.'[186] In later times, with modern industry there would be a direct or at any rate a rapid transition from the land, or craftworking, to the factory: the gap would be too short for a man's taste for work, or resignation to it, to be lost on the way.

What deprived this army of vagrant sub-proletarians of its force, in spite of the fear it inspired, was its lack of cohesion: its spontaneous bursts of violence were isolated. This was not a class but a rabble. A few archers on sentry duty or the *maréchaussée*'s patrol on the country roads would be enough to send it packing. There might be a few brawls and beatings when the seasonal workers arrived, a few cases of arson perhaps, but these were swallowed up in the regular catalogue of petty crime. The 'layabouts and vagrants' lived lives apart, and respectable folk tried to ignore this 'scum of the earth, excrement of the cities, scourge of republics, pack of gallows-birds ... There are so many of them on all sides that it would be hard to count them, and they are good for nothing but the galleys, or to be hanged as an example'. Why waste pity on them?

> I have heard them talk and learnt that those who have grown accustomed to this life cannot leave it off. They have no cares, pay no rents or taxes, have no losses to fear; they are independent, they warm themselves by the sun, sleep and laugh as long as they like, are at home everywhere, have the sky for a blanket, the earth for a mattress; they are birds of passage, following the summer and the fine weather; they go only to prosperous countries where they are given food or can find it ... are free to go anywhere ... in a word, they have no worries.[187]

Thus a bourgeois merchant of Reims explaining to his children the social problems of his time ...

Climbing out of hell

Was it possible to escape from this hell? Occasionally yes, but never unaided, never without accepting some kind of close reliance on other men. One had either to swim to the shore of social organization, of whatever kind, or build an alternative society from scratch, a counter-society with its own laws. The organized bands of criminals – false salt-merchants, forgers, smugglers, brigands and pirates – or those special communities, the army and the huge world of domestic service – were almost the only refuge for those trying to escape from the ranks of the damned. Smuggling and fraud, in order to exist, had to build a disciplined organization, with long chains of solidarity. Banditry had its chiefs, its gangs and its leaders – often noblemen.[188] As for privateering and piracy, they usually depended on the support of at least one city. Algiers, Tripoli, Pisa, Valetta and Segna were the bases of the Barbary corsairs, the Knights of San Stefano, the Knights of Malta and the Uskoks, enemies of Venice.[189] And the army, in spite of its merciless discipline and scornful treatment of recruits[190] never ran short of men: it was a haven of regular life; but the way back to hell was taken by deserters.

Finally there was domestic service: the huge world below stairs was the only labour market with ever-open doors. Every surge of the birth-rate, every economic crisis multiplied the number of recruits. In Lyons in the sixteenth century, depending on the district, servants represented between 19 and 26% of the population.[191] In Paris, or rather the Paris conurbation, says a 'guide' of 1754, 'there are about 12,000 carriages, about a million persons, of whom about 200,000 are domestic servants.'[192] As soon as a family of even modest means was above living in a single room, it began to employ maids and manservants. Even the peasant had his servants. And the duty of the humble was to obey even if the master was but little better off. A judgment of the Paris *Parlement* in 1751 sentenced a servant to be put in irons and banished for insulting his master.[193] And one had little choice of master; one was chosen by him, and any servant who left his employ or was dismissed, unless he very quickly found another position, might be taken for a vagrant. Out-of-work maids, if caught in the street were whipped, and had their hair cropped; the men were sent to the galleys.[194] For theft or even suspected theft, a man was hanged. Malouet[195] the future

This Spanish kitchen has an abundance of servants. Cartoon for tapestry by Francisco Bayen (1736-1795). (Photo Mas.)

member of the Constituent Assembly, relates how, after being robbed by a manservant, he learnt with horror that the man, having been caught and tried, was shortly to be hanged in front of his door. He just managed to save him. It is small wonder in these conditions that those 'below stairs' lent a hand to wrong-doers in outwitting the sentries. Or indeed that poor Malouet was but shabbily repaid by the dishonest servant he had saved from the scaffold.

I have taken my examples from French society, but this was not an exception. Everywhere, the king, the state and the social hierarchy demanded obedience. The pauper was faced with the choice, when he reached the point of begging, between being taken in hand and being abandoned. When Jean-Paul Sartre wrote in April 1974 that the hierarchy ought to be dismantled, that no man should have to be dependent on another man, he seems to me to have put his finger on the crucial point. But is this possible? To say society seems invariably to mean saying hierarchy.[196] All the distinctions which Marx referred to but did not invent – slavery, serfdom, the workers' condition – suggest chains of some kind: it does not always matter greatly that the chains differ in character. If one form of slavery is abolished, another springs up. Yesterday's colonies have all gained their independence, or so we are told in every political speech; but the rattling of chains in the Third World is deafening. Those who live in comfort always seem to accept this with a light heart or at any rate with equanimity. 'If the poor had no children', writes the straight-faced Abbé Claude Fleury in 1688, 'where should we find the workers, soldiers and servants for the rich?'[197] 'The use of slaves in our colonies', writes Melon, 'teaches us that Slavery is contrary neither to Religion nor Morality.'[198] Charles Lion, the honest merchant of Honfleur recruited '*engagés*', 'volunteers', that is free labour for Saint-Domingue. He passed them on to a sea-captain who brought him rolls of tobacco in exchange. But it was a very troublesome business for the poor merchant: boys who would agree to go were hard to find 'and the worst of it is that when you have been feeding these little monkeys for weeks, most of them run away on the day the ship is due to sail'.[199]

The all-pervasive state

The state was a looming presence, the coming together of many things. Outside Europe, it had been imposing its intolerable pressures for centuries. In Europe in the fifteenth century, it embarked upon a determined expansion. The founding fathers of the modern state were the 'Three Wise Men' as Francis Bacon called them, Henry VII of Lancaster, Louis XI of France and Ferdinand of Spain. Their modern state was a new invention – on a par with the modern army, the Renaissance, capitalism and the scientific revolution – an enormous movement which had really begun well before the Three Wise Men. Historians are unanimous in describing the kingdom of the Two Sicilies under Frederick II (1194–

1250) as the first modern state. Ernst Curtius[200] liked to say that Charlemagne was the real pioneer in this field.

The tasks of the state

When it appeared at any rate, the modern state distorted or shattered all previous formations and institutions: provincial states, free cities, *seigneuries*, smaller states. In September 1499, the Aragonese king of Naples knew that he was close to ruin: Milan had just been occupied by the armies of Louis XII, and now it was his turn. He was reported to be swearing 'that he will turn Jew if necessary, but he will not give up his kingdom without a fight. And he even seems to be threatening to call on the Turk'[201] – the desperate words of one on the point of losing everything. There were many in this plight. The new state derived strength from their substance, as it was borne along on the economic upsurge which favoured its growth. But the development never reached full term: neither Spain under Charles V and Philip II, nor France under Louis XIV, despite its imperial ambitions, ever succeeded in restoring and appropriating for itself the former unity of the Christian world. 'Universal monarchy' was a crown that no longer fitted Christendom; one attempt after another was foiled. Perhaps these trumpet-blowing policies were harking back to a vanished era. The age of economic conquests had arrived, although contemporaries were not yet aware of these hidden realities. What the Emperor Charles V never achieved – the conquest of Europe – Antwerp managed easily. Where Louis XIV failed, tiny Holland triumphed, becoming the new centre of the world. Europe had to choose between the old ways and the new – and was now choosing the latter, or more accurately, they were forcing themselves upon her. The rest of the world meantime was still playing by the old rules: the Osmanli Empire in Turkey, surfacing from the depths of history, reproduced the Empire of the Seljuk Turks; the Great Mogul moved into the palaces of the sultanate of Delhi; the Manchus in China perpetuated the China of the Ming dynasty which they had so savagely defeated. Only Europe was innovating in politics (and not in politics alone).

Whether remodelled or built from scratch, the state remained what it had always been, a tangle of functions and varying powers. Its major tasks changed little, though its means were constantly altering.

Its first task was to secure obedience, to gain for itself the monopoly of the use of force in a given society, neutralizing all the possible challenges inside it and replacing them with what Max Weber called 'legitimate violence'.[202]

Its second task was to exert control over economic life, both near and far, to arrange for the circulation of goods, with as much coherence as possible and above all to take possession of a sizeable share of national income to pay for its own expenditure, luxury, 'administration' or wars. Sometimes the prince would immobilize for his own use too great a share of public wealth – one thinks of the treasures of the Great Mogul, the vast palace-storehouse of the Chinese emperors in Peking, or the 34 million ducats' worth of gold and silver found in the sultan's apartments in Istanbul on his death in November 1730.[203]

Lastly the state had to participate in that spiritual life without which no society could remain standing; to derive, if possible, extra strength from powerful religious values, either by choosing among them or by yielding to them. The state also had to keep unceasing watch on significant cultural movements, which often challenged tradition; it had above all not to allow itself to be outflanked by their disturbing new ideas – whether those of the humanists in Lorenzo de Medici's Florence, or of the French philosophers of the Enlightenment before the Revolution.

Maintaining law and order

The state had to maintain order – but what kind of order? The more divided and restless a society, the firmer, for better or worse, has to be the hand of the state, the natural arbiter and policeman.

Law and order was the compromise the state had to find between forces *for* and *against*. When the state intervened *for* someone, it usually meant going to the rescue of the social hierarchy: how would the upper-class minority survive without the state as guarantor of order at its side? But in return, no state could have existed without the collaboration of the dominant class – I cannot imagine Philip II being able to control Spain and the huge Spanish Empire without the help of the Grandees. When the state intervened *against* someone it was inevitably the masses who had to be contained and returned to the path of duty – that is to work.

The state was therefore doing its job when it punished or when it threatened in order to exact obedience. It had 'the right to suppress individuals in the name of the public good'.[204] It was the public executioner – and one absolved of all guilt. If it chose spectacular retribution, this was still legitimate. The crowd that milled around scaffolds and gibbets out of morbid curiosity was never on the side of the victim. Yet another execution was taking place on 8 August 1613 on the Piazza Marina in Palermo, accompanied by the procession of *Bianchi*, the White Penitents. The head of the condemned man was afterwards to be put on display surrounded by twelve black torches. 'All the carriages in Palermo went to this execution', a chronicler tells us, 'and there were so many people there that one could not see the paving-stones', *che il piano non pareva*.[205] In 1633, the crowd that gathered to watch an *autodafé* in Toledo would have stoned the condemned men on their way to the stake, if they had not been surrounded by soldiers.[206] On 12 September 1642, on the Place des Terreaux, 'two gentlemen of quality, Monsieur de Cinq Mars and Monsieur de Thou were beheaded; that day a window in one of the houses facing on to the square could have been rented for about a doubloon'.[207]

In Paris, the Place de Grève was the usual place of executions. In 1974, a film

Dutch gibbets; engraving by Borssum. (Rijksmuseum, Amsterdam.)

was made about the *Place de la République*, which the director described as a microcosm of life in Paris: without wishing to sacrifice too much to the macabre, one can well imagine what a documentary made in the eighteenth century – the Age of Enlightenment – about the Place de Grève would have been like, with its endless succession of execution ceremonies and their gloomy preparations. The people pressed to see Lally-Tollendal executed in 1766. He wished to say a few words on the scaffold – so he was gagged.[208] In 1720, the scaffold was on the Place Dauphine. A haughty parricide feigned indifference; the frustrated crowd greeted with cheers his first cry of pain.[209]

Sensibilities were no doubt blunted by the frequent sight of torture and capital punishment, inflicted only too often for what we should regard as peccadilloes. In 1586, a Sicilian was tempted on the eve of his wedding by a fine cloak which he stole from a lady of quality. He was dragged before the viceroy and hanged within two hours.[210] In Cahors, according to a memorialist who seems to have drawn up a catalogue of all the forms of torture, 'in Lent of the said year 1559, the Rouerguais Caput was burned; Ramon was broken on the wheel; Arnaut was tortured with tongs; Boursquet was quartered; Florimon was hanged, Le Négut hanged near the Valandre bridge in front of Fourié's garden; Pouriot was burned near the Roque des Arcs [about four kilometres outside present-day Cahors]. In the year 1559, during Lent, Me Etienne Rigal was beheaded on the square of the Conque de Cahors.'[211] The gibbets, the corpses dangling from trees whose distant silhouettes stand out against the sky, in so many old paintings, are merely a realistic detail – they were part of the landscape.

Even England offered the same spectacle. In London, executions took place eight times a year with a series of hangings at Tyburn, immediately to the north of Hyde Park, outside the city. A French visitor was present in 1728 when nineteen prisoners were hanged simultaneously. The executions were attended by doctors, waiting for the bodies they had bought from the condemned men themselves – who would already have drunk their 'payment in advance'. Relatives of the condemned were also there, and since the gibbets were low, they pulled on the victims' feet to cut short their agony. However, according to the Frenchman, England was less ruthless than France. He considered 'that justice in England is not rigorous enough. I think', he says, 'that there is a policy of condemning highwaymen to be hanged only to prevent them from going on to murder people, which they do but rarely.' But thefts are frequent, even or rather particularly on the trunk road with its 'flying carriages' between London and Dover. Should these thieves not be tortured and branded as they are in France? Then they would soon 'make themselves scarce'.[212]

Outside Europe, the state showed the same face, an even more frightful one in China, Japan, Siam and India, where executions were an everyday happening – only this time to the accompaniment of public indifference. In Islam, justice was swift and summary. In order to enter the royal palace in Teheran in 1807, a traveller had to step over the bodies of the executed. In the same year in Smyrna, the same traveller, the brother of General Gardanne, went to visit the local pasha, and found 'one man who had been hanged and another who had been beheaded, lying on the doorstep'.[213] A gazette announced on 24 February 1772: 'The new pasha of Salonika has restored calm to the city by his severity. As soon as he arrived a few troublemakers who were disturbing the peace were strangled on his orders; commerce, which had been suspended, has now been restored to full activity.'[214]

But did not the end justify the means? State violence and rough treatment guaranteed internal peace, the safety of the roads, the reliable provisioning of markets and towns, defence against outside enemies and effective conduct of the wars which succeeded each other indefinitely. Domestic peace was a jewel beyond compare. Jean Juvénal des Ursins said in 1440, during the last years of the Hundred Years' War, that 'if a king had come along who could give peace [to the French] even if he was a Saracen, they would have obeyed him'.[215] And much later when Louis XII became the 'Father of the People', it was because he had had the good fortune, with the help of circumstances, to restore quiet to the kingdom and to preserve 'the age of cheap bread'. Thanks to him, wrote Claude

Seyssell (1519) discipline is 'so firmly maintained, on punishment of a few of the most guilty, looting ... so stamped upon, that men-of-arms would not dare to take an egg from a peasant without paying for it'.[216] Was it not in the end because it had preserved those precious and precarious treasures – peace, discipline and order – that the French monarchy, after the Wars of Religion and the serious troubles of the Fronde, so quickly regained its strength and became 'absolute'?

When expenditure exceeded income: borrowing money

For all its tasks, the state needed money – more and more of it as it extended and diversified its powers. It could no longer live, as in the old days, on the personal estate of the prince. It needed access to the wealth in circulation.

So it was within the context of the market economy that a certain capitalism and a certain version of the modern state first appeared. There was more than one point of resemblance between the two developments. The chief similarity was the establishment of a hierarchy in both cases, discreet in the case of capitalism, spectacular and conspicuous in the case of the state. A further resemblance was that the state, like capitalism, resorted to monopoly to raise money: 'in Portugal it is pepper; in Spain, silver; in France, salt; in Sweden, copper; and in the Papal state alum'.[217] Spain also had the *Mesta*, the monopoly of sheep transhumance, and the *Casa de la Contratación*, the monopoly of trading links with the New World.

But just as capitalism, as it developed, did not suppress the traditional activities on which it sometimes supported itself 'as if on crutches',[218] so the state shaped itself around pre-existing political structures, inserting itself among them, forcing upon them wherever it could, its authority, its currency, taxation, justice and language of command. This was a process both of infiltration and super-imposition, of conquest and accommodation. Philip Augustus, on becoming ruler of Touraine, introduced to the whole of the kingdom the *denier tournois*, which would now coexist with the *denier parisis* – the Parisian currency which was not finally ousted until the time of Louis XIV.[219] Saint Louis had decreed in 1262[220] that the royal currency should be used throughout the kingdom, but this victory did not become complete until three hundred years later in the sixteenth century. The spread of taxation took equally long. Philip the Fair who introduced royal taxation on seigniorial lands, did so with prudence and cunning. His instructions to his agents in 1302 were 'Do not levy finances on their lands against the will of the barons'; and 'you must effect these levies and financial requests with as little stir as possible, or coercion of the ordinary people; and be sure to appoint reasonable and courteous sergeants to carry out your bidding'.[221] It was to be nearly a hundred years before taxation was fully effective, under Charles V; compromised under Charles VI, it was restored again under Charles VII: the ordinance of 2 November 1439 once more put the *taille* at the king's discretion.[222]

The tax-collector, drawing, French school, late sixteenth century.
(Paris, Louvre, Photo Larousse.)

In view of the slow growth of fiscal institutions and the imperfect organization of its finances, the state was in a difficult not to say absurd position.
Expenditure regularly exceeded receipts – and the former had to be disbursed
day after day, willy-nilly, whereas the latter always lay in the future and a not
very certain future at that. So the prince could hardly run state business according
to bourgeois housekeeping methods – spending within one's income and not
laying out money until the necessary resources had been found. State expenditure
always ran ahead: all rulers hoped to catch it up, but with very rare exceptions
never succeeded.

Appealing once more to the taxpayers, pursuing them, inventing new taxes
or state lotteries were all in vain: the deficit yawned ever wider. It was simply
not possible to go beyond certain limits – to suck all the currency reserves of the
kingdom into the state coffers. Taxpayers were adept at cheating, and on
occasions were roused to anger. Giovanni di Pagolo Morelli, a fourteenth-
century Florentine advising his heirs on business matters writes: 'Avoid false-
hoods like the plague' – except in matters of taxation, which do not count, 'since
here you are not lying to take someone else's goods, but to prevent your own
from being unjustly seized'.[223] In the times of Louis XIII and Louis XIV, riots in
France almost always originated from over-heavy taxation.

So there was only one solution: the state had to borrow money. Even then,
one had to know how it was done: credit was not an easy thing to master and
public loans did not become widespread in the West until as late as the thirteenth
century: in France it was during the reign of Philip the Fair (1285–1314), in Italy
earlier no doubt, since we do not know the date of the Venetian *Monte Vecchio*.[224] The idea was a late but an original one. In the words of Earl J. Hamilton,
'The national debt is one of the rare phenomena which do not go all the way
back to Greek and Roman antiquity.'[225]

To respond to the forms and requirements of financing, the state was obliged
to develop a policy difficult to conceive of as a whole and even more difficult to
put into practice. If Venice had not chosen the solution of the forced loan, if she
had not obliged the rich to subscribe, and if because of the war, she had not in
the end had difficulty repaying the loans, she might be quoted as a model of
capitalist wisdom. For she had invented, as early as the thirteenth century, a
method of raising money which would be practised successfully by England in
the eighteenth century: Venetian loans, like the later English loans, always
corresponded to the releasing of a set of revenues from which interest and
repayment of the principal would come; and as in England government securities
were transferable and could be sold on the open market, either above, or
generally below face value. A special institution was in charge of running the
loan and paying the twice-yearly-interest (5%, whereas private loans at the same
period carried interest of 20%). This institution was called the *Monte* in Venice,
and in other Italian cities. We know little about the original *Monte Vecchio*,
which was replaced in 1482 by the *Monte Nuovo*;[224] later still came the *Monte*

Nuovissimo. In Genoa, a similar situation was given a different solution. Whereas in Venice the state remained in control of the sources of the revenues which guaranteed the loan, the Genoese moneylenders took over virtually all the Republic's revenues and set up, to administer these for their own benefit, that celebrated state within a state, the *Casa di San Giorgio* (1407).

Not all European states practised these sophisticated financial procedures at first, but there was hardly one that did not borrow money, even in earliest times.[226] The kings of England were borrowing from the Lucchese even before the fourteenth century, then for a longer period from the Florentine bankers; the Valois of Burgundy borrowed from their faithful towns; Charles VII had his private backer, Jacques Cœur; Louis XI borrowed from the Medici in Lyons. In 1522, François I created the *rentes sur l'Hotel de Ville de Paris*, loan bonds on the same pattern as the *Monte*: the king ceded to the Hôtel de Ville certain revenues which would guarantee interest on the bonds. The Pope was from very early days calling on credit to balance the papal finances, which could no longer survive on the income of the Papal State itself, as payments from Christendom were dwindling or disappearing. Charles V had to borrow money on a scale commensurate with his ambitious policies: and consequently surpassed all his contemporaries. His son Philip II was not to be outdone, and public borrowing increased even more in later centuries. Much of the capital accumulated in Amsterdam was finding its way into the coffers of princes in the eighteenth century. But rather than examine this headquarters of international credit, the kingdom of borrowers and lenders, to which we shall return at some length, I would now like to turn to the mechanism by which the state sought to raise money, illustrating them by the little known example of Castile and the classic case of England.

The *juros and* asientos *of Castile*[227]

It was in the fifteenth century that the kings of Castile first instituted government bonds (*juros*) secured on certain revenues released for this purpose. The origin of the revenue in question gave its name to the bonds which might be described as '*juros* on the *Casa de la Contratacion*', on the *Maestrazgos*, the *Puertos Secos*, the *Almojarizfazgo de Indias*, etc. To invest money, says a character in Cervantes,[228] '*como quien tiene un juro sobre las yerbas de Extremadura*', 'like a man who has a *juro* on the grasslands [the *Maestrazgos* pastures] in Estremadura'.

Juros became really widespread in the reigns of Charles V and Philip II, when they could be taken out in various forms: a perpetual annuity (*juro perpetuo*), a life annuity (*de por vida*) or a reimbursable bond (*al quitar*). Depending on the reliability of the particular royal revenues on which it was secured, a *juro* could be a good or a bad bet. There was also a range of interest rates, from 5% to 14% or higher. Although there was no organized market in government stocks such as would be found later in Amsterdam or London, *juros* were bought and sold

Jakob Fugger and his accountant. German engraving of the sixteenth century, at a time when the Augsburg firm, the biggest in the world, was lending enormous sums of money to Charles V. The names of the dossiers are those of the great trading centres of Europe. (Photothèque Armand Colin.)

and the rate varied, but it was generally below face-value. On 18 March 1577, in the middle of a financial crisis it is true, *juros* were selling at no more than 55% of face value.

I should also mention that there were for a while *juros de caución* (guarantee stocks) ceded to the businessmen who undertook by contract (*asiento*) to advance huge sums of money to Philip II. The *asientos*, signed chiefly by Genoese merchants after 1552–1557, soon represented a very large floating debt and the Castilian government on the occasion of its various bankruptcies (1557, 1560, 1576, 1596, 1606, 1627) always proceeded in the same fashion: it converted part of the floating debt into consolidated debt – something that does not surprise us today. Meantime, it is true, it had had to sanction the conversion of the *juros* held by its creditors from being mere pledges (*de caución*) into *juros de resguardo*, which the businessman could sell to the public so long as he paid the interest and returned to the king other *juros* carrying the same interest on the final settlement of accounts.

These practices explain how the Genoese *hombres de negocios* were able to control the *juros* market, buying when prices fell, selling when they rose again, exchanging 'poorly placed' bonds for 'well-placed' ones. Dominating the market, they could hardly lose. All the same, one of the most famous among them, Nicolao Grimaldi, prince of Salerno (who had bought this grand Neapolitan title) went bankrupt in 1575 after playing with fire, precisely in the *juros* market. Moreover, as time went by, the Spanish government realized that the drastic remedy of bankruptcy was not the only means at its disposal: it might suspend the payment of interest on *juros*, reduce the interest rate, or reconvert the bonds. In February 1582, his advisers suggested to Philip II that he alter the interest rate on the *juros* secured on the *alcabalas* of Seville, then at 6 or 7%. Bond-holders would have the choice either of holding on to their stocks at the new rate (which the document does not specify) or of being repaid: 'a million in gold' would be put aside to this end from the next fleet to arrive from the Indies. But the Venetian who is our informant thought that in view of the delay in repayment, stockholders would prefer to sell their *juros* to third parties who would be satisfied with the new interest rate. In the end the scheme did not come off.

The problem with the Spanish finances was that appeals were always having to be made for new *asientos*. In Charles V's time, the chief providers of these advance payments – often at short notice – were the High German bankers, the Welsers and in particular the Fuggers. We need not shed too many tears for these princes of finance – but they had a right to be anxious. They could see solid cash flowing out of their coffers. In order to recover it, inevitably after a long wait, they had to make threats and confiscate pledges: the Fuggers thus became the masters of the *Maestrazgos* (the grazing lands of the Orders of Santiago, Calatrava and Alcantara) and the owners of the Almaden mercury mines. Worse still, in order to recover money already lent, they had to advance more. Although virtually out of the *asiento* market after the bankruptcy of 1557, the Fuggers re-entered it at the end of the century, in the hope of redeeming the irredeemable.

From about 1557 began the reign of the Genoese bankers, the Grimaldi, Pinelli, Lomellini, Spinola and Doria families all *nobili vecchi* of the Republic of Saint George. For their increasingly vast undertakings, they arranged the exchange fairs of Besançon, so-called, but in practice held for many years, after 1579, in Piacenza. From now on, they were not only masters of the fortune of Spain, both public and private (since practically all Spanish investors – nobles, churchmen and above all 'office-holders' – banked with them) but also, by extension, masters of the entire wealth or at any rate the realizable wealth of all Europe. All Italy speculated at the Besançon fairs, lending money to the Genoese without even realizing it; one might of course, like the Venetians in 1596, be in for a nasty shock when the Spanish state declared its bankruptcy.

What made the Genoese merchants so indispensable to the king of Spain was their ability to convert the intermittent flow of silver from America to Seville into a steady stream. After 1567, the Spanish troops fighting in the Netherlands had to be paid regularly every month. They demanded payment in gold coin, and had their way until the end of Philip II's reign (1598). So the Genoese also had to convert American silver into gold. They successfully achieved this double feat and continued to serve the Spanish crown until the bankruptcy of 1627.

It was now their turn to leave the stage: after the German bankers, the Spanish government had exhausted a second golden goose. The challenge was picked up in the years 1620-1630 by the Portuguese New Christians. The Count Duke Olivares knew what he was doing when he gave them their introductions: they were in fact front men for the great Protestant merchants of the Netherlands. Through them, Spain was benefiting from Dutch credit facilities, just as war had once more broken out with the United Provinces, in 1621.

It is unquestionably the case that Spain, in her hour of glory, was an incompetent borrower, allowing herself to be outwitted by her creditors. Sometimes her rulers tried to fight back or even take vengeance: Philip II engineered the bankruptcy of 1575 in an attempt to get rid of the Genoese – without success. It was eventually of their own volition that the latter gave up, or rather refused to renew the *asientos* in 1627. International capitalism could now behave as if it ruled the world.

The English financial revolution: 1688-1756

England in the eighteenth century made a success of her credit policy, and even more so of what P. G. M. Dickson[229] has called her 'financial revolution' – a correct description in the sense that this was evidently something new, but less appropriate if one considers how long the process had taken, beginning in at least 1660, getting into its stride only after 1688, and becoming fully established only at the beginning of the Seven Years' War (1756-1763). It had therefore required a long maturing period (almost a hundred years), favourable circumstances and sustained economic growth.

This financial revolution which culminated in a transformation of public credit was only made possible by a previous thoroughgoing remodelling of the kingdom's finances along clearly determined lines. Generally speaking, in 1640 and still in 1660, English financial structures were very similar to those of France. On neither side of the Channel did centralized public finance, under the exclusive control of the state, exist. Too much had been abandoned to the private initiatives of tax-collectors, who were at the same time official royal moneylenders, to financiers who had their own affairs in mind, and to office-holders who did not depend on the state since they had purchased their posts, not to mention the constant appeals that were made to the City of London, just as the king of France was always calling on the goodwill of Paris. The English reform, which consisted of getting rid of parasitic intermediaries, was accomplished steadily and with discretion, though without any discernible plan of action. The first measures were the bringing under state control (in the form of Crown Commissions) of customs (1671), and excise (1683), a 'tax on internal consumption' copied from Holland; in 1714, the office of Lord Treasurer gave way to a permanent Treasury

Board entrusted with the task of supervising the transit of revenue to the Exchequer. In today's language, we should describe this as the nationalization of public finance, including in this long-drawn-out process the takeover of the Bank of England (a takeover which began only in mid-eighteenth century although the Bank had been founded in 1694) plus the decisive intervention after 1660 of Parliament in voting expenditure or new taxes.

How far-reaching a transformation of the financial bureaucracy this nationalization was, altering all the social and institutional relationships between the agents of the state, can be seen from an incidental – and unfortunately all too brief remark, made by a French observer. Louis XIV's government had twice sent to England (to negotiate a trade agreement which never actually came to anything) two of the Trade deputies, Anisson from Lyons and Fenellon from Bordeaux. On 24 January 1713, they wrote as follows to Desmaretz the *Contrôleur-général des Finances*: 'since the commissioners here are like everyone else, self-interested, we hope to achieve our ends by offering them money, the more so as any gifts we have offered them cannot smack of corruption, since here everything is under government control', *tout est ici en régie*.[230] Was corruption of an official less obvious because in theory he represented the state? It seems doubtful. But certainly to these Frenchmen, the English institutions – not too far removed from a bureaucracy in the modern sense – were original and different from those in France: '*Tout est ici en régie*'.

Without this takeover of the financial machinery of the state, at all events, England would not have been able to develop as she did a credit system that worked – however ill contemporaries spoke of it. One should not attribute too great a role in the process to William III, the *Stadthouder* of Holland who became king of England. He did indeed borrow a great deal 'in the Dutch style' at the beginning of his reign, in order to tie to his still-fragile cause a large number of government stockholders. But the English government was still using traditional, not to say outdated methods of borrowing money to cope with the problems of the War of the League of Augsburg (1689-1697) and later those of the War of the Spanish Succession (1701-1713). The real novelty – the long-term loan – caught on only slowly. The country's rulers gradually realized that there was a possible market for long-term loans at low interest rates; that there was a fixed ratio as it were between the real volume of taxation and the potential volume of loans (the latter could rise to a third of the total without danger), between the size of the short-term debt and that of the long-term debt. The only real danger lay in attaching interest payments to sources of revenue which were uncertain or difficult to estimate in advance. These rules, although long discussed, emerged clearly only when the game began to be played in the open and on the grand scale. Little by little, the dialectic long-term/short-term came to be understood, something which was still not entirely the case in 1713, the year of the Treaty of Utrecht, when long-term loans were said to be 'repayable or self-liquidating'. The long-term debt converted itself almost spontaneously into a perpetual debt. From now on, it did not have to be repaid by the state which, by converting its floating debt into a consolidated debt, did not have to exhaust its credit or cash reserves. As for the subscriber, he could now transfer his title to a third party – this was allowed after 1692 – and thus recover his initial payment at any time. This was the miracle: the state never repaid the loan, but the lender could recover his money whenever he wanted it.

The miracle was not entirely painless. The enemies of the national debt, which soon reached monstrous proportions, had to be defeated in the great debate that took place. The entire system depended on the 'credit-worthiness' of the state, on public confidence in other words. It could therefore exist only thanks to the creation by Parliament of new sources of revenue, all earmarked for the regular payment of interest on the debt. Consequently certain categories of the population – landowners who paid one-fifth of their income to the state in land-tax, consumers or retailers of certain highly-taxed products – considered that they were paying for the whole operation, as opposed to a class of parasites and profiteers – rentiers, moneylenders, businessmen whose income was not taxed, the 'moneyed men' who strutted about and thumbed their noses at the hard-working nation. Did not these profiteers have every inducement to be warmongers, since they stood to gain from any conflict which meant the further raising of state loans and a rise in interest rates? The war with Spain (1739), the first great political division of the century, was very largely their work. It was only natural after this that the consolidated national debt, which we are today inclined to see as the foundation of England's stability, should be bitterly attacked by contemporaries in the name of good housekeeping. In fact it was merely the pragmatic product of circumstances.

It was the rich merchant community, the goldsmiths, the banking houses who specialized in floating loans – in short the London business world, the exclusive and vital heart of the nation – which ensured the success of the government loan policy. But foreigners played their part too. In about the 1720s, as Walpole was coming to power and throughout his period, Dutch capitalism was emerging as a crucial force behind the operation. 'New payments of over £100,000 sterling, to be placed in our funds' were reported in London on 19 December 1719.[231] ('Funds', along with 'securities' and 'annuities', was a term used to describe government stocks.)

How is one to explain the massive purchases of English stocks by the Dutch? The interest rate in England was often (but not always) higher than the usual rates in the United Provinces. And English stocks – unlike Amsterdam annuities – were tax-free, which was also an advantage. Moreover, Holland had a positive trade balance with England. To Dutch firms with offices in London, English stocks represented a convenient and easily convertible investment for their profits. Some of them even reinvested the income from their stocks. So the Amsterdam money market was closely integrated to the City of London by the middle of the century. Speculation in English stocks, cash down or forward trading, was busier and more diversified than in shares in the big Dutch merchant companies. Broadly speaking, although these movements cannot be reduced to a simple pattern, Amsterdam was using the parallel market in English stocks to balance its own short-term credit operations. It has even been claimed that at one time, the Dutch owned one quarter or one-fifth of English stocks – an exaggeration no doubt. 'I know', writes Isaac de Pinto in 1771, 'from all the bankers in London, that foreigners hold no more than one-eighth of the national debt.'[232]

Not that it greatly matters. That England should have grown great at the expense of others, whether Dutch investors or French, Swiss or German, is hardly surprising. The government bond market in Florence, Genoa or Naples in the sixteenth and seventeenth century would not have been so vigorous without foreign subscribers. The Ragusans are said to have held 300,000 ducats' worth of these bonds in about 1600.[233] Capital laughed at frontiers. It flowed towards safe investments. But was it the system itself, the financial revolution, that made the British fortune? The British eventually thought so themselves. In 1769, in the seventh edition of his book, *Every Man his Own Broker*, Thomas Mortimer describes the national debt as the 'standing miracle in politics, which at once astonishes and over-awes the states of Europe'.[234] In 1771, Pinto's treatise, from which I have often quoted, praised it to the skies.[235] Pitt in 1786, said he was persuaded that 'upon this matter of the national debt repose the vigour and even the independence of the Nation'.[236]

However Simolin, the Russian ambassador in London, while himself aware of the advantages of the British consolidated debt, saw it as one of the reasons for the rising cost of living in London, which by 1781 had become 'enormous, passing all imagination'.[237] One cannot help thinking that this escalation of borrowing and prices might have had very different results if Britain had not at the same time become a world power, if she had not for instance ousted the French from North America and India, two regions which were clearly bases of her future greatness.

Budgets, economic change and national product

Public finances make sense only in the context of the overall economic life of a country. But the problem is to find precise figures, clear accounts and verifiable economic data – none of which exists. We do however have records of budgeting – or rather, since the word does not become really meaningful until the nineteenth century, records of government expenditure and receipts. It would be naive to place too much reliance on them, but frivolous to ignore them.

We have for instance, the *Bilanci* of Venice from the thirteenth century to 1797;[238] and the accounts of the House of Valois in Burgundy from 1416 to 1477.[239] It would be possible to reconstruct the figures for Castile (the most thriving area of Spain) in the sixteenth and seventeenth century[240] – the papers are in Simancas. Fairly complete figures survive for England, though they have yet to be closely analysed. For France there is little more than an indication of orders of magnitude.[241] Research is being undertaken at present into the Ottoman Empire.[242] There are even some figures, rather doubtful ones it is true, for China.[243] And the occasional memorandum or traveller's tale hints at the income of the Great Mogul[244] or the 'Czar'.[245]

Even those in charge of financial policy however, had only the vaguest idea about what was happening under their own roof. The notion of budget forecasting was virtually non-existent. The general financial statement drawn up on 1 May 1523 by the French government, which is actually a slightly belated forecast for the year 1523, is a very rare example.[246] So too is the order issued by the king of Spain to the *Sommaria*,[247] the Neapolitan financial council, to draw up a budget forecast as well as a recapitulative budget at the end of the year. This rationalizing zeal on the part of the bureaucracy in Madrid is accounted for by the desire to exploit to the full the resources of the kingdom of Naples. The councillors of the *Sommaria* were even threatened with the suspension of all or half of their emoluments, if they did not comply with the instructions. But the councillors were faced with a near-impossible task. They explained that the tax year was very difficult to relate to the annual budget in Naples: the salt tax was reckoned from 1 January in the Abruzzi, but from 15 November in the harbour warehouses of Calabria. The silk tax was levied from 1 June – and so on. And to crown it all, taxes could vary locally from one part of the kingdom to another. The calculations Madrid wanted would be subject to entirely foreseeable delays, however the officials might storm. And indeed the retrospective financial statement for 1622 did not arrive in Madrid until 23 January 1625; the statement for 1626 came through in 1632, and the one for 1673 in December 1676. Among the conclusions came a word of warning: it was no good thinking of getting rid of the tax-farmers and putting taxes under direct government control – this would be as bad as putting them *in mano del demonio*, in the hands of the devil.

The situation was the same in France. Not until the edict of June 1716 was double-entry auditing introduced into public finance.[248] But this was in any case only a method of checking expenditure, not of determining it in advance. Forecasting was the missing element in these budgets. The only way to keep a check on the rate of expenditure was by observing liquidity rates. The levels in the coffers of the exchequer marked the critical thresholds and dictated the real calendar of financial policy. When Calonne took over as Controller-General of Finance in the dramatic circumstances of 3 November 1783, he had to wait months before finding out the exact situation of the Treasury.

The imperfect budgets that survive, or those that can be reconstructed, are at best only pointers.

They tell us that budgets moved upwards with *rising* price trends: on the whole then, the state did not suffer from these inflationary movements, but followed them. That is, it was not in the same boat as the nobles, whose income

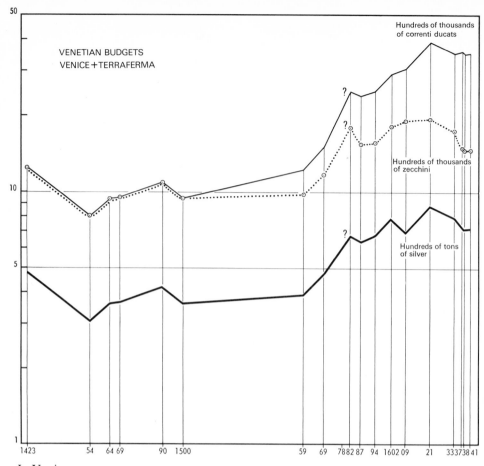

VENETIAN BUDGETS
VENICE+TERRAFERMA

Hundreds of thousands
of correnti ducats

Hundreds of thousands
of zecchini

Hundreds of tons
of silver

I: Venice

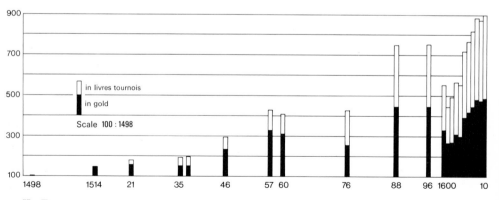

in livres tournois

in gold

Scale 100 : 1498

II: France

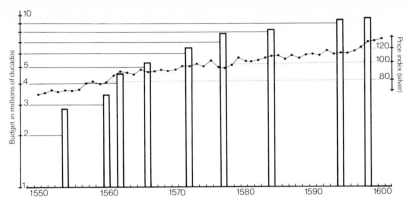

III: Spain

29 BUDGETS AND ECONOMIC TRENDS

I: *Venice*

in *livres tournois*
in gold
Index 100 = 1498

II: *France*

Venice's fiscal revenue came from three sources: the City, the *Terraferma* and the Empire. The Empire is left out of this table since the figures are often imaginary. Graph drawn by Mlle Gemma Miani, using data principally from the *Bilanci generali*. The three graphs correspond to total receipts for Venice and the *Terraferma*: nominal figures (in ducats *correnti*); figures in gold (*zecchini*) and silver (tens of tons). The figures for France, estimated by F. C. Spooner are only of limited value. They are expressed as nominal figures in *livres tournois* and in gold. Imperfect though these estimates are, they do show that budget trends were related to price trends. See Fernand Braudel, *The Mediterranean and the Mediterranean World in the Age of Philip II*, vol. II, pp. 684–685.

III: *Spain*

Budget in millions of *ducados*. Price index (silver)
The index of prices in silver is taken from Earl J. Hamilton. The budgets are expressed in millions of Castilian ducats, a money of account which remained unchanged throughout the period. Budget estimates from unpublished research by Alvaro Castillo Pintado. This time, despite imperfections in the calculations of receipts, the correlation between price trends and the trend in fiscal revenues is much clearer than in the two previous examples. Tentative graphs similar to these could easily be worked out for Sicily and the Kingdom of Naples, or even for the Ottoman Empire, a task already being undertaken by Omar Lufti Barkan's team. Cf. F. Braudel, *The Mediterranean*, *op. cit.*, vol. II, p. 686.

was suddenly left far behind the general index. So a state was never squeezed between incoming revenues at the old rate and outgoing expenses at the new one. This appears to some extent from the French figures in Figure 29, and rather more clearly from the examples of Venice and Spain. E. Le Roy Ladurie, however,[249] suggests on the basis of Languedoc that state revenues may have lagged somewhat behind the rapid price rise in the sixteenth century, but that the gap was closed after about 1585. What is beyond dispute though is the rise of French state revenue in the seventeenth century. If the general economic trend had been the determining factor, one would expect state revenue to have shrunk when prices fell. Yet in Richelieu's time (1624-1642) it doubled or tripled, as if the state were somehow 'the only protected enterprise' during this difficult period, continuing to increase its revenues unhampered. In his will, Richelieu recalled that the *surintendant* of finance used to say 'that the salt tax on the Marais was equal to the Indies of the king of Spain'.[250]

The missing link, which would help to explain more than one anomaly, is that between the sum total of taxation and the national product of which it was only a fraction. According to calculations for Venice[251] – though it must be admitted that Venice is a special case – that fraction might represent something like 10 or 15% of gross national product. If Venice had an income of 1,200,000 ducats in 1600, I think her national product might have been of the order of 8 to 12 million. Experts on Venetian history with whom I have discussed these figures find this estimate rather low, arguing that it makes fiscal tension too high. Whether this is so or not, and without wanting to drag the reader into too many calculations, it is at any rate clear that the fiscal tension in a larger and more extensive and less urbanized territory than Venice would have been lower than this – of the order of 5% say.[252] Was the extension of the territorial state not encouraged precisely by the lower fiscal demands it made, compared to those of city-states operating on a narrower base? Though this is all conjecture, I must stress.

But if historians were to try to carry out these calculations for a number of countries, perhaps it would be possible, by comparing the figures, to find out whether or not this is a way of discovering something about the trend of national product. Without something of the sort, any attempt to apply to the past analyses and perspectives borrowed from present-day studies of growth will be illusory. The calculations have to relate to the whole sum of national income, by which they can be measured. When for example, a historian suggests apropos of western Europe in the fifteenth century that expenditure on wars varied between 5 and 15% of national income, even though these percentages are only guesses rather than strict measurements, this does cast some light on these very old problems.[253] The lower figure of 5% represents roughly the level of a normal budget in those far-off days; but 15% is an excessive figure, which could not be sustained for long without disaster.

The financiers

The double imperfection of the fiscal system and of the administrative organization of the state, and the perpetual need to borrow money explain the preponderant role played from very early days by the financiers. They form a special sector of capitalism, closely and firmly associated with the state, which is why I did not talk about them in the last chapter: it would be wrong to consider them before discussing the state itself.

Cast of sculpture from the private house of Jacques Cœur in Bourges, mid-fifteenth century. It represents one of Jacques Cœur's galleasses; as the king's finance minister he also had interests in the international trade of his time, that of the Levant. (Photo E. Janet-Lecaisne.)

The very word *financier* is not without ambiguity. In the language of the past, it was not the same thing as a *banker*. In theory the 'financier' concerned himself with the state's monetary affairs, the 'banker' looked after his own and in particular those of his clients. But this distinction turns out to be rather unsatisfactory, as does the retrospective distinction between the public and the private financier.[254] In real life, no financier confined himself entirely to 'financial' callings. He always had something else on hand – usually banking – and that something else would be a part of an overall policy which might be very large and diversified.

The trend goes a long way back. Jacques Cœur was Charles VII's finance minister; at the same time he was a merchant, a mining entrepreneur, and a shipowner: in the latter capacity, he ran a Levant trade link from Aigues-Mortes which aimed at independence from the Venetian monopoly. The documents of his trial contain the endless list of his very many affairs and interests.[255] In later times, the *traitants*, *partisans* and *hommes d'affaires* (various categories of tax-farmers) who throng the pages of the financial history of the French monarchy, were similarly only partially engaged in public financing; they were often, without stretching the term in any way, bankers, in the king's service but above all in their own service. The money they lent had naturally to be borrowed from somewhere, and thus they were inevitably caught up in the complex movements of credit. This was true for instance of the Italian financiers called upon by Mazarin: Serantone, Cenami, Contarini, Airoli and Valenti, whom the cardinal had posted, not without good cause, in Genoa or Lyons, and who helped him to operate a steady and fruitful – though sometimes risky – traffic in bills of exchange.[256] Even when the financier was an *officier des finances*, as was often the case in France, so that he was actually lending the king the same money he had collected from the taxpayers, he was not content with his double position as fiscal agent and moneylender. Take for instance the powerful family of money-lenders in Languedoc, the Castaniers in the time of Louis XV.[257] Their fortunes began with the War of the Spanish Succession. Some of them farmed the *taille* in Carcassonne, others were directors of the French Indies Company, their sons and nephews were members of the Toulouse *parlement*, before becoming state ministers. There were Castanier manufactories in Carcassonne. In Paris there was a Castanier bank. Shipowners in Cadiz and Bayonne were in partnership with the Castaniers. In the days of Law's System, there was a Castanier bank in Amsterdam. Later on, Dupleix borrowed from the Castaniers for his Indian policy. Another example of what Chaussinand-Nogaret calls the 'merchant-banker-entrepreneur-shipowner-financiers' are the Gilly or Crozat families. Antoine Crozat, one of the most important lenders of money to the Crown, who wanted to refloat the Indies Company, with Samuel Bernard, participated in the setting-up of the Cape Negro Company, the Guinea Company, the Asiento Treaty (for taking black slaves to Spanish America) and the South Sea Company – in short in all major French international trading. In 1712, he obtained the trade monopoly of Louisiana.

But the situation was different when the financier, instead of lending to his native state, sold his services abroad, to other princes or other states. Was this a different and superior profession? So says at any rate one witness writing from the Dutch point of view: 'One should not', he says, 'confuse the art of the financier with the destructive art which Italy passed on as a poisoned gift to France, the art which created the *partisans*, *traitants* and *fermiers*, expedient persons or tax-farmers as they are known in England, whose astuteness has often been foolishly admired and whose employment ought to be banned by all enlightened governments.'[258] The 'superior' financier of international standing, was becoming a frequent figure in the eighteenth century, in Genoa, Geneva, and especially in Amsterdam.

In the latter city,[259] the distinction between wholesale merchants and banker-financiers grew wider towards the end of the seventeenth century, and once the gap had opened, it rapidly expanded. Responsibility must lie with the very number of borrowers who thronged the Amsterdam money market. The first large state loan with bond issues was 'the Austrian loan of a million and a half florins from the house of Deutz in 1695'.[260] This branch of activity quickly developed, with not only the finance houses who handled loans on a grand scale, but also a multitude of brokers and jobbers offering securities and stocks to the public, and receiving a commission on transactions. When the loan was 'closed', bonds were quoted on the Bourse. It was a common strategy to push their price up and cash at above par bonds one had in any case often acquired in special and advantageous conditions, then to embark upon a similar operation, on condition one was 'no longer left holding part of the last loan'. This was how the colossal bank of Henry Hope & Co., who succeeded the firm of Smeth as moneylenders to Catherine II, managed between 1787 and 1793 to make nineteen Russian loans of three million francs each, a total value of 57 million.[261] It was with Dutch money then, writes J.G. Van Dillen, that Russia was able to conquer a vast territory stretching to the Black Sea at Turkey's expense. Other firms, Hogguer, Horneca & Co., Verbrugge and Goll, Fizeaux, Grand & Co., Smeth, participated in these loans which were of interest to all the powers of Europe or nearly so. Such easy pickings were from time to time interrupted by disasters (but these were occupational risks): an Austrian loan secured on Silesian guarantees in 1736 collapsed in 1763 when Frederick II conquered Silesia; later in the century came the catastrophe of the French loans made after 1780.

This financial stranglehold by Amsterdam was not in itself unprecedented: since the Middle Ages, there had always been in one country or another, a dominant financial group forcing its services on the rest of Europe. I have already described at length how Spain was under the thumb of the merchants of High Germany in the age of the Fuggers, and then of the Genoese *hombres de negocios* after 1552-1557; how France was at the mercy of the astute Italian merchants for centuries on end; how fourteenth-century England was bound hand and foot to the bankers of Lucca and Florence. In the eighteenth century, France finally succumbed to the international Protestant bankers. The same period saw the rise in Germany of the *Hofjuden*, the Court Jews who did their bit to ease the functioning of princely finances, which was often difficult, even for Frederick II.

England, as so often, was a special case. By taking her finances in hand again, she had successfully eliminated the moneylenders who had previously dominated the credit market as they did in France. Thus part of the nation's capital assets

Paying taxes (detail), from a painting by Breughel the Younger (*c.* 1565–*c.* 1637). (Ghent, Fine Arts Museum, Photo Giraudon.)

were diverted into business, especially trade and banking. But public credit did not completely wipe out the financial powers of the past. It is true that the funding system, which quickly became general both for short-term and long-term debts, was open to the public at large. P.G.M. Dickson's admirable study gives a list of categories of subscribers, which ranges from top to bottom of the social hierarchy. But the author has no difficulty in proving that behind this apparently open market, there was in fact a small group of merchants and financiers, all seasoned speculators, who dominated the state loan activities – taking their revenge as it were.[262] In the first place, this was because the large number of small subscribers accounted for only a small proportion of all government loans. And secondly because as in Amsterdam, the money handlers who launched the loans were not content merely to process subscriptions, but bought up large numbers of bonds on their own account, using them almost at once (sometimes even before the registers closed) for speculative ends, and taking advantage of a new loan to speculate in the previous one. Sir John Barnard, who spoke out in Parliament against the monopoly which those he scornfully called 'undertakers' had acquired in state finance, was eventually successful in having the 1747 and 1748 loans made available directly to the public, instead of through these intermediaries. But the speculators easily found their way round the new system of subscription and it was clear once more that the government could not do without the professionals if it wanted to raise a loan.[263] So much so, says P.G.M. Dickson that one must recognize that there was a solid foundation to Tory attacks on financial circles, which cannot be dismissed as mere ignorance or the prejudice of outsiders.[264]

France: *from the* traitants *to the* Ferme générale

France under the monarchy never succeeded in 'nationalizing' state finance. Perhaps it was never seriously tried, despite the efforts of the Abbé Terray, Turgot and above all Necker. But this failure proved to be the death of the monarchy. If the Revolution, by contrast, succeeded in implementing financial reform from the start, this was because the problem was above all social and institutional in character.[265] J.F. Bosher has rightly remarked (1970) that what mattered in the long history of the Crown's finances was less the balance between receipts and expenditure, which did of course play its part, than the structure of a system where for centuries on end, private interests had prevailed.

In fact, France had no public finances at all, no centralized system; so neither control nor forecasting were possible. All the mechanisms were beyond any real government control, since the finances effectively depended on the intermediaries who saw to the collection of taxes, dues and loans. These intermediaries were the towns, above all Paris (with the *rentes sur l'Hotel de Ville*) and Lyons; the provincial estates; the Assembly of the clergy; the tax-farmers who collected indirect taxes; and the finance officers who collected direct taxes. Imagine what it would be like today if the French Treasury did not have at its side the Banque de France, and at its command the army of tax collectors and inspectors, the whole bureaucracy – elephantine empire though it may be – of the rue de Rivoli: if the entire inland revenue system was in private or quasi-private hands. The monarchy was always in this position: it drew effectively on about a hundred funds. What was supposedly the central fund, that of the Royal Treasury, in fact only received about half the king's revenues.[266] If the king needed money, he had to assign a given expenditure to a given fund, but as the proverb put it, 'when the chest is empty, the king has no rights'. Even the *receveurs* and *receveurs-généraux*, who actually controlled the key sectors of direct taxation, were office-holders who had bought their posts and who advanced to the king the sums of money which they recuperated from the *taille*, the *vingtième* and the capitation tax. They were independent and had their own financial affairs.

So the French monarchy was delivered, until the very end of its existence, into the hands of private interests. We may feel sorry for the financiers who were mercilessly prosecuted, from Jacques Cœur to Semblançay, Nicolas Fouquet and even John Law. But how can one fail to recognize the short-term efficacity of the temporary Chambers of Justice set up to investigate and try to recover at least some of the money embezzled by certain handlers of public funds? There were fourteen such bodies set up in all, eight in the sixteenth century, five in the seventeenth and one, the last of all in 1716–1717, soon after the death of Louis XIV.[266] The documents that survive sometimes make it possible to glimpse the state of public finances at the time and the personality of these tax-farmers, known as *traitants* or *partisans* (depending on the wording of the contract they signed with the state).[267]

The judicial inquiry of 1661[268] leading to the prosecution of the *surintendant* Fouquet, provides an opportunity to see the mechanisms and vast ramifications of the system in action. 230 *partisans*, almost all the accused, are on the file. The finances of Louis XIV, in the early days of his reign, were in the hands of these 200 to 300 individuals, of whom the 74 richest of all called the tune. As usual, there was a small group at the top. These people were all interrelated or connected in various ways, by marriage or business association, to each other – effectively forming lobbies. Before long, the Colbert lobby prevailed (ousting incidentally the Mazarin lobby to which Colbert had originally belonged).[269] These *traitants*, in spite of the firmly-held public belief that they were jumped-up nobodies, were in fact all of quite distinguished origins: of 230 *partisans* who have been identified, 176 were nobles (76.5% of the total); of the 74 who headed the list (three of whom are unidentified), 65 were 'secretaries to the king'.

This is the first cause for surprise: these so-called nobodies had long been in the ranks of the aristocracy and many of them had long been in the king's service. It was here, and not in trade, that they had begun their careers. For them, the king's service had been a means of enrichment. (And after all, without inside information, how could they have conducted their affairs?) The second surprise

'Financier in the country, dressed in morning suit'. French caricature, eighteenth century. (Viollet Collection.)

is that the money which these tax-farmers advanced to the king – in cash – had been provided by the great aristocratic landowners of the kingdom. If Fouquet's trial so alarmed high society, it was because it feared possible revelations from the *surintendant*, who in fact held his tongue. But we still have some information about these opulent moneylenders, despite the warnings of discretion and concealment. Mazarin himself in his will, specifically requested that efforts should not be made to discover the origins of his wealth, and that no inquiry be pursued into the accounts and activities of his subordinates, since this concerned 'state property' as he put it. *Raison d'état* could be a powerful alibi. But it is quite true that the entire aristocracy was implicated in the scandal of the royal finances. If the scandal broke, mud would cling to the entire nobility.

So if the aristocracy had allied itself to the tax-farmers, it was because of their social relationships: the fortunes of the noble investors were 'comparable or perhaps superior to those of many of the tax-farmers, whose wealth public report likes to exaggerate, not without a little fantasy'. 'Marriage', concludes Daniel Dessert 'was no longer a bargain in which one exchanged money in return for an ancient name, but rather a capital partnership.' The aristocracy, from the beginning of Louis XIV's personal reign, was thus not outside business affairs:

indeed it had a hand in the most profitable of all, the king's finances, which would be until the end of the *ancien régime*, the fruitful sector *par excellence*, the favoured scene of a vigorous form of capitalism – if a rather doubtful one in our eyes.

The system revealed in 1661 had probably been in existence for some time. It had very ancient roots.[270] Its past pushed it forward. How could it be altered when it was at the very heart of privileged society? If rent from land, which nourished the ruling class, came down from its lofty heights to be invested once more in the nation's life, this was very largely through the advances made by the king's tax-farmers. As the years went by, the system was simply consolidated and institutionalized. In 1669, under Colbert's administration, there were clearly emerging what we should call syndicates (in the stock exchange sense: groups of capitalists) who would be entrusted with the collection of certain categories of taxation. 'But the general tax farms only really begin with the Fauconnet lease of 1680, which grouped together salt-tax, *aides*, *domaines*, *traites* and *entrées*' (all tax-categories) for a real sum of over 63 million *livres tournois*.[271] The *Ferme générale* (the near-monopolistic syndicate of farmers-general) only appeared in its definitive form later, in 1726. It was a late development, which reached full maturity in 1730 when the profitable tobacco monopoly came to swell the already immense domain of the *Ferme*. Every six years the salt-tax contract was knocked down to a straw man, usually one of the Controller-General's footmen. The forty *fermiers-généraux* stood guarantee for the execution of the contract. They had previously deposited huge sums of caution money (up to 1,500,000 *livres* each) on which they received interest. These sums of money represented the first payments anticipated from taxation, but their very size meant that the tax-farmers became virtually irremoveable from their posts. In order to dismiss one – and this did happen occasionally – the Crown had to repay him his deposit and, a further difficulty, find someone equally rich to replace him.

According to the terms of the contract, the *Ferme* paid the king in advance the sum specified in the contract – which in fact represented only a proportion of the annual income from the many taxes whose collection it handled. When the operation was complete, a fantastic share of the nation's wealth remained in the hands of the tax-farmers, who levied tax on salt, tobacco, corn, imports and exports of every kind. Naturally, the state increased its demands on every renewal of the contract: 80 million in 1726; 91 in 1738; 110 in 1755; 138 in 1773. But the profit margin remained enormous.

Membership of this rich man's club was not of course open to all-comers. One had to be extremely rich oneself, to have the approval of the Controller-General, to come from a thoroughly honourable background, to have pursued a career in the offices of finance and perhaps occupied the post of *intendant*, or partner in the Indies Company. Above all, one had to be accepted by the other members. Since the *fermiers-généraux* made appointments, directly or indirectly, to a whole series of vital posts, they were in a position to control the careers of individuals, to promote or block them. Any successful candidature, if one traces it back in time, was accompanied by visits to one's patrons, by patience, protection, back-scratching and bribery. In effect the *Ferme générale* was like a mighty clan, with a network of marriages and old or new blood ties. If a detailed genealogical study were carried out of the forty-odd potentates (44 in 1789 to be precise) with all their family alliances, 'it is quite possible that the exercise would reveal them to be united in two or three families or even in a single family'.[272] To my mind, this is simply one more example of the iron law of minority control, that structural concentration of capitalist activity. What we have here is a financial aristocracy which, naturally, entered the exalted ranks of the high nobility.

The real heyday of the *Ferme générale* can be dated roughly between 1726 and 1776 – about half a century. These dates have their importance. The *Ferme générale* was the apotheosis of the financial system constructed piecemeal by the French monarchy. By creating its ranks of 'officers', it had provided the base from which finance developed. Powerful and tenacious networks linked by kinship had established themselves and become permanent. But Law's system inaugurated a new era of unparalleled prosperity for the tax-farmers. Most of the Mississippi investors who made fortunes overnight were members of the financial establishment rather than lucky speculators. At the same time, the centre of gravity of French economic life shifted from Lyons to Paris. The provincials moved to the capital, made a number of useful connections and expanded the horizon of their interests and activities. The financiers of Languedoc, whom I have already mentioned, are a prime example. Their province represented perhaps a tenth of the kingdom's population; in Paris, in finance in the broad sense (including suppliers to the armies) they formed the most numerous group; they achieved considerable success on a national scale. But then the history of France in every domain (war, literature, politics etc.) has been the story of one province after another coming to the front of the stage.

Needless to say, it was no accident that brought the Languedoc group to the forefront of French finance. Its salt exports (from the salt-marshes of Peccais), grain, wine, cloth, silks, had naturally provided it with external links. Another advantage was that the Languedoc business community was evenly divided between Protestant and Catholic. The Revocation of the Edict of Nantes made only a surface difference. The Protestant links were all external – in Genoa where the Reformation had a foothold, Geneva, Frankfurt, Amsterdam and London. It is hardly surprising that Catholic businessmen smothered their religious susceptibilities: the alliance between Catholics and Protestants in this case was the alliance of internal and external trade. And it was inevitable in all economic centres throughout the kingdom. But in the process, Protestant banking eventually colonized France. It offered its services as a superior order of capitalism, with a span of interests so much greater than that of French finance that it soon outstripped the latter and presently short-circuited it as well. Necker's arrival at the head of the French financial system in 1776 (although he was not formerly appointed Controller-General straight away) was a turning point for the whole of French finance. Necker was the enemy of the *Ferme*: the foreigner was opposed to the indigenous financial community.

Unfortunately for French finance, it was during the same period that it was gradually forsaking its old habits of active investment; it was falling back on its own activities and visibly losing ground, even to the eyes of a lay observer like Sébastien Mercier: 'What is so strange', he writes, 'is that people have sought to excuse finance because it is making less money than in the past, but its profits must still be very great since it is fighting so vigorously to maintain its operations.'[273]

The *Ferme générale* lasted until the Revolution which brought a tragic end for its members: 34 of them were executed in Floréal, Prairial and Thermidor of Year II (May–July 1794). Their conspicuous fortunes, their ties with the high nobility, the immense financial difficulties of the state on the eve of the Revolution had marked them out for popular vengeance. They were not as fortunate as the many businessmen and bankers, in both Paris and the provinces, who were able to conceal their wealth until they became the military suppliers and moneylenders to the new régimes.

State economic policies: mercantilism[274]

Is it possible even to talk about 'the economic policy' of the European states, a term that implies coherence, whereas their actions were inevitably of many kinds and governed by particular or even contradictory circumstances? To envisage such action under a series of clearly-defined and uniform headings would certainly mean giving it a coherence it could never have had – as Sombart does in his quest for the impossible equation of mercantilism.

T.W. Hutchinson[275] is probably right to urge historians and economists to get rid of the word mercantilism altogether: 'one of the vaguest and most irritating "isms" in the language' – and a late derivative of the *mercantile system* against which Adam Smith wrote his celebrated classic in 1776. But with all its faults, this label does conveniently cover a whole series of acts and attitudes, projects and ideas and experiences which mark the first stand of the modern state against the concrete problems facing it, between the fifteenth and eighteenth centuries. In the words of H. Kellenbenz (1965), 'mercantilism was the guiding principle of economic policy (and the related theory) in the age of absolute rulers in Europe'.[276] Perhaps one should say instead of 'absolute rulers' (something of a misnomer) territorial or modern states – so as to put the accent on the development which was pushing them all towards modernity, though by different routes and in different stages. One historian felt sufficiently sure of this to write in 1966 that 'there are as many mercantilisms as there are mercantilists'.[277] With its beginnings in the fourteenth century (or even in the thirteenth with the

Jean-Baptiste Colbert, by C. Lefebvre. (Palace of Versailles, Viollet Collection.)

extraordinary reign of Frederick II of Sicily)[278] and lasting well into the eighteenth, mercantilism over the long-term was certainly not the identifiable and coherent system that Adam Smith described, the better to demolish it.[279]

Close investigation should distinguish between times and places. Richard Häpke for instance identifies three stages between the thirteenth and eighteenth centuries: *Früh-*, *Hoch-* (around Colbert's time) and *Spätmerkantilismus* (after Colbert's death in 1683).[280] Henri Hauser put it the other way round by discovering what he called 'Colbertism before Colbert'.[281] In fact mercantilism was none other than the insistent, egoistic and presently vehement forward thrust of the modern state. 'It was the mercantilists', Daniel Villey assures us, 'who invented the nation'[282] – unless that is it was the nation, or embryonic would-be nation which, by inventing itself, invented mercantilism at the same time. The latter was certainly taking on the trappings of a state religion. In a sarcastic reference to all the official economists, Von Kaunitz, one of Maria Theresa's leading advisers did not hesitate to call himself 'an economic atheist'.[283]

At any rate, as soon as there was a wave of nationalism, of the desire to defend frontiers by customs tolls sometimes of a 'violent' nature,[284] as soon as a form of national self-interest perceptibly emerged, mercantilism came into its own. Castile forebade grain and livestock exports in 1307, 1312, 1371, 1377, 1390;[285] France placed an embargo on grain exports under Philip the Fair in 1305 and 1307.[285] In thirteenth-century Aragon, a Navigation Act, a forerunner of the English one, was introduced. Imports of foreign iron to England were forbidden from 1355[286]; in 1390, the Statute of Employment forbade foreigners to export gold or silver: they had to convert their profits into English goods.[287] And the trade history of the Italian city-states would undoubtedly reveal a host of similar measures, on close examination. So there was nothing new about the major decisions of classic mercantilism: the English Navigation Act of 1651; the duties imposed by Colbert on the tonnage of foreign shipping (1664 and 1667); or the *Produktplakat* which in 1624 established the rights of the Swedish national flag[288] and banned the Dutch vessels which had hitherto carried salt to Sweden from the Atlantic. The quantity of imported salt dropped, and its price rose, but by discriminating against the rival ships, Sweden was able to develop her own merchant navy which would soon be sailing the world's seas. Mercantilism was in other words quite simply a policy of each for himself, as both Montaigne and Voltaire wrote, the first in general terms: 'One man's advantage can only mean another man's loss'; the second more specifically: 'It is clear that one country can only gain if another country loses' (1764).

And the best way to gain advantage, according to the mercantilist states, was to attract to one's shores the greatest possible quantity of the world's stock of precious metals, and thereafter to prevent it from leaving the kingdom. The axiom that a state's wealth consisted of its store of previous metals in fact governed a whole policy with multiple economic consequences and implications. The policy of keeping one's raw materials, using them to manufacture goods which were then exported, and of reducing foreign imports by means of protectionist tariffs – a policy which to us today looks like encouraging growth through industrialization – in fact had other motives. An edict issued by Henri IV (before 1603) called for the development of manufacturing, 'as being the only way to stop transporting out of our kingdom gold and silver to enrich our neighbours'.[289] F.S. Malivsky, the advocate of the territory of Brno, sent to the emperor Leopold I in 1663 a voluminous report in which he argued that 'the Habsburg monarchy was paying millions to foreigners every year for foreign goods which it would have been possible to produce at home'[290] For Le Pottier de La Hestroy (September 1704), the question was childishly simple: if a budget trading deficit was represented by the arrival of foreign goods,

> such goods could only cater to [the people's] luxury and sensual indulgence and in no way enrich the Kingdom, because in the end these goods will be worn out through use. If on the other hand the balance was corrected by means of silver, which does not wear out with use, the silver would have to remain in the Kingdom and, increasing more and more every day, would make the state rich and powerful.[291]

Werner Sombart, following the same line of argument, suggests that 'from the time of the Crusades until the French Revolution' there was a close correlation between the strength of the state and its resources in minerals such as silver and gold: in other words 'the more silver (and later gold) the stronger the state', *so viel Silber (später Gold) so viel Staat!*[292]

States were therefore obsessed with the size of their monetary reserves. Gold and silver are 'tyrants', said Richelieu.[293] In a letter written on 1 July 1669,[294] Louis XIV's ambassador in London (a former *intendant* of Alsace, named Colbert, who was a cousin of the famous minister) commented on the decision of the English government to forbid Ireland to export cattle. This meant depriving France and in particular her navy of a cheap supply of kegs of salt beef. What should be done? Perhaps cattle should be imported from Switzerland and Germany 'as I used to see the butchers do when I was in Alsace'? But,

> it would be better to buy beef produced by the king's subjects, dear though it is, both for the navy and for private individuals, than to buy it at a lower price from foreigners. The money that is spent on the former would remain in the kingdom and would enable His Majesty's poor subjects to pay their taxes, and thus it would return to the King's coffers, while the other [course] would mean money leaving the kingdom.

This was clearly a common sentiment, as was the remark by the writer's more famous cousin that 'everyone ... agrees that the might and greatness of a State are measured entirely by the quantity of silver it possesses'.[295] Fifty years earlier, on 4 August 1616, Don Hernando Carrillo reminded Philip III of Spain that 'everything is kept going by means of silver ... and Your Majesty's strength consists essentially of silver; the day the silver runs out, the war will be lost'.[296] A warning that was perhaps only to be expected from the president of the

Castilian Council of Finance – but similar observations poured from the pens of the contemporaries of Richelieu or Mazarin. Chancellor Séguier received a letter from the *maître de requêtes* Baltazar, whom he had sent on a mission to Montpellier (October 1644), saying, 'You will know, Monseigneur, that the way war is waged nowadays, victory may be determined by the last grain of corn, the last crown and the last man.'[297] Undoubtedly warfare, which was becoming more and more expensive, contributed to the development of mercantilism. With the progress made in artillery, arsenals, battle fleets, standing armies and fortifications, the expenses of the modern state were mounting rapidly. Money and yet more money provided the sinews of war. So money and the accumulation of precious metals became an obsession, the overwhelming consideration that swayed all judgments and counsels.

Should this obsession be dismissed out of hand as naïve? Should we, looking through modern eyes, consider it not only absurd but pernicious to channel home this flow of precious metal and watch over it so intently? Or was mercantilism merely the expression of a basic truth – that precious metals had acted for centuries on end as a guarantee and a driving force for the economy of the *ancien régime*? Only the leading economies of the time allowed specie to circulate freely: seventeenth-century Holland, eighteenth-century England, or in earlier times the trading cities of Italy (silver and gold entered Venice without difficulty and were allowed out again on condition they were re-minted at the Zecca). Should one conclude that allowing the free circulation of precious metals – which was always exceptional – was the intelligent choice made by a leading economy, and one of the secrets of its success? Or on the contrary, *could only a leading economy permit itself the luxury of taking such a liberty, which held no danger for the very rich*?

One historian has suggested that Holland never engaged in any form of mercantilism.[298] This is possible, but perhaps an exaggeration: it is possible because Holland had the freedom of action born of power. Operating an open door policy, afraid of no one, not even needing to ponder overmuch the meaning of her actions, she was an object of reflection for the outside world more than for herself. But the opinion may be exaggerated because the example of other nations' policies was catching, and a spirit of reprisal natural. Holland's strength did not entirely eliminate anxieties, difficult moments or strains. The mercantilist temptation exerted a strong appeal at such moments: Holland took sudden exception for instance to the new modern roads built through the Austrian Netherlands in 1768[299]. And even more telling, when she took in the French Huguenots with their luxury craftsmanship, she took careful steps to protect them.[300] Was this a sensible calculation in the context of Dutch economic activity as a whole? Isaac de Pinto argued that it would have been better to remain faithful to 'a commercial economy', to the open door policy and to the welcome previously accorded without restrictions to the industrial products of Europe and the Indies.[301]

The truth was that Holland could hardly escape the spirit of the times. Her free trade was only skin deep. All her economic activity led to a number of *de facto* monopolies which she guarded jealously. In her overseas empire, she behaved like any other colonial power and worse than some. In theory, all colonies of European powers were considered as private property, subject to the rules of the *Exclusif* or colonial ruling. If the regulation had been strictly observed not a nail would have been hammered, not an inch of fabric woven in Spanish America, say, without express permission from the mother country. Fortunately for the colonies, they were months' or years' travelling distance away from Europe. This distance in itself generated freedom, for some of them at least. The laws of the Indies are spiders' webs, went the saying in Spanish America: they catch the little offenders, but not the big ones.

But to return to our question: was mercantilism merely an error of judgement, an obsession of ignorant people who failed to understand that precious metals were not the essence of value, that the true essence of value lay in labour? We cannot be so sure, since economic life developed on two planes: the circulation of specie and the circulation of 'paper' – if we can conveniently lump all the 'artificial' means of credit under this heading (as eighteenth-century Frenchmen did, to the outrage of Isaac de Pinto). One of these circulations was on a higher plane than the other: the upper level was the realm of paper. The operations of *traitants*, bankers and businessmen were on the whole expressed in this superior language. But in everyday life, it was impossible to proceed without cash currency, however good or bad. At this lower, pedestrian level, paper was not really acceptable and circulated with some difficulty. Little enthusiasm would have been aroused among the small carrying firms who were to transport the French artillery to Savoy in 1601 if they had been offered paper.[302] One could never have enlisted a single soldier or sailor with paper. Already in 1567, when the duke of Alva arrived in the Netherlands with his army, the troops' pay and expenses were invariably being settled in gold, and in gold alone as Felipe Ruiz Martin has long ago established.[303] It was not until after 1598 that the soldier was obliged to accept silver, for want of anything else. But as soon as he received it, he would do his best to change it for gold. To be able to carry one's wealth about in the form of a few coins, easily slipped into purse or belt, was an advantage, indeed a necessity for the soldier. In war, gold or silver coins were as indispensable as bread.

When paper was forced upon ordinary people, whoever they were, it had somehow to be converted into gold, silver or even copper coin. The correspondence of the Paris lieutenant of police, d'Argenson, some of which survives for the years 1706 to 1715, is full of endless references to the small-time sharks, 'the backstreet usurers who negotiate bank notes [issued by the royal government] at fifty per cent under par'.[304] These shady operators were never short of customers, both rich and poor. That this was current practice (in spite of the varying exchange rates which it certainly contributed to exaggerate) clearly emerges

Paying the troops, by Callot. (Photo Bulloz.)

from the merchant correspondence of the period. In the accounts of the Saint-Malo vessels referred to above (pp. 369-70 and 430) there it is in black and white in 1709: 'for 1200 *livres* in bank notes ... allowing for a loss of 40% on the said notes ... we can only give you ... 720 *livres*'. And again in the same year, 'for 16,800 *livres* in bank notes ... at 40% *agio* ... the net result is 10,080 *livres*'.[305]

One might dismiss this as a French peculiarity, in a country rather backward in accepting new economic techniques, since even in the early nineteenth century, the Parisian public only reluctantly accepted the notes issued by the Banque de France. But even in eighteenth-century England, it was sometimes hard to get people to accept paper. The sailors in the Royal Navy for instance, who were paid up to £4 a month, received it in tickets payable at the Navy Office when they put ashore. They were clearly not very pleased with the tickets, since an astute jobber, one Thomas Guy, set himself up a small business in them: he frequented the taverns of Rotherhithe and bought their tickets from sailors for cash – by which means he became one of the richest men in London.[306]

There must have been many people then for whom, as Daniel Dessert puts it, 'metal money [was] the only true measure of all things'.[307] In these circumstances, we might say that mercantilism simply reflected the possibilities of action of newly-emergent and expanding states. Economic needs of the overwhelming everyday kind forced them to set great store by precious metals: without these, the economy would only too often have been paralysed.

The state vis-à-vis *society and culture: an incomplete entity?*

As we approach the conclusion of this analysis, the reader must be aware of the question at issue and choose between two following alternatives.

Either everything depended on the state – the modernity of Europe and, as a consequence, that of the world, including in that modernity capitalism, which was both its cause and its effect. This is the position adopted by Werner Sombart in his two books *Luxus und Kapitalismus* (1912) and *Krieg und Kapitalismus* (1913) – two books which strongly argue the case that capitalism was the product of state power, since luxury was for centuries on end chiefly associated with princely courts and thus with the very heart of the state; and since war, with its ever-increasing expenses and numbers of men in the field was a measure of the vigorous and tumultuous growth of the modern state. This is also the position adopted by the majority of historians – with only a few exceptions[308] – who compare the modern state to the ogre of the fairy tale – Gargantua, Moloch or Leviathan.

Or one could argue, perhaps with more justification, the opposite case: that the state was as yet an unfinished entity, seeking to create its identity, unable to exercise all its rights or to carry out all its tasks, obliged in fact to call on the aid of others as a disagreeable necessity.

If this necessity was forced on the state at every turn, it was above all because it still lacked an adequate administrative apparatus. France under the monarchy is only one example among all the others. In about 1500, if we take the rather optimistic estimate of one historian,[309] France had something like 12,000 persons in government service, out of a population of 15 to 20 million. And the figure of 12,000 is probably a maximum: this was very likely the highest total reached under Louis XIV. In about 1624, Roderigo Vivero,[310] a reliable but somewhat disenchanted observer, suggests that the king of Spain appointed to about '*70,000 plazas, oficios y dignidades*' in a Spain less populated than France but having to administer an enormous empire. The equivalent of Max Weber's modern bureaucracy was this small number of individuals – was it even a bureaucracy in today's sense of the word?[311]

These figures of 12,000 or 70,000 government servants in France or Spain are by no means confirmed. And it is also true that the modern state was constantly seeking to extend the sphere of its action outward from this base, without ever succeeding in reaching the whole nation. But this and other similar efforts were battles lost in advance. In France the *intendant*, who was the government's direct representative in each *généralité*, had hardly any colleagues or subordinates. Consequently as the king's representative, he had to raise his voice to be heard and obeyed, and often had to make examples of people. The army itself was insufficient to the task, even in wartime, and *a fortiori* in peacetime. In 1720, in order to put into position the *cordon sanitaire* round Marseilles, protecting the rest of the country from the plague, all the *maréchaussées* and regular troops had to be called out. The rest of the country and the frontiers were left unprotected.[312] All state actions had to be effected over an area a hundred times greater than that of today in comparative terms. Everything was spread more thinly and consequently weakened.

The French monarchy could save face only by enlisting the service of society (or sections of society) and culture: society in this case meaning those classes which predominated by their prestige, their function and their wealth; culture meaning the millions of voices and millions of ears – everything that was said, thought or repeated from one end of the kingdom to the other.

Social structures changed so slowly that the pattern devised by Georges Gurvitch to analyse the thirteenth century is still a valid guide. Even in 1789, five different societies could still be found at the upper levels of the hierarchy: the king's courtiers, the feudal aristocracy, the seigneurs, the towns – especially the towns – and the Church. With each of these the monarchy had found a compromise, a *modus vivendi*. The Church was well under control – one might even say it has been bought, at least twice and for a high price: by the Concordat of 1516 which brought the appointment of the upper clergy under the Crown (but then the monarchy had had to choose between Rome and the Reformation, a dramatic and perhaps inescapable choice, but one heavy with consequences); and a second time in 1685, with the Revocation of the Edict of Nantes which cost the kingdom a large share of its prosperity. For both the seigniorial nobility and the high nobility, a career of arms was still a promising occupation in an age of constant warfare. And the court and the lure of pensions remained a constant temptation. Independently of these developments, it is hard to say at what point the monarchy was attached to its nobility or rather nobilities. The sociologist Norbert Elias argues that a society is forever marked and determined by its former phases, and no less by its earliest origins. The monarchy had emerged from the feudal swamp. The king of France had been one lord among many, who rose above the rest, marking himself out, using their own language and principles to tower over them. Royalty was thus marked with its origins, 'the nobility was consubstantial with it'. The Crown might fight the nobility but would never break with it: it imprisoned the nobles within the gilded cage of the court – but was itself a prisoner too. The monarchy cut off the nobility from its roots, but did nothing to open up trade to it – on the contrary. As a corollary of this, however, the Crown had to take the nobility under its wing.

Towards the towns, the monarchy was prodigal with favours and privileges, though with the other hand it taxed them heavily and seized a portion of their income. But the towns benefited from the national market which was gradually being established. The patricians and the bourgeoisie of the towns had the monopoly of trade – no little thing. And the king sold to 'the trade interest' part of his power: the king's office-holders came from the towns. They bought their offices and could either sell them again or pass them on to their heirs. Venality of office led to the feudalization[313] of a section of the bourgeoisie. An office was a slice of public authority, handed over by the state, just as once land had been ceded in the form of fiefs. Venality provided the building bricks for a monarchical society constructed in the shape of a pyramid. The upper storeys were formed by the *noblesse de robe*, an ambiguous and important class created not by the caprice of kings but merely by the development (rather slow in fact) of an administrative elite and the requirements of the state.

As purchase of office became more widespread, a whole bourgeois class, especially in France, came into its own. The French state was a wealth-producing machine for these men. A considerable proportion of French fortunes had their origins here. The same could indeed be said of many countries, whether office was venal or not – of England, the United Provinces, the Catholic Netherlands. In Spain, only minor posts in the towns, those of the *regidores* could actually be purchased. But these were precisely the people – nobles or rather ennobled men who were preparing, as the sixteenth century ended, to carve up the established nobility, to take possession of its lands and to move towards the upper levels of society. And who advanced money to the foreign *hombres de negocios*, if not the new rich? Who else refeudalized and half depopulated the Castilian countryside in the seventeenth century if not the same people? In Venice too, office was only venal at lower levels, for the benefit of the *cittadini*, the bourgeoisie. Magistracies exercised by nobles were usually short-term and were occupied in rotation in the antique style as a *cursus honorum*. This did not prevent the nobles from indirect participation in collecting the city's taxes, from practising trade and from running their huge country estates.

That very narrow section of society which occupied state positions derived extra strength from its functions. Office was to the bourgeoisie what the court was to the high nobility – a source of self-satisfaction and a way of succeeding in the world. Such success benefited dynasties of extraordinary durability. Certain groups of families thus came to stand for the state. If the latter was a robust one, the operation might not prove too harmful. This is the sense of J. Van Klaveren's pertinent observation[314] that venality of office, even in France where it was more common than elsewhere, did not automatically lead to corruption nor to the catastrophic disrepute of public authority. Not that office, a transmittable good, was administered with the wisdom of a careful father-figure for the good of all. But a monarch like Louis XIV was able, through office, to reach some of the patrimony of the bourgeoisie: this was effectively a method of taxation; moreover it protected the lower classes from further exactions. Office-holders were quite firmly controlled. After the authoritarian reign of Louis XIV however, things

The young Charles IX of France. (Photo N.D. Roger-Viollet.)

started to go wrong fairly quickly. From the middle of the eighteenth century, enlightened public opinion was protesting against the venality of office. Where once this had benefited the monarchy, now it ceased to help it.[315] Nevertheless in 1746, there was talk in Holland, of setting up a régime on the French model to counter the oligarchies and corruption of the towns.[316]

Thus the monarchy, in France – and indeed throughout the whole of modern Europe, reached the whole of society. Perhaps one should say high society in particular. But then the great mass of subjects were reached through high society.

If the monarchy penetrated the whole of society, it also penetrated the whole culture as well, or very nearly. Culture, from the state's point of view, was the language of ceremony which had to be heard loud and clear. The coronation at Reims, the royal touch for scrofula, the magnificent palaces,[317] were all great assets, guarantees of success. The king's face had to be shown – another ceremonial policy which always worked. From 1563 to 1565, for two long years, Catherine de Medici insisted in travelling the length and breadth of the kingdom in order to show the young king Charles IX to his subjects.[318] What did Castile ask for in 1575?[319] To see the king's face, *'ver el rostro a su rey'*. A Spanish anthology of proverbs dating from 1345 says that 'the King is to the People what rain is to the earth'.[320] And propaganda has always been used, throughout the history of the civilized world. In France there are innumerable examples to choose from: 'We think ourselves tiny mosquitoes compared to the royal eagle' says a pamphleteer of 1619.[321] 'May he smite and tear into shreds and pieces all those who rebel against his commands! Even if they are our wives, our children or our kinsfolk'. The king could hardly ask for more. It is nice to know that there were all the same occasional discordant notes. 'Do you not hear, dear reader, the trumpets and fifes, and the military march of our grand monarch, tantara, tantara! Yes indeed, here comes the invincible, the one and only, to have himself crowned', in Reims, the native city of our bourgeois diarist Maillefer (3 June 1654).[322] Was he perhaps the typical bourgeois whom Ernest Labrousse has described as socially repressed?[323] The bourgeois who was by turns a Leaguer, a Jansenist[324] and a Frondeur? But until the great movement of the Age of Enlightenment, the bourgeois usually muttered behind closed doors.

There are far too many things one could say about this operational territory of culture and propaganda, as well as on the form taken by enlightened opposition: parlementarian, hostile to royal absolutism or noble privilege, but not to the privilege of capital. I shall have more to say later. Nor do I intend at this point to discuss patriotism and nationalism. These were still new ideas in their first flush of youth. They were by no means absent between the fifteenth and eighteenth centuries, particularly since there were always wars on hand to fan the flames. But we should not anticipate, nor should we make the state responsible for creating the nation. As usual, reality is ambiguous: the state creates the nation, providing it with a setting and an identity. But the opposite can also be true: in many ways the nation creates the state, contributing its pulsing lifeblood and its violent passions.

State, economy and capitalism

We have also, on this journey, neglected a whole series of interesting by-ways – but are they really worth stopping at for long? Should I for instance have talked about *bullionism* whenever precious metals were highly sought after, instead of mercantilism – since inevitably the latter assumes the former, which is always, despite appearances, its *raison d'être*? Should I perhaps have talked about *fiscalism* every time I mentioned taxation? But does fiscalism not always go hand in hand with the state, which is as Max Weber used to say,[325] an enterprise like a factory and thus obliged forever to be thinking where its money is coming from – and never finding it adequate as we have seen?

Most important of all, should one go any further without giving a straightforward answer to the question that confronts us time after time: did the state or did it not promote capitalism, further its progress? Even if one has reservations about the degree of maturity of the modern state, and if, with contemporary parallels in mind, one finds it very inadequate, it must be admitted that between the fifteenth and the eighteenth century the state concerned everything and everybody; it was one of the new forces in Europe. But can it *explain* everything, did it govern everything? The answer is quite emphatically no. Indeed one can even argue for a reversal of the terms: the state undoubtedly encouraged capitalism and came to its rescue. But the formula can be reversed: the state also discouraged capitalism which was capable in return of harming the interests of the state. Both statements could be true, one after another or simultaneously since real life is always complicated, in both predictable and unpredictable ways. Whether favourable or unfavourable, the modern state was one of the realities among which capitalism had to navigate, by turns helped or hindered, but often enough progressing through neutral territory. How could things have been otherwise? If the interests of the state and those of the national economy as a whole frequently coincided – since the prosperity of its subjects was in theory a condition of the profits to be made by the state-as-enterprise – capitalism was by contrast always to be found in that section of the economy which sought to participate in the most vigorous and profitable currents of international trade. It was thus engaged in a game played on an infinitely wider plane than that of the ordinary market economy, as we have seen, or than that of the state and its particular preoccupations. Capitalist interests, in the past as in the present, naturally extend beyond the narrow boundaries of the nation; and this prejudices, or at any rate complicates, the dialogue and relationship between state and capital. In Lisbon, which I choose out of a number of possible cities to illustrate the point, the capitalism of the real businessmen, the powerful merchants was quite invisible to the townspeople. This was because the real transactions went on overseas: in Macao, the secret gateway to China, in Goa in India, in London, the source of commands and demands, in far-off Russia (when one wanted to sell an exceptionally large diamond for instance)[326] or in Brazil, the great realm of slaves and plantations, gold-diggers and *garimpeiros* (diamond-hunters). Capitalism always wore seven-league boots. And it is with this dimension above all that the third and last volume of this work will be concerned.

The conclusion to be borne in mind for the present is that the *power apparatus*, the might that pervades and permeates every structure, is something more than the state. It is the sum of the political, social, economic and cultural hierarchies, a collection of means of coercion where the state's presence is always felt, where it is often the keystone of the whole, but where it is seldom if ever *solely* in control.[327] It may even be eclipsed, or destroyed; but it always reconstitutes itself, unfailingly, as if it were somehow a biological necessity of society.

Civilizations do not always put up a fight

Civilizations or cultures – either word can legitimately be used in this context – are great reservoirs of habits, constraints, accumulated lore, accepted practice and statements which may seem, to the individual, personal and sponteneous, but which have really been handed down from a great distance. They are as much our inheritance as the language we speak. Whenever splits and chasms begin to open up in a society, it is the ever-present culture which fills them in, or covers them up, holding us to our tasks. What Necker said of religion – the very heart of civilization: it is, to the poor, 'a heavy chain and a daily consolation'[328] – might equally well be said of civilization and applied to all mankind.

When Europe came to life again in the eleventh century, the market economy and monetary sophistication were 'scandalous' novelties. Civilization, standing for ancient tradition, was by definition hostile to innovation. So it said no to the market, no to profit-making, no to capital. At best, it was suspicious and reticent. Then as the years passed, the demands and pressures of everyday life became more urgent. European civilization was caught in a permanent conflict that was pulling it apart. So with a bad grace, it allowed change to force the gates. And the experience was not peculiar to the West.

Cultural transmission: the Islamic model

A given civilization contains both the permanent and the changing. It is rooted in one place and may survive clinging to its territory for centuries on end. Yet at the same time, it accepts certain borrowings from other civilizations, near or far, and exports its own cultural goods. Imitation and influence operate alongside certain internal pressures working against custom, tradition and familiarity.

Capitalism is governed by precisely the same rules. At every point in its history, it has been the sum of certain methods, instruments, practices, habits of mind, all incontestably cultural goods, which travelled and were exchanged like any other. When Luca Pacioli published his *De Arithmetica* in Venice in 1496, he was summarizing what had long been known about double-entry book-keeping (it had been used in Florence since the late thirteenth century).[329] When Jakob Fugger visited Venice, he studied double-entry book-keeping there and brought the technique back to Augsburg with him. One way or another, it ended up by spreading to a large part of trading Europe.

The bill of exchange also spread from place to place under the influence originally of the Italian cities. But did it perhaps come from even further back? According to E. Ashtor[330] the Islamic *sutfaya* is nothing like the western bill of exchange, differing from it greatly in its juridical construction. Perhaps so. But it was undoubtedly in existence before the European bill of exchange. How could the Italian merchants, who were from very early days travelling to the ports and markets of Islam, have failed to notice this convenient method of transferring a sum of money to distant parts simply by a piece of paper? The bill of exchange, which is supposed to have been an Italian invention, was used in Europe to solve precisely the same problem, even though it did have to adapt, it is true, to conditions not present in Islam, such as the Church's prohibition on lending at interest. But it seems probable to me that it was a borrowing from Islam.

The same could well be true of the association between merchants known as the *commenda*: a long-standing institution in Islam (the Prophet himself and his wife who was a rich widow, had set up a *commenda*)[331] this was the usual way of organizing long-distance trading to India, the East Indies and China. Whether something borrowed or something new, *commenda* certainly appeared in Italy only in the eleventh to twelfth century. It then began to spread from city to city and we are not surprised to find it in the Hanseatic ports in the fourteenth century, though a little modified by local influence. In Italy, the travelling partner, who accompanied the goods, often shared the profits of the operation. But in the Hanseatic contract, the *Diener* normally received a fixed sum from the partner who had put up the capital: he was thus virtually receiving a salary.[332] But there are also examples of profit-sharing.

The model might be altered then. And it sometimes happened that the same solution was adopted simultaneously in different places without borrowing. The still comparatively uncharted history of the early middle ages makes it difficult to pronounce with certainty. But given the itinerant habits of the medieval merchants and the known routes taken by their goods, at least some trading practices must have been borrowed from elsewhere. This is suggested by the Islamic words taken into the western vocabulary: *douane* = customs (Italian *doana*, from the Arabic), *fonduk, magasin, mohatra* (forward selling, immediately followed by resale, which the fourteenth-century Latin texts relating to usury called *contractus mohatrae*). And further evidence comes from the gifts Europe received from the East: silk, rice, sugar cane, paper, cotton, Arabic numerals, the abacus, Greek science rediscovered through Islam, gunpowder, the compass – all of them precious goods which Europe passed on in turn.

To admit the existence of these borrowings means turning one's back on traditional accounts of the history of the West as pioneering genius, spontaneous inventor, journeying alone along the road towards scientific and technical rationality. It means denying the claim of the medieval Italian city-states to have invented the instruments of modern commercial life. And it logically culminates in denying the Roman Empire its role as the cradle of progress. For the much-

Trading in the Levant ports, from a miniature of the Travels of Marco Polo. (Viollet Collection.)

vaunted Empire – centre of the world and of our own history, extending over all the shores of the Mediterranean and here and there penetrating the landmasses – was only one part of an ancient *world economy* much greater than itself, which would outlast it by centuries. Rome was a link in a vast trading zone stretching from Gibraltar to China, a *Weltwirtschaft* in which for centuries men had travelled along interminable routes, carrying in their packs precious goods, ingots, coins, gold and silver objects, pepper, cloves, ginger, lacquer, musk, ambergris, brocades, cottons, muslins, silks, gold-embroidered satins, dye-woods and perfumed woods, Chinese porcelain – for these were being exported long before the celebrated Indies Companies came into being.

And it was on trades such as these, travelling from one end of the world to the other, that the glories of Byzantium and Islam were later built. Byzantium, despite sudden bursts of vigour, was a civilization of relics, trapped in its heavy splendour, using its power to fascinate barbarian princes and to oppress the peoples under its heel; it was willing to exchange goods only for gold. Islam by contrast was in its prime, having been grafted on to the Middle East and its ancient foundations, not on to the world of Greece and Rome. The countries subjugated by the Muslim conquest had played an active role in the trade between the East and the Mediterranean *before* the arrival of the newcomer; they resumed their role as soon as their habits – briefly disturbed by the conquest

– returned to normal. Of the two essential currency instruments of the Muslim economy: the gold *dinar* and the silver *dirhem*, one, the dinar (= *denarius*) was of Byzantine origin, while the other was of Sassanid provenance. Islam had inherited some countries attached to gold (Arabia, North Africa) and others attached to silver (Persia, Spain); the pattern persisted, since this 'territorial' bimetallism was essentially still there, with only occasional variations, centuries later. What we call the Muslim economy was thus the turning to account of an inherited system, a set of links running between the merchants of Spain, North Africa, Egypt, Syria, Mesopotamia, Iran, Abyssinia, Gujerat, the Malabar coast, China and the East Indies. The centres of gravity, or poles of attraction of Muslim life developed of their own accord: Mecca, Damascus, Baghdad, Cairo. The choice between Baghdad and Cairo depended on whether the route to the Far East went by the Persian Gulf, via Basra and Saraf; or by the Red Sea, via Suez and Jeddah, the port of Mecca.

Even before it came into existence Islam was already, by dint of its inheritance, a trading civilization. Muslim merchants enjoyed from earliest times the consideration, at least from their political rulers, which was rarely forthcoming in Europe. The Prophet himself is said to have said: 'The merchant enjoys the felicity both of this world and the next'; 'He who makes money pleases God.' This is almost sufficient in itself to indicate the climate of respectability attaching to commercial life; and there are plenty of concrete examples. In May 1288, the Mamluke government was trying to attract to Syria and Egypt merchants from Sind, India, China and the Yemen. It is hard to imagine in the West anything like the government decree issued on this occasion:

> We extend this invitation to illustrious personages, great merchants desirous of profits, or small retailers ... Whoever arrives in our country will be able to remain or come and go as he pleases ... it is truly a garden of Paradise for those who reside there ... A divine blessing is assured for the journey of any man who inspires charity by borrowing or who accomplishes a good deed by lending.

Two centuries later, the traditional advice given to the prince in the Ottoman Empire (in the late fifteenth century) was:

> Look with favour on the merchants in the land; always care for them; let no one harass them; let no one order them about; for through their trading, the land becomes prosperous and by their wares, cheapness abounds in the world.[333]

Against the weight of these merchant economies, what could religious scruples or reservations achieve? And yet Islam was, like Christendom, prey to a kind of horror of usury, a disease communicated and becoming widespread through the circulation of coin. Although favoured by princes, merchants incurred the enmity of the ordinary people, particularly that of the craft guilds, brotherhoods and the religious authorities. Words originally neutral 'like *bazingun* or *matrabaz*, used in official texts to denote merchants, took on the pejorative sense of profiteers and cheats in popular speech'.[334] But this popular hostility was also a sign of merchant opulence and pride. Without wishing to make too much of the comparison, we may be surprised at the words Islam attributes to Mohammed: 'If God allowed the inhabitants of Paradise to trade, they would deal in fabrics and spices';[335] whereas in Christendom, it was said proverbially that: 'Trade should be free, and unhindered, even into the gates of Hell.'

This image of Islam foreshadows future developments in Europe. The long-distance trade of early European capitalism, carried on by the Italian city-states, was not an inheritance from the Roman Empire. It took over from the great age of Islam in the eleventh and twelfth centuries, from the Islamic civilization which had seen so many industries and products developed for export, and so many economies with thriving foreign trades. The endless sea-voyages, the regular caravans, spoke of an active and efficiently-organized capitalism. Throughout Islam, there were craft guilds, and the changes they underwent (the rise of the master-craftsmen, home-working and craft-working outside the towns) resemble what was to happen in Europe too closely to have been the result of anything but economic logic. There are other resemblances too: there were city-economies which escaped the control of the traditional authorities – Hormuz, the cities on the Malabar coast, rather belatedly Ceuta on the African coast, and even Granada in Spain. These were effectively city-states. And Islam had trading deficits: its purchases from Muscovy, the Baltic, the Indian Ocean, even the Italian cities which quickly put themselves at its service – like Amalfi and Venice – were paid for in gold. In this too, it prefigured European trade, which would also be based on monetary superiority.

This being so, if one had to choose a date to mark the end of Europe's apprenticeship in trade to the cities of Islam and Byzantium, that of 1252 – when the West began once more to mint gold coins[336] – seems as good a date as any, if indeed what was essentially a slow evolution can be dated. At all events, anything in western capitalism of imported origin undoubtedly came from Islam.

Christendom and merchandise: the quarrel over usury

Western civilization did not benefit as Islam did from the bonus of a benevolent religion. It had to start from scratch. From the very beginning, religion (the essence of civilization) and the economy confronted each other. But as they travelled the road together, one of the partners – the economy – became more pressing, made more demands. This was a difficult dialogue between two worlds with little in common, standing for life on earth and life hereafter. Even in a Protestant country like Holland, the Estates waited until 1658 before declaring that 'financial practices' (i.e. usury) were the concern of the civil powers alone.[337] In the Christian countries loyal to Rome, a vigorous reaction led Pope Benedict XIV to reaffirm (in the bull *Vix pervenit*)[338] on 1 November 1745, the ancient restrictions on lending at interest. And in 1769, certain bankers of Angoulême lost their case against their defaulting borrowers on the pretext 'that they had lent at interest'.[339] In 1777, a judgment of the Paris *Parlement* forbade 'any kind of usury [i.e. loan at interest] prohibited by the holy canons'[340] and it continued to be an offence under French law until 12 October 1789. But the debate went on. The law of 1807 fixed the interest rate at 5% in civil loans, 6% in commercial loans; anything above this was deemed usury. And as late as 8 August 1935, a decree-law in France declared excessive interest rates to be usurious, that is legally reprehensible.[341]

So the drama was played out over a long period. If in the end it did not prevent development, it nevertheless corresponded to a deep crisis of conscience as mentalities were changing to face the demands of capitalism.

Benjamin Nelson's original book[342] argues that it is all quite simple: the question of usury, central to western culture, goes back twenty-five centuries to the ancient commandment of Deuteronomy: 'Thou shalt not lend upon usury to thy brother; usury of money, usury of victuals, usury of anything that is lent upon usury. Unto a stranger thou mayest lend upon usury.' A good example of the enduring nature of cultural realities, this distant source, far back in the mists of time, gave rise to an ever-flowing stream. The distinction between lending to one's brother and lending to a stranger did not in fact satisfy the Christian Church whose teachings were universalist. What might have been all right for the tiny Jewish people surrounded by dangerous foes was no longer permissible for Christians: under the new teaching all men were brothers. Lending at usury was forbidden to all, as Saint Jerome (340–420) explained. His contemporary, Saint Ambrose of Milan (340–397) however allowed the practice of usury to one's enemies during a *just* war – *ubi jus belli, ibi jus usurae* – thus opening the door to lending at usury in trade with Islam, something that cropped up again later during the Crusades.

The struggle waged by the Church and the Holy See retained all its rigour, especially since usury was by no means an imaginary evil. The second Lateran Council (1139) decided that the unrepentant usurer would be deprived of the sacraments of the Church and could not be buried in hallowed ground. And the quarrel was taken up from one doctor to another: St Thomas Aquinas (1225–1274), St Bernardino of Siena (1380–1444), St Antonino of Florence (1389–1459). The Church persisted in its persecution but the evil survived.[343]

In the thirteenth century however, the Church *seemed* to receive support from an unexpected quarter. The writings of Aristotle penetrated Christendom in 1240 and were given currency through the work of St Thomas Aquinas. Aristotle is quite unequivocal on usury:

Usury is detested above all and for the best of reasons. It makes profit out of money itself, not from money's natural object ... Money was intended as a means of exchange, not to increase at interest. This term 'interest' (Gk. *tokos* = offspring] which means the birth of money from money is applied to usury because the offspring resembles the parent.[344]

A warning to usurers. Woodcut, fifteenth century. God condemns their evil deeds.
(Library of Congress.)

In short, 'money produces no offspring' – or should not, a formula taken up
many times, by Fra Bernardino and by the Council of Trent in 1563: *pecunia
pecuniam non parit*.

The fact that the same hostility to usury is found in non-Jewish societies –
Greek, West European and Muslim – is revealing. And it could also be found in
India and China. Max Weber, normally a great relativist, does not hesitate to
write: 'the canonical prohibition on interest . . . has an equivalent in almost every
ethical system in the world'.[345] These hostile reactions must all surely be the
result of the intrusion of money – an impersonal means of exchange – into the
closed world of the old agrarian economies. There was an instinctive reaction
against this strange power. But money, the instrument of progress, could not be

dis-invented. And credit was essential to the old agricultural economies, exposed as they were to the recurrent hazards of the calendar, many seasonal disasters and long waiting-periods: one had to plough before one could sow, sow before one could reap, and so it went on, interminably. With the gathering speed of the money economy – which could never find enough gold and silver coins for its needs – it was inevitable that one day 'vituperable' usury would be admitted in the open light of day.

But it took time, and a considerable effort of adaptation. The first decisive step was taken with St Thomas Aquinas, whom Schumpeter considered the first man to have had a general vision of the economic process.[346] The role played by the economic thought of the scholastics, Karl Polanyi remarks, lightheartedly but not inaccurately, was comparable to that of Adam Smith or Ricardo in the nineteenth century.[347] The basic principles however (with Aristotle's support) remained intact: usury, it was still said, was nothing to do with the steepness of the interest rate (as we should think today) nor with the fact that one was lending to a poor man who was entirely at one's mercy. No, usury referred to *any* loan – *mutuum* – which resulted in a profit. The only type of loan not regarded as usury was one where the lender expected nothing but repayment of the original sum after a period of time specified, according to the precept: *mutuum date inde nil sperantes*. Anything else would be equivalent to selling the time during which the money had been lent; and time belongs to God alone. A house may bring in rent or a field crops or dues; but money is barren, and barren it must remain. And indeed such interest-free loans were undoubtedly made: charity, friendship, disinterest, the desire to please God – these must have been motives enough. In Valladolid in the sixteenth century, there are records of loans 'for the sake of honour and good works', *para hacer honra y buena obra*.[348]

But scholastic thought opened up a loophole. The crucial concession was that interest could legitimately be charged when the lender was either running a risk (*damnum emergens*) or failing to gain (*lucrum cessans*). These distinctions opened up plenty of doors. Thus since *cambium*, currency exchange, was merely a transfer of money, the bill of exchange which was its concrete expression could be allowed to travel from place to place since the profit it usually brought was not assured in advance, in other words, there was a risk. Only 'dry exchange' on fictional bills, without any movement from place to place, was considered usurious – not without cause, since *cambio seco* was indeed a disguised form of lending at interest. Similarly, loans to the prince or the state were allowed; and so too were the profits resulting from trading partnerships (the Genoese *commenda*, the Venetian *colleganza*, the Florentine *societas*). Even deposits placed with a banker – *depositi a discrezione* – condemned by the Church, would presently become legitimate, since they could be disguised as participation in an enterprise.[349]

In fact, in an age when economic life was beginning to take off once more, to forbid money from multiplying was attempting the impossible. Agriculture had taken more land into cultivation in this short period than it had in all the centuries since neolithic times.[350] The towns were growing as never before. Trade was increasing in volume and vitality. How could credit have failed to spread across the thriving regions of Europe: Flanders, Brabant, Hainaut, Artois, Ile-de-France, Lorraine, Champagne, Burgundy, Franche-Comté, Dauphiné, Provence, England, Catalonia and Italy? That usury should one day be abandoned in principle to the Jews who were scattered throughout Europe and to whom money-handling was the only means of making a living now left – was one solution, but it was not *the* solution. Or rather, it was one way of using the prohibition in Deuteronomy: if Jews were permitted to practise usury in dealings with non-Jews, Christians could be regarded as 'strangers'. But whenever we have evidence of usury being practised by Jews (in the *banchi* they ran in fifteenth-century Italy for instance) their activities run side by side with those of Christian moneylenders.

The truth was that usury was practised by the whole of society: princes, the rich, merchants, the humble, and even the Church – by a society that tried to conceal the forbidden practice, frowned on it but resorted to it, disapproved of those who handled it, but tolerated them. 'One went as furtively to visit the moneylender as one went to visit a whore'[351] – but one went all the same. 'If I, Marin Sanudo, had been a member of the *Pregadi* as I was last year, I should have spoken out ... to demonstrate that the Jews are as necessary as bakers,'[352] declared a Venetian nobleman in 1519. And the Jews took an undue share of the blame, since the Lombard, Tuscan and Cahors moneylenders, although Christians, openly lent money against pledges and made loans at interest. Here and there however, Jewish moneylenders had cornered the market in usury, in particular north of Rome in the fourteenth century. They had long been kept at arm's length in Florence; but they made their entry in 1396 and settled there in force when Cosimo de Medici returned from exile in 1434; three years later a Jewish group acquired the monopoly of moneylending in the city. A characteristic detail: they set up their practice 'in the same banks and under the same names as the Christian bankers who had preceded them: *Banco della Vacca*, *Banco dei quatro Pavoni* ...'[353]

In any case, both Jews and Christians (not to mention representatives of the Church) used the same methods: fictional sales, false fair bills, invented figures on notarial documents. Such practices became commonplace. In Florence, an early home of capitalism, this much is clear from casual remarks made in the fourteenth century by such men as Paolo Sassetti, the confidant and partner of the Medici. In 1384, he writes apropos of an exchange deal, that his profit was *'piu di f[iorini] quatrocento cinquanta d'interresse, o uxura si voglia chiamare'* – over 450 florins interest, or usury, if you prefer to call it that. Here it is interesting to see how the word 'interest' is clearly separated from the pejorative meaning of 'usury'.[354] Philippe de Commynes, having deposited some money in a branch of the Medici bank in Lyons, complains as if it were the most natural

Capital of a pillar in Autun cathedral, twelfth century. The devil is depicted with a bag of money in his hand. (Photothèque Armand Colin.)

thing in the world, that he has not received enough interest. 'The said gain was a very meagre one for me' (November 1489).[355] Once the ball was rolling, the business world would soon have little to fear from the strictures of the Church. A money-changer in Florence in the fourteenth century was lending money at rates close to 20% – sometimes even higher.[356] The Church had become as disposed to forgive the sins of merchants as it was those of princes.

Not that scruples were not expressed. When a usurer was about to meet his Maker, remorse might lead to repayment of usurious exactions: one usurer alone, a native of Piacenza living in Nice, drew up a list of 200 items.[357] According to Benjamin Nelson, these last-minute repentances and repayments, which filled up so many pages of wills and notarial documents, hardly appear at all after 1330.[358] But even later than this, Jakob Welser the Elder was still refusing, for conscience sake, to take part in the monopolies which afflicted Renaissance Germany. His contemporary Jakob Fugger anxiously consulted Johann Eck, the future adversary of Luther, and paid for him to make a journey to Bologna for consultation.[359] On two occasions, the second in 1532, the Spanish merchants in Antwerp sought the advice of the theologians of the Sorbonne on the same points.[360] In 1577, Lazaro Doria, a Genoese businessman in Spain, retired from business on grounds of conscience, which made a certain stir.[361] In short, mentalities had not changed as quickly as economic practice, as can be seen from the upheaval caused by the bull *In eam* promulgated by Pius V in 1571 on the much-discussed question of exchange and re-exchange: perhaps not entirely intentionally, this implied a return to the most rigorous rules: it simply forbade the *deposito*, that is a loan or deferred payment between two fairs, agreed at the normal rate of 2.5% – the usual method used by merchants who bought and sold goods on credit. The Buonvisi, who were like so many other merchants much inconvenienced by this ruling, wrote from Lyons to Simón Ruiz on 21 April 1571:

> As you must know, His Holiness has forbidden the *deposito*, which was a very convenient way of doing business, but we must be patient, and at this fair, no rate was agreed for the said *deposito*, so we were only able to provide a service for our friends with great difficulty and we had to dissimulate a little. We have done the best we could, but from now on, since everyone will have to obey the ruling, we too wish to do so, and we shall have to use the exchanges of Italy, Flanders and Burgundy.[362]

Since *deposito* has been banned, we shall have to go back to straightforward *cambio*, which is permitted, was the conclusion of the Lucchese firm. One door has been closed, let us try another. We may well believe that they did from Father Laínez (1512-1565) who succeeded Ignatius Loyola as General of the Jesuit order: 'The merchants have so many tricks for inventing ingenious practices that we can hardly see what is going on at the bottom of it all.'[363] The seventeenth century did not invent the *ricorsa* agreement – by which a long-term loan was made through the system of 'exchange and re-exchange', the practice of circulating a bill of exchange for a very long period from one place to another, increasing the repayable amount from year to year – but it certainly brought it into widespread use. When this practice was condemned as pure usury, the Republic of Genoa made long representations and finally persuaded Urban VIII to recognize it as legitimate on 27 September 1631.[364]

The lax attitude of the Church may seem surprising. But how could it fight the combined forces of everyday life? The last of the scholastics, the Spaniards, including the great Luis de Molina, set an example of liberalism.[365] 'How Marx would have enjoyed the Spanish theologians' pronouncements on money-changing, as they lean over backwards to justify profits,' says Pierre Vilar.[366] He would indeed – but could the theologians really have sacrificed the whole economy of Seville (or of Lisbon, which had been temporarily united with it since 1580)?

And the Church was not alone in giving way. The state either preceded or followed it, depending on circumstances. In 1601, Henri IV, by the treaty of Lyons, attached to France the territories of Bugey, Bresse and Gex, which were forcibly confiscated from the duke of Savoy. These little territories had certain privileges and customs, notably in questions of government bonds, interest and usury. The French Crown, which put them under the jurisdiction of the Dijon *parlement*, tried to impose its own regulations upon them. Interest rates on government bonds were almost immediately reduced from one-twelfth (*au denier douze* or 8.3%) to one-sixteenth. Then in 1629, some usurers were prosecuted and several sentences passed. 'The search spread panic, and no one dared sign any interest agreements.' But on 22 March 1642, an edict from the king in Council restored the old usage of the dukes of Savoy, that is the right to 'stipulate the interest which can be charged' as in neighbouring foreign provinces, 'where issuing bonds and stipulating interest is normal'.[367]

As time passed, objections disappeared. In 1771, one observer wondered whether frankly 'a loan-deposit bank (*Mont de Piété*) or a Lombard bank would not be useful in France, and the most effective way to prevent the flagrant usury which is ruining so many individuals'.[368] Just before the Revolution, Sébastien Mercier remarked upon the usury practised by notaries, who made money particularly quickly, and upon the role played by the 'advancers', the small-time moneylenders who were of invaluable aid to the poor after all, since the state tended to monopolize all credit facilities for its many loans.[368] In England, the House of Lords rejected on 30 May 1786 a bill (which had at least got this far) proposing that 'pawnbrokers should be allowed to charge interest of up to 25%, to the great detriment of the people'.[369]

But by this time, the latter half of the eighteenth century, the quarrel was really over. Some latter-day theologians might still fulminate. But on the whole a distinction was made between usury and the regular price of borrowed money. 'I think like you', wrote the rich and honest merchant of Marseilles Jean-Baptiste Roux to his son (29 December 1798) 'that the interest-free loan only concerns a loan made to a man who borrows out of need, and cannot be applied to a merchant who is borrowing money in order to engage in lucrative enterprises and promising speculations.'[370] A quarter of a century earlier the Portuguese financier Isaac de Pinto was already stating unequivocally: 'Interest on money is useful and necessary to all; usury is destructive and blameworthy. To confuse the two is like condemning the useful purposes of fire because it burns and consumes those who venture too near it.'[371]

Puritanism equals capitalism?

The attitude of the Church towards usury must be seen as part of a long process of change in religious attitudes as a whole. What was really taking place was a break with the past – one among many. The *aggiornamento* in our own times – Vatican II – was certainly not the first in this long history. In the view of Augustin of Renaudet,[372] St Thomas Aquinas's *Summa Theologica* was itself the first step towards 'modernism' – and a successful one. Humanism too was in its way an *aggiornamento*: none other than the systematic overhaul within western civilization, of the entire Greco-Latin heritage. It is something we are still living through.

And what about the great break caused by the Reformation? Did this encourage the rise of a capitalism relieved of its anxieties, its scruples, in short of its bad conscience? This is broadly the thesis suggested by Max Weber in the little book he published in 1904, known in English as *The Protestant Ethic and the Spirit of Capitalism.* It is true that after the sixteenth century there is a clear correlation between the countries which welcomed the Reformation and the areas where merchant and later industrial capitalism pursued its successful career, from the glories of Amsterdam to the later glories of London. This must be more than mere coincidence. So was Weber right?

His argument is rather disconcerting: it leads us into a very complex train of thought. Weber seeks to discover a Protestant minority inspired by a very particular ethic, the ideal-type capitalist mentality. This implies a whole series of presuppositions. As an extra complication, the argument works backwards from the present to the past.

We begin with Germany in about 1900. A statistical survey carried out in Baden in 1895 has just established that Protestants are more likely than Catholics to be wealthy and engaged in economic activity. Let us accept for the sake of argument that the results are valid. What do they mean on a wider scale? The man who carried out the survey, Martin Offenbacher, a pupil of Weber's, states unhesitatingly: 'The Catholic ... is of a calmer disposition, with less thirst for profit; he prefers a safe existence, even with a small income, to a life of risks and excitement, even if the latter would bring him wealth and honour. Popular wisdom sums this up as "a man can either eat well or sleep well". In the present example, the Protestant prefers to eat well; while the Catholic prefers to sleep peacefully.' And armed with this slightly comical picture of the Protestants lined up with their spoons and the Catholics turning their back on the table of capitalism, Max Weber proceeds into the past, where he is quickly found at the side of Benjamin Franklin: an excellent witness of course, since in 1748 he had written 'Remember that time is money ... Remember that credit is money ... Remember that money is of a prolific generating nature' (*Advice to a Young Tradesman*).

Weber regards Franklin as standing at the end of a long and privileged line, that of his Puritan ancestors and precursors. Taking another large stride into the past, he introduces us to the preacher Richard Baxter in Cromwell's England. Baxter's teachings can be resumed as follows: we should not waste a moment of our precious brief earthly existence; our only reward must lie in doing our best in the post at which God has placed us; we must work wherever he saw fit to set us. God knows in advance who is to be saved and who is to be damned, but success in one's calling is a sign that one is among the elect (a sort of divine fortune-telling). A merchant who makes his fortune will indeed see in his success proof that God has elected him for salvation. But, warns Baxter, do not use your wealth for luxurious living, for this is the path to damnation. Use your riches for the public good, be of use to the community. Here again, Max Weber is happy to point out, man is a dupe of his own actions: he creates an ascetic form of capitalism, piously condemned to profit maximization, yet he strives to suppress a spirit of lucre. Rational in its consequences, but irrational in its origins, capitalism is the fruit of this unexpected encounter between modern life and the Puritan ethic.

I have summed up far too rapidly and inadequately a line of thought rich in developments, and have over-simplified a subtle and confusing method of argument – to which I must confess to the reader, I am as allergic as Lucien Febvre was. But that is no reason to make Weber say something he did not. Where he saw only coincidence and common ground, he has been accused of declaring Protestantism to be the source of capitalism. Werner Sombart was one of the first historians to exaggerate Weber's thought, the better to destroy his case. Protestantism was after all from the start, Sombart ironically argues, an attempt to return to the poverty of the New Testament, and a real danger for the structures and advanced development of the economy. As for the rules of the ascetic life, these are to be found in the writings of Aquinas and the scholastics. Puritanism is simply a mean and penny-pinching doctrine, fit for small shopkeepers![373] This is frankly ridiculous of course, as most polemics are. It would be equally ridiculous to try to disprove Max Weber's argument from the other end, by quoting the lavish spending of the Dutch in Batavia in the eighteenth century, or the banquets they organized a century earlier in Deshima, to relieve the tedium of the island to which the Japanese carefully confined their activities.

The whole thing would be much easier if the rise of capitalism dated straightforwardly from Calvin's letter on usury (about 1545). This would give us a turning-point. This keen-eyed analysis of the problems of usury by a rigorous mind well-informed about economic life, is clarity itself. For Calvin, a distinction must be made between theology, a sort of indestructible moral infrastructure, and human laws, the judge, the jurist and the letter of the law. Usury is legitimate (provided interest rates are modest, about 5%) between merchants; it is not legitimate when it offends against charity. 'God did not forbid all profits so that a man can gain nothing. For what would be the result? We should have to abandon all trade in goods.' The Aristotelian precept of course holds good: 'I confess what a child can see, that if you shut up money in a chest, it will bear no fruit.' But with money 'one can buy a field … [this time] it cannot be said that money does not engender money'. There is no sense in 'stopping at the words', one must 'look at the realities'. Henri Hauser[374] from whom I have taken these well-chosen quotations from Calvin's thought, concludes that the economic advance of the Protestant countries must have been the result of readier and therefore cheaper credit. 'This is the explanation of the development of credit in countries like Holland or Geneva. It was Calvin who, without realizing it, was making this possible.' Which is another way of agreeing with Max Weber.

Yes, we might say, but what about Genoa, a Catholic city and yet the beating heart of a capitalism already of worldwide dimensions – where interest rates were 1.2%.[375] Where could one find lower? Perhaps capitalism, as it expanded, created low interest rates as much as it was created by them? And in any case, on the question of usury, Calvin was not really breaking any taboos: they had long since been overcome.

Retrospective geography: a good explanation

To take us out of this debate which it would not be helpful to prolong further – not at any rate without quoting from a whole range of amiable polemics from R.H. Tawney to Herbert Lüthy – it may be worth seeing whether there are not some simpler *general* explanations available, less Byzantine and unsupported than this rather misleading retrospective sociology. This is what Kurt Samuelsson has tried to argue (in 1957 and 1971);[376] and I tried the same in 1963.[377] But our arguments were not the same.

It cannot be denied, I would suggest, that Reformation Europe as a whole overtook the Mediterranean economy, brilliant as this was and already long-experienced in the ways of capitalism. (I am thinking of Italy in particular.) But such transfers are the common coin of history; Byzantium declined as Islam rose; Islam made way for Christian Europe; Mediterranean Christendom won the first race to conquer the Seven Seas, but in about 1590, the centre of gravity of Europe swung over to the Protestant North which became the most prosperous region. Until then, and perhaps even until 1610-1620, the word *capitalism* applies primarily to the South – despite Rome and despite the Church. Amsterdam was only beginning to be important at this time. We might also note that the North had made no discoveries – it had not discovered America, nor the route round the Cape, nor the great routes of the world. It was the Portuguese who were the first to reach the East Indies, China and Japan: these spectacular achievements must be credited to 'lazy' southern Europe. Nor did the North invent any of the instruments of capitalism: these all came from the South. Even the Bank of Amsterdam was modelled on the Venetian Bank of the Rialto. And it was by competing with the state monopolies of the southern countries – Spain and Portugal – that the great merchant companies of the North were forged.

That said, if one looks now at a map of Europe and in particular at the course of the rivers Rhine and Danube and if one forgets for the moment the episodic Roman occupation of Britain, the continent can be divided into two: on one side an ancient region, long exploited by men and history and enriched by its efforts; on the other a new Europe, for long centuries uncivilized. The great achievement of the Middle Ages was the colonization, education, development and urbanization of this uncultivated Europe – as far as the Elbe, the Oder and the Vistula, as far as England, Ireland, Scotland and the Scandinavian countries. The words *colony* and *colonialism* would require some qualification perhaps, but broadly speaking northern Europe was a colonial territory, bullied into shape, catechized and exploited by the old Latin culture, the Church and Rome – just as the Jesuits later tried, unsuccessfully, to impose their own pattern upon their reservations in Paraguay. The Reformation, for the countries bordering the North Sea and the Baltic, was among other things, the end of colonialism.

These countries, which were poor, despite the exploits of the Hanseatic towns and the sailors of the North Sea, were left with all the ungrateful tasks, the deliveries of raw materials: English wool, Norwegian timber, Baltic rye. In Bruges and Antwerp, the southern banker and merchant called the tune: their writ ruled and they exasperated rich and poor alike. Note that the Protestant revolution took an even more virulent form on sea than on dry land: the Atlantic had hardly been conquered by Europeans before it became the battleground – only too often forgotten by historians – of fierce religious and material struggles. When the balance finally swung in favour of the North, with its lower wages, its increasingly unbeatable industry, its cheap transport, its fleet of coasters and little sailing ships which could make voyages at low cost, this was a matter of pounds, shillings and pence, of competitive costs. Everything could be produced more cheaply in the North: grain, canvas, woollens, ships, timber, etc. The victory of the North was undoubtedly in a way the victory of the proletarian, the underdog, who had eaten less well, if not less copiously than the south. To this must be added the economic downturn in about 1590, the crisis which, in the past as in the present, strikes first the most advanced countries with their more complex machinery. To the North, this brought a series of good opportunities, perceived and recognized as such, and seized by businessmen who flocked into Holland from Germany, France and indeed Antwerp. The consequence was the powerful rise of Amsterdam, bringing with it general good fortune for the Protestant countries. The victory of the North was the victory of challengers who had more modest requirements than the champions – until the day came, when having ousted all their rivals, they in turn developed the arrogance of the rich; the day when their business network spread far and wide, creating everywhere, in Germany of course but also in Bordeaux and other places, Protestant communities richer, more adventurous and sharper than the local merchants – just as the Italians had once seemed to the countries of the North, in Champagne, Lyons, Bruges and Antwerp, the unrivalled experts on trade and banking.

I find this a persuasive explanation. There are more things in the world than the Protestant ethic. And the same story, played out so often in the past, was to happen again in the eighteenth century. If the industrial revolution had not brought a new deal to Hanoverian England, the world might alternatively have shifted towards rapidly-expanding Russia, or more probably towards the United States, which had forged itself, not without difficulty, into a sort of Republic of the United Provinces, with its proletarian ships not unlike those of the Sea Beggars of the sixteenth century, *mutatis mutandis*. But instead, as a result of technological and political accidents combined with favourable economic circumstances, came the machine revolution, while the Atlantic was reconquered by the British in the nineteenth century thanks to the steamship, an iron vessel propelled by steam-power. This meant the end of the elegant Boston clippers

The northerners begin to rule the waves. A huge Portuguese sailing-ship is attacked off Malacca by small English and Dutch vessels, on 16 October 1602. J. Th. de Bry, *India orientalis, pars septima*. (Photo B.N., Paris.)

with their streamlined wooden hulls. And it was also the moment when America turned away from the sea to devote herself to the conquest of the Frontier and go west.

Does this mean that the Reformation did not heavily influence the behaviour and attitudes of businessmen, with obvious repercussions on the whole of material life? It would be absurd to deny that it did. In the first place, the Reformation created the coherence of the northern countries. It enabled them to stand as a united group against their southern competitors. This was no negligible advantage. And the Wars of Religion left a legacy, born in community of belief, of solidarity between Protestant networks, which played its role in trade for a while at least, until national sentiments overruled all other considerations.

Moreover, unless I am mistaken, the Church where it was maintained and even strengthened in the Catholic Europe of the Counter-Reformation, was a kind of cement holding traditional society together. The various levels of the Church hierarchy, its sinecures which were a sort of social currency, upheld the structure of the past and other hierarchies. They consolidated a social order unlike that of the Protestant countries which was more flexible, less sure of itself. And capitalism in a sense needed a society that could develop in a way favourable to its expansion. So the file on the Reformation and capitalism certainly cannot be closed.

Capitalism equals rationalism?

Another more general explanation sometimes advanced is the progress made by the scientific attitude and rationalism in the West: this is said to have hastened the general economic advance of Europe by furthering at the same time capitalism or rather capitalist intelligence and its constructive breakthrough. This argument too sets much store by an ethic or spirit, by the inventive minds of the entrepreneurs and the justification of capitalism as the spearhead of the economy. This is a very debatable thesis, even if one does not argue as Maurice Dobb has[378] that if the capitalist mentality produced capitalism, where did the capitalist mentality come from? This is not necessarily the way to put it though: it is quite possible to imagine a reciprocal relationship between the mass of realities and the spirit observing and manipulating them.

The most outspoken defender of this thesis is Werner Sombart who sees this as another opportunity to stress the importance of attitudes as against other factors. But the arguments he puts forward do not carry much weight. What is one to make for instance of his dramatic assertion that rationality (which he does not define) is the underlying tendency, the multisecular trend as people might say today, of western development; or as Otto Brunner preferred to put it, its historical destiny;[379] that it was the rationalist spirit which brought us the modern state, the modern city, science, the bourgeoisie and lastly capitalism itself? In short that the capitalist ethic and reason were one and the same thing?

The particular reason in question, in Sombart's mind, was the rationality of the instruments and the means of exchange. He cites for instance the *Liber Abaci*, the book of the abacus written in 1202 by the Pisan Leonardo Fibonacci. This is not a very well-chosen starting point, since the abacus was an Arabic invention; it was in Bougie in North Africa, where his father was a merchant that Fibonacci learnt to use it – along with Arabic numerals, how to judge the value of a currency from the quantity of fine metal, and how to calculate altitude, latitude etc.[380] Fibonacci would be better quoted as evidence of the scientific rationality of the Arabs. Another piece of early evidence is that of the accounts ledgers. The first known example dates from 1211, in Florence. According to the *Handlungsbuch* (kept in Latin) of the Holzschuher (1304–1307)[381] it was the need to keep a record of goods sold on credit rather than an abstract love of order which inspired the first account-books. And in any case, it would be a long time before accounting became the perfect record of transactions. Merchants were often content simply 'to note their affairs on pieces of paper which they stick on the wall', notes Matthaus Schwarz, the very up-to-date book-keeper for the Fuggers from 1517.[382] However by this date, the full technique of double-entry book-keeping had long been revealed by Fra Luca di Borgo (whose real name was Luca Pacioli) in Chapter XI of his *Summa di arithmetica, geometria, proportioni e proportionalità* (1494). Of the two essential registers required for keeping accounts, the *Manuale* or *Giornale* where transactions were recorded in chronological order, and the chief ledger, the *Quaderno*, where each operation was recorded twice, the second, with its double entries, was the novelty. It enabled the merchant to have a precise idea of his assets and his debts at any moment. If the books did not balance, it meant a mistake had been made and could be detected at once.[383]

The usefulness of the *partita doppia* is self-evident. Sombart allows himself a flight of lyricism on the subject: 'It is simply impossible' he writes, 'to imagine capitalism without double-entry book-keeping; they are like form and content', *wie Form und Inhalt.* 'Double-entry book-keeping was born of the same *spirit* [my italics] as the systems of Galileo and Newton, and the modern schools of physics and chemistry ... Without looking too closely [*ohne viel Scharfsinn*, a rather odd precautionary phrase] one might already glimpse in double-entry book-keeping the ideas of gravitation, the circulation of the blood and energy conservation.'[384] One is reminded of Kierkegaard's remark: 'Any truth is only true up to a certain point. When one oversteps the mark, it becomes a non-truth.' Sombart does indeed overstep the mark, and others have followed him, exaggerating in their turn. Spengler compares Luca Pacioli with Christopher Columbus and Copernicus.[385] C.A. Cooke (1950) tells us that the 'importance of the double-entry system of keeping books lies not in its arithmetic but in its metaphysics'.[386] Walter Eucken, a reputable economist, nevertheless declares unhesitatingly (1950) that if the Germany of the Hanseatic League failed to become great in the sixteenth century, it was for lack of adopting *doppelte Buchhaltung* – which was welcomed, along with prosperity, into the ledgers of the merchants of Augsburg.[387]

Any number of objections could be made to these views. To take the smallest ones first, without wishing to belittle Luca Pacioli, one must note that he was not the first in the field. Sombart himself mentions the book on commerce, *Della Mercatura*, written by the Ragusan Cotrugli; although better known in the second edition of 1573, this book dates from 1458.[388] The fact that the second edition was brought out unchanged after a hundred years indicates incidentally how little methods of doing business had changed over these years, despite the considerable economic progress made meantime. In Book I, Chapter XIII of this manual, at any rate, a few pages are devoted to the advantages of orderly book-keeping, which enable one to maintain credit and debit in balance. Federigo Melis, who has read hundreds of merchant registers, tells us that *partita doppia* was already appearing in Florence from very early days, by the end of the thirteenth century in the books of the Compagnia dei Fini and the Compagnia Farolfi.[389]

The man who brought Europe double-entry book-keeping. Painting by Jacopo de Bar, 1495, of the Franciscan friar Luca Pacioli demonstrating plane geometry to one of his pupils, probably Federico de Montefeltre, the son of the duke of Urbino. (Photo Scala.)

But to move on to the real objections, in the first place, this famous double-entry book-keeping did not spread quickly and was by no means universally adopted. In the three hundred years after Luca Pacioli's book, it certainly did not appear as a victorious revolution. The trade manuals mention it, but merchants did not always practise it. Some huge firms did without it for a long time – some of the very biggest like the Dutch East India Company, founded in 1602; and the Sun Fire Insurance Office of London, which only adopted it in 1890 (no, not a misprint, 1890).[390] Historians who are familiar with old-style book-keeping, like Raymond de Roover, Basil S. Yamey and Federigo Melis, do not regard double-entry book-keeping as a necessary substitute for the previous accounting methods sometimes regarded as inefficient. In the days of single-entry accounts, R. de Roover writes,[391] 'medieval merchants found out how to adapt this imperfect instrument to the needs of their own businesses and achieved their ends, sometimes by roundabout ways . . . They hit upon solutions which amaze us today by their flexibility and their extraordinary variety. Nothing could be further from the truth than . . . Sombart's suggestion that the accounts of medieval merchants are such a mess [*Wirwarr*] that it is impossible to decipher them.'

According to Basil Yamey (1962), Sombart exaggerated the importance of accounting in any case. The abstract machinery for reckoning plays a significant role in any business, but it does not dictate the decisions taken by the head of the firm. Even detailed statements (audits) and balance-sheets (which were no easier to draw up by double-entry book-keeping than they were by single-entry, and which were in any case rare in the business world) were not central to the decision-making process, and consequently not central to the operations of capitalism. Balance-sheets usually appeared when a business went into liquidation, rather than in its day-to-day running. And they were difficult to draw up: what should be done about assets that might not materialize? And since a single money of account was being used, how could one record differences in exchange rates – differences which could be very significant? Acts of bankruptcies in the eighteenth century show that even then such difficulties had not really been overcome. As for audits, which were established only at irregular intervals, they made sense only in relation to the previous one. The Fuggers for instance, were able in 1527 to evaluate the capital and profits of their firm since the 1511 audit. But between these two dates, they certainly did not run the business by reference to the 1511 audit.

Finally, when one is considering the range of rational instruments of capitalism, should one not also make room for other instruments besides double-entry book-keeping: bills of exchange, banking, stock exchanges, markets, endorsements, discounting, etc.? But of course all these things were to be found outside the western world and its sacrosanct rationality. And they were in any case an inheritance, a slowly accumulated body of practice which had been simplified and perfected by the day-to-day activities of economic life. More significant than the innovating spirit of entrepreneurship were the increased volume of trade, the frequent inadequacy of the money supply, etc.

But does the readiness of historians to equate capitalism and rationality really stem from admiration for modern trading techniques at all? Does it not rather arise from a general feeling – the word argument is hardly appropriate – that capitalism equals growth; that capitalism is not one stimulus among many, but *the* stimulus, the tiger in the tank, the prime mover of progress? Once more, this is to identify capitalism too closely with the market economy – an arbitrary equation in my view, as I have already explained, though an understandable one, since the two things coexisted and developed simultaneously, one because of the other and vice versa. People have been quick to go one step further and credit capitalism with the 'rationality' which they have seen in the equilibrium of the market, in the operation of the market system. But is there not a contradiction here somewhere? For the famous rational process of the market, about which so much has been written, operates precisely through *spontaneous* exchange,

A Genoese money-changer's bench. Illuminated manuscript, late fourteenth century. (Photothèque Armand Colin.)

trading which is above all free, competitive and in no way directed: whether it is described as the hidden hand (Adam Smith) or the natural computer (Lange) it results from the 'natural order', from the meeting of collective supply and demand, going far beyond individual calculations. *A priori*, this cannot be the same thing as the rational behaviour of the individual entrepreneur who seeks the path of maximum profit to himself. According to Smith, the entrepreneur has no need, any more than the state, to worry about the proper operation of the whole, which is automatically guaranteed. For 'no wisdom or human knowledge' could possibly undertake this task. That capitalism could not exist without rationality, that is without the continual adaptation of means to ends, without an intelligent calculation of probabilities, I will readily agree. But that takes us back to relative definitions of what we mean by rational, which can vary not only from one culture to another but from one set of circumstances to another, from one social group to another, depending in each case on the ends and means. There can be different versions of rationality within a single economy. There is the logic of free competition; and there is the logic of monopoly, speculation and power.

Did Sombart towards the end of his life (1934) become aware of a certain contradiction between the rules of the economy and the action of capitalists? He certainly gives rather a strange picture of the entrepreneur torn between economic calculation and speculation, between rationality and irrationality. He is thus almost at the point of classing capitalism – as I have tended to do in this book – with the 'irrational' behaviour of speculation![392] But I do seriously believe that the distinction between the market economy and capitalism is crucial here. It is important not to attribute to capitalism the virtues and 'rationalities' of the market economy itself – as even Marx and Lenin both do, implicitly or explicitly, by regarding the development of monopolies as an inevitable but *late* development of capitalism. For Marx, the 'capitalist system', when it replaced the feudal system was a 'civilizing' force in that it 'was more favourable to the development of productive forces and social relations' which made for progress, and in that 'it brought about a stage of development from which were absent both coercion and the *monopolization of social progress (including its material and intellectual advantages) by one class of society at the expense of the other*'.[393] If Marx elsewhere condemns 'the illusions of competition', it is in the course of an analysis of the nineteenth-century system of production itself, not in a passage criticizing the behaviour of capitalists. For the latter derive their 'stern ruling authority' entirely from their social function as producers, not as in the past from a hierarchy which made them 'political or theocratic masters'.[394] It is the 'social cohesion of production' which now appears 'as a natural and omnipotent law *vis-à-vis* individual arbitrariness'. My own view is that a case can be argued for the 'external' nature of capitalism both before and after the nineteenth century.

Lenin, in a well-known passage written in 1916[395] argues that capitalism only changed its character (becoming in the early twentieth century 'imperialism') 'at a definite and very high stage of its development, when certain of its fundamental attributes began to be transformed into their opposites.... Economically, the main thing in this process is the substitution of capitalist monopolies for capitalist free competition ... [which had been] the fundamental attribute of capitalism and of commodity production generally.' I do not of course agree on this point. But, Lenin goes on, 'at the same time, monopoly, which has grown out of free competition, does not abolish the latter, but exists over it and alongside it'. And here I am in complete agreement. Putting it in my own words, I would say: 'Capitalism (both past and present, with phases which are monopolistic to a greater or lesser degree) never entirely eliminates the free competition and market economy from which it has grown (and upon which it still draws) but continues to exist over and alongside them.' That is, I would maintain that the economy between the fifteenth and eighteenth century – which consisted essentially of the conquest, from certain long-established 'bases', of a wide area by a flourishing exchange and market economy – also had two levels as distinguished by Lenin in his analysis of late nineteenth-century 'imperialism': monopolies, open or concealed, and free competition; in other words, capitalism as I have been seeking to define it, and the developing market economy.

If I had Sombart's taste for systematic and once-for-all explanations, I might be tempted to suggest that a major element in capitalist development was risk-taking and a taste for speculation. In the course of this book, the reader will have noticed that reference is often made to the underlying notion of gambling, risk-taking, cheating; the rule of the game was to invent a counter-game, to oppose the regular mechanisms and instruments of the market, in order to make it work *differently* – if not in the opposite direction. It might be fun to try and write the history of capitalism within the parameters of a special version of games theory. But the apparent simplicity of the word game (gaming, gambling) would quickly turn out to cover a multitude of different and contradictory realities – forward gambling, playing by the rules, legitimate gambling, reverse gambling, playing with loaded dice. It would be far from easy to make these fit a single theory.

Florence in the Quattrocento: a new art of living

Looking back from the present, it cannot be denied that western capitalism in the long run created a new art of living, new ways of thinking: it developed side by side with them. Can one call this a new civilization? That would I think be putting it too strongly: a civilization is built up over a longer time scale.

But if change there was, when did it come? Max Weber thinks the crucial turning point comes with Protestantism – so not until the sixteenth century; Werner Sombart locates it in fifteenth-century Florence. Otto Hinze[396] remarked that the former favoured the Reformation, the latter the Renaissance.

There is no doubt in my mind: on this point Sombart is right. Thirteenth-century – and *a fortiori* fourteenth-century Florence was a capitalist city, whatever meaning one attaches to the word.[397] The precocious and abnormal picture it presented struck Sombart, quite understandably. What is less understandable is his basing his entire analysis on a single city: Florence (Oliver C. Cox has put up an equally convincing case for Venice as we shall see) and on a single witness – a very illustrious one it is true. Leon Battista Alberti (1404–1472), architect, sculptor, humanist, was the scion of a long-powerful family with an eventful history: members of the Alberti family had economically colonized England in the fourteenth century: indeed so ubiquitous were they that the English documents often refer to them as the *Albertynes* – as if like the Lucchese or indeed the Florentines, they were a nation in themselves. Leon Battista spent many years in exile and with the intention of escaping the troubles of the world entered holy orders. He wrote the first three *Libri della Famiglia* in Rome, in about 1433–1434; the fourth was completed in Florence in 1441. Sombart finds in these books

Panorama of Florence. Detail of fresco *Our Lady of Mercy,* fourteenth century.
(Photo Alinari-Giraudon.)

a new climate: praise of money, recognition of the value of time, the need to live
thriftily – all good bourgeois principles in the first flush of their youth. And the
fact that this cleric came from a long line of merchants respected for their good
faith lent weight to his writings. Money is 'the root of all things'; 'with money,
one can have a town house or a villa; and all the trades and craftsmen will toil

like servants for the man who has money. He who has none goes without everything, and money is required for every purpose.' This was a new attitude towards wealth: previously it had been regarded as a kind of obstacle to salvation. The same was true of time: in the past, time had been considered as belonging to God alone; to sell it (in the shape of interest) was to sell *non suum*, what did not belong to one. But now time was once more becoming a dimension of human life, one of man's possessions which he would do well not to waste. And there was a new approach to luxury: 'Always remember, my sons', writes Alberti 'that your expenditure should never exceed your income' – a new rule which condemned the conspicuous luxury of the nobles. As Sombart says, 'this was introducing a spirit of thrift not into the wretched domestic budgets of humble people who could hardly get enough to eat but into the mansions of the rich'.[398] In other words, the spirit of capitalism.

Not so, says Max Weber, in an intelligent and closely-argued footnote.[399] Alberti was simply repeating the precepts of the wisdom of antiquity: some of the quotations selected for comment by Sombart can be found almost verbatim in Cicero. And it is indeed very tempting to say that Alberti is only talking about household management, *economy* in the etymological sense of the word, and not *chrematistics* – political economy or the flow of wealth through the market. This would place Alberti firmly in the long line of *Hausväterliteratur*, the good housekeeping manuals used by so many well-intentioned German experts until the eighteenth century, to convey a wealth of advice, sometimes of a fascinating character but of only indirect relevance to the world of trade.

Nevertheless, it is Max Weber who is wrong in this case. To realize his mistake, he had only to read the *Libri della Famiglia* of which Sombart's quotations give much too limited an idea. Or he could have listened to evidence from other observers of life in Florence, notably Paolo Certaldo, who would certainly have convinced him.[400] 'If you have money, do not wait, do not keep it lying idle at home, for it is better to work in vain than to be idle for nothing, because even if you gain no profit by working, at least you do not lose the habit of doing business.' Or this: 'Always take trouble and strive to make gains'; or 'It is a fine thing and a great science to know how to make money, but it is even better to know how to spend it sensibly and in the right place.' And one of the speakers in a dialogue written by Alberti comes near to saying: 'Time is money'. If capitalism can be recognized as a 'mentality' and be measured by words, then Weber must surely be wrong. We can however imagine his reply: all this is after all only a desire for lucre. But capitalism is something else again; indeed it is the opposite: it is an inner control 'a brake, a restraint, or at least an attempt at rational restraint of the irrational impulse towards lucre'. This brings us back to square one!

Today's historian may think that such attempts to locate the essence of capitalism are interesting and to some extent worthwhile, but that in no circumstances will they suffice to answer the question. If we really want to discover the origins of the capitalist mentality, we must move out of the charmed circle of words, and look to real life. We must in other words take a good look at the Italian cities of the middle ages – as Marx himself suggests.

Other times, other world views

It is indeed impossible today not to feel that the Sombart-Weber debate has a sense of unreality: it seems to be no more than shadow-boxing. Perhaps what makes it seem faraway and foreign to us is our own historical experience. It was perfectly normal for Max Weber in 1904 and Werner Sombart in 1912 to feel that Europe was the necessary centre of the world, of science, reason, and logic. But we have lost that old self-assurance and superiority complex. After all why should one civilization be more intelligent and rational than another for all time?

Max Weber did consider this question, but after some hesitation, maintained his original position. Any explanation of capitalism, both for him and for Sombart, had to have something to do with the indisputable structural superiority of the western 'mind' – whereas this superiority itself was the result of the accidents and upheavals of history, of the way the world dealt its cards. It is futile to attempt to rewrite world history in support of a cause, let alone an explanation. But what if the Chinese junks *had* sailed round the Cape of Good Hope in 1419, in the middle of the European recession we refer to as the Hundred Years' War – and world domination had fallen to the lot of that huge and distant country, that other pole of the populated world?

The Weber-Sombart debate is marked by another sign of their times: to Max Weber, capitalism appeared as a culmination, the promised land of economic development, the final stage of progress. He never saw it – unless I have missed something in his writing – as a fragile and possibly transitory régime. Today the death, or at any rate series of mutations in what we call capitalism, no longer seems so improbable. We can see them taking place in front of our eyes. Capitalism at any rate 'no longer appears to us to be the last word in historical evolution'.[401]

Capitalism outside Europe

Like Europe, the rest of the world had for centuries had experience of the necessities of production, the laws of trade and movements of currency. Among all the possible combinations, is it absurd to seek for signs heralding or marking a certain form of capitalism? I am tempted to agree with Deleuze and Guattari[402] that 'after a fashion, capitalism has been a spectre haunting every form of society' – capitalism that is as I have defined it. But the fact must be faced that the creation of capitalism succeeded in Europe, made a beginning in Japan, and failed (with some exceptions that prove the rule) almost everywhere else – or perhaps one should say failed to reach completion.

There are two major explanations for this, one to do with economics and geography, the other to do with politics and society. We can do no more than outline these explanations. But however imperfect and in the end negative an investigation like this may be, as one searches through the evidence as yet only partly prospected and collected by European and non-European historians, the clear cases of failure and the near-successes can tell us something about capitalism as a world problem as well as a problem particular to Europe.

The miracles of long-distance trade

The pre-conditions of any form of capitalism have to do with circulation; indeed at first sight one might think them to be exclusively determined by this single factor. The wider circulation stretched its net, the more profitable it was. This elementary determinism was at work everywhere. Recent research by Evelyn Sakakida Pawski shows that in sixteenth-century Fukien and in eighteenth-century Hunan, the coastal strip of these two Chinese provinces, blessed with the gifts of the sea and open to trade, was densely-populated and progressive, with a peasantry apparently quite well off; the inland region, with the same paddy-fields and the same people, was inward-looking and comparatively poor. A thriving economy on one side, stagnation on the other: the rule seems to operate on every level and in every region of the world.

And if this fundamental contrast is particularly striking in China and Asia in these far-off centuries, the reason is that here the distances were enormous; overland journeys, sea-voyages and half-wild zones of under-development were all of exaggerated proportions. Distinctions were marked on a scale very different from that of Europe. By comparison with the great wastes, the thriving zones seemed even narrower, lying along the routes travelled by ships, merchandise and men. So if Japan seems rather different from the rest of eastern Asia, it is in the first place because it is surrounded by the sea, which made communications easier; the Seto no Uchi was a tiny Japanese Mediterranean and a very lively one. (Imagine an inland sea between Lyons and Paris.) I am not seeking to explain the entire development of Japan by the virtues of salt water – but without them, the processes and sequences of events in this singular history would be almost impossible to imagine. And the same is surely true of the southern coast of China with its *rias*, arms of the sea which penetrate the coastal strip from Fu-Chu and Amoy to Canton. Here seagoing and maritime adventure joined forces with a certain form of Chinese capitalism which could only reach its true dimensions if it escaped from the rigid controls of the Chinese mainland. This lively outward-looking side of China contrived, even after 1638 when Japan became almost sealed off from external trade, to keep its hold on the market in copper and silver from the Japanese archipelago, just as the Dutch did, and perhaps more effectively; it sent ships to Manila to pick up silver from the Acapulco galleon; and it had from time immemorial dispatched men, its varied goods, its craftsmen and its unrivalled merchants to every part of the East Indies. Later on, the enthusiasm of Europe for 'the China trade' would turn Canton into a focal market city, stimulating and calling on trade from all over China, and on a higher plane stimulating the skills of its bankers, financiers and moneylenders. The Co-Hong, the group of merchants authorized by the Peking government to set up in competition with the Europeans, founded in 1720 and lasting until 1771, was a rival to the Indies Company and the source of some huge Chinese fortunes.

Very similar observations could be made about other highly active trading cities, such as Malacca before 1510, the year of the Portuguese conquest; or Achem (Atjeh) in Sumatra in about 1600;[403] or Bantam – the Venice or Bruges of the tropics, before the destructive arrival of the Dutch in 1683; or the long-established trading towns of India and Islam. We have a plethora of places to choose from.

Let us suppose then that we choose to look at Surat, on the Gulf of Cambay in India. The English had set up a trading-post here in 1609, the Dutch in 1616, and the French much later but with more lavish equipment in 1665.[404] Towards this last date, Surat was booming. Large vessels put in at the seaward harbour of Swali, on the mouth of the Tapata (Tapti), a small coastal river which was navigable as far as Surat but only for small boats. In Swali the crews of European and non-European ships were lodged in cabins with rush roofs. But large vessels did not stay long, since these were dangerous moorings in bad weather; it was unwise to winter there. Only the merchants stayed behind and lodged in Surat.

According to a French visitor,[405] Surat in 1652 was as big as Lyons – he describes it as having a population of a million, which we may not altogether believe. Trade here was dominated by the Banyan bankers, merchants and commission agents, whose honesty, skill and wealth was widely and accurately reported. 'One could count up to thirty of them who were worth two hundred thousand crowns, and over a third of these had two or three million.' The top fortunes were those of a tax-farmer (30 million) and a merchant 'who lent money at interest to European and Moorish merchants' (25 million). Surat was at this time one of the major ports of the Indian Ocean on the routes between the Red Sea, Persia and the East Indies. It was the gateway to the Mogul Empire, the rendezvous for all India, the chosen centre of shipowners and investors in high-risk maritime trade. Bills of exchange streamed into the town: anyone coming to take a ship there was sure to find money, says Tavernier.[406] It was here that the Dutch came to get the silver rupees they needed for their Bengal trade.[407] Another indication of its importance for international trade was its ethnic and religious cosmopolitanism. As well as the Banyans (who were the most important group as intermediaries) and the huge 'Gentile' artisanal population of the town and its surrounding districts, there was, almost equivalent to the Hindu presence, a

Banyon merchant and his wife from Cambaya, watercolour by a Portuguese resident in Goa and the Indies, sixteenth century. Casanatense Library, Rome. (Photo F. Quilici.)

Muslim trading community which also extended its network from the Red Sea to Sumatra and the rest of the East Indies; and there was an active Armenian colony. Except for the Chinese and Japanese, said a traveller, Gautier Schouten,[408] voyagers from every country and 'merchants from every nation in the Indies' could be found there. 'A prodigious amount of trade is carried on.'

The fortunes of Surat went up and down of course. But in 1758, just after the British conquest of Bengal, the Englishman John Henry Grose was as full of amazement as of admiration at the spectacle of Surat. He does, it is true, express some scepticism at the exaggerated claim that the 'great and truly royal merchant Abdulgafour' alone 'drove a trade equal to the East India Company', but admits that he had been known to 'fit out in a year above twenty sail of ships, between 300 and 800 tons, and none of them had less of his own stock than 20,000 pounds and some of them had 25,000'. He regarded with amazement the Banyans – 'the fairest, openest dealers in the world' moreover – and the scope of their business: 'Many a cargoe from five to ten, twenty, thirty thousand pounds and upwards, has been sold in half an hour's time with very few words.' Their shops 'have a very mean appearance', although 'everything almost that can be asked for is to be found', 'the dealers keeping their goods chiefly in warehouses and selling by samples'. He did not greatly like Indian fabrics, finding fault with their floral patterns and dull red backgrounds, but pick up one of the Cashmere shawls, he says, and you will be delighted at its 'silky' texture; these are of 'exquisite fineness . . . . and so pliant that the fine ones are easily drawn through a common ring for the fingers'.[409] We must imagine dozens of towns almost as active as Surat up and down the coasts of India and the East Indies, with thousands of merchants, entrepreneurs, transporters, brokers, bankers and manufacturers. Was there no capitalism, were there no capitalists? One hesitates to say no. All the typical features of Europe at the same time were present: capital, merchandise, brokers, wholesale merchants, banking, the instruments of business, even the artisanal proletariat, even the workshops very similar to manufactories in big textile centres like Ahmedabad, even domestic working for merchants, handled by special brokers (the machinery for this is described in several articles on the English Bengal trade) – and even, lastly, long-distance trade. But the fact is that this high-tension trading activity was only present in certain places: huge areas were quite untouched by it. It could perhaps be compared to Europe in the thirteenth and fourteenth centuries.

The ideas of Norman Jacobs

Before turning to the second explanation suggested – the political and social one – I should like to open a long parenthesis and I hope a useful one, inspired by Norman Jacobs's book *The Origin of Modern Capitalism and Eastern Asia*, published in Hong Kong in 1958.

Jacobs's argument is at first sight a simple one. In the Far East, he says, only Japan is a capitalist country *today*. To say that Japanese industrial capitalism simply imitated European industrialization is not sufficient explanation. If this were the answer, why should other countries in the Far East not have been capable of similar imitation? It therefore seems likely that some *long-established* structures must be responsible for this propensity, or non-propensity, to welcome capitalism. We should therefore look for the answer in the pre-capitalist structures, seeking to explain the present by the past. With this in mind, one should therefore compare ancient Japan 1) with nearby China: culturally close, but very different; 2) with Europe, culturally very far-removed from Japan, but showing certain similarities. And if the difference between Japan and China is found to be not a cultural one but one of society, social organization and political structures, then Japan's resemblance to Europe will take on significant dimensions. This may cast some new light on capitalism in general and on its social origins in the broad sense.

Jacobs's book wrongly takes it for granted that the essential features of European pre-capitalism are already known; he then proceeds to make a painstaking and elaborate comparison between China and Japan, again taking it for granted (and this is very debatable) that the Chinese case, representing the non-capitalist model, is valid *mutatis mutandis* for India as well. He makes no mention of Islam, which is a glaring omission. But the most serious shortcoming of this reduction to two terms is probably the tendency to make too much of the contrasts between China and Japan. We end up with a black/white reversed image and the danger is that it will lead us to make arbitrary simplications. All the same, the comparison is interesting to follow and instructive throughout.

In making his comparison, Jacobs does not hesitate to set side by side the *entire* history of China and Japan – and I can only applaud him, since I have done much the same thing for Europe, frequently referring back to the great turning-point of the eleventh century or even earlier to explain developments in modern times. Jacobs follows a similar procedure, citing say the decision of the Han dynasty (third century B.C.) on private property in China, or the Japanese edicts of the seventh century exempting from tax land granted to certain social categories – the foundation of Japanese feudalism – or again certain significant incidents from the Ashikaga period (1368–1573) indicating how Japan was already becoming a maritime power, with her pirates scouring the seas of the Far East, while the economy was successfully acquiring its 'liberties' – in the sense of the word used in medieval Europe to mean privileges, barriers against others. Implicitly and explicitly, Norman Jacobs is thus relating the preconditions of capitalism to a very long-term evolution over many centuries; it is by accumulating the historical evidence that he prefers to let the solution emerge. From a sociologist this is showing unusual faith in history.

Jacobs thus traces, over a timespan of centuries, the various *functional* activities of the societies, economies, government policies, religious bodies of Japan and China. He tackles everything: trade, property, political authority, the division of labour, social stratification and mobility, kinship, inheritance systems, the role of religion – in each case watching out for any features in these long-lasting phenomena that resemble European history and could thus be considered as sowing the seeds of a capitalist future. The result is a lengthy and original book, which I shall summarize here in a rather subjective way, adding my own glosses and interpretation as I go along.

In China, the chief obstacle was the state, with its close-knit bureaucracy – and I would add the longevity of the state, which while it might collapse at infrequent intervals was always restored to a position much the same as before: heavily centralized, highly moral, maintaining the strict tradition of Confucian morality, frequently revised but in general faithful to its guiding principles, which committed culture, ideology and religion to its own service; and which committed the state, that is the mandarins of every degree, to the service of the common good. Public works, irrigation, roads, canals, the security and administration of the towns, frontier protection against foreign threats – all this was handled by the state. So too were measures against famine, which meant that the state had to protect and ensure agricultural production, the cornerstone of the entire economy; if necessary, advance payments had to be made to the peasants,

頼
朝

Heroic iconography: the child prodigy Yoritomo (1147–1199) at the age of thirteen kills the robbers who have attacked him. (Tsukioga Nogin Sai Massanobu, *Lives of Famous Men . . .*, 1759, B.N., Paris, Est. DD 161, Photo Giraudon.)

silk-producers and entrepreneurs; the public granaries had to be filled as emergency stores; and as a necessary corollary of this ubiquitous intervention, the state alone had to have the right to levy taxes. If the emperor should forsake the path of morality, then heaven would abandon him and the sovereign would lose his authority. But normally this authority was total and unchallenged and theoretically possessed universal rights. It is true that private land ownership goes back to the Han period, but the government retained in theory the ownership of all land. Peasants and even important landowners might be removed arbitrarily from one part of the empire to another, again in the name of the public good and the need for agricultural colonization. The government as large-scale entrepreneur also retained the right to levy peasant labour. It is true that a landed nobility did establish itself on the backs of the peasants and extracted labour from them, but it did so without any legitimate claim and only to the extent that it undertook, in villages where there was no state functionary exercising direct surveillance, to represent the state and in particular to collect taxes on its behalf. So even the nobility was dependent on the goodwill of the state.

The same was true of the business men or manufacturers whom the lynx-eyed administration could always call to order, controlling and confining their activities. In the ports, all vessels had to be authorized on entry or departure by the local mandarin. Some historians even think that the huge maritime operations of the early fifteenth century were one way in which the state controlled the profits of private foreign trade; this is possible, but not certain. Every town was similarly patrolled, supervised, divided up into districts and streets whose gates were shut at night. Under such conditions, neither the merchants, the usurers, the money-changers, nor the manufacturers whom the state sometimes subsidized for one purpose or another, had much in the way of power. The government had the right to punish or tax anyone it saw fit to, in the name of the common good which condemned excessive wealth on the part of an individual as both immoral and unjust. The offender thus corrected could not complain: he was being chastised by public morality. Only mandarins, bureaucrats or individuals protected by these all-powerful men were above the law – but their privileges could never be taken for granted. Perhaps one should not draw too many conclusions from a single example, but take the case of Heshen the favourite minister of the emperor Qianlong: when the emperor died in 1799, Heshen was put to death by his successor, and his fortune was confiscated. He had been a greedy, corrupt and much-hated man, but his chief crime was that he had too many possessions – a collection of old masters, several houses and pledged property, an enormous stock of gold and jewels; in short, he was too rich and what was more, he was no longer in office . . .

Further prerogatives of the state were the discretionary right to mint poor currencies (the heavy *caixas*, a mixture of copper and lead) which were often counterfeited (but circulated just the same) and which lost in value when the official stamp had worn away or been removed; the state also had the discretionary right to issue paper money, whose holders were not always certain of being reimbursed at a later date. The merchants, the many usurers and the exchange-bankers, who often made a meagre living by collecting state taxes, lived in fear of being pounced on for contributions at the least outward sign of wealth or of being denounced by a rival who wished to turn the egalitarian wrath of the state upon them.

In a system like this, accumulation could only be achieved by the state and within the state apparatus. It could be said in conclusion that China was living under a 'totalitarian' régime (without all the recent terrible connotations of the word). And the Chinese example most opportunely supports my insistence on separating the *market economy* and *capitalism*. For contrary to what is suggested by Jacobs in a rather *a priori* argument – no capitalism, no market economy – China did have a solidly-established market economy to which I have referred several times, with its chains of local markets, its swarming population of small artisans and itinerant merchants, its busy shopping streets and urban centres. So at ground level, trade was brisk and well-provided for, encouraged by a government primarily concerned with agricultural production; but *at upper levels*, the state uncompromisingly controlled everything and expressed unmistakable hostility to any individual making himself 'abnormally' rich. So much so indeed that land near towns (which was in Europe a source of major income and rent for the city-dwellers who paid high prices for it) was heavily taxed in China to compensate for the advantage its proximity to the urban market gave it over land further away. So there could be no capitalism, except within certain clearly-defined groups, backed by the state, supervised by the state and always more or less at its mercy – like the salt-merchants of the thirteenth century or the Co-Hong in Canton. At most one can say that there was a bourgeoisie after a fashion under the Ming dynasty; and a kind of colonial capitalism which has lasted to the present day, among the emigrant Chinese, in particular in the East Indies.

In Japan, and I must be careful not to oversimplify Jacob's thesis, the seeds of capitalism had been sown by the Ashikaga period (1368–1573) with the coming into being of economic and social forces independent of the state (whether the guilds, long-distance trade, free towns, merchant groups who were often answerable to no one). The first signs of the comparative absence of state authority had appeared even earlier, as soon as a solid feudal system had been established. But the early dating is a problem: to say that the feudal system recognizably emerged in 1270, is to be too categorical in an area where over-precise dating may be misleading; and it also means drawing a veil over the early history of this development, the building-up at the expense of the emperor's domains of large individually-owned estates which, even before they became hereditary, were raising armies to preserve themselves and to defend their autonomy. The end result sooner or later would be a set of quasi-independent provinces, powerful, protecting their own towns, merchants, artisan professions and particular interests.

What may have saved China from a feudal régime during the Ming period (1368–1644) and even later, in spite of the disasters of the Mongol conquest (1644–1680) was the permanent presence of a huge population which preserved some kind of continuity and the possibility of a return to normal. I am inclined to think that a feudal system appears out of a zero situation, when population is drastically low, whether as a result of accident, catastrophe, or depopulation; or, in certain circumstances, when a comparatively new country is taking its first steps. Early Japan was an archipelago three-quarters empty. The 'dominant feature' says Michel Vié[410] 'was its backwardness by comparison with the mainland' – that is compared to Korea and above all China. Japan, in those far-off centuries, was chasing the reflection of Chinese civilization, but lacked the weight of population to catch up. Its series of interminable savage wars in which small groups succeeded with difficulty in subjugating one enemy or several, maintained a chronic state of under-development; and the archipelago remained divided into autonomous units which sat together in uneasy alliance under constraint, but which split apart at the first opportunity. The various Japanese societies thus created were chaotic, badly matched and cut off from each other. As against their lack of unity, there was it is true the authority of the *Tennō* (the emperor who lived in Kyoto) but this was more theoretical and spiritual than temporal; and there was also, in various successive capital cities, long- or short-lived, the brutal and hated authority of the *shōgun*, who was something like the Merovingian *maire du palais*. In the end it was the *shōguns* who set up the government of the *bakufu* and who extended this to the whole of Japan under Hideyoshi, the founder of the Tokugawa dynasty (1601–1868) which would rule the country until the Meiji revolution.

Simplifying, one might say that in a kind of anarchy not unlike that of the European Middle Ages, everything developed simultaneously in the diversified arena of Japan as the country gradually formed itself over the centuries: a central government, feudal lords, towns, peasantry, an artisan class, the merchants. Japanese society bristled with 'liberties' like the liberties of medieval Europe, which were privileges behind which one could barricade oneself for protection and survival. And the mixture was never set for good, no unilateral solution was ever successfully imposed. Is this, too, reminiscent of the pluralism of the 'feudal' societies of Europe, which generated conflict and movement? With the eventual arrival in power of the Tokugawa, we must imagine an uneasy balance, forever having to adjust its elements to each other, not a régime organized along totalitarian lines as in China. The triumph of the Tokugawa, which historians have a tendency to exaggerate, could only be a semi-triumph – real but incomplete – like those of the monarchies of Europe.

This triumph was achieved it is true with foot-soldiers and with firearms from Europe (arquebuses in particular, since Japanese artillery caused more noise than damage). Sooner or later, the *daimyō* had to surrender and accept the authority of a quick-thinking government, which had the support of a solid army, and control of a network of main roads with organized halts which made it easier to patrol and intervene wherever necessary. They had to agree to pass one year out of two in Edo (Tokyo) the new, off-centre capital city of the *shōgun* and stay there under a sort of house-arrest, the *sankin-kōtai*. When they went home to their fiefs, they had to leave their wives and children behind as hostages. A relative of the *Tennō* himself also lived in Edo as a hostage. By comparison, the gilded cage in which the French aristocracy was imprisoned in the Louvre or Versailles begins to look like the height of freedom. So the balance of power had shifted in favour of the *shōgun*. Tension remained though and violence was commonplace. Take for example the event which the *shōgun* Iemitsu, a very young man when he succeeded his father in 1632, thought it necessary to stage, to show everyone who was master. He summoned the *daimyō*. When they arrived at the palace and met as usual in the last antechamber, they found no one else there. They waited; it grew very cold; they were brought no food; and night fell. Suddenly, the screens were removed and the *shōgun* appeared to the light of torches. He addressed them as their master: 'I intend to treat all the *daimyō*, even the grandest, as my subjects. If there are any among you who object to this submission, let them go back to their fiefs and prepare to go to war; between them and me, battle shall decide.'[411] This was the same *shōgun* who in 1635 introduced the *sankin* and soon afterwards closed Japan to all foreign trade, except for a few Dutch vessels and Chinese junks. He proposed to keep his merchants on as tight a reign as his nobles.

The feudal nobles were tamed then, but their fiefs remained intact. The *shōgun* proceeded to confiscate certain fiefs, but there was also some redistribution. And the feudal families have lasted down to the present day – a remarkable example of longevity. Dynastic survival was in fact encouraged, particularly by the system of primogeniture, whereas in China an inheritance was divided among all the male children. In the shadow of these powerful families (some of whom successfully negotiated their entry to industrial capitalism) there long survived a lesser client nobility, that of the *samurai*, who would also play a part in the industrial revolution which followed Meiji.

The most important thing from our point of view however was the belated but quickly effective establishment of free markets and free towns – the first of which was the port of Sakai in 1573. The powerful craft guilds extended their networks and monopolies from one town to another; and the merchant associations, formed on the same lines as the guilds, created from the late seventeenth century on and officially recognized in 1721, here and there began to resemble privileged trading companies like those of the West. A final striking feature was that merchant dynasties became established and in spite of some disasters, survived far beyond the time spans suggested by Henri Pirenne, sometimes for centuries on end: the Konoike, Sumitono and Mitsui families for instance. The founder of the last-named, which is still an extremely powerful family even today, was 'a saké manufacturer, who was in 1620 settled in the province of Ise'; his son became 'the financial agent both of the *shōgun* and of the imperial household' in Edo (Tokyo) in 1690.[412]

So these were merchants who lasted, and who exploited the *daimyō*, the *bakufu* and even the *Tennō*; they were well-informed merchants who very soon learnt how to benefit from manipulating money – the multiplier and indispensable agent of modern accumulation. When the government sought to manipulate the currency for its own purposes by devaluing it in the late seventeenth century, it met such determined opposition that it reversed the policy a few years later. And the merchants always came out unscathed, at the expense of the rest of the population.

Society did not systematically favour the merchants however; they received no special social status – on the contrary. The first Japanese economist, Kumazawa Banzan (1619-1691)[413] had little liking for them and, significantly, he held up Chinese society as an ideal. An early form of Japanese capitalism, clearly self-generated and native to the country, did nevertheless appear of its own accord. Through their purchases of rice, supplied to them either by the *daimyō* or

Japanese market in the eighteenth century. By Shunsho, who was one of Hokusai's masters. (Photo Bulloz.)

by the servants of the *daimyō*, the merchants stood at the vital crossroads of the Japanese economy, on the crucial line where rice – the old currency – turned into real money. And while the *price* of rice depended of course on the harvest, it also depended on the merchants who controlled the actual surplus production. They were also in control of the vital axis connecting Osaka, the centre of production, and Edo, the centre of consumption, a huge parasitic capital of over a million inhabitants. And finally, they were the middlemen between a silver centre (Osaka) and a gold centre (Edo) which were played against each other over the heads of the ordinary people who used the old copper coinage – made official in 1636 for lower levels of exchange. As well as this tri-metallic currency, there were also bills of exchange, cheques, bank notes and the trappings of a regular Stock Exchange. And manufactories were emerging from the huge world of artisanal production. So everything conspired to produce a kind of early capitalism which was the product neither of imitation of foreigners, nor of initiatives by any religious community – since the merchants had often eliminated the competition, quite stiff in the early days, from Buddhist monasteries, which the *shōguns* themselves in any case sought to destroy.

In short, this capitalism emerged in the first instance from the development of a market economy which was long-standing, lively and expanding: markets, fairs, sea-voyages, and exchange (if only the redistribution of fish to inland towns) and finally long-distance trade which was also an early development,

particularly with China, and which yielded fantastic rewards (1100 per cent on the first voyages of the fifteenth century).[414] The merchants were moreover extremely generous with their money to the *shōgun* in the 1570s, when they were hoping for a conquest of the Philippines. Unfortunately for them, the necessary and crucial ingredient of a capitalist superstructure – foreign trade – was soon to be lost to Japan. After the closing of the gates in 1638, foreign trade was severely restricted if not suppressed by the *shōguns*. Some historians have argued that the effect of the closure was mitigated by smuggling, particularly from Kyushu, the most southerly island, and from the uninhabited so-called 'Silent Island' in the Korean straits. This is going rather far, even if there is some evidence of active smuggling by the merchants of Nagasaki among others, or by a member of the powerful Shimazu family, the lord of Satsuma who had agents in China in 1691 for the more efficent running of his illegal traffic.[415] It is all the same undeniable that the bans and restrictions in force between 1638 and 1868, for over two hundred years, held back the economic development which had once looked possible. After that however, Japan very quickly caught up, for several reasons, some of which are to do with the world economy. But above all perhaps, because it based its recent industrial takeoff (on the western model) on a long-standing merchant capitalism which it had patiently built by its own efforts. 'The grain was growing under the snow' for a long time – an image from a book written in 1930 by Takekoshi[416] who was also fascinated by the economic and social similarities between Europe and Japan, each of which had developed along its own path, by similar processes, although the results were not exactly the same.

Politics and society – especially society

Let me now close this long parenthesis and return to the problem as a whole. We have now reached a well-known, familiar but fascinating theme. To use Marxist terminology, feudalism prepared the way for capitalism – but as we know Marx never really developed very far his analysis of the transition. And Jacobs only touches on the subject, in the first place to deny that feudalism is a necessary previous stage for capitalism, and in the second place to suggest that 'historically ... the elements which were to help develop capitalism' found in 'certain values, concerning rights and privileges established in the feudal period *for other purposes*', a favourable climate in which to 'institutionalize their own position'. Let me now suggest my own view of what happened. *Except in cities which had developed independently from very earliest times* – such as Venice, Genoa or Augsburg – where a patriciate with merchant-class origins formed the highest tier in society, the top-ranking merchant families, in the West or in Japan, were only a second-best class when the modernizing economy and state pushed them to the fore. They came up against a barrier, like a plant meeting a wall. If the obstacle does not budge, stems and roots will grow along the wall, trying to reach the top. Such was to be the destiny of these bourgeoisies. When the barrier was finally overcome, the victorious family would change its status. In another book I have described this as the betrayal of the bourgeoisie, which is perhaps going too far. In fact the bourgeoisie was never guilty of wholesale betrayal; and it closed ranks again against the obstacle.

These families – contained, barricaded in and aspiring to the sunlit heights of social success – were condemned, as long as the obstacle remained, to practise thrift, calculation, prudence and the virtues of accumulation. And since the members of the nobility, their immediate superiors, were wasteful, ostentatious and economically vulnerable, anything the nobility let fall or abandoned was quickly snapped up by this neighbouring class. Let me give one rapid illustration – but a persuasive one: the usurious policy of the French Séguier family. The fortunes of the bourgeoisie and the *noblesse de robe* (another kind of bourgeoisie) were made, from the sixteenth century onwards, not only by buying up office, estates and properties, by receiving pensions from the king, by regularly collecting dowries; but also by performing a range of services (not all usurious but mostly so) for the high and mighty. The *président* Pierre Séguier (1504–1580) accepted deposits, made advances, collected money, recovered pledges, and lent at interest. He had done some profitable business with Marie Albret, duchess of Nevers: when the time came to settle up, she sold to Séguier 'the *seigneurie* of Sorel near Dreux, for a sum of 9000 *écus*, of which she received only 3600, the rest acting as repayment of debts'.[417] And this was just one affair among many. The *président* was also moneylender to the Montmorencys – who defended themselves reasonably well against him – and to various members of the Sully family. Following these arrangements, there is mention of Pierre Séguier acquiring 'a high stand of trees' near Melun, a share-cropper's estate at Escury near Auneau, and so on.[418] The process was one of parasitism, exploitation and finally absorption. The upper class, a fruit that had slowly ripened with its landed wealth and traditional power, provided a juicy morsel which could be swallowed with a few risks but on the whole to great advantage. The same process occurred in Japan, where the merchant of Osaka took advantage of the misfortunes and wasteful-ness of the *daimyō*. To use Marx's terminology, this was centralization of re-sources for the benefit of one class and at the expense of another. The dominant class would sooner or later provide a meal for those on its heels, just as the Eupatrides in Athens and elsewhere were swallowed up by the cities, the *poleis*. Of course, if this class had the strength to react and defend itself, the rise of others to wealth and power would be difficult or temporarily impeded. Even in Europe, there are examples of this happening. But in any case, social mobility alone was not a sufficient force. In order for one class to be effectively consumed by another, that is consumed steadily over a long period, both the classes in question had to have the faculty of accumulating wealth and of passing on this wealth from generation to generation in a snowball process.

In China, the bureaucracy lay across the top of Chinese society as a single, virtually unbreachable stratum; any damage was spontaneously repaired. No other group or class could approach the immense prestige of the learned man-darins. These representatives of order and public morality were not all above reproach. Many mandarins, particularly in the ports, deposited their money with merchants, who eagerly bought their goodwill. Passing remarks by a European visitor to Canton show us that the local mandarins practised corruption as a matter of course, and grew rich with few pangs of conscience. But what value was an accumulated fortune if it was possessed by a single man? This was merely an accumulation that died with its owner, the reward of office, the fruit of higher education and of the competitive, moderately democratic recruitment proce-dures.[419] The prestige accorded the mandarins often led merchant families to propel their sons towards these brilliant and enviable positions – this was their version of 'betraying' their class. But sons of mandarins did not often become mandarins themselves. The rise of a family could be abruptly cut short. Neither the fortune nor the power of the mandarins was passed on smoothly to create dynasties of dominant families.

In the countries of Islam, the situation was different in its underlying struc-tures, but the results were curiously similar. The difference was that the upper class was constantly *being* changed, by outside agency. The Osmanli sultan in Istanbul is a typical example: he changed his high society as he might his shirt. Think of the recruitment of the janissaries from among Christian boys. The Ottoman 'feudal system' so often evoked was in fact only a pre-feudal régime, of life-grants: the *timars* and *sipahiniks* were estates conceded for a lifetime only. Not until the end of the sixteenth century was a real Ottoman feudal system beginning to appear, with a capitalist policy of land-improvement and of introducing new crops.[420] A feudal aristocracy then became entrenched, particularly in the Balkan peninsula, and succeeded in maintaining its estates and fiefs under family control for many generations. One historian, Nicolai Todorov[421] argues that a struggle for control of the rent from land ended in total victory for the dominant class which already occupied all the high administrative offices of the state. Was it really a total victory? This may need closer examination. But what seems quite certain is that this social upheaval was both the cause and the consequence of a major historical about-turn, the decomposition of the old military, warlike and conquering state, as it was already becoming 'the sick man of Europe'. The more normal and ordinary pattern in Muslim countries was that of a society under firm state control, sometimes under state attack, and cut off from the wealth-producing land for all time. The picture is the same everywhere, in Persia where the khans were lords only in their own lifetime, as in Mogul India in the days of its splendour.

There were no 'great families' forming dynasties in Delhi. François Bernier, a doctor from the faculty of medicine in Montpellier and a contemporary of Colbert, who felt quite lost in the military society surrounding the Great Mogul, graphically conveys to us what he found so disorienting about it. The *omerahs* and *rajahs* were in fact simply mercenaries, lords for life. The Great Mogul appointed them, but did not grant the succession to their children. Why should he? He needed a great army, and he paid his officers with what we would call a living, a *sipahinik* as it was called in Turkey – property which the sovereign – *to whom all land belonged by right* – conceded but took back again on the death of the holder. No nobility could therefore put down roots in land which was regularly confiscated. 'Since all the lands in the kingdom are the Great Mogul's property', Bernier explains, 'it follows that there are no dukes or marquises nor any family of wealthy landowners which lives from its revenues and patrimony.' It was like living under a sort of perpetual New Deal, with the cards being dealt again automatically at regular intervals. These warlords did not have family names like those of the West. 'They only have names worthy of warriors: thunder-bearer, lightning-carrier, breaker of lines, faithful lord, perfect lord, the learned and so on.'[422] So there were none of the picturesque surnames found in the West with their origins in geography and place names. At the pinnacle of the hierarchy were only the prince's favourites – adventurers, hotheads, foreigners, 'men of naught' and even former slaves. That the tip of the pyramid, this strange, insubstantial and temporary construction, should have collapsed with the British conquest is not surprising, since it was held together by the power of the prince and was doomed to fall with him. What is more surprising is that the British presence fabricated a set of family dynasties with hereditary possessions. Without meaning to, the British brought to India their own European perceptions and

The Mogul emperor Akbar (1542–1605) going to war.
(Photo B.N., Paris, Cabinet des Estampes.)

habits. Arriving surrounded by these, they were unable to understand and take seriously the unusual social structure which had so impressed Bernier. The mistake the British made, out of a mixture of ignorance and corruption, was to take the *zamindars* (tax-collectors in villages without a permanent owner) for genuine landowners, and to turn them into a western-style hierarchy devoted to the new masters; these families have often lasted to the present day.

The only class of powerful families which had existed in India – that of the merchants, manufacturers and bankers which had traditionally, father and son, controlled both the economy and the administration of the trading cities, whether sea-ports or a thriving textile centre like Ahmedabad – was to defend itself more effectively and for longer, with the weapon it knew best – money. This class would corrupt the invader, while allowing itself to be corrupted in return.

To illustrate this, let me quote from the dramatic speech made on 30 March 1772 in the House of Commons by Lord Clive,[423] who was defending his honour and his life against accusations of corruption which had piled up against him and which were to drive him to suicide not long after. He describes the case of the young Englishman who arrives in Bengal as a 'writer' or clerk:

> Let us now take a view of one of these writers arrived in Bengal and not worth a groat. As soon as he lands, a Banyan, worth perhaps one hundred thousand pounds, desires he may have the honour of serving this young gentleman, at four shillings and sixpence a month ... The young man takes a walk about the town, he observes that other writers, arrived only a year before him, live in splendid apartments or have houses of their own, ride upon fine prancing Arabian Horses, and in Palanqueens and Chaises, that they keep Seraglios, make Entertainments, and treat with Champagne and Claret. When he returns, he tells the Banyan what he has observed. The Banyan assures him he may soon arrive at the same good fortune; he furnishes him with money; he is then at his mercy. The advantages of the Banyan advance with the rank of his master, who in acquiring one fortune generally spends three. But this is not the worst of it: he is in a state of dependence under the Banyan, who commits such acts of violence and oppression, as his interest prompts him to, under the pretended sanction and authority of the Company's servant. Hence, Sir, arises the clamour against the English gentlemen in India. ... [Clive asserts that] flesh and blood cannot bear [the temptations which are put in the way of the newly arrived Englishman. The Banyan] lays his bags of silver before him today; Gold tomorrow; Jewels the next day; and if these fail, he then tempts him in the way of his profession which is Trade. He assures him that Goods may be had cheap and sold to great advantage up the Country.

This was special pleading of course, but the general picture revealed is not inaccurate. An ancient but lively Indian capitalism was struggling against its 'subordination' to the new masters, piercing through the new fabric of English rule.

Can we not say that examples like these, condensed and too-rapidly presented though they are here, all tend towards a comprehensive explanation which may come near the truth; that is to say, they corroborate each other sufficiently to suggest a satisfactory approach to the problem? Europe's high society was divided into at least two classes which, despite the ups and downs of history, were able to develop dynasties without insuperable difficulties, since they were facing neither a totalitarian tyranny nor the tyranny of an arbitrary despot. Europe thus encouraged the patient accumulation of wealth and the development within its diversified society of various forces and hierarchies whose rivalry could produce a variety of results. As far as European capitalism is concerned, the social order based on economic power no doubt benefited from lying in second place: by contrast with the social order based merely on privileged birth, it was able to gain acceptance as standing for moderation, prudence, hard work and a degree of justification. The politically dominant class attracted hostile attention as church steeples attract lightning. And in this way the privilege of the seigneur once more made people forget about the privilege of the merchant.

By Way of Conclusion

AT THE END OF THIS, my second volume, *The Wheels of Commerce*, it seems clear to me that the capitalist process considered as a whole, was able to develop only out of certain economic and social conditions which either prepared or facilitated its progress:

1 The obvious first condition was a vigorous and expanding market economy. A whole range of factors – geographical, demographic, agricultural, industrial and commercial – contributed to this. It is evident that such development operated world-wide: the population was increasing everywhere, inside and outside Europe, in the countries of Islam, in India, China and Japan, even up to a point in Africa, and before long in America, where Europe made a fresh start. Everywhere there was the same sequence of events, the same creative evolution: fortress-towns, monastery-towns, administrative towns, towns at the crossroads of trade routes or on the shores of rivers and seas. This parallel development proves that the market economy, the same everywhere with only minor variations, was the necessary, spontaneously-developing and in fact normal base of any society over a certain size. Once a critical threshold had been reached, the proliferation of trading, of markets and merchants, occurred of its own accord. But this underlying market economy was only a *necessary*, not a *sufficient* condition for the formation of a capitalist process. China, I would repeat, is the perfect illustration of the fact that a capitalist superstructure did not automatically emerge out of a thriving market economy with all that that implies. Other conditions were also required.

2 Capitalism could only emerge from a certain kind of society, one which had created a favourable environment from far back in time, without being aware in the slightest of the process thus being set in train, or of the processes for which it was preparing the way in future centuries. Of the examples known to us, a society offered a favourable environment to the antecedents of capitalism when, having hierarchies of one kind or another, it encouraged the survival of dynasties and the continuous process of wealth accumulation without which further development would have been impossible. Inheritances had to be passed on,

patrimonies increased, profitable marriages arranged, without hindrance; society had to be divided into groups, some of which were dominant or potentially dominant; and it had to be divided into ranks, with ladders of social mobility which were, if not easy, at any rate possible to climb. In fact, many factors had to be present, of a political or 'historical' character, if one may so call them, rather than specifically economic or social. What was required was a multisecular and general movement of society, as is proved by both Japan and Europe in their own separate ways.

3 But in the last analysis, further development would have been impossible without the special and as it were liberating action of world trade. Long-distance trading was not everything, but it was the only doorway to a superior profit level. In the third and last volume of this work, we shall be looking again at the role of the world-economies, those *enclosed* areas which grew to be special worlds unto themselves, autonomous patches of the planet. They have their own history since their boundaries changed over time; they expanded as Europe embarked upon her conquest of the world. With these world-economies, we shall be moving to a different level of competition, a different scale of domination, one with rules that have been so often repeated that for once we shall be able to follow them without risk of error, through a chronological history of Europe and the world, through a succession of world systems which in fact tell the whole story of capitalism. There is an old expression for this – but it is none the worse for that and says what it means: the international division of labour, and (of course) of the fruits of that labour.

Notes

Translator's note: Wherever possible, when an English-language source is quoted in the text, the original has been traced and the page reference in the notes amended. This has not always been possible. References to works originally published in French have been left unaltered, except where there is a recent and easily available English translation.

Abbreviations used in notes:

A.d.S.   Archivio di Stato.
A.E.   Affaires Etrangères (Foreign Affairs), Paris.
A.N.   Archives Nationales, Paris.
B.M.   British Museum (now British Library), London.
B.N.   Bibliothèque Nationale, Paris.
C.S.A.   Central State Archives, Moscow.
P.R.O.   Public Record Office, London.

NOTES TO FOREWORD

1. Jacques ACCARIAS DE SERIONNE, *Les Intérêts des nations de l'Europe développés relativement au commerce*, 1766, I, esp. p. 270.

2. Frederick W. MAITLAND, *Domesday Book and Beyond*, 2nd edn., 1921, p. 9.

NOTES TO CHAPTER I

1. K. MARX, *Capital*, vol. I, section 7, ch. 23.
2. K. MARX, *Critique of Political Economy*, see ch. on circulation and money.
3. Jean ROMEUF, *Dictionnaire des sciences économiques*, 1956-1958, 'Circulation'.
4. *Oeuvres de Turgot*, ed. G. Schelle, 1913–23, I, p. 29.
5. Cf. the increased estimate of circulation in Guillaume de GREEF, *Introduction à la sociologie*, 2 vols., 1886-89.
6. Gabriel ARDANT, *Théorie sociologique de l'impôt*, 1965, p. 363. 'Production as such is very difficult to estimate'.
7. P. MOLMENTI, *La Vie privée à Venise*, 1896, II, p. 47.
8. Julien FREUND's review of C.B. MACPHERSON's *The Political Theory of Possessive Individualism. Hobbes to Locke*, Oxford, 1962, in *Critique*, 1972, p. 55.
9. In particular in the book co-edited with C.M. ARENSBERG and H.W. PEARSON, *Trade and Market in the Early Empires, Economics in History and Theory*, 1957.
10. Gaston IMBERT, *Des Mouvements de longue durée Kondratieff*, 1959.
11. A description has survived by chance of

the market at Puyloubier, a little village in Provence, during the years 1438-9 and 1459-64. Wheat, oats, wine, sheep, *menons* (castrated goats), hides and leather were on sale here, as well as 'one mule, one donkey, one pony', hogs, fish, vegetables, oil, sacks of lime. Cf. Noël COULET, 'Commerce et marchands dans un village provençal du XVIe siècle. La leyde de Puyloubier', in *Etudes rurales*, nos. 22, 23, 24, July-December 1966. Alan EVERITT, 'The Marketing of Agricultural Produce' in *The Agrarian History of England and Wales*, ed. M.P.R. FINBERG, IV, *1500-1640*, 1967, p. 240.

12. Paul-Louis HUVELIN, *Essai historique sur le droit des marchés et des foires*, 1897, p. 240.

13. In Lucca, there were 144 numbered sites on the marketplace of San Michele, A.d.S. Lucca, Officio sopra la Grascia, 196 (1705).

14. Élie BRACKENHOFFER, *Voyage en France, 1643-1644*, 1927, p. 47.

15. B.N., Ms. Fr., 21633, 133, on the market held in the churchyard of Saint-Jean.

16. Edouard FOURNIER, *Variétés historiques et littéraires*, 1855-1863, V, 249, (1724).

17. B.N., Ms. Fr., 21633, 153.

18. *Variétés*, *op. cit.*, II, p. 124 (1735).

19. G. von BELOW, *Probleme der Wirtschaftsgeschichte*, 1926, p. 373.

20. Etienne BOYLEAUX (dit Etienne Boileau) *Règlemens sur les Arts et Métiers de Paris, redigés au XIIIe siècle et connus sous le nom du Livre des Métiers d'E. Boileau* edited in 1837 in the collection *Documents inédits de l'Histoire de France*, quoted by P. CLAVAL in *Geographie générale des marchés*, 1962, pp. 115, 125.

21. Werner SOMBART, *Der moderne Kapitalismus*, 15th edn., 1928, II, p. 482.

22. Ferdo GESTRIN, *Le Trafic commercial entre les contrèes des Slovènes de l'intérieur et les villes du littoral de l'Adriatique du XIIIe au XVIe siècle*, 1965, summary in French, p. 265.

23. P.-L. HUVELIN, *op. cit.*, p. 18.

24. P. CHALMETTA GENDRON, *'El Señor del Zoco' en España*, 1973, preface by Maxime Rodinson, p. xxxi, note 46; reference to Bernal DIAZ DEL CASTILLO,

Historia verdadera de la conquista de la Nueva España.

25. Father Jean-Baptiste LABAT, *Nouvelle Relation de l'Afrique occidentale*, 1778, II, p. 47.

26. Simon D. MESSING, in *Markets in Africa*, ed. P. BOHANNAN and Georges DALLON, 3rd edn., 1968, pp. 384 ff.

27. Jacques SAVARY DES BRUSLONS, *Dictionnaire universel du commerce*, 1761, III, col. 778.

28. *Diarii della città di Palermo, dal secolo XVI al XIX*, 2, p. 61, in *Biblioteca storica e letteraria di Sicilia*, ed. G. di Marzo.

29. Marcel COUTURIER, *Recherches sur les structures sociales de Châteaudun, 1525-1789*, 1969, p. 191.

30. Information provided by Jean NAGLE, who is working on the faubourg St. Germain in the seventeenth century.

31. A. EVERITT, *art. cit.*, p. 488, note 4.

32. Alberto GROHMANN, *Le Fiere del regno di Napoli in età aragonese*, 1969, p. 28.

33. *The Autobiography of William Stout of Lancaster*, p. 162, quoted by T.S. WILLAN, *Abraham Dent of Kirkby Stephen*, 1970, p. 12.

34. Henri PIGEONNEAU, *Histoire du commerce de la France*, 1889, I, p. 197.

35. Joseph AQUILINA, *A Comparative Dictionary of Maltese Proverbs*, 1972.

36. Roger BASTIDE, Pierre VERGER, 'Contribution sociologique des marchés Nagô du Bas-Dahomey' in *Cahiers de l'Institut de science économique appliquée*, no. 95, November 1959, pp. 33-65, esp. p. 53.

37. B.N., Ms. Fr., 21633, 49, October 1660.

38. *Ibid.*, 20 September 1667.

39. B.N. Ms. Fr., 21782, 191.

40. *Ibid.*, 21633, 43, 19 September 1678.

41. *Ibid.*, 21633, 44, 28 June 1714.

42. *Ibid.*, 21782, 210, 5 April 1719.

43. *Ibid.*, 21633, 46 and 67.

44. Ambroise CONTARINI, *Voiage de Perse en l'année 1473*, col 53, in *Voyages faits principalement en Asie dans les années XIIe-XIIIe-XIVe et XVe siècle*, II, 1785.

45. ATKINSON and WALKER, *Manners and Customs of the Russians*, 1803, p. 10.

46. A.N., A.E., C.P. Angleterre, 122, f° 52, London, 14 January 1677.

47. London, 28 January-7 February 1684, A.d.S., Florence, Mediceo 4213.

48. Edward ROBINSON, *The Early History of Coffee Houses in England*, 1st edn., 1893, 2nd edn. 1972, pp. 176-7.
49. Jean MARTINEAU, *Les Halles de Paris, des origines à 1789*, 1960.
50. Robert CAILLET, *Foires et marchés de Carpentras, du Moyen Age au début du XIXe siècle*, Carpentras, 1953, p. 11.
51. Claude CARRÈRE, *Barcelone, centre économique à l'époque des difficultés, 1380-1462*, 1967, p. 498.
52. W. SOMBART, *Der moderne Kapitalismus*, op. cit., II, pp. 484-485.
53. G.D. RAMSAY, *The City of London*, 1975, p. 37.
54. Georges and Geneviève FRÈCHE, *Le Prix des grains, des vins et des légumes à Toulouse (1486-1868)*, 1967, p. 28.
55. W. SOMBART, *op. cit.*, I, p. 231.
56. A. EVERITT, *art. cit.*, pp. 478 and 482.
57. Pierre DEYON, *Amiens, capitale provinciale. Etude sur la sociologie urbaine au XVIIe siècle*, 1967, p. 181.
58. Marcel BAUDOT, 'Halles, marchés et foires d'Evreux' in *Annuaire du département de l'Eure*, 1935, p. 3.
59. Albert BABEAU, *Les Artisans et les domestiques d'autrefois*, 1886, p. 97.
60. Giuseppe TASSINI, *Curiosità veneziane*, 4th edn., 1887, pp. 75-6.
61. B.N., Ms. Fr., 21557, f°4 (1188).
62. J. MARTINEAU, *op. cit.*, p. 23.
63. *Ibid.*, p. 150.
64. 'Économie et architecture médiévales. Cela aurait-il tué ceci?' in *Annales E.S.C.*, 1952, pp. 433-8.
65. J. MARTINEAU, *op. cit.*, p. 150. Rebuilding of the Halles between 1543 and 1572, according to Léon BIOLLAY, 'Les anciennes halles de Paris' in *Mémoires de la Société de l'histoire de Paris et de l'Ile -de-France*, 1877, pp. 293-355.
66. J. SAVARY DES BRUSLONS, *op. cit.*, III, col. 261.
67. *Journal du voyage de deux jeunes Hollandais* (MM. de Villers), *à Paris en 1656-1658*, ed. A.-P. FAUGÈRE, 1899, p. 87.
68. J.A. PIGANIOL DE LA FORCE, *Description de Paris*, 1742, III, p. 124.
69. Louis BATTIFOL, *La Vie de Paris sous Louis XIII*, 1932, p. 75. Roughly translatable as 'Lady Muck! Cradle-snatcher - after the schoolboys again!

Old bag! Ain't you ashamed of yourself? You're so drunk it's coming out of your ears!' etc.
70. Dorothy DAVIS, *A History of Shopping*, 1966, pp. 74-9 and 89-90.
71. *Voyage en Angleterre*, 1728, Victoria and Albert Museum, 86 NN 2, f° 5.
72. J. SAVARY DES BRUSLONS, III, col., 779. On butter, eggs and cheese, see Abraham du PRADEL, *Le Livre commode des adresses de Paris pour 1692*, ed. E. FOURNIER, 1878, I, pp. 296 ff.
73. J. MARTINEAU, *op. cit.*, p. 204.
74. J. SAVARY DES BRUSLONS, IV, col. 1146.
75. J. BABELON, *Demeures parisiennes sous Henri IV et Louis XIII*, 1965, pp. 15-18.
76. *Journal du voyage de deux jeunes Hollandais*, op. cit., p. 98. 'The horse market at the end of the faubourg St.-Victor', A. du PRADEL, *op. cit.*, I, p. 264.
77. *Journal du citoyen*, 1754, pp. 306-7.
78. A.N., G⁷, 1511.
79. A.N., G⁷, 1668-1670, 1707-1709, cf. *Annales*, I, p. 304.
80. A.N., G⁷, 1511.
81. Jean MEUVRET, in *Revue d'histoire moderne et contemporaine*, 1956.
82. A.N., G⁷, 1701, 222. Paris, 4 December 1713. 'Since the sea has become free, all merchandise comes by Rouen to Paris and is unloaded at the St.-Nicholas port.'
83. P. de CROUSAZ CRETET, *Paris sous Louis XIV*, 1922, pp. 29-31, 47-8.
84. *Voyage en Angleterre*, 1728, f° 36.
85. David R. RINGROSE, 'Transportation and economic stagnation in eighteenth-century Castile' in *The Journal of Economic History*, March 1968.
86. Tirso de MOLINA (Gabriel Tellez), *El Burlador de Sevilla*, ed. J.E. Varey and N.D. Shergold, Cambridge, 1954, p. 28.
87. Although sometimes 'Turkish corsairs capture them off Lisbon', British Museum, Sloane, 1572.
88. Many references, e.g. A.d.S. Venice, Senato Terra 12, March 1494.
89. W. HAHN, *Die Verpflegung Konstantinopels durch staatliche Zwangswirtschaft nach türkischen Urkunden aus dem 16. Jahrhundert*, 1926. On the same subject: DERSCA-BULGARU, 'Quelques données sur le ravitaillement de Constantinople au

XVIe siècle' in *Congrès d'études balkaniques*, Sofia, 1966.

90. Ingomar BOG, 'Das Konsumzentrum London und seine Versorgung' in *Troisiemè Conférence Internationale d'Histoire Economique*, Munich, 1965. Better still, the same author's article under the same title in *Mélanges Lütge*, 1966, pp. 141–82.

91. *The Evolution of the English Corn Market*, 1915.

92. *Ibid.*, p. 122. A.S. USHER, *The History of the Grain Trade in France, 1400–1710*, 1913, pp. 82, 84, 87.

93. Dorothy DAVIS, *A History of Shopping*, 3rd edn., 1967, p. 56.

94. I. BOG, in *Mélanges Lütge, op. cit.*, p. 150.

95. *Ibid.*, p. 147. The highest figure is L. Stone's.

96. Alan EVERITT, 'The Food Market of the English Town', in *Troisiéme Conférence Internationale d'Histoire Economique*, Munich, 1965.

97. *Voyage en Angleterre*, 1728, f°s 14 and 161.

98. On Wales and Scotland, see remarks by Michael HECHTER, *Internal Colonialism: the Celtic fringe in British national development 1536–1966*, 1975, pp. 82–3.

99. Daniel DEFOE, *A Tour through the whole island of Great Britain*, ed. G.D.H. Cole, Everyman edn., 1962, p. 127.

100. A. EVERITT, in *The Agrarian History of England and Wales*, op. cit., IV, pp. 468, 470, 473.

101. Eckart SCHREMMER, *Die Wirtschaft Bayerns*, pp. 613–16.

102. *Ibid.*, p. 608.

103. A. EVERITT, in *The Agrarian History … op. cit.*, IV, p. 469.

104. *Ibid.*, p. 532 ff.

105. *Ibid.*, p. 563.

106. G. von BELOW, *op. cit.*, p. 353.

107. N. DELAMARE, *Traité de police*, 1705, II, p. 654.

108. *Ibid.*, 1710, II, p. 1059, 16 January 1699. Among those found to be stockpiling grain were a draper, a wool merchant, an apothecary, a merchant, a doctor, an excise farmer, a baker and a peasant farmer.

109. M. BAUDOT, *art. cit.*, p. 2.

110. R. CAILLET, *op. cit.*, pp. 23–4.

111. The same thing happened at Saint-Jean-de-Losne in 1712 and 1713, Henri JACQUIN, 'Le ravitaillement de Saint-Jean-de-Losne au XVIIIe siècle', in *Annales de Bourgogne*, 1974, pp. 131–2.

112. Moscow, C.S.A., 50/6, 474, f°s 60 and 61, 13–24 April 1764.

113. A.N., Ms. Fr., 12683.

114. Saint-Malo, 29 June 1713, A.N., G^7, 1701, f° 120.

115. R.L. REYNOLDS, 'In search of a business class in thirteenth-century Genoa', in *The Journal of Economic History*, 1945.

116. Franck SZENURA, *L'Espansione urbana di Firenze nel Dugento*, 1975.

117. Emmanuel LE ROY LADURIE, *The Territory of the Historian*, English transl. 1979, Chapter 5, 'Changes in Parisian rents from the end of the middle ages to the eighteenth century'.

118. Cesena, Bib. Malatestiana, Cassetta XVI, 165, 39.

119. *Variétés*, IV, pp. 105 ff.

120. J. BABELON, *op. cit.*, pp. 15–18.

121. According to unpublished research by J. NAGLE.

122. Museo Correr, P.D., C. 903, f° 12, Andrea Dolfin, Venetian ambassador to Paris, to Andrea Tron, 13 August 1781.

123. G. HUPPERT, manuscript of book later published as *Les bourgeois gentilshommes*, 1977.

124. Wilhelm ABEL, *Agrarkrisen und Agrarkonjunktur*, 2nd edn., 1966, pp. 124 ff.

125. Eugenio ALBERI, *Relazioni degli ambasciatori veneti durante il secolo XVI*, 1839–1863, VIII, p. 257.

126. Jean MEYER, *La Noblesse bretonne au XVIIIe siècle*, 1966, II, p. 897.

127. A. du PRADEL, *op. cit.*, I, p. xxvi, II, pp. 333 ff.

128. Yvonne BEZART, *La Vie rurale dans le Sud de la région parisienne, 1450–1560*, 1929, pp. 68 ff.

129. E. SCHREMMER, *op. cit., passim* esp. pp. 219, 685.

130. *Capital*, II: 'the labour market, which must be distinguished from the slave market'. Among other examples, the slave trade from Istria and Dalmatia towards Florence, Siena and Bologna, A.d.S. Venice, Senato Mar, 6, f° 136 v°, 17 August 1459.

131. Thomas HOBBES, *Leviathan*, Everyman edn., 1924, p. 130.

132. A.N., A.E., B¹, 598, Genoa, 31 March 1783; David RICARDO, *The Principles of Political Economy*, Everyman edn., 1955, p. 52.

133. Eric MASCHKE, 'Deutsche Städte am Ausgang des Mittelalters' in *Die Stadt am Ausgang des Mittelalters*, ed. W. RAUSCH, offprint, p. 20.

134. *Acta Hungarica*, XXIV, p. 30.

135. Marcel POÈTE, *Une Vie de cité, Paris de sa naissance à nos jours*, 1924, I, p. 301.

136. Robert-Henri BAUTIER, 'A propos d'une société lucquoise à Lyon au XIIIe siècle. Les contrats de travail au Moyen Age', in *Bulletin philologique et historique (avant 1610)*, 1964, pp. 162–4.

137. Antonio H. de OLIVEIRA MARQUES, *Daily Life in Portugal in the late Middle Ages*, 1971, pp. 186–8.

138. Marcel DELAFOSSE, 'Les vignerons d'Auxerrois (XIVe–XVIe siècles)', in *Annales de Bourgogne*, vol. 20, no. 77, January–March 1948, pp. 22 ff.

139. Ernst PITZ, in *Wirtschaftliche und soziale Probleme der gewerblichen Entwicklung im 15.–16. Jahrhunderten nach Ansich-Nieder Deutschen Quellen*, ed. F. LÜTGE, 1968, p. 35. Brigit FIEDLER, *Die gewerblichen Eigenbetriebe der Stadt Hamburg im Spätmittelalter*, 1974.

140. A. BABEAU, *Les Artisans et les domestiques d'autrefois*, op. cit., p. 273, note 1, Tallemant des Réaux (1619–1692).

141. Gustave FAGNIEZ, *L'Économie rurale de la France sous Henri IV*, 1897, p. 55.

142. *Le Journal du sire de Gouberville*, 1892, p. 400. Cf., the selections by A. TOLLEMER, *Un Sire de Gouberville*, pp. 27 ff.

143. E. LE ROY LADURIE, *op. cit.*, p. 148.

144. M. BAUDOT, *art. cit.*, p. 8.

145. See below chapter 3, note 90 for the *généralité* of Orleans.

146. According to an article by René GAUCHET.

147. B.N., Ms. Fr., 21672, f° 16 v°.

148. Rolf ENGELSING, 'Der Arbeitsmarkt der Dienstboten im 17., 18. und 19. Jahrhundert' in *Wirtschaftspolitik und Arbeitsmarkt*, ed. Hermann KELLENBENZ, 1974, p. 174.

149. *Op. cit.*, II, p. 49.

150. Peter LASLETT, *The World We Have Lost*, 1965, p. 50. E.H. PHELPS-BROWN and S.V. HOPKINS consider that only a third or so of the population was paid wages, quoted in Immanuel WALLERSTEIN, *The Modern World System*, 1974, p. 82.

151. Herbert LANGER, 'Zur Rolle der Lohnarbeit im spätmittelalterlichen Zunfthandwerk der Hansestädte. Dargestellt haupstsächlich am Beispiel der Hansestadt Stralsund', in *Jahrbuch für Regionalgeschichte*, 3, 1968.

152. Jeffry KAPLOW, *Les Noms des rois*, 1974, pp. 47–8.

153. *Op. cit.*, I, p. 448.

154. See below, chapter 5, sections on strikes in Lyons and Leyden.

155. Quoted by A. BABEAU, *op. cit.*, p. 40.

156. Lorenzo LOTTO, *Libro di spese diverse (1538–1556)*, ed. Pietro ZAMBELLI; Paolo FARINATI, *Giornale 1573–1601*, ed. Lionello PUPPI, 1968, p. xl.

157. P. FARINATI, *ibid.*, p. xliii, note 16.

158. Palermo, 10 December 1704. D. Francisco de Arana to Cardinal Judice. Biblioteca Communale, Palermo, hQq 66, f°s 452 ff. and 476.

159. Benedetto COTRUGLI, *Della mercatura e del mercante perfetto*, Brescia, 1602, p. 50 (the book was originally written in 1458).

160. *Vida y hechos de Estebanillo Gonzalez*, in *La Novela picaresca española*, 1966, p. 1830.

161. 12 April 1679, A.N., G⁷, 491, 505.

162. Yves-Marie BERCÉ, *Histoire des croquants. Étude des soulèvements populaires au XVIIe siècle dans le Sud-Ouest de la France*, 1974, I, p. 41.

163. Louis-Sébastien MERCIER, *Tableau de Paris*, VIII, 1783, pp. 343–5.

164. Y.-M. BERCÉ, *op. cit.*, I, p. 242.

165. Aldo de MADDELENA, Prato conference, April 1975.

166. Bistra A. CVETKOVA, 'Vie économique des villes et ports balkaniques aux XVe et XVIe siècles', in *Revue des études islamiques*, 1970, pp. 277–8, 280–1.

167. Stefan OLTEANU, 'Les métiers en Moldavie et en Valachie (Xe-XVIIe siècles)' in *Revue roumaine d'histoire*, VII, 1968, p. 180, 'Fair' = 'market' clearly in this article.

168. *Young's Travels in France during the*

Years 1787, 1788, 1789, ed. Miss Betham-Edwards, 1913, p. 112.

169. Laszlo MAKKAI, Prato Conference, April 1975.

170. Michelet tells us that a land sale was taking place, 'and no purchaser having appeared, a peasant arrived with his gold coin', *Le Peuple*, 1899 edn., p. 45.

171. Maurice AYMARD, Prato Conference, April 1975, on Sicily.

172. Emiliano FERNÁNDEZ DE PINEDO, *Crecimiento económico y transformaciones sociales del pais vasco 1100-1850*, 1974, esp. pp. 233 ff.

173. F. Sébastián MANRIQUE, *Itinerario de las Missiones*, 1649, p. 59.

174. Michel MORINEAU, 'A la halle de Charleville: fourniture et prix des grains, ou les mécanismes du marché (1647-1821)' in *95e Congrès national des sociétés savantes*, 1970, II, pp. 159-222.

175. Marco CATTINI, 'Produzione, auto-consumo e mercato dei grani a San Felice sul Panaro, 1590-1637', in *Rivista storica italiana*, 1973, pp. 698-755.

176. See above, note 162.

177. *Variétés*, I, 369, note 1.

178. *Journal du voyage de deux jeunes Hollandais, op. cit.*, p. 30.

179. E. BRACKENHOFFER, *op. cit.*, p. 116.

180. Ignace-François LIMOJON de SAINT-DIDIER, *La Ville et la république de Venise*, 1680, p. 68.

181. Charles CARRIÈRE, *Négociants marseillais au XVIIIe siècle*, 1973, I, p. 165.

182. G. William SKINNER, 'Marketing and social structure in China', in *Journal of Asian Studies*, November 1964, p. 6. On markets later in Szechwan, pp. 96-7.

183. Abbé PREVOST, *Histoire générale des voyages . . .* (1750), VIII, p. 533.

184. Marcel MARION, *Dictionnaire des institutions de la France aux XVIIe et XVIIIe siècles*, p. 195, article 'Échoppe'.

185. A. EVERITT, in *The Agrarian History . . ., op. cit.*, IV, p. 484.

186. Robert MARQUANT, *La Vie économique à Lille sous Philippe le Bon*, 1940, p. 82.

187. The image is from Marx, *Capital*, I, section 4, ch 14: 'the worker and his means of production are welded together like a snail and his shell'.

188. R. MARQUANT, *op. cit.*, p. 82.

189. A.H. DE OLIVEIRA MARQUES, *op. cit.*, p. 201.

190. E. BRACKENHOFFER, *op. cit.*, p. 97.

191. B.N., Ms. Fr., 21633, f°s 1, 14, 18, 134.

192. A.d.S. Florence, Mediceo 4709, Paris, 27 June 1718.

193. Friedrich LÜTGE, *Deutsche Sozial- und Wirtschaftsgeschichte*, 1966, *passim* and pp. 143 ff.

194. A.N., G^7 1686, 156. Note on shopkeeper's decorations.

195. A.N., F^{12} 724, 11 April 1788.

196. It was the small shopkeeper, not the merchant, who was the object of social disdain in Italy, in Lucca for example, Marino BERENGO, *Nobili e mercanti nella Lucca del Cinquecento*, 1963, p. 65.

197. Alfred FRANKLIN, *La Vie privée d'autrefois au temps de Louis XIII*, I. *Les Magasins de nouveautés*, 1894, pp. 22 ff.

198. P. BOISSONNADE, *Essai sur l'organisation du travail en Poitou*, I, p. 287.

199. Krakow Archives, correspondence of Federigo Aurelio (3 September 1680-20 March 1683), in Italian Collection 3206.

200. W. SOMBART, *op. cit.*, on a Jewish haberdasher's shop, II, pp. 455 ff., on the question in general.

201. T.S. WILLAN, *Abraham Dent of Kirkby Stephen, op. cit.*

202. According to T.S. WILLAN, *op. cit.*

203. E. SCHREMMER, *op. cit.*, pp. 173-5.

204. A.N., F^{12} 116, f° 58 ff., 28 May 1716.

205. A.N., G^7 1686, 156 - about 1702.

206. *Journal de voyage de deux jeunes Hollandais, op. cit.*, p. 76.

207. E. BRACKENHOFFER, *op. cit.*, p. 117.

208. *Journal de voyage de deux jeunes Hollandais, op. cit.*, p. 50.

209. Tirso DE MOLINA, *El Burlador de Sevilla*, ed. J.E. Varey and N.D. Shergold, Cambridge, 1954, p. 50.

210. Y.-M. BERCÉ, *op. cit.*, I, pp. 222 and 297; see also references to 'cabaret' in the index.

211. Miguel CAPELLA and Antonio MATILLA TASCÓN, *Los Cinco Gremios mayores de Madrid*, 1957, p. 13 and note 23. Cf. LOPE DE VEGA, *La Nueva Victoria de Don Gónzalo de Cordoba*.

212. E. SCHREMMER, *op. cit.*, p. 595.

213. A.N., A.E., C.P. Angleterre, 108, f° 28.

214. *The Complete English Tradesman*, London, 1745, II, pp. 332 and 335.

215. *Voyage en Angleterre, op. cit.*, f° 29.

216. L. BATTIFOL, *op. cit.*, pp. 25–6.
217. See the first edition of Volume I of the present work, 1967, pp. 193–4.
218. W. SOMBART, *op. cit.*, II, p. 465; *Mémoires de la baronne d'Oberkirch*, 1970, p. 348 and note 1, 534.
219. A. FRANKLIN, *La Vie privée ...*, I, *Magasins de nouveautés, op. cit., passim*, pp. 20 and 40.
220. Archives, Malta, 6405, early eighteenth century.
221. Jean-Baptiste SAY, *De l'Angleterre et des Anglais*, 1815, p. 23.
222. A serious study has yet to be done. Here are a few indications. In Valladolid in 1570, there were 1870 artisans' and tradesmen's shops for 40,000 inhabitants, or about one to every 20. (Bartolomé BENNASSAR, *Valladolid au siècle d'or*, 1967). In Rome in 1622, the ratio was about the same: 5578 shops to a population of 114,000 (Jean DELUMEAU, *La Vie économique et sociale de Rome dans la seconde moitié du XVIe siècle*, 1957–1959, I, pp. 377 and 379). On Venice see Daniele BELTRAMI, *Storia della popolazione di Venezia dalle fine del secolo XVI alla caduta dalla Repubblica*, 1954, p. 219, and on Siena a record of all the guilds in the city dating from 1762 (A.d.S. Siena, Archivio Spannochi B 59). On Grenoble in 1723, see E. ESMONIN, *Etudes sur la France des XVIIe et XVIIIe siècles*, 1964, p. 461 and note 80.
223. W. SOMBART, *op. cit.*, II, p. 454.
224. *Wirtschafts- und Sozialgeschichte zentraleuropäischer Städte in neuerer Zeit*, 1963, pp. 183 ff. In Basle, between the sixteenth century and the eighteenth, the number of retail shopkeepers increased by 40% while the number of artisans remained stable or fell slightly.
225. I am indebted to Claude LARQUIÉ for the inventory made on the decease of an *aguardientero* whose shop was on the Plaza Mayor, Archivo de los Protocolos, no. 10598, f°s 372–516, 1667.
226. Surveys made by Maurice AYMARD, 1548, Tribunale del Real Patrimonio 137, Livelli f°s 3561 and 1584; *ibid.*, Privilegiati, f° 8.
227. Moscow, C.S.A., 35/6, 390, 84, London, 7 March 1788.
228. Albert SOBOUL, *Les Sans-Culottes parisiens en l'an II*, 1958, *passim*, esp. pp. 163, 267, 443, 445.
229. A.N., F^12 724.
230. Chanoine François PEDOUE, *Le Bourgeois poli*, 1631.
231. Adam SMITH, *The Wealth of Nations*, Everyman edition, 1937, I, p. 12.
232. Fernand BRAUDEL, *The Mediterranean and the Mediterranean World in the Age of Philip II* (English translation, 1972–3), I, p. 320. All further references are to this edition, which is hereafter abbreviated as *Medit.*
233. Jean-Jacques HÉMARDINQUER, 'La taille, impôt marqué sur un bâton (Landes, Pyrénées, Bourgogne)', in *Bulletin philologique et historique* (until 1610), 1972, pp. 507–12.
234. Lucien GERSCHEL, 'L'Ogam et le nom', in *Etudes celtiques*, 1963, pp. 531–2; and see the 1967 edition of Vol. I of the present work, pp. 357–8.
235. D. DEFOE, *op. cit.*, I, p. 356.
236. A. du PRADEL, *op. cit.*, II, p. 60.
237. A. de PARIS, 3 B 6 27, 26 February 1720.
238. *Variétés*, II, p. 136.
239. *Variétés*, VI, p. 163.
240. A.D. ISÈRE, II E, 621 and 622.
241. *Les Mémoires de Jean Maillefer, marchand bourgeois de Reims (1611–1684)*, 1890, p. 16.
242. A.N., F^12 863–7, 7 October 1728.
243. Information provided by Traian STOIANOVICH.
244. Georges LIVET, 'Les Savoyards à Strasbourg au début du XVIIIe siècle', in *Cahiers d'histoire*, IV, 2, 1959, p. 132.
245. José Luis MARTIN GALINDO, 'Arrieros maragatos en el siglo XVIII', *Estudios y Documentos*, no. 9, 1956; *Medit.*, I, p. 448.
246. M. CAPELLA, A. MATILLA TASCÓN, *op. cit.*, pp. 14 and 22.
247. Marius KULCZYKOWSKI, 'En Pologne au XVIIIe siècle: industrie paysanne et formation du marché national', in *Annales E.S.C.*, 1969, pp. 61–9.
248. D. DEFOE, *op. cit.*, II, p. 300.
249. J. SAVARY DES BRUSLONS, *op. cit.*, the word 'Forain', col. 707.
250. Maurice LOMBARD, 'L'évolution urbaine pendant le Haut Moyen Age' in *Annales E.S.C.*, XII-1957; Édouard PERROY,

Histoire du Moyen Age, 'the Syri, that is Christians and Jews who spoke Greek', p. 20.

251. *Variétés*, III, p. 36.

252. E. SCHREMMER, *op. cit.*, p. 604.

253. Robert MANDROU, *De la culture populaire aux XVIIe et XVIIIe siècles. La Bibliothèque bleue de Troyes*, 1964, p. 56.

254. W. SOMBART, *op. cit.*, II, p. 446.

255. Claude NORDMANN, *Grandeur et liberté de la Suède (1660-1792)*, 1971, p. 36.

256. According to information provided by Andrzej WYCZANSKI.

257. Moscow, C.S.A. 84/2, 420, fᵒˢ 10-11, Leipzig, 6/17 October 1798; and 84/2, 421, fᵒ 3 vᵒ, Leipzig, 8-19 January 1799.

258. A.N., G⁷ 1695, fᵒ 202. Report by Amelot, Paris, 20 September 1710. Jewish pedlars are reported at Toulouse (1695) in Germain MARTIN and Marcel BEZANÇON, *L'Histoire du crédit en France sous le règne de Louis XIV*, 1913, p. 189; and in Valogne (for their misdemeanours) archives of Calvados, C 1419 (1741-1788).

259. E. FOURNIER, *Le Théâtre français aux XVIe and XVIIe siècles*, 1874, II, p. 288.

260. *The Scandinavian Economic History Review*, 1966, no. 2, p. 193.

261. A.d.S., Bologna, II-C, 148-150, 1595.

262. Heinrich BECHTEL, *Wirtschaftsgeschichte Deutschlands*, II, p. 392, note 286.

263. E. BRACKENHOFFER, *op. cit.*, pp. 115 and 144. See LITTRÉ, 'Raisin', on grapes and raisins.

264. Jean GEORGELIN, *Venise au siècle des Lumières*, forthcoming (p. 213 of the manuscript), quoting Gradenigo.

265. Guy PATIN, *Lettres*, III, p. 246.

266. Jacques ACCARIAS DE SÉRIONNE, *La Richesse de la Hollande*, 1778, II, p. 173.

267. B.N., Ms. Fr., 14667, 131.

268. *La Response de Jean Bodin à M. de Malestroit*, 1568, ed. Henri HAUSER, 1932, p. xxxviii.

269. Collection of Dr. Morand, Bonne-sur-Ménoge (Haute-Savoie).

270. J. SAVARY DES BRUSLONS, *op. cit.*, II, col. 679; V. col. 915-16.

271. Morand Collection, Joseph Perollaz to his father, Lucerne, 13 May 1819.

272. *Gazette de France*, Madrid, 24 May 1783, p. 219.

273. See *Il Libro dei vagabondi*, ed. Piero

274. Camporesi, 1973, introduction, many references to European literature.

275. Ernst SCHULIN, *Handelsstaat England*, 1969, pp. 117 and 195. Portuguese pedlars in the early sixteenth century in the Netherlands. J.A. GORIS, *Etude sur les colonies marchandes méridionales ... à Anvers 1488-1567*, 1925, pp. 25-7.

276. David ALEXANDER, *Retailing in England during the Industrial Revolution*, 1970, pp. 63 ff. In 1780, a proposed bill prohibiting peddling, came up against strong opposition from English wool and cotton manufacturers who indicated in their petitions to the Commons the huge volume of merchandise they were handling. D. DAVIS, *op. cit.*, pp. 245-6.

277. Jean DROUILLET, *Folklore du Nivernais et du Morvan*, 1959; Suzanne TARDIEU, *La Vie domestique dans le Mâconnais rural et pré-industriel*, 1964, pp. 190-3.

278. Morand Collection, J.C. Perollaz to his wife, Geneva, 5 August 1834.

279. A.N., F¹² 2175, Metz, 6 February 1813.

280. A.N., F¹² 2175, Paris, 21 August 1813.

281. Basile H. KERBLAY, *Les Marchés paysannes en URSS*, 1968, pp. 100 ff.

282. Jean-Paul POISSON, 'De quelques nouvelles utilisations des sources notariales en histoire économique (XVIIᵉ-XXᵉ siècles)' in *Revue historique*, no. 505, 1973, pp. 5-22.

283. See below, see chapter 4, first section.

284. A.N., F¹² 149, 77.

285. A.N., F¹² 721, Périgueux, 11 June 1783.

286. W. SOMBART, *op. cit.*, II, p. 566. The first one of all was probably the *Hamburger Kommerzdeputation*, created in 1663.

287. J. GEORGELIN, *op. cit.*, p. 86.

288. Piero BARGELLINI, *Il Bicentenario della Camera di commercio fiorentina 1770-1970*, 1970.

289. A.N., G⁷ 1965, 12.

290. A.N., F¹² 151, 195.

291. A.N., F¹² 683, 23 December 1728.

292. Michael MITTERAUER, 'Jahrmärkte in Nachfolge antiker Zentralorte' in *Mitteilungen des Instituts für osterreichische Geschichtsforschung*, 1967, pp. 237 ff.

293. J. SAVARY DES BRUSLONS, *op. cit.*, the word 'Landi', col. 508.

294. Félix BOURQUELOT, *Etudes sur les foires de Champagne*, 1865, p. 10.

294. E. BRACKENHOFFER, *op. cit.*, p. 105, learned this on his way through Lyons; he quotes Eusebius, IV, ch. 3.

295. A.N., F^{12} 1259, D, Livry-sur-Meuse, Vendémiaire, an VIII.

296. LITTRÉ, the word 'Marché'. Markets and fairs could only be established with royal permission. FERRET, *Traité de l'abus*, I, 9.

297. A.N., K 1252.

298. Gérard BOUCHARD, *Un Village immobile, Sennely-en-Sologne au XVIIIe siècle*, 1972, p. 200.

299. J. SAVARY DES BRUSLONS, *op. cit.*, II, col. 668.

300. *Ibid.*, col. 663.

301. *Ibid.*, col. 668.

302. *Ibid.*, col. 671.

303. Jean MERLEY, *La Haute-Loire de la fin de l'Ancien Régime aux débuts de la Troisième République, 1776–1886*, 1974, I, pp. 146–7.

304. See Figure 4.

305. Farnesiane, 668, Valentano, 14 May 1652.

306. R. GASCON, *op. cit.*, 4, I, pp. 241–2.

307. J. SAVARY DES BRUSLONS, *op. cit.*, II, col. 676.

308. Ernst KROKER, *Handelsgeschichte der Stadt Leipzig*, 1925, p. 85.

309. Cristobal ESPEJO, *Las Antiguas Ferias de Medina del Campo*, Valladolid, 1908.

310. Jean BARUZI, *Saint Jean de la Croix et le problème de l'expérience mystique*, 1931, p. 73.

311. H. MAUERSBERG, *Wirtschafts- und Sozialgeschichte zentral-europäischer Städte in neuerer Zeit*, *op. cit.*, p. 184.

312. E. KROKER, *op. cit.*, pp. 113–14.

313. Friedrich LÜTGE, 'Der Untergang der Nürnberger Heiltumsmesse', in *Jahrbucher für Nationalökonomie und Statistik*, Band 178, Heft 1/3, 1965, p. 133.

314. Ruggiero NUTI, *La Fiera di Prato attraverso i tempi*, 1939.

315. R. GAILLET, *op. cit.*, pp. 155 ff.

316. *Vatiétés*, IV, 327 and I, 318, note 2.

317. Moscow, C.S.A., 84/12, 420, 7, Leipzig, 18–29 September 1798.

318. Francisque MICHEL, Édouard FOURNIER, *Le Livre d'or des métiers. Histoire des hôtelleries, cabarets, hôtels garnis et cafés . . .*, Paris, 1851, 2, 10 (1511).

319. R. CAILLET, *op. cit.*, pp. 156 and 159.

320. *Ibid.*, p. 156.

321. A.d.S. Napoli, Affari Esteri, 801, The Hague, 17 May 1768 and 8 May 1769.

322. *Gazette de France*, p. 513, Florence, 4 October 1720.

323. A.d.S. Florence, Fondo Riccardi 309. Leipzig, 18 October 1685, Gio. Baldi to Francesco Riccardi.

324. *Medit.*, I, p. 379 and note 104.

325. P. MOLMENTI, *op. cit.*, II, p. 67, note 1.

326. *Insignia Bologne*, X-8, 1676.

327. Henry MORLEY, *Memoirs of Bartholomew Fair*, London, 1859; J. SAVARY DES BRUSLONS, *op. cit.*, II, col. 679, the word 'Foire'.

328. Quoted by P.-L. HUVELIN, *op. cit.*, p. 30, note 1; reference to LEROUX DE LINCI, *Proverbes*, II, p. 338.

329. J. SAVARY DES BRUSLONS, *op. cit.*, II, col. 656; B.N., Ms. Fr., 21783, 170.

330. *Voyage de deux jeunes Hollandais . . .*, *op. cit.*, p. 75.

331. A. GROHMANN, *op. cit.*, p. 31.

332. R. GASCON, *op. cit.*, I, p. 169.

333. Y.-M. BERCÉ, *op. cit.*, p. 206.

334. E. KROKER, *op. cit.*, p. 132.

335. Lodovico GUICCIARDINI, *Description de tout le Pays-Bas* (1568), 3rd edn., 1625, p. 108.

336. *Gazette de France*, April 1634.

337. Oliver C. COX, *The Foundations of Capitalism*, 1959, p. 27. For an opposite view see P. CHALMETTA GENDRON, *op. cit.*, p. 105.

338. Alfred HOFFMANN, *Wirtschaftsgeschichte des Landes Oberösterreich*, 1952, p. 139.

339. E. KROKER, *op. cit.*, p. 83.

340. Corrado MARCIANI, *Lettres de change aux foires de Lanciano au XVIe siècle*, Paris, 1962.

341. Louis DERMIGNY, 'Les foires de Pézenas et de Montagnac au XVIIIe siècle', in *Actes du congrès régional des fédérations historiques de Languedoc*, Carcassonne, May 1952, esp. pp. 18–19.

342. Robert-Henri BAUTIER, 'Les foires de Champagne', in *Recueils de la Société Jean Bodin*, V: *La foire*, pp. 1–51.

343. F. BOURQUELOT, *Etudes sur les foires de Champagne*, II, *op. cit.*, pp. 301–20.

344. *Medit.*, I, pp. 504–5 and note 283.

345. *Ibid.*, I, p. 343.

346. José Gentil DA SILVA, *Banque et crédit en Italie au XVIIe siècle*, 1969, p. 55.

347. *Ibid.*, see index under *Mercanti di conto*.
348. Domenico PERI, *Il Negotiante*, Genoa, 1638; *Medit.*, I, p. 508.
349. J. GENTIL DA SILVA, *op. cit.*, p. 55.
350. Giuseppe MIRA, 'L'organizzazione fieristica nel quadro dell'economia della "Bassa" Lombardia alla fine del medioevo e nell'età moderna', in *Archivio storico lombardo*, vol. 8, 1958, pp. 289–300.
351. A. GROHMANN, *op. cit.*, p. 62.
352. A. HOFFMANN, *op. cit.*, pp. 142–3.
353. Henri LAURENT, *Un Grand Commerce d'exportation au Moyen Age: la draperie des Pays-Bas en France et dans les pays méditerranéens, XIIe-XVe siècles*, 1935, pp. 37–41.
354. A. GROHMANN, *op. cit.*, p. 20.
355. F. BOREL, *Les Foires de Genève au XVe siècle*, 1892 and attached documents; Jean-François BERGIER, *Les Foires de Genève et l'économie internationale de la Renaissance*, 1963.
356. R. GASCON, *op. cit.*, I, p. 49.
357. A.N., F¹² 149, fᵒ 59, 27 September 1756.
358. TURGOT, article 'Foire' in the *Encyclopédie* of 1757; J. SAVARY DES BRUSLONS, article 'Foire', col. 647.
359. W. SOMBART, *op. cit.*, II, pp. 472 and 479.
360. A.HOFFMANN, *op. cit.*, p. 143; E. KROKER, *op. cit.*, p. 163. NB the word *Messe* (fair) was generally used in Frankfurt but did not become current in Leipzig until the latter half of the seventeenth century when it displaced the words *Jahrmärkte* or *Märkte*, *ibid.*, p. 71.
361. *Medit.*, I, pp. 197–200.
362. W. SOMBART, *op. cit.*, II, p. 473.
363. B.H. KERBLAY, *op. cit.*, pp. 85 ff.
364. Alice Piffer CANABRAVA, *O Comercio português no Rio da Prata (1580-1640)*, 1944, pp. 21 ff. J. SAVARY DES BRUSLONS, *op. cit.*, V, col. 1367 ff. and see also the article on La Vera Cruz and Cartagena.
365. Nicolás SÁNCHEZ ALBORNOZ, 'Un testigo del comerci indiano, Tomás de Mercado y Nueva España', in *Revista de historia de America*, 1959, p. 113.
366. Quoted by E.W. DAHLGREN, *Relations commerciales et maritimes entre la France et les côtes de l'océan Pacifique*, 1909, p. 21.
367. José GENTIL DA SILVA, 'Trafic du Nord, marchés du "Mezzogiorno", finances génoises: recherches et documents sur la conjoncture à la fin du XVIe siècle' in *Revue du Nord*, XLI, no. 162, April-June 1959, pp. 129–52, esp. p. 132.
368. Louis DERMIGNY, in *Histoire du Languedoc*, 196-7, p. 414.
369. A.N., F¹² 1266. The proposal was never accepted. The former Place de la Révolution is now the Place de la Concorde.
370. Werner SOMBART, *Apogée du capitalisme*, 1932, ed. André E. SAYOUS, p. xxv.
371. W. SOMBART, *Der moderne Kapitalismus*, II, *op. cit.*, pp. 488 ff.
372. J. SAVARY DES BRUSLONS, *op. cit.*, III, the word 'Marchand', col. 765.
373. LITTRÉ, *op. cit.*, the word 'Corde', p. 808.
374. W. SOMBART, *Der moderne Kapitalismus*, II, p. 489.
375. Jean-Pierre RICARD, *Le Négoce d'Amsterdam contenant tout ce que doivent savoir les marchands et banquiers, tant ceux qui sont établis à Amsterdam que ceux des pays étrangers*, Amsterdam, 1722, pp. 5-7.
376. Moscow, C.S.A. CENT. 1261-1. 774, fᵒ 18.
377. W. SOMBART, *op. cit.*, II, p. 490.
378. *Histoire du commerce de Marseille*, II, p. 466; IV, pp. 92 ff.; V, pp. 510 ff.
379. W. SOMBART, *op. cit.*, II, p. 490.
380. A.N., F¹² 116, 36.
381. Raymond OBERLÉ, 'L'évolution des finances à Mulhouse et le financement de l'industrialisation au XVIIIe siècle' in *Comité des travaux historiques. Bulletin de la section d'histoire moderne et contemporaine*, no. 8, 1971, pp. 93-4.
382. Cardinal François-Désiré MATHIEU, *L'Ancien Régime en Lorraine et Barrois ... (1658-1789)*, Paris, 1878, p. 35.
383. Jacqueline KAUFMANN-ROCHARD, *Origines d'une bourgeoisie russe, XVIe et XVIIe siècles*, 1969, p. 45.
384. J. SAVARY DES BRUSLONS, *op. cit.*, II, the word 'Entrepôt', col. 329-330.
385. A.N., F¹² 70, fᵒ 102, 13 August 1722.
386. R. GASCON, *op. cit.*, I, p. 158.
387. *Medit.*, I, p. 580.
388. C. CARRÈRE, *op. cit.*, p. 9.
389. Roberto CESSI and Annibale ALBERTI, *Rialto*, 1934, p. 79.
390. Maurice LÉVY-LEBOYER, *Les Banques*

européennes et l'industrialisation internationale dans la première moitié du XIXe siècle, 1964, pp. 254 ff.

391. Mateo ALEMÁN, *Guzmán de Alfarache*, in *La Novela picaresca española, op. cit.*, p. 551.

392. Viera da SILVA, *Dispersos*, III, 340 and IX, 807. The *Real Plaça do Comercio* was built after 1760. Information provided by J. GENTIL DA SILVA.

393. Raimundo de LANTERY, *Memorias*, ed. Alvaro PICARDO Y GOMEZ, Cadiz, 1949. See the article in the *Mélanges Braudel* by Pierre PONSOT, pp. 151–85.

394. R. CESSI and A. ALBERTI, *op. cit.*, p. 66.

395. Richard EHRENBERG, *Das Zeitalter des Fugger*, 3rd edn., 1922, I, p. 70.

396. According to information provided by Guido PAMPALONI.

397. The *loggia dei Mercanti ai Banchi*, is 400m from the Strada Nuova, according to Guiseppe FELLONI (letter of 4 September 1975).

398. R. EHRENBERG, *op. cit.*, I, p. 70.

399. R. MARQUANT, *op. cit.*, p. 61.

400. Jean LEJEUNE, *La Formation du capitalisme moderne dans la principauté de Liège au XVIe siècle*, 1939, p. 27.

401. Claude LAVEAU, *Le Monde rochelais de l'Ancien Régime an Consulat. Essai d'histoire économique et sociale (1744–1800)* unpublished thesis, 1972, p. 146.

402. *Scipta mercaturae*, I, 1967, copperplate engraving by Gaspar Merian between pages 38 and 39.

403. E. KROKER, *op. cit.*, p. 138.

404. A.N., G⁷ 698, 24.

405. *Diarii di Palermo, op. cit.*, II, p. 59.

406. A.d.S., Genoa, Lettere Consoli, 1/26–28.

407. Charles CARRIÈRE, *op. cit.*, I, p. 234.

408. Moscow, C.S.A., 35/6, 744, 9 ff.

409. C. CARRÈRE, *op. cit.*, p. 50.

410. *Ibid.*, p. 51.

411. R. EHRENBERG, *op. cit.*, I, p. 70.

412. Raymond BLOCH, Jean COUSIN, *Rome et son destin*, 1960, p. 126.

413. C. CARRIÈRE, *op. cit.*, I, pp. 232–3.

414. L.-A. BOITEUX, *La Fortune de mer, le besoin de sécurité et les débuts de l'assurance maritime*, 1968, p. 165.

415. D. DEFOE, *op. cit.*, I, 108.

416. J.-P. RICARD, *Le Négoce d'Amsterdam . . ., op. cit.*, pp. 6–7.

417. *Ibid.*, p. 6.

418. See the first edition of Vol. I of the present work, 1967, p. 360. Gino LUZZATTO, *Storia economica di Venezia dall'XI al XVI secolo*, Venice, 1961, pp. 147 ff.

419. Federigo MELIS, *Tracce di una storia economica di Firenze e della Toscana in generale dal 1252 al 1550*, lecture course 1966–7; Alfred DOREN, *Storia economica dell'Italia nel Medio Evo*, 1936, p. 559.

420. Adam WISZNIEWSKI, *Histoire de la Banque de Saint-Georges de Gênes*, Paris, 1865.

421. E. MASCHKE, *art. cit.*, offprint, p. 8.

422. *Medit.*, II, p. 698.

423. Bernard SCHNAPPER, *Les Rentes au XVIe siècle, Histoire d'un instrument de credit*, Paris, 1957; *Registres de l'Hôtel de Ville pendant la Fronde*, ed. LEROUX DE LINCY and DOUET D'ARCQ, 1846–7, II, p. 426.

424. R. SPRANDEL, *Der städtische Rentenmarkt in Nordwestdeutschland im Spätmittelalter*, 1971, pp. 14–23.

425. Armando SAPORI, *Una Compagnia di Calimalo ai primi del Trecento*, 1932, p. 185.

426. Heinrich Johann SIEVEKING, *Wirtschaftsgeschichte*, 1935, p. 87.

427. John FRANCIS, *Chronicles and Characters of the Stock Exchange*, London, 1849, p. 12. N.W. POSTHUMUS, 'The Tulipomania in Holland in the years 1636 and 1637,' in *Journal of Economic and Business History*, I, 1928–9, pp. 434–66.

428. Amsterdam, 1688, re-edited Madrid, 1958.

429. J.G. VAN DILLEN, 'Isaac Le Maire et le commerce des actions de la Compagnie des Indes orientales', in *Revue d'histoire moderne*, January-February and March-May 1935, esp. pp. 24 and 36.

430. J.G. VAN DILLEN, *art. cit.*, pp. 15, 19, 21.

431. A.N., K 1349, 132, fᵒ 82.

432. A.N., A.E., B¹, 757.

433. A.N., K 1349, 132, fᵒ 81.

434. Isaac de PINTO, *Traité de la circulation et du crédit*, 1771, p. 311.

435. C.R. BOXER, *The Dutch Seaborne Empire 1600-1800*, 1965, p. 19.

436. Pierre JEANNIN, *L'Europe du Nord-Ouest et du Nord aux XVIIe et XVIIIe siècles*, 1969, p. 73.

437. J. de LA VEGA, *op. cit.*, p. 322.

438. *Le Guide d'Amsterdam*, 1701, p. 65, mentions the 'Café françois'. The others are indicated by Joseph de LA VEGA, *Die Verwirrung der Verwirrungen*, ed. Otto Pringsheim, 1919, p. 192, note 2, reference to BERG, *Réfugiés*, p. 328.

439. Michele TORCIA, *Sbozzo del commercio di Amsterdam*, 1782.

440. A.N., 61 AQ 4.

441. Herbert LÜTHY, *La Banque protestante en France de la Révocation de l'Edit de Nantes à la Révolution*, 1959-1961, II, p. 515.

442. A.N., 61 AQ 4, Paris, 2 March 1780.

443. H. LÜTHY, *op. cit.*, II, see index.

444. A.N., 61 AQ 4. 'On account at 3/3' means three thirds, divided between Marcet, Pictet and Cramer.

445. A.N., 61 AQ 77 and 88.

446. J. FRANCIS, *op. cit.*, p. 83.

447. *Ibid.*, pp. 26-7.

448. A.N., G⁷ 1699, London, 29 May 1713.

449. J. FRANCIS, *op. cit.*, p. 30.

450. Jean SAVANT, *Tel fut Ouvrard*, 1954, p. 55.

451. Cf. P.G.M. DICKSON, *The Financial Revolution in England*, 1967, pp. 505-510. E.V. MORGAN and W.A. THOMAS, *The Stock Exchange*, 1962, pp. 60-61.

452. *Ibid.*, p. 65.

453. E. SCHULIN, *op. cit.*, pp. 249 and 295.

454. P.G.M. DICKSON, *op. cit.*, p. 504.

455. E.V. MORGAN and W.A. THOMAS, *op. cit.*, p. 17.

456. P.G.M. DICKSON, *op. cit.*, p. 506.

457. Jacob van KLAVEREN, 'Rue de Quincampoix und Exchange Alley. Die Spekulationjahre 1719 und 1720 in Frankreich und England' in *Vierteljahrschrift fur Sozial- und Wirtschaftsgeschichte*, 1963, 48, 3, pp. 331-359.

458. Robert BIGO, 'Une grammaire de la Bourse en 1789' in *Annales d'histoire économique et sociale*, II, 1930, pp. 500 and 507.

459. Marie-Joseph Désiré MARTIN, *Les Étrennes financières*, 1789, pp. 97 ff.

460. *Ibid.*, ch VI, 'Bourse', p. 68.

461. Robert BIGO, *La Caisse d'Escompte (1776-1793) et les origines de la Banque de France*, Paris, 1927, esp. pp. 95-116.

462. *Mémoires du comte de Tilly*, 1965, p. 242.

463. Moscow, C.S.A., 93/6, 428, p. 40, Paris, 15 August 1785.

464. A.N., 61, AQ 4.

465. Roland de LA PLATIÈRE, *Encyclopédie méthodique*, II, p. 2, quoted in C. CARRIÈRE, *op. cit.*, I, p. 244, note.

466. Maurice LÉVY-LEBOYER, *op. cit.*, p. 420, note 17.

467. Jacques GERNET, *Le Monde chinois*, Paris, 1972, p. 231.

468. Pierre GOUBERT, *Beauvais et le Beauvaisis de 1600 à 1730*, Paris, 1960, p. 142.

469. I. de PINTO, *op. cit.*, p. 69.

470. This was the figure suggested for Holland during the 1763 crisis, A.E., Holland, 513, p. 64.

471. M. LÉVY-LEBOYER, *op. cit.*, p. 709; Guy THUILLER, 'Le stock monétaire de la France en l'an X' in *Revue d'histoire économique et sociale*, 1974, p. 253. An anonymous English register from about 1700 distinguishes thirty different categories of paper money. E. SCHULIN, *op. cit.*, p. 287, note 191.

472. A.N., G⁷ 1622.

473. M. TORCIA, *Sbozzo del commercio di Amsterdam*, *op. cit.*, p. 41.

474. *Op. cit.*, I, p. 266.

475. E. MARTINEZ ESTRADA, *Muerte y transfiguración de Martin Fierro*, 1948, *passim* and esp. I, pp. 134-5.

476. Roger LETOURNEAU, *Fès avant le protectorat*, Casablanca, 1949, quoted by P. CHALMETTA, *op. cit.*, p. 128.

477. P. CHALMETTA, *op. cit.*, pp. 133-4, reference to al-MAQRIZI, *Kitab az-Jitat*.

478. S.Y. LABIB, *Handelsgeschichte Ägyptens im Spätmittelalter 1171-1517*, 1965, pp. 277, 290, 323.

479. Nikita ELISSEEFF, *Nur-ad-Din*, III, p. 856, quoted by P. CHALMETTA, p. 176.

480. Carlo A. PINELLI, Folco QUILICI, *L'Alba dell'uomo*, 1974, p. 219.

481. Pierre GOUROU, *Leçons de géographie tropicale*, 1971, p, 106; *Pour une géographie humaine*, 1973, p. 105. Most of the information is in the collective work *Mount Everest*, London, 1963.

482. G.W. SKINNER, *art. cit.*

483. Richard CANTILLON, *Essai sur la nature du commerce en général*, INED, 1952, pp. 5 ff.

484. J.C. VAN LEUR, *Indonesian Trade and*

Society, 1955, pp. 53, 60, 63, etc., and esp. pp. 135-7, 197, 200. Van Leur's interpretation is echoed in Niels STEENSGAARD, *The Asian Trade Revolution of the Seventeenth Century*, 1973. It is challenged by Daniel THORNER, from whom I have a note on the subject, and by the book by M.A.P. MEILINK-ROELSFSZ, *Asian Trade and European Influence in the Indonesian Archipelago between 1500 and about 1630*, 1962. This debate is crucial to world history itself, and I shall be returning to it in chapter 5 of Vol. III of this book.

485. J.C. VAN LEUR, *op. cit.*, pp. 3 ff.

486. A.N., Marine, B⁷ 46, pp. 256 ff.

487. B.N., Lisbon, F.G 7970: translated by Ievon KHACHIKIAN, 'Le registre d'un marchand arménien en Perse, en Inde et au Tibet (1682-1693)', in *Annales E.S.C.*, March-April 1967.

488. Robert MANTRAN, *Istanbul dans la seconde moitié du XVIIe siècle*, 1962.

489. *Russko-indiiskie otnochenyia v XVIII vekye* (Russo-Indian relations in the eighteenth century). Collected documents, pp. 29 ff., 56-65, 74, 82, 95 ff.

490. *Ibid.*, pp. 32, 51-5, 67.

491. *Medit.*, I, p. 287 and p. 641.

492. Luigi CELLI, Introduction à *Due trattati inediti di Silvestto Gozzolini da Osimo, economista e finanziere del sec XVI*, Turin, 1892, pp. 2-6.

493. *Medit.*, II, p. 813.

494. Jacques de VILLAMONT, *Les Voyages du Seigneur de Villamont*, 1600, p. 102, r° and v°.

495. Irfan M. HABIB, 'Banking in Moghul India' in *Contribution to Indian economic history*, I, Calcutta, 1960, pp. 1-20.

496. C.R. BOXER, 'Macao as religious and commercial entrepot in the 16th and 17th centuries' in *Acta asiatica*, 19-74, p. 71.

497. *Voiage de Henri Hagenaar aux Indes orientales* in R.A. Constantin de RENNEVILLE, *Recueil des voiages qui ont servi à l'établissement et au progrès de la Compagnie des Indes orientales*, V, 1706, pp. 294 and 296-7.

498. *Medit.*, II, p. 819.

499. Abbé PRÉVOST, *op. cit.*, VIII, p. 629; W.H.

MORELAND, *From Akbar to Aurangzeb*, 1923, pp. 153-8.

500. Jean-Henri GROSE, *Voyage aux Indes orientales*, 1758, pp. 155 ff. 'The great merchant Abdulgafour, who was said to have built up alone a trade as great as that of the English company...'

501. Jean-Baptiste TAVERNIER, *Les Six Voyages de Jean-Baptiste Tavernier ... qu'il a faits en Turquie, en Perse et aux Indes ...*, Paris, 1676, I, pp. 192, 193.

502. Louis DERMIGNY, *Les Mémoires de Charles de Constant sur le commerce à la Chine*, 1964, pp. 76 and 189-90.

503. Dominique and Janine SOURDEL, *La Civilisation de l'Islam classique*, 1968, p. 584.

504. Robert BRUNSCHVIG, 'Coup d'oeil sur l'histoire des foires à travers l'Islam', in *Recueils de la Société Jean Bodin*, V: *La Foire*, 1953, p. 44 and note 1.

505. J.C. VAN LEUR, *op. cit.*, p. 76.

506. R. BRUNSCHVIG, *art. cit.*, pp. 52-3.

507. Ludovico de VARTHEMA, *Les Voyages de Ludovico di Varthema ou le viateur en la plus grande partie d'Orient*, Paris, 1888, p. 21. 'We took our way and spent three days travelling to a place called Mezeribe. And here we stayed three days while the merchants obtained their wares and bought camels and everything that was necessary to them. The lord of the said Mezeribe, named Zambey, is the lord of the country all about, in other words of the Arabs ... he has forty thousand horses and for his court he has ten thousand mares and three hundred thousand camels'.

508. S.Y. LABIB, *Handelsgeschichte Ägyptens im Spätmittelalter ... op. cit.*, pp. 193-4.

509. *Ibid.*, p. 194.

510. R. BRUNSCHVIG, *art. cit.*, pp. 56-7.

511. S.Y. LABIB, *op. cit.*, p. 197.

512. *Medit.*, I, p. 209 and note 173. Reference to Henry SIMONSFELD, *Der Fondaco dei Tedeschi und die deutsch-venetianischen Handelsbeziehungen*, 1887; Hans HAUSHERR, *Wirtschaftsgeschichte der Neuzeit vom Ende des 14. bis zur Höhe des 19. J.* 3rd edn., 1954, p. 28.

513. William CROOKE, *Things Indian*, 1906, pp. 195 ff.

514. For the following details see Abbé

PRÉVOST, *op. cit.*, I, p. 414 and VIII, pp. 139 ff.

515. W. HEYD, *Histoire du commerce du Levant au Moyen Age*, 1936, II, pp. 662-3.

516. Denys LOMBARD, *Le Sultanat d'Atjeh au temps d'Iskandar Muda, 1607-1636*, 1967, p. 46; reference to John DAVIS, *A briefe relation of Master John Davis, chiefe pilote to the Zelanders in their East India Voyage ... 1598*, London 1625.

517. François MARTIN, *Description du premier voyage faict aux Indes Orientales par les Français de Saint-Malo*, 1604, quoted by D. LOMBARD, *op. cit.*, p. 25 note 4.

518. D. LOMBARD, *op. cit.*, pp. 113-14, reference to Guillaume DAMPIER, *Supplément du voyage autour du monde*, 1723.

519. According to information provided by Michel CARTIER, Denys LOMBARD, and Etienne BALAZS.

520. Etienne BALAZS, 'Les foires en Chine', in *Recueils de la Société Jean Bodin*, V, *La Foire*, 1953, pp. 77-89.

521. *Encyclopedia Britannica*, 1969, XIII, p. 124.

522. Louis DERMIGNY, *La Chine et l'Occident. Le commerce à Canton au XVIIIe siècle*, 1964, I, p. 295, III, p. 1151.

523. *Science and Civilisation in China*, Cambridge, 1954.

524. 'Le marché monétaire au Moyen Age et au début des Temps modernes' in *Revue historique*, 1970, p. 28.

525. C. VERLINDEN, J. CRAEYBECKX, E. SCHOLLIERS, 'Mouvements des prix et des salaires en Belgique au XVIe siècle' in *Annales E.S.C.*, 1955, no. 2, p. 187, note 1: 'In the present state of research, we may even wonder if whether the sixteenth century is not characterized by the concentration of large-scale trade in a few hands'.

526. 'Rue de Quincampoix und Exchange Alley' in *Viertelschrift ... art. cit.*, 1963.

NOTES TO CHAPTER 2

1. I am following the advice of Georges GURVITCH in not using the word 'laws'.

2. I am thinking in particular of the Simon Ruiz archive in Valladolid and the Francesco Datini archive in Prato.

3. J. MAILLEFER, *op. cit.*, p. 102.

4. F. BRAUDEL and A. TENENTI, 'Michiel da Lezze, marchand vénitien (1497-1514) in *Mélanges Friedrich Lütge*, 1956, p. 48.

5. *Ibid.*, p. 64.

6. L. DERMIGNY, *La Chine et l'Occident ...*, II, p. 703 and note 5.

7. A.N., 62 AQ 44, Le Havre, 26 March 1743.

8. F. BRAUDEL and A. TENENTI, *art. cit.*, p. 57.

9. *Medit.*, Eng. transl., I, pp. 621 ff.

10. *Ibid.*, I, pp. 310-11.

11. The following passage is based on a long report made by Daniel Braems in 1687 on his return from the Indies where he had for many years held a senior post in the Company. A.N., B⁷, 463, fᵒˢ 235-236, 253, 284.

12. *Ibid.*, fᵒ 125.

13. See the first edition of Volume I, of this book, 1967, p. 366.

14. Felipe RUIZ MARTIN, *Lettres marchandes échangées entre Florence et Medina del Campo*, Paris, 1965, p. 307.

15. A.N., 62 AQ 33, 12 May 1784.

16. A.N., 62 AQ 33, 29 November 1773. This Dugard was the son of Robert Dugard, founder of the great dye-works in Darnetal who had gone bankrupt in 1763

17. *Ibid.*, 34, 31 October 1775.

18. The adjective is to be understood in the sense of extinction, 'putting an end to, cancelling out an obligation', (LITTRÉ).

19. A.N., 62, AQ 34, 14 March 1793.

20. A.N., 94, AQ 1, file no. 6.

21. A.N., 94, AQ 1, file no. 6, fᵒ 35.

22. Jean CAVIGNAC, *Jean Pellet, commerçant de gros, 1694-1772*, 1967, p. 37.

23. A.N., F¹², 721, 25 February 1783.

24. A.N., 61, AQ 1, fᵒ 28 vᵒ, 4 April 1776.

25. A.N., 94, AQ 1, file no. 11, letter from Pondicherry, 1st October 1729.

26. Pierre BLANCARD, *Manuel de commerce des Indes orientales et de la Chine*, 1806, pp. 40-1.
27. Ferdinand TREMEL, *Das Handelsbuch des Judenburger Kaufmannes Clemens Körbler, 1526-1548*, 1960.
28. J. CAVIGNAC, *op. cit.*, p. 152.
29. *Ibid.*, p. 153.
30. *Ibid.*, p. 154.
31. *Ibid.*, p. 37.
32. Romuald SZRAMKIEWICZ, *Les Régents et censeurs de la Banque de France nommés sous le Consulat et l'Empire*, 1974.
33. Clemens BAUER, *Unternehmung und Unternehmungsformen im Spätmittelalter und in der beginnenden Neuzeit*, 1936, p. 45.
34. Raymond de ROOVER, *The Rise and Decline of the Medici Bank, 1397-1494*, 1963, pp. 86 ff.
35. A.N., 62 AQ 33.
36. Evidently they had decided to go halves with Dugard (represented in the correspondence by the sign 2/2. Similarly 3/3 signified that three parties were in agreement, each for one-third).
37. Fernand BRAUDEL, 'Réalités économiques et prises de conscience: quelques témoignages sur le XVIe siècle' in *Annales E.S.C.*, 1959, p. 735.
38. A.N., G⁷, 1698, 132, 12 April 1713.
39. On *metedores*, E.W. DAHLGREN, *Relations commerciales et maritimes entre la France et les côtes de l'Océan Pacifique*, *op. cit.*, I, p. 42. On *cargadores*, John EVERAERT, *De internationale en coloniale handel der vlaamse Firma's te Cadiz, 1670-1740*, 1973, p. 899.
40. R. GASCON, *op. cit.*, pp. 204-5.
41. Armando SAPORI, *Studi di storia economica*, 3rd edn., 1955, II, p. 933.
42. Jean-Baptiste TAVERNIER, *Voyage en Perse*, ed. Pascal Pia, 1930, p. 69.
43. P.D. de PASSENANS, *La Russie et l'esclavage*, 1822, I, p. 129, note 1.
44. L. BRENTANO, *Le Origini del capitalismo*, 1954, German edn., 1916, p. 9.
45. Hektor AMMAN, 'Die Anfänge des Aktivhandels und der Tucheinfuhr aus Nordwesteuropa nach dem Mittelmeergebiet', in *Studi in onore di Armando Sapori*, 1957, I, p. 276.
46. H. PIGEONNEAU, *op. cit.*, I, p. 253.
47. *Medit.*, I, p. 504.
48. Richard EHRENBERG's expression, *Das Zeitalter der Fugger. Geldkapital und Creditverkehr im 16. J.*, 1896.
49. Pierre VILAR, *La Catalogne dans l'Espagne moderne*, 1962, III, p. 484.
50. Mesroub J. SETH, *Armenians in India from the earliest times to the present day*, 1937.
51. L. DERMIGNY, *Mémoires de Charles de Constant . . .*, *op. cit.*, p. 150, note 5.
52. L. KHACHIKIAN, *art. cit.*, pp. 239 ff.
53. L. DERMIGNY, *La Chine et l'Occident . . .*, *op. cit.*, I, p. 35.
54. Pierre CHAUNU, *Les Philippines et le Pacifique des Ibériques*, 1960, p. 23.
55. V. A. PARSAMIANA, *Relations russo-arméniennes*, Erivan, 1953, doc nos. 44 and 48-50.
56. F. LÜTGE, *op. cit.*, p. 253.
57. *Medit.*, I, p. 288.
58. Malta Archives, Liber Bullarum, 423, fº 230, 1 March and 1 April 1553.
59. *Gazette de France*, 30 January 1649, p. 108, Father Joseph BOUGEREL, *Mémoires pour servir à l'histoire de plusieurs hommes illustres de Provence*, 1752, pp. 144-73.
60. Louis BERGASSE and Gaston RAMBERT, *Histoire du commerce de Marseille*, IV, 1954, p. 65.
61. Simancas, Estado Napoles, 1097, fº 107.
62. The full title translated is: Treasury of measures, weights, numbers and currencies of the entire world; or knowledge of all kinds of weights, measures and currencies which govern trade throughout the whole world, brought together . . . by the humble luminary Lucas of Vanand, at the expense and at the request of Sire Peter, son of the Xac'atur of Julfa. Printed thanks to and with the consent of the most great and sublime doctor and holy bishop Thomas of Vanand of the house of Golt'n. In the year of our Lord 1699, 16 January, At Amsterdam.
63. Alexander WOLOWSKI, *La Vie quotidienne en Pologne au XVIIe Siècle*, 1972, pp. 179-80.
64. L. DERMIGNY, *La Chine et l'Occident*, I, p. 297.
65. Paul SHAKED, *A Tentative Bibliography of Geniza Documents*, 1964; S.D.

GOITEIN, 'The Cairo Geniza as a source for the history of Muslim civilization', in *Studia islamica*, III, pp. 75-91.

66. S.Y. LABIB, in *Journal of Economic History*, 1969, p. 84.
67. H. PIGEONNEAU, *op. cit.*, I, pp. 242-5.
68. *Medit.*, II, p. 821; Attilio MILANO, *Storia degli Ebrei in Italia*, 1963, pp. 218-20.
69. H. INALCIK, in *Journal of Economic History*, 1969, pp. 121 ff.
70. *Sephardim an der unteren Elbe*, 1958.
71. F. LÜTGE, *op. cit.*, pp. 379-80 and more especially H. SCHNEE, *Die Hoffinanz und der moderne Staat*, 3 vols., 1953-1955.
72. Pierre SAVILLE, *Le Juif de Cour, histoire du Résident royal Berend Lehman*, (1661-1730), 1970.
73. Werner SOMBART, *Die Juden und das Wirtschaftsleben*, 1922.
74. H. INALCIK, *art. cit.*, pp. 101-2.
75. Lewis HANKE, 'The Portuguese in Spanish America', in *Rev. de Hist. de America*, June 1961, pp. 1-48; Gonzalo de REPARAZ hijo, 'Os Portugueses no Peru nos seculos XVI e XVII' in *Boletim da Sociedade de Geografia de Lisboa*, January-March 1967, pp. 39-55.
76. Pablo VILA, 'Margarita en la colonia 1550 a 1600' in *Revista nacional de cultura*, Caracas, October 1955, p. 62.
77. A.P. CANABRAVA, *O Comercio portugues no Rio da Prata*, *op. cit.*, pp. 36-8, and references in footnotes to Hanke and others.
78. *Ibid.*, pp. 116 ff; L. HANKE, *art. cit.*, p. 15.
79. L. HANKE, *ibid.*, p. 27.
80. A.P. CANABRAVA, *op. cit.*, pp. 143 ff. Emanuel SOARES da VEIGA GARCIA, 'Buenos Aires e Cadiz, Contribuiçâo ao estudo do comercio livre (1789-1791)' in *Revista de historia*, 1970, p. 377.
81. L. HANKE, *art. cit.*, p. 7.
82. *Ibid.*, p. 14. Quotation from J. TORIBIO MEDINA, *Historia del Tribunal del Santo Oficio de la Inquisición de Cartagena de las Indias*, Santiago, Chile, 1899, p. 221.
83. Gonzalo de REPARAZ, 'Los Caminos del contrabando' in *El Comercio*, Lima, 18 February 1968.
84. Note sent me by Alvaro JARA, information from the accounts of Sebastian Duarte, which are in the Archivo Nacional in Santiago.
85. Jacob van KLAVEREN, *Europäische Wirtschaftsgeschichte Spaniens im 16. und 17. J.*, 1960, p. 151, n. 123.
86. Genaro GARCIA, *Autos da Fe de la Inquisicion de México con extractos de sus causas*, 1910; GUIJO, *Diario*, 1648-1664, Mexico City, 2 vols., 1952, a daily chronicle which describes the *auto da fe* of 11th April 1649, I, pp. 39-47 and 92-3.
87. In the sense in which it is used by João Lucio de Azevedo, *Epocas do Portugal económico, esboços de historia*, 1929; the author is referring to successive periods when first one then another commodity dominated production, - sugar, coffee, etc.
88. L. DERMIGNY, *La Chine et l'Occident*, *op. cit.*, I, p. 77.
89. Johann Albrecht MANDELSLO, *Voyage aux Indes orientales*, 1659, II, p. 197.
90. Baltasar Suárez to Simón Ruiz, 15 January 1590; Simón Ruiz to Juan de Lago, 26 August 1584; S. Ruiz to the Buonvisi in Lyons, 14 July 1569, Ruiz Archives, Archivo historico provincial, Valladolid.
91. See vol. III, chapter 4.
92. M. CAPPELLA and A. MATILLA TASCÓN, *op. cit.*, pp. 181 ff.
93. *Medit.*, I, pp. 214-15.
94. G. AUBIN, 'Bartolomäus Viatis. Ein nürnberger Grosskaufmann vor dem dreissigjährigen Kriege' in *Viertelj. fur Sozial- und Wirtschaftsgeschichte*, 1940, and Werner SCHULTHEISS, 'Der Vertrag der nürnberger Handelsgesellschaft Bartholomäus Viatis und Martin Peller von 1609-15' in *Scripta mercaturae*, I, 1968.
95. Cracow Archives, Ital, 382.
96. Cf. *La Novela picaresca*, *op. cit.*, Estebanillo Gonzalez, pp. 1812, 1817, 1818. Italian merchants in Munich, Vienna and Leipzig, E. KROKER, *op. cit.*, p. 86.
97. *Op. cit.*, p. 361. The article by Charles WILSON referred to in this paragraph is published in *The Anglo-Dutch Contribution to the Civilization of Early Modern Europe* (proceedings of conference held in 1974), Oxford University Press, 1976.
98. *Europe in the Russian mirror*, 1970, pp. 21 ff.
99. *Diarii*, 9 November 1519.
100. H. SIEVEKING, *op. cit.*, p. 76.

101. Francesco CARLETTI, *Ragionamenti sopra le cose da lui vedute ne' suoi viaggi*, 1701, p. 283.

102. François DORNIC, *L'Industrie textile dans le Maine (1650-1815)*, 1955, p. 83.

103. F. LÜTGE, *op. cit.*, p. 235.

104. G. LOHMANN VILLENA, *Las Minas de Huancavelica en los siglos XVI y XVII*, 1949, p. 159.

105. Gérard SIVERY, 'Les orientations actuelles de l'histoire économique du Moyen Age dans l'Europe du Nord-Ouest', in *Revue du Nord*, 1973, p. 213.

106. Jacques SCHWARZ, 'L'Empire romain, l'Egypte et le commerce oriental', in *Annales*, E.S.C., XV (1960), p. 25.

107. A. SAPORI, *Una Compagnia di Calimala ai primi del Trecento*, *op. cit.*, p. 99.

108. Federigo MELIS, 'La civiltà economica nelle sue esplicazioni dalla Versilia alla Maremma (secoli X-XVIII)', in *Atti del 60° Congresso internazionale della 'Dante Aligheri'*, p. 26.

109. Pierre and Huguette CHAUNU, *Séville et l'Atlantique de 1504 à 1650*, 1959, VIII-I, p. 717.

110. R. CANTILLON, *Essai sur la nature du commerce en général*, *op. cit.*, p. 41.

111. F. MELIS, *art. cit.*, pp. 26-7 and 'Werner Sombart e i problemi della navigazione nel medio evo' in *L'opera di Werner Sombart nel centenario della nascita*, p. 124.

112. R. GASCON, *op. cit.*, p. 183.

113. G.F. GEMELLI CARERI, *Voyage autour du monde*, 1727, II, p. 4.

114. *Ibid.*, IV, p. 4.

115. F. CARLETTI, *op. cit.*, pp. 17-32.

116. Condillac, *Le Commerce et le gouvernement*, ed., E. Daire, 1847, p. 262.

117. Michel Morineau kindly sent me a microfilm of the correspondence between the Sardi firm of Leghorn and Benjamin Burlamachi, the originals of which are in the municipal Archives of Amsterdam (Familie-papieren 1, Archief Burlamachi).

118. A.N., 62 AQ 33, Amsterdam, 27 March 1766.

119. Paris Archives, D⁵, B⁶, 4433, f° 48.

120. Vorontsov Archives, Moscow, 1876, vol. 9, pp. 1-2. Venice, 30 December 1783, Simon to Alexander Vorontsov, 'Everything here, except silkstuffs, is prodigiously expensive'.

121. Claude MANCERON, *Les Vingt Ans du Roi*, 1972, p. 471.

122. *Medit.*, I, p. 519.

123. Barthélemy JOLY, *Voyage en Espagne 1603-1604*, ed. L. BARRAU DIHIGO, 1909, p. 17.

124. Bohrepans, London, 7 August 1686 (A.N., A.E., B¹ 757); Anisson, London, 7 March 1714 (A.N., G⁷, 1699); Carlo Ottone, December 1670 (A.d.S. Genoa, Letter Consoli 1-2628); Simolin, London 23 March/3 April 1781 (Moscow, C.S.A., 35/6, 320, f° 167); Hermann, 1791, (A.N., A.E., B¹, 762, f° 461 v°).

125. Fynes MORYSON, *An Itinerary containing his ten years travell*, Glasgow, 1908, vol. IV, p. 70.

126. I de PINTO, *op. cit.*, p. 167: 'Where there is more wealth, everything is more expensive ... That is what makes me think that England is richer than France'; *François Quesnay et la physiocratie*, ed. INED, II, p. 954.

127. Arthur YOUNG, *Travels in France*, ed. M. Betham Edwards, 1890, p. 69.

128. *De la monnaie*, (French trans., by G.M. BOUSQUET and J. CRISAFULLI), 1955, p. 89.

129. Léon DUPRIEZ, 'Principes et problèmes d'interprétation', in *Diffusion du progrès et convergence des prix. Etudes internationales*, 1966, p. 7.

130. See vol. III, chapter 1. J. ACCARIAS DE SERIONNE, *op. cit.*, 1766, I, pp. 270 ff.

131. TURGOT, *Oeuvres*, I, *op. cit.*, pp. 378-9.

132. Pierre DES MAZIS, *Le Vocabulaire de l'économie politique*, 1965, p. 62.

133. H. and P. CHAUNU, *Séville et l'Atlantique de 1504 à 1650*, *op. cit.*, 12 vols.

134. *Ibid.*, VIII-1, p. 260, note 2, 293, note 1.

135. Felipe RUIZ MARTIN, *El Siglo de los Genoveses*, forthcoming; Ruth PIKE, *Enterprise and Adventure. The Genoese in Seville*, 1966.

136. *Gazette de France*, 14 February 1730, report from Madrid, p. 102.

137. I was informed of this important detail by J.-P. BERTHE.

138. Daniel DEFOE, *op. cit.*, I, p. 354.

139. *Thomas Gage's travels in the New World*, ed. Thompson, 1958, pp. 329-30.

140. A.N., F², A, 21.

141. W.L. SCHURZ, *The Manila Galleon*, 1959, p. 363.
142. Ragnar NURSKE, *Problems of capital formation in underdeveloped countries*, 1958.
143. *François Quesnay ...*, *op. cit.*, II, p. 756.
144. *Pierre de Boisguilbert ou la naissance de l'économie politique*, ed. INED, 1966, II, p. 606.
145. *François Quesnay ... op. cit.*, II, pp. 664 and 954-5.
146. 'Dérives', in the sense in which Pierre Gourou uses the expression.
147. *Medit*, I, p. 449.
148. *Ibid.*, I, p. 254.
149. H. and P. CHAUNU, *op. cit.*, VIII-1, p. 445.
150. A.N., G⁷, 1695, p. 252.
151. *Ibid.* Defoe's article cited here is quoted by E. LIPSON, *The Economic History of England*, III, p. 39.
152. J. SAVARY DES BRUSLONS, *op. cit.*, IV, 1762, col. 1023, decisions of 5 September and 28 October 1759, col. 1022 and 1024.
153. Paul BAIROCH, *Révolution industrielle et sous-développement*, Paris, 1963, p. 201.
154. R.M. HARTWELL, *The Industrial Revolution and Economic Growth*, 1971, pp. 181-2.
155. See vol. III, chapter 4.
156. Thomas SOWELL, *Say's Law, an historical analysis*, 1972; Ch. E.L. MEUNIER, *Essai sur la Théorie des débouchés de J.B. Say*, 1942.
157. TURGOT, *Oeuvres, op. cit.*, I, p. 452.
158. Quoted by R. NURSKE, *op. cit.*, p. 16. The quotation is from Mill's *Essay on some unsettled questions of Political Economy*.
159. According to J. ROMEUF, *op. cit.*, I, p. 372.
160. Henri GUITTON, *Les Fluctuations économiques*, 1952, p. 173.
161. I de PINTO, *op. cit.*, p. 184.
162. Eli HECKSCHER, *Mercantilism*, transl. M. Shapiro, 1955, II, p. 208.
163. D. RICARDO, *op. cit.*, 1970, p. 66.
164. *Ibid.*, chapter on profits, especially pp. 88-9.
165. 'Tawney's Century', in *Essays in Economic and Social History of Tudor and Stuart England*, 1961.
166. MICHELET, *Le Peuple*, 1899, pp. 73-4.
167. On the Gianfigliazzi, see Armando

SAPORI, *Studi di storia economica*, 3rd edn., 1955, II, pp. 933 ff. On the Capponi, I consulted the register owned by Armando Sapori, who kindly sent me a microfilm of it.
168. Archives held at the Bocconi University, Milan.
169. B. COTRUGLI, *op. cit.*, p. 145.
170. In *Mélanges Hermann Aubin*, 1965, I, pp. 235 ff.
171. Ernst HERING, *Die Fugger*, 1940, pp. 23 and 27.
172. F. MELIS, *art. cit.*, pp. 21 and 35.
173. F. LÜTGE, *op. cit.*, p. 288.
174. F. GESTRIN, *op. cit.*, p. 116.
175. Hermann KELLENBENZ, 'Le front hispano-portugais contre l'Inde et le role d'une agence de renseignements au service des marchands allemands et flamands', in *Estudia*, XI, 1963; C.R. BOXER, 'Una raridade bibliografica sobre Fernao Cron', in *Boletim internacional de bibliografia lusobrasiliana*, 1971.
176. *Das Meder'sche Handelsbuch und die Welser'schen Nachtrage*, 1974.
177. Johannes MULLER, 'Der Umfang und die Hauptrouten des nürnbergischen Handelsgebietes in Mittelalter', in *V. Jahrschrift fur S. und W. Geschichte*, 1908, pp. 1-38.
178. E. KROBER, *op. cit.*, pp. 71, 163 and *passim*.
179. J.C. PERROT, *op. cit.*, pp. 181 ff.
180. F. MAURETTE, *Les Grands Marchés des matières premières*, 1922.
181. R. GASCON, *op. cit.*, I, p. 37.
182. Cf. vol. I, pp. 220 ff.
183. Cf. the first French edition of vol. I, 1967, p. 162.
184. Cf. vol. I, p. 224.
185. Jacob BAXA and Guntwin BRUHNS, *Zucker im Leben der Völker*, 1967, pp. 24-5.
186. *Ibid.*, p. 27.
187. *Ibid.*, p. 32.
188. See vol. I, p. 225.
189. J. SAVARY DES BRUSLONS, IV, col. 827.
190. J. BAXA and G. BRUHNS, *op. cit.*, p. 27.
191. *Ibid.*, pp. 40-1 and *passim*.
192. 1759, p. 97.
193. *Pierre de Boisguilbert ... op. cit.*, II, p. 621.
194. R. CANTILLON, *Essai sur la nature du commerce en général, op. cit.*, p. 150.

195. Joseph SCHUMPETER, *History of Economic Analysis*, 1954, (8th edn. 1972), p. 317.

196. L. DERMIGNY, *op. cit.*, I, p. 376.

197. B.E. SUPPLE, 'Currency and commerce in the early seventeenth century' in *The Economic History Review*, January 1957, pp. 239–64.

198. G. de MANTEYER, *Le Livre-journal tenu par Fazy de Rame*, 1932, pp. 166–7.

199. Léon COSTELCADE, *Mentalité gévaudanaise au Moyen Age*, 1925, reviewed by Marc BLOCH in *Annales d'histoire économique et sociale*, I, 1929, p. 463.

200. P.R.O., 30/25, Portfolio I, 2 November–2 December 1742.

201. A.d.S. Naples, Affari Esteri, 796, The Hague, 28 May 1756.

202. Moscow, C.S.A., 50/6, 470.

203. *Ibid.*, 84/2, 421, f⁰ 9 v⁰, letter from Facius.

204. Abbé PRÉVOST, *Histoire générale des voyages . . ., op. cit.*, III, p. 641. Voyage of Compagnon in 1716.

205. A.P. CANABRAVA, *O Comércio portugues . . . op. cit.*, p. 13; Lewis HANKE, *La Villa imperial de Potosi. Un Capitulo inédito en la historia del Nuevo Mundo*, 1954.

206. P.V. CAÑETE Y DOMINGUEZ, *Guia histórica*, p. 57, quoted by Tibor WITTMAN, 'La riqueza empobrece; problemas de crisis del Alto Peru colonial en la Guia de P.V. Cañete y Dominguez' in *Acta historica*, Szeged, 1967, XXIV, p. 17.

207. Sergio BUARQUE DE HOLANDA, *Monções*, 1945.

208. J.-B. TAVERNIER, *op. cit.*, II, p. 293.

209. Founder in 1844 of the cacao-producing zone of the Ilheor, Pedro CALMON, *Historia social do Brasil*, 1937, p. 190.

210. Aziza HAZAN, 'En Inde aux XVIe et XVIIe siècles: trésors américains, monnaie d'argent et prix dans l'Empire mogol', in *Annales E.S.C.*, July-August 1969, pp. 835–59.

211. C.R. BOXER, *The Great Ship from Amacom. Annals of Macao and the old Japan trade, 1555-1640*, Lisbon, 1959, p. 6, note 1: 12 September 1633, letter from Manuel da Câmara de Noronha.

212. Antonio de ULLOA, *Mémoires philosophiques, historiques, physiques, concernant la découverte de l'Amérique*, 1787, I, p. 270.

213. J. GERNET, *Le Monde chinois, op. cit.*, p. 423.

214. P. CHAUNU, *Les Philippines, op. cit.*, pp. 268–9.

215. For example in about 1570, the ratio was about 6:1 in China, as against 12:1 in Castile; in 1630 or so it was respectively 8:1 and 13:1, Pierre CHAUNU, 'Manille et Macao' in *Annales E.S.C.*, 1962, p. 568.

216. W.L. SCHURZ, *op. cit.*, pp. 25–7.

217. *Ibid.*, p. 60.

218. Sir George STAUNTON, *An authentic account of an embassy . . . to the Emperor of China*, London, 1797, I, p. 325.

219. *Medit.*, I, p. 594. Better still, the article by Omer L. BARKAN, 'Les mouvements des prix en Turquie entre 1490 et 1655', in *Mélanges Braudel*, 1973, I, pp. 65–81.

220. A.N., 94 AQ 1, file 11, Pondicherry, 1 October 1729.

221. M. CHERIF, 'Introduction de la piastre espagnole ("ryal") dans la régence de Tunis au début du XVIIe siècle' in *Les Cahiers de Tunisie*, 1968, nos. 61–4, pp. 45–55.

222. J. EON (Father Matthias de SAINT-JEAN), *Le Commerce honorable*, 1646, p. 99.

223. A.d.S., Venice, Senato Misti, reg. 43, f⁰ 162.

224. *Ibid.*, reg. 47, f⁰ 175 v⁰. I am grateful to R.C. Mueller for this information.

225. Museo Correr, Donà delle Rose, 26 f⁰ 2.

226. A.N., A.E., B¹¹¹, 235, and Ch. CARRIÈRE, *op. cit.*, II, pp. 805 ff.

227. E. HECKSCHER, *op. cit.*, (Eng. trans.), II, p. 254.

228. *State Papers Domestic, 1660-1661*, p. 411, quoted by E. LIPSON, *The Economic History of England*, 1948, III, p. 73.

229. *Gazette de France*, 16 January, p. 52; 6 March, p. 135; 20 March 1721, p. 139. Similar announcements on 6 March 1730, p. 131; 16 September 1751, p. 464.

230. Moscow, C.S.A., 50/6, 472.

231. *Le Journal d'émigration*, by the Comte d'Espinchal was published in edited form by Ernest d'Hauterive in 1912. The passage quoted here is from the unpublished section of the manuscript in the University Library at Clermont-Ferrand, f⁰ 297.

232. F.C. SPOONER, *L'Économie mondiale et les frappes monétaires en France 1493-1680*, 1956.

233. M. MARION, *Dictionnaire ... op. cit.*, p. 384.

234. Jean-François de BOURGOING, *Nouveau Voyage en Espagne, ou Tableau de l'état actuel de cette monarchie*, Paris, 1788, II, p. 87.

235. Quoted by E. LIPSON, *op. cit.*, III, p. 87. Eli HECKSCHER, in *Mercantilism* attributes this book to John Hales; but according to both Edward Hughes (1937) and Mary Dewar (1964) it should be attributed to Sir Thomas Smith. See E. SCHULIN, *op. cit.*, p. 24.

236. E. SCHULIN, *op. cit.*, p. 94.

237. M.-J. D. MARTIN, *op. cit.*, pp. 105-106.

238. A.d.S. Venice, Inghilterra, 76 and London 13/34, August 1703.

239. B.N. PARIS, Ms. 21779, 176, v° (1713).

240. René GANDILHON, *Politique économique de Louis XI*, 1941, pp. 416-17.

241. N. SANCHEZ ALBORNOZ, 'Un testigo del comercio indiano: Tomás de Mercado y Nueva Espana', in *Revista de historia de América, art. cit.*, p. 122.

242. TURGOT, *op. cit.*, I, p. 378.

243. Moscow, C.S.A., 35/6, 765.

244. Thomas MUN, *A Discourse of trade from England unto the East Indies*, 1621, p. 27. What Mun actually says is: '100,000 l. in money exported may import about the value of 500,000 pounds sterling in wares from the East Indies'.

245. A.N., G⁷, 1686, 53.

246. René BOUVIER, *Quevedo, 'homme du diable, homme de Dieu'*, 1929, pp. 305-6.

247. France-Piedmont, A.N., G⁷ 1568, 108. Sicily-Genoa, Geronimo de USTARIZ, *Théorie et pratique du commerce et de la marine*, 1753, pp. 52-3. Persia-Indies, *Voyage de Gardane*, manuscript in Lenin Library, Moscow, p. 55.

248. A.d.S. Genoa, Lettere Consoli, I, pp. 26-9.

249. Margaret PRIESTLEY, 'Anglo-French Trade and the unfavourable controversy 1660-1685', in *The Economic History Review*, 1951, pp. 37 ff.

250. A.E., C.P., Angleterre, pp. 208, 209.

251. A.N., G⁷ 1699.

252. Moscow, C.S.A., 35/6, 381.

253. E. SCHULIN, *op. cit.*, pp. 308 ff. esp. 319-20. Hume's remark is from his essay *Of the Balance of Trade*, in *Essays ...*, Edinburgh, 1800, I, p. 334.

254. This passage is based on the full correspondence of the Russian consul in Lisbon, J.A. Borchers, between 1770 and 1794, Moscow, C.S.A., from 72/5, 217, 58. The Methuen Treaty lasted until 1836, E. SCHULIN, *op. cit.*, p. 290.

255. Moscow, C.S.A., 725, 226, 73 v°, 10 November 1772; 273, 25 v°.

256. H.E.S. FISHER, *The Portugal Trade*, 1971, pp. 35 and 38.

257. Pierre-Victor MALOUET, *Mémoires*, 1874, I, pp. 10-11.

258. Moscow, C.S.A., 72/5, 226, f° 59, Lisbon, 6 October 1772, Borchers to Ostermann.

259. *Ibid.*, 72/5, 270, f° 52 and v°, 23 April 1782.

260. *Ibid.*, 72/5, 297, f° 22, 13 December 1791.

261. H.E.S. FISHER, *op. cit.*, p. 136.

262. Moscow, *ibid.*, 72/5, 297, f° 25, 20 December 1791.

263. On this question in general, see Ingomar BOG, *Der Aussenhandel Ostmitteleuropas, 1450-1650*, 1971.

264. S.A. NILSSON, *Den ryska marknaden*, quoted by M. HROCH, 'Die Rolle des zentraleuropäischen Handels im Ausgleich der Handelsbilanz zwischen Ost- und Westeuropa, 1550-1650', in I. BOG, *op. cit.*, p. 5, note 1; Arthur ATTMANN, *The Russian and Polish Markets in international Trade, 1500-1600*, 1973.

265. M. HROCH, *art. cit.*, pp. 1-27.

266. L. MAKKAI, Prato conference, April 1975.

267. Ernst KROKER, *op. cit.*, p. 87 is categorical on this point.

268. Cracow Archives, Ital., 382.

269. See volume III, chapter 3.

270. Polish coins were to be found in Georgia (R. KIERSNOWSKI, Prato conference, April 1975). In 1590, Polish carriers brought Spanish reals to Istanbul, (Tommaso ALBERTI, *Viaggio a Constantinopoli*, 1609-1621, Bologna, 1889; *Medit.*, I, pp. 195 ff). Merchants from Poland and Muscovy were known to reach India carrying *rixdales* from Germany (TAVERNIER, *op. cit.*, II, p. 14).

271. See volume III, chapter 5.

272. A.N., G⁷, 1686, 99, 31st August 1701.

273. E. SCHULIN, *op. cit.*, p. 220.

274. R. GASCON, *op. cit.*, p. 48.

275. Albert CHAMBERLAND, 'Le commerce d'importation en France au milieu du

XVIe siècle', in *Revue de géographie*, 1892–1893, pp. 1–32.

276. P. DE BOISGUILBERT, *op. cit.*, II, p. 586, J.J. CLAMAGERAN, *Histoire de l'impôt en France*, II, 1868, p. 147.

277. Henryk SAMSONOWICZ, *Untersuchungen über das danziger Bürgerkapital in der sweiten Hälfte des 15. Jahrhunderts*, Weimar, 1969.

278. Anders CHYDENIUS, 'Le Bénéfice national (1765)' transl., from the Swedish, intro. by Philippe COUTY, in *Revue d'histoire économique et sociale*, 1966, p. 439.

279. Reference unfortunately mislaid, Moscow C.S.A.

280. A.N., A.E., B¹, 762, fᵒ 401, letter from Hermann, French consul in London, 7 April 1791.

281. S. Van RECHTEREN, *Voiage aux Indes Orientales*, 1706, V, p. 124.

282. K.M. PANIKAAR, *L'Asie et la domination occidentale du XVe siècle à nos jours*, pp. 68–72.

283. *Ibid.*

284. *Ibid.*, pp. 95–6.

285. Frédéric MAURO, *L'Expansion européenne*, 1964, p. 141.

286. See William BOLTS, *Considerations on Indian Affairs particularly representing Bengal*, London, 1772 for a full account of Bolts's opinions on the East India Company. The remark referred to here is from the French edition of Bolts's writings, 1775, I, p. xvii.

287. G. UNWIN, 'Indian factories in the 18th century' in *Studies in Economic History*, 1958, pp. 353–73, quoted by F. Mauro, *op. cit.*, p. 141.

288. *Gazette de France*, 13 March 1763, report from London, p. 104.

289. A.E., Asia, 12, fᵒ 6.

290. Moscow, C.S.A., 50/6, 474, fᵒ 23, Amsterdam, 12/33, March 1764.

291. *Gazette de France*, April 1777.

292. K.M. PANIKAAR, *op. cit.*, pp. 120–1.

293. G. D'AVENEL, *Découvertes d'histoire sociale*, 1920, p. 13.

294. In *Finanzarchiv*, I, 1933, p. 46.

295. A. HANOTEAU and A. LETOURNEUX, *La Kabylie et les coutumes kabyles*, 1893, and Pedro CHALMETTA's admirable book, *op. cit.*, pp. 75 ff.

296. Roger BASTIDE and PIERRE VERGER, *art. cit.*

297. Pierre GOUROU, *Les Paysans du delta tonkinois*, 2nd edn., 1965, pp. 540 ff.

298. Personal journeys in 1935.

299. Bronislaw MALINOWSKI, *Les Argonautes du Pacifique occidental*, 1963, p. 117.

300. Karl POLANYI's published works, especially K. POLYANI, C. ARENSBERG, and H. PEARSON, (eds.) *Trade and market in the early empires; economies in history and theory*, Illinois, 1957.

301. See below, chapter 5, first section.

302. Walter C. NEALE, in K. POLANYI and C. ARENSBERG, *op. cit.*, pp. 357 ff.

303. *Ibid.*

304. *Ibid.*

305. 'Markets and other allocation systems in history: the challenge of K. Polyani', in the *Journal of European Economic History*, 6, Winter 1977.

306. W.C. NEALE, *op. cit.*, pp. 357 ff.

307. Maxime RODINSON, in Pedro CHALMETTA, *op. cit.*, p. LIII ff.

308. *Ibid.*, pp. LV ff.

309. In *Annales E.S.C.*, 1974, pp. 1311–12.

310. J.K. GALBRAITH, *The New Industrial State*, 1967.

311. *Ibid.*, pp. 9–10.

312. V.I. LENIN, *Imperialism the highest stage of capitalism*, (in *Selected Works*, 3 vols., Progress Publishing House, Moscow, 1977 reprint, I, pp. 642 ff. *passim.*)

NOTES TO CHAPTER 3

1. François PERROUX, *Le Capitalisme*, 1962, p. 5.

2. Herbert HEATON, 'Criteria of periodization in economic history', in *The Journal of Economic History*, 1955, pp. 267 ff.

3. Notably Lucien FEBVRE, 'Les mots et les choses en histoire économique', in *Annales d'histoire économique et sociale*, II, 1930, pp. 231 ff.

4. For more detailed explanations see the clear, meticulous but unfortunately

rather inaccessible thesis by Edwin
DESCHEPPER, *L'Histoire du mot capital
et dérivés*, typescript, Free University of
Brussels, 1964. I have drawn copiously
on this in the following lines.

5. Prato Archives, no. 700, *Lettere Prato-
Firenze*, document brought to my notice
by F. Melis.

6. Edgar SALIN, 'Kapitalbegriff und
Kapitallehre von der Antike zu den
Physiokraten', in *Vierteljahrschrift fur
Sozial- und Wirtschaftsgeschichte*, 23,
1930, p. 424, note 2.

7. R. GASCON, *Grand Commerce et vie
urbaine, Lyon au XVIe siecle*, 1971, p. 238.

8. E. DESCHEPPER, *op. cit.*, pp. 22 ff.

9. Panurge, in *Pantagruel* (Pléiade edn., p.
383) says, *'Il m'y va du propre cabal. Le
sort, l'usure et les interests je pardonne'*,
where *cabal* clearly means *capital* as
distinct from *interest*.

10. A.N., A.E., B¹ 531, 22 July 1713.

11. J. CAVIGNAC, *op. cit.*, p. 158 (letter from
Pierre Pellet in Martinique, 26 July 1726).

12. François VERON DE FORBONNAIS,
Principes économiques (1767), ed. Daire,
1847, p. 174.

13. A.E., Mémoires et Documents,
Angleterre, 35, f° 43, 4 May 1696.

14. TURGOT, *op. cit.*, II, p. 575.

15. J. SAVARY DES BRUSLONS, *Dictionnaire*,
II, 1760, col. 136.

16. A.N., G⁷, 1705, 121, after 1724.

17. A.N., G⁷, 1706, 1, letter of 6 December
1722.

18. CONDILLAC, *op. cit.*, p. 247.

19. J.-B. SAY, *Cours complet d'économie
politique*, I, 1828, p. 93.

20. SISMONDI, *De la richesse commerciale*,
1803.

21. FORBONNAIS, *op. cit.*, p. 176.

22. DU PONT DE NEMOURS, *Maximes du
docteur Quesnay*, 1846 edn., p. 391,
quoted by Jean ROMEUF, *Dictionnaire
des sciences économiques*, entry for
'capital', p. 199.

23. C. MANCERON, *op. cit.*, p. 589.

24. MORELLET, *Prospectus d'un nouveau
dictionnaire de commerce*, Paris, 1764,
quoted by E. DESCHEPPER, *op. cit.*, pp.
106-7.

25. E. DESCHEPPER, *op cit.*, p. 109.

26. *Ibid.*, p. 124.

27. A.N., K 1349, 132, f° 214, v°.

28. E. DESCHEPPER, *op. cit.*, p. 125.

29. Lucien FEBVRE, 'Pouvoir et privilège',
review of L.-P. MAY, 'L'Ancien Régime
devant le Mur d'Argent', in *Annales
d'histoire économique et sociale*, X, 1938,
p. 460.

30. E. DESCHEPPER, *op. cit.*, p. 128.

31. A.N., Z¹, D 102 B.

32. A.d.S. Naples, Affari Esteri, 801.

33. Pierre-Victor MALOUET, *Mémoires*, 1874,
I, p. 83.

34. A.E., M et D., Angleterre, 35, f°s 67 ff.

35. A.N., F¹², 731, 4 July 1783.

36. Luigi DAL PANE, *Storia del lavoro in
Italia*, 2nd edn., 1958, p. 116.

37. *Cahier de doléances* (complaints register),
Tiers Etat of Garde-Figanières.

38. *Cahier de doléances* of Saint-Pardoux, in
the *sénéchaussée* of Draguignan.

39. D. MATHIEU, *L'Ancien Régime dans la
province de Lorraine et Barrois*, 1879, p.
324.

40. C. MANCERON, *op. cit.*, p. 54.

41. Henry COSTON, *Les Financiers qui mènent
le monde*, 1955, p. 41; 25 September
1790, *Moniteur*, vol. V, p. 741.

42. *Moniteur*, vol. XVII, p. 484.

43. H. COSTON, *op. cit.*, p. 41. RIVAROL,
Mémoires, 1824, p. 235.

44. A. DAUZAT, *Nouveau Dictionnaire
étymologique et historique*, 1964, p. 132. I
was unable to find the passage referred to
in the *Encyclopédie*. Was this perhaps a
mistake?

45. J.-B. RICHARD, *Les Enrichissements de la
langue française*, p. 88.

46. Louis BLANC, *Organisation du travail*,
9th edn., 1850, pp. 161-2, quoted by E.
DESCHEPPER, *op. cit.*, p. 153.

47. J. ROMEUF, *Dictionnaire des sciences
économiques*, entry for '*capitalisme*', p.
203, and J.J. HÉMARDINQUER in *Annales
E.S.C.*, 1967, p. 444.

48. Jean-Jacques HÉMARDINQUER, review of
Jean DUBOIS's book, *Le Vocabulaire
politique et social en France de 1869 à
1872, à travers les œuvres des écrivains, les
revues et les journaux*, 1963, in *Annales
E.S.C.*, 1967, pp. 445-6. But Engels uses
it, and the word *Kapitalismus* was
already being used in 1870 by the
German economist Albert Schäffle
(Edmond SILBENER, *Annales d'histoire
sociale*, 1940, p. 133).

49. H. HEATON, *art. cit.*, p. 268.

50. Lucien FEBVRE, 'L'économie liégeoise au XVIe siècle (Jean LEJEUNE, *La Formation du capitalisme moderne dans la principauté de Liège au XVIe siècle)*', in *Annales E.S.C.*, XII, pp. 256 ff.

51. Andrew SHONFIELD, *Modern Capitalism*, 1965, p. 3.

52. *Annales E.S.C.*, 1961, p. 213.

53. Alexander GERSCHENKRON, *Europe in the Russian Mirror*, 1970, p. 4.

54. K. MARX, *Capital*, I, section 8, ch. 26 on primitive accumulation.

55. *Histoire de la campagne française*, 2nd edn., 1974, pp. 71 ff.

56. D. HUME, 'Essay on Money' in *Essays and Treatises on several subjects*, Edinburgh, 1800, II, p. 302.

57. J. GENTIL DA SILVA, *op. cit.*, I, p. 20.

58. J.-P. CATTEAU-CALLEVILLE, *Tableau de la mer baltique*, II, 1812, pp. 238-9.

59. Ernst PITZ, 'Studien zur Entstehung des Kapitalismus', in *Festschrift Hermann Aubin*, I, 1965, pp. 19-40.

60. A.E., Moscou/A, 35/6, 341/71, v°-72, London, 26 May-6 June 1783.

61. Heinrich Friedrich von STORCH, *Cours d'économie politique*, 1823, I, pp. 246-7.

62. A.d.S. Venice, Notatorio di Collegio, 12, 128, v°, 27 July 1480.

63. Alice HANSON JONES, 'La fortune privée en Pennsylvanie, New Jersey et Delaware (1774)', in *Annales E.S.C.*, 1969, pp. 235-49, and *Wealth estimates for the American middle colonies 1774*, Chicago, 1968.

64. I have drawn principally on his paper given to the Third International Conference of Economic History, Munich 1965, reprinted in S. KUZNETS, *Population, Capital and Growth*, selected essays, 1974, pp. 121 ff.

65. *British Economic Growth 1688-1959*, 2nd edn., 1967.

66. S. KUZNETS, *op. cit.*, p. 130.

67. *Théorie générale de la population*, I, 1954, esp. p. 68.

68. QUIQUERAN DE BEAUJEU, *De laudibus Provinciae*, Paris, 1551 (published in French as *La Provence louée*, Lyons, 1614), quoted by André BOURDE, *Agronomie et agronomes en France au XVIIIe siècle*, p. 50. Cf. also A. PLAISSE, *La Baronnie de Neubourg*, 1961, p. 153, who quotes Charles Estienne: 'The land must be ploughed and ploughed again so many times that it turns into powder if possible'.

69. Jean-Pierre SOISSON, 'Pour une approche économique et sociale du bâtiment. L'exemple des travaux publics à Bruges aux XIVe et XVe siècles', in *Bulletin de la Commission royale des Monuments et des Sites*, vol. 2, 1972, p. 144.

70. Samuel H. BARON, 'The Fate of the *Gosti* in the reign of Peter the Great. Appendix: Gost' Afanasii Olisov's reply to the government inquiry of 1704', in *Cahiers du monde russe et soviétique*, Oct.-Dec. 1973, p. 512.

71. Traian STOIANOVICH, Unesco conference on Istanbul, October 1973, p. 33.

72. S. KUZNETS, *op. cit.*, p. 158.

73. R.S. LOPEZ and H.A. MISKIMIN, 'The economic depression of the Renaissance', in *Economic History Review*, 1962, no. 3, pp. 408-26.

74. Information provided by Felipe RUIZ MARTIN.

75. Mentioned by Alois MIKA, in his article on large estates in Bohemia from the fourteenth to the sixteenth century, in *Sbornik historicky*, I, 1953, and by Josef PETRAN in his study of agricultural production in Bohemia, sixteenth-seventeenth centuries, 1964 (information provided by J. JANACEK).

76. SCHNAPPER, *Les Rentes au XVIe siècle*, Paris, 1957, pp. 109-10.

77. CAVIGNAC, *op. cit.*, p. 212, 13 November 1727.

78. J. MEYER, *op. cit.*, p. 619.

79. D. MATHIEU, *op. cit.*, p. 324.

80. Archivio di Stato, Prato, Arch. Datini Filza 339, Florence, 23 April 1408.

81. According to the many documents in A.d.S. Venice on the failure of this bank, liquidation had still not been completed on 31 March 1592, Correr, Donà delle Rose, 26, f° 107.

82. C. LAVEAU, *op. cit.*, p. 340.

83. H. SOLY, 'The "Betrayal" of the Sixteenth-Century Bourgeoisie: A Myth? Some Considerations of the Behaviour Pattern of the Merchants of Antwerp in the Sixteenth Century', in *Acta Historiae Neerlandicae*, vol. VIII, pp. 31-9.

84. Robert MANDROU, *Les Fugger*,

propriétaires fonciers en Souabe, 1560-1618, 1969.

85. Gilles CASTER, *Le Commerce du pastel et de l'épicerie à Toulouse, 1450-1561*, 1962.
86. A.N., B¹¹¹, 406, long report dated 23 January 1816.
87. G. GALASSO, *Economia e società nella Calabria del Cinquecento*, p. 78.
88. A. BOURDE, *op. cit.*, pp. 1645 ff.
89. Gérard DELILLE, 'Types de développement dans le royaume de Naples, XVIIe-XVIIIe siècle', in *Annales E.S.C.*, 1975, pp. 703-5.
90. Moscow, Dubrovski Papers, Fr. 18-4, f° 86-7.
91. László MAKKAI, in *Histoire de la Hongrie*, Budapest, 1974, pp. 141-2.
92. Georg GRÜLL, *Bauer, Herr und Landesfürst*, 1963, pp. 1 ff.
93. André MALRAUX, *Antimémoires*, 1967, p. 525.
94. A. BOURDE, *op. cit.*, p. 53.
95. Wilhelm ABEL, *Crises agraires en Europe (XIIIe-XXe siècles)*, 1973, p. 182.
96. Wilhelm ABEL, *Geschichte der deutschen Landwirtschaft*, 1962, p. 196.
97. Paul BOIS, *Paysans de l'Ouest*, 1960, pp. 183-4.
98. W. SOMBART, II, p. 1061.
99. F. GESTRIN, *op. cit.*, cf. summary in French, pp. 247-72.
100. A.d.S. Naples, Sommaria Partium 565; GALASSO, *op. cit.*, p. 139.
101. Elio CONTI, *La Formazione della struttura agraria moderna nel contado fiorentino*, Rome, 1965, I, p. VII.
102. Guy FOURQUIN, *Les Campagnes de la région parisienne à la fin du Moyen Age*, 1964, p. 530.
103. Otto BRUNNER, *Neue Wege der Verfassungs- und Sozialgeschichte*, Italian edn., 1970, p. 138.
104. M. GONON, *La Vie familiale en Forez et son vocabulaire d'après les testaments*, 1961, p. 16.
105. *Ibid.*, p. 243.
106. E. JUILLARD, *Problèmes alsaciens vus par un géographe*, 1968, p. 110.
107. *Ibid.*, p. 112.
108. G. FOURQUIN, *op. cit.*, pp. 160 ff.
109. G. GALASSO, *op. cit.*, pp. 76-7.
110. *Ibid.*, p. 76.
111. Georg GRÜLL, *op. cit.*, pp. 30-1.
112. Evamaria ENGEL, Benedykt ZIENTARIA,

Feudalstruktur, Lehnbürgertum und Fernhandel im Spätmittelalterlichen Brandenburg, 1967, pp. 336-8.
113. Marc BLOCH, *Mélanges historiques*, Paris, 1963, II, p. 689.
114. Jacques HEERS, *Le Clan familial au Moyen Age*, Paris, 1974.
115. Vital CHOMEL, 'Communautés rurales et *casanae* lombardes en Dauphiné (1346). Contribution au problème de l'endettement dans les sociétés paysannes du Sud-Est de la France au bas Moyen Age', in *Bulletin philologique et historique*, 1951 and 1952, p. 245.
116. Georges LIVET, *L'Intendance d'Alsace sous Louis XIV, 1648-1715*, 1956, p. 833.
117. André PLAISSE, *La Baronnie de Neubourg*, 1961.
118. G. DELILLE, *art. cit.*, 1975.
119. Yvonne BEZARD, *Une Famille bourguignonne au XVIIIe siècle*, Paris, 1930.
120. J. MEYER, *op. cit.*, p. 780.
121. VAUBAN, *Le Projet d'une dixme royale* (ed. Coornaert, 1933), p. 181, quoted by J. MEYER, *op. cit.*, p. 691, n. 1.
122. A. PLAISSE, *op. cit.*, p. 61.
123. Y. BEZARD, *op. cit.*, p. 32.
124. Gaston ROUPNEL, *La Ville et la campagne au XVIIe siècle*, 1955, p. 314; Robert FORSTER, *The House of Saulx-Tavannes*, 1971.
125. Albert SOBOUL, *La France à la veille de la Révolution*, I, *Economie et Société*, p. 153.
126. A. PLAISSE, *op. cit.*, 1974, p. 114.
127. Louis MERLE, *La Métairie et l'évolution agraire de la Gâtine poitevine*, 1958, pp. 50 ff.
128. G. GRÜLL, *op. cit.*, pp. 30-1.
129. Pierre GOUBERT, *Beauvais et le Beauvaisis*, *op. cit.*, pp. 180 ff.
130. Michel CAILLARD, *A travers la Normandie des XVIIe et XVIIIe siècles*, 1963, p. 81.
131. Vital CHOMEL, 'Les paysans de Terre-basse et la dîme à la fin de l'Ancien Régime', in *Evocations*, 18th year, new series 4th year, no. 4, March-April, 1962, p. 100.
132. Quoted by L. DAL PANE, *op. cit.*, p. 183.
133. Michel AUGÉ-LARIBIÉ, *La Révolution agricole*, 1955, p. 37.
134. Giorgio DORIA, *Uomini e terre di un borgo collinare*, 1968.
135. Aurelio LEPRE, *Contadini, borghesi ed*

operai nel tramonto del feudalesimo napoletano, 1963, p. 27.

136. *Ibid.*, pp. 61–2.

137. Paul BUTEL, 'Grands propriétaires et production des vins du Médoc au XVIIIe siècle', in *Revue historique de Bordeaux et du département de la Gironde*, 1963, pp. 129–41.

138. Gaston ROUPNEL, *op. cit.*, pp. 206–7.

139. Witold KULA, *Théorie économique du système féodal. Pour un modèle de l'économie polonaise, XVIe–XVIIIe siècles*, 1970.

140. J. RUTKOWSKI, 'La genèse du régime de la corvée dans l'Europe centrale depuis la fin du Moyen Age', in *La Pologne au VIe Congrès international des sciences historiques*, 1930; W. RUSINSKI, in *Studia historiae oeconomicae*, 1974, pp. 27–45.

141. L. MAKKAI, in *Histoire de la Hongrie, op. cit.*, p. 163.

142. A. von TRANSEHE-ROSENECK, *Gutsherr und Bauer im 17. und 18. Jahrhundert*, 1890, p. 34, note 2.

143. J. ZIEKURSCH, *Hundert Jahre Schlesischer Agrargeschichte*, 1915, p. 84.

144. F.J. HAUN, *Bauer und Gutsherr in Kursachsen*, 1892, p. 185.

145. Immanuel WALLERSTEIN, *op. cit.*, p. 313 and note 58. At the end of the sixteenth century 'coerced labour' rarely came to 4 days a week; by the eighteenth century, peasant farms of the same size were obliged as a rule to provide 4 to 6 days' labour a week. These figures refer to the largest peasant holdings; less labour was asked of those with smaller holdings since it varied with the size of farm. But the trend towards an increase in the feudal burden, particularly in coerced labour, was general. Cf. Jan RUTKOWSKI, *art. cit.*, pp. 142 and 257.

146. Reference mislaid.

147. Charles d'EZLARY, 'La situation des serfs en Hongrie de 1514 à 1848' in *Revue d'histoire économique et sociale*, 1960, p. 385.

148. J. LESZCZYNSKI, *Der Klassen Kampf der Oberlausitzer Bauern in den Jahren 1635–1720*, 1964, pp. 66 ff.

149. Alfred HOFFMANN, 'Die Grundherrschaft als Unternehmen' in *Zeitschrift für Agrargeschichte und Agrarsoziologie*, 1958, pp. 123–31.

150. W. KULA, *op. cit.*, p. 138.

151. Jean DELUMEAU, *La Civilisation de la Renaissance*, 1967, p. 287.

152. On the question of whether the seigniorial enterprises were capitalist or not, see the controversy between J. NICHTWEISS and J. KUCZYNSKI in *Z. für Geschichtswissenschaft*, 1953 and 1954.

153. Jean de LÉRY, *Histoire d'un voyage faict en la terre de Brésil*, ed. Paul GAFFAREL, II, 1880, pp. 20–1.

154. Gilberto FREYRE, *Casa Grande e Senzala*, 5th edn., 1946.

155. Frédéric MAURO, *Le Portugal et l'Atlantique au XVIIe siècle*, 1960, pp. 213 ff.

156. Alice PIFFER CANABRAVA, *A industriado açucar nas ilhas inglesas e francesas do mar das Antilhas*, unpublished thesis, São Paulo, 1946, pp. 8 ff.

157. Gabriel DEBIEN, 'La sucrerie Galbaud du Fort (1690–1802)' in *Notes d'histoire coloniale*, I, 1941.

158. *Guildiverie* is a word formed from *guildive*, the liquor produced from the 'sugar syrups and the scums of the first boiling'. *Tafia* which is synonymous with it, was the word used by the black slaves and Indians. (LITTRÉ).

159. J. CAVIGNAC, *op. cit.*, p. 173, n. 1.

160. SAVARY, quoted by CAVIGNAC, *op. cit.*, p. 49, n. 3.

161. G. DEBIEN, *art. cit.*, pp. 67–8.

162. G. DEBIEN, 'A Saint-Domingue avec deux jeunes économes de plantation 1777–1778:, in *Notes d'histoire coloniale*, VII, 1945, p. 57. The expression 'piastre gourde' or heavy piastre comes from the Spanish *gorda*.

163. Pierre LÉON, *Marchands et spéculateurs dauphinois dans le monde antillais, les Dolle et les Raby*, 1963, p. 130.

164. François CROUZET in Charles HIGOUNET, *Histoire de Bordeaux*, vol. V, 1968, p. 224; Pierre LÉON in F. BRAUDEL and E. LABROUSSE eds., *Histoire économique et sociale de la France*, II, 1970, p. 502, figure 52.

165. Gaston RAMBERT, in *Histoire du commerce de Marseille*, VI, pp. 654–5.

166. François CROUZET, in *Histoire de Bordeaux, op. cit.*, p. 230, and note 40.

167. Pierre LÉON, *Marchands et spéculateurs . . ., op. cit.*, p. 56.

168. Marten G. BUIST, *At spes non fracta,
     Hope & Co, 1770-1815*, 1974, pp. 20-1.
169. R.B. SHERIDAN, 'The Wealth of Jamaica
     in the Eighteenth Century' in *Economic
     History Review*, vol. 18, no. 2, August
     1965, p. 297.
170. *Ibid.*, p. 296.
171. Richard PARES, *The Historian's Business
     and other essays*, Oxford, 1961, and
     Merchants and Planters, E.H.R.,
     supplement no. 4, Cambridge, 1960,
     quoted by R.B. SHERIDAN, *art. cit.*, p.
     311.
172. R.B. SHERIDAN, *art. cit.*, p. 305.
173. Edmind BURKE, *The Present State of the
     Nation*, quoted by SHERIDAN, *art. cit.*, p.
     304.
174. *Ibid.*, pp. 306 ff.
175. Roland Dennis HUSSEY, *The Caracas
     Company 1728-1784*, 1934.
176. J. BECKMANN, *Beiträge zur Oekonomie,
     Technologie, Polizei und
     Cameralwissenschaft*, 1779-1784, I, p. 4.
     On the variety of land tenure in England,
     cf. Joan THIRSK in *Agrarian history of
     England*, *op. cit.*, *passim* and pp. 8 ff.
177. Diderot's *Encyclopédie*, vol. IV, 1754, col.
     560 ff.
178. K. MARX, *Capital*, vol. III. French trans.,
     Editions sociales, 1950, p. 163.
179. Cf. Jean JACQUART, *La Crise rurale en
     Ile-de-France, 1550-1670*, 1974.
180. André BOURDE, *op. cit.*, I, p. 59.
181. Emile MIREAUX, *Une Province française
     au temps du Grand Roi, La Brie*, 1958.
182. *Ibid.*, p. 97.
183. *Ibid.*, p. 103.
184. *Ibid.*, p. 299.
185. *Ibid.*, pp. 145 ff.
186. V.S. LUBLINSKY, 'Voltaire et la guerre des
     farines' in *Annales historiques de la
     Révolution française*, 1959, pp. 127-45.
187. Pierre GOUBERT, in F. BRAUDEL and E.
     LABROUSSE ed., *Histoire économique et
     sociale de la France*, II, p. 145.
188. Edited by Jean MISTLER, 1968, pp. 40
     and 46.
189. *Mediterranean*, *op. cit.*, I, pp. 78 ff.
190. Jean GEORGELIN, *Venise au siècle des
     Lumières*, 1978, pp. 232 ff.
191. Jean GEORGELIN, 'Une grande propriété en
     Vénétie au XVIIIe siècle: Anguillara'
     Annales E.S.C., 1968, p. 486 and note 1.
192. *Ibid.*, p. 487.

193. MIREAUX, *op. cit.*, pp. 148 ff.
194. P. MOLMENTI, *op. cit.*, pp. 138 ff. and 141.
195. Quoted by J. GEORGELIN, *Venise au siècle
     des Lumières, op. cit.*, pp. 758-9.
196. J.C. Léonard SISMONDE de SISMONDI,
     *Nouveaux Principes d'économie politique
     ou de la richesse dans ses rapports avec
     la population* (1819), 1971 edn., p. 193.
197. A. REUMONT, *Della Campagna di Roma*,
     1842, pp. 34-5, quoted by DAL PANE, *op.
     cit.*, p. 53.
198. DAL PANE, *ibid.*, pp. 104-5 and note 25;
     N.M. NICOLAI, *Memorie, leggi ed
     osservazioni sulle campagne di Roma*,
     1803, quoted by DAL PANE, *ibid.*, p. 53.
199. *Ibid.*, p. 106.
200. Adam SMITH, *The Wealth of Nations*,
     Everyman edition, p. 8.
201. Olivier de SERRES, *Le Théâtre d'agriculture
     et mesnage des champs*, 3rd edn., 1605,
     p. 74.
202. Popular Italian songs, *I dischi del Sole*,
     Edizioni del Gallo, Milan, n.d.
203. Giovanni Di PAGOLO MORELLI, *Ricordi*,
     ed. Vittore BRANCA, 1956, p. 234, a
     personal chronicle (1393-1421).
204. Elio CONTI, *La Formazione della
     struttura agraria moderna nel contado
     fiorentino*, I, p. 13.
205. *Ibid.*, p. 4.
206. Renato ZANGHERI, 'Agricoltura e
     sviluppo del capitalismo' in *Studi storici*,
     1968, no. 34.
207. Information provided by L. MAKKAI.
208. Rosario VILLARI, *La Rivolta
     antispagnola a Napoli*, 1967.
209. Quoted by Pasquale VILLANI, *Feudalità,
     riforme, capitalismo agrario*, 1968, p. 55.
210. *Ibid.*, pp. 97-8.
211. Jean DELUMEAU, *L'Italie de Botticelli à
     Bonaparte*, 1974, pp. 351-2.
212. Pierre VILAR, *La Catalogne dans
     l'Espagne moderne*, II, p. 435.
213. Pierre GOUBERT, in BRAUDEL and
     LABROUSSE, *op. cit.*, pp. 12 and 17.
214. Jean MEYER, *La Noblesse bretonne au
     XVIIIe siècle*, 1966, II, p. 843.
215. Eberhard WEISS, 'Ergebnisse eines
     Vergleichs der grundherrschaftlichen
     Strukturen Deutschlands und
     Frankreichs vom 13. bis zum Ausgang
     des 18. Jahrhunderts' in
     *Vierteljahrschrift fur Sozial- und
     Wirtschaftsgeschichte*, 1970, pp. 1-74.

216. E. LE ROY LADURIE, 'Révoltes et contestations rurales en France de 1675 à 1788' in *Annales E.S.C.*, no. 1, January–February 1974, pp. 6–22.

217. Pierre de SAINT-JACOB, *Les Paysans de la Bourgogne du Nord au dernier siècle de l'Ancien Régime*, 1960, pp. 427–8.

218. Cf. Vol. I, p. 351.

219. René PILLORGET, 'Essai d'une typologie des mouvements insurrectionnels ruraux survenus en Provence de 1596 à 1715', in *Actes du 92e Congrès national des Sociétés savantes, Section d'histoire moderne*, 1967, I, pp. 371–5.

220. P. CHAUNU, *La Civilisation de l'Europe classique*, 1966, p. 353.

221. Paul HARSIN, 'De quand date le mot industrie?' in *Annales d'histoire économique et sociale*, II, 1930.

222. Hubert BOURGIN, *L'Industrie et le marché*, 1924, p. 31.

223. Pierre LÉON, *La Naissance de la grande industrie en Dauphiné (fin du XVIIe siècle–1869)*, 1954, I, p. 56.

224. W. SOMBART, *op. cit.*, II, p. 695.

225. Luigi BULFERETTI and Claudio COSTANTINI, *Industria e commercio in Liguria nell'età del Risorgimento (1700–1861)*, 1966, p. 55.

226. T.J. MARKOVITCH, 'L'industrie française de 1789 à 1964' in *Cahiers de l'ISEA* series AF, no. 4, 1965; nos., 5, 6, 7, 1966, esp. no. 7, p. 321.

227. Federigo MELIS, lecture at the Collège de France, 1970.

228. Hubert BOURGIN, *op. cit.*, p. 27.

229. *Medit.*, I, p. 433–4.

230. See below, section on factories and manufactories.

231. W. SOMBART, *op. cit.*, II, p. 732. For a discussion of these words, see below, section on factories and manufactories.

232. Henri LAPEYRE, *Une Famille de marchands, les Ruiz*, ... 1955, p. 588.

233. Jacques de VILLAMONT, *Les Voyages du seigneur de Villamont*, 1600, f° 4, v°.

234. Hubert BOURGIN, *op. cit.*, p. 31.

235. W. SOMBART, *op. cit.*, II, p. 731.

236. Ortulf REUTER, *Die Manufaktur im frankischen Raum*, 1961.

237. François COREAL, *Relation des voyages de François Coreal aux Indes occidentales ... depuis 1666 jusqu'en 1697*, Brussels, 1736, p. 138.

238. Otto von KOTZEBUE, *Entdeckungs-Reise in die Süd-See und nach der Berings-Strasse ...*, 1821, p. 22.

239. M. CARTIER and TENG T'O, 'En Chine du XVIe au XVIIIe siècle: les mines de charbon de Men-t'ou-kou' in *Annales E.S.C.*, 1967, pp. 54–87.

240. Louis DERMIGNY, *op. cit.*, I, p. 66. Jacques GERNET, *op. cit.*, p. 422.

241. Louis DERMIGNY, *op. cit.*, I, p. 65.

242. *Ibid.*

243. Sir George STAUNTON, *An authentic account of an Embassy ... to the Emperor of China, op. cit.*, II, p. 468. J. GERNET, *op. cit.*, p. 422.

244. P. SONNERAT, *Voyage aux Indes orientales et à la Chine fait par ordre du Roi depuis 1774 jusqu'en 1781*, 1782, I, p. 103.

245. *Ibid.*, pp. 104–5, engravings, pl. XX and XXII.

246. Guy PATIN, *Lettres*, I, p. 2.

247. MONTESQUIEU, *De l'Esprit des lois*, XXIII, p. 15.

248. Marc BLOCH, *Mélanges historiques*, 1963, II, pp. 796–7.

249. A.d.S. Genoa, *Lettere Consoli*, 1/2628.

250. Charles de RIBBE, *Une Grande Dame dans son ménage au temps de Louis XIV, d'après le journal de la comtesse de Rochefort (1689)*, Paris, 1889, pp. 142–7.

251. Witold KULA, *op. cit.*, p. 156, n. 84, Ukraine in 1583–Lithuania in 1788.

252. A.N., F¹², 681, f° 112.

253. J. BECKMANN, *op. cit.*, III, pp. 430–31.

254. Jean LEJEUNE, *op. cit.*, p. 143.

255. C. and S. Suárez to Cosmo Ruiz, Florence, 1 June 1601. Ruiz Archives, Valladolid. '... que todos acuden a la campaña'.

256. A.N., G⁷, 1706, f° 167.

257. Ange GOUDAR, *Les Intérêts de la France mal entendus*, Amsterdam, 1756, III, pp. 265–7, quoted by Pierre DOCKÈS, *L'Espace dans la pensée économique, op. cit.*, p. 270.

258. Roger DION, *Histoire de la vigne et du vin en France des origines au XIXe siècle*, 1959, p. 33.

259. Germain MARTIN, *La Grande Industrie sous le règne de Louis XIV*, (in particular between 1660 and 1715), 1898, p. 84.

260. E. TARLÉ, *L'Industrie dans les campagnes de France à la fin de l'Ancien Régime*, 1910, p. 45, n. 3.

passim.

267. DEFOE, *op. cit.*, I, pp. 253-4.
268. Isaac de PINTO, *op. cit.*, p. 287.
269. A.N., G⁷, 1704, f⁰ 102.
270. MIRABEAU, *L'Ami des hommes ou traité de la population*, 1756-1758.
271. P.S. DUPONT de NEMOURS, *De l'exportation et de l'importation des grains*, 1764, pp. 90-1, quoted by Pierre DOCKES, *L'Espace dans la pensée économique du XVIe au XVIIIe siècle*, 1969, p. 288.
272. François VÉRON de FORBONNAIS, *Principes et observations économiques*, 1767, I, p. 205, quoted by P. DOCKES, *op. cit.*, p. 288.
273. *Mémoires de Oudard Coquault (1649-1668), bourgeois de Reims*, 1875 edn., II, p. 371.
274. *Gazette de France*, 1730, p. 22.
275. Moscow, Lenin Library, Fr. 1100, f⁰ˢ 76-7.
276. Enrique FLORESCANO, *Precios del maiz y crisis agricolas en México (1708-1810)*, 1969, p. 142.
277. Germain MARTIN, *op. cit.*, p. 80.
278. A.N., F¹², 149, f⁰ 80.
279. DEFOE, *op. cit.*, p. 125.
280. E. TARLE, *op. cit.*, p. 43.
281. Prato Conference, April 1968.
282. Domenico SELLA, *European industries (1500-1700)*, 1970.
283. *Ibid.*, pp. 88-9.
284. 'Archéologie de la fabrique: la diffusion des moulins à soie "alla bolognese" dans les Etats vénitiens du XVIe au XVIIIe siècle' in *L'Industrialisation en Europe au XIXe siècle*, ed. P. LÉON, F. CROUZET, R. GASCON, 1972.
285. E. SCHULIN, *op. cit.*, p. 220.
286. 'The unmaking of the Mediterranean trade hegemony' in *Journal of Economic History*, 1975, p. 515.
287. Aloys SCHULTE, 'La lana come promotrice della floridezza economica

nigation à Rouen et au Havre au XVIIIe siècle*, 1966, pp. 108-9.
292. *Gazette de France*, 1783, p. 351.
293. 5 September 1759, SAVARY DES BRUSLONS, IV, col. 1023.
294. Geneviève ANTHONY, *L'Industrie de la toile à Pau et en Béarn de 1750 à 1850* (Etudes d'économie basco-béarnaise, III), 1961, p. 41.
295. A.N., F¹², 151, 148, v⁰, 29 April 1729, *Mignonette* was a striped satinette, *grisette* a cheap grey fabric (worn by the working girls who became known by this name); *burat* a heavy brown cloth.
296. A.N., F¹², 682, 29 August 1726. *Espagnolette* was known as 'Spanish cloth' in England.
297. A.N., G⁷, 1706, f⁰ 81, 19 January 1723.
298. A.N., F¹², 721.
299. A.N., 62 AQ 7.
300. *Variétés*, *op.cit.*, V, p. 345, n. 2.
301. A.N., G⁷, 1700, f⁰ 86.
302. Johann BECKMANN, *op. cit.*, III, introduction.
303. Pierre CHAUNU, *La Civilisation de l'Europe classique*, 1970, p. 332.
304. Bertrand GILLE, *Les Forges françaises en 1772*, 1960, p. XII.
305. The official transporters of wine to Paris for instance had provided almost a million and a half *livres* in six years (1703-1709) and were in difficulties. A.N., G⁷, 1510.
306. LÜTGE, *op. cit.*, pp. 205-6 and 258.
307. Hektor AMMAN, 'Die Anfänge des Activhandels und der Tucheinfuhr aus Nordwesteuropa nach dem Mittelmeergebiet' in *Studi in onore di Armando Sapori*, 1957, I, pull-out p. 308 a.
308. Erich MASCHKE, 'Die Stellung des Reichsstadt Speyer in der mittelalterlichen Wirtschaft Deutschlands' in *Viertelj. für Sozial- und Wirtschaftsgeschichte*, 1967, pp. 435-55, esp. p. 436.

309. *Paris sous Philippe le Bel d'après des documents originaux* ..., ed. H. GÉRARD, 1837.

310. B.N., Fr., 21557, f° 9.

311. F. MELIS, *Aspetti della vita economica medievale, studi nell'Archivio Datini di Prato*, I, p. 458.

312. Municipal archives, Genoa, 572, f° 4.

313. Moscow, Lenin Library, Fr., 374, f° 171.

314. *Ibid.*, f° 121.

315. Diego de COLMENARES, *Historia de la insignia ciudad de Segovia*, 2nd edn., 1640, p. 547.

316. Hermann KELLENBENZ, 'Marchands capitalistes et classes sociales', p. 14, (typescript).

317. Gino LUZZATTO, 'Per la storia delle costruzioni navali a Venezia nei secoli XVe XVI' in *Miscellanea di studi storici in onore di Camillo Manfroni*, pp. 385–400.

318. Museo Correr, Donà delle Rose, 160, f° 53 and v°.

319. Hermann KELLENBENZ, *art. cit.*, note 316.

320. François DORNIC, *L'Industrie textile dans le Maine*, 1955.

321. Raoul de FELICE, *La Basse-Normandie, étude de géographie régionale*, 1907, p. 471.

322. Johann BECKMANN, *op. cit.*, I, pp. 109 ff.

323. F. DORNIC, *op. cit.*, p. 307.

324. Moscow, Lenin Library, Fr., 374, f° 160 v°.

325. London, Victoria and Albert Museum, 86–HH, Box 1, undated.

326. *Barchent* was the German name for fustian.

327. A kind of mining enterprise that went back to the Middle Ages and the *Tridentiner Bergwerkgebrauche* of 1208.

328. Günther v. PROBSZT, *Die niederungarischen Bergstädte*, 1966.

329. Antonina KECKOWA, (*The Salt mines of the Cracow region from the sixteenth to the eighteenth century*), 1969, in Polish.

330. Danuta MOLENDA, *Le Progrès technique et l'organisation économique de l'extraction des metaux non ferreux en Pologne du XIVe au XVIIe siècle*, p. 14. By the same author, *Gornictwo Kruszcowe na terenie zloz slaskokrarowskich do Polowy XVI'wieku*, 1963, p. 410.

331. F. LÜTGE, *op. cit.*, p. 265.

332. J. STRIEDER, *Zur Genesis des modernen Kapitalismus*, 1935.

333. G. LOHMANN VILLENA, *Las Minas de Huancavelica en los siglos XVI y XVII*, pp. 11 ff.

334. A. MATILLA TASCÓN, *Historia de las minas de Almaden*, I (1958), pp. 181-202.

335. F. LÜTGE, *op. cit.*, p. 304; *Enciclopedia Italiana*, entry for 'Idria'.

336. Enrique FLORESCANO, *Precios del maiz y crisis agricolas en Mexico (1708-1810)* 1969, p. 150, note 33.

337. F. LÜTGE, *op. cit.*, p. 378.

338. L.A. CLARKSON, *The pre-industrial economy in England*, 1971, p. 98.

339. *Ibid.*

340. *Gazette de France*, 6 August 1731, p. 594.

341. A.N., F¹², 682, 9 January 1727.

342. Marcel ROUFF, *Les Mines de charbon en France au XVIIIe siècle*, 1922, p. 245, note 1.

343. Germain MARTIN, *La Grande Industrie en France sous le règne de Louis XIV*, 1900, p. 184.

344. A.N., A.E., B¹, 531, 18 February 1713.

345. A.N., F¹², 515, f° 4, 23 May 1738.

346. In the Ardennes *département;* this was the village of Illy, later made famous by the Franco-Prussian war.

347. A.N., F¹², 724.

348. A.N., G⁷, 1692, 101.

349. J.A. ROY, *Histoire du patronat du Nord de la France*, 1968, unpublished.

350. H. SEE, 'L'Etat économique de la Champagne à la fin du XVIIe siècle, d'apres les mémoires des intendants de 1689 et de 1698' in *Mémoires et documents pour servir à l'histoire du commerce et de l'industrie*, general ed. J. HAYEM, 10th series, 1966, p. 265.

351. Guy ARBELOT, *Cinq Paroisses du Vallage, XVIIe-XVIIIe siècles*, 1970, unpublished thesis.

352. Ortulf REUTER, *op. cit.*, p. 14-15.

353. SAVARY DES BRUSLONS, *op. cit.*, III, col. 721.

354. F.L. NUSSBAUM, *A History of the economic institutions of Modern Europe*, 1933, p. 216.

355. Cf. below, section on Van Robais manufactory.

356. F.L. NUSSBAUM, *op. cit.*, pp. 212-13.

357. F. LÜTGE, *op. cit.*, p. 366.

358. DEFOE, *op. cit.*, II, pp. 271-2.

359. Federigo MELIS, *Aspetti della vita economica medievale*, 1962, pp. 286 ff., 455 ff., and *Tracce di una storia economica di Firenze e della Toscana*, p. 249.
360. F. LÜTGE, *op. cit.*, p. 366.
361. Eckart SCHREMMER, *Die Wirtschaft Bayerns*, 1970, p. 502.
362. René GANDILHON, *op. cit.*, p. 176.
363. Quoted by Pierre DOCKES, *op. cit.*, p. 108.
364. Claude PRIS, *La Manufacture royale des glaces de Saint-Gobain, 1665-1830*, unpublished thesis in 5 vols., introduction.
365. A.N., G⁷, 1697, 2, 3 January 1712.
366. A.N., F¹², 682.
367. A.N., G⁷, 1706, 126, March 1723 (for everything in the preceding paragraph).
368. The basic work on this is M. COURTECUISSE, 'La manufacture de draps fins Vanrobais aux XVIIe et XVIIIe siècles' in *Mémoires de la Société d'émulation d'Abbeville*, XXV, 1920.
369. *Voyage d'Angleterre*, doc. cit., f⁰ 4.
370. Georges RUHLMAN, *Les Corporations, les manufactures et le travail libre à Abbeville au XVIIIe siècle*, 1948.
371. F.L. NUSSBAUM, *op. cit.*, p. 215.
372. *Ibid.*, p. 213.
373. *Ibid.*
374. *Ibid.*, p. 216.
375. L.A. CLARKSON, *op. cit.*, p. 99.
376. A.N., G⁷, 1697, 6.
377. *Ibid.*
378. A.N., F¹², 681, 9.
379. A.N., F¹², 516, 13.
380. All the following data are from Claude PRIS's thesis previously quoted.
381. Sidney HOMER, *A History of interest rates*, 1963.
382. The image I have in mind is something like the approximate intersection of bearings in a topographical survey. The converging rays never perfectly coincide.
383. According to W. KULA, information passed on to me by Andrej WICZANSKY.
384. Raymond OBERLÉ, 'L'évolution des fortunes à Mulhouse et le financement de l'industrialisation au XVIIIe siècle' in Comité des travaux historiques, *Bulletin des travaux historiques*, 1971, p. 151 and note 32, reference to *Histoire documentaire de l'industrie de Mulhouse*

et de ses environs au XIXe siècle, 1902, pp. 287 and 698.
385. According to the unpublished study by R. ZUBER, who has been working on the Montgolfier archives (Sorbonne Library).
386. *Handbuch der Deutschen Geschichte*, ed. AUBIN and ZORN, 1971, I, p. 550.
387. J.C. PERROT, *Genèse d'une ville moderne: Caen au XVIIIe siècle*, 1975, I, p. 372.
388. LUDWIG SCHEUERMANN, *Die Fugger als Montanindustrielle in Tirol und Kärnten*, 1929, p. 27.
389. *Daily Life in Portugal in the late Middle Ages*, 1971, esp. p. 198.
390. Walter G. HOFFMANN, *British Industry 1700-1950*, 1955.
391. *Cambridge Economic History of Europe*, IV, 1967, p. 484, fig. 33.
392. Jean-Claude PERROT, *op. cit.*, I, p. 400.
393. *Ibid.*, p. 408.
394. Sidney POLLARD and David CROSSLEY, *The Wealth of Britain*, 1968, pp. 134 ff.
395. Information provided by F. RUIZ MARTIN.
396. *Beauvais et le* Beauvaisis ...' *op. cit.*, p. 327.
397. Orazio CANCILA, 'I prezzi su un mercato dell'interno della Sicilia alla metà del XVII secolo' in *Economia e Storia*, 1966, p. 188.
398. Basile KERBLAY, 'Les foires commerciales et le marché intérieur en Russie dans la première moitié du XIXe siècle' in *Cahiers du monde russe et soviétique*, 1966, p. 424.
399. Vorontsov archives, 10, p. 129. Simon Vorontsov from Southampton, 12-24, September 1801.
400. CANTILLON, *Essai sur la nature du commerce en général*, INED, 1952, p. 36. He not have worried, Pierre Gourou assures me: a lot of horses meant a lot of manure and therefore better crop yields.
401. GALIANI, *Dialogue sur le commerce des blés*, quoted by Pierre DOCKES, p. 321.
402. W. SOMBART, *op. cit.*, II, pp. 357 ff.
403. A.N., G⁷, 1510.
404. DUTENS, *Histoire de la navigation hauturière en France*, 1828, quoted by J.C. TOUTAIN, *Les Transports en France, 1830-1965*, 1967, p. 38.
405. TOUTAIN, *ibid.*, p. 38.
406. A.N., G⁷, 1646, Orleans, 26 December 1708.

407. Jacob STRIEDER, *Aus Antwerpen Notariatsarchiven*, 1930, p. XXV, note 4.
408. Emile COORNAERT, *Les Français et le commerce international à Anvers*, I, pp. 269–70.
409. Aloys SCHULTE, *Geschichte des mittelalterlichen Handels und Verkehrs*, I, pp. 357 ff.
410. A.N., F¹², 721.
411. Stockalper Archiv, Brig, Sch. 31. nos. 2939, 2942, 2966.
412. A.D., Haute-Savoie, C 138–307, f⁰ 92, v⁰.
413. A.N., H 3159/2.
414. W. SOMBART, II, pp. 330–2.
415. *Mediterranean*, I, p. 209.
416. A. EVERITT, in *op. cit.*, IV, p. 559.
417. A.N., G⁷, 1510.
418. Jacques SAVARY, *Le Parfait Négociant*, 1712, I, part 2, pp. 208–9.
419. 'Relazione' of Bernardo BIGONI in *Viaggiatori del '600*, ed. Marziano Guglielminetti, 1967, pp. 309–10.
420. SAVARY DES BRUSLONS, *op. cit.*, IV (1762), col. 1251.
421. SULLY, *Mémoires*, III, p. 42.
422. Wilfrid BRULEZ, *De Firma della Faille en de internationale Handel van vlaamse Firma's in de 16⁰ Eeuw*, 1959, p. 577.
423. H. KELLENBENZ, *Der Meder'sche Handelsbuch und die Welser'chen Nachtrage*, 1974, p. 121.
424. A.N., G⁷, 1685, 77.
425. W. SOMBART, *op. cit.*, II, p. 334.
426. J.P. RICARD, *Le Négoce d'Amsterdam*, p. 218, quoted by W. SOMBART, II, p. 338.
427. Ray Bert WESTERFIELD, *Middlemen in English business, particularly between 1660 and 1760*, 1915.
428. W. SOMBART, *op. cit.*, II, p. 329.
429. J.C. TOUTAIN, *op. cit.*, p. 14.
430. SAVARY DES BRUSLONS, *op. cit.*, I, 1759, col. 429.
431. A.N., G⁷, 1646.
432. A.N., G⁷, 1633.
433. All the following data on Roanne is taken from Denis LUYA's unpublished dissertation, *Batellerie et gens de rivière à Roanne au dernier siècle de l'Ancien Régime*, Lyon, 1972.
434. A.N., H 3156 and H 2933 (in particular a memorandum of 1789 giving a history of the problem).
435. Michel de BOISLILE, *Mémoires des Intendants*, I (1881), pp. 5–6.
436. A.N., K 1352, no. 63, f⁰ 1.
437. SAVARY DES BRUSLONS, I, col. 430.
438. B.N., Fr., 21702, f⁰ˢ 71–3.
439. *Ibid.*, f⁰ˢ 120–6.
440. A.N., G⁷, 1532, August 1705.
441. A.N., F¹², 681, 60 and 44.
442. P. DEYON, *Amiens, capitale provinciale*, 1967, pp. 91 ff.
443. See note 433.
444. DEFOE, *op. cit.*, II, pp. 254–6.
445. SAVARY DES BRUSLONS, *op. cit.*, I, col. 429.
446. H. KELLENBENZ, 'Bäuerliche Unternehmertätigkeit im Bereich der Nord- und Ostsee von Hochmittelalter bis zum Ausgang der neueren Zeit', in *Viertelj. fur Sozial- und Wirtschaftsgeschichte*, March 1962.
447. *Ibid.*
448. *Ibid.*
449. L.A. BOITEUX, *La Fortune de mer, le besoin de sécurité et les débuts de l'assurance maritime*, pp. 45 ff.
450. *Ibid.*, p. 48.
451. Ralph DAVIS, *Aleppo and Devonshire Square*, p. 34, note 2.
452. A.N., K 1351. (It has been impossible to trace the original English version.)
453. SEIGNELAY, *Journal de voyage en Hollande*, 1867 edn., pp. 293 and 297.
454. A.N., F¹², 724.
455. A.N., F¹², 724, 25 September 1788.
456. A.N., A.E., B¹, 627, 2 August 1725.
457. A.N., Colonies, F², A 16.
458. Yosaburo TAKEKOSHI, *Economic aspects of the political history of Japan*, 1930, I, pp. 223–4.
459. Documents communicated to me by Jean MEYER.
460. Frederio C. LANE, 'Progrès technologiques et productivité dans les transports maritimes de la fin du Moyen Age au début des Temps modernes' in *Revue historique*, April–June, 1974, pp. 277–302.
461. Germain MARTIN, *La Grande Industrie sous le règne de Louis XIV*, p. 213.

1. MENENDEZ PIDAL, *Historia de España*, III, pp. 171-2.
2. In *Boll. Senese di Storia Patria*, VI, 1935.
3. H. PIGEONNEAU, *Histoire du commerce en France*, 1885, p. 237.
4. *Op. cit.*, p. 230.
5. Georg von BELOW, *Probleme der Wirtschaftsgeschichte*, 1926, p. 381. See also for confusion between *négociants* and *négociants détailleurs*, J. ACCARIAS DE SERIONNE, *Les Intérêts des nations de l'Europe*, 1766, II, p. 372.
6. P. CHALMETTA, *op. cit.*, pp. 103 and 117.
7. F. Sebastiàn MANRIQUE, *Itinerario de las Missiones*, 1649, p. 346.
8. On *tradesman* and *merchant*, see Daniel DEFOE, *The Complete English Tradesman*, *op. cit.*, I, pp. 1-3. On *mercatura* and *mercanzia*, cf. COTRUGLI, *op. cit.*, p. 15.
9. CONDILLAC, *op. cit.*, p. 306.
10. On the Genoese in Madrid, cf. *Mediterranean*, *op. cit.*, I, p. 509, note 301, on Charles Lion, cf. Paul DECHARME, *Le Comptoir d'un marchand au XVIIe siècle d'après une correspondance inédite*, 1910, p. 11.
11. Florence EDLER, 'The Vandermolen, commission merchants of Antwerp; trade with Italy, 1538-1544', in *Essays in honour of J.W. Thompson*, 1938, p. 90, note 34, (Antwerp, 7 December 1539).
12. DEFOE, *op. cit.*, II, p. 135.
13. B.N., Fr., 21702, f°s 14 and 40.
14. TURGOT, *Oeuvres*, *op. cit.*, I, p. 262.
15. F. RUIZ MARTÍN, *Lettres marchandes ... op. cit.*, pp. xxxvi-xxxvii.
16. Pierre VILAR, *op. cit.*, III, *passim*, and p. 384-422.
17. Jean-Claude PERROT, *op. cit.*, I, pp. 435-7.
18. On the firm of A. Greppi, cf. Bruno CAIZZI, *Industria, commercio e banca in Lombardia nel XVIII secolo*, 1968, pp. 203, 206, 210; on the firm of Tripp, cf. P.W. KLEIN, *De Trippen in de 17º Eeuw*, 1965, pp. 474 ff.
19. *Middlemen in English Business*, 1915.
20. C. CARRIERE, *op. cit.*, I, p. 251.
21. D. DEFOE, *op. cit.*, I, p. 102.
22. S. POLLARD and D.W. CROSSLEY, *op. cit.*, p. 169, note 65.
23. *Variétés*, *op. cit.*, III, pp. 41 and 56-7.
24. A.N., G⁷, 1686, f⁰ 156.
25. Claude CARRÈRE, *Barcelone, centre économique ...*, 1967, I, p. 143.
26. Claude-Frédéric LEVY, *Capitalistes et pouvoir au siècle des Lumières*, 1969, p. 354.
27. Jean SAVANT, *Tel fut Ouvrard*, 1954, pp. 11 ff.
28. Remy Bensa to P.F. Delessart, Frankfurt, 14 September 1763, A.N., 62, AQ 34.
29. M.G. BUIST, *op. cit.*, p. 13.
30. *Oeuvres*, I, p. 264.
31. 1759, p. 57.
32. DEFOE, *op. cit.*, I, pp. 354-7.
33. *Ibid.*, p. 368.
34. *Ibid.*, p. 364.
35. *Ibid.*, p. 358.
36. *Ibid.*, p. 46.
37. *Ibid.*, II, p. 10.
38. K.N. CHAUDHURI, *The Trading World of Asia and the English East India Company*, 1978.
39. K. MARX, *Capital*, I, section 7, ch. 24, iii.
40. Ch. CARRÈRE, *op. cit.*, II, pp. 916-20.
41. *Ibid.*, I, p. 88.
42. *Variétés*, V, p. 256.
43. Robert BIGO, 'Une grammaire de la Bourse en 1789', in *Annales*, 1930, p. 507.
44. G.B. CARDINALE di LUCA, *Il Dottor vulgare*, 1673, V, p. 29.
45. Daniel DESSERT, 'Finances et société au XVIIe siècle: à propos de la chambre de justice de 1661', in *Annales*, *E.S.C.*, 1974, no. 4, pp. 847-85.
46. Museo Correr, exact reference mislaid.
47. C. LAVEAU, *op. cit.*, p. 154.
48. Violet BARBOUR, *Capitalism in Amsterdam in the seventeenth century*, 1950, p. 44.
49. S. POLLARD and D.W. CROSSLEY, *op. cit.*, pp. 149-50.
50. Isaac de PINTO, *op. cit.*, pp. 44-5, 77 ff., 95-6.
51. A.N., 62 AQ, Dugard papers.
52. *Ibid.* Literally 'we must walk past upright', *il faut passer debout*, i.e., without stopping.
53. C. CARRIÈRE, *op. cit.*, II, p. 918.
54. A.P. USHER, *The Early History of Deposit Banking in Mediterranean Europe*, 1943, p. 6.

55. Federigo MELIS, 'Origines de la Banca moderna' in *Moneda y credito*, no. 116, 1971, pp. 3-18, notably p. 4.
56. Cf. above, chapter 1, on fairs.
57. M. MORINEAU, in *Anuario de historia económica y social*, 1969, pp. 289-362.
58. P.R.O. London, 30/25, 4 January 1687.
59. 9 August 1613, quoted by J. GENTIL da SILVA, *op. cit.*, p. 350, note 46.
60. Carlo M. CIPOLLA, 'La prétendue "Révolution des prix"; réflexions sur l'expérience italienne', in *Annales E.S.C.*, 1955, pp. 513-16.
61. Isaac de PINTO, *op. cit.*, pp. 46 and 77-8.
62. Quoted by POLLARD and CROSSLEY, *op. cit.*, p. 169.
63. A.N., G⁷, 1691, 35 (6 March 1708).
64. A.N., A.E., B¹, 331, 25 November 1713.
65. A.d.S., Venice, Consoli Genova, 6, 98, Genoa, 12 November 1628.
66. A.G., Warsaw, Radziwill papers, Nantes, 20 March 1726.
67. A.N., G⁷, 1622.
68. *Ibid.*, 'Memorandum on bank notes', 1706 (?).
69. Marcel ROUFF, *Les Mines de charbon en France au XVIIIe siècle*, 1922, p. 243.
70. C. CARRIÈRE, *op. cit.*, II, pp. 917 ff.
71. B. CAIZZI, *Industria, commercio e banca in Lombardia . . . op. cit.*, pp. 149, 206.
72. Guy CHAUSSINAND-NOGARET, *Les Financiers du Languedoc au XVIIIe siècle*, 1970, pp. 40 and 103-4; *Gens de finance au XVIIIe siècle*, 1972, *passim* and pp. 68 ff., review of Yves DURAND's book in *Annales E.S.C.*, 1973, p. 804.
73. Pierre VILAR, *op. cit.*, II, pp. 482-91.
74. TURGOT, *Oeuvres*, *op. cit.*, I, p. 381.
75. L. DERMIGNY, *Le Commerce à Canton*, *op. cit.*, II, p. 774.
76. C. GLAMANN, *Dutch Asiatic Trade, 1620-1740*, 1958, p. 261.
77. LA BRUYERE, *Caractères . . .*, VI, 39.
78. Léon SCHICK, *Un Grand Homme d'affaires au début du XVIe siècle, Jakob Fugger*, 1957, p. 416.
79. Pierre VILAR, in *L'Industrialisation en Europe au XIXe siècle*, 1972, ed. LEON, CROUZET and GASCON.
80. J. CAVIGNAC, *op. cit.*, p. 156, 12 April 1725.
81. Jean MAILLEFER, *op. cit.*, p. 179.
82. MABLY, *Oeuvres*, XIII, *Du commerce des grains*, pp. 291-7.
83. Jean-Baptiste SAY, *op. cit.*, I, p. 176.
84. Jacques HEERS in *Revue du Nord*, Jan. 1964, pp. 106-7; Peter MATHIAS, *The First Industrial Nation, an economic history of Britain, 1700-1914*, 1969, p. 18.
85. F. LÜTGE, *op. cit.*, p. 294.
86. *Mediterranean*, I, p. 422.
87. Pierre GOUBERT, *Louis XIV et vingt millions de Français*, 1966.
88. Enrique OTTE, 'Das Genuesische Unternehmertum und Amerika unter den Katholischen Königen', in *Jahrbuch für Geschichte von Staat, Wirtschaft und Gesellschaft Latein-amerikas*, 1965, Bd 2, pp. 30-74.
89. Maurice DOBB, *Studies in the development of capitalism*, 4th edn., 1950, pp. 109 ff., 191 ff.
90. A.N., G⁷, 1865, 75.
91. H.H. MAURUSCHAT, *Gewürze, Zucker und Salz im vorindustriellen Europe . . .*, quoted by Wilhelm ABEL, *Einige Bemerkungen zum Land Stadtprobleme im spätmittelalter*, p. 25.
92. Baltasar Suàrez to Simón Ruiz, 26 February 1591, Ruiz Archives, Valladolid.
93. *Encyclopedia britannica*, 1969, XIII, p. 524.
94. SAVARY DES BRUSLONS, V, col. 668.
95. Moscow, Central Archives, Alex. Baxter to Vorontsov . . ., 50/6, 1788.
96. C.R. BOXER, *The Great Ship from Amacon*, 1959, pp. 15-16.
97. Abbé de BELIARDY, *Idée du Commerce*, B.N., Fr., 10759, f° 310, v°.
98. G.F. GEMELLI CARERI, *op. cit.*, IV, p. 4.
99. Denys LOMBARD, *op. cit.*, p. 113.
100. Johan Albrecht MANDELSLO, *op. cit.*, II, p. 346.
101. F. GALIANI, *Dialogues sur le commerce des bleds*, ed. Fausto Nicolini, 1959, pp. 178-80 and 252.
102. Simón Ruiz to Baltasar Suàrez, 24 April 1591, Ruiz Archives, Valladolid.
103. D. DEFOE, *op. cit.*, II, pp. 149 ff.
104. For the following details see Christian BEC, *Les Marchands écrivains à Florence, 1375-1434*, 1967, pp. 383 ff.
105. Richard EHRENBERG, *Das Zeitalter der Fugger*, 1922, I, p. 273, n. 4.
106. J.-P. PALEWSKI, *Histoire des chefs d'entreprise*, 1928, pp. 103 ff.
107. Ralph DAVIS, *Aleppo and Devonshire Square*, 1967, p. 66.

108. Edited by V. von KLARWILL, *The Fugger News-Letters*, 1924-1926, 2 vols.
109. Paolo da CERTALDO, quoted by C. BEC, *op. cit.*, p. 106.
110. A.N., A.E., B¹, 623.
111. A.N., 61 AQ 4, fᵒ 19.
112. *Ibid.*
113. A.N., 61 AQ 2, fᵒ 18, letter of 18 December 1777.
114. Text by Paolo da CERTALDO, quoted by C. BEC, *op. cit.*, p. 106.
115. A.E., C.P., Angleterre 532, fᵒˢ 90-1, Beaumarchais to Vergennes, Paris, 31 August 1779.
116. Bonvisi to S. Ruiz, quoted by J. GENTIL DA SILVA, *op. cit.*, p. 559.
117. On this prolonged crisis see Pomponne's correspondence, A.N., A.E., B¹, Hollande 619 (1669).
118. James BOSWELL, *Life of Samuel Johnson*, Everyman edn., I, p. 607.
119. An expression used by the author of a pamphlet of 1846 attacking the French minister of Public Works who had granted the licence for the northern region railway to Rothschild's Bank, fraudulently, by allowing it to be the only bidder. Quoted by Henry COSTON, *Les Financiers qui mènent le monde*, 1955, p. 65.
120. See above, chapter 1, on markets.
121. A.N., F¹², 681.
122. A.N., G⁷, 1707, p. 148.
123. A.N., G⁷, 1692, pp. 34-6.
124. *Ibid.*, fᵒ 68.
125. A.N., F¹², 662-70, 1 February 1723.
126. A.N., G⁷, 1692, fᵒ 211, vᵒ (1707 or 1708). The Biesme valley is in Argonne.
127. A.N., F¹², 515, 17 February 1770.
128. A.N., G⁷, 1685, p. 39.
129. A.N., F¹², 681, fᵒˢ 48, 97, 98, 112 and A.N., G⁷, 1706, & nᵒˢ 237 and 238. A letter of 26 December 1723 refers to government measures of 1699 and 1716, annulling all past deals, in order to prevent 'this kind of hoarding' in the wool trade.
130. A.N., F¹², 724, nᵒ 1376.
131. SAVARY DES BRUSLONS, *op. cit.*, IV, col. 406, for the respective weight of the different *razières* or *rasières*: 280-90 pounds to 245.
132. A.N., G⁷, 1678, fᵒ 41 and fᵒ 53, November and December 1712.
133. Jean EON (Father Mathias de Saint-Jean), *Le Commerce honorable*, *op. cit.*, pp. 88-9.
134. 'John NICKOLLS' (pseud. of Plumard de Dangeul), *Remarks on the advantages and disadvantages of France and Great Britain*, English edn., Leyden, 1754, pp. 168-9.
135. Henri PIRENNE, *Histoire économique de l'Occident médiéval*, 1951, p. 45, note 3.
136. Joseph HÖFFNER, *Wirtschaftsethik und Monopole*, 1941, p. 58, note 2.
137. Hans HAUSHERR, *Wirtschaftsgeschichte der Neuzeit*, 1954, pp. 78-9.
138. Ulrich von HÜTTEN, *Opera*, 1859-1862 edn., pp. 302 and 299, quoted by HÖFFNER, *op. cit.*, p. 54.
139. Violet BARBOUR, *op. cit.*, p. 75.
140. *Ibid.*, p. 89. (Declaration by De Witt to the States-General in 1671. This grain was stored not only in Amsterdam but in several towns in Holland).
141. Samuel LAMBE, *Seasonable observations . . .*, 1658, pp. 9-10, quoted by V. BARBOUR, *op. cit.*, p. 90.
142. J. SAVARY, *Le Parfait Négociant*, *op. cit.*, 1712 edn., II, pp. 135-6.
143. A.N., A.E., B¹, 619, The Hague, 25th September 1670.
144. *Ibid.*, 4 July 1669.
145. *Ibid.*, 26 September 1669.
146. J. SAVARY, *op. cit.*, II, pp. 117-19.
147. A.N., G⁷, 1686-99.
148. Marten G. BUIST, *op. cit.*, pp. 431 ff.
149. P.W. KLEIN, *op. cit.*, pp. 3-15, 475 ff.
150. Jacob van KLAVEREN, *Europäische Wirtschaftsgeschichte Spaniens*, *op. cit.*, p. 3. '. . . Erstens ist es für die Wirtschaft an sich von keiner Bedeutung, ob das Geld aus Silber, Gold oder aus Papier besteht'.
151. Marcel MARION, *Dictionnaire des institutions*, p. 384, 2nd col. Louis DERMIGNY, 'La France à la fin de l'Ancien Régime, une carte monétaire' in *Annales E.S.C.*, 1955, p. 489.
152. MALESTROIT, 'Mémoires sur le faict des monnoyes . . .', 1567 in *Paradoxes inédits*, ed. L. EINAUDI, 1937, pp. 73 and 105.
153. F.C. SPOONER, *L'Economie mondiale et les frappes monétaires en France, 1493-1680*, 1956, pp. 128 ff.
154. C.M. CIPOLLA, *Studi di storia della moneta: i movimenti dei cambi in Italia*

dal sec. XIII al XV, 1948, and review by R. de ROOVER in *Annales*, 1951, pp. 31-6.

155. Geminiano MONTANARI, *Trattato del valore delle monete*, ch. III, p. 7, quoted by J. GENTIL DA SILVA, *op. cit.*, p. 400.

156. C.M. CIPOLLA, *Mouvements monétaires de l'Etat de Milan (1580-1700)*, p. 1952, pp. 13-18.

157. Marquis d'ARGENSON, *Mémoires et Journal inédit*, 1857-8 edn., II, p. 56. A *sol* was worth 12 *deniers*, and a *liard* 3 *deniers*: so a coin worth 24 *deniers* had been devalued by 6 *deniers*, that is 25%.

158. J. GENTIL DA SILVA, *Banque et crédit en Italie au XVIIe siècle*, I, pp. 711-16.

159. Gio. Domenico PERI, *Il Negotiante*, 1666 edn., p. 32.

160. F. RUIZ MARTÍN, *Lettres marchandes de Florence*, *op. cit.*, p. xxxviii.

161. R. GASCON, *op. cit.*, I, p. 251.

162. J. GENTIL DA SILVA, *op. cit.*, p. 165.

163. Jean EON, *op. cit.*, p. 104.

164. Isaac de PINTO, *op. cit.*, pp. 90-1, note 23.

165. *États et tableaux concernant les finances de France depuis 1758 jusqu'en 1787*, 1788, p. 225.

166. J. BOUVIER, P. FURET and M. GILLET, *Le Mouvement du profit en France au XIXe siècle*, 1965, p. 269.

167. M.G. BUIST, *op. cit.*, pp. 520-5 and notes.

168. Louis DERMIGNY, *Cargaisons indiennes. Salier et Cie, 1781-1793*, 1960, II, p. 144.

169. Giorgio DORIA in *Mélanges Borlandi*, 1977, pp. 377 ff.

170. F. RUIZ MARTÍN, *El Siglo de los Genoveses*, unpublished.

171. J. MEYER, *L'Armement nantais, op. cit.*, pp. 220 ff.

172. *Ibid.*, p. 219.

173. Jacob M. PRICE, *France and the Chesapeake*, 1973, I, pp. 288-9; calculations passed on to me by J.J. Hémardinquer.

174. A.N., 94, AQ 1, f° 28.

175. L. DERMIGNY, *Cargaisons indiennes, op. cit.*, pp. 141-3.

176. J. MEYER, *op. cit.*, pp. 290-1.

177. M. BOGUCKA, *Handel zagraniczny Gdanske ...*, 1970, p. 137.

178. A.N., Colonies, F² A 16.

179. Thomas MUN, *A Discourse of Trade from England into the East Indies*, London, 1621, p. 55, quoted by P. DOCKES, *op. cit.*, p. 125.

180. HAKLUYT (1885 edn.), pp. 70-1, quoted by J.C. VAN LEUR, *op. cit.*, p. 67.

181. Jean GEORGELIN, *Venise au siècle des Lumières (1669-1797)*, p. 436 (typescript).

182. *Ibid.*, p. 435.

183. Cf. how capital liberated by the abandonment of industry in Caen was re-invested elsewhere, J.C. PERROT, *op. cit.*, I, pp. 381 ff.

184. Stephan MARGLIN, in *Le Nouvel Observateur*, 9 June 1975, p. 37.

185. J. KULISCHER, *op. cit.*, Italian edn., I, p. 444.

186. Cf. below, vol. III, chapter 2.

187. J. KULISCHER, *op. cit.*, I, p. 446.

188. J. GENTIL DA SILVA, *op. cit.*, p. 148.

189. Jean MAILLEFER, *op. cit.*, p. 64.

190. C. BAUER, *op. cit.*, p. 26.

191. F. MELIS, *Tracce di una storia economica ..., op. cit.*, p. 29.

192. A.E. SAYOUS, 'Dans l'Italie à l'intérieur des terres: Sienne de 1221 à 1229' in *Annales*, 1931, pp. 189-206.

193. Hermann AUBIN, Wolfgang ZORN, *Handbuch ..., op. cit.*, p. 351.

194. J. KULISCHER, *op. cit.*, German edn., I, pp. 294-5.

195. A. SCHULTE, *Geschichte der grossen Ravensburger Handelsgeschellschaft, 1380-1530*, 1923, 3 vols.

196. H. HAUSHERR, *op. cit.*, p. 29.

197. Françoise BAYARD, 'Les Buonvisi marchands banquiers à Lyon 1575-1629' in *Annales E.S.C.*, Nov.-Dec. 1971, p. 1235.

198. Jean MEYER, *L'Armement nantais ..., op. cit.*, p. 105, note 8.

199. *Ibid.*, p. 112, note 2.

200. *Ibid.*, pp. 107-15.

201. F. MELIS, *Tracce di una storia economica, op. cit.*, pp. 50-1.

202. Jean MEYER, *L'Armement nantais ... op. cit.*, p. 107 and note 6.

203. Archives de la Ville de Paris (AVP), 3 B 6, 21.

204. J.P. RICARD, *op. cit.*, p. 368.

205. Title IV, article 8, quoted by Ch. CARRIÈRE, *op. cit.*, II, p. 886.

206. *Ibid.*, p. 887.

207. J. SAVARY, *Le Parfait Négociant*, 1712 edn., part 2, pp. 15 ff.

208. Eric Maschke, 'Deutsche Städte am Ausgang des Mittelalters' in *Die Stadt am Ausgang des Mittelalters*, 1974, offprint, pp. 8 ff.

209. The organization in Toulouse is admirably set out in Germain Sicard, *Aux origines des sociétés anonymes: les moulins de Toulouse au Moyen Age*, 1953.

210. *Ibid.*, p. 351, note 26.

211. E.F. Heckscher, *op. cit.*, English trans., I, p. 334, and *passim*.

212. A.V.P., 3 B 6, 66.

213. A.N., Z¹ D 102 A, f⁰ˢ 19–20.

214. Jean-François Melon, *Essai politique sur le commerce*, 1734, pp. 77–8.

215. Jean Meyer, *L'Armement nantais . . .*, *op. cit.*, p. 275.

216. A.N., Z¹ D 102 A.

217. Jean Meyer, *L'Armement nantais*, *op. cit.*, p. 113.

218. Ch. Carrière, *op. cit.*, II, pp. 879 ff.

219. D. Defoe, *op. cit.*, I, p. 215.

220. The word was only just appearing. Littré's dictionary gives a quotation from Fénelon, *Télémaque*, XII, 1699.

221. According to a remark in Isaac de Pinto, *op. cit.*, p. 335.

222. Guy Antonetti, *Greffulhe, Montz et Cie, 1789–1793*, p. 96; cf. J. Everaert, *op. cit.*, p. 875. German firms in Cadiz in about 1700 were not numerous.

223. George Lillo, *The London merchant*, ed. W.H. Burney, 1965, p. 29.

224. W. Sombart, *op. cit.*, II, p. 580.

225. Manuel Nuñes Diaz, O *Capitalismo monarquico poàtuguès (1415–1549)*, São Paulo, 1957, doctoral thesis.

226. Charles Verlinden, *Les Origines de la civilisation atlantique*, 1966, pp. 11–12 and 164.

227. Louis Dermigny, *La Chine et l'Occident, Le commerce à Canton . . .*, *op. cit.*, I, p. 86.

228. A.N., A.E., B¹ 760, London, July 1713.

229. Charles Wilson, *England's Apprenticeship, 1603–1763*, 3rd edn., 1967, pp. 172–3.

230. On this subject see the discussion and long bibliography in Jurgen Wiegandf, *Die Merchants Adventurers Company auf dem Kontinent zur Zeit des Tudors und Stuarts*, 1972.

231. E.F. Heckscher, Eng. trans., 1955, I, p. 328.

232. *Ibid.*, p. 423.

233. M.M. Postan, *Medieval Trade and Finance*, 1973, pp. 302–4.

234. F. Lütge, *op. cit.*, p. 342.

235. According to J.U. Nef, K.W. Taylor, I. Wallerstein and T.K. Rabb in *Enterprise and Empire*, 1967, pp. 19 ff., and 26 ff.

236. For the French Northern Company, cf. A.N., G⁷, 1685, I; for the French West Indies Company, cf. A.E., M. and D., 16.

237. *Etudes d'histoire économique*, 1971, p. 33.

238. S. Pollard and D.W. Crossley, *op. cit.*, pp. 150–1.

239. *Ibid.*, pp. 143, 146, 147, 163.

240. P. Jeannin, *L'Europe du Nord-Ouest et du Nord aux XVIIe et XVIIIe siècles*, 1969, p. 192.

241. S. Pollard and D.W. Crossley, *op. cit.*, p. 149.

242. Letter from Pontchartrain to Tallard (6 August 1698), cf. A.E., CP, Ang. 208, f⁰ 115; letter from Tallard to Pontchartrain (21 August 1698), cf. A.N., A.E., B¹ 759.

243. Peter Laslett, *The World we have lost*, 1965, p. 156.

244. Charles Boxer, *The Dutch Seaborne Empire, 1600–1800*, 1965, p. 43.

245. Maurice Dobb, *Studies in the Development of Capitalism*, 4th edn., 1950, p. 191, note 1.

246. A.N., G⁷, 1686, f⁰ 85.

247. A.N., Marine B⁷, 230, quoted by Charles Frostin, 'Les Pontchartrain et la pénétration commerciale française en Amérique espagnole (1690–1715)', in *Revue historique*, 1971, p. 311, note 2.

248. A.N., K 1349, f⁰ 14 and 15.

249. Paul Kaeppelin, *La Compagnie des Indes Orientales et François Martin*, 1908, pp. 135–6.

250. *Ibid.*, p. 593.

251. A.N., G⁷, 1699.

252. Charles Montagne, *Histoire de la Compagnie des Indes*, 1899, pp. 223–4.

253. M. Levy-Leboyer, *op. cit.*, p. 417, note 2.

254. See Vol. I, Introduction.

255. Walter Achilles, 'Getreidepreise und Getreidhandelsbeziehungen europäischen Raum in XVI und XVII Jahrh.' in *Zeitschrift für Agrargeschichte*, 59, pp. 32–55.

256. E. Maschke, *art. cit.*, p. 18.

257. J.P. Ricard, *Le Négoce d'Amsterdam,*
1722, p. 59.
258. *Schriften,* 1800, I, p. 264, quoted by W.
Sombart, 2, p. 500.

259. E. Zola, *L'Argent,* ed. Fasquelle, 1960,
p. 166, quoted by P. Miquel, *L'Argent,*
1971, pp. 141–2.
260. Galiani, *op. cit.,* pp. 162–8, 178–80, 152.

NOTES TO CHAPTER 5

1. Quoted by Louis Dumont in *Homo
hierarchicus,* 1966, p. 18.
2. I am thinking of a conversation in
November 1937.
3. Emile Durkheim (1858–1917) presented
his thesis *De la division du travail social*
in 1893 and founded *L'Année sociologique*
in 1896; I refer here to the latter.
4. *Revue de synthèse,* 1900, p. 4.
5. Despite the attempts by Alfred Weber,
Kulturgeschichte als Kultursoziologie,
1935, or Alfred von Martin, *Soziologie
der Renaissance . . .,* 1932; and more
recently an impressive work of synthesis
by Alexander Rustow, *Ortsbestimmung
der Gegenwart,* 3 vols., 1950–7.
6. *Op. cit.,* p. 9.
7. J. Schumpeter, *op. cit.,* Italian edn., I, p.
23.
8. Novalis, *Encyclopédie,* 1966, p. 43.
9. Similar remarks can be found in the
writings of René Clemens, Raymond
Aron, Wilhelm Ropke, Jacques Attali,
Joseph Klatzmann, Marcel Mauss.
10. *English Social History,* 1942.
11. Many people think the opposite, e.g.
Edward J. Nell, 'Economic relationships
in the decline of feudalism: an economic
interdependence' in *History and Theory,*
1957, p. 328: 'the relations between the
variables should be considered rather
than the variables themselves'. Evans-
Pritchard's view is that social structure
can be reduced to the inter-relationships
between groups, according to S.F.
Nadel, *La Théorie de la structure sociale,*
1970, p. 30.
12. I. Wallerstein, *op. cit.,* p. 157.
13. Jack H. Hexter, *Reappraisals in
History,* 1963, p. 72.
14. *Variétés,* III, p. 312, *Advis de Guillaume
Hotteux ès Halles.*
15. *L'idéal historique,* 1976.
16. Karl Bosl, 'Kasten, Stände, Klassen in
mittelalterlichen Deutschland', in *ZBLG*

32, 1969. It is impossible to use the word
in a strict sense.
17. On caste in India, see Claude
Meillassoux, 'Y a-t-il des castes aux
Indes' in *Cahiers internationaux de
sociologie,* 1973, pp. 5–29.
18. *La Vocation actuelle de la sociologie,*
1963, I, pp. 365 ff.
19. *Pour la sociologie,* 1974, p. 57.
20. Prévost, *op. cit.,* I, p. 8.
21. Van Rechteren, *Voyages,* 1628–1632,
V, p. 69.
22. A.N. K 910, 27 *bis.*
23. See for example Arthur Boyd Hibbert in
Past and Present, 1953, no. 3, and Claude
Cahen, in *La Pensée,* July 1956, pp. 95–6:
feudalism does not mean the negation of
trade. For the orthodox view see Charles
Parain and Pierre Vilar, 'Mode de
production féodal et classes sociales en
système précapitaliste', 1968, *Les Cahiers
du Centre d'Etudes et Recherches
marxistes,* no. 59.
24. It dates from 1815 at earliest: the word is
not in *La Néologie* by L.S. Mercier,
1801; see N. Landais, *Dictionnaire général
et grammatical,* 1934, II, p. 26.
25. Armando Sapori and Gino Luzzatto,
for instance.
26. Georges Gurvitch, *Déterminismes
sociaux et liberté humaine,* 2nd edn.,
1963, pp. 261 ff.
27. Marc Bloch, *La Société féodale,* 2 vols.,
1939–1940.
28. Jacques Heers, *Le Clan familial au
Moyen Age,* 1974.
29. A. Thiers, *De la propriété,* 1848, p. 93.
30. Jean-Francois Melon, *op. cit.,* p. 126.
31. Charles Wright Mills, *The Power
Elite,* 1959.
32. *Delle lettere di Messer Claudio Tolomei,*
Venise, 1547, f°s 144 v°–145. (This
passage was pointed out to me by Sergio
Bertelli.)
33. Frederic C. Lane, *Venice, a maritime*

republic, 1973, p. 324; see also K.J. BELOCH, *Bevölkerungsgeschichte Italiens*, vol. III, 1961, pp. 21-2.

34. F.C. LANE, *op. cit.*, pp. 429-30.
35. SAINTOLON, *Relazione della Republica di Genova*, 1684, Venice, Marciana, 6045, c. II-8.
36. Gerald STRAUSS, 'Protestant dogma and city government. The case of Nuremberg', in *Past and Present*, n° 36, 1967, pp. 38-58.
37. C.A.B.F. de BAERT-DUHOLAND, *Tableau de la Grande-Bretagne*, An VIII, IV, p. 7.
38. C.R. BOXER, *The Dutch seaborne Empire, 1600-1800*, 1965, p. 11.
39. R. GASCON, *op. cit.*, I, p. 407.
40. G.D. RAMSAY, *The City of London*, 1975, p. 12.
41. E.W. DAHLGREN, *Les Relations commerciales et maritimes entre la France et les côtes du Pacifique*, I, 1909, pp. 36-7, note 2.
42. François DORNIC, *op. cit.*, p. 178.
43. Jacques TENEUR, 'Les Commerçants dunkerquois à la fin du XVIIIe siècle et les problèmes économiques de leur temps', in *Revue du Nord*, 1966, p. 21.
44. Quoted by Charles CARRIÈRE, *op. cit.*, I, pp. 215-16.
45. *Ibid.*, p. 265.
46. Reference mislaid.
47. Emilio NASALLI ROCCA, 'Il Patriziato piacentino nell'età del principato. Considerazioni di storia giuridica, sociale e statistica', in *Studi in onore di Cesare Manaresi*, 1952, pp. 227-57.
48. J.M. ROBERTS, in *The European Nobility in the Eighteenth Century*, ed. A. GOODWIN, 1953, p. 67.
49. J. GENTIL DA SILVA, *op. cit.*, pp. 369-70, note 92.
50. Phyllis DEANE, W.A. COLE, *British economic growth*, 2nd edn., 1967, pp. 2 ff.; S. POLLARD, D.W. CROSSLEY, *op. cit.*, pp. 153 ff.
51. S. POLLARD, D.W. CROSSLEY, *op. cit.*, p. 169.
52. André PARREAUX, *La Société anglaise de 1760 à 1810*, 1966, p. 8.
53. Pierre GOUBERT, *L'Ancien Régime*, 1969, I, pp. 158-9.
54. P. LÉON, in *Histoire économique et sociale de la France*, II, 1970, p. 607; Jean

MEYER, *La Noblesse bretonne au XVIIIe siècle*, p. 56.
55. W. DWOERACZEK, 'Perméabilité des barrières sociales dans la Pologne du XVIe siècle', in *Acta Poloniae Historica*, 1971, 24, pp. 30, 39.
56. M.N. PEARSON, 'Decline of the Moghol Empire', in *The Journal of Asian Studies*, Feb. 1976, p. 223: There were 8000 privileged men in an Empire of 60 to 70 million inhabitants. 'The 8000 men were the Empire.'
57. *Op. cit.*, I, p. VIII.
58. Quoted in Julien FREUND, *op. cit.*, p. 25.
59. Lawrence STONE, 'The anatomy of the Elizabethan aristocracy', in *The Economic History Review*, 1948, pp. 37-41.
60. H. KELLENBENZ, *Der Merkantilismus in Europa und die soziale Mobilität*, 1965, pp. 49-50.
61. Peter LASLETT, *op. cit.*, p. 44.
62. Pierre GOUBERT, *L'Ancien Régime, op. cit.*, I, p. 105.
63. *Handbuch der deutschen Wirtshafts- und Sozialgeschichte, op. cit.*, p. 371.
64. On Venice, *La Civiltà veneziana nell'età barocca, op. cit.*, p. 307, February 1685; *La Civiltà Veneziana del Settecento*, pp. 244, 274.
65. *Ibid.*, p. 244.
66. On Longleat, *cf. New Encyclopedia Britannica*, 15th edn., VI, p. 319; on Wollaton Hall, *ibid.*, X, p. 729; on Burghley House, *cf.* J. Alfred GOTCH, *Architecture of the Renaissance in England*, I, 1894, pp. 1-3; on Holdenby, *cf.* Henry SHAW, *Details of Elizabethan Architecture*, 1839, p. 8.
67. Peter LASLETT, *op. cit.*, 1965 edn., p. 150.
68. *Cf.* H.R. TREVOR-ROPER, 'The General crisis of the seventeenth century', in *Past and Present*, n° 16 (Nov. 1959), pp. 31-64, and the debate between E.H. KOSSMANN, E.J. HOBSBAWM, J.H. HEXTER, R. MOUSNIER, J.H. ELLIOTT, L. STONE, with reply by H.R. TREVOR-ROPER, in *Past and Present*, n° 18 (Nov. 1960), pp. 8-42. See also Lawrence STONE, *The Causes of the English Revolution*, 1972; J.H. HEXTER, *Reappraisals in History*, 1963, pp. 117 ff.
69. P. BOURDIEU , J.C. PASSERON, *La*

Reproduction. Éléments pour une théorie du système d'enseignement, 1970.

70. In *Histoire de la Savoie*, ed. GUICHONNET, 1974, p. 250.

71. Daniele BELTRAMI, *Storia della popolazione di Venezia*, 1954, pp. 71, 72, 78. In 1581, nobles were 4.5% of the population, *cittadini* 5.3%. In 1586 the figures are 4.3% and 5.1% respectively.

72. Werner SCHULTHEISS, 'Die Mittelschicht Nürnbergs im Spätmittelalter', in *Städtische Mittelschichten*, ed. E. MASCHKE and J. SYDOW, Nov. 1969.

73. 'Marchands capitalistes et classes sociales', typescript, p. 9. In sixteenth-century Lübeck, the *Fernhändler* represented 50 or 60 family-firms in a town of 25,000 inhabitants.

74. *Verfassungs- und Wirtschaftsgeschichte des Mittelalters*, 1928, p. 329.

75. Th. K. RABB, *Enterprise and Empire*, 1967, pp. 26 ff.

76. According to André PIETTRE, *Les Trois Ages de l'économie*, 1955, p. 182, quoted by Michel LUTFALLA, *L'État stationnaire*, 1964, p. 98.

77. G. CHAUSSINAND-NOGARET, 'Aux origines de la Révolution: noblesse et bourgeoisie', in *Annales E.S.C.*, 1975, pp. 265–77.

78. [Burgundy]: Henri DROUOT, *Mayenne et la Bourgogne, étude sur la Ligue (1587–1596)*, 1937, I, pp. 45, 51; [Rome]: Jean DELUMEAU, *op. cit.*, I, p. 458: 'As the seventeenth century began, the great lords of the old days, [in the Roman Campagna] weighed down by their debts, sold up their landed properties and declined in favour of a new more manageable aristocracy with no warlike past'.

79. B.N., F. Esp., 127, c. 1610.

80. *Beauvais et le Beauvaisis . . .*, p. 219: F. BRAUDEL, in *Annales E.S.C.*, 1963, p. 774.

81. Raymond CARR, 'Spain', in *The European Nobility in the Eighteenth Century*, *op. cit.*, p. 44.

82. Henri PIRENNE, *Les Périodes de l'histoire sociale du capitalisme*, Brussels 1922.

83. H. KELLENBENZ, typescript, *op. cit.*, p. 17.

84. Claude CARRÈRE, *op. cit.*, I, p. 146.

85. Friedrich LÜTGE, *op. cit.*, p. 312.

86. J.H. HEXTER, *op. cit.*, pp. 76 ff.

87. G. TAYLOR, 'Non-capitalist Wealth and the Origins of the French Revolution', in *American Historical Review*, 1967, p. 485.

88. Pierre DARDEL, *op. cit.*, pp. 154–5.

89. ACCARIAS DE SÉRIONNE, *La Richesse de la Hollande*, *op. cit.*, II, p. 31.

90. F. DORNIC, *op. cit.*, p. 161.

91. R. de ROOVER, *The Medici Bank*, 1948, p. 20, note 50.

92. Guy CHAUSSINAND-NOGARET, *Les Financiers du Languedoc au XVIIIe siècle*, 1970.

93. Paolo NORSA, 'Una famiglia di banchieri, la famiglia Norsa (1350–1950)', in *Bollettino dell'Archivio storico del banco di Napoli*, 1953.

94. André RAYMOND, *Artisans et commerçants au Caire au XVIIIe siècle*, 1973, II, pp. 379–80.

95. The original title of the book which I consulted in typescript. It was published in 1977 under the title *Les bourgeois gentilshommes: an essay on the definition of élites in Renaissance France*, University of Chicago Press, 1977.

96. Guy PATIN, *op. cit.*, II, p. 196.

97. Romain BARON, 'La bourgeoisie de Varzy au XVIIe siècle', in *Annales de Bourgogne*, 1964, p. 173.

98. M. COUTURIER, *op. cit.*, pp. 215–16. Tanners for instance were divided into 'master-tanners' and 'merchant tanners'. Only the latter were 'honorables hommes'.

99. C. LOYSEAU, *Cinq Livres du Droict des Offices*, 1613, p. 100.

100. *Op. cit.*, p. 35.

101. G. HUPPERT, *op. cit.*, typescript.

102. *Op. cit.*, pp. 128–9.

103. Edited by L. Raymond LEFEBVRE, 1943, pp. 131–3.

104. Joseph NOUAILLAC, *Villeroi, Sécrétaire du roi*, 1909, p. 33.

105. His astrologer, Primi Visconti, if we can believe H. MERCIER, *Une Vie d'ambassadeur du Roi-Soleil*, 1939, p. 22.

106. G. HUPPERT, *L'Idée de l'histoire parfaite*, 1970.

107. R. MANDROU, *La France aux XVIIe et XVIIIe siècles*, 1970, p. 130.

108. In the *Cayer présenté au roy par ceux du tiers estat de Dauphiné*, Grenoble, 1re éd.

1603, quoted by Davis BITTON, *The French Nobility in crisis – 1560-1644,* 1969, pp. 96 and 148, note 26.

109. Quoted by BANCAL, *Proudhon,* I, p. 85, no. 513.

110. A.N., G⁷, 1686, 156.

111. SAINT-CYR, *Le Tableau du siècle,* 1759, p. 132, quoted by Norbert ÉLIAS, *La Société de Cour,* 1974, p. 11.

112. Manuel FERNÁNDEZ ALVAREZ, *Economia, sociedad y corona,* 1963, p. 384.

113. *Variétés,* V, 235 [1710].

114. See below, vol. III, ch. 3.

115. Witold KULA, 'On the typology of economic systems,' in *The Social sciences, Problems and Orientations,* 1968, p. 115.

116. Tommaso CAMPANELLA, *Monarchia di Spagna,* in *Opere,* 1854, II, p. 148, quoted by Carlo de FREDE, in *Studi in onore di Amintore Fanfani,* V, pp. 5-6 and 32-3.

117. Giuseppe GALASSO, *op. cit.,* p. 242.

118. FÉNELON, *Dialogues des Morts,* II, 1718, p. 152.

119. R. PERNOUD, *Histoire de la bourgeoisie en France,* II, 1962, p. 10.

120. Paolo CARPEGGIANI, *Mantova, profilo di una città,* 1976, Appendix: *Sabbioneta,* pp. 127 ff. The word *casino,* p. 139, refers to the prince's private villa and garden.

121. For the preceding paragraph, A.d.S., Venice, for example *Senato Terra,* 24, 9 January 1557; 32, Padua, 9 January 1562; P. MOLMENTI, *op. cit.,* II, p. 111.

122. Jürgen KUCZINSKI, *op. cit.,* p. 71.

123. Vorontsov Archives, VIII, p. 34, 18-29 December 1796.

124. André PARREAUX, *La Société anglaise de 1760 à 1810,* 1966, p. 12.

125. Between 1575 and 1630, about half the peerage was investing in trade, that is one in two, whereas the proportion is one in fifty taking the nobility and gentry as a whole, T.K. RABB, *Enterprise and Empire,* 1967, note 16 and p. 27.

126. R. GASCON, *op. cit.,* I, p. 444.

127. Pierre VILAR's paper at the International Congress of Historical Sciences, Rome 1955.

128. P. MOLMENTI, *op. cit.,* II, p. 75.

129. Jerónimo de ALCALÁ, *El donador hablador,* 1624, in *La Novela picaresca española,* 1966, p. 1233.

130. For the following examples see Y.M.

131. *Les Soulèvements populaires en France de 1623 à 1648,* 1963.

132. Carlo de FIDE, in *Mélanges Fanfani,* V, 1962, pp. 1-42.

133. Ingomar BOG, in *Z. für Agrargeschichte,* 1970, pp. 185-96.

134. *Variétés,* VII, p. 330, 7 June 1624.

135. Y.-M. BERCÉ, *op. cit.,* p. 300.

136. B.N., Fr., 21773, f° 31.

137. Henri GACHET, 'Conditions de vie des ouvriers papetiers en France au XVIIIᵉ siècle', *Communication à l'Institut français d'histoire sociale,* 12 June 1954.

138. The following paragraph is based on Nathalie ZEMON DAVIS: 'Strikes and salvation at Lyons', in *Archiv für Reformationgeschichte,* LVI (1965), pp. 48-64, and Henri HAUSER, *Ouvriers du temps passé,* 1927.

139. H. HAUSER, *op. cit.,* p. 180, note 1.

140. *Ibid.,* pp. 203, 234, note 1 and A. FIRMIN-DIDOT, *Aldo Manuce et l'hellénisme à Venise,* 1875, p. 269.

141. N.W. POSTHUMUS, *De Geschiedenis van de Leidsche lakenindustrie,* 3 vols., 1908-1939; Émile COORNAERT, 'Une capitale de la laine: Leyde', in *Annales E.S.C.,* 1946.

142. A.N., A.E., B¹, 619, 8 and 29 October 1665.

143. For the next three paragraphs, see POSTHUMUS, *op. cit.,* III, pp. 721-9, 656-7, 674, 691-6, 869 ff., 722-4, 876-8.

144. Paul MANTOUX, *La Révolution industrielle au XVIIIᵉ siècle,* 1959, pp. 57-9. Carlos GUILHERME MOTA's article 'Conflitos entre capital e trabalho; anatoçoes acerca de uma agitaçao no Sudo-este inglês en 1738' in *Revista de Historia,* São Paulo, 1967, drew my attention to the incident described here.

145. Peter LASLETT, *Un Monde que nous avons perdu* (French edn.), 1969, p. 172-3. A. VIERKAND, Die *Stetigkeit im Kulturwandel,* 1908, p. 103: 'The less advanced man is, the more likely he is to be influenced by the traditional model and suggestion.' Quoted by W. Sombart. *Le Bourgeois,* French edn. p. 27. But how

BERCÉ, *op. cit.,* II, p. 681 (Aquitaine); E. MASCHKE, *art. cit.,* p. 21 (German cities); René FEDOU, 'Le cycle medieval des révoltes lyonnaises' in *Cahiers d'histoire,* 3, 1973, p. 240 (Lyons).

is one to explain the violence of popular movements in Russia?

146. E. Coornaert, *Les Corporations en France avant 1789*, 10th edn., 1941, p. 167.
147. *Ibid.*, pp. 168-9.
148. R. Zangheri in *Studi Storici*, 1968, p. 538; Jérôme Blum, 'The condition of the European peasantry on the eve, of emancipation', in *Journal of Modern History*, 1974.
149. Roland Marx, *La Révolution industrielle en Grande-Bretagne*, 1970, p. 19.
150. Sully, *Mémoires . . .*, *op. cit.*, III, p. 107; *Variétés*, V, p. 129. The *hampones* in Spain, J. Van Klaveren, *op. cit.*, p. 187, note 36; and the *oziosi* in Italy, Aurelio Lepre, *op. cit.*, p. 27.
151. 21 June 1636, *Civiltà Veneziana*, *op. cit.*, p. 285.
152. *Mémoires*, *op. cit.*, 1875, I, p. 215.
153. A.N., G⁷, 1647, 1709.
154. Unpublished master's thesis by Mme Buriez, *L'Assistance à Lille au XVIIIe siècle*, Faculty of Arts, Lille University.
155. Richard Gascon, 'Economie et pauvreté aux XVIe et XVIIe siècles: Lyon, ville exemplaire et prophétique' in *Etudes sur l'histoire de la pauvreté*, ed. M. Mollat, II, 1974, pp. 747 ff. See also R. Egelsing, *art. cit.*, p. 27.
156. P. Laslett, *op. cit.*, pp. 45-6.
157. F. Lütge, *op. cit.*, p. 382.
158. Information provided in Cracow by MM. Kulczykowsy and Francic.
159. Mme Buriez's thesis *op. cit.* In Cahors in 1546, there were 3400 paupers in a population of 10,000, M.-J. Prim, unpublished master's thesis, Toulouse, p. 53. In the Causses, at Chanac, there were 60 beggars for 338 taxpayers, Paul Marres, 'L'économie des Causses du Gévaudan au XVIIIe siècle', in *Congrès de Mende*, 1955, p. 167. In La Rochelle in 1776, there were 3668 poor to 14,271 inhabitants, Laveau, *op. cit.*, p. 72. In Avallon in 1614, the poor were one sixth of the population, Y. Durand, *op. cit.*, p. 42. On the *Habenichtse*, the 'have-nots' of Augsburg in 1500, see H. Bechtel, *op. cit.*, II, p. 52, note 6. See also for a general survey, Olwen Hufton, 'Towards an understanding of the poor of eighteenth-century France' in *French government and society, 1500-*

1850, ed. J.F. Bosher, 1975, pp. 145 ff.
160. There are many references for 1749, 1759, 1771, 1790 in the departmental archives of Haute-Savoie, C 143, fᵒˢ 29-38; C 135, H.S.; C 142, 194, fᵒ 81; C 165, fᵒ 81 vᵒ; IC, III, 51, fᵒˢ 40-7.
161. Who existed in very large numbers, M. Couturier, *op. cit.*, Châteaudun, 1697; A. Poitrineau, *op. cit.*, p. 608: 'beggars made up the bottom layer of every village population'.
162. Vauban, *Projet d'une dîme royale*, Daire edn., 1843, p. 34.
163. Yves Durand, in *Cahiers de doléances des paroisses du bailliage de Troyes pour les Etats généraux de 1614*, 1966, pp. 39-40. The distinction between the poor who were beggars and those who were merely unemployed must not be lost sight of. J. van Klaveren, 'Población y ocupación', in *Ecónomica*, 1954, no. 2, rightly points out that Malthus was talking about paupers not the unemployed.
164. In German towns in 1384, 1400, 1442, 1446, 1447.
165. E. Coyecque, 'L'Assistance publique à Paris au milieu du XVIe siècle', in *Bull. de la Soc. de l'Histoire de Paris et de l'Ile de France*, 1888, p. 117.
166. *Ibid.*, pp. 129-230, 28 January 1526: 500 of the Parisian poor were sent to the galleys.
167. *Variétés*, VII, p. 42, note 3 (1605). Irish 'beggars' in Paris were sent to Canada. Vagrants in Seville were sent to the Magellan Straits. A.d.S. Venice, Senato Spagna, Zane to the Doge Madrid, 30 October 1581.
168. C.S.L. Davies, 'Slavery and Protector Somerset; the Vagrancy Act of 1547' in *Economic History Review*, 1966, pp. 533-49.
169. Ogier Ghiselin de Busbecq, *The Turkish Letters*, p. 101.
170. CF. Olwen Hufton, *The Poor of 18th Century France*, 1974, pp. 139-59.
171. A.N., A.E., B¹ 521, 19 April 1710. Cf. AD XI, 37 (1662). Around Blois 'there are few roads without corpses lying at the side of them'.
172. A.d.S. Venice, Senato Terra 1 (Venice); Delamare, *op. cit.*, 1710, p. 1012 (Paris). There were 3000 poor outside Chambéry, François Vermale, *Les Classes rurales*

en Savoie au XVIIIe siècle, 1911, p. 283.

173. Suzanne CHANTAL, *La Vie quotidienne au Portugal après le tremblement de terre de Lisbonne de 1755*, 1962, p. 16. There are many mentions in the letters sent by the Russian consul in Lisbon, see Moscow, Central Archives 72/5, 260, 54, vº Lisbon, 30 May 1780.

174. C. MANCERON, *op. cit.*, I, pp. 298-9, according to P. GROSCLAUDE, *Malesherbes*, p. 346.

175. J.-P. GUTTON, *La Société et les pauvres, L'exemple de la généralité de Lyon*, 1970, pp. 162 ff.

176. J.-P. GUTTON, 'Les mendiants dans la société parisienne au début du XVIIIe siècle, in *Cahiers d'Histoire*, XIII, 2, 1968, p. 137.

177. *Variétés*, V. p. 272.

178. The two centres – the French consulates in Rotterdam and Genoa – for rescuing sailors 'dismissed the service' who had been put ashore, provide a copious correspondence: A.N., AE B¹, 971-3 (Rotterdam) and 530 ff (Genoa). These were wretched men, put ashore in rags, without shoes or shirts; in the hope of being helped and repatriated, various adventurers or 'coureurs' would try to slip into their ranks, Bⁱ 971, fº 45, 31 December 1757: 'many were covered in vermin, they had to be cleaned and their rags put in the oven'.

179. *Variétés*, V, p. 222.

180. A.d.S. Napoli, Affari Esteri, 796.

181. *Ibid.*

182. Comte de LA MESSELIÈRE, *Voyage à Saint-Pétersbourg, an XI-1803*, pp. 262-3.

183. A.N., Marine, B¹, 48, fº 113.

184. Nina ASSODOROBRAJ, *The Origins of the Working Class* (in Polish) 1966; summary in French, pp. 321-5.

185. Quoted by J.-C. PERROT, *op. cit.*, I, p. 423, note 232.

186. Robert MOLIS, 'De la mendicité en Languedoc (1775-1783)', in *Revue d'hist. écon. et sociale*, 1974, p. 483.

187. J. MAILLEFER, *Mémoires*, pp. 120-2.

188. Gaston ZELLER, *Aspects de la politique française sous l'Ancien Régime*, 1964, pp. 375-85.

189. *Medit.*, Eng. trans., see index references for Uskoks, pirates, Knights of St Stephen, etc.

190. De LINGUET, quoted by MANCERON, *op. cit.*, I, p. 169: 'In the army, a pioneer (sapper) is valued less than a gun-carriage horse, because such a horse is expensive, whereas the soldier can be had for nothing....' It would be better to have figures than impressions, but the figures are hard to come by. To give some idea of scale, according to a report from Frankfurt of 9 August 1783, the total troops in Europe amounted to two million men, or just over 1.3% of the population, if the total population of Europe is taken to be about 150 million. *Gazette de France*, p. 307.

191. R. GASCON, *op. cit.*, I, p. 400.

192. JÈZE, *Journal du Citoyen*, 1754, p. 1.

193. Extract from the Registers of the Paris Parlement, years 1750-1, fº 427. Judgment of 14 August 1751, sentencing the servant Pierre Pizel.

194. Marius MITTRE, *Les Domestiques en France*, p. 14. *Variétés*, V, p. 253, note; ref. to *Traité de la Police*, 9, ch. 3.

195. P.-V. MALOUET, *Mémoires de Malouet*, 1874, I, pp. 48-9.

196. Claude VEIL, 'Phénoménologie du travail', in *L'Évolution psychiatrique*, no. 4, 1957, p. 701. 'Even when he is tied to a machine, a man is never the slave of the machine. He can only be the slave of other men. In this respect, and *mutatis mutandis*, there are always galleys.'

197. Abbé C. FLEURY, *Les Devoirs des maîtres et des domestiques*, 1688, p. 73. Similar sentiments were expressed almost a century later by I. de PINTO, *op. cit.*, p. 257: 'Let us imagine for a moment a state in which everyone was rich; it would not be able to subsist without sending for foreign immigrants to work for it' – a prophetic sentence. But already in the eighteenth century and before, the poor were already tending to migrate in large numbers.

198. *Op. cit.*, p. 58. Similar remarks, much later in BAUDRY DES LOZIERES, *Voyage à Louisiane*, 1802, pp. 103 ff.

199. P. DECHARME, *op. cit.*, p. 119.

200. *Literatura europea y Edad Media*, 1955, I, p. 40.

201. A.d.S. Mantua, Archivio Gonzaga, Donatus de Bretis to the marquis of Mantua, B. 1438.

202. *Le Savant et le Politique*, 1963, p. 101.

203. *Gazette de France*, p. 599.

204. Max Weber, *Economia e società*, Italian edn., 2, p. 991.

205. *Diarii, op. cit.*, I, pp. 184, 196.

206. British Museum, Mss Sloane, 42.

207. Élie Brackenhoffer, *op. cit.*, p. 111.

208. Louis-Sébastien Mercier, *op. cit.*, III, p. 278.

209. *Ibid.*, p. 279.

210. *Diarii, op. cit.*, 1, p. 111.

211. *Livre de main des Du Pouget (1522–1598)*, critical edn. by M.J. Prim, D.E.S., Toulouse, 1964, typescript.

212. Anonymous traveller, 1728, Victoria and Albert Museum, 86 NNZ, fos 196 ff.

213. According to the copy in the French manuscripts section of the Lenin Library in Moscow, fos 5 and 54.

214. *Gazette de France*, 29 February 1772, p. 327.

215. Françoise Autrand, *Pouvoir et société en France, XIVᵉ–XVᵉ siècles*, 1974, p. 12.

216. R. Gascon in *Histoire économique et sociale de la France*, Braudel-Labrousse (eds.) 1976, I, p. 424; Claude Seyssel, *Histoire singulière du roy Loys XII*, 1558, p. 14.

217. L. Stone, *An Elizabethan: Sir Horatio Pallavicino*, 1956, p. 42.

218. Marx's expression.

219. Jean Imbert, *Histoire économique*, 1965, p. 206.

220. *Ibid.*, p. 207 and Le Blanc, *Traité historique des monnoyes de France*, 1692, pp. 175–6.

221. *Ordonnances des Rois de France de la troisième race*, Laurière edn., 1723, vol. 1, p. 371 (instructions accompanying ordinance on money raised for the Flanders war, 1302).

222. Gabriel Ardant, *Histoire de l'impôt*, 1971, 1, p. 238.

223. C. Bec, *op. cit.*, p. 62.

224. G. Luzzatto, *Storia economica di Venezia, op. cit.*, p. 208.

225. 'Origin and growth of the national debt in Western Europe', in *American Economic Review*, n° 2, mai 1947, p. 118.

226. Even in the twelfth century, H. Pirenne, *op. cit.*, p, 35, note 2. The first really large loan in France was the one in 1295 for the Guyenne campaign against the English: C. Florange, *Curiosités financières . . .*, 1928, p. 1.

227. Rather than give a large number of references to *The Mediterranean*, I leave the reader to follow them up, as they are easy to find. More details in *El siglo de los Genoveses* by Felipe Ruiz Martin which I consulted several years ago (unpublished manuscript).

228. In *La Gitanilla, Novelas ejemplares*, Nelson edn., p. 100.

229. P.G.M. Dickson, *The Financial Revolution in England. A study in the development of public credit, 1688–1756*, 1967.

230. A.N., G⁷, 1699.

231. Warsaw, A.G., Radziwill Collection, 26 December 1719.

232. I. de Pinto, *op. cit.*, p. 1, note 2.

233. Information from Jorjo Tadić.

234. Thomas Mortimer, *Every Man His Own Broker*, 1775, p. 165.

235. I. de Pinto, *op. cit.*, in 1771 flattered himself (p. 13) that he was the first man to have maintained that 'the national debt had enriched England'; he explains the advantages of the system admirably, comparing it to that of France; he notes that the English in general, including some eminent persons 'are ignorant of its nature' and stupidly oppose it (p. 43).

236. Moscow, State Archives, 35/6, 390, 114.

237. *Ibid.*, 320, 167, letter from Simolin, London 23 March–3 April 1781.

238. *Bilanci generali*, Seria seconda, Venice, 1912.

239. M. Mollat, *Comptes généraux de l'État bourguignon entre 1416 et 1420*, 1964.

240. *Medit.*, II, pp. 684 and 686.

241. *Ibid.*

242. See S.J. Shaw's translation, *The Budget of Ottoman Egypt, 1596–7*; and especially current research by Omer Lufti Barkan.

243. Staunton, *op. cit.*, II, p. 615, 36 million tahels (=oz of silver). R. Vivero, British Museum, Add. 18287, f° 49, 1632, 130 million gold crowns.

244. Abbé Prévost, *Voyages, op. cit.*, X, pp. 238 ff.

245. A.N., K 1352 (1720) ou A.E., Russie M.D., 7, fos 298–305 (c. 1779).

246. Roger Doucet, *L'État des finances de 1523*, 1923.

247. Francesco CARACCIOLO, *Il regno di Napoli nei secoli XVI e XVII*, 1966, I, p. 106.
248. VÉRON DE FORBONNAIS, *Recherches ... sur les finances de France*, 1758, pp. 429 ff.
249. Emmanuel LE ROY LADURIE, *Les Paysans du Languedoc*, 1966, I, pp. 295-6.
250. Cardinal de RICHELIEU, *Testament politique*, ed. Louis ANDRÉ, 1947, p. 438. Text quoted by [J.-F. MELON], *Essai politique sur le commerce*, 1734, p. 37.
251. Cf. vol. III, chapter 2.
252. Selon C.M. CIPOLLA, Prato Conference, May 1976.
253. Philippe CONTAMINE, Prato Conference, April 1974.
254. François PIETRI, *Le Financier*, 1931, p. 2.
255. Michel MOLLAT, *Les Affaires de Jacques Cœur. Journal du Procureur Dauvet*, 2 vol., 1952.
256. Germain MARTIN and Marcel BESANÇON, *op. cit.*, p. 56.
257. G. CHAUSSINAND-NOGARET, *Les Financiers du Languedoc au XVIIIe siècle*, 1970, et *Gens de finance au XVIIIe siècle*, 1972. Many references: see 'Castanier' in the index.
258. *Richesse de la Hollande*, *op. cit.*, II, p. 256.
259. J.G. van DILLEN, *Munich V*, pp. 181 sq.
260. *Ibid.*, p. 182.
261. *Ibid.*, p. 184.
262. P.G.M. DICKSON, *op. cit.*, pp. 253-303.
263. *Ibid.*, pp. 289-90.
264. *Ibid.*, p. 295.
265. J.F. BOSHER, *French Finances 1770-1795. From Business to Bureaucracy*, 1970. On Necker's institutional reforms, see p. 150 ff.
266. *Ibid.*, pp. 304, and 17, note 2.
267. M. MARION, *Dictionnaire*, *op. cit.*, p. 236.
268. Daniel DESSERT, 'Finandes et société au XVIIe siècle à propos de la chambre de justice de 1661', in *Annales E.S.C.*, n° 4, 1974.
269. Daniel DESSERT et Jean-Louis JOURNET, 'Le *lobby* Colbert: un royaume ou une affaire de famille?', in *Annales E.S.C.*, 1975, pp. 1303-1337.
270. But there had been a series of incidents in its history: the execution of Semblançay in 1522 and the boycott of financial office-holders; appeals for capital to the Paris and Lyons money-markets; bankruptcy in 1558 leading to the return at the end of the century of an oligarchy of financiers, etc. Cf. R. GASCON in *Histoire économique et sociale de la France*, ed. BRAUDEL and LABROUSSE, vol. I, pp. 296 ff.
271. Marcel MARION, *op. cit.*, p. 232.
272. G. CHAUSSINAND-NOGARET, *op. cit.*, p. 236.
273. L.-S. MERCIER, *op. cit.*, III, p. 201.
274. On the question generally see Pierre DEYON's excellent little book, *Le Mercantilisme*, 1969.
275. In *Z. für Nationalökonomie XVII*.
276. *Der Merkantilismus*, 1965, p. 5.
277. Henri CHAMBRE, 'Pososkov et le mercantilisme', in *Cahiers du monde russe*, 1963, p. 358.
278. The word was mentioned in this context by Paul MANSELLI, Prato Conference 1974.
279. Adam SMITH, *The Wealth of Nations*.
280. H. BECHTEL, *op. cit.*, II, p. 58.
281. Henri HAUSER, *Les Débuts du capitalisme*, 1931, pp. 181 ff.
282. In *Revue d'histoire économique et sociale*, 1959, p. 394.
283. Franz von POLLACK-PARNAU, 'Eine österreischiche-ostendische Handels-Compagnie 1775-1785', in *Vierteljahrschrift für Sozial- und Wirtschaftsgeschichte*, 1927, p. 86.
284. A.N., G⁷, 1698, f⁰ 154, 24 June 1711.
285. Werner SOMBART, *op. cit.*, I, p. 364.
286. J. KULISCHER, *op. cit.*, German edn., II, p. 203.
287. H. HAUSHERR, *op. cit.*, p. 89.
288. Eli F. HECKSCHER, *op. cit.*, p. 480.
289. ISAMBERT, *Recueil général des anciennes lois françaises*, 1829, XV, p. 283 (Edict establishing a manufactory of cloth coats and cloth of gold, silver and silk, Paris, August 1603).
290. A. KILMA, J. MACUREK, 'La question de la transition du féodalisme au capitalisme en Europe centrale (XVIe–XVIIe siècles)', in International Conference of Historical Sciences, Stockholm, 1960, IV, p. 88.
291. A.N., G⁷, 1687.
292. W. SOMBART, *op. cit.*, I, p. 366.
293. Cardinal de RICHELIEU, *Testament politique*, 1947 edn., p. 428.

294. A.N., W.E., B¹, 754, London, 1 July 1669.

295. Ch. W. COLE, *Colbert and a century of French mercantilism*, 1939, I, p. 337.

296. SIMANCAS, *Consultas y junitas de hacienda*, leg. 391, f⁰ 542.

297. A.D. LUBLINSKAYA, *Lettres et mémoires adressés au chancelier Séguier (1633-1649)*, 1966, II, p. 88.

298. H. KELLENBENZ, *Der Merkantilismus*, *op. cit.*, p. 65.

299. A.d.S. Naples, Affari Esteri, 801, The Hague, 2 September, 15 November 1768.

300. Isaac de PINTO, *op. cit.*, p. 247.

301. *Ibid*, p. 242.

302. See above, chapter 3, section on transport.

303. *El siglo de los Genoveses*, still unfortunately unpublished.

304. A.N., G⁷, 1725, 121, 6 February 1707.

305. A.N., 94 A Q 1, 28.

306. John FRANCIS, *op. cit.* pp. 67-8.

307. D. DESSERT, *art. cit.*

308. Exceptions that prove the rule: LAVISSE, *Histoire de France*, VII, 1, pp. 5 ff. *Medit.*, II, pp. 687 ff.

309. R. MOUSNIER, *Les XVIe et XVIIe siècles*, 1961, p. 99.

310. British Museum, Add. 18287, f⁰ 24.

311. J.F. BOSHER, *op. cit.*, pp. 276 ff.; the word *bureaucratie* (bureaucracy) may have been used for the first time by GOURNAY, 1745, cf. B. LESNOGORSKI, International Congress of Historical Sciences, Moscow, 1970.

312. Warsaw, Archives, Radziwill Collection.

313. Or refeudalization, in the sense in which the word is used by G. GALASSO, *op. cit.*, p. 54 – that is a return to some extent to a previous state of feudalization.

314. J. van KLAVEREN, 'Die historische Erscheinung der Korruption . . .' in *Vierteljahrschrift für Sozial- und Wirtschaftsgeschichte*, 1957, pp. 304 ff.

315. According to MOUSNIER and HARTUNG, it was only after the War of the Austrian Succession that venality in France reached intolerable proportions, *International Congress of Hist. Sciences*, Paris, 1950, quoted by I. WALLERSTEIN, *op. cit.*, p. 137 note 3.

316. J. van KLAVEREN, *art. cit.*, p. 305.

317. See the brilliant description by Régine PERNOUD, *op. cit.*, II, pp. 8 ff.

318. Pierre CHAMPION, *Catherine de Médicis présente à Charles IX son royaume 1564-1566*, 1937.

319. British Museum, Add. 28368, f⁰ 24, Madrid, 16 juin 1575.

320. L. PFANDL, *Philipp II. Gemälde eines Lebens und einer Zeit*, 1938.

321. *Variétés*, II, p. 291.

322. *Op cit.*, p. 55.

323. E. LABROUSSE, *Le XVIIIe siècle*, in *Hist. générale des civilisations*, ed. M. CROUZET, 1953, p. 348.

324. Cf. Pierre GOUBERT, *Beauvais . . .*, *op. cit.*, p. 338.

325. *Op. cit.*, II, 698.

326. Moscow State Archives, 72/5-299, 22, Lisbon, 22 February 1791.

327. On the fragmentation of the power apparatus, see F. FOURQUET, *op. cit.*, esp. pp. 36-7.

328. 'De l'importance des idées religieuses', in *Oeuvres complètes de M. Necker*, edited by his grandson the Baron de Staël, 1820, vol. XVII, quoted by M. LUTFALLA, 'Necker ou la révolte de l'économie politique circonstancielle contre le despotisme des maximes générales', in *Revue d'hist. econ. et soc.*, 1973, no. 4, p. 586.

329. F. MELIS, *Tracce di una storia economica . . .*, *op. cit.*, p. 62.

330. E. ASHTOR, Prato Conference, 1972.

331. S. LABIB, 'Capitalism in medieval Islam', in *Journal of Economic History*, 1969, p. 91.

332. Hans HAUSHERR, *op. cit.*, p. 33; Philippe DOLLINGER, *La Hanse*, 1964, pp. 207, 509.

333. Halil INALCIK, 'Capital formation in the Ottoman Empire', in *The Journal of Economic History*, 1969, p. 102.

334. *Ibid.*, pp. 105-6.

335. M. RODINSON, *Islam et capitalisme*, *op. cit.*, p. 34.

336. This was the date when the gold florin was coined (Cf. F. MELIS, article 'Fiorino' in *Enciclopedia Dantesca*, 1971, p. 903.

337. H. DU PASSAGE, article 'Usure' in *Dictionnaire de théologie catholique*, vol. XV, 1950, col. 2376.

338. *Ibid.*, col. 2377-2378.

339. TURGOT, *Mémoire sur les prêts d'argent*, Daire ed., 1844, p. 110. In *Œuvres*, ed. Schelle, III, pp. 180-3.

340. Ch. CARRIÈRE, 'Prêt à intérêt et fidélité religieuse', in *Provence historique*, 1958, p. 107.

341. Law of 3 September 1807 and decree-law of 8 August 1935. Cf. *Nouveau Répertoire Dalloz*, 1965, 'Usure', IV, p. 945.

342. Benjamin N. NELSON, *The Idea of usury from tribal brotherhood to universal otherhood*, 1949. Gabriel LE BRAS, H. DU PASSAGE, article 'Usure', in *Dictionnaire de théologie catholique*, vol. xv, 1950, col. 2336-2390.

343. G. LE BRAS, art. cit., col. 2344-2346.

344. ARISTOTLE, *Politics*, Everyman edn., pp. 20-1.

345. Max WEBER, *L'Éthique protestante et l'esprit du capitalisme*, French edn., 1964, p. 76, note 27.

346. SCHUMPETER, *Storia dell'analisi econimica*, p. 10, note 3.

347. Karl POLANYI in K. POLANYI et Conrad ARENSBERG, *Les Systèmes économiques dans l'histoire et dans la théorie*, 1975, p. 94.

348. B. BENNASSAR, *Valladolid au siècle d'or*, p. 258.

349. R. de ROOVER, *The Medici Bank*, 1948, p. 57.

350. Marc BLOCH, *Les Caractères originaux de l'histoire rurale française*, 1952, I, p. 5.

351. Léon POLIAKOF, *Les Banchieri juifs et le Saint-Siège, du XIIe siècle*, 1965, p. 81.

352. *Diarii*, 9 November 1519, quoted by L. POLIAKOF, *op. cit.*, p. 59, note 5.

353. L. POLIAKOF, *op. cit.*, p. 96.

354. C. BEC, *Les Marchands écrivains à Florence, 1355-1434*, p. 274.

355. R. de ROOVER, *op. cit.*, p. 56, note 85.

356. Charles de LA RONCIÈRE, *Un Changeur florentin du Trecento ...*, 1973, pp. 25, 97, 114, note 5, 172, 197.

357. B. NELSON, 'The Usurer and the Merchant Prince: Italian businessmen and the ecclesiastical law of restitution, 1100-1550', in *The Tasks of economic history* (supplement to *The Journal of economic history*), VII (1947), p. 116.

358. *Ibid.*, p. 113.

359. G. Von PÖLNITZ, *Jakob Fugger*, 1949, I, p. 317. B. NELSON, *The Idea of usury, op. cit.*, p. 25.

360. J.A. GORIS, *Les Colonies merchandes méridionales à Anvers*, 1925, p. 507.

361. Pierre JEANNIN, *Les Marchands au XVIe siècle*, 1957, p. 169.

362. Archivo provincial Valladolid, Ruiz Collection, quoted by H. LAPEYRE, *Une Famille de marchands, les Ruiz*, 1955, p. 135 and note 139.

363. Père LAÍNEZ, *Disputationes tridentinae ...*, vol. II, 1886, p. 228 (... subtilitas mercatorum, ducentes eos cupiditate ... tot technas invenit ut vix facta nuda ipsa perspici possint ...).

364. Giulio MANDICH, *Le Pacte de Ricorsa et le marché italien des changes au XVIIe siècle*, 1953, p. 153.

365. J. HÖFFNER, *Wirtschaftsethik und Monopole*, 1941, p. 111; B. NELSON, *Idea of usury*, p. 61, note 79.

366. In conversation.

367. Ph. COLLET, *Traité des usures ...*, 1690, 'Avertissement'.

368. Isaac de PINTO, *Traité de la circulation et du crédit*, 1771, p. 36; L.-S. MERCIER, *Tableau de Paris*, 1782, III, pp. 49-50.

369. Moscow State Archives, 35/6, 370, p. 76.

370. C. CARRIÈRE, art. cit., p. 114.

371. I. de PINTO, *op. cit.*, pp. 213-14.

372. A. RENAUDET, *Dante humaniste*, 1952, pp. 255-6.

373. Werner SOMBART, *Le Bourgeois*, 1926, p. 313.

374. H. HAUSER, *Les Débuts du capitalisme*, 1931, pp. 51, 55.

375. C. M. CIPOLLA, 'Note sulla storia del saggio d'interesse, corso, dividendi e sconto dei dividendi del Banco di S. Giorgio nel sec. XVI', in *Economia internazionale*, vol. 5, May 1952, p. 14.

376. *Économie et religion, une critique de Max Weber*, Swedish edn. 1957, French edn. 1971.

377. F. BRAUDEL, *Le Monde actuel*, 1963, pp. 394-5.

378. *Studies in the development of capitalism*, 1946, p. 9.

379. O. BRUNNER, *op. cit.*, pp. 16-17.

380. Aldo MIELI, *Panorama general de historia de la Ciencia*, 11, pp. 260-5.

381. Ed. by H. PROESLER, 1934.

382. W. SOMBART, *op. cit.*, II, p. 129, note 1.

383. F. MELIS, *Storia della Ragioneria*, 1950, pp. 633-4.

384. W. SOMBART, *op. cit.*, II, p. 118.

385. Oswald SPENGLER, *The Decline of the West*.

386. G.A. COOKE, *Corporation Trust and Company*, 1950, p. 185.
387. Basil S. YAMEY, 'Accounting and the rise of capitalism', in *Mélanges Fanfani*, 1962, t. VI, pp. 833-4, note 4. It was slow to catch on in France, R. GASCON, *op. cit.*, I, pp. 314 ff.
388. W. SOMBART, *op. cit.*, II, p. 155.
389. F. MELIS, *Tracce di una storia economica di Firenze e della Toscana dal 1252 al 1550*, 1966, p. 62.
390. B. S. YAMEY, art. cit., p. 844, note 21.
391. R. de ROOVER, in *Annales d'hist. économique et sociale*, 1937, p. 193.
392. W. SOMBART, *Die Zukunft des Kapitalismus*, 1934, p. 8, quoted by B.S. YAMEY, art. cit., p. 853, note 37.
393. K. MARX, *Capital*, III section 7, ch. 27, on competition, and conclusion (fragments).
394. *Ibid.*, fragments on relations of distribution and production. (French edn., *Oeuvres*, Pléiade, II, 1968, pp. 1480 ff).
395. LENIN, *Imperialism, the highest stage of capitalism, op. cit.*
396. Otto HINTZE, *Staat und Verfassung*, 1962, II, pp. 374-431: *Der moderne Kapitalismus als historisches Individuum. Ein kritischer Bericht über Sombarts Werk.*
397. W. SOMBART, *Le Bourgeois*, p. 129.
398. *Ibid.*, pp. 132-3.
399. M. WEBER, *L'Éthique protestante et l'esprit du capitalisme*, French edn., p. 56, note 11.
400. C. BEC, *Les Marchands écrivains à Florence 1375-1434*, pp. 103-4.
401. Otto BRUNNER, *op. cit.*, pp. 16-17.
402. Gilles DELEUZE, Félix GUATTARI, *Capitalisme et schizophrénie. L'anti-Œdipe*, 1972, p. 164.
403. Denys LOMBARD, *Le Sultanat d'Atjeh au temps d'Iskandar Muda (1607-1636)*, 1967.
404. J. SAVARY, V, col. 1217.
405. PRÉVOST, *op. cit.*, VIII, p. 628.
406. TAVERNIER, *op. cit.*, II, p. 21.
407. A.N., Marine, B 7 46, 253. Report by the Dutchman Braems.
408. Gautier SCHOUTEN, *Voiage ... aux Indes Orientales, commencé en l'an 1658 et fini en l'an 1665*, II, pp. 404-5.
409. John Henry GROSE, *Voyage to the East Indies*, I, pp. 105, 111-12, 118.
410. Michel VIÉ, *Histoire du Japan des origines à Meiji*, 1969, p. 6.
411. DE LA MAZELIÈRE, *Histoire du Japan*, 1907, III, pp. 202-3.
412. D. et V. ELISSEEFF, *La Civilisation japonaise*, 1974, p. 118.
413. N. JACOBS, *op. cit.*, p. 65.
414. Y. TAKEKOSHI, *Economic aspects of the political history of Japan*, 1930, I, p. 226.
415. N. JACOBS, *op. cit.*, p. 37.
416. Y. TAKEKOSHI, *op. cit.*, I, p. 229.
417. Denis RICHET, *Une Famille de robe à Paris du XVIᵉ au XVIIIᵉ siècle, les Séguier*, unpublished thesis, p. 52.
418. D. RICHET, *ibid.*, p. 54. George HUPPERT in his book *The Bourgeois Gentilshommes* gives a number of examples, chapter V.
419. PING-TI HO, 'Social Mobility in China', in *Comparative Studies in society and history*, I, 1958-1959.
420. *Medit.*, II, pp. 718 ff.
421. Nicolaï TODOROV, 'Sur quelques aspects du passage du féodalisme au capitalisme dans les territoires balkaniques de l'Empire ottoman', in *Revue des études sud-est européennes*, vol. I, 1963, p. 108.
422. François BERNIER, *Voyages ... contenant la description des États du Grand Mogol*, 1699, I, pp. 286-7.
423. Lord CLIVE, Speech to House of Commons in *The Debates and Proceedings of the British House of Commons*, April 1772-July 1773, (Almon's Debates) London, 1774, p. 1 ff. (out of order).

Index

abacus, 572
Abbas the Great, Shah, 154, 159
Abbeville, 330, 333, 335, 338
Abdulgafour (Abd ul Ghafur), 124, 584
Abel, Wilhelm, 227
Académie française: *Dictionnaire*, 234, 238
Accarias de Serionne, J., 114
Acciaioli, Alessandro, 54
accounting, *see* book-keeping
Adam, Paul, 460
Affaitadi (firm), 150
Africa Company (English), 447, 449
Agricola, 302
griculture, 178, 180, 183, 256-7, 270, 272, 281-97
Ahmad al Badawi, 128
Airoli, House of, 534
Alberti, Leon Battista, 410, 578, 580
Alembert, Jean le Rond d', 313
Alexandria (Egypt), 128-9, 140
Alexandria della Palea, 85-8
Almaden, 326
Almoshof, 251-2
Alsace, 258
Alva, Fernando Alvarez de Toledo, Duke of, 547
Amalric, 434
Ambrose of Milan, St, 560
America, 272-8, 325-7
America, Latin: markets, 114; Portuguese
merchants in, 160-2, 164, 405; silver, 175, 194,
196-9; supply and demand, 175-6; trade deficit,
205; plantations, 272, 302-3; autonomous
enterprise, 280
American War of Independence, 206, 275, 410
Amiens, 35
Amsterdam: Bourse, 26, 92, 94, 99-106, 110, 112,
125, 135, 146-7; shops, 63; and wholesale trade,
96-7; and sugar market, 193; shipbuilding, 366;
shipping, 368; Bank of (and credit), 388, 390,

395, 569; and information, 411; and
monopolies, 421, 423; and merchant companies,
450-1; social style, 490; and English money
loans, 527-8; international financiers, 535, 537;
rise to power, 570
André (Caen lace-maker), 379
Anguillara, 284
Anisson, 209, 454, 526
Anne, Queen of England, 452
Ansbach, 301-2, 330
Antonietti, Guy, 104
Antonino of Florence, St, 560
Antwerp: market, 56-7; fairs, 90, 92, 135, 448; and
wholesale trade, 96; Exchange, 99; sugar
market, 193; and merchant companies, 448, 451;
Farnese captures, 451
apprenticeships and training, 408-9
Aquinas, St Thomas, 560, 562, 566, 568
Aquitaine, 90
Aragon, 294
Ardant, Gabriel, 165
Aretino, Pietro, 26
Argenson, Marc Rene Voyer d', Marquis, 430, 547
Argentina, 114
aristocracy, *see* nobility; privilege
Aristotle, 560
Armenians, 122-4, 154-9, 163, 165
army, 550; *see also* soldiers
Arnould, Ambroise-Marie, 295
Arpaia (Naples), 254
artisans, 60, 62, 298, 307-9, 318
artists, 54
Ashkenazim (Jews), 159
Ashtor, E., 556
Asia, 447; *see also* individual countries
asientos (Castile), 522-4
Assodorobraj, Nina, 511

651